THE MAKING

OF *American History*

THE MAKING

OF *American*

History VOLUME II

DEMOCRACY IN AN INDUSTRIAL WORLD

Third Edition

EDITED BY DONALD SHEEHAN

SMITH COLLEGE

HOLT, RINEHART
AND WINSTON

NEW YORK · CHICAGO ·
SAN FRANCISCO · TORONTO

Preface to the Third Edition

Since this collection was first published, the main current of interpretation of the American past has followed a new course. The liberal-progressive school of historians which dominated the previous decades has been subject to massive attacks on all sides. From Charles Beard's *An Economic Interpretation of the Constitution* in 1912 to Arthur Schlesinger, Jr.'s *The Age of Jackson* in 1945, themes of division and conflict had been emphasized. American society and especially its political life were characterized by a fierce struggle between rich opponents of democracy and coalitions of the less privileged—farmers, laborers, and small businessmen oppressed by mounting industrial monopolies and the lengthening tentacles of eastern financiers.

The present revision reflects the rejection of this central thesis by a growing number of influential writers who argue that unity and continuity have been at the core of American development. Louis Hartz has analyzed the widespread acceptance of the ideas associated with John Locke and the absence of vigorous aristocratic and socialist traditions. Arthur Link, Arthur Schlesinger, Jr., and, more particularly, Richard Hofstadter have examined the nostalgic content of twentieth-century reform movements. The internal conflicts previously alleged to have underlain the Revolution and the federal Constitution have been denied by Robert Brown.

The other additions to this edition are of several kinds. Representing both the increasing reliance of historians on the concepts of the social scientists and the importance of their studies to an understanding of the modern period are David Riesman's *The Lonely Crowd* and John Kenneth Galbraith's *The Affluent Society*. Older historical traditions are seen in the vigorous and graceful pages of Samuel Eliot Morison's *Maritime History of Massachusetts*, first published in 1921, and in the magnificent synthesis of the Civil War era emerging from Allan Nevins. Finally, there is the stimulating blend of literature and history found in Henry Nash Smith's *Virgin Land*.

Once again, an attempt has been made to include excerpts from books of lasting importance and to introduce them by short comments on the general character of their contribution to the continuing evolution of historical interpretation.

DONALD SHEEHAN

Northampton, Massachusetts
October 1962

Preface

This anthology is offered with the hope that it will form a useful supplement to textbooks in American history. Significant excerpts have been culled from the outstanding studies of several generations of our best scholars and combined into a whole illustrating the major developments in American society and government. At each focal point in the narrative of our national development, a selection is presented from the work of an expert whose special insight or ability will contribute to both understanding and interest. Although these specialists may have highly personalized views, an effort has been made to include only those writings which have gained a general acceptance among historians.

The purposes of such an anthology are several. It may, first of all, provide a solution for teachers whose desire to assign "outside" readings is thwarted by the inadequacies of the accessible libraries. Most college libraries contain individual copies of the books from which the selections in this anthology were taken, but it is manifestly futile to require three hundred readers to use a single copy. Today's students are often impatient with a course in American history which is limited to a textbook presentation. Most teachers would agree that some attempt should be made to add significance and meaning to a factual summary. It is hoped that this anthology will help to satisfy the demands of both students and teachers.

Further, students of American history should have some sense of the cumulative process of learning, some notion of how our present concepts have evolved from earlier ones. This is sometimes apparent in the selections themselves, but each introduction offers a summary of previous interpretations of the same subject and attempts to relate those interpretations to the general trends in historical analysis.

Even among scholars seeking to present an unbiased picture of the past there may be substantial disagreement. One group may find the explanation of events in political differences; another will emphasize philosophic or religious divergencies; a third will seek an economic basis for its analysis. Whether slavery was cruel or humane, whether the social contribution of Commodore Vanderbilt outweighed his ethical delinquencies—these and dozens of other specific questions continue to induce a variety of answers. These differences, and the willing acceptance of conflicting points of view, give health and vitality to American scholarship. Individual historians may seek to explain all causation in terms of an isolated group of facts, but scholarship as a whole is not confined to the rigid dimensions of doctrinaire theory of any kind.

Some word must be said to explain why these secondary accounts are offered in preference to so-called "primary source materials." The editor feels that the average beginning student has neither the time nor the experience to depend upon contemporary documents. In a survey course, there is time for only the most elementary sampling of such material, and the fraction to which the student is exposed may not be representative of the whole. Obviously, there is much value in acquainting students with the nature of basic historical materials, but it is chiefly an illustrative value. In any case, familiarity with the most vital of the analytical studies made over a long period of years by the best hisorians is an essential part of historical study.

Since only works of outstanding importance have been included in this collection, the criticisms which the editor has offered in the introductions are not intended to cast doubt upon the value of the selections, but are included as a guide for the student whose ability to read critically is limited by his lack of knowledge of alternative points of view. Although many would disagree with the criticisms raised, the editor has made an attempt to avoid a personal judgment and to mention only those limitations which have been generally commented on.

Here, then, are the classical studies of our national past. All historical scholars know them, and textbook writers have built upon them. It is hoped that they will help to stimulate in students the lasting interest in history for which all teachers of the subject strive.

DONALD SHEEHAN

New York, N. Y.
February 28, 1950

Contents

VOLUME II

I · The Aftermath

II · The Rise of Industrial America

III · *Voices in Respectful Protest*

IV · *The Second Aftermath*

V · *The New Deal and the World Divided*

VI · *Affluence and Conformity*

CONTENTS

PART I

THE AFTERMATH

VERNON L. PARRINGTON

ABOUT FIFTY YEARS AGO many historians believed that the writing of history could be reduced to an objective science into which the personality of the author need not enter. This theory presupposed that historical "facts," like chemical elements, could be individually isolated, then joined by some automatic and mechanical process into useful combinations which would reveal impartial "truths" about the past.

Although a desire for maximum objectivity remains a working principle of their profession, many historians now feel that it is substantially impossible for an author to divorce himself entirely from his own ideals and preconceptions. There is also a general agreement that a work is not invalidated or rendered useless simply because a historian's personal preferences have influenced his choice and interpretation of materials.

One of the best illustrations of a successful combination of strong personal convictions and unusually penetrating insight is offered by Vernon L. Parrington's *Main Currents in American Thought.* The author made clear in his introduction that he was well aware that his objectivity was limited. Further, he contended that it was in part because he did have preferences differing from those of his predecessors that he felt justified in presenting his work. Whereas previous historians had tended to be Hamiltonians and had emphasized the conservatives' contribution to American development, Parrington willingly acknowledged his devotion to liberal principles and anticipated some distortion in his views in favor of those who could be identified with the Jeffersonian tradition.

Parrington's liberalism appears to be related to his early environment. Born in Illinois, he began his teaching career in Kansas during the years of distress in the early 1890's which saw the birth of the Populist party and the rise of a national Progressive movement which continued until the First World War. Neither his undergraduate years at Harvard nor the golden haze of Coolidge prosperity at the end of his career seems to have softened his criticism of propertied interests and their literary allies. With Charles Beard, he gave voice to the historical expression of the reforming mood that produced the social indictments of Lincoln Steffens and Jacob Riis and the political programs of Woodrow Wilson and Robert La Follette.

Although it is chiefly to students of history that his work now appeals, Parrington spent most of his academic life as a professor of English. The materials out of which he fashioned his *Main Currents in American Thought,* which appeared in 1927, belong in general to literature rather than to politics and economics. Yet he had no concern with belles-lettres and only a secondary interest in literary values of any kind. The creative uniqueness of a writing was less important to him than its relation to the general intellectual climate which fostered it. It was to the main stream of America's characteristic ideas—to their origin and their evolution—that he devoted his analytical efforts. Having determined to view literature as a vehicle for ideas rather than for esthetics, Parrington removed intellectual history from philosophic abstractions and linked it with economic and social developments.

Regardless of whether its subject matter was religious, political, philosophic, or economic, Parrington related each writing to the basic theme of the continuing battle between democracy and its opponents. His virtues, ranging from the brilliance of his prose to the breadth of his knowledge and the keenness of his insight, impress themselves readily upon the reader. It is difficult to find in historical literature a more persuasive exposition than his of the case for humanitarian liberalism in America.

So often are his deficiencies overlooked by enthusiastic admirers that it seems appropriate to give them some emphasis. Probably most criticisms of Parrington derive from the lack of balance resulting from his rampant liberalism. Although he was too conscientious a scholar to indulge in caricature, he tended to magnify the virtues of his Jeffersonian heroes and to minimize the contributions of men with whom he did not agree. To fit better into his general theme, figures such as John Adams became more conservative than they were, and others such as the New England theologian Thomas Hooker were transformed by his enthusiasm into zealous democrats. The same inclination to extremes he applied to historical eras as well. The buoyancy and productiveness of the period following the Civil War cannot be seen because the focus is concentrated on the materialism and corruption, which became for Parrington the whole truth of the era. Perhaps a more fundamental complaint can be made of his tendency to apply late-nineteenth- and twentieth-century concepts to earlier times when they may not be applicable. For example, Parrington appeared to assume that Thomas Jefferson's conception of democracy had been identical with his own.

Like other historians who emphasize the economic basis of politics, Parrington is more successful in dealing with his villains than with his heroes. If Alexander Hamilton's economic and social loyalties led to his aristocratic ideas of government, why were not Jefferson's defined by his place in a plantation, slaveholding economy? When one defends the author by referring to his description of strong liberalizing factors such as free land or the "natural rights" doctrine of John Locke, one is led to the further complaint of being left without an explanation of why such things influenced some men but not others to whom they were equally accessible. Why did liberal religious thought pass Cotton Mather by and fasten itself upon Roger Williams?

Students of literature have criticized Parrington's disparagement of the literary contribution of such prominent men of letters as Nathaniel Hawthorne and Edgar Allan Poe. Although he may be defended by his own statement that he was not engaged in making esthetic judgments, it seems true that he was occasionally guilty of an unjust distortion because of his insistence upon subjecting every piece of writing, regardless of its purpose, to the same sociological standards.

These few criticisms by no means exhaust the possibilities. Yet the endless multiplication of negative comments could not outweigh the legitimate praise to which Parrington is entitled. Few American writers have combined the infectious enthusiasm and sustained diligence which he displayed; even fewer have been able to stimulate the widespread interest in history with which he must be credited.

The American Scene

I

FREE AMERICA

THE POT was boiling briskly in America in the tumultuous post-war years. The country had definitely entered upon its freedom and was settling its disordered household to suit its democratic taste. Everywhere new ways were feverishly at work transforming the countryside. In the South another order was rising uncertainly on the ruins of the plantation system; in the East an expanding factory economy was weaving a different pattern of industrial life; in the Middle Border a recrudescent agriculture was arising from the application of the machine to the rich prairie soil.

All over the land a spider web of iron rails was being spun that was to draw the remotest outposts into the common whole and bind the nation together with steel bands. Nevertheless two diverse worlds lay on the map of continental America. Facing in opposite directions and holding different faiths, they would not travel together easily or take comfort from the yoke that joined them. Agricultural America, behind which lay two and a half centuries of experience, was a decentralized world, democratic, individualistic, suspicious; industrial America, behind which lay only a half a dozen decades of bustling experiment, was a centralizing world, capitalistic, feudal ambitious. The one was a decaying order, the other a rising, and between them would be friction till one or the other had become master.

Continental America was still half frontier and half settled country. A thin line of homesteads had been thrust westward till the outposts reached well into the Middle Border—an uncertain thread running through eastern Minnesota, Nebraska, Kansas, overleaping the Indian Territory and then running west into Texas—approximately halfway between the Atlantic and the Pacific. Behind these outposts was still much unoccupied land, and beyond stretched the unfenced prairies till they merged in the sagebrush plains, gray and waste, that stretched to the foothills of the Rocky Mountains. Beyond the mountains were other stretches of plains and deserts, vast and forbidding in their alkali blight, to the wooded coast ranges and the Pacific Coast. In all this immense territory were only scattered settlements—at Denver, Salt Lake City, Sacramento, San Francisco, Portland, Seattle, and elsewhere—tiny outposts in the wilderness, with scattered hamlets, mining camps, and isolated homesteads lost in the great expanse. On the prairies from Mexico to Canada—across which rumbled great herds of buffalo—roved powerful tribes of hostile Indians who fretted against the forward thrust of settlement and disputed the right of possession. The urgent business of the times was the subduing of this wild region, wresting it from Indians and buffalo and wilderness; and the forty years that lay between the California Gold Rush of '49 and the Oklahoma Land Rush of '89 saw the greatest wave of pioneer expansion—the swiftest and most reckless—in all our pioneer experience. Expansion on so vast a scale necessitated building, and the seventies became the railway age, bonding the future to break down present barriers of isolation, and opening new territories for later exploitation. The reflux of the great movement swept back upon the Atlantic coast and gave to life there a fresh note of spontaneous vigor, of which the Gilded Age was the inevitable expression.

It was this energetic East, with its accumulations of liquid capital awaiting investment and its factories turning out the materials needed to push the settlements westward, that profited most from the conquest of the far West. The impulsion from the frontier did much to drive forward the industrial revolution. The war that brought devastation to the South had been more friendly to northern interests. In gathering the scattered rills of capital into central reservoirs at Philadelphia and New York, and in expanding the factory system to supply the needs of the armies, it had opened to capitalism its first clear view of the Promised Land. The bankers had come into control of the liquid wealth of the nation, and the industrialists had learned to use the machine for production; the time was ripe for exploitation on a scale undreamed-of a generation before. Up till then the potential resources of the continent had not even been surveyed. Earlier pioneers had only scratched the surface—felling trees, making crops, building pygmy watermills, smelting a little iron. Mineral wealth had been scarcely touched. Tools had been lacking to develop it, capital had been lacking, transportation lacking, technical methods lacking, markets lacking.

In the years following the war, exploitation for the first time was provided with adequate resources and a competent technique, and busy prospectors were daily uncovering new sources of wealth. The coal and oil of Pennsylvania and Ohio, the copper and iron ore of upper Michigan, the gold and silver, lumber and fisheries, of the Pacific Coast, provided limitless raw materials for the rising industrialism. The Bessemer process quickly turned an age of iron into an age of steel and created the great rolling mills of Pittsburgh from which issued the rails for expanding railways. The reaper and binder, the sulky plow and the threshing machine, created a large-scale agriculture on the fertile prairies. Wild grass-lands provided grazing for immense herds of cattle and sheep; the development of the corn-belt enormously increased the supply of hogs; and with railways at hand the Middle Border poured into Omaha and Kansas City and Chicago an endless stream of produce. As the line of the frontier pushed westward new towns were built, thousands of homesteads were filed on, and the speculator and promoter hovered over the prairies like buzzards seeking their carrion. With rising land-values money was to be made out of unearned increment, and the creation of booms was a profitable industry. The times were stirring and it was a shiftless fellow who did not make his pile. If he had been too late to file on desirable acres he had only to find a careless homesteader who had failed in some legal technicality and "jump his claim." Good bottom land could be had even by late-comers if they were sharp at the game.

This bustling America of 1870 accounted itself a democratic world. A free people had put away all aristocratic privileges and conscious of its power went forth to possess the last frontier. Its social philosophy, which it found adequate to its needs, was summed up in three words—preëmption, exploitation, progress. Its immediate and pressing business was to dispossess the government of its rich holdings. Lands in the possession of the government were so much idle waste, untaxed and profitless; in private hands they would be developed. They would provide work, pay taxes, support schools, enrich the community. Preëmption meant exploitation and exploitation meant progress. It was a simple philosophy and it suited the simple individualism of the times. The Gilded Age knew nothing of the Enlightenment; it recognized only the acquisitive instinct. That much at least the frontier had taught the great American democracy; and in applying to the resources of a continent the lesson it had been so well taught the Gilded Age wrote a profoundly characteristic chapter of American history.

II

FIGURES OF EARTH

In a moment of special irritation Edwin Lawrence Godkin called the civilization of the seventies a chromo civilization. Mark Twain, with his slack western standards, was equally severe. As he contemplated the slovenly reality beneath the gaudy exterior he dubbed it the Gilded Age. Other critics with a gift for pungent phrase have flung their gibes at the ways of a picturesque and uncouth generation. There is reason in plenty for such caustic comment. Heedless, irreverent, unlovely, cultivating huge beards, shod in polished top-boots—the last refinement of the farmer's cowhides—wearing linen dickeys over hickory shirts, moving through pools of tobacco juice, erupting in shoddy and grotesque architecture, cluttering its homes with ungainly walnut chairs and marble-topped tables and heavy lambrequins, the decade of the seventies was only too plainly mired and floundering in a bog of bad taste. A world of triumphant and unabashed vulgarity without its like in our history, it was not aware of its plight, but accounted its manners genteel and boasted of ways that were a parady on sober good sense.

Yet just as such comments are, they do not reach quite to the heart of the age. They emphasize rather the excrescences, the casual lapses, of a generation that underneath its crudities and vulgarities was boldly adventurous and creative—a generation in which the democratic freedoms of America, as those freedoms had taken shape during a drab frontier experience, came at last to spontaneous and vivid expression. If its cultural wealth was less than it thought, if in its exuberance it was engaged somewhat too boisterously in stamping its own plebeian image on the work of its hands, it was only natural to a society that for the first time found its opportunities equal to its desires, a youthful society that accounted the world its oyster and wanted no restrictions laid on its will. It was the ripe fruit of Jacksonian leveling, and if it ran to a grotesque individualism—if in its self-confidence it was heedless of the smiles of older societies—it was nevertheless by reason of its uncouthness the most picturesque generation in our history; and for those who love to watch human nature disporting itself with naïve abandon, running amuck through all the conventions, no other age provides so fascinating a spectacle.

When the cannon at last had ceased their destruction it was a strange new America that looked out confidently on the scene. Something had been released by the upheavals of half a century, something strong and assertive that was prepared to take possession of the continent. It did not issue from the loins of war. Its origins must be sought elsewhere, further back in time. It had been cradled in the vast changes that since 1815 had been reshaping America: in the break-up of the old domestic economy that kept life mean and drab, in the noisy enthusiasms of the new coonskin democracy, in the romanticisms of the California gold rush, in the boisterous free-doms discovered by the forties and fifties. It had come to manhood in the battles of a tremendous war, and as it now surveyed the con-tinent, discovering potential wealth before unknown, it demanded only freedom and opportunity—a fair race and no favors. Every-where was a welling-up of primitive pagan desires after long repres-sions—to grow rich, to grasp power, to be strong and masterful and lay the world at its feet. It was a violent reaction from the narrow poverty of frontier life and the narrow inhibitions of backwoods religion. It had had enough of skimpy, meager ways, of scrubbing along hoping for something to turn up. It would go out and turn it up. It was consumed with a great hunger for abundance, for the good things of life, for wealth. It was frankly materialistic and if material goods could be wrested from society it would lay its hands heartily to the work. Freedom and opportunity, to acquire, to possess, to enjoy—for that it would sell its soul.

Society of a sudden was become fluid. With the sweeping-away of the last aristocratic restraints the potentialities of the common man found release for self-assertion. Strange figures, sprung from obscure origins, thrust themselves everywhere upon the scene. In the reac-tion from the mean and skimpy, a passionate will to power was issuing from unexpected sources, undisciplined, confused in ethical values, but endowed with immense vitality. Individualism was being simplified to the acquisitive instinct. These new Americans were primitive souls, ruthless, predatory, capable; single-minded men; rogues and rascals often, but never feeble, never hindered by petty scruple, never given to puling or whining—the raw materials of a race of capitalistic buccaneers. Out of the drab mass of common plebeian life had come this vital energy that erupted in amazing abundance and in strange forms. The new freedoms meant diverse things to different men and each like Jurgen followed after his own wishes and his own desires. Pirate and priest issued from the com-mon source and played their parts with the same picturesqueness. The romantic age of Captain Kidd was come again, and the black flag and the gospel banner were both in lockers to be flown as the needs of the cruise determined. With all coercive restrictions put away the democratic genuis of America was setting out on the road of manifest destiny.

Analyze the most talked-of men of the age and one is likely to find a splendid audacity coupled with an immense wastefulness. A note of tough-mindedness marks them. They had stout nippers. They fought their way encased in rhinoceros hides. There was the Wall Street crowd—Daniel Drew, Commodore Vanderbilt, Jim Fisk, Jay Gould, Russell Sage—blackguards for the most part, railway wreckers, cheaters and swindlers, but picturesque in their rascality. There was the numerous tribe of politicians—Boss Tweed, Fernando Wood, G. Oakey Hall, Senator Pomeroy, Senator Cameron, Roscoe Conkling, James G. Blaine—blackguards also for the most part, looting city treasuries, buying and selling legislative votes like railway stock, but picturesque in their audacity. There were the professional keepers of the public morals—Anthony Comstock, John B. Gough, Dwight L. Moody, Henry Ward Beecher, T. De Witt Talmage—ardent proselytizers, unintellectual, men of one idea, but fiery in zeal and eloquent in description of the particular heaven each wanted to people with his fellow Americans. And springing up like mushrooms after a rain was the goodly company of cranks— Victoria Woodhull and Tennessee Claflin, "Citizen" George Francis Train, Henry Bergh, Ben Butler, Ignatius Donnelly, Bob Ingersoll, Henry George—picturesque figures with a flair for publicity who tilled their special fields with splendid gestures. And finally there was Barnum the Showman, growing rich on the profession of humbuggery, a vulgar greasy genius, pure brass without any gilding, yet in picturesque and capable effrontery the very embodiment of the age. A marvelous company, vital with the untamed energy of a new land. In the presence of such men one begins to understand what Walt Whitman meant by his talk of the elemental.

Created by a primitive world that knew not the machine, they were marked by the rough homeliness of their origins. Whether wizened or fat they were never insignificant or commonplace. On the whole one prefers them fat, and for solid bulk what generation has outdone them? There was Revivalist Moody, bearded and neckless, with his two hundred and eighty pounds of Adam's flesh, every ounce of which "belonged to God." There was the lyric Sankey, afflicted with two hundred and twenty-five pounds of human frailty, yet looking as smug as a banker and singing "There were ninety and nine" divinely through mutton-chop whiskers. There was Boss

Tweed, phlegmatic and mighty, overawing rebellious gangsters at the City Hall with his two hundred and forty pounds of pugnacious rascality. There was John Fiske, a philosophic hippopotamus, warming the chill waters of Spencerian science with his prodigious bulk. There was Ben Butler, oily and puffy and wheezy, like Falstaff larding the lean earth as he walked along, who yearly added more flesh to the scant ninety-seven pounds he carried away from Waterville College. And there was Jim Fisk, dressed like a bartender, huge in nerve as in bulk, driving with the dashing Josie Mansfield down Broadway—prince of vulgarians, who jovially proclaimed, "I worship in the Synagogue of the Libertines," and who on the failure of the Erie coup announced cheerfully, "Nothing is lost save honor!"

Impressive as are the fat kine of Egypt, the lean kine scarcely suffer by contrast. There were giants of puny physique in those days. There was Uncle Dan'l Drew, thin as a dried herring, yet a builder of churches and founder of Drew Theological Seminary, who pilfered and cheated his way to wealth with tobacco juice drooling from his mouth. There was Jay Gould, a lone-hand gambler, a dynamo in a tubercular body, who openly invested in the devil's tenements as likely to pay better dividends, and went home to potter lovingly amongst his exotic flowers. And there was Oakey Hall, clubman and playwright, small, elegant, and unscrupulous; and Victoria Woodhull who stirred up the Beecher case, a wisp of a woman who enraged all the frumpy blue-stockings by the smartness of her toilet and the perfection of her manners; and little Libby Tilton with her tiny wistful face and great eyes that looked out wonderingly at the world—eyes that were to go blind with weeping before the candle of her life went out. It was such men and women, individual and colorful, that Whitman and Mark Twain mingled with, and that Herman Melville—colossal and dynamic beyond them all—looked out upon sardonically from his tomb in the Custom House where he was consuming his own heart.

They were thrown up as it were casually out of the huge caldron of energy that was America. All over the land were thousands like them, self-made men quick to lay hands on opportunity if it knocked at the door, ready to seek it out if it were slow in knocking, recognizing no limitations to their powers, discouraged by no shortcoming in their training. When Moody set out to bring the world to his Protestant God he was an illiterate shoe salesman who stumbled over the hard words of his King James Bible. Anthony Comstock, the roundsman of the Lord, was a salesman in a drygoods shop, and as careless of his spelling as he was careful of his neighbors' morals. Commodore Vanderbilt, who built up the greatest fortune of the time, was a Brooklyn ferryman, hard-fisted and tough as a burr-oak, who in a lifetime of over eighty years read only one book, *Pilgrim's Progress,* and that after he was seventy. Daniel Drew was a shyster cattle-drover, whose arid emotions found outlet in periodic conversions and backslidings, and who got on in this vale of tears by salting his cattle and increasing his—and the Lord's—wealth with every pound of water in their bellies—from which cleverness is said to have come the Wall Street phrase, "stock-watering." Jim Fisk was the son of a Yankee peddler, who, disdaining the unambitious ways of his father, set up for himself in a cart gilded like a circus-wagon and drove about the countryside with jingling bells. After he had made his pile in Wall Street he set up his own opera house and proposed to rival the Medici as a patron of the arts—and especially of the artists if they were of the right sex. A surprising number of them—Moody, Beecher, Barnum, Fisk, Comstock, Ben Butler—came from New England; Jay Gould was of Connecticut ancestry; but Oakey Hall was a southern gentleman; Fernando Wood, with the face of an Apollo and the wit of an Irishman, was the son of a Philadelphia cigar-maker and much of his early income was drawn from sailors' groggeries along the waterfront; Tweed was a stolid New Yorker, and Drew was a York State country boy.

What was happening in New York was symptomatic of the nation. If the temple of Plutus was building in Wall Street, his devotees were everywhere. In Chicago, rising higgledy-piggledy from the ashes of the great fire, Phil Armour and Nelson Morris were laying out stockyards and drawing the cattle and sheep and hogs from remote prairie farms to their slaughter-houses. In Cleveland, Mark Hanna was erecting his smelters and turning the iron ore of Michigan into dollars, while John D. Rockefeller was squeezing the small fry out of the petroleum business and creating the Standard Oil monopoly. In Pittsburgh, Andrew Carnegie was applying the Bessemer process to steel-making and laying the foundations of the later steel trust. In Minneapolis, C. C. Washburn and Charles A. Pillsbury were applying new methods to milling and turning the northern wheat into flour to ship to the ends of the earth. In San Francisco, Leland Stanford and Collis P. Huntington were amassing huge fortunes out of the Southern Pacific Railway and bringing the commonwealth of California to their feet. Everywhere were boom-town and real-estate promoters, the lust of speculation, the hankering after quick and easy wealth.

In the great spaces from Kansas City to Sacramento the frontier spirit was in the gaudiest bloom. The experiences of three centuries of expansion were being crowded into as many decades. In the fifties the highway of the frontier had run up and down the Mississippi River and the golden age of steamboating had brought a motley life to Saint Louis; in the seventies the frontier had passed far beyond and was pushing through the Rocky Mountains, repeating as it went the old frontier story of swagger and slovenliness, of boundless hope and heroic endurance—a story deeply marked with violence and crime and heart-breaking failure. Thousands of veterans from the disbanded armies, northern and southern alike, flocked to the West to seek their fortunes, and daily life there soon took on a drab note from the alkali of the plains; yet through the drabness ran a boisterous humor that exalted lying to a fine art—a humor that goes back to Davy Crockett and the Ohio flatboatmen. Mark Twain's *Roughing It* is the epic of this frontier of the Pony Express, as *Life on the Mississippi* is the epic of the preceding generation.

The huge wastefulness of the frontier was everywhere, East and West. The Gilded Age heeded somewhat too literally the Biblical injunction to take no thought for the morrow, but was busily intent on squandering the resources of the continent. All things were held cheap, and human life cheapest of all. Wild Bill Hickok with forty notches on his gun and a row of graves to his credit in Boot Hill Cemetery, and Jesse James, most picturesque of desperadoes, levying toll with his six-shooter on the bankers who were desecrating the free spirit of the plains with their two per cent. a month, are familiar heroes in Wild West tales; but the real plainsman of the Gilded Age, the picturesque embodiment of the last frontier, was Captain Carver, the faultless horseman and faultless shot, engaged in his celebrated buffalo hunt for the championship of the prairies. Wagering that he could kill more buffalo in a day than any rival hero of the chase, he rode forth with his Indian marker and dropping the miles behind him he left an endless trail of dead beasts properly tagged, winning handsomely when his rival's horse fell dead from exhaustion. It was magnificent. Davy Crockett's hundred and five bears in a season was but 'prentice work compared with Captain Carver's professional skill. It is small wonder that he became a hero of the day and his rifle, turned now to the circus business of breaking glass balls thrown from his running horse, achieved a fame far greater than Davy's Betsy. With his bold mustaches, his long black hair flying in the wind, his sombrero and chaps and top-boots, he was a figure matched only by Buffalo Bill, the last of the great plainsmen.

Captain Carver was picturesque, but what shall be said of the thousands of lesser Carvers engaged in the same slaughter, market-hunters who discovered a new industry in buffalo-killing? At the close of the Civil War the number on the western plains was estimated at fifteen millions. With the building of the Union Pacific Railroad they were cut asunder into two vast herds, and upon these herds fell the hunters with the new breech-loading rifles, shooting for the hide market that paid sixty-five cents for a bull's hide and a dollar and fifteen cents for a cow's. During the four years from 1871 to 1874 nearly a million head a year were slain from the southern herd alone, their skins ripped off and the carcasses left for the coyotes and buzzards. By the end of the hunting-season of 1875 the vast southern herd had been wiped out, and with the building of the Northern Pacific in 1880 the smaller northern herd soon suffered the same fate. The buffalo were gone with the hostile Indians—Sioux and Blackfeet and Cheyennes and a dozen other tribes.[1] It was the last dramatic episode of the American frontier, and it wrote a fitting climax to three centuries of wasteful conquest. But the prairies were tamed, and Wild Bill Hickok and Captain Carver and Buffalo Bill Cody had become romantic figures to enthrall the imagination of later generations.[2]

1 See Allan Nevins, "The Taming of the West," in *The Emergence of Modern America*.

2 It is the same story in the matter of the passenger pigeon. In early days the flights of these birds ran to untold millions. The last great nesting was at Petoskey, Michigan, in 1878, covering a strip forty miles long and from three to ten miles wide. Upon the nests fell the market-hunters and a million and a half

It was an abundant harvest of those freedoms that America had long been struggling to achieve, and it was making ready the ground for later harvests that would be less to its liking. Freedom had become individualism, and individualism had become the inalienable right to preëmpt, to exploit, to squander. Gone were the old ideals along with the old restraints. The idealism of the forties, the romanticism of the fifties—all the heritage of Jeffersonianism and the French Enlightenment—were put thoughtlessly away, and with no social conscience, no concern for civilization, no heed for the future of the democracy it talked so much about, the Gilded Age threw itself into the business of money-getting. From the sober restraints of aristocracy, the old inhibitions of Puritanism, the niggardliness of an exacting domestic economy, it swung far back in reaction, and with the discovery of limitless opportunities for exploitation it allowed itself to get drunk. Figures of earth, they followed after their own dreams. Some were builders with grandiose plans in their pockets; others were wreckers with no plans at all. It was an anarchistic world of strong, capable men, selfish, unenlightened, amoral—an excellent example of what human nature will do with undisciplined freedom. In the Gilded Age freedom was the freedom of buccaneers preying on the argosies of Spain.

III

POLITICS AND THE FAIRY GODMOTHER

Certainly the Gilded Age would have resented such an interpretation of its brisk activities. In the welter of change that resulted from the application of the machine to the raw materials of a continent, it chose rather to see the spirit of progress to which the temper of the American people was so responsive. Freedom, it was convinced, was justifying itself by its works. The eighteenth century had been static, the nineteenth century was progressive. It was adaptable, quick to change its ways and its tools, ready to accept whatever proved advantageous—pragmatic, opportunist. It was not stifled by the dead hand of custom but was free to adapt means to ends. It

---

squabs were shipped to New York by rail, besides the thousands wasted. Within a generation the passenger pigeon had become extinct. See W. B. Mershon, *Outdoor Life and Recreation*, February, 1929, p. 26 ff.

accepted progress as it accepted democracy, without questioning the sufficiency of either. The conception accorded naturally with a frontier psychology. Complete opportunism is possible only amongst a people that is shallow-rooted, that lives in a fluid society, scantily institutionalized, with few vested interests. In a young society it is easy, in a maturing society it becomes increasingly difficult.

Dazzled by the results of the new technique of exploitation applied on a grand scale to unpreëmpted opportunities, it is no wonder the Gilded Age thought well of its labors and confused the pattern of life it was weaving with the pattern of a national civilization. It had drunk in the idea of progress with its mother's milk. It was an inevitable frontier interpretation of the swift changes resulting from a fluid economics and a fluid society in process of settling into static ways. It served conveniently to describe the changes from the simplicities of social beginnings to the complexities of a later order. It was made use of following the War of 1812 to explain the stir resulting from the westward expansion and the great increase in immigration; but it was given vastly greater significance by the social unsettlements that came with the industrial revolution. With the realization of the dramatic changes in manner of living—the added conveniences of life, release from the laborious round of the domestic economy, ease of transportation—that resulted from the machine order, it was inevitable that the idea of progress should have been on every man's tongue. The increase of wealth visible to all was in itself a sufficient sign of progress, and as the novelty of the industrial change wore off and the economy of America was more completely industrialized, it was this augmenting wealth that symbolized it.

In such fashion the excellent ideal of progress that issued from the social enthusiasms of the Enlightenment was taken in charge by the Gilded Age and transformed into a handmaid of capitalism. Its duties were narrowed to the single end of serving profits and its accomplishments came to be exactly measured by bank clearings. It was unfortunate but inevitable. The idea was too seductive to the American mentality not to be seized upon and made to serve a rising order. Exploitation was the business of the times and how better could exploitation throw about its activities the sanction of idealism than by wedding them to progress? It is a misfortune that America has never subjected the abstract idea of progress to critical

examination. Content with the frontier and capitalistic interpretations it has confused change with betterment, and when a great
idealist of the Gilded Age demonstrated to America that it was
misled and pointed out that the path of progress it was following
was the highway to poverty, he was hooted from the market-place.

Having thus thrown the mantle of progress about the Gold Dust
twins, the Gilded Age was ready to bring the political forces of
America into harmony with the program of preëmption and exploitation. The situation could hardly have been more to its liking. Postwar America was wholly lacking in political philosophies, wholly
opportunist. The old party cleavage between agriculture and industry had been obscured and the logic of party alignment destroyed by
the struggle over slavery. Democrat and Whig no longer faced each
other conscious of the different ends they sought. The great party
of Jefferson and Jackson was prostrate, borne down by the odium
of slavery and secession. In the North elements of both had been
drawn into a motley war party, momentarily fused by the bitterness
of conflict, but lacking any common program, certain indeed to split
on fundamental economic issues. The Whig Republican was still
Hamiltonian paternalistic, and the Democrat Republican was still
Jeffersonian *laissez faire,* and until it was determined which wing
should control the party councils there would be only confusion.
The politicians were fertile in compromises, but in nominating
Lincoln and Johnson the party ventured to get astride two horses
that would not run together. To attempt to make yoke-fellows of
democratic leveling and capitalistic paternalism was prophetic of
rifts and schisms that only the passions of Reconstruction days could
hold in check.

In 1865 the Republican party was no other than a war machine
that had accomplished its purpose. It was a political mongrel, without logical cohesion, and it seemed doomed to break up as the Whig
party had broken up and the Federalist party had broken up. But
fate was now on the side of the Whigs as it had not been earlier. The
democratic forces had lost strength from the war, and democratic
principles were in ill repute. The drift to centralization, the enormous development of capitalism, the spirit of exploitation, were
prophetic of a changing temper that was preparing to exalt the
doctrine of manifest destiny which the Whig party stood sponsor for.

The middle class was in the saddle and it was time to bring the political state under its control. The practical problem of the moment was to transform the mongrel Republican party into a strong cohesive instrument, and to accomplish that it was necessary to hold the loyalty of its Democratic voters amongst the farmers and working-classes whilst putting into effect its Whig program.

Under normal conditions the thing would have been impossible, but the times were wrought up and blindly passionate and the politicians skillful. The revolt of Andrew Johnson came near to bringing the party on the rocks; but the undisciplined Jacksonians were overthrown by the appeal to the Bloody Flag and put to flight by the nomination of General Grant for the presidency. The rebellion of the Independent Republicans under Horace Greeley in 1872 was brought to nothing by the skillful use of Grant's military prestige, and the party passed definitely under the control of capitalism, and became such an instrument for exploitation as Henry Clay dreamed of but could not perfect. Under the nominal leadership of the easygoing Grant a loose rein was given to Whiggish ambitions and the Republican party became a political instrument worthy of the Gilded Age.

The triumph of Whiggery was possible because the spirit of the Gilded Age was Whiggish. The picturesque embodiment of the multitude of voters who hurrahed for Grant and the Grand Old Party was a figure who had grown his first beard in the ebullient days before Secession. Colonel Beriah Sellers, with his genial optimism and easy political ethics, was an epitome of the political hopes of the Gilded Age. With a Micawber-like faith in his country and his government, eager to realize on his expansive dreams and looking to the national treasury to scatter its fructifying millions in the neighborhood of his speculative holdings, he was no other than Uncle Sam in the boisterous days following Appomattox. The hopes that floated up out of his dreams were the hopes of millions who cast their votes for Republican Congressmen who in return were expected to cast their votes for huge governmental appropriations that would insure prosperity's reaching certain post-office addresses. Citizens had saved the government in the trying days that were past; it was only fair in return that government should aid the patriotic citizen in the necessary work of developing national resources. It was paternalism as understood by speculators and subsidy-hunters, but was it not a part of the great American System that was to make the country rich and self-sufficient? The American System had been talked of for forty years; it had slowly got on its feet in pre-war days despite the stubborn planter opposition; now at last it had fairly come into its own. The time was ripe for the Republican party to become a fairy godmother to the millions of Beriah Sellerses throughout the North and West.

It is plain as a pikestaff why the spirit of Whiggery should have taken riotous possession of the Gilded Age. With its booming industrial cities America in 1870 was fast becoming capitalistic, and in every capitalistic society Whiggery springs up as naturally as pigweed in a garden. However attractive the disguises it may assume, it is in essence the logical creed of the profit philosophy. It is the expression in politics of the acquisitive instinct and it assumes as the greatest good the shaping of public policy to promote private interests. It asserts that it is a duty of the state to help its citizens to make money, and it conceives of the political state as a useful instrument for effective exploitation. How otherwise? The public good cannot be served apart from business interests, for business interests are the public good and in serving business the state is serving society. Everybody's eggs are in the basket and they must not be broken. For a capitalistic society Whiggery is the only rational politics, for it exalts the profit-motive as the sole object of parliamentary concern. Government has only to wave its wand and fairy gifts descend upon business like the golden sands of Pactolus. It graciously bestows its tariffs and subsidies, and streams of wealth flow into private wells.

But unhappily there is a fly in the Whiggish honey. In a competitive order, government is forced to make its choices. It cannot serve both Peter and Paul. If it gives with one hand it must take away with the other. And so the persuasive ideal of paternalism in the common interest degenerates in practice into legalized favoritism. Governmental gifts go to the largest investments. Lesser interests are sacrificed to greater interests and Whiggery comes finally to serve the lords of the earth without whose good will the wheels of business will not turn. To him that hath shall be given. If the few do not prosper the many will starve, and if the many have bread who would begrudge the few their abundance? In Whiggery is the fulfillment of the Scriptures.

Henry Clay had been a prophetic figure pointing the way America was to travel; but he came a generation too soon. A son of the Gilded Age, he was doomed to live in a world of Jacksonian democracy. But the spirit of Henry Clay survived his death and his followers were everywhere in the land. The plain citizen who wanted a slice of the rich prairie land of Iowa or Kansas, with a railway convenient to his homestead, had learned to look to the government for a gift, and if he got his quarter-section and his transportation he was careless about what the other fellow got. A little more or less could make no difference to a country inexhaustible in resources. America belonged to the American people and not to the government, and resources in private hands paid taxes and increased the national wealth. In his favorite newspaper, the *New York Tribune,* he read daily appeals for the adoption of a patriotic national economy, by means of which an infant industrialism, made prosperous by a protective tariff, would provide a home market for the produce of the farmer and render the country self-sufficient. Money would thus be put in everybody's pocket. Protection was not robbing Peter to pay Paul, but paying both Peter and Paul out of the augmented wealth of the whole.

The seductive arguments that Horace Greeley disseminated amongst the plain people, Henry Carey purveyed to more intelligent ears. The most distinguished American economist of the time, Carey had abandoned his earlier *laissez-faire* position, and having convinced himself that only through a close-knit national economy could the country develop a well-rounded economic program, he had become the most ardent of protectionists. During the fifties and later he was tireless in popularizing the doctrine of a natural harmony of interests between agriculture and manufacturing, and to a generation expanding rapidly in both fields his able presentation made great appeal. It was but a step from protectionism to governmental subsidies. Beriah Sellers and Henry Clay had come to be justified by the political economists. (Note that amongst Carey's converts were such different idealists as Wendell Phillips and Peter Cooper.)

IV

THE GREAT BARBECUE

Horace Greeley and Henry Carey were only straws in the wind that during the Gilded Age was blowing the doctrine of paternalism about the land. A Colonel Sellers was to be found at every fireside talking the same blowsy doctrine. Infectious in their optimism, naïve in their faith that something would be turned up for them by the government if they made known their wants, they were hoping for dollars to be put in their pockets by a generous administration at Washington. Congress had rich gifts to bestow—in lands, tariffs, subsidies, favors of all sorts; and when influential citizens made their wishes known to the reigning statesmen, the sympathetic politicians were quick to turn the government into the fairy godmother the voters wanted it to be. A huge barbecue was spread to which all presumably were invited. Not quite all, to be sure; inconspicuous persons, those who were at home on the farm or at work in the mills and offices, were overlooked; a good many indeed out of the total number of the American people. But all the important persons, leading bankers and promoters and business men, received invitations. There wasn't room for everybody and these were presumed to represent the whole. It was a splendid feast. If the waiters saw to it that the choicest portions were served to favored guests, they were not unmindful of their numerous homespun constituency and they loudly proclaimed the fine democratic principle that what belongs to the people should be enjoyed by the people—not with petty bureaucratic restrictions, not as a social body, but as individuals, each free citizen using what came to hand for his own private ends, with no questions asked.

It was sound Gilded Age doctrine. To a frontier people what was more democratic than a barbecue, and to a paternalistic age what was more fitting than that the state should provide the beeves for roasting. Let all come and help themselves. As a result the feast was Gargantuan in its rough plenty. The abundance was what was to be expected of a generous people. More food, to be sure, was spoiled than was eaten, and the revelry was a bit unseemly; but it was a fine spree in the name of the people, and the invitations had been written years before by Henry Clay. But unfortunately what was intended to be jovially democratic was marred by displays of plebeian temper. Suspicious commoners with better eyes than manners discovered the favoritism of the waiters and drew attention to the difference between their own meager helpings and the heaped-up plates of more favored guests. It appeared indeed that there was gross discrimination in the service; that the farmers' pickings from the Homestead Act were scanty in comparison with the speculators' pickings from the railway land-grants. The *Crédit Mobilier* scandal and the Whisky Ring scandal and divers other scandals came near to breaking up the feast, and the genial host—who was no other than the hero of Appomattox—came in for some sharp criticism. But after the more careless ones who were caught with their fingers where they didn't belong, had been thrust from the table, the eating and drinking went on again till only the great carcasses were left. Then at last came the reckoning. When the bill was sent in to the American people the farmers discovered that they had been put off with the giblets while the capitalists were consuming the turkey. They learned that they were no match at a barbecue for more voracious guests, and as they went home unsatisfied, a sullen anger burned in their hearts that was to express itself later in fierce agrarian revolts.

What reason there was for such anger, how differently rich and poor fared at the democratic feast, is suggested by the contrast between the Homestead Act and the Union Pacific land-grant. Both were war-time measures and both had emerged from the agitations of earlier decades. By the terms of the former the homesteader got his hundred and sixty acres at the price of $1.25 an acre; by the terms of the latter the promoters got a vast empire for nothing. It was absurd, of course, but what would you have? The people wanted the railway built and Collis P. Huntington was willing to build it on his own terms. The government was too generous to haggle with public-spirited citizens, and too Whiggish to want to discourage individual enterprise. Ever since the cession of California there had been much talk of a continental railway to tie the country together. In the first years the talk in Congress had all been of a great national venture; the road must be built by the nation to serve the common interests of the American people. But unfortunately sectional jeal-

ousies prevented any agreement as to the route the survey lines were
to run, and the rising capitalism was becoming powerful enough to
bring into disfavor any engagement of the government in a work
that promised great rewards. Under its guidance political opinion
was skillfully turned into the channel of private enterprise. The
public domain backed by the public credit, it was agreed, must pay
for the road, but the government must not seek to control the enterprise or look to profit from it directly; the national reward would
come indirectly from the opening-up of vast new territories.

The definite shift in policy came about the year 1855. In 1837
Stephen A. Douglas had been the driving force behind the state
enterprise of building the Illinois Central Railway. In 1853 he proposed that the Pacific Railroad should be built by private enterprise.
With the change promptly came a request for a patriotic land-grant.
The government was expected to provide the road, it appeared, but
private enterprise was to own it and manage it in the interest of
speculators rather than the public. For old-fashioned souls like
Thomas A. Benton, who still remembered the Jeffersonian concern
for the common well-being, it was a bitter mess to swallow.

> I would have preferred [he said] that Congress should have made
> the road, as a national work, on a scale commensurate with its grandeur
> and let out the use of it to companies, who would fetch and carry on
> the best terms for the people and the government. But that hope has
> vanished . . . a private company has become the resource and the
> preference. I embrace it as such, utterly scouting all plans for making
> private roads at national expense, of paying for the use of roads built
> with our land and money, of bargaining with corporations or indi-
> viduals for the use of what we give them.[3]

With this speech the old Jeffersonianism pulled down its flag and
the new Whiggery ran up its black banner. The Gilded Age had
begun and Old Bullion Benton had outlived his time. In the tumultuous decades that followed there was to be no bargaining with
corporations for the use of what the public gave; they took what they
wanted and no impertinent questions were asked. The hungriest
will get the most at the barbecue. A careless wastefulness when the
supply is unlimited is perhaps natural enough. There were hard-

[3] Quoted in J. P. Davis, *The Union Pacific Railway*, pp. 67-68.

headed men in the world of Beriah Sellers who knew how easy it was to overreach the simple, and it was they who got most from the common pot. We may call them buccaneers if we choose, and speak of the great barbecue as a democratic debauch. But why single out a few, when all were drunk? Whisky was plentiful at barbecues, and if too liberal potations brought the Gilded Age to the grossest extravagancies, if when it cast up accounts it found its patrimony gone, it was only repeating the experience of a certain man who went down to Jericho. To create a social civilization requires sober heads, and in this carousal of economic romanticism sober heads were few— the good Samaritan was busy elsewhere.

The doctrine of preëmption and exploitation was reaping its harvest. The frontier spirit was having its splurge, and progress was already turning its face in another direction. Within the next half-century this picturesque America with its heritage of crude energy— greedy, lawless, capable—was to be transformed into a vast uniform middle-class land, dedicated to capitalism and creating the greatest machine-order known to history. A scattered agricultural people, steeped in particularistic jealousies and suspicious of centralization, was to be transformed into an urbanized factory people, rootless, migratory, drawn to the job as by a magnet. It was to come about the more easily because the American farmer had never been a land-loving peasant, rooted to the soil and thriving only in daily contact with familiar acres. He had long been half middle-class, accounting unearned increment the most profitable crop, and buying and selling land as if it were calico. And in consequence the vigorous individualism that had sprung from frontier conditions decayed with the passing of the frontier, and those who had lost in the gamble of preëmption and exploitation were added to the growing multitude of the proletariat. It was from such materials, supplemented by a vast influx of immigrants, that was fashioned the America we know today with its standardized life, its machine culture, its mass psychology— an America to which Jefferson and Jackson and Lincoln would be strangers.

T. HARRY WILLIAMS

THE PASSING years have seen a deepening of understanding of the Reconstruction period. But added penetration has revealed new complexities in the subject matter, and historians have as much difficulty as ever in agreeing upon the facts and their meaning. Sectional biases have declined in intensity, but equally compulsive ideologies have taken their place.

The first historical accounts of the Reconstruction period were animated by the same passions which had accompanied the Civil War. The Northerns were certain that Congressional policy was wise and just; southern writers attacked the same policy as vindictive and unconstitutional. These partisan interpretations gradually lessened as the memory of the war receded and its participants died of old age. By the turn of the century, William A. Dunning began to establish at Columbia University a school of Northern scholars who could deal sympathetically with the South.

Dunning's pioneer work is notable not only because of its reappraisal of Northern leadership but also because of its attempt to place Reconstruction politics in a broader context. Forward-looking in conception and conciliatory in mood, his work was sufficiently attractive to dominate Reconstruction scholarship for several decades and to establish an interpretative norm.

However, this unity gradually disappeared. Criticisms of Dunning multiplied as a new generation of "revisionists" began a re-examination of every phase of postwar culture. His effort to furnish a national economic background for Southern Reconstruction was condemned as superficial and inadequate. Some scholars suggested that in breaking through the cobweb of Northern prejudice, Dunning had made assumptions involving another kind of distortion—the idea of the racial inferiority of Negroes. Indeed, it has been argued that he did not arrive at an essentially new interpretation but had simply accepted the Southern position.

Despite these attacks, the influence of Dunning has continued, and many scholars continue to share his point of view, emphasizing the evils of "Radical Reconstruction." His critics have usually been more sympathetic to the actions of Congress, although the degree of approbation has varied greatly. At the extreme left are the historians who applaud what was done but do not think that the federal government was radical enough. There is a middle stand which finds merit in some of the Reconstruction legislation, yet condemns the use of military means to enforce it.

These brief remarks scarcely suggest, let alone summarize, the variety and the heat which characterize the current investigation of this difficult subject. In the article that follows, T. Harry Williams has reviewed many of the recent trends in interpretation, and skillfully compared the differences among them. Much of the material he discusses first appeared in journals which are relatively inaccessible to the student. In addition, Williams offers some penetrating suggestions in the still undeveloped field of the motivations of significant groups in the Reconstruction drama. Although the motives of Northern politicians and influential businessmen have been examined, relatively little attention has been given to the reasoning of the planters, the middle-class whites, and the Negroes, whose votes were so important in determining the direction of Southern government.

If Williams and the scholars whose work he describes have

raised more problems than they have solved, they have at least gathered sufficient evidence to destroy the familiar stereotypes and to indicate the main lines upon which a more accurate picture of the Reconstruction period must be drawn.

An Analysis of Some Reconstruction Attitudes

IN LATE YEARS revisionist historians have done much to correct the existing and often distorted picture of the Reconstruction period in American history. Earlier writers on Reconstruction, whether they were Republican politicians or southern polemicists, journalists, or historians, exhibited a number of historical deficiencies, but in general it may be said that they told a story that was too simple and naïve. It was simple in that the terrible complexities of Reconstruction were presented in the easy terms of stereotypes—the good white Southern Democrats fighting against the bad colored Republicans and their insidious northern allies, or vice versa. It was naïve in that virtually no analysis was made to explain why people acted as they did. Thus carpetbaggers were dishonest because they were bad men or Republicans, but no attempt was made to describe the forces which contributed to their dishonesty. The revisionists have forced several modifications in the Reconstruction story. They have demonstrated, among other things, that the corruption of the Reconstruction state governments has been exaggerated and that in any case corruption was a national, not a purely southern, phenomenon, with an expanding capitalism as the chief corrupting agent; that Democrats were quite as willing as Republicans to be bought by business; that the supposed astronomically high appropriations of the Reconstruction governments seem so only in

From *The Journal of Southern History*, XII (1946), 469-486, by permission of the editor of the journal and of the author.

comparison with the niggardly budgets of the planter-controlled governments of the ante-bellum period; that although the Reconstruction governments were corrupt and dishonest, they must be credited with definite progress in the fields of popular education and internal improvements; and that the national reconstruction program was radical only in a superficial sense in that it gave political power to the Negro but failed to provide economic power through the promised confiscation and ownership of land, and thus that because the position of the Negro had no lasting basis his rule was easily overthrown.[1]

These new viewpoints have provided a desirable balance and proportion to the traditional historical treatment of Reconstruction. Still debated and in part unexplored in research are the motives of the northern and southern people during this period. Who supported Reconstruction and why; and who opposed it, and why? In analyzing the motivation of Reconstruction, historians have devoted most of their attention to northern political and economic groups and have produced certain conclusions which have been generally accepted. What may be termed the Beale thesis, because it has been most competently developed by Professor Howard K. Beale, offers a sectional-class explanation of Reconstruction. According to this thesis, Reconstruction was a successful attempt by northeastern business, acting through the Republican party, to control the national government for its own economic ends: notably, the protective tariff, the national banks, a "sound" currency. To accomplish its program, the business class had to overthrow from the seats of power the old ruling agrarian class of the South and West. This it did by inaugurating Reconstruction, which made the South Republican, and by selling its policies to the voters wrapped up in such attractive vote-getting packages as northern patriotism or the bloody

[1] Francis B. Simkins, "New Viewpoints of Southern Reconstruction," in *Journal of Southern History* (Baton Rouge, 1935-   ), V (1939), 49-61; Howard K. Beale, "On Rewriting Reconstruction History," in *American Historical Review* (New York, 1895-   ), XLV (1940), 807-27; Horace Mann Bond, "Social and Economic Forces in Alabama Reconstruction," in *Journal of Negro History* (Washington, 1916-   ), XXIII (1938), 290-348. These writers do two things that so many writers on the subject have not done: they treat Reconstruction as a national development rather than as something happening in an insulated South, and they relate it to southern forces before and after Reconstruction.

shirt.[2] Another student of the period, while accepting the Beale thesis, points out that northern business men supported Reconstruction not only because of national issues but also because they thought it would enable them to exploit the South through protected capital investments, and that Republican bosses supported Reconstruction because they believed that if the South could be made Republican they could stay in power.[3]

The Negro author, W. E. Burghardt Du Bois, conceding the part played by industry in formulating the Reconstruction program, contends that there was in the North a substantial mass opinion of liberal idealism, which he calls "abolition-democracy," that stood for a democratic reconstruction plan, including equal rights for Negroes. This group, he insists, represented in politics by men like Thaddeus Stevens, was equally influential with business in determining the nature of Reconstruction.[4] The existence of such a body of opinion cannot be disputed. That it was as extensive as Du Bois thinks or that it was animated by as much idealism for the Negro may well be doubted; unfortunately there is no way to document accurately its numbers or influence. One thing is certain. The leaders of abolition-democracy did not succeed in incorporating their ideas into the Republican reconstruction scheme. They demanded universal suffrage, universal amnesty, and confiscation of the land of rich Southerners and its distribution among the freedmen. The Republican politicos, being economic reactionaries, discarded confiscation because they had no interest in bringing about a social revolution, and they rejected universal amnesty because it would

[2] Howard K. Beale, *The Critical Year: A Study of Andrew Johnson and Reconstruction* (New York: 1930), 1, 8, 115, 143-45; Beale, "On Rewriting Reconstruction History," *loc. cit.,* 813.

[3] William B. Hesseltine, "Economic Factors in the Abandonment of Reconstruction," in *Mississippi Valley Historical Review* (Cedar Rapids, 1914-   ), XXII (1935), 191-210. See also, Hesseltine, *The South in American History* (New York, 1943), 488-89.

[4] W. E. Burghardt Du Bois, *Black Reconstruction: An Essay toward a History of the Part which Black Folk Played in the Attempt to Reconstruct Democracy in America, 1860-1880* (New York, 1938), 182, 185-87. Beale, in his article, "On Rewriting Reconstruction History," *loc. cit.,* 818-19, admitted that there were minority elements of democratic idealism in the Republican party and that Stevens and Charles Sumner were representatives of these elements. For the contrary view that Stevens thought solely in terms of power for his class and party, see Richard N. Current, *Old Thad Stevens: A Story of Ambition* (Madison, 1942).

have made a Republican South improbable. It would seem that the party bosses, instead of being influenced to any considerable degree by abolition-democracy, used it for whatever it was worth to marshal support for a program designed to benefit a plutocratic minority.

An interpretation of northern motivation that differs in part from both Beale and Du Bois has come from Marxist historians and writers.[5] The Marxian thesis has been elaborately presented by James S. Allen,[6] who regards Reconstruction as a plan formulated and carried through by big business to enable it to dominate the nation. Up to a point, this is only the Beale thesis dressed up in Marxian jargon. Allen, however, proceeds to advance the claim that the business program was "democratic," because industry, in achieving power, smashed the old, feudal planter class of the South and thus helped prepare the way for the coming of the industrial state which, after business itself was smashed, would evolve into a perfect democracy of the Marxist variety.[7] In recent years writers of Marxist persuasion have dropped Allen's emphasis on the class struggle, and have presented Reconstruction as a straight-out plan of equalitarian democracy. The new departure has been most strikingly expressed, in fictional form, by Howard Fast, who flatly states that the Reconstruction acts of 1867 were intended "to create a new democracy in the South."[8] The Marxian thesis in any of these forms has little validity. No amount of historical legerdemain can transform the economic reactionaries of the Republican party into great liberals or make the protective tariff and the gold standard into items of the democratic faith. Furthermore, as will be shown, the Marxists are wrong when they try to develop the corollary that Reconstruction was also a democratic process in the South.[9]

[5] The term Marxist is here applied to those writers who frankly state that they are interpreting history according to the laws and predictions of Karl Marx and to those who without acknowledging Marx write history that conforms to the Marxian pattern.

[6] James S. Allen, *Reconstruction: The Battle for Democracy, 1865-1867* (New York, 1937).

[7] *Ibid.*, 18, 22, 81, 89.

[8] Howard Fast, *Freedom Road* (New York, 1944), 71.

[9] It is significant that those Negroes who envisioned Reconstruction as a real social revolution for their people saw little idealism in the Republican party. Thus the New Orleans *Tribune*, a Negro newspaper, said: "The Republican party of the North was not formed upon the true basis of justice and equality, as the history of abolition and slavery plainly shows; and it has only the right to

The sectional-class thesis of Beale would seem to be the most nearly correct analysis of northern motivation, although Beale did not fully explain how northeastern business persuaded agrarian Republicans from the Middle West to support industrial measures and a reconstruction policy designed to insure the rule of business in the South. It has since been demonstrated that this was done in part by giving the Middle West exceptionally generous appropriations for internal improvements and in effect buying its support;[10] and to this should be added such other inducements as free land, pensions, and railroads, as well as such emotional and psychological appeals as habitual use of the bloody shirt. Du Bois was also undoubtedly correct in contending that idealistic forces played a part in shaping reconstruction policy, and his point is a good, although minor, corrective to the purely economic analysis. But the major fact remains that the men who made Reconstruction were moved by issues of economic and political power far more than by democratic idealism.

While the question of northern motivation has been fairly well established, there has been little attempt to prepare a systematic analysis of southern attitudes toward Reconstruction. Most of the professional historians writing on southern reconstruction have been members of or followers of the so-called Dunning school. They are largely responsible for the familiar stereotypes of Reconstruction. According to their interpretation, Reconstruction was a battle between two extremes: the Democrats, as the group which included the vast majority of the whites, standing for decent government and racial supremacy, versus the Republicans, the Negroes, alien carpetbaggers, and renegade scalawags, standing for dishonest government and alien ideals. These historians wrote literally in terms of white and black. This is not to say that they did not recognize the fact that there were differences between Southerners on such issues as

claim credit for having abolished slavery as a political necessity and of having given the ballot to the black men as an arm of defence to the loyal white men. Emergency, nay necessity, had more to do with the abolition of slavery and the passage of the Military Bill than had philanthropy and love for the negro." Quoted in New Orleans *Times*, July 4, 1873.

10 Helen J. and T. Harry Williams, "Wisconsin Republicans and Reconstruction, 1865-1870)," in *Wisconsin Magazine of History* (Madison, 1917-   ), XXIII (1939), 17-39.

Negro suffrage. But they explained the differences in terms of individual motivation. Thus Southerners who advocated the vote for Negroes were either bad men, or wartime Unionists who hated "rebels," or kindly planters who knew Negroes well and wanted to control their votes in the right direction. Although the Dunning writers sensed an apparent disagreement between the planter-business class and the small farmers on the Negro question, with the planters being willing to accept a position of greater equality for the Negro, they did not explore the difference or try to ascertain whether there were economic and social causes for its existence.[11]

No such reluctance characterizes Du Bois. He boldly proclaims that Reconstruction was a labor movement, an attempt by the white and black proletariat to control the South, "a vision of democracy across racial lines."[12] A basic error invalidates most of his thesis. There was no white proletariat of any significant numbers; the great mass of the whites were yeoman farmers who thought in terms of racial supremacy instead of class solidarity. Furthermore, he exaggerates the readiness of the former non-slaveholding whites to unite with the Negroes. He himself recognizes that there are factual weaknesses in his theory. He knows that the common whites furnished the power by which the Republican state governments were overthrown; but he explains this disturbing fact by claiming that the planters cut off the developing interracial co-operation of the proletariat by appealing to the prejudices of the poorer whites and organizing them on the color line.[13] Closely paralleling Du Bois' interpretation, and even going beyond it, is that of the Marxists.

[11] The views of the Dunning school are in William A. Dunning, *Reconstruction: Political and Economic, 1865-1877* (New York, 1907), especially pp. 116-17, 213; Walter L. Fleming, *The Sequel of Appomattox: A Chronicle of the Reunion of the States* (New Haven, 1921), especially pp. 47-48, 50-52, 87-88. These criticisms of Dunning and Fleming are not made in any carping spirit. It is recognized that they and other members of the Dunning school were pioneers in the study of Reconstruction and made important factual contributions to its history. It should also be noted that Fleming was aware that many planters were for Negro suffrage and that most farmers were against it. See his *Civil War and Reconstruction in Alabama* (New York: 1905), 387-88. But he ascribed the planters' attitude merely to a desire to control the Negro vote in order to maintain their power in the legislature.

[12] Du Bois, *Black Reconstruction,* 346-47, 350.

[13] *Ibid.,* 130-31. These criticisms of Du Bois do not detract from the fact that his book was a valuable contribution to Reconstruction history. In some respects he got closer to the truth of Reconstruction than any other writer.

They, too, present Reconstruction as a biracial movement of the laboring class which was finally destroyed by a counter-revolution of the planters.[14] According to Howard Fast, the Negroes and poor whites joined hands in the Republican party and created "a fine, a just, and a truly democratic civilization," but the reactionary planter class refused to permit this experiment in social democracy and wiped it out with force.[15] That the validity of such assertions is open to serious question can be shown by examining the attitude of the planters and business men in Louisiana toward Reconstruction and the Negro and placing the results in the larger setting of what is known about the general attitudes of the southern whites in other parts of the region.

First of all, despite the opinions of the Marxists, the overwhelming mass of the people—the yeoman farmers, middle class whites, and poor whites—were fiercely opposed to Negro suffrage and to any condition of equality for the Negro. The evidence on this point, while not voluminous because of the general inarticulateness of the common whites, is strong; it is best expressed by the fact that the small-farmer, white-belt areas of the southern states voted heavily against Republicans and Republican measures in election after election.[16] As Horace Mann Bond puts it, the farmers hated equally slavery, planters, and Negroes.[17] The attitude of the common whites of Reconstruction is consonant with the known attitude of the poorest whites, economically, today; that is, racial antipathy toward Negroes is always sharpest when accentuated by economic competition. The teachings of social psychology can be adduced to support the generalization concerning the reaction of the whites. In a caste

[14] Allen, *Reconstruction*, 111-15, 126, 183-84, 193. On different pages Allen states that a significant portion of the common whites joined the Republican party and again that practically all of them did. The book as a whole gives the impression that the poorer whites as a class became Republicans.

[15] Fast, *Freedom Road*, 263.

[16] Paul Lewinson, *Race, Class, and Party: A History of Negro Suffrage in the South* (New York, 1932), 23, 37, 52; Roger W. Shugg, *Origins of Class Struggle in Louisiana: A Social History of White Farmers and Laborers during Slavery and After, 1840-1875* (Baton Rouge, 1939), 230; Hesseltine, *South in American History*, 485; Dunning, *Reconstruction*, 213; Fleming, *Sequel of Appomattox*, 47-48, 50, 87-88; Fleming, *Civil War and Reconstruction in Alabama*, 387-88.

[17] Bond, "Social and Economic Factors in Alabama Reconstruction," *loc. cit.*, 294-95. Bond finds that at the beginning of Reconstruction there was some political co-operation between poor whites and Negroes.

system based on a fixed status for groups, any attempt by a sub-
ordinated element—in this case the Negroes—to achieve a higher
status unlooses feelings of tension and fear in the next higher
group, which will exert itself, often violently, to keep the sub-
ordinated group down.[18]

The most powerful group in the South was the planter-business
class and its professional allies; its position on Reconstruction was
of decisive importance. In the beginning days of Reconstruction, the
planters and business men strongly opposed the central proposal
of the Radical Republican program—suffrage for the Negro. But
they opposed it for economic rather than racial reasons. This fact is
crucially important in understanding their reactions. To use modern
terms, they feared that the grant of the ballot to the Negro would
add to the strength of the liberal or progressive vote. This is not
to say that they did not regard the Negro as an inferior being of an
entirely separate race. But it is to say that they reacted to a proposal
to enfranchise a laboring class as would any propertied minority
in any society—they opposed it because they believed it would lead
to an attack upon property.[19] A few quotations selected from many
statements appearing in conservative New Orleans newspapers
which were spokesmen of the planter-business interests will demonstrate the point. Terming universal suffrage a menace to property,
the New Orleans *Times* said: "The right to vote should be given
to those only who can use it with discretion and sound judgment,
and as our electoral privileges are already too wide, it would be the
maddest folly to extend them at once to a class who have always
been under control, and who—without the ability to form a correct
judgment for themselves—would be left to the tender mercies of
party tricksters." Let the Negro wait until he acquired property be-

18 Kimball Young, *Social Psychology* (New York, 1944), 262-63, 269.
19 There was logic in this position. Many of the Negro leaders were exponents
of radical agrarianism. Said the New Orleans *Tribune*: "There is no more room
in the organization of our society, for an oligarchy of slaveholders, or property
holders"; and again, "There is in fact, no true republican government, unless
the land, and wealth in general, are distributed among the great mass of the inhabitants." Quoted in Du Bois, *Black Reconstruction*, 458-59. This agrarianism
never secured any significant victories because the carpetbaggers, scalawags, and
professional Negro politicians, interested mainly in corruption and power, choked
it off. See Shugg, *Origins of Class Struggle in Louisiana*, 243-44.

fore he became a voter.[20] In a fuller and more philosophical exposition of its views, the *Times* stated:

> Wherever voters greatly outnumber property holders, property will assuredly be unsafe. When voters have property and intelligence, there is some hope that they may "find their interest in the interest of the community" and be anxious to secure a consistent, honest, economical and straight-forward administration. But the selfish interest of the non-property holding voter lies in an altogether different direction. He wishes to secure rich pickings, and, too frequently, soils his fingers by base bribes. Were universal negro suffrage to be added to the white universal suffrage now existing in the South, the security of both life and property would be greatly weakened. . . . With our present too widely extended suffrage it is difficult even now to steer between the rocks of the political Scylla and the whirlpool of its Charybdis, and with universal negro suffrage added, the task would be wholly hopeless.[21]

Becoming frankly specific, the *Times* later declared that "If representative institutions are to be preserved in this country, the control of taxes must be left to those who pay them, and the protection of property to those who own it."[22] The New Orleans *Crescent*, endorsing the proposal of South Carolina's planter leader, Wade Hampton, to extend the vote to Negroes who had acquired property and an education,[23] asserted: "Southern conservatives ask nothing more on the subject of suffrage than that its distribution shall be determined by the test of character and intelligence. They have asked for nothing more from the time that, by one of the irreversible results of war, the Southern negroes became a part of the free population of the country. It is not their fault if such a test has been rejected in favor of another that proscribes a large proportion of the highest intelligence on the one hand, and opens all political functions to the maximum of ignorance on the other."[24] Expressing the conserva-

20 New Orleans *Times*, August 13, 1865.

21 *Ibid.*, December 24, 1866.

22 *Ibid.*, February 2, 1868. There are similar statements in the issues of November 26, 30, 1866, January 26, 1867.

23 Hampton, Alexander H. Stephens, Benjamin F. Perry, and other leaders had suggested a limited Negro suffrage based on property and education, thus permitting only those Negroes to vote who were conscious of property rights. Hampton believed the planters could easily control such voters. Lewinson, *Race, Class, and Party*, 37-39; Fleming, *Sequel of Appomattox*, 50-52.

24 New Orleans *Crescent*, October 23, 1867.

tives' fear of the economic implications of Negro suffrage, the *Crescent* said: "It seems to be practically absurd and dangerous to commit the decisions of those difficult questions to numbers of extemporized citizens incapable of forming any accurate or rational opinions; and likely to imagine that the right to vote means the right to live without work, and to rob the industrious classes for the benefit of the idle and thriftless."[25] The *Picayune* denounced Negro suffrage because it did not believe that common men of any color should vote; manhood suffrage was "the unlimited suffrage of the ignorant, landless and lawless."[26] "We look upon it [voting] as a duty rather than a right," said the *Picayune,* "and regret that there is so much of it among the whites."[27] To the *Picayune,* Reconstruction was a process that proscribed "intelligence, probity and property" and elevated propertyless nobodies to power.[28]

To the testimony of conservative newspapers can be added representative statements of conservative planter-business leaders. In 1867, when Congress was considering the radical reconstruction acts, various southern newspapers asked prominent individuals to give their reactions to the proposed measures. More frank and philosophical than most was J. W. Robb of Mississippi. He warned conservatives that all republics in history had fallen when they had extended the ballot to a laboring class, "an ignorant horde of stupid and besotted men." "I believe," he continued, "that from the introduction of negro suffrage, the worst form and spirit of agrarianism will arise to disturb the peace and order of the State, and that it will require our utmost exertions to keep it down, and retain for ourselves political existence and individual security."[29] Francis T. Nicholls, who became governor of Louisiana in 1877 when white supremacy supposedly was restored, told a Congressional committee that conservatives were opposed to Reconstruction because it had endangered property interests by placing ignorance in power. Before Reconstruction, he said, there had been a relatively small group of ignorant white voters whom the rich could control, but Reconstruc-

25 *Ibid.,* May 14, 1868.
26 New Orleans *Daily Picayune,* May 10, 1868.
27 *Ibid.,* May 23, 1868.
28 *Ibid.,* May 24, 1868.
29 J. W. Robb, in Jackson *Clarion,* March 19, 1868, quoted in New Orleans *Times,* March 22.

tion had made ignorance "the dominating power." He favored a law that in the interest of property would disfranchise the ignorant of both races.[30]

Congress ignored the opposition to Negro suffrage of the planter-business class, based primarily on economic grounds, and of the common whites, based primarily on racial grounds. In 1867 it passed the reconstruction laws of the Radical Republicans; and Negro suffrage and, in many states, Negro rule became a reality. There followed a period of years, varying in different states, in which the Republican party, led by white carpetbaggers and scalawags and composed predominantly of the Negro masses, controlled the South. The political record of its rule was a compound of blatant corruption and forward social legislation. It was an expensive program. Money was needed to gratify the desires of the white and colored politicians for graft and of the colored masses for social services furnished by the state. The Republicans had to resort to higher and higher taxation, and necessarily they laid the heaviest taxes upon real property. While taxation affected all property holders, large and small, the brunt of it fell upon the large holders. This, as Du Bois points out, is a crucial fact in Reconstruction history—a war-impoverished propertied class was being compelled by the votes of poor men to bear an almost confiscatory tax burden.[31]

Faced with extinction by taxation, the planter-business class reacted again and characteristically in economic rather than racial terms. Negro votes had imposed the tax burden. Negro votes could lift it. If in order to persuade the Negroes to do so it was necessary to grant them political and civil equality or even to let them run the state, well and good. Get the tax rate down, cried one New Orleans conservative, "even if every office in the State, from Governor to the most insignificant constable, were filled by a negro."[32] Urged another: "We must get rid of party hacks and political jobbers, and satisfy the reasonable demands of the negroes. This accomplished, Louisiana will again blossom as the rose. It is our only salvation."[33] A prominent merchant declared: "I am in favor, in case we ever have another election, of giving to the colored

[30] *House Reports,* 43 Cong., 2 Sess., No. 261, Part 3, pp. 646-47.
[31] Du Bois, *Black Reconstruction,* 590-91.
[32] Letter of Archibald Mitchell, in New Orleans *Picayune,* June 18, 1873.
[33] New Orleans *Times,* May 29, 1873.

people the bulk of the lucrative positions. . . . I am not afraid that they will, in any considerable degree abuse their privileges, and, for ourselves, we want nothing but peaceful government."[34] "You want civil equality; you shall have it," a leading business man pledged the Negroes, "if you forsake the Northern adventurer who has plundered poor Louisana until she is penniless."[35] On with political cooperation with Negroes, exclaimed a property holder, "for God's sake if it will give us an honest government; our present lot is insupportable."[36] A blunt Natchitoches planter asserted that is was imperative that the whites detach the Negroes from the Republicans: "When the war was over we wouldn't have anything to do with the niggers, and let the Radicals gobble them up. . . . I am in favor of anything to get them. Drop the name of Democracy, I say, and go in for the niggers."[37]

What practical political action did the planter-business class take during Reconstruction to protect itself from excessive taxation and to foster its economic interests? In local elections in New Orleans, for example, the business men contemplated putting up Negro candidates for Congressional and city offices to compete with white Republicans. On Carondelet Street, the city's great busines center, it was planned to nominate a colored foreman of one of the leading cotton presses for Congress. Such a man, asserted the business reporter of the New Orleans *Times,* "Will protect and do more for the South than any white Radical which can be selected to run against him. Carondelet street will go for the gentlemen with the cotton press."[38] The business men, this journalist explained, "are taking an unusual interest in being represented in Congress by a representative born in the South. The nearer approach to a real African, black in color, the more confidence will be placed in him."[39] Since the records do not show that the Carondelet magnates got their foreman nominated, it is probable that the Democratic leaders in New Orleans refused to take a Negro candidate, or even

34 *Ibid.,* May 30, 1873.
35 *Ibid.,* June 6, 1873.
36 *Ibid.,* June 23, 1873.
37 *Ibid.,* June 9, 1873.
38 *Ibid.,* August 13, 1867. "On 'Change" column. The business columns of the newspapers contain much information about the activities of business men in Reconstruction. Historians have overlooked this important source.
39 *Ibid.,* August 17, 1867. See also issue of September 5.

more probable that the cotton press gentleman, if he had political ambitions and an eye for the future, became a Republican. Regardless of the outcome, however, the episode demonstrated that these hardheaded business men placed their economic interests above racial differences and that they preferred to entrust those interests to an understanding and amenable Negro rather than to an untried white.

A second device adopted by the conservatives was to enter the Republican party and seek to control it. A recent study by David H. Donald illustrates how this was done in Mississippi.[40] After Radical Reconstruction went into effect most of the former Whigs, in antebellum times the party of the big slaveholders, became Republicans. "Such action is not hard to understand," writes Donald. "The Whigs were wealthy men—the large planters and the railroad and industrial promoters—who naturally turned to the party which in the state as in the nation was dominated by business interests."[41] At first these planters, or scalawags, to use a familiar term, dominated the party, but they lost their leadership to the carpetbaggers who, in the struggles for power within the party, were willing to promise more to the Negroes. Donald points to the planters' fruitless opposition to the Republican program of big budgets and high taxes and their revulsion against the social equality claimed by the Negroes as sources of their difficulties. Finally, repudiated by people they could not control, they drifted "slowly and reluctantly over to the Democratic camp."[42]

Still a third device employed by the planters and business men was to invite the Negroes to leave the Republicans and join with them in a new political organization separate from the Democratic party. The conservatives promised in such case to respect the Negro's civil equality and his right to vote and to hold office. Such movements were tried in several states,[43] the most elaborate being

[40] David H. Donald, "The Scalawag in Mississippi Reconstruction," in *Journal of Southern History*, X (1944), 447-60.

[41] *Ibid.*, 449-50.

[42] *Ibid.*, 453-55.

[43] Francis B. Simpkins and Robert H. Woody, *South Carolina during Reconstruction* (Chapel Hill, 1932), 447-54; Alrutheus A. Taylor, *The Negro in South Carolina during the Reconstruction* (Washington, 1924), 195-97; John S. Reynolds, *Reconstruction in South Carolina, 1865-1877* (Columbia, 1905), 139-43; James W. Garner, *Reconstruction in Mississippi* (New York, 1901), 238-43.

the so-called "Louisiana Unification Movement."[44] Inaugurated in 1873, this movement was headed by General Pierre G. T. Beauregard and was supported by the flower of the wealth and culture of New Orleans and South Louisiana.[45] Its platform advocated complete political equality for the Negro, an equal division of state offices between the races, and a plan whereby Negroes would become landowners. The unifiers denounced discrimination because of color in hiring laborers or in selecting directors of corporations, and called for the abandonment of segregation in public conveyances, public places, railroads, steamboats, and the public schools.[46] The Louisiana movement, like the others, failed for lack of support from the white masses. The unification program was popular in New Orleans and in the plantation belt of South Louisiana, but in the small-farmer areas of other parts of the state it was received with loathing and execration.

It is evident that a basis existed for an alliance of the planter-business class and the Negroes. "If they [the planters] had wished," writes Du Bois, "they could have held the Negro vote in the palm of their hands."[47] Why did such an alliance fail to materialize? In the first place, the leaders of the unification movements could not persuade any significant number of whites to support the concessions which the planters were willing to accord the colored people. The common whites, animated by racial motives, refused to follow planter leadership, and without any mass white support the unification movements could not succeed. In Louisiana the movement failed to develop much mass support even from the Negroes

[44] T. Harry Williams, "The Louisiana Unification Movement of 1873," in *Journal of Southern History*, XI (1945), 349-69.

[45] Beauregard believed that in the long run Negro suffrage would increase the political power of the South. The whites could control the Negroes "with a little education and some property qualifications" and "defeat our adversaries with their own weapon." Quoted in New York *Tribune*, April 1, 1867. For other expressions of a similar view, see *ibid.*, April 4, 1867, quoting Mobile *Tribune* and Wilmington (N. C.) *Dispatch*.

[46] Williams, "Louisiana Unification Movement," *loc. sit.*, 359-61. It is to be noted that rich whites could ask for the destruction of segregation without having to encounter many of the results of non-segregation. This was particularly true in education. As a North Louisiana newspaper pointed out, the rich sent their children to private white schools; the poorer whites had to send theirs to public schools which the rich proposed to make biracial. Shreveport *Times*, quoted in Monroe *Ouachita Telegraph*, June 28, 1873.

[47] Du Bois, *Black Reconstruction*, 611.

because professional Negro politicians, secure in their place in the Republican party, advised their followers to shun co-operation and because those Negro leaders who favored co-operation could not suppress their suspicion of the sincerity of the planter-business class. "We know that, by an alliance with you, we can have more privileges than we now enjoy," one Negro spokesman told the conservatives. "We will not then have to cling to the carpet-baggers for protection, but can ourselves take whatever share of office and representation falls to us fairly. Still, we have *some* rights now, and we don't intend to give them up. Rather than do that, we will cling to the carpet-bagger forever, and let him share our power."[48]

In the second place, the planters and business men, while willing to make far-reaching concessions to the Negroes, did not make them because they believed in the principles of racial equality. They made them because of pressing economic reasons and because they wanted to control the Negro vote. They never ceased to regard the Negroes as inferior creatures who by an unfortunate turn of fate had become politically powerful in the state. Hence there was a limit to their concessions, its line marked by anything that seemed to suggest social equality. The carpetbaggers, unhampered by such reservations, could always outbid the conservatives. Thus in states like Mississippi, where the planter tried to dominate the Republican party, the carpetbaggers took the leadership of the Negroes away from the scalawags. Finally, the differing economic aspirations of the wealthy whites and the Negroes prevented any lasting alliance of the two. The Negroes demanded a program of social services financed by the state, which meant high taxes. The planters wanted to control the colored vote in order to reduce these services and lower taxes which they considered almost confiscatory. The Negroes wanted higher wages and shorter hours; the planters wanted a serf-like system of sharecropping. The planter simply lacked the capital to finance the Negro's social or labor program;[49] but in view of the obvious conflict between the desires of the two groups it is doubtful whether such a program would have received support from the

48 New Orleans *Times*, May 28, 1873
49 This point is well developed in Du Bois, *Black Reconstruction*, 611-12.

planters even if they had possessed the necessary means for financing it.

And so the planters and business men, unable to prevent the establishment of Negro suffrage and unable to control it after it was established, joined with the common whites to overthrow the Republican state governments. By 1877 the Democrats controlled every southern state, and what the textbooks call white supremacy was restored. Actually, Negroes continued to vote, although in reduced numbers, and white supremacy was not restored until the 1890's. As Professor C. Vann Woodward has ably demonstrated, the men who came to power after Reconstruction were not in the old agrarian, planter tradition. They were often of the planter class, but in reality they were industrialists or would-be industrialists. They preached the industrialization of the South through the importation of Yankee capital, a policy of low taxes to attract business, and a political alliance with the Northeast instead of with the South's traditional ally, the West.[50] These men reacted to Negro suffrage as had men of their class during Reconstruction. As the vote of labor, it was something to be feared and kept in hand, but as the vote of an inferior people, it was also something that might be manipulated for the benefit of the wealthy. As events developed, the bosses of the New South sometimes found that they could use the colored vote to beat down attempts of the farmers to take over control of the Democratic party. In the election of 1880 in Georgia, for example, the rich defeated the farmers through a combination of a minority of the white votes and a majority of the colored ones.[51] The southern champions of industrialism, therefore, took no

---

[50] C. Vann Woodward, *Tom Watson: Agrarian Rebel* (New York, 1938), 58-72. For similar developments in other states, see Francis B. Simkins, *Pitchfork Ben Tillman, South Carolinian* (Baton Rouge, 1944), 79-80; Willie D. Halsell, "The Bourbon Period in Mississippi Politics, 1875-1890," in *Journal of Southern History*, XI (1945), 519-37.

[51] Woodward, *Tom Watson*, 80-81; Judson C. Ward, "The Republican Party in Bourbon Georgia, 1872-1890," in *Journal of Southern History*, IX (1943), 200. See, also, Simkins, *Pitchfork Ben Tillman*, 164, 167. The planters also employed the Negro vote against the Republicans. In 1884 Edward Gay, Democrat, was running for Congress from a South Louisiana district against Republican William P. Kellogg. Edward N. Pugh, Democratic leader of Ascension Parish, outlined for the sugar planters methods of swinging the colored vote behind Gay. Let owners and managers tell the Negro workers to vote for Gay, he advised: "They naturally receive with deference the expression of opinion by their employers on

action to disfranchise the Negro; they used him to maintain the supremacy of a few white men over other white men. Disfranchisement finally came as a result of the efforts of small-farmer leaders like Ben Tillman.[52]

Placed in the general setting, therefore, the interests and activities of the Louisiana planter-capitalist group serve to confirm the fact that the Reconstruction period was one of the most complex in American history. It witnessed the ending of a great civil struggle and the travail of postwar adjustment, the consummation of a momentous economic revolution, and a wrenching change in race relations. No less complex than the times were the motives that impelled people—northern and southern, white and black, rich and poor—to act as they did. No simple or generic explanation cast in the form of sectional stereotypes will supply the key to what happened. Economic, social, and political stimuli affected groups in the South in different ways, and Southerners differed among themselves on the issues of Reconstruction in about the same degree as did groups in the North. The planter-capitalist class of the South thought and acted in terms of economic self-interest in a fashion similar to the industrial magnates of the North. The important difference was that the business men carried the northern people with them while the planters were unable to convince the white masses in the South that economics transcended racial supremacy.

---

all subjects. . . . Nearly all the leading colored men are with us and they need only the offer of substantial moral support from the employers to swell the number of the supporters of Mr. Gay from the ranks of the colored employees." Edward N. Pugh to William Porcher Miles, October 30, 1884, in W. P. Miles Papers (Southern Historical Collection, University of North Carolina).

[52] Although the impetus for disfranchisement generally came from farmer leaders, the rich whites acquiesced in the movement. They did so partly out of a desire to placate the white masses and partly because the farmers, particularly during the agrarian unrest of the 1890's, sometimes tried to vote the Negroes on their side. The competition for the colored vote frightened many whites and forced the wealthy whites to pay out large monetary sums to retain their Negro supporters. Undoubtedly the planter-business class saw in disfranchisement a chance to eliminate a purchasable vote that was steadily becoming more expensive. See George M. Reynolds, *Machine Politics in New Orleans, 1897-1926* (New York, 1936), 21, 26-27, 29-30, 35. "As the situation had developed," writes Reynolds, "it seemed best to take the Negro vote off the market and leave only the white electorate with its comparatively small venal vote to be traded in on election day" (p. 26). For an itemized account of how much it cost the planters in one Louisiana parish to buy Negro votes in the election of 1892, and a complaint about the price, see Henry McCall to William Porcher Miles, May 4, 1892, in

PART II

THE RISE OF INDUSTRIAL AMERICA

ALLAN NEVINS

THE UNINITIATED may wonder why today's historians so often find it necessary to write new books on subjects about which so many old books have already been produced. When one surveys the catalogue of a large library, it is difficult to believe that there is any aspect of American history that has not been examined many times over.

Often this rewriting has its origin in the interests of the historian rather than in the discovery of new facts. A reshuffling of the historical records will bring to the top those aspects of the past which have most meaning today. Although this increases the "timeliness" of a work, it may lead to distortion as well. For example, it is possible that the religious motivation of the Puritans of Massachusetts Bay may be too much de-emphasized by current writers who concentrate on the development of our economic institutions or political democracy.

Part of the need for new books results from the fact that the definition of history has gradually broadened. A good deal of today's writing comes as a corrective to studies made at a time when history was considered merely a record of past politics. When historians discovered the necessity for relating political institutions to their economic and social environment, they found that previous writers had done comparatively little to supply a factual basis for such an analysis. A penetrating description of how the average American had lived, what forces motivated him, and how his needs were supplied simply did not exist.

The writing of social history presented special problems which even now are not completely resolved. Past generations have more often retained records of the outstanding than of the typical. The famous men made an indelible imprint, but the average citizen was consigned to oblivion. While the homes of Washington and Jefferson may be inspected, the rude shacks in which most of their contemporaries lived have disappeared. Even where extant materials are plentiful, there can be no assurance that the part of the past which remains is an accurate reflection of the whole. A proper appraisal requires techniques which are more the equipment of the sociologist than of the historian. Such men as Allan Nevins have made important contributions to the solution of these problems, but the ultimate answers lie in the future.

The first comprehensive effort to meet the need for social histories is contained in a series of thirteen volumes collectively called *A History of American Life*. It was completed, significantly enough, only within the last few years. Nevins' *The Emergence of Modern America*, which appeared in 1927, forms the seventh volume of the series; it concerns itself with the dominant social characteristics of the years immediately following the Civil War.

Nevins' extensive historical writings reflect a career which began in journalism and moved on to the field of academic scholarship. As a former journalist, Nevins has ever been mindful of the need for making history readable and intelligible. But unlike some others who consider it their task to make the presentation of history attractive rather than formidable, lively rather than pedantic, Nevins has not used his emphasis upon readability as an excuse for a superficial knowledge of his subject matter.

Nevins' reputation rests upon two kinds of writing. Twice awarded the Pulitzer Prize for biography, he has achieved lasting recognition for his lives of Grover Cleveland, Hamilton Fish, Abraham Hewitt, John Fremont, and John D. Rockefeller. Although his emphasis is upon the men rather than their times, the specific problems with which his political figures were concerned receive a detailed analysis. His accounts of businessmen describe in popular terms the industrial progress which helped to determine their course of action.

If Nevins is not associated with any new general theory of historical interpretation, he has shown a special talent for the difficult task of synthesizing the material of countless specialized studies into an understandable whole. *The Emergence of Modern America* displays this ability to give collective significance to thousands of isolated facts. In contrast to Parrington's approach, Nevins' is positive rather than negative; it is concerned with the constructive aspects of these years rather than with the moral deficiencies of the men who participated in them. While this approach does not lead him to omit mention of the unsavory atmosphere of the Grant administration and the criminality of such men as Jim Fiske and Jay Gould, it has been partly responsible for the criticism perhaps most often voiced of Nevins' work: that he has tended to point too favorable a picture of our national past.

Yet if this positivism constitutes a basis for criticism, it is also a source of the insight underlying his contribution. Living in an age of different social values, today's historian has many obstacles in the way of an appreciation of the crude, expansive years after the Civil War. Nevins has succeeded in offering convincing evidence that vulgarity and avariciousness did not preclude constructive achievement.

The Industrial Boom in the North

MEANWHILE the industrial North was pressing forward with a speed which seemed to leave all old landmarks behind and which year by year wrought new social changes. David A. Wells wrote in 1889 that to a generation whose memory covered only the years following 1860, "the recitation of the economic experiences and industrial conditions of the generation next preceding is very much akin to a recurrence to ancient history."[1] Economically the nation of 1865—a nation which had hardly advanced to the Missouri, which used iron alone, which had a modest railway system and but one and a half billion dollars invested in manufacturing—was a world away from the nation of 1878—a nation which had pressed to the Pacific, which was producing huge quantities of steel, which had the finest railway system in the world and which had invested nearly three billions in manufacturing. The impetus behind this stride was at its greatest in the years 1865-1873; Northern industry was booming when the war ended and the boom had eight years to run.

The victorious end of the war and the return of labor from the armies gave increased buoyancy to enterprise in every field. A leading Northern manufacturer, testifying under oath, said that his rate of profit in 1865 had been "painfully large;" and the special commissioner of revenue reported at the end of the following year that the returns of business had been almost unprecedently high.[2] Scarcely a record in industry escaped being broken during the next five years. More cotton spindles were set revolving, more iron furnaces were

From *The Emergence of Modern America* by Allan Nevins, copyright 1927 by The Macmillan Company and used with their permission.

[1] D. A. Wells, *Recent Economic Changes* (N. Y., 1889), 65.

[2] Special Commissioner of Revenue, *Report* (Dec., 1869). See also *Scientific American*, Sept. 15, 1866: "There are more men in New York today whose annual incomes reach $100,000 than there were twenty-five years ago of those whose entire possessions amounted to as much."

lighted, more steel was made, more coal and copper were mined, more lumber was sawed and hewed, more houses and shops were constructed and more manufactories of different kinds were established, than during any equal term in our earlier history.[3] Moreover, the improvements in the quality of manufactures equaled the increase in quantity.

The high prices which war-time demands and the issue of greenbacks had brought about continued in nearly all markets. The elation of Northern victory, the feeling of recuperative power, the sense of enormous Western wealth waiting only to be unlocked, were reflected in industry. "The truth is," John Sherman wrote his brother in the fall of 1865, "the close of the war with our resources unimpaired gives an elevation, a scope to the ideas of leading capitalists, far higher than anything ever undertaken in this country before. They talk of millions as confidently as formerly of thousands."[4] Sherman himself thought of leaving politics to engage in railroading, banking or manufacturing in Ohio. The home market was steadily expanding, partly through the inflow of immigrants from Europe, partly through the rapid settlement of the Western prairies. The war had tended to break down the previous economic dependence upon Europe, and behind a high tariff wall a host of new manufactories were making articles formerly shipped from abroad. In 1859 there had been one hundred and forty thousand manufacturing establishments; in 1869 there were two hundred and fifty-two thousand with a commensurate increase in the number of employees.[5] A succession of foreign wars, beginning with the Austro-Prussian War of 1865-1866 and the coalition of Brazil, Argentina and Uruguay against Paraguay, also benefited American trade.

Although the modern steel age was born in 1856, when Henry Bessemer in England invented his process, it did not gain a real foothold in America for a decade. Till after the Civil War steel was rare and costly, used chiefly in cutlery and fine tools. The demands of the conflict gave manufacturers no taste or time for experimenting, so that not until 1864 was the Bessemer process first used, at a short-lived plant in Wyandotte, Michigan, and even in 1867 only two

---

[3] Special Commissioner of Revenue, *Report* (Jan., 1869).
[4] John and W. T. Sherman, *Letters* (Rachel S. Thorndike, ed., N. Y., 1894), 258.
[5] *Abstract of the Census of Manufactures, 1919* (Wash., 1923), 13, table 3.

thousand six hundred tons of steel ingots were produced.[6] Then, steel making expanded with striking speed. The new process excited the wonder of all who witnessed it: the pouring of the molten iron into a great converter, the dazzling shower of sparks as the air was forced through the incandescent mass and the drawing off of the flaming metal as white-hot steel. The first steel king arose in the person of Captain Eber S. Ward of Detroit, who at the close of the war began making and selling steel under the American patents of William Kelly.[7] He soon found his chief rival in Alexander M. Holley of Troy, New York, who had bought the Bessemer rights. Since neither could make steel satisfactorily without infringing upon the legal prerogatives of the other, Ward, who was growing old, surrendered his patents to Holley, a dashing young industrialist still in his early thirties, in return for a thirty-per-cent share in the consolidation. Holley thus for a time stepped forth as the leading steel-and-iron maker of America.[8]

Steel speedily became as cheap as cast iron and its cheapness created such a keen demand that by 1875 a dozen important Bessemer works had been established. Before the war the iron business of the nation had been widely diffused, with bloomeries and furnaces scattered from the Adirondacks and Berkshires to Virginia and Tennessee. Now the greatest steel works, including the Cambria Works, which Daniel J. Morrell established in Johnstown (1871), the Bethlehem Works (1873) and the J. Edgar Thomson Steel Works (1875), as Carnegie called his establishment near Pittsburgh, rose in Pennsylvania alone. When the first proposal came to Carnegie to use the Bessemer process, the young ironmaster demurred, saying that "Pioneering doesn't pay a new concern: we must wait until the process develops." But he soon afterwards saw it demonstrated in England, and hurried home to organize the firm of Carnegie, McCandless & Co., to develop the new methods with a capital of seven hundred thousand dollars.[9] Meanwhile smaller works were flourishing in

6 C. D. Wright, *The Industrial Evolution of the United States* (N. Y., 1901), chap. xiv; H. U. Faulkner, *American Economic History* (N. Y., 1924), 574.

7 V. S. Clark, *History of Manufactures in the United States, 1607-1860* (Carnegie Inst., *Contribs. to Am. Econ. Hist.*, Wash., 1916), 512 ff.

8 H. N. Casson, *The Romance of Steel* (N. Y., 1907), 1-60.

9 Andrew Carnegie, *Autobiography* (J. C. Van Dyke, ed., Boston, 1920); Casson, *Steel*, 73 ff.

Cleveland, Chicago and St. Louis. The American production of steel rose steadily to three hundred and seventy-five thousand tons in 1875 and nine hundred and twenty-nine thousand in 1879, even the Panic of 1873 producing little visible check. Hard on the heels of the Bessemer process came that of the open hearth, but its progress was slow, for it required more time and the more careful instruction of the steel workers. A Siemens regenerative furnace was installed by John Fritz at the Bethlehem plant in 1872, and about nine thousand tons of open-hearth steel were being made two years later.[10] Thousands of men found work and high wages in the steel plants, producing a commensurate development of the Michigan iron mines.[11] But the social importance of steel production lay beyond all comparison in its contribution to the improvement of transportation, engineering and building construction. The greater part of the steel went into rails, the output of which exceeded two hundred and ninety thousand tons in 1875 and nine hundred and fifty thousand tons in 1880. Their durability as compared with iron rails was an indispensable quality. The huge crops of the Middle West and the growing volume of manufactured goods from the Mississippi Valley could never have been carried without them.[12]

The years 1865-1873 also witnessed the emergence of the four factors whose combination made possible the development of the American meat-packing business upon an international scale. These were the tidal overflow of the plains by the cattle ranchers, the ramification of railways throughout the cattle country, the invention of refrigeration and the appearance of men astute enough to organize the distribution of livestock and meats in an efficient way. In the first year of peace the railway reached Kansas City, a cattle market and shipping point was established at Abilene, and some thirty-five thousand cattle were sent East from this terminus. It was

[10] John Fritz, *Autobiography* (N. Y., 1912), 166 ff.; J. M. Swank, *History of the Manufacture of Iron in All Ages* (Phila., 1884), chap. xvi.

[11] Mine owners raised their prices, whereupon some steel mills acquired their own mines. *N. Y., Eve. Post*, Aug. 21, 1873.

[12] Barbed-wire fencing became commercially important by 1874 when Joseph H. Glidden and Jacob Haish began a battle over patent rights; wire nails, in 1875 when Joseph Goebbles founded the Kentucky Wire Nail Works in Covington. Industrial Museum of American Steel and Wire Company (Worcester, Mass.), *Book*, no. 2

clear to farsighted men that the West would shortly become one vast livestock range, crying for a market.

Already in Milwaukee and Chicago two of the great packers of the future, Philip D. Armour and Nelson Morris, had established themselves in readiness for this rich opportunity.[13] Armour, an adventurous New Yorker, had risen during the war to be partner in Jacob Plankinton's packing house in Milwaukee, then the fourth largest of its kind in America. The business, thanks to large war contracts and to Armour's careful watch upon price fluctuations, expanded rapidly, throwing out branches in Chicago and Kansas City; and he determined to head a firm of his own. A flood of cattle and hogs had poured in war times into the Chicago slaughterhouses, becoming so unmanageable that the Illinois legislature was compelled in 1865 to incorporate the Union Stockyards, which on Christmas day of that year opened its new facilities—three hundred and forty-five rather swampy acres just south of the city limits—to the livestock shippers. Two years later Armour and Company, an enterprise in which Philip Armour was assisted by several able brothers, began meat packing in Chicago, and it was not long before the Armour brand was known in all parts of the world. Nelson Morris, a young Bavarian Jew, had been even earlier in entering the Chicago field. He went into meat packing at twenty-two, in the first days of the Civil War, and had no difficulty in securing large army contracts. When the conflict ended his business was flourishing. By 1870 Armour and Nelson Morris in Chicago and Jacob Plankinton in Milwaukee had emerged as the foremost Western packers, and were already taking the leadership from the older Eastern houses, like those of Jacob Dold in Buffalo and the Cordukes in Cincinnati.[14]

One Eastern packer possessed a driving energy equal to their own —Gustavus F. Swift.[15] A Cape Cod Yankee, Swift had risen so rapidly from the position of a local butcher that by the middle seventies he was conducting one of the largest dressed-beef businesses in New

13 R. A. Clemen, *The American Livestock and Meat Industry* (N. Y., 1923), 149 ff.
14 F. W. Gunsaulus, "Philip D. Armour," *Am. Rev. of Revs.*, XXIII (1901), 167-176; A. Warren, "Philip D. Armour," *McClure's*, II (1894), 260; T. W. Goodspeed, "Gustavus Franklin Swift," *Chicago University Record* (new ser.), VII (1921), 96-116.
15 Clemen, *Livestock and Meat Industry.* 159 ff.

England. He knew that his natural sphere was the West and the year 1875 found him cautiously looking about for a site for a plant. In a very short time he had a large slaughterhouse in Chicago and was packing meats in competition with Armour and Morris. It was he who saw that beef might be fully dressed in Chicago and sent East, perfectly fresh, in refrigerator cars; and in initiating this fresh dressed-beef business on a large scale, he revolutionized the packing industry.[16] The industry now concentrated itself in a few great cities to an extent previously impossible, with large resulting gains in the cheapness and quality of the meat served on American tables. The local butcher, especially in the East, was thrust to the wall,[17] and even large Eastern slaughterhouses faced a competition from the Mississippi Valley which they had difficulty in meeting. Kansas City, with her packing houses still closer than Chicago to the range, sent two carloads of refrigerated meats to New York and one to Boston in the fall of 1875, thus opening a business which increased steadily. By the end of the seventies a general effort was being made by Western packers, and with success, to develop an Eastern market for all the beef and pork they could dress.[18]

As the control of the meat-packing business passed to Chicago and Kansas City, simultaneously the seats of the milling industry were transferred to Minneapolis and in lesser degree to St. Louis and Chicago, with direct benefits both to wheat growers and customers. Its Western development heralded the ultimate extinction of the small gristmills scattered by thousands over the nation and it made possible the rapid settlement of Minnesota wheatlands and the overflow of farmers into the Dakota valleys. Here, too, we meet picturesque and aggressive figures in the persons of three Minneapolis millers: Cadwallader C. Washburn, Charles A. Pillsbury and George M. Christian. The two former were New Englanders by birth, Washburn being one of a group of Maine brothers who achieved a singu-

16 Commissioner of Agriculture, *Report for 1870*, 250 ff.; L. F. Nickerson, "Refrigeration," *National Provisioner*, III (1891), no. 8; L. D. H. Weld, *Private Freight Cars and American Railways* (Columbia Univ., *Studies*, XXI, no. 1), 16.

17 Board of Health (N. Y. City), *Report of Sanitary Committee on Slaughtering for 1874*.

18 Clemen, *Livestock and Meat Industry*, chap. ii; Charles Winans, *Evolution of a Vast Industry* (Chicago, n. d.).

larly varied eminence.[19] while Pillsbury had worked his way through Dartmouth College in the class of 1863. Christian was an Alabamian who came North after the war in search of opportunities lacking at home, and in 1869 was made a partner in Washburn's establishment.[20] With wheat fields, railways and water power all at hand in Minneapolis, these men were further aided by the introduction of new mechanical processes. They adopted the "gradual reduction" method brought to them in 1870 by a Minnesotan named Edward La Croix, which preserved much of the gluten previously lost with the bran. This process was of cardinal importance to the Northern wheat belt, for whereas previously winter wheat had made the best flour, now the hard spring wheat furnished as good a product. But men like Pillsbury were still not satisfied. Early in the seventies he and other Northwesterners went to Europe to investigate the milling processes of various nations, but particularly of Hungary, where for decades wheat had been reduced to flour by slowly passing it through a series of chilled iron rollers. In 1874 the Hungarian system was adopted, with modifications, in the Washburn and Pillsbury establishments and gradually extended to other American mills. The result was a fine flour which attracted every buyer by its snowy whiteness and made better bread than Americans had ever before eaten.[21]

Even more Aladdin-like was the development of the Pennsylvania oil fields. Petroleum was destined to be the foundation for a host of new industries, and though few of its uses were discovered between 1865 and 1878, these few were important in themselves and still more important for the vistas they opened up.[22] At the beginning of our period only six years had elapsed since Colonel E. L. Drake sank the first oil well near the village of Titusville in western Pennsylvania. In 1864 it was a district of more than four hundred square miles dotted over with derricks and producing during the twelve months

[19] Gaillard Hunt, *Israel, Elihu and Cadwallader Washburn, a Chapter in American Biography* (N. Y., 1925), *passim*.

[20] For biographies see *Northwestern Miller*, Sept. 10, 1924.

[21] Hester M. Pollock, *Our Minnesota* (N. Y., 1917), 196 ff.; *Northwestern Miller*, March 12, 1924.

[22] Waldemar Kaempffert, ed., *A Popular History of American Invention* (N. Y., 1924), II, 83.

more than two million one hundred thousand barrels. Already some of the uses of the new product, which a half-dozen years earlier had been a quack Indian medicine, were known through half the world. It lubricated machinery in Manchester and Lyons; Swiss peasants and English noblemen illuminated their abodes with its mellow rays; it was used to light mariners in the wild Indian Ocean and along the South American coasts. Many New Bedford mariners, reading the fate of their trade, had abandoned whale fishing to seek the oil fields.[23] There was no lack of a market, and the rapidity with which oil lamps sold in homes, rich and poor alike, assured it of a steady expansion.

The hold which petroleum had gained upon the popular imagination in the East was illustrated by the speculative mania of 1865, precipitated by the sudden opening in January of a new basin on Pithole Creek. Within six weeks an almost untouched sylvan district became the site of Pithole City and its ten thousand inhabitants, which steadily increased until it held five thousand more. The typical evolution of the mining or oil town was crowded into a few months: tents and shanties gave way to good frame residences, to long streets of restaurants, saloons, land offices and stores. For a time Pithole City, which not many years later reverted to an open wheat field, had a postal business outrivaling all cities in the state except Philadelphia.[24] Stimulated by the new discovery, a fever of speculation seized the large Eastern centers. The capital of the oil companies of public record, which had been computed early that year at three hundred and twenty-six million dollars, rose by midsummer to at least five hundred million dollars, with new companies springing into life every hour. The rush of population lifted numerous hamlets almost overnight into small cities; the almost continuous loss of life due to carelessness and lawlessness proved no deterrent.

The chief initial difficulty of the industry, which despite constant vicissitudes and disappointments kept on growing, was to store and

23 E. P. Oberholtzer, *United States since the Civil War* (N. Y., 1917-1926, in progress), I, 255.
24 G. S. Montague, *Rise and Progress of the Standard Oil Company* (N. Y., 1904), 5. See also Andrew Cone and W. R. Johns, *Petrolia: a Brief History of the Pennsylvania Petroleum Region* (Walter Jones, ed., N. Y., 1870); G. W. Brown, *Old Times in Oildom* (Oil City, Penn., 1909); S. G. Bayne, *Derricks of Destiny, an Autobiography* (N. Y., 1924), 34-84.

transport the oil. The expedients of the early days were pictur-
esquely crude. Oil Creek had been navigable to the Allegheny in
freshets and the desperate producers resorted for a time to artificial
floods. That is, they repaired the old mill dams, collected water
behind them and loosed it at prearranged hours, sweeping a
crowded flotilla of oil boats—sometimes six hundred—down to the
river. More commonly they relied upon teamsters who were as rough
and undependable as the muddy roads.[25] Naturally it was not long
before inventive men hit upon the remedy, and in 1865 the first
extensive pipe line, carrying eighty barrels of oil every hour over a
stretch of seven miles, was placed in operation despite the teamsters'
protests. It was followed by others, and the price of delivering oil
to the Allegheny River boats was reduced from two dollars and fifty
cents or three dollars a barrel to one dollar or even fifty cents. At
the same time the tank car, invented by Charles P. Hatch, began to
take the place of ordinary cars loaded with barrels. Before 1870 long
lines of wooden tank cars became familiar in Pennsylvania and Ohio,
and soon afterwards these leaky and inflammable carriers were
replaced by tubular iron cars.[26]

As the oil fields developed, a great new refining industry sprang
up, offering work to thousands. By 1865 there were a number of
large refineries, producing benzine, gasoline, coal oil, paraffin and
tar. Very shortly the refineries began to mass themselves at two
points, Cleveland and Pittsburgh. The former city in 1865 had
thirty such businesses and at the end of the following year sixty. For
some time the two centers ran neck and neck, but at the beginning
of the seventies the superior position of Cleveland became evident,
for having the Great Lakes and Erie Canal as well as the New York
Central, it lay upon competitive transportation lines, while Pittsburgh was completely dependent upon the Pennsylvania Railroad.[27]
A centralization of the refining business was inevitable. The keen
competition in refining methods, which were susceptible of great
improvement, alone sufficed to drive many small manufactories from
the arena.

[25] Bayne, *Derricks of Destiny*, 66-67.
[26] Kaempffert, *Invention*, II, 93-94; Ida M. Tarbell, *History of the Standard Oil
Company* (N. Y., 1904), I, chap. i.
[27] Tarbell, *Standard Oil Company*, I, 38 ff.; Montague, *Standard Oil Company*,
19.

It was at this moment that there appeared upon the scene the decisive factor in the sweep toward unification: a leader sufficiently astute, aggressive and merciless to drive it to its logical conclusion, the erection of a monopoly. In 1865 John D. Rockefeller, a young Cleveland commission dealer of twenty-six, launched into the oil trade under the firm name of Rockefeller & Andrews.[28] The Civil War had given him, as it did Armour and others, the capital needed for commercial undertakings on a large scale. Rockefeller saw that the necessary economies in refining were beyond the reach of any firm which had less than a half million in capital, and that the larger the unit the greater would be its efficiency. He pursued a policy of steady expansion. A second refinery was established. H. M. Flagler was accepted as partner, a New York office was opened, and one rival manufactory after another was absorbed. In June, 1870, there appeared the Standard Oil Company of Ohio, with a capital of a million dollars and a position of towering strength in the industry. It was the largest company in the largest refining center of the country, with a daily output of one thousand five hundred barrels, or about one seventh of the whole production of Cleveland. Rockefeller's ambition, however, was far from satisfied.[29]

Thus the oil industry stood at a crucial point in 1870. Petroleum was being pumped from a large district of northwestern Pennsylvania, and wells were being sunk from West Virginia to Missouri in the hope of finding new fields. A business of which nobody had dreamed ten years earlier was giving the world more than five million barrels of oil annually, of which one hundred and fifty million gallons were going abroad, together with millions of gallons of gasoline, naphtha and benzine.[30] Hardly less than two hundred million dollars was invested in the business. The refineries had to keep pace with the oil harvest: Pittsburgh was now refining almost six thousand barrels a day, New York City more than nine thousand, the oil fields about nine thousand and Cleveland about twelve thousand.[31] The leading railways reaching the oil region, the Penn-

---

[28] J. D. Rockefeller, *Random Reminiscences of Men and Events* (N. Y., 1909), gives an excellent impression of the oil magnate's personality.

[29] Montague, *Standard Oil Company*, 6-7.

[30] See *Scientific American,* July 1, 1865, for beginnings of the coal-tar dye industry.

[31] Tarbell, *Standard Oil Company*, I, 51.

sylvania, New York Central and Erie, were keenly aware of the rich prize at stake and were bending every effort to gain the central stream of the traffic. It was under these circumstances that Rockefeller, who had already for two or three years insisted that the Erie and New York Central systems grant him secret freight rebates, planned a new coup. This was nothing less than the formation of a great pool of refiners which, by using the weapon of discriminatory freight rates, should take control of the oil market. The story of this attempt, its temporary failure and eventual success, must be left to a later time.

Meanwhile industries which could not be called new were exhibiting a large-scale standardization, involving also a concentration of capital, which gave them an appearance of entire novelty. In this roster the manufacture of men's clothing and of boots and shoes stood preëminent. During the Civil War a farsighted Scotchman, Gordon McKay, built up a huge business in supplying the army with machine-made shoes. Manufacturers East and West adopted the new machinery, which was rapidly improved, until it was hardly a fiction to say that leather was put in at one end and came out finished footwear at the other. Not only were shoes cheapened by the new process, but they were made more attractive and comfortable than the product of the ordinary artisan at the bench.[32] A single workman was able to turn out three hundred pairs in one day, and a single factory in Massachusetts was soon producing as many shoes as thirty thousand Paris bootmakers.

The manufacture of ready-made clothes had as striking a growth just after the Civil War. The first thought of the discharged soldier was to obtain good civilian clothes and this demand was sustained by the development of the West and the heavy immigration. Since it was difficult for garment cutters to keep pace with the sewing machines, inventors brought out mechanical cloth cutters, the first of which was made on Staten Island in 1872.[33] Few sights struck foreign travelers so forcibly as the enormous piles of ready-made suits exposed in shop windows at surprisingly low prices.

But this consolidation of industrial enterprises was evident in almost every field of business. Not until the Civil War did any cot-

[32] Andrew Carnegie, *Triumphant Democracy* (N. Y., 1887), 226-227.
[33] Kaempffert, *Invention*, II, 395.

ton mill have a hundred thousand spindles, or any iron furnace produce more than three hundred tons a week.[34] The success of the Waltham enterprise in making watches by factory methods instead of slowly and expensively by hand led to the establishment of the American Watch Factory at Elgin, Illinois, in 1865. The sewing-machine factory, the farm-implement factory, the piano and organ factory, all improved their processes, their subdivision of labor and their capacity for quantity production in these flush years. Many small businesses sprang into a hothouse life, for money was abundant,[35] but all the while the principal manufactories—those at the top—grew astonishingly. Less and less did the American people consume goods made in small and simple establishments managed by individual proprietors; more and more did they use goods from large factories managed by corporate boards.

A pronounced westward thrust of industry became evident quite apart from the birth of the meat-packing and flour-milling undertakings of the Northwest. Besides the Elgin watch factory and the Union Stock Yards in Chicago, the first year of peace saw large pottery works started at Peoria, woolen mills at Atchison, a farm-implement factory at Moline, and an important stove foundry at Quincy, Illinois.[36] Two years later George Pullman founded the Pullman Palace Car Company in Chicago. William H. Seward remarked of McCormick's reaper that through its use "the line of civilization moves westward thirty miles each year," and it was natural that the makers of agricultural machinery should move west too. McCormick's own factory stood on the north bank of the Chicago River. In Akron and Canton, Ohio, during 1865 about ten thousand mowing machines were made, though the price averaged one hundred and twenty-five dollars each. Two of the heritages of the war were a beet-sugar industry in Illinois and Wisconsin, and a flourishing tobacco industry in the latter state. Particularly interesting was the progress of the brewing business in St. Louis and Milwaukee, with their large German population, for the nation was beginning to appreciate the fact that beer was less harmful than ale or spirits, while the excise tax placed upon it was comparatively

[34] Clark, *History of Manufactures in the United States*, 415, 456.
[35] See *Statistical Abstract of the United States, 1921* (Wash., 1922), 868.
[36] *American Annual Cyclopedia* (N. Y., 1861-1903), V. (1865), 432, 458.

small. In 1865 Milwaukee, where the Schlitz and Pabst companies were active, was producing fifty-five thousand barrels of beer, while in 1873 the sale had risen to two hundred and sixty thousand.[37]

This westward march of manufacturing was plainly indicated by the census of 1870. It showed that in the nation as a whole the number of establishments had increased in the decade almost eighty per cent. But in Indiana they had more than doubled, in Illinois they had trebled, and in Missouri they had more than trebled. Before the war the great states along the upper Mississippi had been almost wholly agricultural and their cities had depended upon the trade of the farms; now the smoke of factory chimneys showed that they were definitely passing out of the pioneer stage. In the East, the agglutination of industry in strategically placed centers interested every observer. Bridgeport, Connecticut, for example, was just rising to a place of prominence as the seat of the Wheeler & Wilson Sewing-Machine Company; the Simpson Waterproof Cloth Company, which had made trainloads of raincoats for the soldiers; the Hotchkiss Company, which had turned from shells to general hardware; and the newly established Mallory Hat Company.[38]

Financial institutions responded to the buoyant expansion of the time like vegetation to a tropical sun. The inflation of credit made banking a business which tyros could enter with success. The federal government having established a great new national banking system, between the fall of 1864 and the fall of 1865 the number of such banks rose from five hundred and eighty-four to 1,566.[39] But even more remarkable was the multiplication of savings banks. The workmen were enjoying what seemed high pay, and needed repositories for it. In Massachusetts there were ninety-three savings banks in 1862, and one hundred and eighty in 1875; in New York State in the same period the number increased from seventy-four to one hundred and fifty-eight. Costly offices were hired and fitted up, high rates of interest were promised and extravagant salaries were

[37] Frederick Merk, *Economic History of Wisconsin during the Civil War Decade* (State Hist. Soc. of Wis., *Studies*, I, 1916), 145, 154; F. F. Cook, *Bygone Days in Chicago* (Chicago, 1910), 196 ff.

[38] *Scientific American*, July 8, 1865; *Compendium of the Ninth Census* (Wash., 1872), 796 ff.

[39] W. O. Scroggs, *Century of Banking Progress* (Garden City, N. Y., 1924), 203.

granted.[40] Insurance companies, many of them speculative ventures with insufficient capital, incompetent management and a shocking inattention to sound actuarial principles, rose on every hand. Until these years trust companies had been almost unknown in the United States, but now there sprang up a sudden realization of their usefulness and opportunities, and between 1864 and 1875 no fewer than forty came into existence.[41] Many observers became alarmed by the disturbance of the former balance between production and consumption, pointing to the huge growth of all businesses of exchange—trade agencies, commission houses, brokerage, banking, retailing—as not wholly legitimate but in large part the forced fruit of inflation. When the census of 1870 was taken, it was found that while the population had been increasing twenty-two and one-half per cent, the trading classes, including those engaged in transportation, had increased forty per cent. Francis A. Walker computed that the nation was maintaining a useless array of middlemen and retailers equivalent to the standing armies of the British Empire and with a greater number of dependents.[42]

In answer to the heavy demands of industry upon the labor market, and to the alluring spectacle of prosperity, comfort and opportunity presented by American life, the stream of European immigration rose rapidly to a torrent. The Fenian movement and land troubles in Ireland, the panic of 1866 in England and the Austro-Prussian conflict gave tens of thousands of Europeans a special incentive to emigrate to the United States. For the first time American manufacturers combined in considerable numbers to send agents to Europe to stimulate emigration, and their efforts advertised the opportunities open to active men. The increasing speed and cheapness of transatlantic travel was also a factor of importance. In 1856 a mere handful of European newcomers, some five thousand in a total of one hundred and thirty-one thousand, had arrived in steamships, the others using sailing vessels; but in 1865 the great majority were transported by steam. Not quite a quarter of a million immigrants were admitted in 1865, and thereafter the number rose year

[40] *Commercial and Financial Chronicle*, April 25, 1874.
[41] *Com. and Fin. Chron.*, Aug. 3, 1878; H. W. Lanier, *A Century of Banking in New York, 1822-1922* (N. Y., 1922), chap. x.
[42] F. A. Walker, "Some Results of the Census," *Journ. of Soc. Sci.*, V, 71-97.

by year until in 1873 it reached the then amazing total of four hundred and sixty thousand.[43]

In this fresh surge of Old World population certain novel, interesting and valuable elements appeared prominently. When in 1850 Fredrika Bremer, the Swedish novelist, visited the Northwest, she found a large advance-guard of Scandinavians; now the central host was coming, and by 1870 there were almost forty-five thousand of them in Illinois alone. The first Swedish secular journal, the *Svenska Amerikanaren*, was established in Minnesota in 1866, edited by Colonel Hans Mattson who became known as an active agent in Europe to induce Scandinavians to migrate.[44] About one hundred and twenty-five thousand Scandinavians entered the republic in the first half of the seventies. Some Slavs, German-Russian Mennonites, and Bohemians also arrived. Decidedly more important was the accession of Italians from Sicily and Naples; for in the same half decade slightly more than a hundred thousand people of Latin blood, most of them Italians seeking work in the construction gangs on the railroads and other rough employment, were admitted. But it was the British, Irish and German immigration which continued the heaviest, these nationalities leading in the order named. The result of the inflow was that by 1875 the nation had about seven and a half million of foreign-born among its forty million people.[45]

The building of railways, to which the nation turned with characteristic energy just after the war, was urgently needed. Not only was the meager Southern system now largely in ruins, but the railways from the East to the Middle West were quite inadequate. The produce of the Mississippi Valley had increased faster than the means of carrying it, and the corn growers of Iowa, the meat packers of Chicago and the oil shippers of Pennsylvania were especially vociferous in complaint.[46] The congestion on the trunk lines was accentuated by seasonal difficulties, for at the close of the war one third of the freight annually carried from the central valley to the

[43] Philip Davis, *Immigration and Americanization* (Boston, 1920), 66, presents the figures by years. See *Com. and Fin. Chron.*, Sept. 1, 1866, for comment.

[44] R. E. Park, *The Immigrant Press and Its Control* (N. Y., 1922), 320; Pollock, *Our Minnesota*, 333.

[45] See *Am. Ann. Cyclop.*, XVII (1877), 386, for general review.

[46] Sir S. M. Peto, *The Resources and Prospects of America* (London, 1866), 227, 278, 294.

Atlantic was still conveyed by the lakes and canals, and when they were frozen, the rail blockade often became disastrous. These transportation difficulties depressed the inland markets and kept land values unduly low. The need for new arteries grew steadily more acute, for every year a hundred thousand settlers poured across the Mississippi.

This task of construction was made the easier because railway profits had been high during the war and capital was easy to obtain, while the spirit of national self-confidence also played a large rôle.[47] At the close of the conflict the whole American system totaled about thirty-five thousand miles and had cost a little more than a billion. Then came an amazing leap forward, and by the end of 1872 the railway mileage had doubled.[48] Everyone looked upon this growth with rejoicing. It was estimated that the existing lines created more wealth each year than was absorbed by the cost of extensions and H. V. Poor concluded in 1868 that the gross earnings of the railways amounted in a little over four years to as much as their cost.[49]

The proudest achievement of the railway builders, the completion of a transcontinental line, had everywhere been regarded as an urgent task even before the fighting ended. The Far West pointed to its farming possibilities, its mineral wealth, and to a world's commerce with the Orient waiting only for the steel highway. Samuel Bowles in his trip to the Pacific in 1865 found that the one question of a yearning population was, "When will the railroad be built?"[50] Eastern wealth wanted the opportunities for investment, Eastern labor wanted those for employment. National leaders were apprehensive lest a new generation should arise on the Pacific Coast without any warm attachment to the Union; while some social observers believed that the West was suffering from the excessively rapid growth of communities far removed from the conventional and religious restraints found in the rest of America and that the influence of these communities upon American manners, letters and politics was vulgarizing.[51] Every year the pressure of goods and passengers

[47] *Nation*, March 11, 1869.
[48] *Com. and Fin. Chron.*, Jan. 11, 1873.
[49] H. V. Poor, *Influence of the Railroads of the United States in the Creation of its Commerce and Wealth* (New York, 1869).
[50] Samuel Bowles, *Across the Continent* (Springfield, Mass., 1865), 255 ff.
[51] *Nation*, Jan. 11, 1866.

upon the slender means of communication with the Far West became more excessive.

What were these means? The West in 1865 was served beyond the Mississippi Valley railheads by a fast growing network of freighter and stage lines, and already it boasted of one highly developed system, that of Benjamin Holladay.[52] This system, which covered a distance of three thousand three hundred miles in all, was a product of government patronage under a federal contract for the carriage of the transcontinental mails and included branch lines to such new mining towns as Virginia City in Montana and Boise City, Idaho. Though Holladay's rates were high (for the costs and risks were great), yet just after the war his stages were crowded with passengers who paid a fare of one hundred and seventy-five dollars from the Missouri River to Denver, three hundred and fifty dollars to Salt Lake City and from four hundred to five hundred dollars to California.[53] In answer to the constantly increasing demands there occurred in 1866 a general reorganization and consolidation of the Western stage lines. The Wells Fargo Company, with its huge capital, took over Holladay's stages, paying him two million five hundred thousand dollars, and also acquired the Pioneer Stage Company and all other stage and express properties between the Missouri River and the Pacific. It bought new coaches, improved their speed and opened fresh lines. Like Holladay himself, the company, with its chain of fortified storehouses, was not wholly popular and was frequently denounced as monopolistic.[54]

Though the stagecoach was a rude, uncomfortable and, at times, uncertain mode of travel, it served its purpose remarkably well and sometimes the speed attained was surprising. Schuyler Colfax, Samuel Bowles and Albert D. Richardson in 1875 covered the distance from Atchison to Denver, an arc-shaped route of six hundred and fifty-three miles, in four and a half days.[55] Bowles tells us that he

52 F. A. Root and W. E. Connelly, *The Overland Stage to California* (Topeka, 1901); G. D. Bradley, *The Story of the Pony Express* (Chicago, 1913); S. L. Clemens (Mark Twain, *pseud.*), *Roughing It* (Hartford, 1872).

53 Holladay's investment was two million dollars. *Senate Miscel. Doc.*, 47 Cong., 2 sess., no. 19.

54 F. L. Paxson, *The Last American Frontier* (N. Y., 1910), chap. xi.

55 See letters of A. D. Richardson in *N. Y. Tribune*, June, July and Aug., 1865. For impressions by travelers see W. H. Dixon, *New America* (5th edn., rev., London, 1867), I, chap. iv; J. F. Rushing, *Across America* (N. Y., 1877), 150 ff.

found the food at the early stopping places better than that at the ordinary hotels and restaurants along the railway west of Chicago. On the stretch between Denver and Salt Lake City, where hostile Indians had been troublesome, they were not so well fed, the canned fruits and vegetables disappearing along with the tablecloths, and antelope meat becoming the staple dish. At every station fresh horses took the place of the jaded teams with a delay of only from two to four minutes, and every fifty miles a new driver climbed into the box.[56]

The Union Pacific Railroad, begun during 1864, was easily the greatest engineering feat that America had undertaken, and next to the Suez Canal and the Mont Cenis tunnel, completed almost at the same time, it might fairly have been rated the world's greatest engineering achievement. Mountain gorge, umbrageous wilderness and arid plain, amounting in all to one thousand eight hundred miles from Omaha to Sacramento, had to be traversed; and hostile Indians had to be fought back. To house, feed and direct the thousands of laborers was a formidable problem, for the railway passed through only two small settled areas, Carson City and the Salt Lake district, and near a third, Denver. Foundries and machine shops had to be erected as the work progressed. The Central Pacific—the western portion—gained at the start, but when they met at Promontory Point in 1869, the Union Pacific—the eastern line—had laid 1,086 miles against 689 by its rival.

Despite the difference in the amount of mileage laid, the business enterprise displayed by the Central Pacific was far superior to that of its rival.[57] The Californians who undertook this line were merchants past middle age who had acquired a generous competence without ever interesting themselves in railways. Leland Stanford, the foremost figure, had, after a brief career as a lawyer in Wisconsin, become a wholesale grocer in San Francisco, where he thrust himself forward in politics and in 1861 was elected governor. He was a man of great tenacity and strength of purpose, of imposing physique and masterful mien. Collis P. Huntington, a Connecticut Yankee who had established a large hardware business in California, was one of

[56] Bowles, *Across the Continent*, letters 3-5, 14-17.
[57] H. H. Bancroft, *The Pacific States of North America* (San Fran., 1882-1890), XIX, 543 ff.

the keenest merchants in the West, cool, energetic and quick-sighted. Charles Crocker, a self-made man who had built up a large dry-goods trade, had shown himself an indefatigable pusher and an adroit manager of gangs of workmen. These three, all living in Sacramento in the early sixties, were converted to enthusiastic belief in the transcontinental railway by a promoter named T. D. Judah, the engineer of the Sacramento Valley and other rail lines. Their aim at first was simply to reach the rich Nevada mines and gain control of the Nevada trade; and in June of 1861 they had organized the Central Pacific Railroad Company, with Stanford as president, Huntington vice-president and Judah the chief engineer. When Congress authorized the transcontinental road, they hastened to accept the terms of the government for the western extremity. They did their own work, dismissing all subcontractors and organizing the firm of Crocker and Company to secure all the profits from construction.[58]

A huge task it was. There was little white labor, and coolies were imported from China until by 1865 some five thousand were at work and in 1866 more than ten thousand. Iron, machinery, rolling stock and other supplies came by sea, a hazardous journey of months around Cape Horn or across Panama. The road had to traverse the Sierras at a height of more than seven thousand feet and in a space of sixty miles it passed through fifteen tunnels. Trestles, culverts, snowsheds, tanks and drainage systems must be built at enormous expense. Skeptics were loud in ridicule, yet the construction was rapidly and efficiently carried forward. In the first three years (1863-1865) about twenty miles were built annually; about thirty in 1866 and in 1867, when the state line was reached, forty-six miles. The company had long since resolved not to stop at the Nevada mines, but to push into Utah and meet the Union Pacific as far east as possible, perhaps at Salt Lake. Despite the hurry, the road was built for permanence.[59] Nor did it suffer from any scandal like the Credit Mobilier affair.

On the east, the Union Pacific met fewer difficulties. It had plenty

[58] The standard general works on the Central and Union Pacific lines are: J. P. Davis, *The Union Pacific Railway* (Chicago, 1894), and Nelson Trottman, *History of the Union Pacific* (N. Y., 1923).

[59] Charles Nordhoff, *California for Health, Pleasure and Residence* (new ed., rev., N. Y., 1882), 32 ff.

of labor, the Irish workingmen available in 1864 being supplemented the next year by large bodies of discharged soldiers. With General G. M. Dodge as its chief engineer, the laborers had a semi-military organization as they crossed the Indian-troubled prairies, and more than once dropped their picks to deploy as skirmishers.[60] At the height of the undertaking, with more than twelve thousand men busy, the actual construction was a scene to quicken the pulse: the light cars bringing up the rails, the builders hurrying them into place, the gaugers, spikers and bolters following close behind and swinging to the grand anvil chorus of the sledge hammers. A city that Samuel Bowles appropriately called "Hell on wheels" staggered forward with the railway across the plains—a terminal that every few weeks was packed upon a long string of freight cars, with houses, furniture, clothes, tents, gambling machines, bar equipment and rubbish, and transported to a new site.[61]

Almost before the nation knew it, the two iron bands met fifty-three miles west of Ogden, Utah. Here on May 10, 1869, while the entire country seemed to stand in expectation, the last spike was driven. As the smoke of the two engines facing each other mingled and the final three strokes went home, the telegraph in every city of the Union clicked off: "One, two, three—done!" East and West were joined and the frontier had begun to disappear from American history.[62] This iron girdle was, by modern standards, a precarious link. East of Ogden it was a hastily graded, ill-ballasted, poorly equipped railway of a single track, with few decent stations, shops or round-houses; it had been built by the dizzy methods of the Credit Mobilier, and had cost three times as much as it should.[63] Yet it closed an old era and opened a new one.

East of this slight transcontinental thread a new network of lines spread rapidly throughout the Middle West. In Illinois alone the years 1870-1871 saw one thousand eight hundred and thirty-five miles

[60] Slason Thompson, *A Short History of American Railways, Covering Ten Decades* (N. Y., 1925), 174 ff.

[61] J. H. Beadle, *The Undeveloped West* (Phila., 1873), 87 ff., pictures the rough town of Benton. See also W. A. Bell, *New Tracks in North America* (London, 1869), I, 17 ff.

[62] *Nation*, VIII, May 13, 1869.

[63] J. B. Crawford, *The Credit Mobilier of America* (Boston, 1880); Rowland Hazard, *The Credit Mobilier of America* (Providence, 1881).

of railway constructed, most of the routes running east and west across the state. The counties here and in other states were allowed to bond themselves heavily and sometimes foolishly in aid of railway enterprises. One railway after another, meanwhile, debouched from Illinois across Iowa or Missouri to tap the Great Plains.[64] The Chicago & Northwestern crossed the Mississippi at Clinton, Iowa, and pushed rapidly west till early in 1867 the first train rolled into Council Bluffs. The St. Joseph & Council Bluffs line, spanning northern Missouri, reached the latter town in December, 1867. Work at the same time was proceeding on the Chicago, Rock Island and Pacific, which had thrown the first bridge across the Mississippi at Rock Island as early as 1856, and which reached the Missouri at Council Bluffs in the early summer of 1869. The Chicago, Burlington and Quincy entered Nebraska in 1869, and in 1871 purchased a small railway which gave it a terminus in Omaha.[65] It was clear that Omaha and Kansas City would be the two great transportation centers west of Chicago, yet it was not until March, 1873, when the Union Pacific completed a two-thousand-seven-hundred-and-fifty-foot structure, that the Missouri River was bridged at the former point. Until that day all freight and passengers had to be carried across in ferryboats, against the uncertainties of a strong current and shifting bottom.[66]

The northern country, so recently a solitude, was now being pierced in every direction. In Wisconsin the railway mileage more than doubled in the years 1868-1873 inclusive, bringing the peninsular wilderness within sound of the locomotive whistle. Minnesota sent Edward Rice, whom it pleasantly called its Chesterfield for his fine bearing and genial manners, to London to obtain capital for construction, and by 1872 a web of lines was being spun over the southern and eastern sections. There was a two-hundred-and-seventeen-mile railway from St. Paul westward across the entire state to Breckinridge; there were lines southwest from Minneapolis to Fari-

64 E. L. Bogart and C. M. Thompson, *The Industrial State, 1870-1893* (C. W. Alvord, ed., *The Centennial History of Illinois, Illinois Centennial Series, Springfield, Ill.*, 1898-1920, IV), 318 ff.

65 A. C. Wakeley, *History of Omaha: the Gate City, and Douglas County, Nebraska* (Chicago, 1917), 252 ff.

66 A. C. Wakeley, *History of Omaha and Douglas County*, 253; Alfred Sorensen, *Story of Omaha from Pioneer Days* (Omaha, 1889), chap. xxxi.

bault and southeast from Minneapolis to Winona; and a new railway of great value wound through forest and over ravine to connect the Mississippi at St. Paul with the Great Lakes at Duluth.[67] In Nebraska a railway was completed to the new capital at Lincoln in the summer of 1870, and two years later the Chicago, Burlington and Quincy formed a junction with the Union Pacific at Kearney. Branch lines were overspreading western Missouri and thrusting out into Kansas.[68]

Of especial importance was the commencement of a series of great new trunk lines roughly parallel to the Union Pacific. Only one of these lines lay to the north of Omaha and Denver—the Northern Pacific. As early as 1864 it had received a charter from Congress, the incorporators including many prominent Northern financiers and politicians; the route authorized lay from the head of Lake Superior to Puget Sound. Money was hard to obtain and until 1870, when Jay Cooke and his associates took up the enterprise, no actual construction was begun. But Cooke set to work with irresistible energy. By June, 1873, the railway had been extended four hundred and fifty miles westward to Bismarck on the Missouri River, and was giving a heavy impetus to Minnesota settlement. Then the Panic blasted the green plant, and its growth abruptly and totally stopped.[69] Similarly unfortunate was the history of the Southwestern Pacific, or Southern Pacific, which was extended from a point near St. Louis southwest to Vinita in Indian Territory when the Panic of 1873 caused it to default and ended construction. The ambitious Texas & Pacific hardly became more than a mere paper railroad, though under John C. Frémont it sufficed as a foundation for much gilded and rather reprehensible speculation.

Happily, some other trunk lines did far better. One was the Missouri Pacific, pushing from St. Louis to Kansas City. Another was the Kansas Pacific, which cut westward from Kansas City through the new towns of Wichita and Topeka to Denver, which it reached in the summer of 1870. Most interesting of all the great southwestern lines was the Atchison, Topeka and Santa Fé system, which flourished

[67] E. P. Oberholtzer, *Jay Cooke, Financier of the Civil War* (Phila., 1907), II, 96 ff.; J. G. Pyle, *Life of James J. Hill* (Garden City, 1917), I, 103 ff.
[68] Secretary of the Interior, *Report for 1875*, 113.
[69] Oberholtzer, *Jay Cooke*, II, chaps. xv-xvi.

like a green bay tree between 1868 and the Panic. Following the old Santa Fé trail, this railway, under the guidance of an indefatigable free-soil pioneer and promoter named Cyrus L. Holliday, reached Emporia in the summer of 1871, and by the close of the following year a furious spurt had carried it across the Colorado boundary. The shock of the Panic arrested it at Pueblo, at the foot of the Rockies, but the road opened various Kansas branches, and the Centennial year found it one of the important trunk arteries of the nation. Other railways whose names have long since become familiar, such as the Missouri, Kansas and Texas, and the Denver and Rio Grande, were being prosecuted in these years with greater or less success.[70]

Was all this feverish railway expansion really healthy, well-planned or profitable? The element of speculative mania was evident to everyone. Thousands of miles of railway were being constructed in advance of real need and by the most questionable financial methods.[71] With six or eight lines planned to cross the continent from east to west and as many more to connect the Great Lakes with the Gulf, the investing public was being fed by roseate dreams of an utterly unrealizable character. Altogether too much was being made of the supposed ability of any railway to create traffic in a virgin district. The competition among the lines tapping the West was growing keener and keener and was certain ultimately to force down their receipts. The stock of many companies had been recklessly watered; and the frequency with which dividends were declared in stock and scrip, not in cash, suggested that earnings were small. Year by year the method of financing new railway lines seemed to grow worse.[72] At first the companies constructing them had sold for cash sufficient stock to pay for the work; but later the promoters

[70] Stuart Daggett, *Railroad Reorganization* (*Harvard Economic Studies*, IV), chaps. vi, ix; M. S. Snow, ed., *History of the Development of Missouri, and particularly of Saint Louis* (St. Louis, 1908), II, 332 ff. For Texas railway building, see Bancroft, *Pacific States*, XI, 570 ff.

[71] For a thorough discussion of financial aspects of the "railmania," see *Com. and Fin. Chron.*, March 11, 1869. The astonishing activity in building and rebuilding Southern railways is set forth in the *Com. and Fin. Chron.*, Aug. 10, 1867; Dec. 19, 1868; Jan. 18, 1869. By the close of 1868 there were nearly five thousand miles under construction in this section.

[72] See the *Nation*, VI, May 21, 1868, for a vivid characterization of dishonest methods of railroad financing.

had found a way of lining their pockets well by appropriating most or all of the stock to themselves and juggling it to high levels, while they paid for the road by reckless bond issues. Even where financial operations were well-intentioned, the recklessness was often astounding. Jay Cooke's Northern Pacific railway was a comparatively well-managed enterprise, yet some of his methods of pushing it would now be deemed fantastic, if not insane. The first step of his firm was to organize a gigantic lobby to obtain the patronage of the government. Governors of Pennsylvania and Minnesota, congressmen, financiers and politicians were enlisted; money was used freely, and shares in the project were discreetly bestowed upon leaders who wanted *douceurs*; while Cooke himself argued with several refractory representatives. An enormous selling campaign was organized. Schuyler Colfax was offered a lucrative position if he would resign the vice-presidency; agents were granted territorial districts; squads of lecturers were organized and advertising was undertaken on the costliest scale. The road was bitterly attacked as a fraud and a thievish raid upon the public lands and Cooke spared no expense in replying to these assaults. As for the bonds, they bore an interest rate of seven and three tenths per cent, and the selling agents were to receive a commission of six per cent in cash and ten per cent in stock. In this manner was a golden millstone hung about the neck of the infant Northern Pacific.[73]

So long as the country enjoyed its flush of after-war prosperity, the roads which were thus being built paid. For a time the profits of some seemed magnificent. Thus in 1867, fourteen of the leading lines of the nation showed aggregate earnings of more than sixty-five million dollars, and in the next year of almost seventy million dollars. The gross revenues of the railways of the whole country in 1867 were about twenty-seven per cent of their cost.[74] The generosity of the federal and state governments in land grants and cash subsidies assured at least a temporary affluence to a majority of the new railways. Even in the devastated South the roads returned to a dividend-paying basis with astonishing celerity. During 1867, for example, it

73 Oberholtzer, *Jay Cooke*, II, 225 ff.
74 "Our existing railroads are computed to create more wealth every year than is absorbed for the construction of new railroads." *Com. and Fin. Chron.*, Jan. 11, 1873.

was found that one thousand three hundred and thirty-three miles of railway in Georgia earned five thousand two hundred and eighty-seven dollars gross for every mile, which was more than one tenth of the cost of the lines and which permitted dividends of from two and a half to ten per cent.[75]

Yet all the while there were ominous indications of the probable inability of many great railways to weather such a storm as burst in 1873. The chief of these was perhaps the difficulties into which the Union Pacific fell within a few years after its completion.[76] It and the Central Pacific charged excessively high rates on transcontinental freight, reaching at first ten or eleven cents in gold for every ton-mile: they demanded all that the traffic would bear. The same tea that was shipped from China to New York for two cents a pound by sea was carried from San Francisco to New York by rail for thirteen cents. To carry a ton of flour from San Francisco to Chicago cost one hundred and twenty-six dollars, while to transport it from Chicago to New York, a distance one third as great, the charge was only ten dollars. Passenger rates, which at the outset were almost equally exorbitant, were later reduced to a more tolerable level.[77] While the Central Pacific, carefully built and financed, flourished, the Union Pacific, wastefully built and recklessly financed, languished. It was burdened with interest payments on seventy-four million dollars in bonds and, if any thing were left, dividend payments on thirty-six million dollars in stock. Moreover, the Credit Mobilier scandal struck a heavy blow at its prestige. By 1872, when it was in the hands of a coterie headed by Commodore Vanderbilt's son-in-law, Horace F. Clark, it was in sore traits.

The land-grant railways naturally made every effort to people their wide holdings and the colonizing activities of the Santa Fé furnish an interesting example of the work of nearly all Western roads in scattering the seeds of future millions.[78] It held alternate sections in a ten-mile strip on each side of the main Kansas line. In 1870 the railway established a land department and invited the editors of between three hundred and four hundred newspapers to

[75] *Com. and Fin. Chron.*, Oct. 3, 1868.

[76] Anna Youngman, *The Economic Causes of Great Fortunes* (N. Y., 1909), chap. iii.

[77] Oberholtzer, *United States since the Civil War*, II, 482-483.

[78] Cy Warman, *Story of the Railroad* (N. Y., 1898), 113 ff.

come to Kansas, transportation free. Homeseekers were carried at half rates, and if any man bought land, his whole fare was refunded. Sometimes European agents of the railway recruited homeseekers in large groups, which were discharged from the trains at a suitable station, so that there was soon a community of Swedes at one spot, Englishmen at another, and Irishmen or even Russians at a third.[79]

Not less important than the new railway construction was the establishment of long-distance trunk lines by the amalgamation of short railroads, the building of extensions or the conclusion of leasing arrangements. Hitherto travel from New York to Chicago had meant the use of eight or a dozen independent lines with repeated changes. In the East the New York Central led the way. In 1868 Commodore Vanderbilt combined the New York Central and the Hudson River railroads, furnishing a single road from New York to Buffalo; it was a logical step to arrange with the Lake Shore and Michigan Southern for through service to Chicago and in 1873 he made this line an integral part of the Central system.[80] Not merely that, but as early as May, 1870, he came to terms with the Rock Island and the Chicago & Northwestern, so that he could advertise an uninterrupted carriage of New York passengers as far west as Omaha. The Vanderbilt group of railways thus held control of four thousand five hundred miles of track and a capital of not less than a quarter billion dollars. The Pennsylvania, one of the most powerful lines in the country, having for years monopolized the traffic between Philadelphia and Pittsburgh, was hardly behind in the race; its shrewd head, J. Edgar Thomson, used the Pennsylvania legislature as he needed it. Turning westward he reached Chicago by an agreement with the Columbus, Chicago and Indiana Central; at the same time he prevented the Erie from making a connection with the Western metropolis.[81] Jay Gould, however, did shortly obtain a direct and unbroken communication between New York on the east, and Cleveland, Cincinnati and St. Louis on the west. In April, 1869, the Erie was able to advertise: "1,400 miles under one management; 860 miles without change of cars; the broad-gauge, double-track

79 W. E. Miller, *The Peopling of Kansas* (Columbus, 1906).

80 Daggett, *Railroad Reorganization*, 2 ff.

81 E. H. Mott, *Between the Ocean and the Lakes; the Story of Erie* (N. Y., 1899), 173, 177.

route between New York, Boston, and New England cities and the West." This made three main routes between the coast and the Middle West, and when the Baltimore & Ohio reached Chicago in 1874, there were four. Competition for passengers and freight was keen.

In the Mississippi Valley a similar consolidation took place under pressure of the demand for through trunk lines joining Chicago with the transcontinental roads built or planned to the Pacific. The Chicago & Northwestern, under the presidency of William B. Ogden, the greatest figure in Western railway affairs, was one of these lines; the Rock Island and the Chicago, Burlington & Quincy were others.[82] The Illinois Central lost no time after the conflict in completing a through route, nine hundred and fifty miles almost as the crow flies, from Chicago to the Gulf. At the South also the tendency toward the formation of long trunk highways was irresistible. The organization of the Chesapeake and Ohio in 1868, a direct line from Norfolk to Cincinnati, furnished the shortest route from the Ohio Valley to tidewater. Both Norfolk and Charleston were joined at the same time with the Tennessee railways, so that they enjoyed easy communication with Memphis. The South, it should be said, was building railways rapidly during these years—more than twelve hundred miles of track in 1870, more than one thousand in 1871, and in 1873, nearly thirteen hundred miles.[83]

One result of the tremendous railway expansion of the time was a sharp check upon the commerce of the Great Lakes and the inexorable conquest of much lake and canal business in grain carrying. Lake transportation had flourished during the war, coming out of the conflict with a great fleet of more than six hundred thousand tons; yet its essential weaknesses were evident.[84] During the winter months the vessels were icebound and idle, their capital charges meanwhile steadily mounting. Moreover, ships from Milwaukee and

[82] Slason Thompson, *Cost, Capitalization and Estimated Value of American Railways* (3d edn., Chicago, 1908), 187; J. W. Cary, *The Organization and History of the Chicago, Milwaukee, and St. Paul Railway Company* (Milwaukee, 1892); W. H. Stennett, *Yesterday and Today; History of the Northwestern Railway System* (Chicago, 1910).

[83] *Com. and Fin. Chron.*, Feb. 15, 1873; J. L. Ringwalt, *Development of Transportation Systems in the United States* (Phila., 1888).

[84] C. R. Fish, "Some Phases of the Economic History of Wisconsin," Wis. Hist. Soc., *Proceeds.*, LV, 204-216.

Chicago had to round the Michigan peninsula, an indirect and wasteful route, and transfer charges added to the cost. The railways struck hard at these weaknesses through their ability to make long continuous hauls in all seasons. Almost as important was the development just after the war of "through freight" or "fast freight" companies, owning large numbers of freight cars, which, by contract with the railways, they sent express from shipper to consignee in every part of the nation.[85]

Slowly but surely lake vessels were being driven out of existence, and many of the shipping centers of the Great Lakes felt their prosperity threatened. Chicago, already one of the greatest railway centers of the world, was quite safe; but Buffalo, at one extremity of the lakes and Milwaukee at the other, with Detroit and other ports between, were in grave danger. In 1869, through a convention of the boards of trade of all the principal lake ports, they took steps to meet the situation. Their plan was to enable the captains of all the lake freighters to offer lower rates, by reducing the transfer and terminal charges and by getting the marine insurance companies to cut their premiums. To a noteworthy extent they realized this program. Buffalo, Oswego and Toledo sliced their transfer charges by one half or three fourths, and the railway companies running between Lake Michigan and the Mississippi River struck one half off their charges for wheat and flour; while, as the most important stroke of all, the New York legislature in 1870 reduced the tolls for wheat on the Erie Canal from six to three cents a bushel.[86]

The stubborn tenacity of the owners of the schooners, the new screw steamers and the steam barges not only conserved the prosperity of the Lake cities, but was of indispensable value to the Middle West as a competitive check upon the railways. Whenever they could avoid this competition, the trunk lines shamelessly gouged the farmers and other shippers. Year after year they shoved up their freight rates, as soon as November came and ice closed the ports, by from one third to two thirds; and year after year they reverted to an honest competitive level when April released the vessels.[87] The war between the two transportation agencies steadily

[85] Merk, *Economic History of Wisconsin*, 384.
[86] Merk, *Economic History*, chap. xv.
[87] These were also the years in which sailing ships were being steadily crowded out by steam vessels. J. C. Mills, *Our Inland Seas* (Chicago, 1910), 158.

continued, and though the rail rates never reached so low a point, in general, as the water rates, the quickness and safety of land transit gave it an advantage. Finally, by 1875, a fair balance had been reached. By that year the carriage of ores had attained a volume which gave the lake vessels a great new field of employment.

Much more complete was the railway conquest of the Mississippi.[88] Before the war ten million bushels of Western wheat had been annually shipped from New Orleans, while millions of dollars of Western corn, pork and beef went down the river to be sold in Southern markets. In those years St. Louis often showed the visitor a solid mile of steamboats lying in two or three tiers. The scene at New Orleans was one never to be forgotten. Now these days were as utterly gone as those of the Roman triremes. Mark Twain, crossing under the shadow of the mighty Eads bridge at St. Louis early in the seventies, saw only a half-dozen inert steamboats, a mile of empty wharves and a drunken Negro. From the long reach of plank wharves at New Orleans the steamboats had almost vanished.[89] In the sixties the tonnage plying the Mississippi fell from 468,210 to 398,296, and it became far more largely than before a commerce of the upper river, not of the entire channel from Dubuque to New Orleans. The river boats acted merely as local carriers, distributing their cargoes to the railway terminals scattered along the banks. The river, in other words, became a mere feeder to dozens of railways. With some exaggeration Mark Twain summarized the contrast between the old days and the new:

> Boat used to land . . . captain on hurricane roof . . . mighty stiff and straight . . . iron ramrod for a spine . . . kid gloves, plug tile, hair parted behind . . . man on shore takes off hat and says: "Got twenty-eight tons of wheat, capt'n . . . be great favor if you can take them." Captain says: "I'll take two of them . . ." and don't even condescend to look at him. But nowadays the captain takes off his old slouch, and smiles all the way round to the back of his ears, and gets off a bow which he hasn't got any ramrod to interfere with, and says: "Glad to see you, Smith, glad to see you—you're looking well—haven't

[88] For river steamboating see G. B. Merrick, *Old Times on the Upper Mississippi* (Cleveland, 1908); same author, "Joseph Reynolds and the Diamond Jo Line of Steamers, 1862-1911," Miss. Valley Hist. Assoc., *Proceeds.*, VIII 217-261; E. W. Gould, *Fifty Years on the Mississippi* (St. Louis, 1889).

[89] S. L. Clemens (Mark Twain, *pseud.*), *Life on the Mississippi* (Hartford, 1874), chap. xxii.

seen you looking so well for years—what you got for us?" "Nuth'n," says Smith; and keeps his hat on, and just turns back and goes to talking with somebody else.[90]

For years the old-time interests nourished by Mississippi commerce refused to accept the doom which had fallen upon them. They declared that all would be well if the rapids near Keokuk were overcome and the silt bars at the mouth of the river cleared away; they persuaded Congress to dredge and light the channel as never before, and it spent millions on the Eads jetties. St. Louis even erected elevators on the river and established a barge line to New Orleans. Several powerful corporations were formed to place large fleets upon the river and to handle them with all the economy of large-scale management. Among these were the famous "Diamond Jo" line, organized by Joseph Reynolds near the close of the sixties, and the Northwestern Union Packet Company, which came into existence in 1866 through the exertions of Commodore William F. Davidson. But the position of all these lines was essentially weak and even the barging business was more and more heavily invaded by the railroads. The Mississippi by 1873 had ceased to be a great highway.

It would be expected that the position of labor, in this period of thriving industry, would be one of great prosperity; and viewed superficially, this seemed the fact. Work was abundant and wages were firm or rising. Men talked with wonder of the high pay which skilled employees were receiving. Rumor exaggerated the returns obtained by labor, while employers, as ever in flush periods, had much to say of the money the working class spent on liquor, fine clothes, jewelry and parlor organs.[91] But when investigators looked beneath this bright surface they found a very different state of affairs. It can be summarized in Commissioner Wells's succinct statement at the close of 1866 that while the average wage had risen about sixty per cent since 1860, the increase in the cost of commodities was about ninety per cent, while in computing the cost of living a still greater rise in house rents had to be considered. Wells found that only a single working group, the copper miners, enjoyed the advantage of doubled wages in facing a doubled cost of living. Innumerable workmen—the ready-made clothing workers, the farm laborers of the North and West, and so on—obtained only half again as much

[90] Mark Twain, *Life on the Mississippi* (N. Y., 1911), 433.
[91] *N. Y. Eve. Post*, July 13, 1865; *Am. Ann. Cyclop.*, IX (1869), 260 ff.

as before the war.[92] Nor was this a merely transient pinch. Two years later, when a momentary depression was making business men uneasy, it was still more evident that the workingmen had actually suffered a loss from the economic changes produced by the war. For all their apparently enhanced reward, skilled employees could be found living in shabbier and less sanitary homes than formerly—sometimes eating plainer fare. Commissioner Wells again asserted that the great majority of wage-earners were worse off than in 1860.[93]

Ordinary workmen of intelligence in the larger cities were glad to get $2 a day. The whistles everywhere sounded at seven a.m., at noon an hour was allowed and at six in the evening the ten-hour day was finished. In some trades the hours were a little shorter, but in others a good deal more. Thus in New York the drivers of horse cars and stages labored, in blazing heat or biting cold, twelve or even sixteen hours a day for two dollars, while hotel or livery drivers toiled an equal period for from ten dollars and fifty cents to twelve dollars a week. The lot of women employees was often bitterly hard. When peace came, New York had not less than fifteen thousand working women whose weekly pittance did not rise above three dollars and fifty cents or four dollars. They were employed in shops, factories and large stores and they had reason to count themselves happier than the thousands of wretched women, sisters to Tom Hood's slaving seamstress, who carried materials home and made shirts and overalls for seventy-five cents a dozen. Girls in the drygoods stores of the great Eastern cities, where civilization was proudest of its achievements, toiled from seven thirty in the morning till the closing hour of nine or ten, without seats, without rest rooms or facilities for a quiet lunch, without more consideration than dumb animals received; and for this health-ruining drudgery many were paid five dollars a week.[94]

It was therefore no impulse of perversity, as some employers suggested, which led at once to a concerted movement for shorter hours and better pay. Ira Steward, a self-educated Boston machinist, indignant at the overwork he saw all about him and imbued with the ideas of John Stuart Mill, became the foremost apostle of a wide-

92 Special Commissioner of Revenue, *Report for December, 1866*, 14 ff.; *N. Y. Eve. Post and N. Y. Herald*, Jan. 4, 1867, for comment.
93 Special Commissioner of Revenue, *Report for December, 1868; Nation*, IX, July 15, 1869.
94 *N. Y. Eve. Post*, July 13, 1865.

spread agitation for an eight-hour day.[95] Eight Hour Leagues were formed in various states, a national congress met at Baltimore in 1866, and labor pressure carried through six legislatures laws which established eight hours as the legal day, unless other hours were agreed upon. These statutes proved futile, but the movement, by calling forcible attention to some of the grave abuses which labor endured, had its decided value. Another expression of the growing labor discontent lay in the vigorous movement for distributive coöperation on the Rochdale plan, an outgrowth of Socialistic and Fourieristic philosophy. Coöperative stores were set up to sell groceries, meat, drygoods and footwear to workmen, while many workers, in the years 1866-1869, tried to open small factories and produce wares coöperatively. Bakers went into the breadmaking business; coach makers combined to make and sell vehicles; coal miners, shipwrights, glass blowers, hat makers, tailors, printers and many others embarked in business for themselves. Most important of all were the coöperative stove foundries established in Rochester, Troy, Pittsburgh, Louisville, Cleveland, Chicago and other cities in 1866-1867 under the leadership of William H. Sylvis, president of the Molders' International Union.[96] Some of these undertakings were financially successful, but the basic difficulty was that they tended to turn into old-style capitalistic enterprises, the owners hiring new workmen on a wage basis.

The best weapon of underpaid, overworked labor was after all, not legislative action nor coöperation but a trade union powerful enough to call an effective strike. Though by 1870 there were more than thirty national unions with a total membership of perhaps three hundred thousand, and though the year 1866 witnessed the formation of the National Labor Union as a result of Sylvis's efforts, there was still little militant labor action. Strikes were few in number, frowned upon by public opinion, and for the most part abortive. Many organizations fell into quick decay, the National Labor Union going to pieces in the years 1870-1872.[97] In many respects the most

[95] J. R. Commons and Associates, *History of Labour in the United States* (N. Y., 1921), II, 87 ff.; 124 ff., 138-139; F. T. Carlton, *The History and Problems of Organized Labor* (N. Y., 1921), 63; J. R. Commons and others, *Documentary History of American Industrial Society* (Cleveland, 1910-1911), IX, 26.

[96] J. C. Sylvis, *The Life, Speeches, Labors and Essays of William H. Sylvis* (Phila., 1872); Commons and Associates, *Labour in the United States*, II, 111.

[97] Mary Beard, *A Short History of the American Labor Movement* (N. Y., 1920), 72 ff.; Commons and Associates, *Labour in the United States*, II, chap. iv.

impressive of the bodies formed in the first decade after the war was the Knights of St. Crispin, the shoemakers' organization. It was a natural response to the introduction of the factory system into the shoe industry and its chief initial object was to protect the skilled journeyman against the competition of green hands and apprentices. Established in Milwaukee early in 1867, it spread like a prairie fire before a gale, until by the spring of 1872 there were no fewer than three hundred and twenty-seven lodges. The Crispins for a time conducted strikes with impressive success, waging a series of victorious battles in Lynn, Worcester, Philadelphia and San Francisco; but after an unsuccessful strike at Lynn in 1872, the order was gradually beaten back by the employers.[98] Throughout these years the organization of unions and the conduct of strikes were grievously hampered by the inrush of immigrant workers, many of them skilled and all ready to accept employment under conditions which American labor found unsatisfactory.

This sullen discontent on the part of a great mass of workers, these attempts to seize upon one remedy after another—of one, the organization of the Knights of Labor in 1869, we shall hear a great deal more—represented part of the dark reverse of the bright shield of industrial prosperity and expansion. Another gloomy aspect of the business rush and whirl lay in the frequent dishonesty, the sharp manipulation and the ever-growing tendency toward speculative excesses, which accompanied it. Still another lay in the private extravagance, the relaxation of moral standards and the vulgarization of taste which it encouraged from Boston to Omaha. The war, which had done so much to create the era of inflation and abounding prosperity, had also introduced many elements of confusion and recklessness into American life and thrown off old restraints. But for the time the great body of Americans, intent upon dipping their cups into the golden stream, overlooked all this. They thought only of the humming mills, the smoking factories, the magic birth of new cities and towns all over the West, the throng of immigrants from Europe, the atmosphere of optimism and cheer. The nation had never seemed so busy, its future never so bright. There was faith everywhere; but after the stunning disasters of 1873, so suddenly to follow, men wondered how they could have been so credulous.

[98] D. D. Lescohier, *The Knights of St. Crispin, 1867-1874* (Univ. of Wis., *Econ. and Pol. Sci. Series*, VII, 1910, no. 1).

C. VANN WOODWARD

∿∿

THE FOCUS of historians tends to follow the most dramatic action on the historical stage. Among historians more concerned with sociological trends than climactic events, there is an equivalent inclination to minimize the inchoate in favor of the strongly developed. It is no accident, therefore, that the culture of the pre-Civil War South has been examined minutely but that the years after Reconstruction have been relatively neglected. The attractiveness of the ante-bellum South requires little explanation. Although it scarcely had the unity suggested by the careless generalization "slave culture," it has seemed to many to be an integrated and somewhat exotic whole. Southern writers have had the added inducement of feeling, consciously or unconsciously, that it was an act of sectional faith to provide satisfactory accounts of the "Old South" in full flower.

Having laid the Confederacy to rest and withdrawn the last of the federal troops from the occupied South, historians have customarily shifted their interest to the industrial progress of the victorious North. When Southern developments have re-entered the general historical narrative, they have usually appeared as subdivisions of the "agrarian protest" or "the rise of regional literature."

C. Vann Woodward's *Origins of the New South, 1877–1913,* is a brilliant and long-needed study in a neglected field. Out of scattered monographs, original research, and a penetrating understanding, Woodward has fashioned a broad synthesis which attempts to integrate all the important phases of Southern

C. VANN WOODWARD 83

society into a coherent whole. It is a difficult task, made more demanding by Woodward's steady refusal to accept many of the traditional concepts his predecessors used to organize the material. Indeed, the primary purpose of the book may be considered as an effort to redefine the term "the New South," which others have used so glibly.

If one set of circumstances may be said to dominate the others within this culture, Woodward seems reasonably certain that it is the economic. Just as the country as a whole was dominated in the last quarter of the nineteenth century by the rise of industry, so the key to Southern development—political and ideological as well as economic—must be sought in the ways in which the region was affected by the shift away from an agriculturally oriented economy. The same representatives of big business moved into positions of political power, believing in the doctrines of social Darwinism which held sway in Northern thought. But what gives especial distinction to Woodward's work is his searching analysis of the impact of these general trends on a section less prepared than the North to receive them.

It is not a pretty story, and the author certainly cannot be accused of making it less grim than it was. The ruthless selfishness of business interests, the continued frustration of the spirit of the Thirteenth Amendment, the demoralizing agrarian poverty, and the brutality of factory life—all these are set down with what seems an almost excessive severity. In any case, if the "New South" of industry and grimy cities did not arrive overnight, it was not for want of Northern examples and of Southern leaders eager to duplicate them. The failure to achieve a full-fledged industrial society may be attributed partly to the same circumstances which had kept the region in a colonial status throughout its history. The North proved no less exacting a creditor than Great Britain had been in the eighteenth century; and absentee ownership increased in direct ratio with industrial expansion.

The least satisfactory part of the book deals with the persistence of "Old South" within the new. Woodward appears to regard the former primarily as a legend useful to appease Southern vanity and to titillate the advocates of the new industrial order. But there was a substance as well as a myth. The continuing force of agrarian economic institutions and ideologies must be explained rather than dismissed. Resentment of a commercial culture took more important, even if less attractive, forms than the novels of Thomas Nelson Page. Woodward is, of course, well aware of this, although his description of the triumph of Whiggery sometimes makes less than an adequate allowance for it. The reconciliation of new industrial hopes with sectional realities is still far from complete.

Not the least noteworthy feature of this book of many distinctions is the fact that its author is a Southerner. Sectional historians are noted more for their loyalties than for their objectivity. In dealing fearlessly and honestly with the South, Woodward has not only written what is destined to become a classic in its own right; he may very well have set the standard by which future regional historians will judge their success in disengaging facts from feelings.

The Divided Mind of the New South

CANVASSING the Southern problem in 1880, Edwin L. Godkin felt that he had hit upon the essence of the matter. "The conversion of the Southern whites to the ways and ideas of what is called the industrial stage in social progress, which is really what has to be done to make the South peaceful, is not a more formidable task than that which the anti-slavery men had before them fifty years ago," he wrote. He believed that the conversion could be effected "by the kind of speaking which persuades men and not that which exasperates them." Admittedly there were obstacles. "The South," he said, "in the structure of its society, in its manners and social traditions, differs nearly as much from the North as Ireland does, or Hungary, or Turkey." The common religion, language, and law were important, "but they are only a basis."[1]

Godkin was not the first to entertain such ideas. They seemed especially common, in fact, among critics of foreign or New England extraction. Alexis de Tocqueville had thought that the perverse South would be "assimilated" by "the civilization of the North."[2] Ralph Waldo Emerson, the New England sage, shared his views. Speaking at Washington in 1862 to an audience that included President Lincoln and members of his cabinet, Emerson asked, rhetorically: "Why cannot the best civilization be extended over the whole country, since the disorder of the less-civilized portion menaces the existence of the country?"[3] Once Lincoln's policy of moderation was overthrown, the idea of revolutionizing Southern society in the image of the North became the avowed policy of

From *Origins of the New South* by C. Vann Woodward, by permission of the Louisiana State University Press.

[1] *Nation*, XXXI (1880), 126.

[2] Alexis de Tocqueville, *Democracy in America*, trans. by Henry Reeve (New York, 1904), II, 444.

[3] Ralph Waldo Emerson, quoted in Charles and Mary Beard, *The American Spirit* (New York, 1942), 310.

the party in power. In the words of Thaddeus Stevens, "It is intended to revolutionize their principles and feelings . . . [to] work a radical reorganization in Southern institutions, habits, and manners." For Governor Horatio Seymour that revolution would not be complete "until their ideas of business, industry, money making, spindles and looms were in accord with those of Massachusetts."[4]

Inhabitants of "the less-civilized portion," from the days of Thomas Jefferson down to the period under consideration, had shown little hospitality toward these conceptions and some truculence in rejecting them. As late as 1880, only a week after Godkin's analysis of the situation appeared, Whitelaw Reid despaired of converting the refractory Southerners. "To us," he wrote, "the principles to which they cling are heresies not to be entertained after such bloody refutation as they have had. . . . [Yet] no facts, no statistics, no arguments, can make them comprehend that the Northern masses are their superiors, intellectually, physically, numerically, and financially."[5] Had Reid and Godkin scanned the Southern scene more carefully, however, they would have discovered much to inspire hope.

In comparing the difficulties of converting the South to "the industrial stage of social progress" with those encountered by the abolitionists, Godkin might have taken heart in reflecting that whereas the abolitionists had been met with resolute hostility, their tracts having been banned from the mails and their sympathizers summarily ejected, the new revolutionists were able to penetrate the South's borders with ease. Their tracts filled Southern journals, and their Southern converts stormed and took whole cities.

Among the spokesmen of Northern industry who caught the ear of the South was the Boston capitalist Edward Atkinson. Although one of the aims of Atkinson's mission, as spokesman of New England's cotton manufacturers, was to divert the South into primary industries and the preparation of raw materials, he was listened to eagerly and read widely. His biographer describes him as "a former Abolitionist who had his first Southern contact in helping

4 Quoted in Howard K. Beale, *The Critical Year* (New York, 1930), 149, 276.
5 New York *Tribune*, August 30, 1880.

to equip John Brown's raiders with Sharp's rifles."[6] But whereas Atkinson's armed emissary had been dealt with harshly, Atkinson himself was given an honorary degree by a leading Southern university, and was much sought after as a speaker. Speaking in Atlanta in 1880 he said: "When we, who are business men take a firm hold upon political questions, and try men and measures by their effect on industry and commerce, a great advance in the true science of politics will have been made." North and South would then be "one in faith, and one in hope." He was "warmly congratulated" upon his speech by Governer Colquitt, former Governor Bullock, Kimball, and the two Inman brothers—now presumably all "one in faith."[7]

William D. Kelley, often called "Pig Iron" because of his advocacy of protection, performed the mission from the Pennsylvania ironmasters to the Southern mineral region that Atkinson performed for the New England manufacturers in the textile South. Back in 1867 the Radical Republican Kelley had appeared at Mobile to preach his doctrines to a mixed group of whites and blacks and precipitated a riot that threatened his life. Less than twenty years later, however, in an extended speaking tour in the same region Kelley professed himself touched by "The eager desire of these energetic, hopeful, and courteous people" to hear a man they once "regarded as the chief apostle of a system of oppressive sectional taxation, which had reduced the Southern people to the condition of hewers of wood and drawers of water."[8]

The South gave willing ear to other Northern evangelists, but far more influential than the Northerners were their Southern apostles. Some of them, not old enough to recall the Old Order, combined the zeal of the new convert with the impetuosity of youth. Richard H. Edmonds was only twenty-five when he founded the *Manufacturers' Record* of Baltimore in 1882, and William Wadley Yonge was twenty-three when he helped launch the *Tradesman* of Chattanooga. Born in Augusta, Georgia, in 1856, Yonge, with the support of Adolph S. Ochs, started the *Tradesman* in 1879. Yonge

6 Harold F. Williamson, *Edward Atkinson; The Biography of an American Liberal, 1827-1905* (Boston, 1934), 176.
7 Quoted in Hannibal I. Kimball, *International Cotton Exposition, 1881 . . .* (New York, 1882), 12-14, 26.
8 Kelley, *Old South and the New,* 138-39.

died at the age of twenty-nine, but his journal continued to expand in influence. The young Virginian Edmonds gained greater influence, not only through the Baltimore journal, but through pamphlets, books, and speeches. Spread on the pages of the *Manufacturers' Record* were weekly reports on the triumphs of the Southern capitalism: investments, new establishments, letters, and speeches of Northern capitalists. The journal described itself as "a thoroughly Southern paper," "thoroughly identified with the New South."[9] Edmonds employed statistics for hortatory purposes, with something of the orator's license. A businessman himself, and eventually director in several large corporations, Edmonds scorned politics and politicians and, as he said, "labored persistently to impress upon the people of the South the importance of giving every possible encouragement to Northern and foreign capitalists to invest their money in the South." He inveighed against "demagogues and blatherskites," who provoked "the agrarian spirit against railroads," and he pressed the protests of Northeast capitalists against "local taxation and other shortsighted but sugar-coated communism in many Southern states."[10] Inspired by the *Record,* many similar journals were founded in the South. One of them, the *Texas Trade Review,* declared that "Mr. Edmonds has set an example that may well and profitably be followed by others."[11]

In a day when newspapers were regarded as the voice of their editors, the editors of city dailies—Francis W. Dawson of the Charleston *News and Courier,* Henry Watterson of the Louisville *Courier-Journal,* Henry W. Grady of the Atlanta *Constitution*— were public figures of supreme importance. Their organs were regarded in the eighties as "metropolitan and unprejudiced," as distinct from small papers that reflected "local surroundings and interests" and were therefore "prejudiced"[12]—a distinction, incidentally, which sounds, more surely than volumes of statistics, the depths of change in the New South. The country editors themselves, eager to keep up with the city oracles, "echoed them with tiny peals in the local weeklies."[13]

9 *Manufacturers' Record,* VI (August 16, 1884), 7; IX (February 13, 1886), 7.
10 *Ibid.,* VII (May 2, 1885), 359; VIII (December 5, 1885), 544.
11 Quoted *ibid.,* XXXIV (December 16, 1898), 349.
12 New Orleans *Times Democrat,* quoted *ibid.,* VII (June 13, 1885), 556.
13 Thomas D. Clark, *The Southern Country Editor* (Indianapolis, 1948), 28-29.

Dawson, the romantic Anglo-Southerner who had enlisted in the Confederate navy at Southampton in the opening year of the Civil War, began his persistent campaign for Southern capitalism and industry in the early seventies from the columns of the *News and Courier*. In Dawson's metropolitan and unprejudiced eyes there was nothing in old Charleston that could not be improved with an eye to Pittsburgh. "As for Charleston," he wrote, "the importation of about five hundred Yankees of the right stripe would put a new face on affairs, and make the whole place throb with life and vivid force." He preferred "a cross between the Bostonian and the Chicagoan."[14] Although Dawson and his compatriot Godkin, who preceded him to the New World by five years, chose opposing sides in the Civil War of their adopted land, they saw eye to eye on the deeper consequences of that unpleasantness. If Atkinson and Kelley were the emissaries of Boston and Philadelphia, Dawson and Godkin spoke with the voice of Manchester to the New South.

There was a magic in Henry Grady's name that still has potency. "What a radiant and charming and accomplished man he was!" exclaimed Josephus Daniels half a century after Grady's death.[15] To his own times Grady was "a genius born for an era—a marvel of inspiration to every faltering industry."[16] He came by his businessman's philosophy honestly, for he sprang not from planter stock but from ante-bellum tradesmen, promoters, and gold prospectors, and he married into a pioneer cotton-manufacturing family. Grady's business associates and friends included John H. Inman, Major Burke, and Victor Newcomb, young president of the Louisville and Nashville. Hard luck stalked his newspapers, three of which failed within five months. His luck turned in 1880, however, when Cyrus W. Field loaned him $20,000 to buy a quarter interest in the Atlanta *Constitution*, and Newcomb guided him in stock speculation to pay off the loan. By 1887 the weekly edition of his paper was claiming the largest subscription list in the South, and the following year it was acknowledged to have the largest circulation of any paper of its kind in the United States. But Grady

14 Charleston *News and Courier*, August 11, 1882.
15 Daniels, *Tar Heel Editor*, 382.
16 Walter G. Cooper, *The Piedmont Region* . . . (Atlanta, 1895), 97.

became more famous and influential than his paper. As a practical political with the wires of a powerful machine in his hands, he helped see to it that Georgia was governed by the new industrialists. As an orator of national fame he advertised opportunities for investment in his region, celebrated the self-made man, and preached "reconciliation" with the Northeast. Both Grady and Dawson died in 1889, still young men, yet men who had lived to see their message accepted as the creed of their people.[17]

Rarely were the new captains of industry sufficiently articulate to speak their message directly to their people. Yet not only was Daniel Augustus Tompkins a great industrialist, but he was also supremely articulate, and fired with a zeal to proselytize his unregenerate countrymen. Brought up in the county of Edgefield, South Carolina, Tompkins was educated at Rensselaer Polytechnic Institute in New York, served his apprenticeship as engineer at the Bethlehem Iron Works, and in 1882 moved to Charlotte, North Carolina, to open his own business. This included, according to his biographer, the work of "industrial missionary and apostle of the New South." His business prospered wonderfully. He became "chief owner and president of three large cotton mills, director of eight mills, and stockholder in many more," besides a manufacturer and distributor of cotton-mill machinery and machinery for other kinds of mills all over the South. Edmonds quickly discovered in young Tompkins a kindred spirit and invited him to write for the *Manufacturers' Record*. As owner of three newspapers and writer of innumerable pamphlets and articles, Tompkins became a publicist in his own right. In his papers he "made use of all possible material that could be used either to point the moral or adorn the tale of industrialism. . . . Anything, everything, and everybody—all the world—was grist in the voracious Tompkins mill of industrialism. He ground it out and gave it to Piedmont Carolina for its meal." Capable of some subtlety, the propagandist realized that "these changes had to be carefully expressed and worked out to keep from offending the delicate sensibilities of a fine race of people." Like some modern Augustine, Tompkins elaborated a whole theory of the history of his people to justify his faith. "In the early days of the republic," ran the theory, "the

17 Nixon, *Henry W. Grady*, 26-32, 45, 122, 167-69, 183, 238, 257-58, 262.

South was the manufacturing end of the union." Then arose false prophets—"Mr. Jefferson," with his "mistaken theory," for example, not to mention Tompkins' distant relative Calhoun—and there followed years of wandering in the wilderness. The new gospel, then, was not recantation but asseveration. Like Carnegie a reader of Herbert Spencer, Tompkins believed that "the survival of the fittest is, has been, and will always be the law of progress." In his papers he fought child-labor legislation and sought to save "Democracy from Communistic Populism," and capitalist enterprise from governmental regulation of any sort.[18]

It is perhaps worth observing of Tompkins, as well as of all the apostles of his persuasion so far mentioned, that it is a mistake to view them merely as advocates of "industrialism"—of which there were several ante-bellum examples in the South. What is more important, they were preaching laissez-faire capitalism, freed of all traditional restraints, together with a new philosophy and way of life and a new scale of values.

Influences of other kinds brought to bear on the dominant minority in the South were changing the region's character more subtly and powerfully than it could be altered by frank propaganda. Recalling that in the old days "the Lowndeses, Randolphs, Rutherfords and so on married right and left into the Knickerbocker blood," a Richmond newspaper in the nineties was not surprised to observe that more recently "intermarriage has given New York's best society a distinctly southern blend."[19] Both Cornelius Vanderbilt and Collis P. Huntington, in their second marriages, chose young brides from Alabama. Henry M. Flagler at seventy-one married a young North Carolina belle and built her a $2,500,000 palace at Palm Beach. For these aging buccaneers the South was a belated romance upon which they lavished endowments, investments, and the devotion of dotage.

Charles Dudley Warner remarked in 1889 that "society becomes yearly more and more alike North and South. It is becoming more and more difficult to tell in any summer assembly—at Newport, the White Sulphur, Saratoga, Bar Harbor—by physiognomy, dress

18 Winston, *Builder of the New South . . . Daniel Augustus Tompkins*, 12-16, 75-78, 126, 234, 242-44, 253, 299.
19 Richmond *Dispatch*, June 9, 1895.

or manner, a person's birthplace."[20] Irene Langhorne of Virginia established her claim to the title of the all-American "Gibson girl" by marrying Charles Dana Gibson in 1895. About Miss Langhorne there was said to be "no trace of languor." She was "in tune with the times," "capable and energetic." Even Southern belles could be brisk and businesslike. And over the gilded court of New York's exclusive Four Hundred, as arbiter of a thousand fine points ("One is taken, the other left"), presided the renegade Georgian, Ward McAllister. On his arm Irene Langhorne led the grand march at the New York Patriarch's Ball in 1893.

> He does not reign in Russia cold,
> Nor yet in far Cathay,
> But o'er this town he's come to hold
> All undisputed sway.[21]

New Southerners invaded not only Fifth Avenue but Wall Street, where there were "several Aladdins who came from the South." Some ancient names appeared in these alien courts: a Beverley Tucker, "for many years a successful counsel before congressional committees for large railroad corporations,"[22] or a John C. Calhoun, railroad speculator. But most of the names were new: John H. Inman, from broker's clerk to Fifth Avenue mansion. "What an exemplar is here for our young men," exclaimed Henry Grady over Inman's rise. "What a brilliant promise to draw them away from the arid ways of politics . . . at thirty-six worth a million and a half."[23] Some were found useful as presidents of Southern firms controlled from Wall Street: Samuel Spencer, from section boss to president of Morgan's Southern Railway. "Being found exceedingly faithful over a very few things," it was said of him, "he was soon given authority over many."[24]

One evidence of the South's acceptance of Northern ideas as the "national" standard was its pathetic eagerness for Northern ap-

---

[20] Warner, *Studies in the South and West*, 35-36.
[21] Ward McAllister, *Society as I Have Found It* (New York, 1890, 162, 232; Fairfax Downey, *Portrait of an Era as Drawn by C. D. Gibson* (New York, 1936), 215, 222.
[22] Richmond *Dispatch*, July 5, 1890.
[23] Quoted in Russell F. Terrell, *A Study of the Early Journalistic Writings of Henry W. Grady* (Nashville, 1927), 163.
[24] Richmond *Dispatch*, June 9, 1895.

proval: A little Mississippi weekly paper, quoting the Detroit *Free Press,* congratulating Mississippians on their "push"; a Baltimore journal basking in the approval of Henry Ward Beecher; the Galveston *News* snatching at a compliment from Jay Gould; Atlantans rejoicing in a donation to their Cotton Exposition from General William T. Sherman. "We wanted commendation at that time from our conquerors," remembered a New Orleans woman, "and we needed it."[25]

Northern families were sometimes important elements in the new dominant society. Especially in the mineral region were they prone to make of some towns not only economic, but political outposts of empire. Writing to Secretary William E. Chandler, who had inquired about prospects for the Republican party in Alabama, a Northern immigrant replied: "Large manufacturing interests have sprung up at Birmingham just outside; and all in this District: Alabama Furnace; Anderson Furnace, controlled by Genl. Tyler of Pennsylvania, Tecumpsa [*sic*] Furnace controlled by Ohio people, Shelby *Iron* Furnace, the largest in the state—some millions of Capital, controlled by *Hartford Connecticut people*—The Stonewall Furnace, the Aetna Furnace, Cedar Creek Furnace, & other large manufacturing interests—*all controlled by Northern men* who will cooperate if the proper influences are brought to bear."[26]

Within the little islands of industrialism scattered through the region, including the old towns as well as the new, was rising a new middle-class society. It drew some recruits from the old planter class, but in spirit as well as in outer aspect it was essentially new, strikingly resembling the same class in Midwestern and Northeastern cities.[27] Richmond, former capital of the Confederacy, observed the social revolution within its walls with complacency: "We find a new race of rich people have been gradually springing up among us, who owe their wealth to successful trade and espe-

---

[25] King, *Memories of a Southern Woman of Letters,* 53.
[26] W. E. Horne, Talladega, Ala., to Chandler, September 15, 1882, in Chandler Papers. A similar instance was that of a Pennsylvanian who wrote Chandler: "While not wishing to be egotistical I think I can control the Electoral vote of Florida in the coming national contest." He explained: "I am the man who originated the Disston scheme which has put several millions of dollars in that state and put them on their feet." A. B. Linderman to Chandler, December 19, 1883, *ibid.*
[27] *Figaro* (New Orleans), I, (1883-1884), 8.

cially to manufacturers. . . . [They] are taking the leading place not only in our political and financial affairs, but are pressing to the front for social recognition. . . . 'The almighty dollar' is fast becoming a power here, and he who commands the most money holds the strongest hand. We no longer contemn the filthy lucre. . . . They may be parvenuish, and want something of the polish which is the heritage of birth or only acquired by many generations of refining influences; but these are trifling matters. . . . Our provincial characteristics are fast disappearing, and we are not only advancing towards metropolitan development, but are losing our petty, narrow prejudices and becoming truly cosmopolitan. . . . We are not longer a village but a city."[28]

The *Industrial South* asked in the title of an editorial, "Shall We Dethrone Our Idols?" and answered with a thumping affirmative. It seems that "the founders of our American system . . . forgot to consider that the American public was to be peculiarly a community of business men, and that what it would most need was the practical wisdom of business men in the administration of its affairs. And so from the beginning the places of trust and honor were filled by warriors and orators." The inference was plain: "Beyond all question we have been on the wrong tack and should take a new departure."[29] With Virginia leading the way, this heedless iconoclasm swept the South. "If proselytism be the supreme joy of mankind," declared Henry Watterson in 1877, "New England must be pre-eminently happy, for the ambition of the South is to out-Yankee the Yankee."[30] There were even breaches in that irreducible citadel of Southernism—Mississippi. "We are in favor," announced a Vicksburg paper to a hushed Delta, "of the South, from the Potomac to the Rio Grande, being thoroughly and permanently Yankeeized."[31]

The facts of the record would not seem to warrant the contention that "whereas in England many from the middle class became captains of industry, here [in the South] the characteristic leadership proceeded from the aristocracy." According to this inter-

28 Richmond *Whig and Advertiser*, April 4, 1876.
29 *Industrial South*, V (1885), No. 3, p. 2.
30 From a speech delivered in New York, quoted in New York *Tribune*, November 21, 1877.
31 Vicksburg *Herald*, quoted in *American*, II (1881), 166.

pretation, the English industrialists were "small men who struck it lucky," whereas the Southern mill men were "gentlemen."[32] A study of the background of 254 industrialists in the South of this period reveals that "about eighty per cent came of nonslaveowning parentage." Out of a total of 300 studied only 13 per cent were of Northern birth.[33] Professor John Spencer Bassett, the historian, who took a peculiar delight in the rise of the new and the decline of the old ruling class, wrote that "The rise of the middle class has been the most notable thing connected with the white population of the South since the war. . . . Everywhere trade and manufacturing is almost entirely in the hands of men who are sprung from the non-planter class, and . . . the professions seem to be going the same way." As for the old planters, a decadent class, Bassett thought, "They have rarely held their own with others, and most frequently they have been in the upper ranks of those who serve rather than those who direct business. . . . But the captains of industry . . . are men who were never connected with the planter class."[34] A shrewd New England observer corroborated the Southerner's view when he wrote in 1890: "now, like a mighty apparition across the southern horizon, has arisen this hope or portent of the South,—the Third Estate,—to challenge the authority of the old ruling class." He advised his section against "exclusive observation of the old conflict of races" in the South. "For the coming decade, the place to watch the South is in this movement of the rising Third Estate. What it demands and what it can achieve in political, social, and industrial affairs . . . on these things will depend the fate of this important section of our country for years to come."[35]

Mark Twain on a Southern junket in the eighties was brought face to face with these men of the New South: "Brisk men, energetic of movement and speech; the dollar their god, how to get it their religion."[36] Somewhat awkwardly, but with great show of

32 Mitchell and Mitchell, *Industrial Revolution in the South*, 32, 106.

33 George W. Adams, unpublished paper quoted in Schlesinger, *Rise of the City*, 15 n. The industrialists studied were "random instances" from Virginia, North Carolina, South Carolina, Georgia, Alabama, and Tennessee.

34 John S. Bassett, "The Industrial Decay of the Southern Planter," in *South Atlantic Quarterly* (Durham), II (1903), 112-13.

35 A. D. Mayo, "The Third Estate of the South," in *New England Magazine* (Boston), N.S., III (1890-1891), 300.

36 Twain, *Life on the Mississippi*, 412.

self-assurance, this new man adjusted to his shoulders the mantle of leadership that had descended from the planter. Some considerable alteration was found necessary: less pride and more "push," for example. Punctilio was sacrificed to the exigencies of "bustle," and arrogance was found to be impracticable in the pursuit of the main chance.

Up and down the ranks of society the professions began to cut their garments to the new pattern. "The way of the successful author is pointed out by the successful business man," affirmed Bassett of Trinity College, an institution already associated with the Duke fortune. Professor Bassett found it to be "in harmony with the general social development here" that "the future of authorship in the South will be in the hands of the new men," men unburdened by the incubus of "the blood of a dozen generations of slaveowners." The businessman was the Southern author's best model, because he had "no prejudices against work, no habits of extravagance, and no false loyalty to the worn out ideas of a forgotten system."[37] Even the college student, paragon of conservatism, was reported to be abandoning "the pleasant vices, the midnight brawl, the lawless pranks, the roystering vagabondism of the old days," and, at least in Nashville, to be "earnestly intent upon business, preparing to promote a new progress."[38] Edmonds could report with a degree of truth that "the easy-going days of the South have passed away, never to return. . . . The South has learned that 'time is money.' "[39]

For the ambitious if backward Southerner there were manuals of instruction in the new morals and manners. One, for example, entitled *The Law of Success,* appeared in 1885 under the imprint of the Southern Methodist Publishing House. The Southern author adduced his maxims empirically "from the crystallized experiences of twelve hundred successful men," for the most part Southerners who were "all self-made." His rules, "in harmony with all moral obligations," were primarily laid down for "success in private business." But they were also the assured "means by which to accomplish any purpose," including those of "artists, authors, bankers,

[37] John S. Bassett, "The Problems of the Author in the South," in *South Atlantic Quarterly,* I (1902), 207-208.
[38] Nashville *Daily American,* September 19, 1880.
[39] *Manufacturers' Record,* XIV (November 3, 1888), 11.

dentists, editors." The reader was instructed in "selecting a wife with a view to making his life a success," and in "the commercial value of the Ten Commandments and a righteous life." The theory was advanced that "even social calls and visiting the club-room may prove paying investments of one's time." Allegedly an educator himself, the author evidently kept up with the "trend" and perhaps was a little in advance. "The educator of the future," he wrote, "will teach his pupils what will pay best. He will teach them the art of thinking, which, for the purpose at hand, I may define to be the art of turning one's brains into money. He will not teach dead languages, obsolete formulas, and bric-a-brac sciences . . . which are never used in the ordinary transactions of the forum, the office, the shop, or the farm." The proof, again, was empirical: "The richest man in Arkansas never had any schooling whatever."[40]

Well might Bishop Atticus G. Haygood ask, "Does History record an example in any race or age, where a people of strong character went so far in fifteen years as the Southern people—a race of Anglo-Saxon blood—have gone since 1865 in the modification of opinions, in the change of sentiments that had been, through generations, firmly fixed in all their thinking and feeling? The change in the opinions and sentiments of the Southern people since 1865 is one of the most wonderful facts of history."[41]

Perhaps the most curious aspect of the revolution in values, manners, and institutions that was daily leveling those distinctive traits that Godkin believed set the South as far apart from the Norh as Ireland was the romanticism that accompanied and partially obscured the process. For along with the glittering vision of a "metropolitan" and industrial South to come there developed a cult of archaism, a nostalgic vision of the past. One of the most significant inventions of the New South was the "Old South"—a new idea in the eighties, and a legend of incalculable potentialities.

The first step was the Lost Cause itself. In 1880, in the earlier and more abject stage of the Great Recantation, Watterson's paper could say blandly that "The 'bonny blue flag' is the symbol of nothing to the present generation of Southern men. . . . The

[40] William S. Speer, *The Law of Success* (Nashville, 1885), 5-8, 14, 19-20, 43, 84-85, 226.
[41] Atticus G. Haygood, *Our Brother in Black: His Freedom and His Future* (Nashville, 1881), 101.

Southern Confederacy went down forever fifteen years ago. Its issues and ensigns went down with it."[42] An exaggeration, to be sure, but such a statement, even a suggestion of it, ten years later would have been well-nigh unthinkable. By that time the official position on the progress of the Lost Cause was typified by the editor who declared simply, "It is not lost! On earth it may be lost forever. But might never did make right."[43] The deeper the involvements in commitments to the New Order, the louder the protests of loyalty to the Old.

Jefferson Davis, hardly the most popular Confederate official, was resurrected from his plantation exile in 1886 by Henry Grady (as one means of repairing the political fortunes of General Gordon) and borne in triumph up and down his old domain. Watterson's paper reported the progression "a continuous ovation." Standing on the spot in Montgomery where he had taken his oath as Confederate President twenty-five years before, Davis said, "Your demonstration now exceeds that which welcomed me then. This shows that the spirit of southern liberty is not dead."[44] An observer from Lowell, Massachusetts, declared the ovations were such "as no existing ruler in the world can obtain from his people, and such as probably were never before given to a public man, old, out of office, with no favors to dispense, and disfranchised!" He reported to Lowell that there must be "something great, and noble, and true in him and in the cause to evoke this homage."[45] Thus Yankeedom took to its heart the Lost Cause—a favorite theme in Northern theaters in the nineties, and one not unknown to later generations. The composer of "Carry Me Back to Old Virginny," which glorified the old slave regime, was a native of Long Island and a descendant of slaves.[46] Southern romanticism was highly contagious.

Local reunions of Confederate brigades were known earlier, but it was not until 1889, in New Orleans, that the United Confederate Veterans was organized, with General Gordon "unanimously

[42] Louisville *Courier-Journal*, September 7, 1880.
[43] Richmond *Times*, May 29, 1890.
[44] Richmond *Dispatch*, April 29, 1886; Louisville *Courier-Journal*, May 3, 1886.
[45] Lowell *Weekly Sun*, quoted in *Industrial South*, VI, (1886), 333.
[46] There was an ante-bellum song of the same name, but the familiar one was composed by James A. Bland in 1878.

elected general commander." Lacking the lucrative incentive of Corporal James Tanner's billions extracted from the public treasury for the G.A.R., the commanders of the U.C.V. nevertheless mobilized hosts of ragged Confederates, who thronged to the annual reunions. At the reunion in Richmond in 1896 thousands, many without money, slept in "all the parks, on roofs, on doorsteps, in yards, and even in the streets." Upwards of 10,000 veterans attended, 444 from Texas, and spent the day cheering Mrs. Davis and her daughter ("the chivalric Gordon at the head of the procession") and listening to oratory. The "Adjutant General" reported to Gordon at this session that his office had "now become a vast bureau, with an enormous accumulation of books and papers," conducting an immense correspondence. To the reunion in the same city eleven years later were attracted 80,000 people.[47]

In 1895 the United Daughters of the Confederacy was organized in the capital of the New South, Atlanta. Only then, when the movement was taken into custody by Southern Womanhood, did the cult of the Lost Cause assume a religious character. Monuments were planted in courthouse squares—usually the figure of a soldier facing North, gun in hand. "Our Confederate Column" of the Richmond *Dispatch* had its manifold counterparts, filled with reminiscences, dying words, heroes of godlike mold, battles, skirmishes, and alarums, often giving the impression of news fresh from the front. A week before Bryan was nominated in Chicago, on the occasion of a veterans' reunion, the Richmond *Times* devoted nineteen of its twenty-four pages to the Confederacy and the Old South, and its rival, the *Dispatch,* not to be outdone, twenty of its twenty-four pages. It is a matter for speculation whether any lost cause in modern history, from that of Bonnie Prince Charlie to that of Wilhelm's legions, has received the devotion lavished upon the Stars and Bars.

The romanticism and sentimentality of that generation of Southerners, however, was too copious to spend itself upon the Lost Cause. Genealogy became the avocation of thousands. Its more esoteric branches yielded their treasures to seekers after the heritage of grandeur. The fabled Southern aristocracy, long on its last legs,

[47] Richmond *Times*, July 2, 1896; Richmond *Dispatch*, June 30, 1896; Richmond *Times-Dispatch*. June 5, 1907.

was refurbished, its fancied virtues and vices, airs and attitudes ex-humed and admired. Homage even from the plain man, who for ages had been unimpressed by doings of the upper crust, was added in this period. Drippings from the plantation legend overflowed upon race and labor relations, public charities, and even the organ-ization of factory villages. The Natchez Cotton Mills were adorned with "three spires or turrets of mansard style to give them grace and beauty," and the Female Institute of Columbia, Tennessee, boasted in an advertisement of "its resemblance to the old castles of song and story, with its towers, turreted walls, and ivy-mantled porches."

Mark Twain saw the paradox, but only through the glasses of his age and therefore darkly: "practical common-sense, progressive ideas, and progressive works, mixed up with the duel, the inflated speech, and the jejune romanticism of an absurd past that is dead."[48] Henry James came closer with a cast of one of his loose, netlike sentences. "The collapse of the old order," he speculated, "the humiliation of defeat, the bereavement and bankruptcy in-volved, represented, with its obscure miseries and tragedies, the social revolution the most unrecorded and undepicted, in propor-tion to its magnitude, that ever was; so that this reversion of the starved spirit to the things of the heroic age, the four epic years, is a definite soothing salve."[49]

In addition, the South suffered from a prevailing sense of in-feriority and a constant need for justifying a position. But the really curious thing is that oftener than not this archaic romanticism, this idealizing of the past, proceeded from the mouths of the most active propagandists for the New Order. And this with no apparent sense of inconsistency, certainly none of duplicity. It is true, as al-ready pointed out, that Tompkins (who penned romantic pictures of "Life in the Old South") elaborated a theory to prove that the New South was merely a revival of the "true" genius of the Old South, as it existed prior to certain heresies. Edmonds went so far as to scorn the very name "New South," insisting that it was "simply a revival of the South as it existed thirty-five years ago," that is, in

[48] Twain, *Life on the Mississippi*, 468.
[49] Henry James, *The American Scene* (New York, 1907), 371.

1860![50] But such strained rationalizations did not embarrass the oratory of Henry Grady, of the young Woodrow Wilson, or even of Walter Hines Page, all of whom paid reverent homage to ancestral shrines. Joel Chandler Harris worked for Grady in the Atlanta *Constitution*'s editorial hatchery with no consciousness of serving two masters. After all, if the United Confederate Veterans could follow John B. Gordon as the living embodiment of the legend, what need was there for awkward rationalizations!

The bitter mixture of recantation and heresy could never have been swallowed so readily had it not been dissolved in the syrup of romanticism. Political servants of the New Order used this formula to advantage. In 1894, when the tide of Populism was rising fearfully, Senator Matt W. Ransom's political fortunes were foundering in North Carolina. The mayor of Charlotte wrote him that "The country people, as it seems to us, are at present against you." Then he proposed a well-tested stratagem: "getting Genl Gordon to deliver his lecture on 'the last days of the Confederacy' inviting the country people, and getting him to make an allusion to you!"[51]

No paradox of the New South was more conspicuous than the contrast between the earnestly professed code of shopkeeper decorum and sobriety and the continued adherence to a tradition of violence. For violence was, if anything, more characteristic of the new society than of the old. In the place of the code duello, the traditional expression of violence in the Old South, gunplay, knifing, manslaughter, and murder were the bloody accompaniments of the march of Progress. The old state of South Carolina, with less than a quarter of the six New England states' population, reported nearly three times their number of homicides in 1890. For all its cities and slums and unassimilated immigrants, Massachusetts had only 16 homicides as compared with 65 in Virginia, 69 in North Carolina, 88 in Kentucky, 92 in Georgia, and 115 in Tennessee. Yet none of the Southern states mentioned came within a quarter of a million of the population of Massachusetts, and all were among those having the highest percentage of native, rural

50 Quoted indirectly in New Orleans *Times-Democrat*, November 10, 1895.
51 R. J. Brevard to M. W. Ransom, July 3, 1894, in M. W. Ransom Papers (University of North Carolina Library, Chapel Hill).

population. In the western tiers of states, Michigan had 31 homicides and Alabama 108, Wisconsin 20 and Mississippi 106, Minnesota 21 and Louisiana 98. Kansas and Nebraska were no further removed from frontier conditions than was Texas, but the Northern states reported respectively 34 and 23 homicides and Texas 184. Yet the census figures were admittedly unreliable, since they fell far short of the actual number of homicides, especially those of the rural, sparsely settled areas.[52] A Kentucky editor published figures in 1885 demonstrating that there had been an average of 223 murders a year for the past six years in Kentucky, though the census returned only 50 for 1880; and a Mississippi paper declared in 1879 that there was an average of a murder a day in that state, while the census of the following year reported only 57.[53] It is not improbable that the amount of homicide was two or three times that reported.[54] Italy, with what appeared to be the highest homicide rate in Europe, did not have in her prisons in 1890 as many convicts charged with murder as did the South Central states, which had less than a third of Italy's population.[55] The South seems to have been one of the most violent communities of comparable size in all Christendom.

The record of violence should not be hastily attributed to the Negro, for at least in South Carolina, Kentucky, and Texas white men killed much more often, in proportion to their numbers, than did Negroes. Race violence there was, undoubtedly, but it was only a part of the general milieu of Southern violence and can be understood best against that background. Nor could lower-class whites bear disproportionate blame, for the newspapers of the day were crowded with homicidal frays between lawyers, planters, railroad presidents, doctors, even preachers, and particularly editors. Guns blazed in banks, courtrooms, and schoolhouses as well as in bars

[52] On the unreliability of homicide data, see Bureau of the Census, *Special Reports, Mortality Statistics, 1900-1904* (Washington, 1906), cv-cvi; for the above figures, see *Eleventh Census, 1890, Vital and Social Statistics,* Pt. III, *Statistics of Deaths,* 27-425; to compare 1880, see *Tenth Census, 1880,* XII, *Mortality and Vital Statistics,* Pt. II, 388-427.

[53] Hardinsburg (Ky.) *Breckinridge News,* in Clark, *Southern Country Editor,* 223; Vicksburg *Herald,* May 25, 1879.

[54] Horace V. Redfield, *Homicide, North and South* (Philadelphia, 1880), 172.

[55] Burr J. Ramage, "Homicide in the Southern States," in *Sewanee Review* (Sewanee, Tenn.), IV (1895-1896), 221.

and ginhouses. Casualties were fewer in the spectacular mountain feuds than in bustling towns of the lowlands. And the immediate causes were often absurdly trivial. Of the quarrels resulting in the shooting of five men on one day in a Mississippi county, two arose over the opening of doors and two over petty debts. Dueling persisted, but in diminishing proportions. In one year there were 128 homicides and only 3 duels in South Carolina. In place of the relatively civilized duel there arose the barbarous custom of "shooting-on-sight." According to Southern editors dedicated to reform, the practice of toting a pistol was "almost universal" in some parts. The state auditor of Alabama in 1881 reported the valuation of tools and farming implements in his state to be $305,613; that of guns, pistols, and dirks, $354,247.[56] Turning the chronicles of Southern communities—Edgefield, Vicksburg, Memphis—one is reminded forcefully at times of Marlowe's London, or the Highlands of the wild Scots.

Another anachronism from the Old Order that contrasted queerly with the new society was a lingering grace and simplicity of life. Even its detractors could not quite deny the persistence of this heritage from the country life of ante-bellum Virginia, Carolina, and the Bluegrass. Of the two relics—the heritage of violence and that of grace—the former undoubtedly had more to feed upon in the new society and proved the hardier tradition. Grace and gallantry were more vulnerable to the new climate of push and progress and survived only in sheltered places. Specious varieties of the genuine article were, of course, cultivated for the tourist trade, adopted sedulously by the ancestor societies and the *nouveaux riches* (of Northern as well as Southern origins), and associated in numerous ways known to the advertiser's art with brands of tobacco, liquor, stage beauties, and politicians. When the New South was personified by the cartoonist it was, significantly, in the garb of the ante-bellum planter.

[56] *Nation*, XXXVI (1883), 14; also Redfield, *Homicide, North and South*, 90, 95-96, 101, 151-52, 159, 202; Ramage, "Homicide in the Southern States," *loc. cit.*, 215-19, 222-23; Clark, *Southern Country Editor*, 218-23; Nathaniel S. Shaler, "The Peculiarities of the South," in *North American Review*, CLI (1890), 487. In 1913 the homicide rate in Southern cities was 21.2 per 100,000 population and in Eastern cities 5.6. Frederick L. Hoffman, *The Homicide Problem* (Newark, 1925), 23.

Distressed at the poverty of Southern achievement in the arts and sciences during this period, Nathanial Southgate Shaler speculated on the reasons for "the failure of the Kentucky people to make good their promise." He ascribed it to "a peculiar combination of circumstances, of which the Civil War was the most potent," especially the resulting sacrifice of life. "This sacrifice," he wrote, "was in peculiarly large measure from the intellectual, the state-shaping class," and it was made in the South "in far larger proportion than the Northern states." Before the war he had seen evidence that "men and women were seeking, through history, literature, the fine arts, and in some measure through science, for a share in the higher life. Four years of civil war . . . made an end of this and set the people on a moral and intellectual plane lower than they occupied when they were warring with the wilderness and the savages."[57]

As a matter of fact, Shaler's own career, filled with achievement and renown in geology, was partial refutation of his picture of intellectual barrenness. In his own bluegrass South there was an unusual burst of scientific activity in the eighties. A thriving group of geologists, among them Robert Peter and John R. Proctor, flourished in Kentucky. Lucien Carr, another Kentuckian, won high praise among ethnologists for his studies of the Mound Builders of the Mississippi Valley, and Ellen Churchill Semple of Louisville later became a pioneer in human geography. Edward E. Barnard of Tennessee achieved international fame as an astronomer, and J. Lawrence Smith of Louisville made significant contributions in chemistry. Alert surgeons of the region maintained productive medical schools and flourishing professional journals and established the first state board of health in Tennessee in 1877 and in Kentucky in 1878.[58]

Apart from the sciences and the more practical arts the picture was darker. Even those creative spirits who survived the ordeal of

[57] *The Autobiography of Nathaniel Southgate Shaler* (New York, 1909), 76-77. Mr. Justice Holmes wrote a concurring opinion: "the best part of the South was simply wiped out." Oliver Wendell Holmes to Sir Frederick Pollock, April 25, 1920, in Mark A. de Wolfe (ed.), *Holmes-Pollock Letters* (Cambridge, 1941), II, 40-41.
[58] F. Garvin Davenport, "Scientific Interests in Kentucky and Tennessee, 1870-1890," in *Journal of Southern History*, XIV (1948), 500-21.

war and clung to their purpose found the odds heavily against them. Sidney Lanier's nightmarish struggle against poverty and hemorrhages was only one of the tragedies of the period. Lanier, however, was more fortunate than some; he found a berth for the last three years of his life, first at the Peabody Institute and then (from 1879 to 1881) at the newly founded Johns Hopkins University. A mixture of the Old and the New Order, Baltimore was at one and the same time the last refuge of the Confederate spirit in exile and a lying-in hospital for the birth of the New Order. There William H. Browne's *Southern Magazine* expired in 1875 and Albert T. Bledsoe's *Southern Review*, in 1879; there also the first number of Edmond's *Manufacturers' Record* appeared in 1882; and there Basil L. Gildersleeve wrote his *Creed of the Old South*. To Baltimore came the young Southerners—Walter Hines Page, Woodrow Wilson, and scores of others—to hesitate between the Old and the New. Gildersleeve and about a third of the Hopkins faculty were Southerners.

Others found no refuge. Paul Hamilton Hayne lived in this period near Augusta, Georgia, in a shack furnished with goods boxes and papered by his wife with pictures cut from magazines, like the shacks of Negro croppers. Praise for his verse came from Tennyson and Swinburne, and he continued to write at the carpenter's bench that served him as a desk. Virtually his only associates were the illiterate crackers who worked at a nearby sawmill. He lived in the shack until his death in 1886.

Perhaps Shaler's gloomy analysis and Edward King's belief that "a generation has been doomed" were overstatements of the case. Yet multiple instances of frustration could be cited to support those views. "There's failure in the very air," declared one of Ellen Glasgow's young Virginians. And he echoed a hundred aspirations when he exclaimed, "No, I want to get away, not to spend my life as a missionary to the broomsedge."[59]

Flight was an all-too-common impulse. The swelling migration of Southern talent to the Northeast began quite early. Shaler himself was one instance. The leading American architect of the period, Henry Hobson Richardson, was born on a Louisiana plantation and educated in New Orleans, Harvard, and Paris. In the

[59] Ellen Glasgow, *Barren Ground* (New York, 1925), 112.

seventies and eighties his buildings sprinkled the entire country
—with the exception of his native region. Likewise, John Wellborn
Root of Georgia won his fame as an architect entirely in the North.
Joseph Le Conte and his brother John, Georgians, gained high
distinction as scientists in California but found no opportunity at
home after 1865. The South of the eighties was a bleak place for the
young scholar. "The studious man is pronounced impractical and
is suspected as a visionary," wrote young Woodrow Wilson from
Atlanta in 1883.[60] Wilson soon left for the Johns Hopkins to prepare for a teaching career, a career he pursued outside the South.
Walter Hines Page took his departure for the golden cities about the
same time, flinging back a farewell to the "mummies" of North
Carolina. The South could have its own golden cities and sky-
scrapers, he prophesied, if it would only forget "constitutional
questions which have been irrevocably settled."[61] Page left for New
York "dead broke." In ten years he had put the *Forum* on its feet,
become editor of the *Atlantic Monthly,* and, to keep a hand in the
work of converting his unregenerate homeland, acquired part
ownership of the *Manufacturers' Record.*[62] His headquarters, however, remained in Boston and New York.

Withdrawal of the artist or critic sometimes became a secession
that was spiritual as well as physical, and resulted not only in the
alienation of the writer from his people but in a schism within the
spirit of the man himself. A recurrent tragedy in the intellectual
history of the South, this phenomenon had its cruder prototype in
Hinton Rowan Helper, and its clearest example from this period
in George W. Cable, the novelist. Cable's story, complicated by
psychological crosscurrents, by the heritage of a hapless Virginian
father and a mother of New England stock against a Creole background of New Orleans, presents too many complexities to unravel
here. The crisis of the conflict within him, however, is described
in his own words. As he watched the "great Reconstruction agony

60 Woodrow Wilson to Robert H. Dabney, May 11, 1883, in Ray S. Baker,
Woodrow Wilson; Life and Letters (Garden City, 1927-1939), I, 169.
61 Burton J. Hendrick, *The Training of an American; The Earlier Life and
Letters of Walter H. Page, 1855-1913* (Boston, 1928), 146.
62 In 1895 Page was the second largest stockholder, Edmonds the largest. "List
of Stockholders, May 23, 1895," filed under the name of Richard H. Edmonds in
Walter Hines Page Papers (Houghton Library, Harvard University, Cambridge).

from its first day to its last," Cable found his emotions deeply torn —"with his sympathies ranged upon the pro-Southern side of the issue, and his convictions drifting irresistibly to the other," he wrote. The pull of his convictions and of New England eventually asserted themselves. In 1885, the year Page left for New York, Cable published *The Silent South,* the most radical indictment of Southern racial policy written by a Southerner in that period, and in 1885 he moved his family to Northampton, Massachusetts. He had the right, as he said, to speak as "a native of Louisiana, an ex-Confederate soldier, and a lover of my home, my city, and my State."[63] Yet he never again lived in the South. Both Cable and his people were losers—the writer, of his art, which never fulfilled its rich promise; the South, of a fearless critic and a point of view that could thenceforth be more readily dismissed complacently as foreign. Later Cable would look homeward and melt with ruth: "I felt that I belonged still," he wrote, "peculiarly to the South."[64]

It was in the field of fiction that the postwar generation found fullest expression. The Southern literary revival of the eighties came with a concentration and suddenness that made it unique in the region's history. There were a few transitional figures—the poets Hayne and Lanier, the story-writer Richard M. Johnston— but all of the new major writers burst upon the national consciousness about the same time. Whatever lasting fame these writers were to earn was to depend, with striking similarity and quite regardless of the extent of later publication, upon one or two books, in each case their earliest. All of these books appeared between 1879 and 1887. Cable's *Old Creole Days* was published in 1879, *The Grandissimes* in 1880, and *Madame Delphine* in 1881. Irwin Russell of Mississippi, precursor of the dialect school, died in 1879 at the age of twenty-six. Joel Chandler Harris' *Uncle Remus* appeared in 1881 and his *Mingo* in 1884, Thomas Nelson Page's *In Ole Virginia* in 1887,[65] "Charles Egbert Craddock's" *In the Tennessee Mountains* and *Where the Battle Was Fought* in 1884. A dozen lesser

---

[63] George W. Cable, *The Silent South* (New York, 1885), 25, 47.

[64] Lucy L. C. Biklé, *George W. Cable: His Life and Letters* (New York, 1928), 162; see also Arlin Turner, "George W. Cable, Novelist and Reformer," in *South Atlantic Quarterly,* XLVIII (1949), 539-45.

[65] "Marse Chan," the most famous story in the collection, was first published in 1884, after the publisher had held it four years.

luminaries, among them Grace King and Kate Chopin, took their first bows within the same years.

It was a propitious moment to gain the national eye. The decline of New England's long dominance, New York's neglect of Melville and Whitman, and the subsidence of the vogue enjoyed by the West in the seventies had cleared the stage for the New South. The ninth edition of the *Encyclopedia Britannica,* 1886, in a badly outdated article on "American Literature," said that Southern letters, "mainly by their connection with the North," had been "saved from sinking to the level of Mexico or the Antilles." Yet the following year the New York *Critic* declared that "Southern literature is a sort of craze" and complained of the "excessive praises" lavished on it.[66] In 1888 Albion W. Tourgée, hardly a pro-Southern critic, observed in the *Forum* that "A foreigner studying our current literature, without knowledge of our history, and judging our civilization by our fiction would undoubtedly conclude that the South was the seat of intellectual empire in America, and the African the chief romantic element of our population." As evidence, he pointed out that a few months before "every one of our great popular monthlies presented a 'Southern story' as one of its most prominent features; and during the past year nearly two-thirds of the stories and sketches furnished to newspapers by various syndicates have been of this character." The Southern revival, then, was a national as well as a regional phenomenon, called forth, in part, by a freakishly romantic turn of Northern fancy. Indeed, according to Tourgée, "it cannot be denied that American fiction to-day, whatever its origin, is predominantly Southern in type and character"; not only that, but "distinctly Confederate in sympathy."[67]

If credit for the revival be assigned in the South, it would be a mistake to overlook Joel Chandler Harris. "What strange habitations does genius choose among men," observed the sleekly groomed

[66] Anonymous, "Literature in the South," in *Critic* (New York), VII (1887), 322-23.

[67] Albion W. Tourgée, "The South as a Field for Fiction," in *Forum,* VI (1888-1889), 406-407. According to Shields McIlwaine, *The Southern Poor-White from Lubberland to Tobacco Road* (Norman, 1939), 100, "Between 1882 and 1887, the annual average of articles published on the South was about ten times that during the preceding eighty years."

Walter Hines Page, noting the "red unkempt hair," "the freckled face and freckled hands" of "Joe Harris."[68] This shy, inveterate countryman, illegitimate son of an itinerant Irish laborer, could write unflattering truths of literacy criticism. "The stuff we are in the habit of calling Southern literature," he wrote in 1879, "is not only a burlesque upon true literary art, but a humiliation and a disgrace to the people whose culture it is supposed to represent. . . . The truth might as well be told: we have no Southern literature worthy of the name."[69] Writing across a desk from where Henry Grady was exhorting the South to exploit her "mountains stored with exhaustless treasures," Harris was telling the Southerner with idle literary capital that "all around him, untouched, undeveloped, undisturbed, unique and original, as new as the world, as old as life" were literary materials of unparalleled richness. "But they must be mined. They must be run through the stamp mill," he added.[70]

With a zeal approaching that of the speculators who were combing the Piedmont for mining stakes, the literary prospectors began a veritable gold rush to the unexplored corners of the region—and much they unearthed that glittered. Scratch the surface, they believed, and one would find "local color," picturesqueness, quaintness. Provided with the divining rod of current literary fashion, they could not have wished for richer deposits of the material they sought. Where else could one unearth such a variety of "types": cove-locked mountaineers of the Smokies, ex-slaves who practiced voodoo and told African fables that were philological nuggets, picturesque poor whites, decadent aristocrats, homespun provincials, romantic Creoles, and Cajuns along every bayou? Harris' success with Negro dialect in *Uncle Remus* precipitated a national flood of dialect literature. Again Southern resources led the boom. Did not "our contemporary ancestors" still speak "Shakespeare's English"? Not to mention Sea-Island Gullah, Cajun patois, and poor-white English!

It would be stretching a point to claim Lafcadio Hearn for the

---

[68] Hendrick, *Earlier Life and Letters of Walter H. Page*, 149.
[69] Atlanta *Constitution*, quoted in *Harper's Weekly*, XXIV (1880), 19.
[70] Quoted in Cary McWilliams, "Localism in American Criticism," in *Southwest Review* (Dallas), XIX (1933-1934), 422-23.

Southern revival, in spite of his ten years in New Orleans, from 1877 to 1887, several of them on Major Burke's *Times-Democrat*. In fact, both of these strange birds of passage took flight about the same time—Major Burke to seek the gold of Honduras, Lafcadio in quest of the golden women of Martinique. It was in his New Orleans years that Hearn achieved his first recognition, however, and *Chita* (1889) was not unrelated to the milieu of "Marse Chan" (1884). Nor did Hearn misrepresent the mood of his Southern contemporaries when he exclaimed, "I have pledged me to the worship of the Odd, the Queer, the Strange, the Exotic, the Monstrous" —with the possible exception of the last named of his idols.[71]

Not that the outpourings of the eighties were alien to the spirit of the New South. On the contrary they gave expression to many of its moods, especially its florid romanticism. "And the Southerner, be he never so progressive," wrote progressive Professor Edwin Mims of Thomas Nelson Page, "cannot but now and then sigh, amid some of the raw expressions of the new South, for the charm and leisure of the old."[72] And what delectable sighs! What bittersweet tears washed Nashville's grimy cheeks over Page's *In Ole Virginia*! "Dem wuz good ole times, marster—de bes Sam ever see! Dey wuz in fac'l Niggers didn' hed nothin' 'tall to do." Embarrassing race conflict dissolved in liquid dialect, angry Populist farmers became merely quaint in Billy Sanders' vernacular, depression rolled aside, and for a moment, "de ole times done come back again."

Boston and New York shared the illusion and cheered the dashing Confederates. Even the polemical literature of the South in ante-bellum years had not lavished such praise upon the plantation legend. Yankee imitators of the Dixie school sought to outdo it in sentimentality. Maud Howe, daughter of the composer of "The Battle Hymn of the Republic," declared in her novel *Atalanta in the South* (1886) that the Negro was happier in slavery than in freedom; Thomas Wentworth Higginson, onetime militant abolitionist and commander of a Negro regiment, dissolved in tears over "Marse Chan." A favorite theme of the Southern school and its Northern imitators was "reconciliation," preached with

71 Lafcadio Hearn to W. D. O'Connor, June 29, 1884, in Elizabeth Bisland, *Life and Letters of Lafcadio Hearn*, 2 vols. (Boston, 1906), I, 328.

72 Edwin Mims, "Thomas Nelson Page," in *Atlantic Monthly*, C (1907), 113.

little more subtlety than in Grady's orations or Edmonds' editorials. The conventional ending of their novels was a union between Confederate heroine and true-blue Federal hero. Bronson Howard outdid the novelists by uniting *five* such lovelorn pairs in his play *Shenandoah* (1889). By 1892 it seemed entirely appropriate for the Boston *Atlantic Monthly* to publish Gildersleeve's "Creed of the Old South," an uncompromising panegyric.[73]

The Southern school, like the rest of the country, was, of course, inundated by Victorian prudery—all except Hearn, who complained of "a Sunday-school atmosphere" about Cable. Harris assured his publisher that "In all my writings you will find nothing that cannot be read and explained to a young girl." *The White Rose of Memphis*, a novel by Colonel William Falkner[74] of Mississippi, was characterized by another Mississippian in 1882 as "hallowed with an atmosphere of purity and sweetness." It probably was.

For all their shortcomings and the comparative brevity of the revival (it reached its peak by 1887), the Southern writers undeniably possessed solid virtues. Among them, however, one will search in vain for a realistic portrayal of their own times. But for an occasional interest of Harris and Cable, the writers were too preoccupied with their quaint "types" of the hinterland to notice what was going on in their own parlors. The importation of shoddy standards from the North and the encroachment of rank indigenous evils, the preachment of an alien ethics, and the spreading helotry among the farmers went largely unchallenged in their pages. "Life, as a whole," philosophized the rising Kentucky novelist James Lane Allen in 1885, "presents a scene of happiness and success; shall the novel of life present a spectacle of wretchedness and failure?"[75]

[73] These and other illustrations of Yankee acquiescence are ably discussed in Buck, *Road to Reunion*, 220-35. See also, Francis P. Gaines, *The Southern Plantation: A Study in the Development and the Accuracy of a Tradition* (New York, 1924), 81-82.

[74] The grandfather of the novelist, William Faulkner, though he spelled his name differently. A veteran of General Nathan B. Forrest's raiders, Colonel Falkner, besides writing a novel, found time to build a local railroad, fight many duels, and kill his quota of opponents. He was finally shot dead in the main street of his home town by a former friend and business associate in a shoot-on-sight fray for which he refused to arm himself. *Mississippi, A Guide to the Magnolia State* (New York, 1938), 456-58.

[75] Quoted in Grant C. Knight, *James Lane Allen and the Genteel Tradition* (Chapel Hill, 1935), 53.

Joel Harris knew better than that, but he clung tenaciously to the doctrine of neighborly love that among his Middle Georgia countrymen ("the most democratic people the world has ever seen," he thought) proved the talisman against all evil. Why not, then, among sections and races and classes, however estranged? On that theory, at least, he tried to believe that Atlanta was only an enlargement of Snap Bean Farm.[76]

As acknowledged shepherds of Southern folds, the Protestant clergy enjoyed a position that was unchallenged in this period. "There is no part of the world in which ministers of the Gospel are more respected than in the Southern States," declared a distinguished minister in 1885.[77] This was more fact than boast. Bishop Haygood was on equally safe ground when he observed that since the Civil War "The controlling sentiment of the Southern people in city and hamlet, in camp and field, among the white and the black, has been religious."[78]

Observers from outside the region were struck by Southern religiosity. "The South is by a long way the most simply and sincerely religious country that I was ever in," wrote an English traveler. "In other countries men are apt to make a private matter of their religion . . . ; but the Southerner wears his upon his sleeve."[79] Northerners were prone to account for the trait after the manner of Warner, who wrote that "Life in the South is still on simpler terms than in the North, and society is not so complex." He found the people "more frank and impulsive . . . it may be less calculating." A New York journalist wrote that "There is everywhere much of primitive-simplicty in their methods of life and in their manners and character." On all hands he heard talk of "things marvelous, supernatural and impossible generally . . . the same as that

[76] John Donald Wade, "Profits and Losses in the Life of Joel Chandler Harris," in *American Review* (New York), I (1933), 17-35.

[77] Dr. O. P. Fitzgerald, quoted in Hunter D. Farish, *The Circuit Rider Dismounts; A Social History of Southern Methodism, 1865-1900* (Richmond, 1938), 105.

[78] Atticus G. Haygood, *The New South: Gratitude, Amendment, Hope . . .* (Oxford, Ga., 1880), 9-10.

[79] Sir William Archer, *Through Afro-America: An English Reading of the Race Problem* (London, 1910), 73-74.

which was heard a quarter of a century ago in the log cabins of . . . Indiana."[80]

Evangelical fervor, revivalism, camp meetings, mass conversions were no new phenomena in the South. But in this period, religious zeal was abnormally intensified. Membership in the Southern Methodist Church, lower in 1866 than in 1854, doubled in the fifteen years following the war. The greatest gains were made when revivalism was at highest pitch, and the eighties were "a time of extraordinary revivals." Net gain in members of the Methodist Church in 1885 was the highest in its history, and a rapid rate of growth was maintained throughout the century.[81] Scenes recalling the Wesleyan revivals of early industrial England were not unknown to the New South. It was the heyday of such masters of pulpit demagogy as Sam Jones. "When I get up to preach," said the Reverend Mr. Jones, "all I do is to KNOCK OUT THE BUNG and let nature cut her caper." Thousands thronged the special trains that ran to his performances to witness these wonders of nature. "His power is felt not only by the lower classes . . . but by the purely intellectual as well," it was reported.[82]

To a remarkable degree this religious ferment was the work of only two Protestant sects, the Methodists and the Baptists, which in the middle eighties were said to have "very nearly a monopoly of church membership" in eight Southern states. "In Alabama and Mississippi the members of these two sects . . . [made up] 95 per cent. of the total church membership; in Georgia, 94 per cent.; in Florida, 93; in South Carolina, 91; in North Carolina, 86; in Virginia, 81"—this, as compared with a little over 47 per cent accounted for by the two sects in church membership of the nation as a whole. Thus the Methodists and Baptists had about twice the relative strength in the South that they had in the whole country.[83]

Edwin A. Alderman, president of the University of Virginia, contended that "The fancied home of the cavalier is the home of

80 Warner, *Studies in the South and West,* 32; New York *Tribune,* March 11, 1881.
81 Farish, *Circuit Rider Dismounts,* 69, 74-76.
82 Nashville *Daily American,* June 6, 1887; Jackson *Clarion,* April 28, 1886.
83 *Nation,* XLI (1885), 211.

the nearest approach to puritanism and to the most vital protestant evangelicalism in the world to-day."[84]

Further evidence of the strength of Southern puritanism—or perhaps, more accurately, the surrender to the middle class—was the increase of blue laws, and restrictions of various sorts aimed at the saloon, the prize fight, and what a leading Methodist journal called "one of the antechambers of hell," the theater. Even before the Civil War all the Southern states except Virginia and Tennessee had experimented with local prohibition of saloons through special state legislation, a method peculiar to the South. In 1874 Arkansas, Kentucky, and North Carolina, and in 1876, Texas, supplemented their special laws with general local-option laws for townships. The eighties saw a burst of prohibition activity. This took the form of general county local-option laws in Arkansas, Florida, Georgia, Louisiana, Mississippi, and North Carolina, and local option for townships in South Carolina and Virginia. "Blind tiger" and "scientific temperance education" laws were becoming popular.[85] An editor in sinful New Orleans might denounce "the Medieval bigotry and religious tyranny" of Sunday blue laws in adjacent states, but it is the conclusion of a scholar that Sabbath observance prevailed "to a greater extent in the South than in any other section."[86]

The rupture between North and South had come earliest in the great Protestant sects, and there it was slowest to heal. The Northern branches sought to imitate the state during Reconstruction in using force to effect union, sometimes seizing Southern churches and their funds by force. They were bitterly and effectively resisted by Southern churchmen. The Northern "connections" then established their own churches in the South and the struggle continued. "We claim the South," declared the New York *Christian Advocate* in 1879, "because the Republic which we have recently saved by Methodist conscience and Methodist bayonets, now demands at our hands another salvation by Methodist ideas and faith."

84 Edwin A. Alderman, *The Growing South* (New York, 1908), 20.

85 Leonard S. Blakey, *The Sale of Liquor in the South*, in Columbia University *Studies in History, Economics and Public Law*, LI, Whole No. 127 (New York, 1912), 12, and Table I, 39.

86 New Orleans *Times-Democrat*, November 8, 1895; Farish, *Circuit Rider Dismounts*, 340.

Missionaries established Northern journals in the South, one of which in New Orleans based its right to leadership on the theory "that New England has developed a stronger arm, a more active brain, a greater love of freedom, and a higher form of civilization." Another in Atlanta announced in 1881: "There is a struggle now going on as to the character of the Methodism of the future in this section. Shall it be under American or southern ideas? This is the bone of contention between us and the Southern Church."[87]

As a result of the continuation of a temporal struggle on an ecclesiastical plane, and of the clerical championship of the Southern cause after the surrender and defection of its secular defenders, the Southern churches became for a time centers of resistance to the invasion of Northern culture. "All through the South," noted a Northern observer in 1881, "the ministers appear to view 'progress' with a degree of alarm, and certainly with decided reprobation. I should say that Southern ministers very generally appear to feel instinctively that it brings new dangers to religious institutions."[88] The attitude was expressed in the leading religious journals. "Let us have a rest on this sort of talk we have had about the New South," demanded one. "It begins to sound like cant. It seems to cast unjust reproaches upon the dead." And again, "When Mammonism thus possesses the people they soon become prepared to make almost any concession of moral principle to the demands of commercial expediency. . . . Cursed be the wealth which comes to us at such a price! Blessed be the poverty which gives us immunity from such temptations."[89] A churchman of Chapel Hill, warning the flock against "the perils in the New South," wrote, "Nothing is surer than that much of the lauded change in the South consists mainly in the *money-mania*. . . . The standard of character erected by the blatant portion of the New South—that portion that reviles the Old South—is the *brazen* standard of money making."[90]

[87] Quoted in Farish, *Circuit Rider Dismounts*, 108-109, 117-18. For evidence of a similar struggle in the Presbyterian Church, see Thomas Cary Johnson, *The Life and Letters of Benjamin Morgan Palmer* (Richmond, 1906), 440, 457, 472-74.

[88] New York *Tribune*, March 11, 1881.

[89] Nashville *Christian Advocate*, March 5, 26, 1887.

[90] A. W. Mangum, letter, *ibid.*, May 14, 1887.

For a time the churches showed a disposition to take up cudgels against "mammonism" in its secular entrenchments. "Nearly all the necessaries of life," affirmed the Nashville *Christian Advocate*, in 1888, "are now controlled by 'the trusts,' even to the medicine for the healing of the sick, the oil that feeds the light. . . . Nothing escapes the extortion of these worst publicans the world ever saw."[91] Increasingly, however, as the churches, with their huge publishing houses, their large investments in colleges, universities and schools, and their private endowments became vested interests, and as they became dependent upon the "publicans" North and South—the tobacco trust, for example, and various Northern philanthropic endowments—the earlier tendency faded. The "blessed poverty" that gives "immunity from temptations" seemed less important than a suitable endowment. Old-fashioned sins, like that of the bottle, came to absorb the attention of the churches with crusades for temperance and prohibition. Presidents of handsomely endowed church universities, and publications, such as the *Biblical Recorder* of the North Carolina Baptists, became defenders of the trusts. Publicans and sinners of the newer type had less to fear from ecclesiastical wrath in later years, and the New Order and its standards and values received little more criticism from the clergy than it had from the writers.

In the dustbins of the eighties—where the eighties hastily swept them—are the remains of an elaborately reasoned critique of the Brave New South. The critique was identified with the Lost Cause, since the men who proclaimed it, men like Robert L. Dabney of Virginia and Charles Colcock Jones of Georgia, wore the uniform of the Confederacy and spoke in its name and memory. The doctrines they pronounced, however, like the style in which they pronounced them, were closer to the eighteenth than to the nineteenth century, closer to Thomas Jefferson than to Jefferson Davis. They were more like the polemics of John Taylor of Caroline against the Federalists than those of Robert Barnwell Rhett against the Abolitionists. They linked "plutocracy" and "communism" in a way Taylor would have understood, and spat the word "privilege" with his special vehemence. They regarded huge cities not as "metropolitan and unprejudiced" but as "sores on the body politic." They were

91 Quoted in Farish, *Circuit Rider Dismounts*, 334.

unimpressed by the splendors of the "new equality": "the regal luxury of a Vanderbilt, in his gaudy palace, beside the hireling laborer in his sordid tenement-lodging, who is his theoretical EQUAL!" Nor did they fancy the new "free enterprise": "Capital is collected in commanding masses, at whose bidding the free-holding citizen is sunk into the multitudinous hireling proletariat." Nor the "free press": "Its sheets come up, like the frogs of Egypt, into our houses, our bed chambers, our very kneading troughs . . . a deluge of perversions . . . the creatures of money." As for the great twin gods Mass and Speed, they were really demons in disguise, and would end by swallowing their foolish worshipers. These gentry were, in short, more old-fashioned than the Lost Cause itself: they were not only incorrigibly "unprogressive," they were "reactionary," and Walter Hines Page would have pronounced them "mummies" without a moment's hesitation.[92]

In his address "The New South," Robert L. Dabney, Stonewall Jackson's chief of staff and biographer, warned against the "special temptations to which a subjugated people are exposed while passing of necessity under a new and conquering system," particularly the temptation "to become like your conquerors." He said: "I hear our young men quote to each other the advice of the wily diplomat Gortstschacoff to the beaten French: 'Be strong.' They exclaim: Let us develope! develope! develope! Let us have like our conquerors, great cities, great capitalists, great factories and commerce and great populations; then we shall cope with them. . . . To exclaim as so many do of factories, and mines, and banks, and stock boards, and horse-powers of steam, and patent machines, 'These be thy gods, O Israel!' This would be a deadly mistake."

Never, of course, was there the remotest chance of Dabney's goose quill prevailing against the clattering presses of Grady and Dawson, Tompkins and Edmonds. Anyway, the New South had no ear for pessimism—not with Georgia boasting eleven millionaires in 1892, and Kentucky twenty-four, and New Orleans alone thirty-

92 Robert L. Dabney, *The New South. A Discourse* . . . (Raleigh, 1883), *passim;* Charles C. Jones, Jr., *The Old South. Addresses Delivered before the Confederate Survivors Association* (Augusta, Ga., 1887), *passim;* John Donald Wade, "Old Wine in a New Bottle," in *Virginia Quarterly Review* (University, Va.), XI (1935), 239-52.

five![93] Not with Edmonds proclaiming that throughout "the real South"—the urbanized, capitalistic South—could be heard "a continuous and unbroken strain of what has been termed 'the music of progress—the whirr of the spindle, the buzz of the saw, the roar of the furnace and the throb of the locomotive.' " Not until the New South was confronted by the Populists did it meet with a challenge that set it back on its heels for a spell.

[93] Shugg, *Origins of Class Struggle in Louisiana,* 291 and note.

IDA M. TARBELL

ALTHOUGH THE IMPORTANCE of an intimate knowledge of past business activities is now recognized by scholars, the lack of accurate and detailed analyses of representative corporations remains a serious obstacle to a proper understanding of American history as a whole. The absence of such studies is a special handicap for anyone concerned with the formative years after the Civil War when the national economy began to take on its modern industrial form. No other period illustrates so well the characteristics of free enterprise and of a government dominated by the wishes of business leaders. To attempt to write a history of this era without understanding the problems which business encountered and its attitude toward them is as futile as to explain the American Revolution without reference to British mercantilism.

Yet the historians who were contemporaries of Vanderbilt, Rockefeller, and Carnegie did not consider it their duty to record industrial developments. Their interest was in politics, and even political history was isolated in its own vacuum. Before professional historians rid themselves of this limited conception, business history had entered the field of scholarship through a side door opened by crusading journalists such as Ida M. Tarbell. Even though Miss Tarbell hoped that her work would be judged as a serious historical study, it should not have surprised her that when *The History of the Standard Oil Company* was published, in 1904, it was immediately identified with the muckraking movement which had arisen in the periodical literature of the time. Not only was Ida Tarbell associated on the staff of *McClure's Magazine* with such reformers as Ray Stannard Baker and Lincoln Steffens; she also shared their social ideals and their purpose of exposing corporate and trust malpractices.

Although Miss Tarbell's assumption of the Standard Oil Company's guilt interfered with her investigation and helped to predetermine her ultimate conclusions, her methods of research were more like those of the scholar than of the journalist. The numerous inquiries conducted by state and federal governments into the affairs of the company and the lawsuits to which it had been a party had created a considerable body of documentary evidence, a good deal of which consisted of transcripts of testimony taken under oath. Miss Tarbell devoted many months to examining these scattered documents. Then, much to her surprise and pleasure, she found that an official of the Standard Oil Company, Henry Rogers, was interested in her work and eager to have the company represented in the best possible light. After making clear her intention to paint as dark a picture as the facts indicated, Miss Tarbell engaged in repeated conversations with Rogers for more than two years. Each important point was argued by the two, and material in the company's files was made available for Miss Tarbell's inspection. Her first article on the Standard Oil Company was not published until a year after she had made Rogers' acquaintance.

Although Miss Tarbell did devote space to the company's constructive achievements, her conclusions were not substantially different from those reached a few years earlier by Henry Demarest Lloyd in his *Wealth Against Commonwealth*. She believed that Rockefeller's genius for efficient organization and his insistence upon service to the customer were more than offset by the destruction of morals and men caused by his ruthless methods of achieving monopoly and exploiting control over the market. Disclaiming any intention to criticize mere size, she condemned the Standard Oil Company because of its practices and as an example of the fact that trusts did not conduct business according to the rules of fair play.

Her judgment was thus essentially ethical rather than economic. Her censure was concentrated not on what big business was doing but on the way it was doing it. Her point of departure was an assumption of what the proper rules of business should be rather than an analysis of the conditions which produced the practices she condemned. If she could not be expected to devote much time to the general business setting, she causes legitimate surprise with her failure to give adequate attention to the oil industry itself. Her initial chapter, dealing with conditions in western Pennsylvania before Rockefeller's company entered the scene, strikes the note of eulogistic praise for the constructive achievements of the independent producers rather than of concern for the chaos and confusion which provided the Standard Oil Company with its opportunity for exploitation. This idealization of small business leads her, perhaps unintentionally, to represent Rockefeller's enterprise as an isolated source of evil and to assign to it a monopoly on unscrupulousness within the oil industry. The most severe of its modern critics would make no such claim for the Standard Oil Company. In brief, a different point of departure might have led Miss Tarbell to the same conclusions but might have given her a more convincing basis for them.

Although Miss Tarbell was aware of the importance of individuals in the history of the Standard Oil Company, her work has been criticized for its neglect of personalities. While this can be explained by the documentary nature of her evidence, it cannot be denied that the deficiency makes the work less readable and the narrative less understandable. Since the author intended to make ethical judgments, the need to know and make known to the reader the men who established policy seems evident. Yet such important figures as Henry Flagler and John D. Archbold flit in and out of the pages before the reader can become acquainted with them; even Rockefeller himself remains a silhouette, a distinct but incomplete man.

Ida Tarbell's history has the strength of a pioneer study written while the trusts it wanted to expose were still in full strength. As an indictment of contemporary methods, it may lack the patience of historical scholarship, but its indignation gives it a virility, even an insight, which a mood of calm appraisal cannot reproduce. Further, although Miss Tarbell was trained as a journalist, she helped academic historians to realize the vital role of business history in the study of the American past.

Cutting to Kill

To know every detail of the oil trade, to be able to reach at any moment its remotest point, to control even its weakest factor—this was John D. Rockefeller's ideal of doing business. It seemed to be an intellectual necessity for him to be able to direct the course of any particular gallon of oil from the moment it gushed from the earth until it went into the lamp of a housewife. There must be nothing—*nothing* in his great machine he did not know to be working right. It was to complete this ideal, to satisfy this necessity, that he undertook, late in the seventies, to organise the oil markets of the world, as he had already organised oil refining and oil transporting. Mr. Rockefeller was driven to this new task of organisation not only by his own curious intellect; he was driven to it by that thing so abhorrent to his mind—competition. If, as he claimed, the oil business belonged to him, and if, as he had announced, he was prepared to refine all the oil that men would consume, it followed as a corollary that the markets of the world belonged to him. In spite of his bold pretensions and his perfect organisation, a few obstinate oil refiners still lived and persisted in

From *The History of the Standard Oil Company* by Ida M. Tarbell. First published in 1902 by the S. S. McClure Company.

doing business. They were a fly in his ointment—a stick in his wonderful wheel. He must get them out; otherwise the Great Purpose would be unrealised. And so, while engaged in organising the world's markets, he incidentally carried on a campaign against those who dared intrude there.

When Mr. Rockefeller began to gather the oil markets into his hands he had a task whose field was literally the world, for already, in 1871, the year before he first appeared as an important factor in the oil trade, refined oil was going into every civilised country of the globe. Of the five and a half million barrels of crude oil produced that year, the world used five millions, over three and a half of which went to foreign lands. This was the market which had been built up in the first ten years of business by the men who had developed the oil territory and invented the process of refining and transporting, and this was the market, still further developed, of course, that Mr. Rockefeller inherited when he succeeded in corralling the refining and transporting of oil. It was this market he proceeded to organise.

The process of organisation seems to have been natural and highly intelligent. The entire country was buying refined oil for illumination. Many refiners had their own agents out looking for markets; others sold to wholesale dealers, or jobbers, who placed trade with local dealers, usually grocers. Mr. Rockefeller's business was to replace independent agents and jobbers by his own employees. The United States was mapped out and agents appointed over these great divisions. Thus, a certain portion of the Southwest—including Kansas, Missouri, Arkansas and Texas—the Waters-Pierce Oil Company, of St. Louis, Missouri, had charge of; a portion of the South—including Kentucky, Tennessee and Mississippi—Chess, Carley and Company, of Louisville, Kentucky, had charge of. These companies in turn divided their territory into sections, and put the subdivisions in the charge of local agents. These local agents had stations where oil was received and stored, and from which they and their salesmen carried on their campaigns. This system, inaugurated in the seventies, has been developed until now the Standard Oil Company of each state has its own marketing department, whose territory is divided and watched over in the above fashion. The entire oil-buying territory of the country is thus covered by local agents reporting to division headquarters. These report in turn to the head of the state marketing department, and his reports go to the general marketing headquarters in New York.

To those who know anything of the way in which Mr. Rockefeller does business, it will go without saying that this marketing department was conducted from the start with the greatest efficiency and economy. Its aim was to make every local station as nearly perfect in its service as it could be. The buyer must receive his oil promptly, in good condition, and of the grade he desired. If a customer complained, the case received prompt attention and the cause was found and corrected. He did not only receive oil; he could have proper lamps and wicks and burners, and directions about using them.

The local stations from which the dealer is served to-day are models of their kind, and one can easily believe they have always been so. Oil, even refined, is a difficult thing to handle without much disagreeable odour and stain, but the local stations of the Standard Oil Company, like its refineries, are kept orderly and clean by a rigid system of inspection. Every two or three months an inspector goes through each station and reports to headquarters on a multitude of details—whether barrels are properly bunged, filled, stencilled, painted, glued; whether tank wagons, buckets, faucets, pipes, are leaking; whether the glue trough is clean, the ground around the tanks dry, the locks in good condition; the horses properly cared for; the weeds cut in the yard. The time the agent gets around in the morning and the time he takes for lunch are reported. The prices he pays for feed for his horses, for coal, for repairs, are noted. In fact, the condition of every local station, at any given period, can be accurately known at marketing headquarters, if desired. All of this tends, of course, to the greatest economy and efficiency in the local agents.

But the Standard Oil agents were not sent into a territory back in the seventies simply to sell all the oil they could by efficient service and aggressive pushing; they were sent there to sell all the oil that was bought. "The coal-oil business belongs to us," was Mr. Rockefeller's motto, and from the beginning of his campaign in the markets his agents accepted and acted on that principle. If a dealer bought but a barrel of oil a year, it must be from Mr. Rockefeller. This ambition made it necessary that the agents have accurate knowledge of all outside transactions in oil, however small, made in their field. How was this possible? The South Improvement scheme provided perfectly for this, for it bound the railroad to send daily to the principal office of the company reports of all oil shipped, the name of shipper, the quantity and kind of oil, the name of consignee, with the destination and the cost of freight.[1] Having such knowledge as this, an agent could immediately locate each shipment of the independent refiner, and take the proper steps to secure the trade. But the South Improvement scheme never went into operation. It remained only as a beautiful ideal, to be worked out as time and opportunity permitted. The exact process by which this was done it is impossible to trace. The work was delicate and involved operations of which it was wise for the operator to say nothing. It is only certain that little by little a secret bureau for securing information was built up until it is a fact that information concerning the business of his competitors, almost as full as that which Mr. Rockefeller hoped to get when he signed the South Improvement Company contracts, is his to-day. Probably the best way to get an idea of how Mr. Rockefeller built up this department, as well as others of his marketing bureau, is to examine it as it stands to-day. First, then, as to the methods of securing information which are in operation.

Naturally and properly the local agents of the Standard Oil Company are watchful of the condition of competition in their districts, and naturally and properly they report what they learn. "We ask our salesmen and our agents to keep their eyes open and keep us informed of the situation in their respective fields," a Standard agent told the Industrial Commission in 1898. "We ask our agents, as they visit the trade, to make reports to us of whom the different parties are buying; principally to know whether our agents are attending to their business or not. If they are letting too much business get away

1 The Eighth Section of Article Second of this contract, defining the duties of the railroads reads: "To make manifests or way-bills of all petroleum or its products transported over any portion of the railroads of the party of the second part or its connections, which manifests shall state the name of the consignor, the place of shipment, the kind and actual quantity of the article shipped, the name of the consignee, and the place of destination, with the rate and gross amount of freight and charges, and to send daily to the principal office of the party of the first part duplicates of all such manifests or way-bills."—Proceedings in Relation to Trusts, House of Representatives, 1888. Report Number 3,112, page 360.

from them, it looks as if they were not attending to their business. They get it from what they see as they go around selling goods." But there is no such generality about this part of the agent's or salesman's business as this statement would lead one to believe. As a matter of fact it is a thoroughly scientific operation. The gentleman who made the above statement, for instance, sends his local agents a blank like the following to be made out each month:

EXHIBIT "B—R."[2]

MONTHLY REPORT.

U.S. COPYING PENCIL	Town_____			Date_____			1897.	
DEALER	ADDRESS	Estimated Sales per month of		Brand or Kind of Goods	Price	If by Tank Wagon mark "T"	BUY FROM	
		R. Oil	Gaso.				Name	Point of Shipment

_____ Salesman or Agent.

The local agent gets the information to fill out such a report in various ways. He questions the dealers closely. He watches the railway freight stations. He interviews everybody in any way connected with the handling of oil in his territory. All of which may be proper enough. When, in the early eighties, Howard Page, of the Standard Oil Company, was in charge of the Standard shipping department in Kentucky, his agents visited the depots once a day to see what oil arrived there from independent shippers. A record of these shipments was made and reported monthly to Mr. Page. He was able to tell the Interstate Commerce Commission, in 1887, almost exactly what his rivals had been shipping by rail and by river. Mr. Page claimed that his agents had no special privileges; that anybody's

[2] Record of pleadings and testimony in Standard Oil Trust quo warranto cases in the Supreme Court of Ohio, 1899, page 681.

agents would have been allowed to examine the incoming cars, note the consignor, contents and consignee. It did not appear in the examination, however, that anybody but Mr. Page had sent agents to do such a thing. The Waters-Pierce Oil Company, of St. Louis, once paid one of its Texas agents this unique compliment: "We are glad to know you are on such good terms with the railroad people that Mr. Clem (an agent handling independent oil) gains nothing by marking his shipments by numbers instead of names." In the same letter the writer said: "Would be glad to have you advise us when Clem's first two tanks have been emptied and returned, also the second two to which you refer as having been in the yard nine and sixteen days, that we may know how long they have been held in Dallas. The movement of tank cars enters into the cost of oil, so it is necessary to have this information that we may know what we are competing with."[3]

The superior receiving the filled blanks carefully follows them by letters of instructions and inquiries, himself keeping track of each dealer, however insignificant, in the local agent's territory, and when one out of line has been brought in, never failing to compliment his subordinate. But however diligent the agent may be in keeping his eyes open, however he may be stirred to activity by the prodding and compliments of his superiors, it is of course out of the question that he get anything like the full information the South Improvement scheme insured. What he is able to do is supplemented by a system which compares very favourably with that famous scheme and which undoubtedly was suggested by it. For many years independent refiners have declared that the details of their shipments were leaking regularly from their own employees or from clerks in freight offices. At every investigation made these declarations have been repeated and occasional proof has been offered; for instance, a Cleveland refiner, John Teagle, testified in 1888 to the Congressional Committee that one day in 1883 his bookkeeper came to him and told him that he had been approached by a brother of the secretary of the Standard Oil Company at Cleveland, who had asked him if he did not wish to make some money. The bookkeeper asked how, and after some talk he was informed that it would be by his giving information concerning the business of his firm to the Standard.

[3] Trust Investigation of Ohio Senate, 1898, page 370.

The bookkeeper seems to have been a wary fellow, for he dismissed his interlocutor without arousing suspicion and then took the case to Mr. Teagle, who asked him to make some kind of an arrangement in order to find out just what information the Standard wanted. The man did this. For twenty-five dollars down and a small sum per year he was to make a transcript of Mr. Teagle's daily shipments with net price received for the same; he was to tell what the cost of manufacturing in the refinery was; the amount of gasoline and naphtha made and the net price received for them; what was done with the tar; and what percentage of different grades of oil was made; also how much oil was exported. This information was to be mailed regularly to Box 164 of the Cleveland post-office. Mr. Teagle, who at that moment was hot on the tracks of the Standard in the courts, got an affidavit from the bookkeeper. This he took with the money which the clerk had received to the secretary of the Standard Oil Company and charged him with bribery. At first the gentleman denied having any knowledge of the matter, but he finally confessed and even took back the money. Mr. Teagle then gave the whole story to the newspapers, where it of course made much noise.

Several gentlemen testified before the recent Industrial Commission to the belief that their business was under the constant espionage of the Standard Oil Company. Theodore Westgate, an oil refiner of Titusville, told the Commission that all of his shipments were watched. The inference from his testimony was that the Standard Oil Company received reports direct from the freight houses. Lewis Emery, Jr., of Bradford, a lifelong contestant of the Standard, declared that he knew his business was followed now in the same way as it was in 1872 under the South Improvement Company contract. He gave one or two instances from his own business experience to justify his statements, and he added that he could give many others if necessary. Mr. Gall, of Montreal, Canada, declared that these same methods were in operation in Canada. "When our tank-cars come in," Mr. Gall told the Commission, "the Standard Oil Company have a habit of sending their men, opening a tank-car, and taking a sample out to see what it contains." Mr. Gall declared that he knew this a long time before he was able to get proof of it. He declared that they knew the number of cars that he shipped and the place to which they went, and that it was their habit to send salesmen after every shipment. Mrs. G. C. Butts, a daughter of George Rice, an independent refiner of Marietta, Ohio, told the Ohio Senate Committee which investigated trusts in 1898 that a railroad agent of their town had notified them that he had been approached by a Standard representative who asked him for a full report of all independent shipments, to whom and where going. The agent refused, but, said Mrs. Butts: "We found out later that someone was giving them this information and that it was being given right from our own works. . . . A party writing us from the Waters-Pierce office wrote that we had no idea of the network of detectives, generally railroad agents, that his company kept, and that everything that we or our agents said or did was reported back to the managers through a regular network of detectives who were agents of the railroads and oil company as well."

But while the proofs the independents have offered of their charges show that such leaks have occurred at intervals all over the country, they do not show anything like a regular system of collecting information through this channel. From the evidence one would be justified in believing that the cases were rare, occurring only when a not over-nice Standard manager got into hot competition with a rival and prevailed upon a freight agent to give him information to help in his fight. In 1903, however, the writer came into possession of a large mass of documents of unquestionable authenticity, bearing out all and more than the independents charge. They show that the Standard Oil Company receives regularly to-day, at least from the railroads and steamship lines represented in these papers, information of *all* oil shipped. A study of these papers shows beyond question that somebody having access to the books of the freight offices records regularly each oil shipment passing the office—the names of consignor and consignee, the addresses of each, and the quantity and kind of oil are given in each case. This record is made out usually on a sheet of blank paper, though occasionally the recorder has been indiscreet enough to use the railroad company's stationery. The reports are evidently intended not to be signed, though there are cases in the documents where the name of the sender has been signed and erased; in one case a printed head bearing the name of the freight agent had been used. The name had been cut out, but so carelessly that it was easy to identify him. These reports had evidently been sent to the office of the Standard Oil Company, where they had received a careful examination, and the information they contained had been classified. Wherever the shipment entered was from one of the distributing stations of the Standard Oil Company, a line was drawn through it, or it was checked off in some way. In every other case in the mass of reports there was written, opposite the name of the consignee, the name of a person *known* to be a Standard agent or salesman in the territory where the shipment had gone.

Now what is this for? Copies of letters and telegrams accompanying the reports show that as soon as a particular report had reached Standard headquarters and it was known that a carload, or even a barrel, of independent oil was on its way to a dealer, the Standard agent whose name was written after the shipment on the record had been notified. "If you can stop car going to X, authorise rebate to Z (name of dealer) of three-quarters cent per gallon," one of the telegrams reads. There is plenty of evidence to show how an agent receiving such information "stops" the oil. He *persuades* the dealer to countermand the order. George Rice, when before the House Committee on Manufactures in 1888, presented a number of telegrams as samples of his experience in having orders countermanded in Texas. Four of these were sent on the same day from different dealers in the same town, San Angelo. Mr. Rice investigated the cause, and, by letters from the various firms, learned that the Standard agent had been around "threatening the trade that if they bought of me they would not sell them any more," as he put it.

Mrs. Butts in her testimony in 1898 said that her firm had a customer in New Orleans to whom they had been selling from 500 to 1,000 barrels a month, and that the Standard representative made a contract with him to pay him $10,000 a year for five years to stop handling the independent oil and take Standard oil! Mrs. Butts offered as evidence of a similar transaction in Texas the following letter:

"LOCKHART, TEXAS, November 30, 1894.

"Mr. Keenan, who is with the Waters-Pierce people at Galveston, has made us several visits and made us propositions of all kinds to get us out of the business. Among others, he offered to pay us a monthly salary if we would quit selling oil and let them have full control of the trade, and insisted that we name a figure that we would take and get out of the business, and also threatened that if we did not accept his proposition they would cut prices below what oil cost us and force us out of business. We asked him the question, should we accept his proposition, would they continue to sell oil as cheap as we were then selling it, and he stated most positively that they would advance the price at once should they succeed in destroying competition.

"J. S. LEWIS AND COMPANY."

In the Ohio Investigation of 1898 John Teagle, of Cleveland, being upon his oath, said that his firm had had great difficulty in getting goods accepted because the Standard agents would persuade the dealers to cancel the orders. "They would have their local man, or some other man, call upon the trade and use their influence and talk lower prices, or make a lower retail price, or something to convince them that they'd better not take our oil, and, I suppose, to buy theirs." Mr. Teagle presented the following letter, signed by a Standard representative, explaining such a countermand:

"DES MOINES, IOWA, January 14, 1891.
"JOHN FOWLER,
    Hampton, Iowa.
"Dear Sir:—Our Marshalltown manager, Mr. Ruth, has explained the circumstances regarding the purchase and subsequent countermand of a car of oil from our competitors. He desires to have us express to you our promise that we will stand all expense provided there should be any trouble growing out of the countermand of this car. We cheerfully promise to do this; we have the best legal advice which can be obtained in Iowa, bearing on the points in this case. An order can be countermanded either before or after the goods have been shipped, and, in fact, can be countermanded even if the goods have already arrived and are at the depot. A firm is absolutely obliged to accept a countermand. The fact that the order has been signed does not make any difference. We want you to absolutely refuse, under any circumstances, to accept the car of oil. We are standing back of you in this matter, and will protect you in every way, and would kindly ask you to keep this letter strictly confidential. . . .
                    "Yours truly,
                              E. P. PRATT."

Peter Shull, of the Independent Oil Company of Mansfield, Ohio, testified before the same committee to experiences similar to those of Mr. Teagle.

"If I put a man on the road to sell goods for me," said Mr. Shull, "and he takes orders to the amount of 200 to 300 barrels a week, before I am able to ship these goods possibly, the Standard Oil Company has gone there and compelled those people to countermand those orders under a threat that, if they don't countermand them, they will put the price of oil down to such a price that they cannot afford to handle the goods."

In support of his assertion Mr. Shull offered letters from firms he has been dealing with. The following citations show the character of them:

"TIFFIN, OHIO, February 1, 1898.

"INDEPENDENT OIL COMPANY,
    Mansfield, Ohio.

"*Dear Sirs:*—The Standard Oil Company, after your man was here, had the cheek to come in and ask how many barrels of oil we bought and so forth, then asked us to countermand the order, saying it would be for our best; we understand they have put their oil in our next door and offer it at six cents per gallon, at retail. Shall we turn tail or show them fight? If so, will you help us out any? . . .

"Yours truly,
                                "TALBOTT AND SON."

"TIFFIN, OHIO, January 24, 1898.

"INDEPENDENT OIL COMPANY.

"*Dear Sirs:* . . . I am sorry to say that a Standard Oil man from your city followed that oil car and oil to my place, and told me that he would not let me make a dollar on that oil, and was dogging me around for two days to buy that oil, and made all kinds of threats and talked to my people of the house while I was out, and persuaded me to sell, and I was in a stew what I should do, but I yielded and I have been very sorry for it since. I thought I would hate to see the bottom knocked out of the prices, but that is why I did it—the only reason. The oil was all right. I now see the mistake, and that is of getting a carload—two carloads coming in here inside of a week is more than the other company will stand. . . .

"Yours truly,
                                "H. A. EIRICK."

In case the agent cannot persuade the dealer to countermand his order, more strenuous measures are applied. The letters quoted above hint at what they will be. Many letters have been presented by witnesses under oath in various investigations showing that Standard Oil agents in all parts of the country have found it necessary for the last twenty-five years to act at times as these letters threaten. One

of the most aggressive of these campaigns waged at the beginning
of this war of exterminating independent dealers was by the Standard marketing agent at Louisville, Kentucky—Chess, Carley and
Company. This concern claimed a large section of the South as its
territory. George Rice, of Marietta, Ohio, had been in this field for
eight or ten years, having many regular customers. It became Chess,
Carley and Company's business to secure these customers and to
prevent his getting others. Mr. Rice was handicapped to begin with
by railroad discrimination. He was never able to secure the rates of
his big rival on any of the Southern roads. In 1888 the Interstate
Commerce Commission examined his complaints against eight different Southern and Western roads, and found that no one of them
treated him with "relative justice." Railroad discriminations were
not sufficient to drive him out of the Southwest, however, and a war
of prices was begun. According to the letters Mr. Rice himself has
presented he certainly in some cases began the cutting, as he could
well afford to do. For instance, Chess, Carley and Company were
selling water-white oil in September, 1880, in Clarksville, Tennessee,
at twenty-one cents a gallon delivered in carloads—export oil was
selling in barrels in New York at that date at 10⅝ cents a gallon.
Rice's agent offered at eighteen cents. The dealer to whom he made
the offer, Armstrong by name, wished to accept, but as he had been
buying of Chess, Carley and Company, went first to see them about
the matter. He came back "scared almost out of his boots," wrote the
agent to Rice.

"Carley told him he would break him up if he bought oil of anyone
else; that the Standard Company had authorised him to spend $10,000
to break up any concern that bought oil from anyone else; that he
(Carley) would put all his drummers in the field to hunt up Armstrong's customers and sell his customers groceries at five per cent.
below Armstrong's prices, and turn all Armstrong's trade over to
Moore, Bremaker and Company, and settle with Moore, Bremaker
and Company for their losses in helping to break Armstrong up,
every thirty days.

"That if Armstrong sent any other oil to Clarksville, Tennessee,
he (Carley) would put the price of oil so low in Clarksville as to make
the party lose heavily, and that they (the Standard) would break up
anyone that would sell him (Armstrong) oil, and that he (Carley) had
told Stege and Reiling the same thing. Did you ever? What do you
think of that?"

Very soon after this, Chess, Carley and Company took in hand a Nashville firm, Wilkinson and Company, which was buying of Rice. "It is with great reluctance," they wrote, "that we undertake serious competition with any one, *and certainly this competition will not be confined to coal-oil or any one article, and will not be limited to any one year.* We always stand ready to make reasonable arrangements

with any one who chooses to appear in our line of business, and it will be unlike anything we have done heretofore if we permit any one to force us into an arrangement which is not reasonable. Any loss, however great, is better to us than a record of this kind." And four days later they wrote: "If you continue to bring on the oil, it will simply force us to cut down our price, and no other course is left to us but the one we have intimated." Wilkinson and Company seem to have stuck to Rice's oil, for, sixteen months later, we find

Chess, Carley and Company calling on the agent of a railroad, which already was giving the Standard discriminating rates, to help in the fight.

The screw was turned, Mr. Rice affirms, his rate being raised fifty per cent. in five days.

Rice carried on his fight for a market in the most aggressive way, and everywhere he met disastrous competition. In 1892 he published a large pamphlet of documents illustrating Standard methods, in which he included citations from some seventy letters from dealers in Texas, received by him between 1881 and 1889, showing the kind of competition his oil met there from the Waters-Pierce Oil Company, the Standard's Texas agents. A dozen sentences, from as many different towns, will show the character of them all:

"I have had wonderful competition on this car. As soon as my car arrived the Waters-Pierce Oil Company, who has an agent here, slapped the price down to $1.80 per case 110."

". . . Oil was selling at this point for $2.50 per case, and as soon as your car arrived it was put down to $1.50, which it is selling at to-day."

"The Waters-Pierce Oil Company reduced their prices on Brilliant oil from $2.60 to $1.50 per case and is waging a fierce war."

"Waters-Pierce Oil Company has our state by the throat and we would like to be extricated."

"I would like to handle your oil if I could be protected against the Waters-Pierce Oil Company. I am afraid if I would buy a car of oil from you this company would put the oil way below what I pay and make me lose big money. I can handle your oil in large quantities if you would protect me against them."

"The Waters-Pierce Oil Company has cut the stuffing out of coal-oil and have been ever since I got in my last car. They put the price to the merchants at $1.80 per case."

"We have your quotations on oil. While they are much lower than what we pay, yet unless a carload could be engaged it would pay no firm to try and handle, as Waters-Pierce Oil Company would cut below cost on same."

"The day your oil arrived here, their agent went to all my customers and offered their Eupion oil at ten cents per gallon in barrels and $1.50 per case, and lower grades in proportion, and told them if they did not refuse to take the oil he would not sell them any more at any price, and that he was going to run me out of the business, and then they would be at his mercy."

"Now we think Waters-Pierce Oil Company have been getting too high a price for their oil. They are able and do furnish almost this entire state with oil. They cut prices to such an extent when any other oil is offered in this state that they force the parties handling the oil to abandon the trade."

"Trace and hurry up car of oil shipped by you. We learn it is possible that your oil is side-tracked on the line, that Waters-Pierce might get in their work."

"If we were to buy a car or more, the Waters-Pierce Oil Company would manage to sell a little cheaper than we could, and continue doing so until they busted me up."

"In regard to oil, we are about out now, and Waters-Pierce have put their oil up again and quote us at the old price."

"Jobbers say when they take hold of another oil they are at once boycotted by Waters-Pierce Oil Company, who not only refuse to sell them, but put oil below what they pay for it, and thus knock them out of the oil trade, unless they sell at a loss."

"If I find I can handle your oil in Texas without being run out and losing money by this infernal corporation, the Waters-Pierce Oil Company, I want to arrange with you to handle it extensively. I received verbal notice this morning from their agent that they would make it hot for me when my oil got here."

Mr. Rice claims, in his preface to the collection of letters here quoted from, that he has hundreds of similar ones from different states in the Union, and the writer asked to examine them. The package of documents submitted in reply to this request was made up literally of hundreds of letters. They came from twelve different states, and show everywhere the same competitive method—cutting to kill. One thing very noticeable in these letters is the indignation of the dealers at the Standard methods of securing trade. They resent threats. They complain that the Standard agents "nose" about their premises, that they ask impudent questions, and that they generally make the trade disgusting and humiliating. In Mississippi, in the eighties, the indignation of the small dealers against Chess, Carley and Company was so strong that they formed associations binding themselves not to deal with them.

These same tactics have been kept up in the Southwest ever since. A letter, dated April 28, 1891, from the vice-president of the Waters-Pierce Oil Company, A. M. Finlay, to his agent at Dallas, Texas, says bluntly: "We want to make the prices at Dallas and in the neighbourhood on Brilliant and water-white oil, that will prevent Clem (an independent dealer) from doing any business." And Mr. Finlay adds: "Hope you will make it a point to be present at the next meeting of the city council, to-morrow night, and do everything possible to prevent granting a permit to build within the city limits, unless building similar to ours is constructed, for it would not be fair to us to allow someone else to put up constructions for the storage of oil, when they had compelled us to put up such an expensive building as we have."[4]

Mr. Rice is not the only independent oil dealer who has produced similar testimony. Mr. Teagle and Mr. Shull, in Ohio, have furnished considerable. "The reason we quit taking your oil is this," wrote a Kansas dealer to Scofield, Shurmer and Teagle, in 1896: "The Standard Oil Company notified us that if we continued handling your oil they would cut the oil to ten cents retail, and that we could not afford to do, and for that reason we are forced to take their oil or do business for nothing or at a loss." "The Standard agent has repeatedly told me that if I continued buying oil and gasoline from your wagon," wrote an Ohio dealer to the same firm in 1897, "they would have it retailed here for less than I could buy. I paid no attention to him, but yesterday their agent was here and asked me decidedly if I would continue buying oil and gasoline from your wagon. I told him I would do so; then he went and made arrangements with the dealers that handle their oil and gasoline to retail it for seven cents."

Mr. Shull summed up his testimony before the same committee to which Mr. Teagle gave the above, by declaring: "You take $10,000 and go into the business and I will guarantee you won't be in business ninety days. Their motto is that anybody going into the oil business in opposition to them they will make life a burden to him. That is about as near as you can get to it."

Considerable testimony of the same sort of practices was offered in the recent "hearing before the Industrial Commission," most of

[4] Trust Investigation of Ohio Senate, 1898, page 370.

it general in character. The most significant special case was offered by Mr. Westgate, the treasurer of the American Oil Works, an independent refinery of Titusville, Pennsylvania.

The American Oil Works, it seems, were in 1894 shipping oil called "Sunlight" in barrels to South Bend, Washington. This was in the territory of the Standard agents at Portland, Oregon, one of whom wrote to a South Bend dealer when he heard of the intrusion: "We will state for your information that never a drop of oil has reached South Bend of better quality than what we have always shipped into that territory. They can name it 'Sunlight,' 'Moonlight,' or 'Starlight,' it makes no difference. You can rest assured if another carload of 'Sunlight' arrives at your place, it will be sold very cheap. We do not purpose to allow another carload to come into that territory unless it comes and is put on the market at one-half its actual cost. You can convey this idea to the young man who imported the carload of 'Sunlight' oil."

When John D. Archbold, of the Standard Oil Company, had his attention called to this letter by Professor Jenks, of the Industrial Commission, Mr. Archbold characterised the letter as "a foolish statement by a foolish and unwise man" and promised to investigate it. Later he presented the commission with an explanation from the superior of the agent, who declared that the writer of the letter did not have any authority to say that oil would be sold on the basis mentioned. "The letter," he continued, "was intended to be written in a jocular manner to deny a claim that he was selling oil inferior in quality to that sold by others." It is hard for the mere outsider to catch the jocularity of the letter, and it must have been much more difficult for the dealer who received it to appreciate it.

Independent oil dealers of the present day complain bitterly of a rather novel way employed by the Standard for bringing into line dealers whose prejudices against buying from them are too strong to be overcome by the above methods. This is through what are called "bogus" oil companies. The obdurate dealer is approached by the agent of a new independent concern, call it the A B C Oil Company, for illustration. The agent seeks trade on the ground that he represents an independent concern and that he can sell at lower prices than the firm from which the dealer is buying. Gradually he works his way into the independent's trade. As a matter of fact, the new company is merely a Standard jobbing house which makes no oil, and which conceals its real identity under a misleading name. The mass of reports from railroad freight offices quoted from in this article corroborate this claim of the independents. The A B C Oil Company is mentioned again and again as shipping oil, and in the audited reports it is always checked off in the same fashion as the known Standard companies, and none of its shipments is referred to Standard agents. Independents all over the country tell of loss of markets through underselling by these "bogus" companies. The lower price which a supposedly independent concern gives to a dealer who will not, under any condition, buy of the Standard, need not demoralise the Standard trade in the vicinity if the concession is made with caution. After the trade is secure, that is, after the genuine independent is ousted, the masquerading concern always finds itself obliged to advance prices. When the true identity of such a company becomes known its usefulness naturally is impaired, and it withdraws from the field and a new one takes its place.

There is never a dealer in oil too small to have applied the above methods of competition. In recent years they have frequently been applied even to oil peddlers. In a good many towns of the country oil is sold from door to door by men whose whole stock in trade is their peddling wagons. Many of these oil peddlers build up a good trade. As a rule they sell Standard oil. Let one take independent oil, however, and the case is at once reported. His customers are located and at once approached by a Standard tank wagon man, who frequently, it is said, not only sells at a lower price than they have been paying, but even goes so far as to clean and fill the lamps! In these raids on peddlers of independent oil, refined oil has been sold in different cities at the doors of consumers at less than crude oil was bringing at the wells, and several cents per gallon less than it was selling to wholesale dealers in refined. It is claimed by independents that at the present time the "bogus" companies generally manage this matter of driving out peddlers, thus saving the Standard the unpopularity of the act and the dissatisfaction of the rise in price which, of course, follows as soon as the trade is secured.

The general explanation of these competitive methods which the Standard officials have offered is that they originate with "over-zealous" employees and are disapproved of promptly if brought to the attention of the heads of the house. The cases seem rather too universal for such an explanation to be entirely satisfactory. Certainly the system of collecting information concerning competitive business is not practised by the exceptional "over-zealous" employee, but is a recognised department of the Standard Oil Company's business. In the mass of documents from which the reports of oil shipments referred to above were drawn, are certain papers showing that the system is nearly enough universal to call for elaborate and expensive bookkeeping at the headquarters of each Standard marketing division. For instance, below is a fragment illustrating the page of a book kept at such a headquarters.

Basis Reports	Date Sup'd	Date Rec'd	SHIPPER	FROM	CONSIGNEE	DESTINATION	Refined Barrels	Naphtha Barrels	Lubiting Barrels	CAR Initial	CAR No.	REMARKS
5/20	5/14	1	Penn Mfg Co	Oil City	L. M O Co	Georgeville		93		L. M	7741	
5/22	5/15	16	Warren L. M Co	Strathco	A. Spence Co	"		76		P L M	432	
5/7	5/2	7	Crystal Oil Co	Oil City	Hamilton Oil Co	"	64		12	S. K	1684	
5/12	5/6	9	Clew Lenix Co	Strathco	X 4 3. Oil Co	"	112			L M	43	
		1	Empire Oil Ins.	Reno	Boston Mat Co	"	63			P L M	64 328	
5/27	5/23	25	Warren L. M Co	Strathco	"	"		87		S K	637 48	
5/7	5/1	4	Tiona Refg Co	Clarendon	"	"	75			S K	66 042	
5/14	5/30	30	Titusville Oil Mc	Titusville	Long Martin Co	"		92		B ro	374 21	
	5/22	22	Pittsburg Refg Co	Craspolis	Henry Whitehead	"		92		"	94	
5/11	27	9/1	Emery Mfg Co	Bradford	X 4 3 Oil Co	"		122		S K	496	
5/16	5/26	26	Cumins H Co	Titusville	"	"		126		P L M	643	

The figures, dates, consignees and destination on the above are fictitious. The names of shippers were copied from the original in possession of the writer.

What does this show? Simply that every day the reports received from railroad freight agents are entered in records kept for the purpose; that there is on file at the standard Oil headquarters a detailed list of the daily shipments which each independent refiner sends out, even to the initials and number on the car in which the shipment goes. From this remarkable record the same set of documents shows that at least two sets of reports are made up. One is a report of the annual volume of business being done by each particular independent refiner or wholesale jobber, the other of the business of each individual local dealer, so far as the detectives of the Standard have been able to locate it. For instance, among the documents is the report on a well-known oil jobbing house in one of the big cities of the country—reproduced on the next page.

Statement showing Receipts and Deliveries for December

	Barrels			
	1901	1902	1901	1902
	Coal	Oil	Gasoline	
Total Receipts of Competitor	3540	5070	1102	2214
Less shipments not in our District	420	1849	198	562
Net Shipments in our District	3120	3221	904	1652

	Old Places	New Places	Car Load	Less Car Load			
Territory covered by Competitor Oil (	2140		2140	927	3067		
(	2412	63	2475	742		3217	
Gaso)			361				361
	1051	411					1462
Balance					53	4	543	190
Not accounted for							211	87
					53	4	332	103

	For Year	1901	1902	1901	1902
		Coal	Oil	Gasoline	
Receipts		23787	26742	8764	13141
Less Shipments not in our territory		1410	1921	1262	2167
		22377	24821	7502	10974

	Old Places	New Places	Car Load	Less Car Load			
Territory covered by competitor Oil (	8146	1179	9325	6127	15452		
(	9691	487	10178	1129		11307	
				678			678
Gaso.)	729	11	623	849			2212
					6925	13514	6827	8762
Not accounted for						3122	196	2171
					6925	10392	6628	6591

The above is similar to the form compiled by the Standard Oil Company.

A comparison of this report with the firm's own accounts shows that the Standard came within a small per cent. of an accurate estimate of the X Y Z's business.

Another curious use made of these reports from the freight offices is forming a card catalogue of local dealers. (See form below.) Oil is usually sold at retail by grocers. It is with them that the local agents deal. Now the daily reports from the freight offices show the oil they receive. The competition reports from local agents also give more or less information concerning their business. A card is made out for each of them, tabulating the date on which he received oil, the name and location of the dealer he got it from, the quality, and the price he sells at. In a space left for remarks on the card there is

Date Shipped	Year	Shipped by	From	No. Bbls.	Kind of Oil	Price	Remarks
5/14	1901	B r Co	Pasadena	2	Refd		Formerly dealt altogether
5/19		"	"	3	"		with X.Y. Co.—a it
5/26		"	"	3	"		was shan him away
6/3		"	"	3	"		from what prejudices
6/10		X.Y 3.Co	"	3	L M. N		have some to against this a
6/20		"	"	3	"		disposed to send of our S.O Co
6/26		B. r Co	"	2	Refd		won't buy of Merrill
7/4		X.Y. 3 Co	"	4	L M N		
7/16		B r Co	"	3	Refd		

Name __E. C. Link__   Town __Georgeville.__
P. O. _____ Sh. Pt. _____   Salesman __Merrill__   Nearest Tank Wagon Station _____   Rate _____

The names, figures, and locations on the above form are fictitious
The remarks are copied from cards in possession of the writer.

written in red ink any general information about the dealer the agent may have picked up. Often there is an explanation of why the man does not buy Standard oil—not infrequently this explanation reads: "Is opposed to monopolies." It is impossible to say from documentary evidence how long such a card catalogue has been kept by the Standard; that it has been a practice for at least twenty-five years the following quotation from a letter written in 1903 by a prominent Standard official in the Southwest to one of his agents shows: "Where competition exists," says the official, "it has been our custom to keep a record of each merchant's daily purchase of bulk oil; and I know of one town at least in the Southern Texas Division where that record has been kept, whether there was competition or not, for the past fifteen years."[5]

The inference from this system of "keeping the eyes open" is that the Standard Oil Company knows practically where every barrel shipped by every independent dealer goes; and where every barrel bought by every corner-grocer from Maine to California comes from. The documents from which the writer draws the inference do not, to be sure, cover the entire country, but they do cover in detail many different states, and enough is known of the Standard's competitive methods in states outside this territory to justify one in believing that the system of gathering information is in use everywhere. That it is a perfect system is improbable. Bribery is not as dangerous business in this country as it deserves to be—of course nothing but a bribe would induce a clerk to give up such information as these daily reports contain—but, happily, such is the force of tradition that even those who have practised it for a long time shrink from discovery. It is one of those political and business practices which are only respectable when concealed. Naturally, then, the above system of gathering information must be handled with care, and can never have the same perfection as that Mr. Rockefeller expected when he signed the South Improvement Company charter.

The moral effect of this system on employees is even a more serious feature of the case than the injustice it works to competition. For a "consideration" railroad freight clerks give confidential information concerning freight going through their hands. It would certainly be quite as legitimate for post-office clerks to allow Mr. Rockefeller to read the private letters of his competitors, as it is that the clerks of a railroad give him data concerning their shipments. Everybody through whose hands such information passes is contaminated by the knowledge. To be a factor, though even so small a one, in such a transaction, blunts one's sense of right and fairness. The effect on the local Standard agent cannot but be demoralising. Prodded constantly by letters and telegrams from superiors to secure the countermand of independent oil, confronted by statements of the amount of sales which have gotten away from him, information he knows only too well to have been secured by underhand means, obliged to explain why he cannot get this or that

[5] Trust Investigation of Ohio Senate, 1898, page 371.

trade away from a rival salesman, he sinks into habits of bullying and wheedling utterly inconsistent with self-respect. "Is there nothing you independents can do to prevent our people finding out who you sell too?" an independent dealer reports a hunted Standard agent asking him. "My life is made miserable by the pressure brought on to chase up your sales. I don't like such business. It isn't right, but what can I do?"

The system results every now and then, naturally enough, in flagrant cases of bribing employees of the independents themselves. Where the freight office does not yield the information, the rival's own office may, and certainly if it is legitimate to get it from one place it is from the other. It is not an unusual thing for independent refiners to discharge a man whom they have reason to believe gives confidential information to the Standard. An outrageous case of this, which occurred some ten years ago, is contained in an affidavit which has been recently put at the writer's disposition. It seems that in 1892 the Lewis Emery Oil Company, an independent selling concern in Philadelphia, employed a man by the name of Buckley. This man was discharged, and in September of that year he went into the employ of the leading Standard refinery of Philadelphia, a concern known as the Atlantic Refining Company. According to the affidavit made by this man Buckley, the managers of the Standard concern, some time in February, 1893, engaged him in conversation about affairs of his late employer. They said that if they could only find out the names of the persons to whom their rival sold, and for what prices, they could soon run him out of business! And they asked Buckley if he could not get the information for them. After some discussion, one of the Standard managers said: "What's the matter with the nigger?" alluding to a coloured boy in the employment of the Lewis Emery concern. Buckley told them that he would try him. "You can tell the nigger," said one of the men, "that he needn't be afraid, because if he loses his position there's a position here for him."

Buckley saw the negro and made a proposition to him. The boy agreed to furnish the information for a price. "Starting from February, 1893," says Mr. Buckley, "and lasting up to about August of the same year, this boy furnished me periodically with the daily shipments of the Lewis Emery concern, which I took and handed personally, sometimes to one and sometimes to the other manager. They took copies of them, and usually returned the originals." The negro also brought what is known as the price-book to Buckley, and a complete copy of this was made by the Standard managers. "In short," says Mr. Buckley in his affidavit, "I obtained from the negro all the inside facts concerning the Lewis Emery Oil Company's business, and I furnished them all to the Standard managers." In return for this information the negro lad was paid various sums, amounting in all to about ninety dollars. Buckley says that they were charged upon the Standard books to "Special Expenses." The transaction was ended by the discharge of the coloured boy by the Lewis Emery concern.

The dénouement of this case is tragic enough. The concern was finally driven out of business by these and similar tactics, so Mr. Emery and his partner both affirm. The negro was never taken into the Atlantic Refinery, and Buckley soon after lost his position, as he of course richly deserved to. A man who shows himself traitorous, lying, thieving, even for the "good of the oil business," is never kept long in the employment of the Standard Oil Company. It is notorious in the Oil Regions that the people who "sell" to the Standard are never given responsible positions. They may be shifted around to do "dirty work," as the Oil Regions phrase goes, but they are pariahs in the concern. Mr. Rockefeller knows as well as any man ever did the vital necessity of honesty in an organisation, and the Buckleys and negroes who bring him secret intelligence never get anything but money and contempt for their pains.

For the general public, absorbed chiefly in the question, "How does all this affect what we are paying for oil?" the chief point of interest in the marketing contests is that, after they were over, the price of oil has always gone back with a jerk to the point where it was when the cutting began, and not infrequently it has gone higher —the public pays. Several of the letters already quoted in this chapter show the immediate recoil of the market to higher prices with the removal of competition. A table was prepared in 1892 to show the effect of competition on the price of oil in various states of the Union. The results were startling. In California, oil which sold at non-competitive points at $26\frac{1}{2}$ cents a gallon, at competitive points brought $17\frac{1}{2}$ cents. In Denver, Colorado, there was an "Oil War" on in the spring of 1892, and the same oil which was selling at Montrose and Garrison at twenty-five cents a gallon, in Denver sold at seven cents. This competition finally killed opposition and Denver thereafter paid twenty-five cents. The profits on this price were certainly great enough to call for competition. The same oil which was sold in Colorado in the spring of 1892 at twenty-five cents, sold in New York for exportation at 6.10 cents. Of course the freight rates to Colorado were high, the open rate was said to be nine cents a gallon, but that it cost the Standard Oil Company nine cents a gallon to get its oil there, one would have to have documentary proof to believe, and, even if it did, there was still some ten cents profit on a gallon—five dollars a barrel. In Kansas, at this time, the difference between the price at competitive and non-competitive points was seven cents; in Indiana six cents; in South Carolina four and one-half cents.

In 1897 Scofield, Shurmer and Teagle, of Cleveland, prepared a circular showing the difference between prices at competitive and non-competitive points in Ohio, and sent it out to the trade. According to this circular the public paid from 25 to 33⅓ per cent. more where there was no competition. The fact that oil is cheaper where there is competition, and also that the public has to pay the cost of the expensive "Oil Wars" which have been carried on so constantly for the last twenty-five years all over the country, is coming to be recognised, especially in the Middle West of this country, by both dealers and communities. There is no question that the attempts of Standard agents to persuade or bully dealers into countermanding orders, or giving up an independent with whose oil they are satisfied, meet with much less general success than they once did. It even happens now and then that communities who have had experience with "Oil Wars" will stand by an independent dealer for months at a time, resisting even the temptation to have their lamps cleaned and filled at next to nothing.

Briefly put, then, the conclusion, from a careful examination of the testimony on Standard competitive methods, is this:

The marketing department of the Standard Oil Company is organised to cover the entire country, and aims to sell all the oil sold in each of its divisions. To forestall or meet competition it has organised an elaborate secret service for locating the quantity, quality, and selling price of independent shipments. Having located an order for independent oil with a dealer, it persuades him, if possible, to countermand the order. If this is impossible, it threatens "predatory competition," that is, to sell at cost or less, until the rival is worn out. If the dealer still is obstinate, it institutes an "Oil War." In late years the cutting and the "Oil Wars" are often intrusted to so-called "bogus" companies, who retire when the real independent is put out of the way. In later years the Standard has been more cautious about beginning underselling than formerly, though if a rival offered oil at a less price than it had been getting—and generally even small refineries can contrive to sell below the non-competitive prices of the Standard—it does not hesitate to consider the lower price a declaration of war and to drop its prices and keep them down until the rival is out of the way. The price then goes back to the former figure or higher. John D. Archbold's testimony before the Industrial Commission in 1898 practically confirms the above conclusion. Mr. Archbold said that the Standard was in the habit of fighting vigorously to hold and advance its trade—even to the extent of holding prices down to cost until the rival gives way—though he declared it to be his opinion that the history of the company's transactions would show that the competitor forces the fight. Mr. Archbold told the commission that he personally believed it was not advisable to sell below cost for the sake of freezing out a smaller rival, save in "greatly aggravated cases," though he admitted the Standard sometimes did it. The trouble is that, accepting Mr. Rockefeller's foundation principle that the oil business belongs to him, any competition is "an aggravated case." All that is reassuring in the situaation has come from the obstinate stand of individuals—the refiners who insisted on doing an independent business, on the theory that "this is a free country"; the grocers who resented the prying and bullying of Standard agents, and asserted their right to buy of whom they would; the rare, very rare, community that grasped the fact that oil sold below cost temporarily, meant later paying for the fight. These features of the business belong to the last decade and a half. At the period we have reached in this history—that is, the completion of the monopoly of the pipelines in 1884 and the end of competition in transporting oil—there seemed to the independents no escape from Mr. Rockefeller in the market.

The sureness and promptness with which he located their shipments seemed uncanny to them. The ruthlessness and persistency
with which he cut and continued to cut their prices drove them to
despair. The character of the competition Mr. Rockefeller carried
on in the markets, particularly of the South and Middle West of this
country, at this time, aggravated daily the feeble refining element,
and bred contempt far and wide among people who saw the cutting,
and perhaps profited temporarily by it, but who had neither the
power nor the courage to interfere. The knowledge of it fed greatly
the bitterness in the Oil Regions. Part of the stock in conversation
of every dissatisfied oil producer or ruined refiner became tales of
disastrous conflicts in markets. They told of crippled men selling
independent oil from a hand cart, whose trade had been wiped out
by a Standard cart which followed him day by day, practically giving away oil. They told of grocers driven out of business by an attempt to stand by a refiner. They told endless tales, probably all
exaggerated, perhaps some of them false, yet all the them believed,
because of such facts as have been rehearsed above. There came to
be a popular conviction that the "Standard would do anything."
It was a condition which promised endless annoyance to Mr. Rockefeller and his colleagues. It meant popular mistrust, petty hostilities,
misinterpretations, contempt, abuse. There were plenty of people
even willing to deny Mr. Rockefeller ability. That the Standard was
in a venture was enough in those people's minds to damn it. Anything the Standard wanted was wrong, anything they contested was
right. A verdict for them demonstrated the corruption of the judge
and jury; against them their righteousness. Mr. Rockefeller, indeed,
was each year having more reason to realise monopoly building had
its trials as well as it profits.

HENRY DAVID

THE TRADITIONAL UNPOPULARITY of radical thought in America has been reflected in the reluctance which historians have shown to describe its occurrence in our national past. Yet without an analysis of radical doctrines, important historical incidents could never be completely understood. This was especially true of the Haymarket Affair, which convulsed the nation in 1886. It remained for Henry David, a half century later, to describe the role of philosophic anarchism in that great upheaval and the reverberations of the doctrine on American society.

The neglect which radical philosophies have experienced at the hands of historical writers has characterized also, but to a lesser degree, the treatment accorded the serious labor turmoils of the last quarter of the nineteenth century. It was natural for historians, as for other Americans, to stress national prosperity rather than depression and harmony rather than the domestic strife resulting from economic distress. Yet the passing of time made possible a more objective appraisal, and the broadening of the definition of history permitted an increasing emphasis on sociological subject matter. Modern historians such as David assume that it is their function to explain rather than to glorify the past; they would assert that to gloss over significant circumstances merely because they are unpleasant serves the purposes of neither scholarship nor patriotism.

The History of the Haymarket Affair attempts to achieve several goals. First, it sketches with broad strokes the general position of labor in the industrial expansion following the Civil

War. Whereas other writers have concentrated on the crudity of general business ethics and the ferocious competition which existed in the oil industry or among such railroad buccaneers as Jay Gould and Jim Fiske, David is concerned with the effect which this unrestrained quest for profits had upon the newly created masses of industrial workers. He finds that, while the laborers of the preceding era had both their skills and personal associations with their employers to protect them, the 1880's saw machines substituted for special training and huge impersonal corporations for individual entrepreneurs. Labor had become a commodity—and so cheap a commodity that many who had nothing else to sell lived in desperate poverty.

The major part of David's book is devoted to the immediate circumstances of the Haymarket Affair. The scene is laid in Chicago. Although attention is given to the physical background of suffering and unemployment and to the contemporary agitation for an eight-hour day, what helps to make this book unique is its penetrating analysis of the role played by social-revolutionary doctrines. This analysis includes not only a description of the propaganda circulated in Chicago but also a careful exposition of how the doctrines of anarchism and Marxian socialism were brought to this country and spread among American radicals. To his difficult task, David brought both a wide knowledge and a penetrating insight.

After a brief narrative dealing with the scene in which the bomb was actually thrown, David proceeds to his second major concern, the aftermath of the Haymarket Affair. He finds himself in complete disagreement with such venerable historians as James Ford Rhodes and Ellis Paxson Oberholtzer, who approved of the verdict reached in the trial of the anarchist leaders. That these men should have been sentenced to death for murder for no reason other than their advocacy of anarchist doctrines seems to David a travesty on justice. His detailed exposition of the conduct of the trial by a prejudiced judge and a biased jury gives substance to his conclusion that this had been a war on ideas and not an honest search for a just decision.

To give an objective appraisal of so dramatic a series of events constitutes a difficult problem for any historian. Anarchism is hardly a subject to inspire the neutral position for which most historians strive. Yet the kind of sympathy which David has for labor as a whole provided him with the background necessary for rewriting so important an episode in American history. Unless David had fully appreciated the legitimate grievances of labor in this period, it would have been difficult for him to treat seriously this invasion of radical doctrines which became important only because of the large-scale social distress of the times. But the reasons for the success of David's study are less important to the student of history than the study itself, which will continue to enjoy a well-deserved esteem.

The Labor Scene

IN AMERICAN labor history the tumultuous years of the middle 'eighties have long been marked as exceptional. The occurrences that packed the years 1884-1886 constitute what Selig Perlman calls the "great upheaval."[1] They are more deserving of this title than even the convulsive events of 1877 and the bitter struggles of 1893-1894. Norman J. Ware speaks of 1886 as a "revolutionary year,"[2] and it is significant that in 1887 George E. McNeill[3] wrote with insight that the previous twelvemonth

[1] John R. Commons and Associates, *History of Labour in the United States,* 2 vols., New York, 1926, vol. 2, title of Chap. IX.

[2] Norman J. Ware, *The Labor Movement in the United States, 1860-1895. A Study in Democracy,* New York, 1929, p. 302.

[3] George E. McNeill, 1836-1906, a respected labor leader of the 'seventies and 'eighties, was active in the eight-hour movement of the 'sixties and played a leading rôle in the establishment of the Massachusetts Bureau of Labor Statistics, of which he was deputy chief for several years.

"will be known as the year of the great uprising of labor. The future historian will say: Trades-unions increased their membership and their powers as never before. The Knights of Labor, who had for seventeen years struggled against all adverse influences, added to their membership by tens of thousands weekly. Trades and occupations that had never before been organized joined the . . . assemblies of the order. . . . Laboring men who had heretofore considered themselves as scarcely more than serfs, without rights or privileges, fearing to organize, or failing to do so because of the hopelessness of their condition, seemed imbued with a new spirit. . . . Strikes prevailed everywhere. Thousands of grievances were settled by peaceful arbitration. Every branch of labor was affected. . . . The skilled and the unskilled, the high-paid and the low-paid, all joined hands. . . . The press was filled with labor news."[4]

It is not strange that the decade of the 'eighties should have witnessed a pulsating labor movement accompanied by struggles of a vigor and scope which had hitherto been absent from nineteenth century America. They were the fruit of the sweeping industrialization of the country which characterized the Civil War years and the period following. Though the basis for the Industrial Revolution in America had been laid much earlier, it was not until after 1865 that the implications of the change in industrial technique became fully apparent. Concurrently, new areas in the trans-Mississippi West were being opened to agriculture, while the development of transcontinental railroads and the consolidation of trunk lines served to create a domestic market of national scope.

The half century following the Civil War witnessed the refashioning not only of American industry, but of the whole structure of American society. Manufacturing broke away from its dependence upon commerce. Changes in technology were paralleled by changes in the organization of industry and business enterprise in general. Through the corporate form huge "combinations" came to dominate industrial activity. Immense fortunes, far greater than those of earlier days, were founded. Urban centers were multiplying in number and mounting in population. In them a true industrial proletariat was growing rapidly. The stream of cheap European labor entering the country was becoming wider and creating new problems.

4 George E. McNeill, editor, *The Labor Movement, The Problem of To-Day, Comprising a History of Capital and Labor, and Its Present Status*, New York, 1887, pp. 170-171.

The 'eighties themselves were unmistakably marked by a definite quickening in the extension of the factory and machine technique. Not only was there an increase in the number of machines, but they also invaded fields in which they had been relatively absent. Factories and shops in general grew vastly in number, and the amount of capital invested in foundries and machine-shops alone increased two and one-half times in the decade. This, together with the notable increase in the number of patents issued during the 'eighties, offers further evidence of the tendency toward the completer mechanization of production.

This process characterized the whole field of American industry. It was constantly asserted during this period that rapid mechanization was responsible for an over-production of goods which in turn caused industrial depressions. Carroll D. Wright, the first Commissioner of Labor, stated in his annual report of 1886, that manufacturers estimated that in the production of agricultural implements, machines had displaced fully one-half of the "muscular" labor necessary fifteen or twenty years earlier. In the shoe-making and textile industries, there was an equal reduction in the manual labor formerly employed. In the manufacture of small arms, one man with the use of power machinery and with a division of labor "turns out and fits the equivalent of 42 to 50 stocks in ten hours as against 1 stock in the same length of time by manual labor, a displacement of 44 to 49 men in this one operation."

By the 'eighties, striking evidence of the accelerated tempo of industrial life was available. Between 1874 and 1882, the production of Bessemer steel ingots jumped from 191,933 tons to 1,696,450. In Pennsylvania alone, in the ten-year period 1875-1885, it mounted from 148,374 to 1,109,034 tons. In 1884, there were 125,739 miles of railroad in operation, almost a four-fold increase since 1865. The total production of iron and steel rails in 1880, 1,461,847 tons, was more than double that of 1874. In 1860, 14,000,000 tons of coal were mined. In 1884 almost 100,000,000 tons of bituminous and anthracite coal were being extracted from the earth. Regardless of the field, evidences of the phenomenal growth of America industry abound. In Massachusetts, for example, 2,633,075 cases of boots and shoes were manufactured in 1885, compared with the 718,660 cases annually produced two decades earlier. The total value of manufactures estimated at $1,019,000,000 for 1849, came to $3,386,000,000 in 1869 and to $9,372,000,000 twenty years later. The economic expansion of the two decades after the Civil War was reflected in the growth of international commerce. Exports and imports of the United States, totalling $687,192,176 in 1860, rose to $828,730,176 in 1870, and to more than one and a half billion dollars in 1880. Between 1876 and 1885, the country enjoyed an unbroken annual excess of exports over imports. In the twenty year period 1860-1880, the total value of American imports and exports increased at a more rapid rate than that of the British Isles or France.[5]

In 1884, the *Commercial and Financial Chronicle* pointed out that "this country has already a commerce with the countries south of us on the American continent by no means inconsiderable, and not contemptible in comparison with that of England and France. It is quite equal to that of our rivals in point of variety, and, excepting a few great classes of articles like textiles, iron manufactures, boots, hats and clothing, it is also equal in amount." It urged that these markets be further developed for the consumption of American manufactures, and recommended that "Americans . . . establish foreign houses, and place them in charge of active, intelligent and pushing agents." American manufacturing had reached a point where it was imperative to seek foreign markets "not merely with the purpose of disposing of an occasional surplus of goods which temporary over-production or under-consumption leave undisposed of, but for the permanent supply of great populations which are to be clothed and fed and transported from place to place."[6] These observations clearly indicate that American industry had already outgrown its swaddling clothes.

The changes in industrial technique led to the increase of factory laborers, who in contrast to the handicraft worker, may be regarded

[5] For the statistical and quoted material in this section on economic development, see *The First Annual Report of the Commissioner of Labor, March, 1886. Industrial Depressions,* Washington, 1886, pp. 67-71, 72-73, 80-87; Commons, *op. cit.,* vol. 2, pp. 358-359. Excellent textbook treatments of the period of industrialization are Fred Albert Shannon, *Economic History of the People of the United States* New York, 1934, Chaps. XXII-XXIV; Louis M. Hacker and Benjamin B. Kendrick *The United States since 1865,* Revised Edition, New York, 1934, Chap. X.

[6] Vol. 39, no. 999, August 16, 1884, p. 171.

as semi-skilled or unskilled. Differentiation between employer and employee became more striking, and the dominant conception of the worker as an impersonal commodity became more sharply confirmed. In M. A. Foran's *The Other Side, A Social Study Based on Fact,* published in 1886, a noteworthy though poorly conceived labor novel which is strongly pro-working class, but not opposed to capitalism as such, social cleavage between employers and employees is a constant theme. Antagonistic to radical doctrines, the novel nevertheless presents the average employer of the period just as unfavorably as did the revolutionary of the day, describing him as a domineering "master."[7]

The gulf which separated workingman and employer, either individual or corporate, was produced by the economic changes which the country had experienced. In some occupations it was a comparatively recent development. A brass-worker discussing this question in 1883, remarked: "Well, I remember that fourteen years ago the workmen and foremen and the boss were all as one happy family; it was just as easy and as free to speak to the boss as anyone else, but now the boss is superior, and the men all go to the foremen; but we would not think of looking the foreman in the face now any more than we would the boss. . . . The average hand growing up in the shop now would not think of speaking to the boss, would not presume to recognize him, nor the boss would not recognize him either."[8] Employers "adopt a superior standpoint," complained another workingman. "The employer has pretty much the same feeling towards the men that he had toward his machinery. He wants to get as much as he can out of his men at the cheapest rate. . . . That is all he cares for the man generally."[9]

[7] Published in Washington, D. C., and dedicated "To the Working Men and Women of America . . ." It has been overlooked by Parrington and Hicks in their studies of the literature of the period. See especially, pp. 75, 158-159.

[8] *Report of the [Education and Labor] Committee of the Senate upon the Relations between Labor and Capital, and Testimony Taken by the Committee,* 4 vols., Washington 1885, vol. 1, p. 473 (cited hereafter as *Rep. of the Sen. Com. on Lab.*). Senator Henry W. Blair of New Hampshire was chairman. The resolution as a result of which the Committee was appointed contemplated an inquiry concerning the relations between labor and capital hours and wages of labor, the share of labor and capital in the national income, the causes of strikes, etc. The Report contains a mine of valuable information. A fifth volume containing the report of the Committee was probably suppressed. It never appeared.

[9] *Ibid.,* vol. 1, pp. 681, 682.

One manufacturer bluntly declared, according to Samuel Gompers, "I regard my employés as I do a machine, to be used to my advantage, and when they are old and of no further use I cast them in the street."[10] The indifference to human values here displayed was neither an invention of Gompers nor wholly exceptional. A New England wool-manufacturer, complacently observed that when workers "get starved down to it, then they will go to work at just what you can afford to pay."[11] Such views accompanied the conviction that it is, as Jay Gould said, an "axiom . . . that labor is a commodity that will in the long run be governed absolutely by the law of supply and demand,"[12]—an argument which justified adequately the manner in which workers were commonly treated. Labor was a commodity—though sometimes a peculiar and troublesome one—and there was no reason why it should be dealt with differently from other commodities. ". . . I never do my talking to the hands," said a New England mill owner, "I do all my talking with the overseers."[13]

As long as these attitudes were taken by a considerable body of employers, it is no wonder that the feeling between them and the workers was generally one of steadily increasing "distrust and dissatisfaction," as Joseph Medill, publisher of the Chicago *Tribune*, put it.[14] P. J. McGuire, a labor leader, was no less aware of the absence of amicable relations between workers and employers. Their respective activities and wealth—or lack of it—drove a powerful wedge between them. They had no social contacts. "They do not know each other on the street."[15] The more poorly paid workers, observed W. H. Foster, general secretary of the Federation of Organized Trades and Labor Unions, in 1883, exhibited an attitude of "sullen discontent" toward those who employed them. "They do not seem to have the courage to express openly what they think all the time, unless they are under the influence of liquor."[16]

In pre-Civil War days industry was smaller in scope; less of it was corporately organized; the independent artisan was still an impor-

10 *Ibid.*, vol. 1, p. 288.
11 *Ibid.*, vol. 3, p. 288.
12 New York *Times*, April 30, 1886.
13 *Rep. of the Sen. Com. on Lab.*, vol. 3, p. 38.
14 *Ibid.*, vol. 2, p. 990.
15 *Ibid.*, vol. 1, pp. 357-358.
16 *Ibid.*, vol. 1, p. 410.

tant industrial factor; and escape from working-class ranks was less difficult. The relationship of employer and employee of that period had almost vanished by the 'eighties. As one writer sympathetic to labor observed of the 'eighties and 'nineties, "the old liberality of American employers is on the wane. Competition compels them to be close-fisted and to inaugurate a policy of aggressive resistance against the demands of organized labor."[17] As labor, becoming increasingly conscious of its condition, boldly voiced its complaints and demands, and resorted more widely to industrial action to gain its objectives, capital developed not only the normal defense mechanisms but a definite militancy. In an age dedicated to the business exploitation of the vast resources of America it would have been strange had there not been an aggressive capitalist class. The spirit of the Gilded Age can be understood when it is remembered that the business men of the period were pioneers—pioneers in industry, pioneers in the pursuit of wealth.[18]

The idealization of property so characteristic of the period was a natural result of the intensive pursuit of material possessions. Walt Whitman declared that "Democracy looks with suspicious, ill-satisfied eyes upon the very poor and on those out of business; she asks for men and women with occupations, well off, owners of houses and acres, and with cash in the bank."[19] John Hay's *The Bread-Winners,* with its hostile treatment of discontented labor, its "odor of property-morality," was a natural and early literary manifestation of this attitude.[20] Josiah Strong remarked that the "Christian man who is not willing to make the largest profits which an honest regard for the laws of trade permits is a rare man."[21] To the charge that the

[17] Henry W. Cherouny, *The Burial of the Apprentice: A True Story from Life in a Union Workshop . . . and Other Essays on Present Political and Social Problems,* New York, 1900, p. 118.

[18] Van Wyck Brooks, *The Ordeal of Mark Twain,* new and revised edition, New York, 1933, pp. 83 *ff.*

[19] Quoted in *ibid.,* p. 82.

[20] Vernon Louis Parrington, *The Beginnings of Critical Realism in America, 1860-1920,* New York, 1930, pp. 173 *et seq.;* Granville Hicks, *The Great Tradition, An Interpretation of American Literature since the Civil War,* New York, 1933, pp. 78-84; Tyler Dennett, *John Hay. From Poetry to Politics,* New York, 1933, Chap. X, *passim.*

[21] Josiah Strong, *Our Country. Its Possible Future and Its Present Crisis,* revised edition, New York, 1891, p. 259; *cf.* p. 166.

Vanderbilts' wealth was a monstrous injustice in a democratic republic, one writer replied that "Mr. Vanderbilt is receiving a propor-
tionally small, and a well earned part of the profits of the greatest
economical device of modern times." He was merely being rewarded
for his father's great services to mankind and more particularly to
American society.[22]

That tremendous appetite for wealth, which showed its worst side
in the operations of Jay Gould, was amusingly satirized in the following bit of doggerel:

"JAY GOULD'S MODEST WANTS
My wants are few; I scorn to be
A querulous refiner;
I only want America
And a mortgage deed of China;
And if kind fate threw Europe in,
And Africa and Asia,
And a few islands of the sea,
I'd ask no other treasure.
Give me but these—they are enough
To suit my notion—
And I'll give up to other men
All land beneath the ocean."[23]

The arrogance of wealth is illustrated by the words attributed to
an American millionaire of the 'eighties who said of his class: "We
are not politicians or public thinkers; we are the rich; we own America; we got it, God knows how, but we intend to keep it if we
can. . . ."[24] The cry that American labor shared inadequately in the
industrial wealth of the nation and that a large portion of the laboring class was impoverished was either never heard or flatly denied
by capital. Andrew Carnegie, addressing the Nineteenth Century
Club at the close of 1887, exclaimed, "I defy any man to show that
there is pauperism" in the United States.[25] William Graham Sumner,
closing his eyes to incontrovertible evidence, declared that pauper-

[22] M. L. Scudder, Jr., *The Labor-Value Fallacy*, third edition, Chicago, 1887,
pp. 76-79.
[23] S. W. Foss in *Tid-Bits*, undated clipping, New York Public Library Scrap-
Books on Labor.
[24] Quoted in Virginius Dabney, *Liberalism in the South*, Chapel Hill, 1932,
[25] Quoted in *Social Science Review*, vol. 1, no. 2, December 14, 1887, p. 9.
p. 203.

ism did not characterize the American wage-earning class. "It is constantly alleged in vague and declamatory terms," he wrote, "that artisans and unskilled laborers are in distress and misery, or are under oppression. No facts to bear out these assertions are offered."[26]

If they admitted the existence of poverty among a considerable portion of the working-class, business men were ready to ascribe it to inadequate education,[27] drink, laziness, and improvidence. Occasionally, they placed part of the responsibility upon the activities of manipulators and gamblers who were not to be confused with sober, honest industrialists.[28] Joseph Medill declared that the primary "cause of the impecunious condition of millions of the wage classes of this country is due to their own improvidence and misdirected efforts. Too many are trying to live without labor . . . and too many squander their earnings on intoxicating drinks, cigars and amusements, who cannot afford it."[29] It was easy to place the responsibility for inadequate wages and penury upon unalterable economic laws which determined the share that labor received. Thus, the Commercial Club of Boston was informed that

"There is certainly a very general complaint just now that labor does not get its share, that capital gets more than its share, that things ought not to go on as they have gone. . . . But complaints are not always well founded. Men as well as children often desire what they cannot and ought not to have. And complaining settles nothing. The existing mode of division is the work of certain natural laws. . . .

"It is perfectly right for the wage earner to get all he can. The employer will pay as little as he can. . . . It is the duty of the employer to sedulously regard the interests of those he employs, to deal fairly by them. Above all, every man imbued with the spirit of Christianity, the Christian in deed as well as in name, will strive to do as he would be done by.

26 W. G. Sumner, "Industrial War," *Forum,* vol. 2, September, 1886, p. 3.

27 See, however, the statement of a New England mill owner who in 1883 declared: "There is such a thing as too much education for working people sometimes. I don't mean to say by that that I discourage education . . . or that I think that with good sense any amount of education can hurt anyone, but I have seen cases where young people were spoiled for labor by being educated to a little too much refinement." *Rep. of the Sen. Com. on Lab.,* vol. 3, p. 15.

28 R. Heber Newton, *The Present Aspect of the Labor Problem. Four Lectures Given in All Souls Church, New York, May 1886,* New York, 1886, pp. 21-25. The Rev. Newton's second lecture gives capital's view of the labor problem and of the existing economic order, pp. 21-36.

29 *Rep. of the Sen. Com. on Lab.,* vol. 2, p. 959.

"But after all, one inexorable law finally settles this as it does so many other economic questions, and that is the law of demand and supply."[30]

Not everyone, however, denied that the American worker had just ground for complaint, or ascribed such unfortunate conditions as existed to the operation of natural laws. In his first annual report in 1886, Commissioner Wright, discussing the effect of the industrial revolution upon the worker, declared that "if the question should be asked, has the wage-worker received his equitable share of the benefits derived from the introduction of machinery, the answer must be no. In the struggle for industrial supremacy in the great countries devoted to mechanical production, it probably has been impossible for him to share equitably in such benefits."[31] Some of the State bureaus of labor or labor statistics pointed to evidences of the maldistribution of wealth, and concluded that labor did not receive a fair share in the returns of industry. Such assertions were made by the bureau of New Jersey in 1881 and 1883, of Illinois in 1882, and of Michigan in 1884.[32] Some writers charged that State and Federal laws favored the few at the expense of the many. In an article in the *Contemporary Review,* Prof. Charles Kendall Adams reported that in 1886 a "very large proportion of our thoughtful writers were inclined to take it for granted that the wage-workers had a grievance that could, in some way, be corrected. The opinion was very general that . . . the masses of the people did not receive their fair share . . ."[33] When Francis A. Walker asserted that the "real labor problem of today" turned on the question of how the self-assertiveness of the working-class could be tempered, he made it clear that it was "rightful," and that it would make for an "equitable and beneficial distribution of wealth" which was then lacking.[34]

Labor's grievances sprang from the privileges and corruption of

[30] A. S. Wheeler, *The Labor Question. A Paper Read before the Commercial Club of Boston, October 16, 1886. Reprinted from the Andover Review for November, 1886,* Boston, 1886, pp. 3, 8.

[31] *First Annual Report of the Commissioner of Labor,* pp. 88-89.

[32] Cited in Richmond Mayo Smith, "American Labor Statistics," *Political Science Quarterly,* vol. 1, no. 1, March, 1886, p. 53.

[33] "Contemporary Life and Thought in the United States," *Contemporary Review,* vol. 52, November, 1887, pp. 731-732.

[34] Francis A. Walker, *The Labor Problem of Today. An Address Delivered before the Alumni Association of Lehigh University, June 22d, 1887,* New York, 1887, pp. 8, 14.

the American political system, the growth of a small, immensely wealthy class, the results of corporate industrial organization, and the economic and social condition of the wage-earners at large and certain groups of them in particular. Protests against monopolies and large corporations filled the air during the period. The latter were denounced as sources of "outrage" and "corruption" and destroyers of human rights. National and State governments, it was charged, had been captured by corporate interests, for whose benefit they legislated at the expense of the many. The courts were stigmatized as subservient tools of the vested interests. A contributor to the *Catholic Quarterly Review* summed up current attitudes in the assertion that "it is futile for the public press to be constantly preaching platitudes respecting patience and regard for the rights of the employers and respect for law, whilst evasions and defiant violations, constantly practised by mammoth capitalists and corporations, are ignored, condoned and tacitly approved."[35]

If one examines the economic and social condition of the American working-class during the 'eighties, one can understand why labor was restive and discontented.

Though statistical information on pauperism in the United States before 1890 is lacking, there is sufficient evidence to leave no doubt concerning its existence. It is safe to say that a considerable number of American wage-earners lived below the poverty level. Estimates for the early 'nineties indicate that ten per cent of the total population of urban districts was poverty-stricken.[36] This would probably be true, roughly speaking, for the preceding decade. Samuel Gompers offered, in 1883, some interesting conjectures on the extent of pauperism in the United States. Taking the census statistics of 1870 for

[35] George D. Wolff, "The Wage Question," *The Catholic Quarterly Review,* vol. 11, no. 42, April, 1886, pp. 343-344. For characteristic and different types of protest in behalf of labor, see the *Rep. of the Sen. Com. on Lab.,* vol. 1-4, *passim; Newton, op. cit.,* pp. 3-20, *passim;* Richard T. Ely, *The Labor Movement in America,* new and revised edition, New York, 1905, p. 61, Appendix I, No. VIII, pp. 371-373; The Hon. Stewart L. Woodford, *The Labor Problem. Annual Oration Before the New York Delta of Phi Beta Kappa* (New York, 1886), *passim;* McNeill, *op. cit.,* chap. XVII, *passim;* Walter B. Hill, *Anarchy, Socialism, and the Labor Movement. An Address Delivered Before the Literary Societies of the University of Georgia, July 19, 1886,* Columbus, Ga., 1886, pp. 23-25, 37 *et seq.*

[36] Thomas Sewall Adams and Helen L. Sumner, *Labor Problems,* eighth edition, New York, 1911, p. 150.

the five greatest manufacturing States, New York, Massachusetts, Ohio, Pennsylvania and Illinois, he showed that the average annual wages for industrial workers came to about $405.64. With five individuals in the average family, the amount for the support of each one was $81.149. There were in those five States in 1870, Gompers pointed out, "62,494 paupers, maintained by the States at a cost of $6,161,354, or a fraction over $95 per individual. Thus it appears that the workingman was compelled to support himself above the degree of 'pauperism' on $14 less per annum than the State spent to support paupers as paupers. These figures are, of course, old, but they can be depended upon, except that the wage of the workingmen is less now than it was in 1870."[37] Gompers' argument is open to serious objections, but it is not incorrect in its insistence upon the existence of a pauper class. It was said more than once that "dire want" and "superfluity"[38] were characteristic of the American scene.

Implicit in the statistics of the distribution of national wealth and income is the fact that a considerable part of the American working-class lived neither far from nor securely above the poverty line. On the basis of the census of 1890, Charles B. Spahr concluded that 200,000 families had an annual income of $5,000 and over; 1,300,000 families an income of from $1,200 to $5,000; 11,000,000 families an income under $1,200. The average annual income from labor per family for the last group was $380. He computed that one per cent of the families received nearly a fourth of the national income, while fifty per cent of the families received barely a fifth. More than half of the aggregate income of the country was enjoyed by one-eighth of the families, and the richest one per cent received a larger total income than the poorest fifty per cent. The great majority of small property owners, both urban and rural, possessed barely one-eighth of the national wealth, and one per cent of the families had more wealth than the remaining ninety-nine per cent. Of the twelve million families in the country, about five and one-half million could be classed as propertyless.[39]

"I have a brother who has four children, besides his wife and him-

37 *Rep. of the Sen. Com. on Lab.*, vol. 1, pp. 291-292.

38 Strong, *op. cit.*, p. 174.

39 Charles B. Spahr, *An Essay on the Present Distribution of Wealth in the United States*, New York, 1896, pp. 68-69, 128-129, 158-159; *cf.* pp. 50-52; *Free Society*, May 6, 1900, p. 2; Strong, *op. cit.*, p. 174.

self," reported a workingman in 1883. "All he earns is $1.50 a day."
This was the abbreviated life history of thousands. He continued:
"He works in the ironworks at Fall River. He only works about nine
months out of twelve. There is generally about three months of stop-
page, taking the year right through, and his wife and his family all
have to be supported for a year out of the wages of nine months—
$1.50 a day for nine months out of the twelve, to support six of them.
It does not stand to reason that those children and he himself can
have natural food or be naturally dressed."[40] Speaking of the industrial population of Fall River, especially of the mill operatives, a
physician of that city declared that as a class they were "dwarfed
physically," and that their careworn attitude always impressed visi-
tors. ". . . most of them," he asserted, "are obliged to live from hand
to mouth, or, at least, they do not have sufficient food to nourish
them as they need to be nourished." If they drank, it was to find
escape from the realities of life and its oppressive ennui.[41] A Chicago
printer, active in labor circles, made it clear in 1883 that the workingmen of his city bitterly resented their condition. "The very fact
of their living in the squalor and wretchedness they do live in," he
said, "has provoked discontent in their minds; and in all our labor
agitations, wherever there is any particular excitement aroused, these
men who feel that they are oppressed are ready for almost any
remedy. Even if it reached a revolution, if you chose, they are ripe
for it." The lower class workers found it impossible to save money.
"They don't receive enough wages . . ." he explained. "Instead of
laying up money or anything of that kind, they are not able to earn
enough to support themselves and their families."[42]

This picture of the poorer working people of Chicago is perhaps
overdrawn, but it is not entirely misleading. What was true of the
pushing Lake City was roughly true of practically every urban center
in the country. Careful investigation of the tenement areas of the
city in 1883-1884, undertaken by the Citizens' Association of Chicago
—interested not only in civic improvement,[43] but also in lower rents,
which would mean reduced wages and a source of profitable real

40 *Rep. of the Sen. Com. on Lab.*, vol. 3, p. 452.
41 *Ibid.*, vol. 3, pp. 408-415, *passim*.
42 *Ibid.*, vol. 1, pp. 574-576, *passim*. The statements were made by P. H. Logan.
43 The Citizens' Association was a civic reform organization.

estate investment—disclosed the existence of frightful conditions. The report which followed the investigation speaks of "the wretched condition of the tenements into which thousands of workingmen are huddled, the wholesale violation of all rules for drainage, plumbing, light, ventilation and safety in case of fire or accident, the neglect of all laws of health, the horrible condition of sewers and outhouses, the filthy dingy rooms into which they are crowded, the unwholesome character of their food, and the equally filthy nature of the neighboring streets, alleys and back lots filled with decaying matter and stagnant pools."[44] For these "unwholesome dens" into which they were crowded, working-class families paid extravagant rents in proportion to the wages they received.[45] In many cases, they were "fleeced at a rate which returns 25 to 40 per cent per annum of the value of the property."[46] Those with small incomes had to live on the outskirts of the city—which was perhaps why Chicago spread like quicksilver—to secure decent housing, or else occupy "pigsties" in the city proper.[47] Chicago, it may be noted, with an average of over eight persons to a dwelling, and with about seventeen per cent of the dwellings containing three or more families, appears to have had housing facilities which were superior to other urban centers.[48]

There is little wonder that many of Chicago's inhabitants displayed "sullen discontent." Of a population of approximately 630,000 in 1884, a quarter of a million were classed as adult wage-earners, and the vast majority of these, caught between low wages and high rents for bad dwellings, had good ground for complaint. Dissatisfaction was keen among large groups of the foreign born. Slightly less than half of Chicago's inhabitants were of foreign origin, with the Germans far in the lead and the Bohemians following with about 35,000 to 40,000. Many of both nationalities had come to the United States hoping to find both a haven and an earthly heaven.

[44] *Report of the Committee on Tenement Houses of the Citizens' Association of Chicago, September, 1884,* Chicago, 1884, p. 3.
[45] *Ibid.,* p. 4.
[46] *Ibid.,* p. 9.
[47] *Ibid.,* p. 15.
[48] Marcus T. Reynolds, *The Housing of the Poor in American Cities. The Prize Essay of the American Economic Association for 1892. (Publications of the American Economic Association,* vol. 8, nos. 2 and 3), London, March and May, 1893, pp. 19, 30; Strong, *op. cit.,* p. 184.

Among the Bohemians, largely low-paid laborers who lived in a wretched quarter of the city, dissatisfaction ran high.[49]

Jane Addams' *Twenty Years at Hull House*, though it treats essentially of the years after 1889, is an indictment of the social conditions under which tens of thousands of the inhabitants of Chicago lived and labored during the entire decade.[50] In it is the story of Chicago's squalid and crowded tenements, of the lack of the necessary sanitation provisions, adequate municipal legislation, charitable organizations, and relief facilities, of the thousands sunk in dire poverty, of the conditions that make for a diseased community, and of the unawareness of all this. Nor was Chicago unique in this. America of the 'eighties may not have been conscious of its Chicagos—Jane Addams writes of the "unfounded optimism that there was no real poverty among us"[51]—but they existed.

Standard of living and particular living conditions are, of course, causally related to wages, both money and real. Especially during the 'eighties, did the American worker insist that he was being underpaid. He did not receive enough for his labor as such, and he did not receive enough to lead a decent existence. The industrial depression which was first felt in 1882, made available a large labor surplus in certain occupations by 1883, led to keen competition for employment, and tended to depress wages.[52] In the textile industry, for example, this was the case. "I stand every morning in my factory," said a New England manufacturer, "and am obliged to refuse the applications of men who want to come to work for a dollar a day . . . and women begging for the opportunity to work for 50

---

[49] *Rep. of the Com. on Ten. Houses of the Cit. Assn. of Chicago*, p. 10; *The University*, Chicago, February 6, 1886, clipping, Labadie Scrap-Book; *Hull House Maps and Papers. A Presentation of Nationalities and Wages in a Congested District of Chicago, together with Comments and Essays on Problems Growing Out of the Social Conditions*, New York, 1895; Josepha Humpal Zeman, "The Bohemian People in Chicago," pp. 115-119 *passim*; Claudius O. Johnson, *Carter Henry Harrison I, Political Leader (Social Science Studies Directed by the Local Community Research Committee of the University of Chicago)*, Chicago, 1928, p. 189.

[50] New York, 1911, *passim* and especially pp. 99-100, 158, 194-195, 198-199, 201-202, 281; Strong, *op. cit.*, p. 186.

[51] *Op. cit.*, p. 158.

[52] For the causes of the depression, see *First Annual Report of the Commissioner of Labor*, pp. 291-292. Wages in Massachusetts in 1885, were about five per cent lower than they were in 1880, Spahr, *op. cit.*, p. 98 note.

cents a day. . . . It is evident . . . that there are a large number of men who desire to be employed at the low rates of wages now prevailing, and who cannot find employment."[53]

Despite the fact that the wage statistics gathered in the period are not always reliable, it appears that hourly money wages, recovering in 1880 from the effects of the depression beginning in 1873, rose to 1883, dropped somewhat in the following year and, after slight upward and downward movements in 1886, started to climb again in 1887. A more optimistic, but probably less accurate version of wage movements for the years 1883-1886 gives the same index figure for hourly wages for four solid years. That is to say, money wages at best remained at a fixed point for 1883-1886.[54]

A glance at actual money wages has value. In a number of New England textile mills, the daily earnings for all types of employees, male and female, ranged from $.50 to $1.80. This was for a working day running somewhat above ten hours. Most of the skilled male hands earned slightly better than one dollar a day, while women, of course, received less. Average weekly wages of $7.50-8.00 were considered better than fair, and in general the average monthly income was not much above $20. Only in comparatively few cases did it reach twice that sum. The wages of carpenters in 1883 averaged $1.45 a day for the entire year, although their actual money wage for time worked came to about one dollar more than that. Compositors in Massachusetts in the same year earned, on the basis of piecework, an average weekly wage of $7-9, which was probably what their income was elsewhere. The daily average wage of machine shop workers in 1883 was $2.00, although many earned as little as $1.25, and in some cases men were paid $4.00 a day. Certain classes of skilled shipyard mechanics received lower daily wages than the same class of labor in New England. In Delaware they earned from $10-12 a week, while in New York their wages ran higher at $2.60-3.50 a day. P. J. McGuire, General Secretary of the Brotherhood of Carpenters and Joiners, claimed on the basis of government fig-

[53] *Rep. of the Sen. Com. on Lab.*, vol. 2, p. 1117.

[54] Willford Isbell King, *The Wealth and Income of the People of the United States*, New York, 1923, table XXXVII, p. 198; *Handbook of Labor Statistics, 1929 Edition. Bulletin of the United States Bureau of Labor Statistics, Miscellaneous Series, No. 491*, Washington, 1929, p. 760. For movements of mining wages bearing out these generalizations, see Spahr, *op. cit.*, p. 114.

ures, that in 1883 the average earnings of workingmen throughout the United States came to slightly more than a dollar a day.[55]

Inadequate and incomplete statistical returns for the State of Illinois in 1884, show that yearly earnings of heads of families ranged between $210 and $1,608. The average earnings were $525.27, and this sum was increased on the average, by the income of other members of the family to $588. Yearly average living expenses were estimated at $507.56. Of the wage-earning heads of families investigated, twenty-four per cent failed to make a living, nine per cent barely made ends meet, and sixty-seven per cent enjoyed some surplus.[56] In Massachusetts, the average annual living costs of a workingman's family in 1883 were put at $754.42. The average income of wage-earning heads of families was $558.68. The difference between the two figures had to be supplied by the earnings of wives and children if the family was not to fall below the poverty line. This placed almost a third of the support of the average family upon others than its head.[57]

Broadly speaking, wages in Illinois were higher in 1882 than they were in 1886. Of 114 organized occupations for which there are adequate statistics, seventy-one show a decrease in average weekly wage between 1882 and 1886, twenty-three show an increase, and twenty remained the same. Excluding the occupations which experienced a drop in wages of five per cent or less, almost sixty per cent of the trades examined suffered wage decreases. The average weekly wages for all 114 occupations came to $15.34 in 1882 and to $14.51 in 1886. Since the workers were employed only seventy-five per cent of full time during the year, the average yearly wage came to $566.19. This was approximately $50 more than the annual average for the unorganized employees in the same occupations. The only trades which could boast of wage increases for the years 1882-1886 were those which were well organized; and trade unions reported greater success in maintaining or even increasing wages than assemblies of the Knights of Labor.[58]

[55] These wage figures come from *Rep. of the Sen. Com. on Lab.*, vol. 3, pp. 4, 28, 74, 125; vol. 1, pp. 320, 552-553, 757, 838-839.
[56] Smith, *loc. cit.*, p. 70; *cf.* Strong, *op. cit.*, pp. 147-148.
[57] Strong, *op. cit.*, p. 147. Compare with the earnings in Massachusetts in 1890, Spahr, *op. cit.*, pp. 97-98.
[58] *Fourth Biennial Report of the Bureau of Labor Statistics of Illinois, 1886*, Springfield, 1866, tables XXXI-XXXV, pp. 335-361.

Wage levels in these years in the State of Illinois appear representative of the country at large. An investigation of the earnings of almost 140,000 employees in 552 establishments scattered throughout twenty-eight States and covering some forty industries in 1886, shows that the average daily wage of male workers was almost two dollars. With an average of 282.6 working days a year, this gives an annual average income of $565.20. The income of women and children in industry was strikingly lower. The average daily wage of the first came to $1.11, and of the second to $.70. Though the figures cover a relatively small portion of the six million wage-earners in the country,[59] the industries and States considered are so representative that the conclusions may be safely accepted.[60]

For those employed with some regularity, the tendency of wages to remain fixed or move downward was more than equalized before 1886 by changes in commodity prices and the general cost of living. Commodity prices, recovering from the depression of 1873-78, had risen more rapidly than wages between 1879 and 1882. They began to fall precipitately after the last year, and did not move upward again until 1886. In purchasing power wages declined in 1880, only to be followed by a gradual upward movement in the next year which continued until 1885. The slight drop in real wages in 1886 became more pronounced in 1887, but in the following year there was again a recovery.[61]

Labor, however, did not gain as much as might be expected from the rise in real wages between 1881-1885, because of the irregularity of employment. While precise statistics for unemployment are lacking, there can be no doubt that a considerable portion of the wage-earning class were always unemployed for a part of the year, and that practically all workers experienced some irregularity of employment. These generalizations are supported by the findings in Massachusetts. In 1885, the industrial population of that State lost on the average 1.16 working months during the year. At the same time, almost thirty per cent of the industrial wage-earners were unemployed at their particular trades for 4.11 months during the year.

---

[59] Paul H. Douglas, "An Analysis of Strike Statistics," 1881-1921, *Journal of American Statistical Association*, n. s. no. 143 (vol. 18), September, 1923, p. 869. Douglas gives 6,905,000 as the average number of industrial workers for 1886-1890.

[60] *First Annual Report of the Commissioner of Labor*, p. 226.

[61] King, *op. cit.*, table XXXVII, p. 198; *cf.* Adams and Sumner, *op. cit.*, p. 514.

The Massachusetts Commissioner of Labor concluded that about one-third of the persons engaged in remunerative labor were unemployed at their principal occupation for about one-third of the working time.[62] Statistics covering more than 85,000 industrial wage-earners in the State of Illinois for 1885-1886 show that they were employed, on the average, 37.1 weeks in the year. Three per cent received twenty or less weeks of work during the year; thirty-two per cent received between twenty and thirty weeks' work; thirty per cent received between thirty and forty weeks' work; and thirty-five per cent between forty and fifty-two weeks' work. These figures show that the average worker was normally idle about one-fourth of the possible working time during the year.[63]

If, in the best of times, there was a constant unemployed class of two and one-half per cent of the total wage-earners in the country, as was asserted at the time, Carroll D. Wright's estimate of almost one million unemployed persons in 1885 in agriculture, trade, transportation, mining, manufacturing, and mechanical occupations, may be regarded as conservative. Since the depression of 1882-1886 hit industry in particular, the vast majority of the unemployed were industrial wage-earners. This unemployment, it was computed, accounted for a daily loss of consumptive power of one million dollars. Other contemporary estimates of unemployment set much higher figures. Terence V. Powderly, General Master Workman of the Knights of Labor, spoke of the widespread unemployment that affected the country from 1883 on, and declared that from one and a half to two million men were out of work in 1885. It was shortly after asserted that the unemployed reached two million in 1886.[64] Inevitably the

[62] Cited in Adams and Sumner, *op. cit.*, pp. 160-161; Spahr, *op. cit.*, pp. 100-102.

[63] *Fourth Biennial Report of the Bureau of Labor Statistics of Illinois*, table XXVII, pp. 318-319.

[64] *First Annual Report of the Commissioner of Labor*, pp. 65-66; Terence V. Powderly, "The Army of the Discontented," *North American Review*, vol. 140, April, 1885, p. 369; *Record of the Proceedings of the Ninth Regular Session of the General Assembly, Held at Hamilton, Ont., Oct. 5-13, 1885*, n. p., 1885, p. 11; *Labor: Its Rights and Wrongs. Statements and Comments by the Leading Men of Our Nation on the Labor Question of To-Day* . . . Washington, 1886, pp. 305-306; McNeill, *op. cit.*, pp. 575-576. S. B. Elkins put the number of unemployed in 1885 at 350,000; Hon. S. B. Elkins, *The Industrial Question in the United States. Address Delivered before the Alumni Association of the University of the State of Missouri, June 3, 1885*, New York (1885), p. 7.

feeling became widespread among American workers that a decrease in hours would reduce unemployment, and that they were not adequately paid for the goods and values they produced during the normal working day.[65]

Most industrial problems and most labor discontent arose in connection with the primary questions of employment, wages and hours. There were, however, other sources of antagonism between employer and worker in the secondary conditions of labor in a number of industrial practises to which employers resorted. The latter include the black-list, the iron-clad oath and the practise of assessing fines and charges. While these affected only some workers, they called forth protests from American labor at large.

Fining, most common in retail stores, hotels, and restaurants, was also found in factories, generally only in those employing large numbers of women and children. Workers were fined for coming late, for being absent without permission, for singing or talking with one another during working hours, for unusual noise, for imperfections in the work, and for a host of arbitrary reasons. Fines were sometimes assessed to the extent of two and three per cent of the weekly wages, without any statement of the reasons for their imposition. It is true, of course, that fining affected industry to a minor extent at this time, and there was almost none of it among male factory workers. It was most in evidence in the older manufacturing States, but was spreading to all. In severely condemning the system in 1886, the Bureau of Labor Statistics of Illinois pointed out that fining was a development of the past five years, and that while it had not yet made deep inroads, the practise was growing rapidly.[66]

A series of investigations by the Chicago *Times* of the factories of Chicago, especially those employing women and children, disclosed in 1888 that the fining practise had spread. Frequently employees lost a considerable portion of the $3-4 weekly they received for a ten hour day through fines.[67]

Other burdensome charges were levied upon employees. Female operatives, especially in the clothing industry, were sometimes forced

[65] For hours, see below pp. 34-35, 159-160 [in *History of the Haymarket Affair*].
[66] *Fourth Biennial Report of the Bureau of Labor Statistics of Illinois,* pp. 501-506, 507-509, 510-526.
[67] John P. Altgeld, *Live Questions: Including Our Penal Machinery and Its Victims,* Chicago, 1890, pp. 80-89 ("Slave Girls in Chicago").

to contribute a certain per cent of the weekly wage to pay for the machines upon which they worked. If the worker left her employ before the machine was paid for, she usually forfeited her "contributions." Payments for needles and thread were common, and frequently workers were required to cover the expense of repairing machines. In at least one instance, the employer levied a charge of twenty-five cents weekly upon each operative for the steam by which the factory was run. There were authenticated instances where female operatives lost one-half of their weekly wages—which generally came to about five dollars—because of such charges.[68] Another practise, also found widely among female workers, compelled new hands to turn over a portion of the first week's wages as surety against quitting the factory before the expiration of a six months' period or without giving two weeks' notice. If the proper notice were given or six months had elapsed, the money was returned. Where this rule was rigidly enforced, an employee would lose the sum deposited for failing to report to work on any one day before the half year was up.[69]

The iron-clad oath, comparable to the yellow-dog contract of the present day, was employed to prevent the unionization of factories and shops. The oath affirmed that the signer was not a member of a labor organization, did not contemplate joining and would never join one. In its broadest sense it prohibited the members of a shop from collective action or even consultation of any kind. It was usually accompanied by a pernicious system of spying which employers were informed of infractions of the oath. Membership in a labor organization of any sort was, for one who had signed it, cause for instant dismissal. Where labor organizations were weak or were in process of formation, the iron-clad oath was a particularly potent weapon. Workers had no legal redress against it. It was successfully used on many occasions to drive workers out of their organizations, or at least make such membership secret.[70]

[68] *Proceedings of the General Assembly of the Knights of Labor of America. Eleventh Regular Session, Held at Minneapolis, Minnesota, October 4 to 19, 1887*, n. p., 1887 (cited hereafter as *Proceedings of G. A., K. of L., 1887*), pp. 1584-1588.

[69] *Fourth Biennial Report of the Bureau of Labor Statistics of Illinois*, pp. 507-508.

[70] *Proceedings of G. A., K. of L., 1887*, pp. 1715, 1737, 1776; *Alarm*, December

Against the black-list the worker was given statutory protection by some States and in practically all of them its use could be prosecuted as a conspiracy punishable at common law.[71] Few wage-earners were cognizant of this, however, and court action was rarely taken in essence, the black-list was the employers' method of boycotting obnoxious workers. Names on the list were circularized among employers within the same trade, and workers thus distinguished found it impossible to secure employment within a given district or even in other regions. Commonly regarded by workers as the cause of the labor boycott, to which it was analogous, the black-list was employed almost solely against men engaged in union activities. It served, therefore, as a supplementary weapon to the iron-clad oath. In the 'eighties, and especially by 1886, it was increasingly popular among employers. It was most bitterly resented in organized labor circles, which regarded its employment as a blanket declaration of war against union labor by the employer.[72] Employers also often imported foreign and colored workers into a troublesome locality to prevent the formation of labor organizations or destroy those which already existed.[73]

A limited number of workers found a grievance in the fact that they received their wages partly in cash and partly in goods or orders for goods. This practise obtained largely in the coal industry, where the company store system was frequently found with it. In Illinois, about one-fifth of the wage-earners in the coal industry were subject to the burdens of the system. In most instances, these stores sold goods at prices above those prevailing in the locality, and frequently they profiteered to the extent of twenty per cent above normal prices.[74] In many regions, reported Carroll D. Wright in 1886, "employment depends partially upon taking goods out of the companies' stores."[75] Large numbers of workers likewise found the custom of

17, 1887 (contains reprint of typical iron-clad oath); *A Summary of the Third Annual Report of the Bureau of Labor Statistics of New York, January 21, 1886*, Albany, 1886, p. 25; *Newton, op. cit.*, pp. 39-40.

[71] See below, pp. 42 *et seq.* [in *The History of the Haymarket Affair*].

[72] Newton, *op. cit.*, p. 17; Hill, *op. cit.*, p. 47; *Proceedings of G. A., K. of L., 1887*, pp. 1408, 1666, 1667.

[73] *Proceedings of G. A., K. of L., 1887*, pp. 1669-1670.

[74] *Fourth Biennial Report of the Bureau of Labor Statistics of Illinois*, pp. 321-327, 333-334.

[75] *First Annual Report of the Commissioner of Labor*, p. 244.

paying wages at fortnightly or monthly intervals burdensome,[76] and some States passed laws to protect the worker from employers who withheld his earnings for too long a time.

Obviously, not all American workers were being subjected to the unjust conditions which produced the working-class discontent of the period. But the unpleasant elements in the industrial scene cannot be glossed over, and the latter cannot be presented in the roseate light in which many of its contemporaries saw it. The American worker, it is true, was less rigidly fixed in his economic class and function than the European; passage into another class was easier for him; he enjoyed a degree of social equality and freedom, as well as material advantages, which the European did not. All this was frequently pointed out at the time.[77] Yet it does not follow that the American workingman had no reason for complaint, or that he was not conscious of the inequalities in American society. In 1888, James Bryce observed that

> "There are no struggles between privileged and unprivileged orders, not even that perpetual strife of rich and poor. . . . No one of the questions which now agitate the nation is a question between rich and poor. Instead of suspicion, jealousy, and arrogance embittering the relations of classes, good feeling and kindliness reign. Everything that government, as the Americans have . . . understood the term, can give them, the poorer class have already. . . . Hence the poorer have had little to fight for, no grounds for disliking the well-to-do, few complaints to make against them."

Bryce placed upon the shoulders of foreigners who brought "their Old World passions with them," responsibility for the cries of protest which were raised and the labor disturbances which occurred.[78]

His judgment, however, cannot be accepted as either adequate or accurate. The elements which disturbed the serenity of the industrial scene were not exceptional to it—they cannot be regarded as rare abnormalities—and it was not alone the "foreigner" who was cognizant of them. If the worker aired his grievances, it was because he had full reason. America had reached a stage in economic development where a tranquil industrial life and a contended working class were practical impossibilities.

[76] *Fourth Biennial Report of the Bureau of Labor Statistics of Illinois*, p. 326.
[77] James Bryce, *The American Commonwealth*, 2 vols., new edition, New York, 1927, vol. 2, pp. 300 ff., 647-649, Chap. CXIX, *passim*.
[78] *Ibid.*, vol. 2, pp. 647-648.

JULIUS W. PRATT

~~~~~~

THE SPANISH-AMERICAN WAR is often used by historians to mark
the entrance of the United States upon the stage of world politics. Yet the events of the war itself offer a less than satisfactory
explanation of our change in national foreign policy. It is difficult, for example, to see at first glance how a sincere effort to
bring freedom to the oppressed Cubans could result in the formation of an American empire.

The task of explaining the psychological background of the
war and the changes in attitude which undermined our traditional disinterestedness in global affairs fell into the capable
hands of Julius W. Pratt. When Pratt undertook his study, he
had already established an enviable reputation with a book on a
similar theme, called *Expansionists of 1812*. Whereas previous
historians had attributed the War of 1812 to maritime grievances against Great Britain, Pratt broke new ground by asserting
that the conflict stemmed from an expanionist urge on the part
of the United States which was being frustrated by British agitation among the western Indians.

The connection between these two studies is suggested by the
title of the first chapter in *Expansionists of 1898:* "The New
Manifest Destiny." Pratt implies that the same kind of impulse
which carried Americans into the War of 1812 and eventually
across the continent also sent them to Cuba and planted the
American flag in the Philippines. But this "manifest destiny" of
the Spanish-American War period had its own characteristics
which required separate investigation.

Although Pratt's analysis of American thought at the close of the nineteenth century is hardly flattering to the national ego, it is not built solely upon the narrow economic determinism which other critics have used in condemning the war's imperialistic aftermath. It is his contention that the expansionist urge in America was compounded of many elements. In the foreground he places religious figures such as Josiah Strong and intellectual figures such as John W. Burgess, who talked and wrote about the desirability of expansion when businessmen were apathetic to it. Instead of having economic motives, these leaders urged a spread of American influence in the name of humanity, asserting that the benefits of Christianity and of the Anglo-Saxon genius for political organization justified imperialistic behavior and outweighed any evils which might result from it. The "white man's burden" was to spread and maintain a superior civilization. To differentiate this attitude from that which sought conquest for reasons of exploitation, a new phrase, "the imperialism of righteousness," was ultimately coined and publicized.

As the trouble with Spain increased, Pratt found the business community sitting on the side lines, fearful lest the popular clamor for assistance to the starving and persecuted Cubans would bring on a war which might upset the prosperity returning under President William McKinley. Except for a few scattered investors, the only people eager for colonial acquisitions for economic purposes appeared to be politicians and intellectuals such as James Blaine, Albert Beveridge, and Alfred Mahan. Then, with Dewey's victory at Manila, Pratt noted a quick conversion in the business community. The explanation lay in China rather than in the West Indies. A Wall Street which had been unwilling to intervene in Cuba either for the sake of the natives or of American investments became suddenly interested in a war with Spain because of the opportunity it presented of obtaining a "gateway to the Orient." The peace treaty, in which Spain yielded the Philippines and Guam as well as Puerto Rico, gave substance to this concern for trade in the East and reflected a quickly developing interest in colonial markets.

Little criticism has been made of Pratt's exposition of the role of the nonbusiness groups in preparing the way for the Spanish-American War and for a wider role for America in world affairs. In his focus upon the quick change in business opinion and its relation to the acquisition of the Philippines, Pratt throws considerable light upon the immediate situation; but at the same time he may have inadvertently minimized long-range trends arising from America's growing ability to supply the world with her products. American exports preceded the idea that imperialism could be righteous; and the assumption that the government would foster and protect the national commerce dated at least as far back as the day when Thomas Jefferson went to war with the Barbary pirates.

Such observations do not imply that Pratt's work is not essentially valid. Rather, his book remains an effective and lasting rebuttal both to those who see in the Spanish-American War simply the result of idealistic compassion and to those who deny America any humanitarian impulse and see only the pursuit of profitable investments. Neither an apologist nor a cynic, Pratt illustrates admirably the balance for which historians strive.

The New Manifest Destiny

O N MARCH 24, 1895, there died obscurely in New York a one-time journalist and diplomat, John Louis O'Sullivan by name. Fifty years before, he had enriched the national vocabularly with the potent phrase, "manifest destiny," and had, as editor of the *Democratic Review* and as an acquaintance of Presidents Polk, Pierce, and Buchanan, urged energetically the policy of

From *Expansionists of 1898* by Julius W. Pratt, by permission of the Johns Hopkins Press.

expansion which the phrase embodied.[1] Thereafter, both he and his idea had fallen upon evil times. O'Sullivan had been a Democrat and a Southern sympathizer, and the idea for which he stood had been too frequently connected with the cause of slavery-extension to escape a share of the discredit suffered by the latter. The close of the Civil War found O'Sullivan an exile in Europe. The efforts of Seward as Secretary of State and Grant as President to revive the expansionist policy of pre-war days met with little popular support.[2]

But while the passing years only deepened the obscurity surrounding the man, they brought a surprising resurrection of the idea which he had advocated and even of the phrase which he had coined. Before O'Sullivan's death, "manifest destiny" was again in the air. There was new talk of expansion, which now found its chief support not as formerly among Democrats but in the other political camp—in what O'Sullivan had once described as the party of "wicked and crazy Republicanism." It was the Republican party which in 1892 pledged its belief in "the achievement of the manifest destiny of the republic in its broadest sense."[3] It was a Republican administration which gave most sympathetic support to the project of an American-controlled isthmian canal and which sought naval bases for the United States in Hawaii and Samoa and in various Caribbean islands. It was a Republican Senator who proclaimed, in an article which O'Sullivan may well have read just before his death, that the United States should extend its limits from the Rio Grande to the Arctic Ocean, should build a Nicaraguan canal, control Hawaii, maintain its influence in Samoa, and own Cuba; that, since "the great nations [were] rapidly absorbing for their future expansion and their present defence all the waste places of the earth," the United States, as one of the great nations, "must not fall out of the line of march."[4] In fact, the United States was about to embark, under Republican

1 Julius W. Pratt, "John L. O'Sullivan and Manifest Destiny," *New York History*, XIV, 213-234. Dr. Albert K. Weinberg in his *Manifest Destiny: A Study of Nationalist Expansionism in American History*, has made an elaborate study of the ideas advanced at various periods in justification of the acquisition of new territory by the United States.

2 T. C. Smith, "Expansion after the Civil War, 1865-1871," *Political Science Quarterly*, XVI, 412-436.

3 E. Stanwood, *A History of the Presidency from 1788 to 1897*, p. 496.

4 H. C. Lodge, "Our Blundering Foreign Policy," *The Forum*, XIX, 8-17.

leadership, upon a new career of expansion, which was to be justified if not motivated by new interpretations of "manifest destiny."

The manifest destiny of the 1840's had been largely a matter of emotion. Much of it had been simply one expression of a half-blind faith in the superior virility of the American race and the superior beneficence of American political institutions. In the intervening years, much had been done to provide this emotional concept with a philosophic backing. The expansionists of the 1890's were able to cite the lessons of science and of history in support of their doctrine. Far-fetched and fallacious as their reasoning may appear to us, it nevertheless carried conviction to some of the best minds of the period.

Prominent among the conceptions which contributed to the new expansionist philosophy was the Darwinian hypothesis of evolution through natural selection. If the continuous struggle for existence among biological forms resulted in the elimination of the unfit and the emergence of higher types, why might not the same law hold good in human society? If the survival of the fittest was the law of nature and the path of progress, surely the more gifted races need offer neither apologies nor regrets when they suppressed, supplanted, or destroyed their less talented competitors. And who could doubt that the Anglo-Saxon race, especially in its American branch, possessed those superior talents which entitled it to survive? Certainly not Charles Darwin, the founder of the creed. In his second great work, *The Descent of Man*, the English scientist included a passage well calculated to flatter American self-esteem.

There is apparently much truth [he wrote] in the belief that the wonderful progress of the United States, as well as the character of the people, are the results of natural selection; the more energetic, restless, and courageous men from all parts of Europe having emigrated during the last ten or twelve generations to that great country, and having there succeeded best. Looking to the distant future, I do not think that the Rev. Mr. Zincke takes an exaggerated view when he says: "All other series of events—as that which resulted in the culture of mind in Greece, and that which resulted in the empire of Rome—only appear to have purpose and value when viewed in connection with, or rather as subsidiary to, . . . the great stream of Anglo-Saxon emigration to the west."[5]

[5] Charles Darwin, *The Descent of Man, and Selection in Relation to Sex*, I, 179.

In thus hailing the American as "the heir of all the ages, in the foremost files of time," Darwin was merely recording what seemed to him a scientific fact. He was not preaching a message or advocating a policy. It was not difficult, however, to derive a practical lesson from such a premise, and this task was gladly undertaken by certain of Darwin's disciples in the United States. Among the foremost of these was the historian, John Fiske. A convert to the theory of evolution since his undergraduate days at Harvard—where he had been threatened with expulsion for his unorthodox opinions—he became one of its chief popularizers in the United States.[6] In an essay entitled "Manifest Destiny," which he published in *Harper's Magazine* in 1885, it is easy to detect the working of the evolutionary theory. After stressing the superior character of Anglo-Saxon institutions and the overwhelming growth of Anglo-Saxon numbers and power, Fiske remarked:

> It is enough to point to the general conclusion that the work which the English race began when it colonized North America is destined to go on until every land on the earth's surface that is not already the seat of an old civilization shall become English in its language, in its religion, in its political habits and traditions, and to a predominant extent in the blood of its people. The day is at hand when four-fifths of the human race will trace its pedigree to English forefathers, as four-fifths of the white people of the United States trace their pedigree to-day. The race thus spread over both hemispheres, and from the rising to the setting sun, will not fail to keep that sovereignty of the sea and that commercial supremacy which it began to acquire when England first stretched its arm across the Atlantic to the shores of Virginia and Massachusetts.

Even the English language, he believed, would "ultimately become the language of mankind."[7]

Another widely read author whose ideas closely resembled Fiske's and whose indebtedness to Darwin was no less obvious was the Congregational clergyman, Josiah Strong. In 1885 he published a small

---

The passage quoted and endorsed by Darwin is from Rev. F. B. Zincke, *Last Winter in the United States*, p. 29.

[6] See the sketch of Fiske by J. T. Adams in *Dictionary of American Biography*, VI, 420-423.

[7] John Fiske, "Manifest Destiny," *Harper's New Monthly Magazine*, LXX, 578-590. This essay was also published in Fiske's *Amerian Political Ideas Viewed from the Standpoint of Universal History*, pp. 101-152.

volume entitled *Our Country: Its Possible Future and Its Present Crisis*, in which appeared a chapter on "The Anglo-Saxon and the World's Future." The Anglo-Saxon, he asserted, as the chief representative of two great ideas—civil liberty and "a pure *spiritual* Christianity"—was "divinely commissioned to be, in a peculiar sense, his brother's keeper. Add to this the fact of his rapidly increasing strength in modern times, and we have well-nigh a demonstration of his destiny." God, it appeared to Mr. Strong, was training this favored race for the final competition of races—the struggle for existence—which would arise from the continued pressure of population upon the means of subsistence.

> Then this race of unequaled energy, with all the majesty of numbers and the might of wealth behind it—the representative, let us hope, of the largest liberty, the purest Christianity, the highest civilization— having developed peculiarly aggressive traits calculated to impress its institutions upon mankind, will spread itself over the earth. If I read not amiss, this powerful race will move down upon Mexico, down upon Central and South America, out upon the islands of the sea, over upon Africa and beyond. And can any one doubt that the result of this competition of races will be the "survival of the fittest"?

The extinction of weaker races before the all-conquering Anglo-Saxon might appear sad to some, but to Mr. Strong it seemed almost inevitable. Only adverse climatic conditions could hold the Anglo-Saxon in check, and the areas where he could not thrive were not extensive. "Is there room for reasonable doubt," he asked in conclusion, "that this race, unless devitalized by alcohol and tobacco, is destined to dispossess many weaker races, assimilate others, and mold the remainder, until, in a very true and important sense, it has Anglo-Saxonized mankind?"[8]

The reader may be tempted to attribute the rather sophomoric generalizations and prophecies of Fiske and Strong to their lack of broad and systematic scholarly training. Yet one of their contemporaries who possessed these advantages to a degree unusual among American scholars of his time arrived by a different road at quite similar conclusions. Professor John W. Burgess, after completing his undergraduate work at Amherst, had spent two years in the study of

---

[8] Josiah Strong, *Our Country: Its Possible Future and Its Present Crisis*, chap. xiv, pp. 208-227.

history and political science at Göttingen, Leipzig, and Berlin. Thence he returned to teach, first at Amherst and later at Columbia, where in 1880 he took a leading part in founding the School of Political Science.

It is significant that the two German scholars to whom Burgess acknowledged the heaviest debt were Gustav Droysen, historian of the rise of the Prussian state, and Rudolph von Gneist, profound student of the development of English constitutional law.[9] Whether the admiration for the political talents of the Teutonic race which Burgess must have derived from study under these men was strengthened by an acquaintance with Count Arthur Gobineau's work on the superiority of the Nordic stock can only be conjectured.[10] In any event, his most ambitious work, *Political Science and Comparative Constitutional Law,* published in 1890, contains a remarkable chapter on "National Political Character," in which Burgess virtually assigned world dominion to Germans and Anglo-Saxons.[11]

After analyzing the political character of Greek, Slav, Celt, Roman, and Teuton as exhibited in their political institutions, Burgess concluded that all but the last were deficient in the highest political talent. The successes of Greek, Celt, and Slav had been confined to the organization of local communities; the genius of the Roman was for world empire. Only Teutons had developed the true national state, which was, in Burgess's opinion, "the most modern and the most complete solution of the whole problem of political organization which the world has as yet produced." The fact that the national state was a Teutonic creation stamped the Teutonic nations "as the political nations *par excellence,* and authorize[d] them, in the economy of the world to assume the leadership in the establishment and administration of states.[12]

Having thus assigned the Teutons to their proper place in the hierarchy of races, Burgess proceeded, in the next chapter, to draw

[9] John W. Burgess, *Reminiscences of an American Scholar,* pp. 126, 131.

[10] Gobineau's *Essai sur l'inégalité des races humaines* (4 vols., Paris, 1853-1855) was translated into English with the title *Moral and Intellectual Diversity of Races* (Philadelphia, 1856).

[11] John W. Burgess, *Political Science and Comparative Constitutional Law,* I, 30-39.

[12] *Ibid.,* p. 39.

certain "conclusions of practical politics."[13] It followed easily from what had been said,

> that the Teutonic nations are particularly endowed with the capacity for establishing national states, and are especially called to that work; and, therefore, that they are intrusted, in the general economy of history, with the mission of conducting the political civilization of the modern world.[14]

This meant, among other things,[15] that the Teutonic nations were "called to carry the political civilization of the modern world into those parts of the world inhabited by unpolitical and barbaric races; *i.e., they must have a colonial policy.*"[16] To North Americans, who were reluctant to undertake such responsibility and inclined to regard it as "unwarrantable interference in the affairs of other states," Burgess pointed out that

> by far the larger part of the surface of the globe is inhabited by populations which have not succeeded in establishing civilized states; which have, in fact, no capacity to accomplish such a work; and which must, therefore, remain in a state of barbarism or semi-barbarism, unless the political nations undertake the work of state organization for them. This condition of things authorizes the political nations not only to answer the call of the unpolitical populations for aid and direction, but also to force organization upon them by any means necessary, in their honest judgment, to accomplish this result. There is no human right to the status of barbarism.[17]

To justify such interference in the interests of civilization, it was not necessary that the inferior race be wholly barbaric. In the case of

13 *Ibid.,* pp. 40-48.
14 *Ibid.,* p. 44.
15 Of some modern interest are Burgess's conclusions as to the proper attitude of the Teutonic rulers to alien elements within their own borders. In a state with heterogeneous population, he wrote, "the Teutonic element, when dominant, should never surrender the balance of political power, either in general or local organization, to the other elements. Under certain circumstances it should not even permit participation of the other elements in political power . . . the participation of other ethnical elements in the exercise of political power has resulted, and will result, in corruption and confusion most deleterious and dangerous to the rights of all, and to the civilization of society." *Ibid.,* pp. 44-45. Burgess was likely thinking of the South during the carpet-bag régime. The passage might, however, have been taken as a text by the rulers of the Third Reich.
16 *Ibid.,* p. 45. Italics mine.
17 *Ibid.,* pp. 45-46.

populations "not wholly barbaric, which have made some progress in state organizations, but which manifest incapacity to solve the problem of political civilization with any degree of completeness," interference by the political nations would be justifiable.

No one can question that it is in the interest of the world's civilization that law and order and the true liberty consistent therewith shall reign everywhere upon the globe. A permanent inability on the part of any state or semi-state to secure this status is a threat to civilization everywhere. Both for the sake of the half-barbarous state and in the interest of the rest of the world, a state or states, endowed with the capacity for political organization, may righteously assume sovereignty over, and undertake to create state order for, such a politically incompetent population.

To undertake such interference was not only a right but an obligation. "Indifference on the part of Teutonic states to the political civilization of the rest of the world is, then, not only mistaken policy, but disregard of duty."[18]

Modern imperialism could ask for no more sweeping justification than Professor Burgess gave it. To a reviewer in the *Nation* this portion of Burgess's work seemed a surprising endorsement of "the political morality of Omar and Pizarro." "The war-cry of the modern State," remarked this writer, "is not 'The sword of the Lord and of Gideon,' it is true, but it conquers in the name of its 'world-duty,' which is practically the same thing."[19] It is little wonder that, as Burgess complained later, his discussion of the colonial question was widely condemned in Continental Europe and in America "as a justification of the existing system of British colonial empire and of its farther extension in Asia and Africa, if not elsewhere, as a permanent world condition. The British publicists," he remarked naively,

[18] *Ibid.*, pp. 47-48. It is interesting to compare portions of the above passage with language subsequently used by one of Burgess's students at Columbia. In his annual message of December 6, 1904, President Theodore Rooevelt wrote, with reference to the Dominican Republic: "If a nation shows that it knows how to act with reasonable efficiency and decency in social and political matters, if it keeps order and pays its obligations, it need fear no interference from the United States. Chronic wrongdoing, or an impotence which results in a general loosening of the ties of civilized society, may in America, as elsewhere, ultimately require intervention by some civilized nation, . . ." *Congressional Record*, 58th Cong., 3d sess., p. 19. This was, of course, part of the famous Roosevelt Corollary to the Monroe Doctrine.
[19] *Nation*, LIII, 240 (September 24, 1891).

understood me better and defended this part of my book with distinct appreciation."[20] Why, one may ask, should they have done otherwise?

It may be remarked here, parenthetically, as a curious fact, that when in 1898 the United States embarked upon a war which led directly to the assumption of a portion of the "world-duty" which Burgess had held before its eyes, he himself heatedly opposed that course. The war with Spain was to him "the first great shock" that he had experienced since the founding of the School of Political Science, which he had looked upon as an agency for international peace. The atrocity stories which preceded the war he set down as the insidious work of British statesmen, who wished to embroil the United States in a war with Spain; and the extension of American authority over subject peoples he regarded as "disastrous to American political civilization" and as "a fatal move . . . bound to reach farther and finally compromise the liberties of all American citizens."[21] Burgess apparently saw no inconsistency between this attitude and his earlier advocacy of a colonial policy. To the student any attempt to reconcile the two seems hopeless.

From Burgess, who planted the seed of an expansionist policy only to abjure the ripened fruit, we may turn to a philosopher whose thought on this subject was consistent and who never shrank from the responsibilities which his ideas entailed for his country. In the same year in which Burgess's treatise on political science saw the light there also appeared *The Influence of Sea Power upon History*, by Alfred Thayer Mahan, at that time a captain in the United States Navy. The embodiment of a series of lectures on naval history which Mahan had been detailed to give at the Naval War College at Newport, Rhode Island, the volume put forth the thesis which Mahan was further to illustrate and defend through the remainder of his active life. This thesis was, in short, that sea power was the most potent factor in the making or breaking of nations, that without sea power no people, however gifted, had attained or could attain the fullest measure of well-being or of influence and importance in world affairs. This volume, which told the story of the rise of British sea power in the years from 1660 to 1783, was followed by others which

20 Burgess, *Reminiscences*, p. 249.
21 *Ibid.*, pp. 312-316.

carried the narrative to the close of the Napoleonic wars, with excursions into other periods and into the naval history of the United States.[22]

But Mahan was always the preacher as well as the historian. What he perhaps had most at heart, and what certainly most concerns us here, was his indoctrination of his own countrymen with the gospel of sea power. A patriotic American, he wished to see his nation profit by the lessons which he had discovered in history and which he drove home at every opportunity, in his books and in the numerous articles which he contributed to American periodicals.

The history of sea power, wrote Mahan in 1890, embraces "in its broad sweep all that tends to make a people great upon the sea or by the sea."[23] While it is "largely a military history," its fundamental significance is economic. Sea power exists chiefly for the sake of commerce; it includes all that goes to make sea-borne commerce secure and profitable—a merchant marine, that trade may not be in alien hands; a navy capable of defending the merchant marine and keeping the trade routes open in time of war; colonies, which may both serve the interests of commerce directly and also provide naval vessels with secure bases and coaling stations the world over.

These things, in Mahan's mind, were the essential foundations of national prosperity and national greatness. How desperate to him, in 1890, must have appeared the prospects of his own country! There was, indeed, a growing foreign trade, but it was carried in ships flying alien flags. There was the beginning—a very feeble beginning— of a modern navy. A dozen light cruisers were built or being built as well as the two second-class battleships, "Maine" and "Texas"; and in the year of the publication of *The Influence of Sea Power upon History*, Congress authorized the construction of three first-class battleships. These small beginnings did not impress Mahan. Without a great merchant marine, of which he saw little prospect, he doubted whether an adequate navy would or could be built.

Even had the United States a great national shipping, it may be doubted whether a sufficient navy would follow; the distance which

---

[22] For a partial bibliography of Mahan's writings see C. C. Taylor, *The Life of Admiral Mahan, Naval Philosopher*, pp. 336-338.
[23] *The Influence of Sea Power upon History, 1660-1783*, p. 1.

separates her from other great powers, in one way a protection, is also a snare.[24]

As for colonies, which "afford . . . the surest means of supporting abroad the sea power of a country,"—

> Such colonies the United States has not and is not likely to have. . . . Having therefore no foreign establishments, either colonial or military, the ships of war of the United States, in war, will be like land birds, unable to fly far from their own shores. To provide resting-places for them, where they can coal and repair, would be one of the first duties of a government proposing to itself the development of the power of the nation at sea.[25]

But Mahan was not without hope for the future. For a quarter of a century, it is true, America had turned her eyes inward, away from the sea—an attitude which, in the historian's mind had spelled disaster for France in the seventeenth and eighteenth centuries.[26] There were signs now, however, that the nation might be forced to "the turning of the eyes outward, instead of inward only, to seek the welfare of the country." The growing productivity of its farms and factories would compel a search for foreign markets and induce relations to the world "radically distinct from the simple idea of self-sufficingness." The competition for markets and colonies being carried on by the seaboard powers of Europe, especially the aggressiveness shown of late by Germany in the Pacific, in Africa, in South America, might bring those powers into collision with the United States; had, in fact, already done so in the recent Samoan complication. The prospective piercing of the Isthmus of Panama, which would be, "nothing but a disaster to the United States, in the present state of her military and naval preparation"; the unsettled political conditions prevalent in Haiti, Central America, and the Hawaiian Islands, places of great military or commercial importance, whose control might be productive of international quarrels—all these things might perhaps jar the United States from her wonted complacency, might lead her to "look outward" and to build up her sea power.[27]

---

[24] *Ibid.*, pp. 87-88.   [25] *Ibid.*, p. 83.   [26] *Ibid.*, p. 87.
[27] Mahan, "The United States Looking Outward," *Atlantic Monthly*, December, 1890, reprinted in *The Interest of America in Sea Power, Present and Future*, pp. 3-27.

In preparation for the day when such a change of attitude should come about, Mahan sketched the outlines of a program. In addition to constructing a modern navy and adequate coast defenses, the United States must be ready to take, when opportunity offered, such outlying positions as would confer mastery of the essential water routes. Of preeminent importance, when the isthmian canal should have been opened, would be the control of the Caribbean. Upon such control would depend freedom of interoceanic transit. What, then, were the necessary measures?

> Control of a maritime region is insured primarily by a navy; secondarily, by positions, suitably chosen and spaced one from the other, upon which as bases the navy rests, and from which it can exert its strength. At present the positions of the Caribbean are occupied by foreign powers, nor may we, however disposed to acquisition, obtain them by means other than righteous; but a distinct advance will have been made when public opinion is convinced that we need them, and should not exert our utmost ingenuity to dodge them when flung at our head.[28]

Next to the isthmus and the Caribbean area, Mahan was concerned with the Pacific. That ocean was destined to be the scene not only of a thriving commerce but of a gigantic struggle of faces, civilizations, and religions—of Orient against Occident. The day was approaching "when the vast mass of China—now inert—[might] yield to one of those impulses which have in past ages buried civilization under a wave of barbaric invasion. The great armies of Europe, whose existence is so frequently deplored, may be providentially intended as a barrier to that great movement, if it come." But China might "burst her barriers eastward as well as westward, toward the Pacific as well as toward the European Continent"; in that event, to be confronted not by the armies of Europe but, God willing, by the navy of the United States.

> Whate'er betide, Sea Power will play in those days the leading part which it has in all history, and the United States by her geographical position must be one of the frontiers from which, as from a base of operations, the Sea Power of the civilized world will energize.[29]

[28] *Ibid.*, pp. 102-103 (from "The Isthmus and Sea Power," originally published in the *Atlantic Monthly*, September, 1893).

[29] *Ibid.*, pp. 31-32 (letter to New York *Times*, January 30, 1893); pp. 123-124 (from "Possibilities of an Anglo-American Reunion," *North American Review,*

In that approaching Armageddon, the United States would need not only the unobstructed use of the isthmian canal, but outposts in the Pacific as well, and the most logical outpost was in the Hawaiian Islands. As early as 1890 Mahan had remarked that for the defense of the west coast it was essential that no foreign power should acquire a lodgment in those islands.[30] Three years later he predicted that the outcome of the contest between East and West in the Pacific might be determined by "a firm hold of the Sandwich Islands by a great, civilized, maritime power," and that the United States was "naturally indicated as the proper guardian for this most important position."[31]

While Mahan's arguments for expansion looked primarily to the national interest, he did not hesitate to identify that interest with the welfare of the world at large. With her frontage on the Pacific, the United States stood guard over the preservation of Western civilization. But it was her rôle not only to defend but to extend the blessings of that civilization. "How much poorer would the world have been," he exclaimed, "had Englishmen heeded the cautious hesitancy that now binds us reject every advance beyond our shorelines!"[32] Indeed, such a policy of beneficent expansion seemed to him a part of divine destiny. When one reflects, he wrote, upon the chains of accidents by which Great Britain had taken and held both Gibraltar and Jamaica,—

one marvels whether incidents so widely separated in time and place, all tending towards one end—the maritime predominance of Great Britain—can be accidents, or are simply the exhibition of a Personal Will, acting through all time, with purpose deliberate and consecutive, to ends not yet discerned.[33]

Even more than Burgess's, Mahan's message seemed to sound the battle-cry: "The sword of the Lord and of Gideon!"

The basic ideas of all these men—Darwin, Fiske, Strong, Burgess, and Mahan—were in current circulation at the beginning of the 1890's, though Mahan's thesis was broadened as the decade advanced. In 1894 appeared another contribution to the new expansionist

---

November, 1894). The "yellow peril" idea was more fully elaborated in "A Twentieth Century Outlook," *Harper's Magazine*, September, 1897. See *infra*, chap. vi, p. 222.

[30] *Ibid.*, p. 26.   [32] *Ibid.*, p. 50.
[31] *Ibid.*, p. 32.   [33] *Ibid.*, pp. 307-308.

philosophy in Benjamin Kidd's *Social Evolution*. Kidd, an English sociologist, belonged, like Fiske, to the Darwinian school and, also like Fiske, attempted to apply the Darwinian formula to society. The part of his book that concerns us here is a chapter dealing with the relation of the white man to the tropics.[34] In the near future, Kidd predicted, the European races were certain to have utilized all available agricultural lands in the temperate zone. It would then be imperative that, in the interest of the food supply, the immense resources of the tropics should be developed. But since it was evident that the native peoples of the tropics had not the requisite "social efficiency" to insure such development, it would be necessary for the more efficient races (preeminently the Anglo-Saxons) to take control. The spirit of altruism and social responsibility which, since the Reformation, had developed to a high degree in England, was a guarantee that such Anglo-Saxon control would be exercised not for purposes of human exploitation but for the common good. The partition of Africa seemed to Kidd evidence that Europe realized the future importance of the tropics. In the western hemisphere—where Haiti and the Central American states were cited as horrible examples of "social inefficiency"—the same realization might be perceived,

> even in the United States, where the necessity for the future predominance of the influence of the English-speaking peoples over the American Continents is already recognised by a kind of national instinct that may be expected to find clearer expression as time goes on.[35]

All of these writers contributed to the "intellectual climate" of the United States in the decade in which it inaugurated a program of overseas expansion. How far they influenced the popular thought of the period cannot, obviously, be determined with any high degree of exactitude. They were all, however, well known and widely read.

---

[34] Benjamin Kidd, *Social Evolution*, pp. 303-329.

[35] *Ibid.*, p. 324. The thesis set forth in this chapter Kidd elaborated at greater length in his *The Control of the Tropics* (1898). Another application of the evolutionary concept to society, which has significance for this study is found in Professor Simon N. Patten's *The Theory of Social Forces* (supplement to *Annals* of American Academy of Political and Social Science, VII, 1896). "The earth," he wrote (pp. 131-132), "has but one general environment and can bring to perfection but one type of man. Attempts to preserve lower types of men, or to bring them into organic relations with higher types, tend to make a society static and thus check its progress."

John Fiske's lectures on "American Political Ideas"—of which that on "Manifest Destiny" was the conclusion—were given orally many times in the United States. In print, they enjoyed a circulation as wide as that of *Harper's Magazine;* and they were subsequently published in book form. Fiske was, according to one reliable student of his career, "one of the most important intellectual influences in America in the last quarter of the nineteenth century."[36] Josiah Strong's volume, *Our Country,* had a circulation of 170,000 copies in English, besides being translated into several foreign languages.[37]

Burgess's treatise was not written for popular consumption, but in the opinion of President Butler of Columbia University, it "made a most profound impression at the time of its publication, both in Europe and in the United States. It served as the basis of the lectures and interpretations which Professor Burgess gave at Columbia University for a generation to thousands of eager and interested students of law and political science."[38] Among these students was young Theodore Roosevelt, some of whose ideas bear more than a fancied resemblance to Burgess's teachings.[39] At least one newspaper cited Burgess's work in support of the annexation of Hawaii.[40]

Of Mahan's influence upon his contemporaries there is no dearth of evidence. His books were widely noticed.[41] Unlike the other

---

[36] Adams, *loc. cit.*

[37] *National Cyclopaedia of American Biography,* IX, 416-417.

[38] Nicholas Murray Butler's "Foreword" to John W. Burgess, *The Foundations of Political Science,* p. v. This volume is a reprinting of certain of the chapters of *Political Science and Comparative Constitutional Law,* including those considered above. The republication was suggested by President Butler in 1917, in the hope that it might "be of commanding service for the guidance of public opinion when the issues of the great war . . . were presented for settlement upon its termination." *Ibid.* Professor Burgess relates that arrangements to that end were made with the publishers of the original work, but that the plan was suspended when a typesetter in the publishing establishment discovered that "everything done by the Germans in the present war found its justification in that book." *Reminiscences of an American Scholar,* pp. 256-257. The reprint was finally brought out in 1933 by the Columbia University Press. Professor Burgess died in January 1931.

[39] [Resemblance of Roosevelt Corollary previously noted—Ed.]

[40] New York *Commercial Advertiser,* February 11, 1893. For Burgess's influence on President Dole of Hawaii, see *infra,* chap. vi, note 8.

[41] E. g., *Literary World,* XXI, 218 (July 5, 1890); *Harper's New Monthly Magazine,* LXXXVII, 962 (November, 1893); *Political Science Quarterly,* IX, 171-173 (March, 1894).

writers, he addressed himself directly to the problems in hand, contributing to such periodicals as the *Atlantic Monthly*, the *Forum*, the *North American Review, Harper's Magazine*, and *McClure's Magazine* articles urging naval preparedness, the annexation of Hawaii, the control of the Caribbean, and related policies.[42] His arguments were repeatedly cited in Congress, by Henry Cabot Lodge and other expansionist Senators and Congressmen,[43] and printed in reports of Congressional committees.[44] Theodore Roosevelt reviewed his books with high appreciation,[45] praised his magazine articles,[46] and corresponded with him in regard to annexing Hawaii and the Virgin Islands.[47] Other expansionist publicists went to Mahan for their arguments.[48] To a British observer, on the eve of the Spanish-American War, it seemed that the spirit of America had been remade through Mahan's influence. Mahan's teaching, wrote "The Looker-on," in *Blackwood's*,

> was as oil to the flame of "colonial expansion" everywhere leaping into life. Everywhere a new-sprung ambition to go forth and possess and enjoy read its sanction in the philosophy of history ennobled by the glory of conquest. . . . I doubt whether this effect of Mahan's teachings has gone deeper anywhere than in the United States.[49]

Controvert as it may current fashions in historical interpretation, the observation must be made that the rise of an expansionist philosophy in the United States owed little to economic influences. Of the writers mentioned, only Mahan had much to say of expansion as an

[42] See the thirteen essays, all published 1890 to 1899, collected in the two volumes, *The Interest of America in Sea Power, Present and Future*, and *Lessons of the War with Spain*.

[43] E. g., *Cong. Record*, 51st Cong., 2d sess., p. 1856; 53d Cong., 2d sess., pp. 1844-1849; 53d Cong., 3d sess., pp. 3082-3084, 3111, 3113. In not all of these speeches is Mahan mentioned by name, but in all the debt to his ideas is perfectly obvious.

[44] *Senate Report* No. 681, 55th Cong., 2d sess., p. 99.

[45] *Pol. Sci. Quart.*, IX, 171-173.

[46] H. C. Lodge (ed.), *Selections from the Correspondence of Theodore Roosevelt and Henry Cabot Lodge*, I, 274.

[47] H. F. Pringle, *Theodore Roosevelt, a Biography*, pp. 171, 293.

[48] E. g., Lt. F. L. Winn, U. S. A., in *Overland Monthly*, XXIII, 496 (May, 1894); Truxton Beale, in *North American Review*, CLXVI, 760 (June, 1898).

[49] *Blackwood's Edinburgh Magazine*, CLXIII, 563-565 (April, 1898). For a recent appraisal of Mahan's influence, see L. M. Hacker, "The Incendiary Mahan: a Biography," *Scribner's Magazine*, XCV, 263-268, 311-320.

aid to commerce, and Mahan's ideas were derived from the study of history, not from my contemporary economic pressure. In fact, as will be shown later,[50] business interests in the United States were generally opposed to expansion, or indifferent to it, until after May 1, 1898. The need of American business for colonial markets and fields for investment was discovered not by business men but by historians and other intellectuals, by journalists and politicians.

Among the public men who espoused expansion largely in the supposed interest of trade was James G. Blaine, Secretary of State during three and one-quarter years of Benjamin Harrison's administration. In Congress, twenty years before, Blaine had predicted with approval the "expansion of our flag and our sovereignty over insular or continental possessions, north or south."[51] But by the time of his first appointment as Secretary of State (under Garfield in 1881), his idea of expansion had, according to Professor Lockey, "suffered a radical change." He had already begun to formulate his Pan-American policy, of which one of the chief purposes was, in his own words, "to cultivate such friendly, commercial relations with all American countries as would lead to a large increase in the export trade of the United States, by supplying fabrics in which we are abundantly able to compete with the manufacturing nations of Europe."[52] Like President Hoover in later years, Blaine had come to realize that, in the words of Professor Lockey, "territorial aggrandizement at the expense of the neighbors, whose friendship was essential to the success of that policy, was no longer to be thought of." Hence, assurances that the United States would scrupulously respect the independence and territorial integrity of its southern neighbors.[53]

Yet the assumption of this attitude of friendliness and forbearance toward Latin America did not prevent Blaine from contemplating the eventual dominance of the United States in the Caribbean. He believed it essential to the welfare of the United States that there should be an isthmian canal under American control. His energetic efforts to secure, for that purpose, a modification of the Clayton-

[50] *Infra,* chap. vii.
[51] Quoted by Joseph B. Lockey, *James Gillespie Blaine,* in S. F. Bemis (ed.), *The American Secretaries of State and Their Diplomacy,* VIII, 116.
[52] *Ibid.,* VII, 275.   [53] *Ibid.,* VIII, 116-117.

Bulwer Treaty are well known.[54] Cuba, because of its relation to the future canal and the Gulf trade, must never be permitted to pass out of the "American system." The actual possession of Cuba might not be necessary, or even desirable, he wrote in 1881;[55] yet ten years later he believed that the United States would one day need to annex both Cuba and Puerto Rico,[56] if not, indeed, all the West India islands.[57] That he was keenly interested in acquiring a naval base in the Caribbean we shall presently see.

Blaine showed no less interest in the Pacific than in the Caribbean. Like Mahan and others of his day, he saw in that ocean the great theater of American trade in the years to come. Two diverging lines, drawn from San Francisco to the Aleutian Islands and to Honolulu, would mark "the natural limit of the ocean belt within which our trade with the oriental countries must flow." The southern side of this triangle would be, moreover, "the direct line of communication between the United States and Australasia. Within this line lies the commercial domain of our western coast."[58] Hawaii, obviously, if held by a strong naval power, would dominate this area. Blaine considered it, like Cuba, a part of the American system, but because of both the actual existence of international rivalries in Hawaii, and its close cultural and commercial ties with the United States, he regarded the annexation of Hawaii as more natural and more imperative than the acquisition of Cuba. Should the maintenance of the independence of Hawaii prove impracticable, he wrote in 1881, the United States would "unhesitatingly meet the altered situation by seeking an avowedly American solution for the grave issues presented."[59] A decade later he wrote to President Harrison:

> I think there are only three places that are of value enough to be taken; one is Hawaii and the others are Cuba and Porto Rico. Cuba and Porto Rico are not imminent and will not be for a generation.

[54] For a recent treatment of this subject see D. S. Muzzey, *James G. Blaine,* pp. 197-201. A standard account is in M. W. Williams, *Anglo-American Isthmian Diplomacy, 1815-1915.*
[55] *Papers Relating to the Foreign Relations of the United States, 1881,* p. 638. The volumes in this series will hereafter be cited in the abbreviated form, *U. S. For. Rel.* with the appropriate year.
[56] Muzzey, *op. cit.,* p. 394.
[57] C. C. Tansill, *The Purchase of the Danish West Indies,* p. 191.
[58] *U. S. For. Rel., 1881,* p. 636.
[59] *Ibid.,* p. 639.

Hawaii may come up for decision at any unexpected hour, and I hope we shall be prepared to decide it in the affirmative.[60]

Such was the man who, in March, 1889, became Harrison's first Secretary of State. To what extent Blaine shaped the foreign policy of the Harrison administration is difficult if not impossible to determine.[61] Yet Harrison's foreign policy, so far as they concern us here, were in accord with ideas which Blaine had previously expressed. It seems safe to assume that in their desire to promote American interests and even American sovereignty in the Caribbean and the Pacific, Harrison, Blaine, and John W. Foster, who succeeded Blaine in June 1892, worked harmoniously.[62] Whoever was chiefly responsible, the Harrison administration adopted an expansionist policy which, though barren of results, foreshadowed in its purposes the "large policy" of 1898.

No attempt will be made here to present in detail all the features of this policy, most of which have been treated in other studies. It is important, however, to view them in relation to one another.

In the settlement of the Samoan question—the first problem that confronted the new administration in the field of foreign relations—Harrison and Blaine succeeded in preserving the nominal independence of the islands under the tripartite protection of the United States, Germany, and Great Britain, and in safeguarding American rights at Pago-Pago under the treaty of 1878. Though Blaine was acclaimed for having taken a stronger tone than his Democratic predecessor and thus having brought Germany to terms, it has been

[60] *Gail Hamilton* (pseudonym for Mary Abigail Dodge), *Biography of James G. Blaine*, p. 692.

[61] *Cf.* Prof. A. T. Volwiler's review of Muzzey's *James G. Blaine, in American Historical Review*, XLI, 554-557.

[62] Two other men who are known to have been very close to Harrison and who may have influenced his foreign policy were Whitelaw Reid of the New York *Tribune*, an enthusiastic expansionist, and B. F. Tracy, Secretary of the Navy. Tracy was insistent upon a vigorous defense of American interests on the isthmus and in the Pacific. In his annual report for December, 1892, he complained that "the aggressive policy of foreign nations . . . has continued, and this country, whether it will or not, will soon be forced into a position where it cannot disregard measures which form a standing menace to its prosperity and security. On the Isthmus our commerce is engaged in a desperate fight to maintain its foothold. In the South Pacific repeated annexations and protectorates are extending the power and influence of the maritime states of the Old World. . . . *House Exec. Doc.* No. 1, Pt. III, 52d Cong., 2d Sess., p. 37.

shown that he found the German Government disposed toward a
reasonable compromise and that he did, in fact, little more than push
ahead to a settlement along lines already sketched by Bayard.[63] That
Harrison, at any rate, did not consider the Samoan question as one
of first magnitude we may perhaps infer from the conservative tone
of editorials on the subject in the New York *Tribune*, which, in the
hands of Harrison's friend Whitelaw Reid, may almost be considered
an administration organ. Samoa, according to the *Tribune*, lay "entirely outside the circle of American interests." It might well be a
matter of concern to Australia and New Zealand, but not to us.

> There has been a scramble for territorial acquisition in that quarter
> during the last decade, England, France, and Germany having either
> coveted or seized one island after another. America ought not to com-
> pete with those powers in rivalries that lie outside of its own sphere
> of activity.[64]

Not in the Samoan incident are the evidences of a new policy to be
found, but in the administration's attitude to the canal question, to
the Caribbean, and to Hawaii.

A treaty negotiated by Secretary Frelinghuysen with Nicaragua in
December, 1884, had, in plain disregard of the restrictions of the

[63] For several recent accounts of the Samoan affair see Muzzey, *op. cit.*, pp.
394-402; G. H. Ryden, *The Foreign Policy of the United States in Relation to
Samoa;* Alice Felt Tyler, *The Foreign Policy of James G. Blaine*, chap. ix.

[64] N. Y. *Tribune*, January 11, January 18, 1889. After the disastrous hurricane
of March, 1889, however, the *Tribune* insisted upon retention of all American
rights in the land-locked harbor of Pago-Pago. "Pago-Pago should neither be
neglected nor surrendered, but intelligently and sagaciously utilized." *Ibid.*,
March 31, 1889. While the Samoan incident is not particularly significant as an
indication of the new administration's policy, it did call forth, in Congress and
the press, some expressions which give an interesting foretaste of the expansionist
talk which was to be heard in the next ten years. Senator Frye, of Maine, asserted
that Pago-Pago was destined to be of the most vital importance to the commerce
of the United States in the South Pacific. *Cong. Record*, 50th Cong., 2d sess., pp.
108, 1374. Senator Dolph, of Oregon, and Mr. G. H. Bates, invoked the Monroe
Doctrine for the protection of Samoa against European covetousness. *Ibid.*, pp.
1325-1337, G. H. Bates, "Some Aspects of the Samoan Question," *Century Magazine, XV*, 945-949. Mr. U. S. Eddy, member of a New York exporting firm, declared
that American policy in Samoa had "created a profound impression in Europe,
where it was rightly regarded as the indication of a changed attitude." The
United States, he thought, was "about to begin an aggressive movement in the
campaign of commerce." U. S. Eddy, "Our Chance for Commercial Supremacy,"
Forum, XI, 419-428.

Clayton-Bulwer Treaty, proposed to give to the United States exclusive rights in the construction and control of a Nicaraguan canal.[65] This treaty had not been acted upon by the Senate and had been withdrawn by Cleveland in December, 1885. The project of a Nicaraguan canal to rival the French canal under construction at Panama had then been taken up by American capitalists and promoters, who on February 20, 1889, secured from Congress a charter under the name of the Maritime Canal Company of Nicaragua.[66] But as the company met with difficulty in raising the money, the proposal arose to have the United States guarantee the bonds of the company and in return receive possession of all or a majority of the stock, thus securing indirectly, as the principal stockholder in the corporation, that control over the canal which, by the Clayton-Bulwer Treaty, it was estopped from securing directly.[67] To this scheme, certainly contrary to the spirit if not to the letter of the nation's treaty obligations, Harrison gave his cordial support, expressing the opinion, in December, 1891, that the completion of the canal was "a matter of the highest concern to the United States.[68] A year later he again recommended that Congress give " prompt and adequate support" to the Maritime Canal Company, and added:

> It is impossible to overstate the value from every standpoint of this great enterprise, and I hope that there may be time, even in this Congress, to give to it an impetus that will insure the early completion of the canal and *secure to the United States its proper relation to it when completed.*[69]

Whether the isthmus was to be pierced by an American canal at Nicaragua or a French canal at Panama, the control of the approaches to it was a matter of vital importance to the United States, and no sooner had Captain Mahan begun publishing his admoni-

[65] P. M. Brown, *Frederick T. Frelinghuysen*, in Bemis, *op. cit.*, VIII, 30-31.

[66] *U. S. Statutes at Large*, XXV, 673-675. J. B. Henderson, *American Diplomatic Questions*, pp. 75-101. There is a MS Master's thesis, The Maritime Canal Company of Nicaragua, by Margaret Stern Wilkinson, in the University of Buffalo Library.

[67] *Cong. Record*, 51st Cong., 2d sess., p. 1123. See *Senate Report*, No. 1944, 51st Cong., 2d sess., a report from the Senate Committee on Foreign Relations, January 10, 1891, recommending the government guarantee of the bonds.

[68] James D. Richardson (ed.), *A Compilation of the Messages and Papers of the Presidents*, IX, 189.

[69] *Ibid.*, p. 317. Italics mine.

tions upon this subject, than the Harrison administration was fishing in the troubled waters of the Caribbean with that object in view. The first opportunity to present itself was in Haiti, where a new president, Hyppolite, had come into power encumbered with certain supposed obligations to the United States. Frederick Douglass was sent as minister to Haiti, evidently with verbal instructions to press upon Hyppolite the mutual advantages to be derived from a lease of Môle St. Nicholas to the United States for a naval station; and when Hyppolite proved obstinate, Harrison dispatched Rear Admiral Gherardi as a special envoy to assist Douglass. Gherardi was instructed to point out to Hyppolite that the presence of a part of the United States fleet in Haitian waters would "be equivalent to a guaranty of the autonomy and independence of the Haytian government without any treaty relations which might appear as a subordination of one Republic to the other."[70] Gherardi went even further than this, promising the Haitian foreign minister the protection of the United States against any attempts at revolution that might be provoked by a grant of the coveted lease.[71] Unable to convince the Haitian government with these arguments, Gherardi suggested to Blaine that the United States might seize Môle St. Nicholas in order to "relieve the Haitian government of responsibility and embarrassment."[72]

The drastic policy suggested by Admiral Gherardi was not followed. Instead, the Washington government turned to the Dominican Republic, where Samana Bay presented a site for a naval base equally eligible with Môle St. Nicholas. In opening negotiations for a reciprocity treaty in May, 1891, the Dominican minister in Washington let it be known that he was empowered also to negotiate a lease for such part of Samana Bay as the United States might need for a naval station. As negotiations proceeded, President Heureaux intimated that he would need a cash payment of $200,000 immediately upon the execution of the treaty, in order to suppress possible armed opposition to such an infringement of Dominican sovereignty.

[70] Tyler, *op. cit.*, p. 94. The whole incident is treated in *ibid.*, pp. 91-98. See also Frederick Douglass, "Haiti and the United States: Inside History of the Negotiations for the Môle St. Nicholas," *North American Review*, CLIII, 337-345, 450-459 (Sept., Oct., 1891).

[71] Tyler, *op. cit.*, p. 96.

[72] *Ibid.*, pp. 96-97, note 22, citing Gnerardi to Blaine, February 9, 1891, MS *Dispatches, Haiti*, XXV.

This information was made known confidentially to the proper committees of Congress, and that body incorporated in the Sundry Civil Appropriation Bill of August 5, 1892, an item of $250,000 "for providing coaling and naval stations, . . . to be expended under direction of the President."[73] A convention was drawn up providing for a lease to the United States for 99 years, renewable for a like period, of the island of Carenero in Samana Bay, with free use and occupancy of the waters and shores of the bay and the right to erect any necessary defenses, the United States to pay $250,000 within thirty days, $50,000 annually for five years, and $25,000 annually thereafter.

Unhappily for the success of the plan, rumors of what was afoot leaked out, and their reverberations in the Dominican Republic compelled Heureaux to break off negotiations. Subsequent efforts to secure action, in Secretary Foster's words, met with "delays, subterfuges, and broken promises."[74]

Môle St. Nicholas and Samana Bay did not exhaust the list of possible naval bases in the Caribbean. In the summer of 1891, certain Danish officials sounded the United States minister to Denmark, Mr. C. E. Carr, upon the possibility of reviving Seward's old project —the sale of the islands of St. Thomas and St. John to the United States.[75] Upon receipt of Carr's report, Blaine wrote Harrison that he was opposed to this purchase until the United States should be in possession of the larger islands, since the Danish islands lacked both commercial and strategic importance and would be difficult to defend. "They are destined to become ours," he wrote, "but among the last of the West Indies that would be taken."[76]

Blaine's refusal may have been due to the fact that at this time the prospects of obtaining Samana Bay seemed good. When Carr brought the matter anew to Foster's attention in the fall of 1892,

[73] U. S. Statutes at Large, XXVII, 349.

[74] Memorandum by Secretary John W. Foster, February 23, 1893, accompanied by copies of the proposed treaty. Miscellaneous Letters, 1893, Department of State. Before becoming Secretary of State in June, 1892, Foster had been in charge of the reciprocity negotiations authorized by the McKinley Tariff act of 1890. (W. R. Castle, Jr., John Watson Foster, in Bemis, op. cit., VIII, 191). Apparently he had handled the negotiations with the Dominican Republic from start to finish. There is an excellent account of this episode in Sumner Welles, Naboth's Vineyard, I, 468-495.

[75] Tansill, op. cit., p. 190.

[76] Ibid., p. 191. Blaine to Harrison, August 10, 1891. Gail Hamilton, loc. cit.

he found Foster friendly to the idea but doubtful whether the transaction could be consummated before March 4, 1893, when the Harrison régime would terminate. Foster wrote Carr:

> The question of the acquisition of the Islands is one of far-reaching
> importance, the extent of which is appreciated by no one more than
> the President. As his administration is, however, drawing to its close,
> he considers it inadvisable to express any views or indicate any policy,
> the consummation of which he could not effect.[77]

Thus the Harrison administration was fated to pass into history
without having materially strengthened the position of the United
States in the Caribbean. Its purposes, however, now that the facts
are revealed, are clear enough.

> There is very good reason for believing [wrote a reporter for the
> Washington *Star*, February 1, 1893] that if he [Harrison] had been
> re-elected an aggressive foreign policy would have been the most
> marked feature of his administration and that the end of another
> four years would have found this country in possession of strong
> points of advantage, from a naval point of view, in the South Atlantic
> and in the Pacific, placing us in a position both to foster and protect
> American commerce and to check foreign aggression in this hemi-
> sphere.

This seems like an accurate characterization. It was called forth,
however, by the arrival of the news that a revolution in Hawaii had
overthrown the royal government and that the United States would
be invited to annex the islands. Thus, thought the *Star* reporter,
there was even yet a chance that what Harrison had failed to accomplish in the Caribbean he might be able to achieve in the Pacific
before laying down the cares of office.

Upon Harrison's Hawaiian policy, the subject of much writing
but little real understanding, we must now dwell at considerable
length.

[77] Foster to Carr, December 20, 1892. Tansill, *op. cit.*, p. 195.

PART III

VOICES IN RESPECTFUL PROTEST

JOHN D. HICKS

THE PERIOD of the 1890's has been called "the watershed of American history." Behind lay decades of expansion when the unexploited wealth of the country waited free for the asking of enterprising men; in the future would come the test of the nation's ability to conserve and distribute wisely its dwindling assets. While the philosophy of rugged individualism continued to characterize a good deal of business activity, the realization that pioneer virtues were hardly suitable to a complex industrial society was producing the first gestures of public regulation. The Jeffersonian idea that a small government of limited power was the best defense of individual liberties lingered tenaciously, but began to give way to an increased confidence in the ability of democratic government to defend the rights of the weaker members of society.

What was true for the nation as a whole had special meaning for the agricultural population. The census report of 1890 declaring the end of an official frontier represented the cold fact that farmers could no longer turn to the free land which had been the traditional remedy for their ills. In an economy increasingly dominated by industrial interests, the farmers considered themselves forgotten, a minority fragment associated more with the past than the present. Yet the means of salvation which they sought to employ through the Populist party forecast the future. The grievances were old, but the program of government intervention was new.

For many years it was as difficult for historians to appraise correctly the significance of these new trends in American life as it was for politicians. The program of the Populist party, calling for regulated currency, even for the public ownership of railroads, appeared to come not from grass-roots agrarianism but from European radicalism. The supporters of William Jennings Bryan were characterized as revolutionists rather than as reformers, more deserving of jail sentences than of terms in office. When the Populist party disintegrated, many conservatives hailed the passing of a pernicious and sinister force in American politics.

Such misconceptions need not be shared by anyone to whom John D. Hicks's definitive study of the Populist movement, which appeared in 1931, is available. Tracing the source of the movement to specific economic grievances rather than to foreign ideologies, Hicks follows the course of the farmers' protest from the feeble Alliances of the 1880's to the years of decline following fusion with the Democrats in the "free silver" campaign of 1896. Where others saw an early effort to collectivize the national economy. Hicks detects the complaint of small business striving to maintain itself while retaining an essentially individualistic philosophy. Some critics did recognize the traditional pattern of the protest, but failed to assign any value to the Populists' program. In the final chapter of his book Hicks shows how virtually every reform demanded by the Populist party subsequently made its way into the platforms of the major parties and then into legislation passed before Franklin Roosevelt took office.

As a description of the agricultural opposition to the industrialists' dictation in business and government, Hicks's study is both exhaustive and accurate. Its deficiencies lie in its omissions, chiefly in its failure to emphasize sufficiently the relation of the Populist party and its principles to the more general Progressive movement of the quarter century before the First World War. For example, the Democrats' repudiation of Grover Cleveland in 1896 showed the strength of the farmers' group, but resulted also from the urban opposition represented by Governor John

Altgeld, the liberal governor of Illinois. In relating the ultimate success of Populist demands, Hicks does not make clear that they were effectuated because they were so widely shared by nonfarming elements. Bryan failed as a presidential candidate, but became Secretary of State for Woodrow Wilson, who had been the reform governor of an industrial state.

Perhaps it may be argued with equal truth that for Hicks to have given more attention to the other reform movements of the period would have been to suggest interrelations which did not exist. The Populist party represented an unsuccessful rather than a successful fusion of labor and agrarian demands. Subsequent years witnessed the effectual union of discontented groups that the 1890's failed to achieve.

In any event, John D. Hicks's *The Populist Revolt* takes its place on any shelf of highly recommended readings in American history.

The Populist Contribution

EARLY in 1890, when the People's party was yet in the embryo stage, a farmer editor from the West set forth the doctrine that "cranks always win." As he saw it,

The cranks are those who do not accept the existing order of things, and propose to change them. The existing order of things is always accepted by the majority, therefore the cranks are always in the minority. They are always progressive thinkers and always in advance of their time, and they always win. Called fanatics and fools at first, they are sometimes persecuted and abused. But their reforms are generally righteous, and time, reason and argument bring men to their

From *The Populist Revolt* by John D. Hicks, by permission of the University of Minnesota Press.

side. Abused and ridiculed, then tolerated, then respectfully given a hearing, then supported. This has been the gauntlet that all great reforms and reformers have run, from Galileo to John Brown.[1]

The writer of this editorial may have overstated his case, but a backward glance at the history of Populism shows that many of the reforms that the Populists demanded, while despised and rejected for a season, won triumphantly in the end. The party itself did not survive, nor did many of its leaders, although the number of contemporary politicians whose escutcheons should bear the bend sinister of Populism is larger than might be supposed; but doctrines showed an amazing vitality.

In formulating their principles the Populists reasoned that the ordinary, honest, willing American worker, be he farmer or be he laborer, might expect in this land of opportunity not only the chance to work but also, as the rightful reward of his labor, a fair degree of prosperity. When, in the later eighties and in the "heart-breaking nineties," hundreds of thousands—perhaps millions—of men found themselves either without work to do or, having work, unable to pay their just debts and make a living, the Populists held that there must be "wrong and crime and fraud somewhere." What was more natural than to fix the blame for this situation upon the manufacturers, the railroads, the money-lenders, the middlemen—plutocrats all, whose "colossal fortunes, unprecedented in the history of mankind," grew ever greater while the multitudes came to know the meaning of want. Work was denied when work might well have been given, and "the fruits of the toil of millions were boldly stolen."[2]

And the remedy? In an earlier age the hard-pressed farmers and laborers might have fled to free farms in the seemingly limitless lands of the West, but now the era of free lands had passed. Where, then, might they look for help? Where, if not to the government, which alone had the power to bring the mighty oppressors of the people to bay? So to the government the Populists turned. From it they asked laws to insure a full redress of grievances. As Dr. Turner

[1] *Farmers' Alliance* (Lincoln), February 15, 1890. This chapter follows in the main an article on "The Persistence of Populism," *Minnesota History*, 12:3-20 (March, 1931).
[2] Donnelly's preamble to the St. Louis and Omaha platforms stated not un fairly the Populist protest.

puts it, "the defences of the pioneer democrat began to shift from free land to legislation, from the ideal of individualism to the ideal of social control through regulation by law."[3] Unfortunately, however, the agencies of government had been permitted to fall into the hands of the plutocrats. Hence, if the necessary corrective legislation were to be obtained, the people must first win control of their government. The Populist philosophy thus boiled down finally to two fundamental propositions; one, that the government must restrain the selfish tendencies of those who profited at the expense of the poor and needy; the other, that the people, not the plutocrats, must control the government.

In their efforts to remove all restrictions on the power of the people to rule, the Populists accepted as their own a wide range of reforms. They believed, and on this they had frequently enough the evidence of their own eyes, that corruption existed at the ballot box and that in a fair count was often denied. They fell in line, therefore, with great enthusiasm when agitators, who were not necessarily Populists, sought to popularize the Australian ballot and such other measures as were calculated to insure a true expression of the will of the people.[4] Believing as they did that the voice of the people was the voice of God, they sought to eliminate indirect elections, especially the election of United States senators by state legislatures and of the president and the vice president by an electoral college. Fully aware of the habits of party bosses in manipulating nominating conventions, the Populists veered more and more in the direction of direct primary elections, urging in some of their later platforms that nominations even for president and vice president should be made by direct vote. Woman suffrage was a delicate question, for it was closely identified with the politically hazardous matter of temperance legislation, but, after all, the idea of votes for women was so clearly in harmony with the Populist doctrine of popular rule that it could not logically be denied a place among genuinely Populistic reforms. Direct legislation through the initiative and referendum and through the easy

[3] Turner, *Frontier in American History*, 277.

[4] At St. Louis in December, 1889, the Northern Alliance demanded the Australian system of voting. Thereafter nearly every Alliance or Populist platform gave the subject favorable mention.

amendment of state constitutions naturally appealed strongly to the Populists—the more so as they saw legislatures fail repeatedly to enact reform laws to which a majority of their members had been definitely pledged. "A majority of the people," said the Sioux Falls convention, "can never be corruptly influenced."[5] The recall of faithless officials, even judges, also attracted favorable attention from the makers of later Populist plafforms.

To list these demands is to cite the chief political innovations made in the United States during recent times. The Australian system of voting, improved registration laws, and other devices for insuring "a free ballot and a fair count" have long since swept the country. Woman suffrage has won an unqualified victory. The election of United States senators by direct vote of the people received the approval of far more than two-thirds of the national House of Representatives as early as 1898; it was further foreshadowed by the adoption, beginning in 1904, of senatorial primaries in a number of states, the results of which were to be regarded as morally binding upon the legislatures concerned; and it became a fact in 1913 with the ratification of the seventeenth amendment to the constitution.

The direct election of president and vice president was a reform hard to reconcile with state control of election machinery and state definition of the right to vote. Hence this reform never made headway; but the danger of one presidential candidate receiving a majority of the popular vote and another a majority of the electoral vote, as was the case in the Cleveland-Harrison contest of 1888, seems definitely to have passed. Recent elections may not prove that the popular voice always speaks intelligently; but they do seem to show that it speaks decisively.

In the widespread use of the primary election for the making of party nominations, the Populist principle of popular rule has scored perhaps its most telling victory. Tillman urged this reform in South Carolina at a very early date, but on obtaining control of the Democratic political machine of his state, he hesitated to give up the power that the convention system placed in his hands. At length, however, in 1896 he allowed the reform to go through.[6]

[5] See Stanwood, *History of the Presidency*, 2:39-42, for the Sioux Falls platform.
[6] Simkins, *Tillman Movement*, 239-243.

Wisconsin, spurred on by the La Follette forces, adopted the direct primary plan of nominations in 1903, and thereafter the other states of the Union, with remarkably few exceptions, fell into line. Presidential preference primaries, through which it was hoped that the direct voice of the people could be heard in the making of nominations for president and vice president, were also adopted by a number of states, beginning with Oregon in 1910.

Direct legislation by the people became almost an obsession with the Populists, especially the middle-of-the-road faction, in whose platforms it tended to overshadow nearly every other issue; and it is perhaps significant that the initiative and referendum were first adopted by South Dakota, a state in which the Populist party had shown great strength, as close on the heels of the Populist movement as 1898. Other states soon followed the South Dakota lead, and particularly in Oregon the experiment of popular legislation was given a thorough trial.[7] New constitutions and numerous amendments to old constitutions tended also to introduce much popularly made law, the idea that legislation in a constitution is improper and unwise receiving perhaps its most shattering blow when an Oklahoma convention wrote for that state a constitution of fifty thousand words. The recall of elected officials has been applied chiefly in municipal affairs, but some states also permit its use for state officers and a few allow even judges, traditionally held to be immune from popular reactions, to be subjected to recall. Thus many of the favorite ideas of the Populists, ideas that had once been "abused and ridiculed," were presently "respectfully given a hearing, then supported."[8]

Quite apart from these changes in the American form of government, the Populist propaganda in favor of independent voting did much to undermine the intense party loyalties that had followed in the wake of the Civil War. The time had been when for the Republican voter "to doubt Grant was as bad as to doubt Christ,"[9]

[7] Ellis P. Oberholtzer, *The Referendum in America together with Some Chapters on the Initiative and the Recall.*

[8] For satisfactory general discussions of these reforms see Charles A. Beard, *American Government and Politics,* 4th ed., ch. 24; Charles A. and Mary R. Beard, *The Rise of American Civilization,* Vol. 2, ch. 27; and David S. Muzzey, *The United States of America,* Vol. 2, ch. 7.

[9] Barr, in *Kansas and Kansans,* 2:1194.

when the man who scratched his party ticket was regarded as little, if any, better than the traitor to his country. The Alliance in its day had sought earnestly to wean the partisan voter over to independence. It had urged its members to "favor and assist to office such candidates only as are thoroughly identified with our principles and who will insist on such legislation as shall make them effective." And in this regard the Alliance, as some of its leaders boasted, had been a "great educator of the people." The Populist party had to go even further, for its growth depended almost wholly upon its ability to bring voters to a complete renunciation of old party loyalties. Since at one time or another well over a million men cast their ballots for Populist tickets, the loosening of party ties that thus set in was of formidable proportions.

Indeed, the man who became a Populist learned his lesson almost too well. When confronted, as many Populist voters thought themselves to be in 1896, with a choice between loyalty to party and loyalty to principle, the third-party adherents generally tended to stand on principle. Thereafter, as Populism faded out, the men who once had sworn undying devotion to the Omaha platform, were compelled again to transfer their allegiance. Many Republicans became Democrats via the Populist route; many Democrats became Republicans. Most of the Populists probably returned to the parties from which they had withdrawn, but party ties, once broken, were not so strong as they had been before. The rapid passing of voters from one party to another and the wholesale scratching of ballots, so characteristic of voting today, are distinctly reminiscent of Populism; as are also the nonpartisan ballots by which judges, city commissioners, and other officers are now frequently chosen, wholly without regard to their party affiliations.

In the South the Populist demands for popular government produced a peculiar situation. To a very great extent the southern Populists were recruited from the rural classes that had hitherto been politically inarticulate. Through the Populist party the "wool hat boys" from the country sought to obtain the weight in southern politics that their numbers warranted but that the Bourbon dynasties had ever denied them. In the struggle that ensued, both sides made every possible use of the negro vote, and the bugaboo of negro domination was once again raised. Indeed, the experience of North

Carolina under a combination government of Populists and Republicans furnished concrete evidence of what might happen should the political power of the negro be restored. Under the circumstances, therefore, there seemed to be nothing else for the white Populists to do but return to their former allegiance until the menace of the negro voter could be removed.

With the Democratic party again supreme, the problem of negro voting was attacked with right good will. Indeed, as early as 1890 the state of Mississippi, stimulated no doubt the agitation over the Force Bill, adopted a constitution that fixed as a prerequisite for voting a two years' residence in the state and a one year's residence in the district or town. This provision, together with a poll tax that had to be paid far in advance of the dates set for elections, diminished appreciably the number of negro voters, among whom indigence was common and the migratory propensity well developed. To complete the work of disfranchisement an amendment was added to the Mississippi constitution in 1892 that called for a modified literary test that could be administered in such a way as to permit illiterate whites to vote, while discriminating against illiterate, or even literate, blacks. The Tillmanites in South Carolina found legal means to exclude the negro voter in 1895; Louisiana introduced her famous "grandfather clause" in 1898; North Carolina adopted residence, poll-tax, and educational qualifications in 1900; Alabama followed in 1901; and in their own good time the other southern states in which negro voters had constituted a serious problem did the same thing. Some reverses were experienced in the courts, but the net result of this epidemic of anti-negro suffrage legislation was to eliminate for the time being all danger that negro voters might play an important part in southern politics.[10]

With this problem out of the way, or at least in the process of solution, it became possible for the rural whites of the South to resume the struggle for a voice in public affairs that they had begun in the days of the Alliance and had continued under the banner of Populism. They did not again form a third party, but they did contend freely in the Democratic primaries against the respectable

[10] Paul Lewison, "The Negro in the White Class and Party Struggle," *Southwestern Political and Social Science Quarterly*, 8:358-382. For an excellent brief statement see Holland Thompson, *The New South*, ch. 3.

and conservative descendants of the Bourbons. The Tillman machine in South Carolina continued for years to function smoothly as the agency through which the poorer classes sought to dominate the government of that state. It regularly sent Tillman to the United States Senate, where after his death his spirit lived on in the person of Cole Blease.[11] In Georgia the struggle for supremacy between the two factions of the Democratic party was a chronic condition, with now one side and now the other in control. Former Populists, converted by the lapse of time into regular organization Democrats, won high offices and instituted many of the reforms for which they had formerly been derided. Even Tom Watson rose from his political deathbed to show amazing strength in a race for Congress in 1918 and to win an astounding victory two years later when he sought a seat in the United States Senate.[12]

For better or for worse, the political careers of such southern politicians as James K. Vardaman and Theodore G. Bilbo of Mississippi, the Honorable "Jeff." Davis of Arkansas, and Huey P. Long of Louisiana demonstrate conclusively the fact that the lower classes in the South can, and sometimes do, place men of their own kind and choosing in high office. In these later days rural whites, who fought during Populist times with only such support as they could obtain from Republican sources, have sometimes been able to count as allies the mill operatives and their sympathizers in the factory districts; and southern primary elections are now apt to be as exciting as the regular elections are tame. Populism may have had something to do with the withdrawal of political power from the southern negro, but it also paved the way for the political emancipation of the lower class of southern whites.

The control of the government by the people was to the thoughtful Populist merely a means to an end. The next step was to use the power of the government to check the iniquities of the plutocrats. When the Populists at Omaha were baffled by the insistence of the temperance forces, they pointed out that before this or any other such reform could be accomplished they must "ask all men to first help us to determine whether we are to have a republic to adminis-

11 Simkins, *Tillman Movement*, ch. 10.
12 Arnett, *Populist Movement in Georgia*, 220-226; Brewton, *Thomas E. Watson*, chs. 44, 45.

ter." The inference is clear. Once permit the people really to rule, once insure that the men in office would not or could not betray the popular will, and such regulative measures as would right the wrongs from which the people suffered would quickly follow. The Populist believed implicitly in the ability of the people to frame and enforce the measures necessary to redeem themselves from the various sorts of oppression that were being visited upon them. They catalogued in their platform the evils from which society suffered and suggested the specific remedies by which these evils were to be overcome.

Much unfair criticism has been leveled at the Populists because of the attitude they took towards the allied subjects of banking and currency. To judge from the contemporary anti-Populist diatribes and from many subsequent criticisms of the Populist financial program, one would think that in such matters the third-party economists were little better than raving maniacs. As a matter of fact, the old-school Populists could think about as straight as their opponents. Their newspapers were well edited, and the arguments therein presented usually held together. Populist literature, moreover, was widely and carefully read by the ordinary third-party voters, particularly by the western farmers, whose periods of enforced leisure gave them ample opportunity for reading and reflection. Old-party debaters did not tackle their Populist antagonists lightly, for as frequently as not the bewhiskered rustic, turned orator, could present in support of his arguments an array of carefully sorted information that left his better-groomed opponent in a daze. The appearance of the somewhat irrelevant silver issue considerably confused Populist thinking, but even so many of the old-timers kept their heads and put silver in its proper place.

The Populists observed with entire accuracy that the currency of the United States was both inadequate and inelastic. They criticized correctly the part played by the national banking system in currency matters as irresponsible and susceptible of manipulation in the interest of the creditor class. They demanded a stabilized dollar, and they believed that it could be obtained if a national currency "safe, sound, and flexible" should be issued direct to the people by the government itself in such quantities as the reasonable demands of business should dictate. Silver and gold might be issued as well as paper, but the value of the dollar should come from the fiat of government and not from the "intrinsic worth" of the metal.

It is interesting to note that since the time when Populists were condemned as lunatics for holding such views legislation has been adopted that, while by no means going the full length of an irredeemable paper currency, does seek to accomplish precisely the ends that the Populists had in mind. Populist and free-silver agitation forced economists to study the money question as they had never studied it before and ultimately led them to propose remedies that could run the gauntlet of public opinion and of Congress. The Aldrich-Vreeland Act of 1908 authorized an emergency currency of several hundred million dollars, to be lent to banks on approved securities in times of financial disturbance. A National Monetary Commission, created at the same time, reported after four years' intensive study in favor of a return to the Hamiltonian system of a central Bank of the United States. Instead Congress in 1914, under Wilson's leadership, adopted the federal reserve system. The Federal Reserve Act did not, indeed, destroy the national banks and avoid the intervention of bankers in all monetary matters, but it did make possible an adequate and elastic national currency, varying in accordance with the needs of the country, and it placed supreme control of the nation's banking and credit resources in the hands of a federal reserve board, appointed not by the bankers but by the president of the United States with the consent of the Senate. The Populist diagnosis was accepted, and the Populist prescription was not wholly ignored.[13]

Probably no item in the Populist creed received more thorough castigation at the hands of contemporaries than the demand for subtreasuries, or government warehouses for the private storage of grain; but the subtreasury idea was not all bad, and perhaps the Populists would have done well had they pursued it further than they did. The need that the subtreasury was designed to meet was very real. Lack of credit forced the farmer to sell his produce at the time of harvest, when the price was lowest. A cash loan on his crop that would enable him to hold it until prices should rise was all

[13] E. W. Kemmerer, *The A B C of the Federal Reserve System*, 5th ed.; H. Parker Willis, *The Federal Reserve System, Legislation, Organization, and Operation.*

that he asked. Prices might thus be stabilized; profits honestly earned by the farmers would no longer fall to the speculators. That the men who brought forward the subtreasury as a plan for obtaining short-term rural credits also loaded it with an unworkable plan for obtaining a flexible currency was unfortunate; but the fundamental principle of the bill has by no means been discredited. Indeed, the Warehouse Act of 1916 went far towards accomplishing the very thing the Populists demanded. Under it the United States Department of Agriculture was permitted to license warehousemen and authorize them to receive, weigh, and grade farm products, for which they might issue warehouse receipts as collateral. Thus the owner might borrow the money he needed—not, however, from the government of the United States.[14]

In addition to the credits that the subtreasury would provide, Populist platforms usually urged also that the national government lend money on farm lands directly at a low rate of interest. This demand, which received an infinite amount of condemnation and derision at the time, has since been treated with much deference. If the government does not now print paper money to lend the farmer, with his land as security, it nevertheless does stand back of an elaborate system of banks through which he may obtain the credit he needs. Under the terms of the Federal Reserve Act national banks may lend money on farm mortgages—a privilege they did not enjoy in Populist times—and agricultural paper running as long as six months may be rediscounted by the federal reserve banks. From the farm loan banks, created by an act of 1916, the farmers may borrow for long periods sums not exceeding fifty per cent of the value of their land and twenty per cent of the value of their permanent improvements. Finally, through still another series of banks, the federal intermediate credit banks, established by an act of 1923, loans are made available to carry the farmer from one season to the next or a little longer, should occasion demand; the intermediate banks were authorized to rediscount agricultural and live-stock paper for periods of from six months to three years. Thus the government has created a comprehensive system of rural credits through which the farmer may obtain either short-term loans, loans of inter-

14 *Federal Statutes Annotated, Supplement,* 1918, pp. 1057-1065. See also Wiest, *Agricultural Organization in the United States,* 467-469.

mediate duration, or long-term loans, as his needs require, with a minimum of difficulty and at minimum interest rates.[15]

It would be idle to indulge in a *post hoc* argument in an attempt to prove that all these developments were due to Populism; but the intensive study of agricultural problems that led ultimately to these measures did begin with the efforts of sound economists to answer the arguments of the Populists. And it is evident that in the end the economists conceded nearly every point for which the Populists had contended.

More recent attempts to solve the agricultural problem, while assuming, as readily as even a Populist could have asked, the responsibility of the government in the matter, have progressed beyond the old Populist panacea of easy credit. Agricultural economists now have their attention fixed upon the surplus as the root of the difficulty. In industry, production can be curtailed to meet the demands of any given time, and a glutted market with the attendant decline in prices can be in a measure forestalled. But in agriculture, where each farmer is a law unto himself and where crop yields must inevitably vary greatly from year to year, control of production is wellnigh impossible and a surplus may easily become chronic. Suggestions for relief therefore looked increasingly towards the disposal of this surplus to the greatest advantage.[16]

The various McNary-Haugen bills that have come before Congress in recent years proposed to create a federal board through which the margin above domestic needs in years of plenty should be purchased and held, or disposed of abroad at whatever price it would bring. Through an "equalization fee" the losses sustained by "dumping" the surplus in this fashion were to be charged back upon the producers benefited. Although this proposition was agreeable to a majority of both houses of Congress, it met opposition from two successive presidents, Coolidge and Hoover, and was finally set aside for another scheme, less "socialistic." In 1929 Congress passed and the president signed a law for the creation of an appointive federal farm

15 H. Parker Willis and William H. Steiner, *Federal Reserve Banking Practice*, chs. 10-14; W. S. Holt, *The Federal Farm Loan Bureau, Its History, Activities, and Organization*; Herbert Myrick, *The Federal Farm Loan System*; A. C. Wiprud, *The Federal Farm Loan System in Operation*.

16 The Agricultural Crisis and Its Causes. Report of the Joint Commission of Agricultural Inquiry, 1921, *House Report* No. 408, 67 Congress, Session 1.

board, one of whose duties it is, among others, to encourage the organization of cooperative societies through which the farmers may themselves deal with the problem of the surplus. In case of necessity, however, the board may take the lead in the formation of stabilization corporations, which under its strict supervision may buy up such seasonal or temporary surpluses as threaten to break the market and hold them for higher prices. A huge revolving fund, appropriated by Congress, is made available for this purpose, loans from this fund being obtainable by the stabilization corporations at low interest rates. There is much about this thoroughly respectable and conservative law that recalls the agrarian demands of the nineties. Indeed, the measure goes further in the direction of government recognition of and aid to the principle of agricultural cooperation than even the most erratic Alliancemen could have dared to hope. Perhaps it will prove to be the "better plan" that the farmers called for in vain when the subtreasury was the best idea they could present.[17]

To the middle western Populist the railway problem was as important as any other—perhaps the most important of all. Early Alliance platforms favored drastic governmental control of the various means of communication as the best possible remedy for the ills from which the people suffered, and the first Populist platform to be written called for government ownership and operation only in case "the most rigid, honest, and just national control and supervision" should fail to "remove the abuses now existing." Thereafter the Populists usually demanded government ownership, although it is clear enough from their state and local platforms and from the votes and actions of Populist officeholders that, pending the day when ownership should become a fact, regulation by state and nation must be made ever more effective.

Possibly government ownership is no nearer today than in Populist times, but the first objective of the Populists, "the most rigid, honest, and just national control," is as nearly an accomplished fact as carefully drawn legislation and highly efficient administration can make it. Populist misgivings about governmental control arose from the knowledge that the Interstate Commerce Act of 1887, as well as

17 E. R. A. Seligman, *Economics of Farm Relief*; R. W. Kelsey, *Farm Relief and Its Antecedents*.

most regulatory state legislation, was wholly ineffectual during the nineties; but beginning with the Elkins Act of 1903, which struck at the practice of granting rebates, a long series of really workable laws found their way into the statute books. The Hepburn Act of 1906, the Mann-Elkins Act of 1910, and the Transportation Act of 1920, not to mention lesser laws, placed the Interstate Commerce Commission upon a high pinnacle of power. State laws, keeping abreast of the national program, supplemented national control with state control; and through one or the other agency most of the specific grievances of which the Populists had complained were removed.[18] The arbitrary fixing of rates by the carriers, a commonplace in Populist times, is virtually unknown today. If discriminations still exist between persons or places, the Interstate Commerce Commission is apt to be as much to blame as the railroads. Free passes, so numerous in Populist times as to occasion the remark that the only people who did not have passes were those who could not afford to pay their own fare, have virtually ceased to be issued except to railway employes. Railway control of state governments, even in the old Granger states, where in earlier days party bosses took their orders directly from railway officials, has long since become a thing of the past. The railroads still may have an influence in politics, but the railroads do not rule. Governmental control of telephones, telegraphs, and pipe lines, together with such later developments as the radio and the transmission of electric power, is accepted today as a matter of course, the issues being merely to what extent control should go and through what agencies it should be accomplished.

For the trust problem, as distinguished from the railroad problem, the Populists had no very definite solution. They agreed, however, that the power of government, state and national, should be used in such a way as to prevent "individuals or corporations fastening themselves, like vampires, on the people and sucking their substance."[19] Antitrust laws received the earnest approval of Alliancemen and Populists and were often initiated by them. The failure of such laws to secure results was laid mainly at the door of the courts, and when

18 William Z. Ripley, *Railroads; Rates and Regulation;* Homer B. Vanderblue and Kenneth F. Burgess, *Railroads. Rates—Service—Management;* David Philip Locklin, *Railroad Regulation since 1920.*
19 See the Cincinnati platform in the *American,* 27:167 (September 10, 1898).

Theodore Roosevelt in 1904 succeeded in securing an order from the United States Supreme Court dissolving the Northern Securities Company, it was hailed as a great victory for Populist principles. Many other incidental victories were won. Postal savings banks "for the safe deposit of the earnings of the people" encroached upon the special privileges of the bankers. An amendment to the national constitution in 1913, authorizing income taxes, recalled a contrary decision of the Supreme Court, which the Populists in their day had cited as the best evidence of the control of the government by the trusts; and income and inheritance taxes have ever since been levied. The reform of state and local taxation so as to exact a greater proportion of the taxes from the trusts and those who profit from them has also been freely undertaken. Labor demands, such as the right of labor to organize, the eight-hour day, limitation of injunctions in labor disputes, and restrictions on immigration were strongly championed by the Populists as fit measures for curbing the power of the trusts and were presently treated with great consideration. The Clayton Antitrust Act and the Federal Trade Commission Act, passed during the Wilson régime, were the products of long experience with the trust problem. The manner in which these laws have been enforced, however, would seem to indicate that the destruction of the trusts, a common demand in Populist times, is no longer regarded as feasible and that by government control the interests of the people can best be conserved.[20]

On the land question the Populist demands distinctly foreshadowed conservation. "The land," according to the Omaha declaration, "including all the natural resources of wealth, is the heritage of all the people and should not be monopolized for speculative purposes." Land and resources already given away were of course difficult to get back, and the passing of the era of free lands could not be repealed by law, but President Roosevelt soon began to secure results in the way of the reclamation and irrigation of arid western lands, the enlargement and protection of the national forests, the improvement of internal waterways, and the withdrawal from entry of lands bearing mineral wealth such as coal, oil, and phosphates.

[20] Eliot Jones, *The Trust Problem in the United States;* Henry R. Seager and Charles A. Gulick, *Trust and Corporation Problems;* Myron W. Watkins, *Industrial Combinations and Public Policy.*

At regular intervals, since 1908, the governors of the states have met together in conference to discuss the conservation problem, and this once dangerous Populist doctrine has now won all but universal acceptance.[21]

It would thus appear that much of the Populist program has found favor in the eyes of later generations. Populist plans for altering the machinery of government have, with but few exceptions, been carried into effect. Referring to these belated victories of the Populists, William Allen White, the man who had once asked, "What's the matter with Kansas?" wrote recently, "They abolished the established order completely and ushered in a new order."[22] Mrs. Mary E. Lease looked back proudly in 1914 on her political career:

> In these later years I have seen, with gratification, that my work in the good old Populist days was not in vain. The Progressive party has adopted our platform, clause by clause, plank by plank. Note the list of reforms which we advocated which are coming into reality. Direct election of senators is assured. Public utilities are gradually being removed from the hands of the few and placed under the control of the people who use them. Woman suffrage is now almost a national issue. . . . The seed we sowed out in Kansas did not fall on barren ground.[23]

Thanks to this triumph of Populist principles, one may almost say that, in so far as political devices can insure it, the people now rule. Political dishonesty has not altogether disappeared and the people may yet be betrayed by the men they elect to office, but on the whole the acts of government have come to reflect fairly clearly the will of the people. Efforts to assert this newly won power in such a way as to crush the economic supremacy of the predatory few have also been numerous and not wholly unsuccessful. The gigantic corporations of today, dwarfing into insignificance the trusts of yesterday, are, in spite of their size, far more circumspect in their conduct than their predecessors. If in the last analysis "big business" controls, it is because it has public opinion on its side and not merely the party bosses.

To radicals of today, however, the Populist panaceas, based as

21 Theodore Roosevelt, *Autobiography*, ch. 11; Charles R. Van Hise, *The Conservation of Natural Resources in the United States.*
22 White, in *Scribners' Magazine*, 79:564.
23 *Kansas City Star*, March 29, 1931.

they were upon an essentially individualistic philosophy and designed merely to insure for every man his right to "get ahead" in the world, seem totally inadequate. These latter-day extremists point to the perennial reappearance of such problems as farm relief, unemployment, unfair taxation, and law evasion as evidence that the Populist type of reform is futile, that something more drastic is required. Nor is their contention without point. It is reasonable to suppose that progressivism itself must progress; that the programs that would provide solutions for the problems of one generation might fall far short of meeting the needs of a succeeding generation. Perhaps one may not agree with the view of some present-day radicals that only a revolution will suffice and that the very attempt to make existing institutions more tolerable is treason to any real progress, since by so doing the day of revolution is postponed; but one must recognize that when the old Populist panaceas can receive the enthusiastic support of Hooverian Republicans and Alsmithian Democrats these once startling demands are no longer radical at all. One is reminded of the dilemma that Alice of Wonderland encountered when she went through the looking-glass into the garden of live flowers. On and on she ran with the Red Queen, but however fast they went they never seemed to pass anything.

"Well, in our country," said Alice, still panting a little, "you'd generally get to somewhere else—if you ran very fast for a long time as we've been doing."

"A slow sort of country!" said the Queen, "Now here, you see, it takes all the running you can do to keep in the same place. If you want to get somewhere else, you must run twice as fast as that!"

RICHARD HOFSTADTER

RICHARD HOFSTADTER has gradually assumed the status of a major figure among contemporary historians of America. Writing with clarity and wit, he has re-examined the main stream of the American past from a perspective combining an independent judgment with a sure grasp of the techniques of modern scholarship.

His viewpoint is based upon an explicit rejection of the spirit of "sentimental appreciation" that has dominated much of the historical work about America. "I have no desire," he has written, "to add to a literature of hero-worship and national self-congratulation." Many have shared this antipathy. But unlike some "objective" scholars who use facts as a substitute for judgment, and popular "debunkers" who associate truth with unpleasantness, he has been both committed and informed. His final purpose has been not to destroy myths but to reveal an unperceived reality, even if he would prefer to be "overcritical" rather than "overindulgent."

His first major work was *The American Political Tradition and the Men Who Made It,* published in 1948. It has become a landmark in the writing of American history, one of the first major breaks with the "Progressive School of Interpretation," which had dominated historical scholarship for several decades. That view of the American past had been epitomized by such works as Charles Beard's *An Economic Interpretation of the Constitution,* and, at the end, Arthur Schlesinger, Jr.'s *The Age of Jackson.* Essentially, it saw the national development as a struggle between two groups of interests: the democratic common man—farmer, laborer, and mechanic—and the somewhat sinister representatives of property and privilege.

Hofstadter both reflected and led a movement away from this basic conception. Instead of genuine struggle, he saw the unity of one nation under John Locke. Political divisions had been superficial and had resulted only in sham battles that tended to obscure the common national philosophy of faith in the virtues of private property. Thus, Andrew Jackson was not a leader of the western democrats or the eastern laborers, but rather a spokesman for entrepreneurial freedom, for a democratic capitalism in which all could hope to become employers and property owners.

The Age of Reform, published in 1955, presented a development from and continuation of these ideas. Concerned chiefly with the twentieth century, it attempted to destroy the Progressives' view of themselves and to redefine the objectives and achievements of the political reformers from the Populists to the New Deal.

Taken as a whole, the Progressive movement is assigned a nostalgic ideal—to preserve the individualistic values and to return to the economic modes of the past. The denunciation of monopoly and economic privilege was not a new rallying cry, but a traditional one to which the followers of Jefferson had responded. But in the twentieth century such reforms had very limited meaning. Commercialized farmers could not seek salvation in the dream of a self-sufficient yeomanry. Modern industrialism and mass production had made comparatively meaningless the Jacksonian ideal of a land of small businesses. Remedies for the failures in American society that grew out of such thinking were almost doomed to failure.

Such ideas had been expressed before. But Hofstadter placed them within an analytical framework that was clearer and more comprehensive. And in dealing with the Populists and agrarian

reform, he pierced the myth of the virtuous independent yeoman to reveal the harsh realities of rural self-interest.

Even more original is his analysis of the motivations of the
leaders of the Progressive movement, which grows out of his
own general thesis and from concepts borrowed from psychology.
He is primarily concerned not with the "externals" of the
period—that is, with the economic realities—but with the "in-
ternals," the psychological effect of those realities on individuals.
Especially, he analyzes the group that supplied much of Progressive leadership—not militant laborers but spokesmen for
small businesses, the professions, and skilled artisans. All of
these had lost "status" to the new rulers of industrial America,
men with more money, lower morals, and cruder tastes. The
"Progressive movement" emerged, then, as the reaction of an
older middle-class America with roots in the past but a willingness to use state economic intervention in a way not envisioned
by their spiritual predecessors, the moralistic "Mugwumps" of
the 1880's.

By adding the findings of the social psychologist to historical
facts of a somewhat familiar sort, Hofstadter has produced a
new insight that not only has contributed to his attack on the old
interpretation of the Progressive movement as a democratic
upsurge against exploitation, but has also offered a plausible
answer to the puzzling question of why widespread reform
occurred in a period of prosperity.

It has been Hofstadter's self-appointed task to break ground,
not in the sense of providing fresh facts, but in setting forth new
explanations of old facts. In this, he has unquestionably succeeded. But he has not written to analyze what is, or has been,
right or admirable about the American system and its leaders.
Instead he has supplied a counterbalance to the "literature of
hero-worship and national self-congratulation." For example, in
commenting about his own treatment of Jefferson in an earlier
book, he acknowledges that "a great deal more than I have
chosen to say . . . might be said . . . about Jefferson's de-

mocracy. . . ." It would be a mistake, then, to accept an admittedly incomplete account as a complete concept.

Similarly, there is much that he chooses to omit from *The Age of Reform*. He does not explore the successes of the Progressive movement or what was new about it. The focus is largely on the nostalgic content and the motives of a group of reformers most of whom wished to turn back the clock. His theme is not the dynamic quality of American political life but its inflexibility.

The lesson of both the *American Political Tradition* and *The Age of Reform* is that our political past offers an inadequate guide for the future. Franklin Roosevelt is praised "for his sense of the failure of a tradition," but criticized for not seeking a comprehensive plan for a stable economy and "distributive justice." Hofstadter concludes that at the end of several decades of reform, there remained too much misplaced belief in private enterprise and individualistic values.

It is curious that he should protest against any intimation that he be included among the "New Conservatives." Many who have profited from his sharp perceptions and informative theses will not wish to share his estimate of the efficiency and viability of the American economic and political system. One could conclude, for example, that the Progressives did demonstrate the adaptability of the system and that Franklin Roosevelt should be remembered for his belief in it rather than for a sense of its failure.

These alternatives should not obscure Hofstadter's success in achieving his objective. He has put important and original questions to his material and has provided answers that have enlarged the perspective of his readers.

The Status Revolution and Progressive Leaders

I. THE PLUTOCRACY AND THE MUGWUMP TYPE

POPULISM had been overwhelmingly rural and provincial. The ferment of the Progressive era was urban, middle-class, and nationwide. Above all, Progressivism differed from Populism in the fact that the middle classes of the cities not only joined the trend toward protest but took over its leadership. While Bryan's old followers still kept their interest in certain reforms, they now found themselves in the company of large numbers who had hitherto violently opposed them. As the demand for reform spread from the farmers to the middle class and from the Populist Party into the major parties, it became more powerful and more highly regarded. It had been possible for their enemies to brand the Populists as wild anarchists, especially since there were millions of Americans who had never laid eyes on either a Populist or an anarchist. But it was impossible to popularize such a distorted image of the Progressives, who flourished in every section of the country, everywhere visibly, palpably, almost pathetically respectable.

William Allen White recalled in his *Autobiography,* perhaps with some exaggeration, the atmosphere of the Greenback and Populist conventions he had seen, first as a boy, then as a young reporter. As a solid middle-class citizen of the Middle West, he had concluded that "those agrarian movements too often appealed to the ne'er-do-wells, the misfits—farmers who had failed, lawyers and doctors who were not orthodox, teachers who could not make

Reprinted from *The Age of Reform* by Richard Hofstadter, by permission of Alfred A. Knopf, Inc. Copyright 1955 by Richard Hofstadter.

the grade, and neurotics full of hates and ebullient, evanescent enthusiàsms." Years later, when he surveyed the membership of the Bull Moose movement of 1912, he found it "in the main and in its heart of hearts *petit bourgeois*": "a movement of little businessmen, professional men, well-to-do farmers, skilled artisans from the upper brackets of organized labor . . . the successful middle-class country-town citizens, the farmer whose barn was painted, the well-paid railroad engineer, and the country editor."[1]

White saw himself as a case in point. In the nineties he had been, in his own words, "a child of the governing classes," and "a stouthearted young reactionary," who rallied with other young Kansas Republicans against the Populists and won a national reputation with his fierce anti-Populist diatribe: "What's the Matter with Kansas?" In the Progressive era he became one of the outstanding publicists of reform, a friend and associate of the famous muckrakers, and an enthusiastic Bull Mooser. His change of heart was also experienced by a large portion of that comfortable society of which he was a typical and honored spokesman, a society that had branded the Populists and Bryan as madmen and then appropriated so much of the Populist program, as White said of its political leaders, that they "caught the Populists in swimming and stole all of their clothing except the frayed underdrawers of free silver."[2]

Clearly, the need for political and economic reform was now felt more widely in the country at large. Another, more obscure process, traceable to the flexibility and opportunism of the American party system, was also at work: successful resistance to reform demands required a partial incorporation of the reform program. As Bryan Democracy had taken over much of the spirit and some of the program of Populism, Theodore Roosevelt, in turn, persistently blunted Bryan's appeal by appropriating Bryan's issues in modified form. In this way Progressivism became nationwide and bipartisan, encompassing Democrats and Republicans, country and city, East, West, and South. A working coalition was forged between the old Bryan country and the new reform movement in the cities, without which the broad diffusion and strength of Progressivism would

[1] *Autobiography*, pp. 482-3.
[2] Quoted by Kenneth Hechler: *Insurgency* (New York, 1940), pp. 21-2

have been impossible. Its spirit spread so widely that by the time of the three-cornered presidential contest of 1912 President Taft, who was put in the position of the "conservative" candidate, got less than half the combined popular vote of the "Progressives," Wilson and Roosevelt.

After 1900 Populism and Progressivism merge, though a close student may find in the Progressive era two broad strains of thought, one influenced chiefly by the Populist inheritance, the other mainly a product of urban life. Certainly Progressivism was characterized by a fresh, more intimate and sympathetic concern with urban problems—labor and social welfare, municipal reform, the interest of the consumer. However, those achievements of the age that had a nationwide import and required Congressional action, such as tariff and financial legislation, railroad and trust regulation, and the like, were dependent upon the votes of the Senators from the agrarian regions and were shaped in such a way as would meet their demands.

While too sharp a distinction between Populist and Progressive thinking would distort reality, the growth of middle-class reform sentiment, the contributions of professionals and educated men, made Progressive thought more informed, more moderate, more complex than Populist thought had been. Progressivism, moreover, as the product of a more prosperous era, was less rancorous. With the exception of a few internally controversial issues of a highly pragmatic sort, the Populists had tended to be of one mind on most broad social issues, and that mind was rather narrow and predictable. The Progressives were more likely to be aware of the complexities of social issues and more divided among themselves. Indeed, the characteristic Progressive was often of two minds on many issues. Concerning the great corporations, the Progressives felt that they were a menace to society and that they were all too often manipulated by unscrupulous men; on the other hand, many Progressives were quite aware that the newer organization of industry and finance was a product of social evolution which had its beneficent side and that it was here to stay. Concerning immigrants, they frequently shared Populist prejudices and the Populist horror of ethnic mixture, but they were somewhat more disposed to discipline their feelings with a sense of some obligation to the immigrant and the recognition that his Americanization was a practical problem that must be met with a humane and constructive program. As for labor, while they felt, perhaps more acutely than most Populists of the nineties, that the growth of union power posed a distinct problem, even a threat, to them, they also saw that labor organization had arisen in response to a real need among the urban masses that must in some way be satisfied. As for the bosses, the machines, the corruptions of city life, they too found in these things grave evils; but they were ready, perhaps all too ready, to admit that the existence of such evils was in large measure their own fault. Like the Populists the Progressives were full of indignation, but their indignation was more qualified by a sense of responsibility, often even of guilt, and it was supported by a greater capacity to organize, legislate, and administer. But lest all this seem unfair to the Populists, it should be added that the Progressives did not, as a rule, have the daring or the originative force of the Populists of the 1890's, and that a great deal of Progressive political effort was spent enacting proposals that the Populists had outlined fifteen or even twenty years earlier.

Curiously, the Progressive revolt—even when we have made allowance for the brief panic of 1907 and the downward turn in business in 1913—took place almost entirely during a period of sustained and general prosperity. The middle class, most of which had been content to accept the conservative leadership of Hanna and McKinley during the period of crisis in the mid-nineties, rallied to the support of Progressive leaders in both parties during the period of well-being that followed. This fact is a challenge to the historian. Why did the middle classes undergo this remarkable awakening at all, and why during this period of general prosperity in which most of them seem to have shared? What was the place of economic discontents in the Progressive movement? To what extent did reform originate in other considerations?

Of course Progressivism had the adherence of a heterogeneous public whose various segments responded to various needs. But I am concerned here with a large and strategic section of Progressive leadership, upon whose contributions the movement was politically and intellectually as well as financially dependent, and whose members did much to formulate its ideals. It is my thesis that men of this sort, who might be designated broadly as the Mugwump type, were Progressives not because of economic deprivations but primarily because they were victims of an upheaval in status that took place in the United States during the closing decades of the nineteenth and the early years of the twentieth century. Progressivism, in short, was to a very considerable extent led by men who suffered from the events of their time not through a shrinkage in their means but through the changed pattern in the distribution of deference and power.

Up to about 1870 the United States was a nation with a rather broad diffusion of wealth, status, and power, in which the man of moderate means, especially in the many small communities, could command much deference and exert much influence. The small merchant or manufacturer, the distinguished lawyer, editor, or preacher, was a person of local eminence in an age in which local eminence mattered a great deal. In the absence of very many nationwide sources of power and prestige, the pillars of the local communities were men of great importance in their own right. What Henry Adams remembered about his own bailiwick was, on the whole, true of the country at large: "Down to 1850, and even later, New England society was still directed by the professions. Lawyers, physicians, professors, merchants were classes, and acted not as individuals, but as though they were clergymen and each profession were a church."[3]

In the post-Civil War period all this was changed. The rapid development of the big cities, the building of a great industrial plant, the construction of the railroads, the emergence of the corporation as the dominant form of enterprise, transformed the old society and revolutionized the distribution of power and prestige. During the 1840's there were not twenty millionaires in the entire country; by 1910 there were probably more than twenty millionaires sitting in the United States Senate.[4] By the late 1880's

[3] *The Education of Henry Adams* (New York, Modern Library ed., 1931), p. 32; cf. Tocqueville: *Democracy in America* (New York, 1912), Vol. I, pp. 40-1.
[4] Sidney Ratner: *American Taxation* (New York, 1942), pp. 136, 275.

this process had gone far enough to become the subject of frequent, anxious comment in the press. In 1891 the *Forum* published a much-discussed article on "The Coming Billionaire," by Thomas G. Shearman, who estimated that there were 120 men in the United States each of whom was worth over ten million dollars.[5] In 1892 the *New York Tribune,* inspired by growing popular criticism of the wealthy, published a list of 4,047 reputed millionaires, and in the following year a statistician of the Census Bureau published a study of the concentration of wealth in which he estimated that 9 per cent of the families of the nation owned 71 per cent of the wealth.[6]

The newly rich, the grandiosely or corruptly rich, the masters of great corporations, were bypassing the men of the Mugwump type—the old gentry, the merchants of long standing, the small manufacturers, the established professional men, the civic leaders of an earlier era. In a score of cities and hundreds of towns, particularly in the East but also in the nation at large, the old-family, college-educated class that had deep ancestral roots in local communities and often owned family businesses, that had traditions of political leadership, belonged to the patriotic so-cieties and the best clubs, staffed the governing boards of philan-thropic and cultural institutions, and led the movements for civic betterment, were being overshadowed and edged aside in the making of basic political and economic decisions. In their personal careers, as in their community activities, they found themselves checked, hampered, and overridden by the agents of the new cor-

[5] Thomas G. Shearman: "The Coming Billionaire," *Forum,* Vol. X (January 1891), pp. 546-57; cf. the same author's "The Owners of the United States," ibid., Vol. VIII (November 1889), pp. 262-73.

[6] Ratner, op. cit., p. 220. Sidney Ratner has published the *Tribune's* list and one compiled in 1902 by the *New York World Almanac,* together with a valuable introductory essay in his *New Light on the History of Great American Fortunes* (New York, 1953). The *Tribune's* list was compiled chiefly to prove to the critics of the tariff that an overwhelming majority of the great fortunes had been made in businesses that were not beneficiaries of tariff protection. For an analysis of the *Tribune's* list, see G. P. Watkins: "The Growth of Large Fortunes," *Publications of the American Economic Association,* third series, Vol. VIII (1907), pp. 141-7. Out of the alarm of the period over the concentration of wealth arose the first American studies of national wealth and income. For a review of these studies, see C. L. Merwin: "American Studies of the Distribution of Wealth and Income by Size," in *Studies in Income and Wealth,* Vol. III (New York, 1939), pp. 3-84.

porations, the corrupters of legislatures, the buyers of franchises, the allies of the political bosses. In this uneven struggle they found themselves limited by their own scruples, their regard for reputation, their social standing itself. To be sure, the America they knew did not lack opportunities, but it did seem to lack opportunities of the highest sort for men of the highest standards. In a strictly economic sense these men were not growing poorer as a class, but their wealth and power were being dwarfed by comparison with the new eminences of wealth and power. They were less important, and they knew it.

Against the tide of new wealth the less affluent and aristocratic local gentry had almost no protection at all. The richer and better-established among them found it still possible, of course, to trade on their inherited money and position, and their presence as window-dressing was an asset for any kind of enterprise, in business or elsewhere, to which they would lend their sponsorship. Often indeed the new men sought to marry into their circles, or to buy from them social position much as they bought from the bosses legislation and franchises. But at best the gentry could only make a static defense of themselves, holding their own in absolute terms while relatively losing ground year by year. Even this much they could do only in the localities over which they had long presided and in which they were well known. And when everyone could see that the arena of prestige, like the market for commodities, had been widened to embrace the entire nation, eminence in mere localities ceased to be as important and satisfying as once it had been. To face the insolence of the local boss or traction magnate in a town where one's family had long been prominent was galling enough;[7] it was still harder to bear at a time

[7] In the West and South it was more often the absentee railroad or industrial corporation that was resented. In more recent times, such local resentments have frequently taken a more harmful and less constructive form than the similar resentments of the Progressive era. Seymour M. Lipset and Reinhard Bendix have pointed out that in small American cities dependent for their livelihood upon large national corporations, the local upper classes, who are upper class only in their own community, resent their economic weakness and their loss of power to the outsiders. "The small industrialist and business man of the nation is caught in a struggle between big unionism and big industry, and he feels threatened. This experience of the discrepancy between local prominence and the decline of

when every fortune, every career, every reputation, seemed smaller and less significant because it was measured against the Vander-derbilts, Harrimans, Goulds, Carnegies, Rockefellers, and Morgans.[8]

The first reaction of the Mugwump type to the conditions of the status revolution was quite different from that later to be displayed by their successors among the Progressives. All through the seventies, eighties, and nineties men from the upper ranks of business and professional life had expressed their distaste for machine politics, corruption, and the cruder forms of business intervention in political affairs. Such men were commonly Republicans, but independent enough to bolt if they felt their principles betrayed. They made their first organized appearance in the ill-fated Liberal Republican movement of 1872, but their most important moment came in 1884, when their bolt from the Republican Party after the nomination of James G. Blaine was widely believed to have helped tip the scales to Cleveland in a close election.

While men of the Mugwump type flourished during those decades most conspicuously about Boston, a center of seasoned wealth and seasoned conscience, where some of the most noteworthy names in Massachusetts were among them,[9] they were also prominent in

---

local economic power provides a fertile ground for an ideology which attacks both big business and big unionism." "Social Status and Social Structure," *British Journal of Sociology*, Vol. II (June 1951), p. 233.

[8] It may be significant that the era of the status revolution was also one in which great numbers of patriotic societies were founded. Of 105 patriotic orders founded between 1783 and 1900, 34 originated before 1870 and 71 between 1870 and 1900. A high proportion of American patriotic societies is based upon descent and length of family residence in the United States, often specifically requiring family participation in some such national event as the American Revolution. The increase of patriotic and genealogical societies during the status revolution suggests that many old-family Americans, who were losing status in the present, may have found satisfying compensation in turning to family glories of the past. Of course, a large proportion of these orders were founded during the nationalistic outbursts of the nineties; but these too may have had their subtle psychological relation to status changes. Note the disdain of men like Theodore Roosevelt for the lack of patriotism and aggressive nationalism among men of great wealth. On the founding of patriotic societies, see Wallace E. Davies: *A History of American Veterans' and Hereditary Patriotic Societies, 1783-1900,* unpublished doctoral dissertation, Harvard University, 1944, Vol. II, pp. 441 ff.

[9] Notably Charles Francis Adams, Jr., Edward Atkinson, Moorfield Storey, Leverett Saltonstall, William Everett, Josiah Quincy, Thomas Wentworth Higginson.

a metropolis like New York and could be found in some strength in such Midwestern cities as Indianapolis and Chicago. None the less, one senses among them the prominence of the cultural ideals and traditions of New England, and beyond these of old England. Protestant and Anglo-Saxon for the most part, they were very frequently of New England ancestry; and even when they were not, they tended to look to New England's history for literary, cultural, and political models and for examples of moral idealism. Their conception of statecraft was set by the high example of the Founding Fathers, or by the great debating statesmen of the silver age, Webster, Sumner, Everett, Clay, and Calhoun. Their ideal leader was well-to-do, well-educated, high-minded citizen, rich enough to be free from motives of what they often called "crass materialism," whose family roots were deep not only in American history but in his local community. Such a person, they thought, would be just the sort to put the national interest, as well as the interest of civic improvement, above personal motives or political opportunism. And such a person was just the sort, as Henry Adams never grew tired of complaining, for whom American political life was least likely to find a place. To be sure, men of the Mugwump type could and did find places in big industry, in the great corporations, and they were sought out to add respectability to many forms of enterprise. But they tended to have positions in which the initiative was not their own, or in which they could not feel themselves acting in harmony with their highest ideals. They no longer called the tune, no longer commanded their old deference. They were expropriated, not so much economically as morally.

They imagined themselves to have been ousted almost entirely by new men of the crudest sort. While in truth the great business leaders of the Gilded Age were typically men who started from comfortable or privileged beginnings in life,[1] the Mugwump mind

---

[1] See William Miller: "American Historians and the Business Elite," *Journal of Economic History*, Vol. IX (November 1949), pp. 184-208; "The Recruitment of the American Business Elite," *Quarterly Journal of Economics*, Vol. LXIV (May 1950), pp. 242-53. C. Wright Mills: "The American Business Elite: a Collective Portrait," *Journal of Economic History*, Vol. V (Supplemental issue, 1945), pp. 20-44. Frances W. Gregory and Irene D. Neu: "The American Industrial Elite in the 1870's," in William Miller, ed.: *Men in Business* (Cambridge, 1952), pp. 193-211.

was most concerned with the newness and the rawness of the corporate magnates, and Mugwumps and reformers alike found satisfaction in a bitter caricature of the great businessman. One need only turn to the social novels of the "realists" who wrote about businessmen at the turn of the century—William Dean Howells, H. H. Boyesen, Henry Blake Fuller, and Robert Herrick, among others—to see the portrait of the captain of industry that dominated the Mugwump imagination. The industrialists were held to be uneducated and uncultivated, irresponsible, rootless and corrupt, devoid of refinement or of any sense of noblesse. "If our civilization is destroyed, as Macaulay predicted," wrote Henry Demarest Lloyd in an assessment of the robber barons, "it will not be by his barbarians from below. Our barbarians come from above. Our great money-makers have sprung in one generation into seats of power kings do not know. *The forces and the wealth are new, and have been the opportunity of new men. Without restraints of culture, experience, the pride, or even the inherited caution of class or rank,* these men, intoxicated, think they are the wave instead of the float, and that they have created the business which has created them. To them science is but a never-ending repertoire of investments stored up by nature for the syndicates, government but a fountain of franchises, the nations but customers in squads, and a million the unit of a new arithmetic of wealth written for them. They claim a power without control, exercised through forms which make it secret, anonymous, and perpetual. The possibilities of its gratification have been widening before them without interruption since they began, and even at a thousand millions they will feel no satiation and will see no place to stop."[2]

Unlike Lloyd, however, the typical Mugwump was a conservative in his economic and political views. He disdained, to be sure, the most unscrupulous of the new men of wealth, as he did the opportunistic, boodling, tariff-mongering politicians who served them. But the most serious abuses of the unfolding economic order of the Gilded Age he either resolutely ignored or accepted com-

[2] Henry Demarest Lloyd: *Wealth against Commonwealth* (New York, 1894, ed. 1899), pp. 510-11; italics added. For some characteristic expressions on the plutocracy by other writers, see the lengthy quotations in Lloyd's article: "Plutocracy," in W. D. P. Bliss, ed.: *Encyclopedia of Social Reform* (New York, 1897), pp. 1012-16.

placently as an inevitable result of the struggle for existence or the improvidence and laziness of the masses.[3] As a rule, he was dogmatically committed to the prevailing theoretical economics of *laissez faire*. His economic program did not go much beyond tariff reform and sound money—both principles more easily acceptable to a group whose wealth was based more upon mercantile activities and the professions than upon manufacturing and new enterprises —and his political program rested upon the foundations of honest and efficient government and civil-service reform. He was a "liberal" in the classic sense. Tariff reform, he thought, would be the sovereign remedy for the huge business combinations that were arising. His pre-eminent journalist and philosopher was E. L. Godkin, the honorable old free-trading editor of the *Nation* and the New York *Evening Post*. His favorite statesman was Grover Cleveland, who described the tariff as the "mother of trusts." He imagined that most of the economic ills that were remediable at all could be remedied by free trade, just as he believed that the essence of government lay in honest dealing by honest and competent men.

Lord Bryce spoke of the Mugwump movement as being "made more important by the intelligence and social position of the men who composed it than by its voting power."[4] It was in fact intellect and social position, among other things, that insulated the Mugwump from the sources of voting power. If he was critical of the predatory capitalists and their political allies, he was even more contemptuously opposed to the "radical" agrarian movements and the "demagogues" who led them, to the city workers when, led by "walking delegates," they rebelled against their employers, and to the urban immigrants and the "unscrupulous bosses" who introduced them to the mysteries of American civic life. He was an impeccable constitutionalist, but the fortunes of American politics had made him an equally firm aristocrat. He had his doubts, now that the returns were in, about the beneficence of universal suffrage.[5] The last thing he would have dreamed of was to appeal

[3] For a cross-section of the views of this school, see Alan P. Grimes: *The Political Liberalism of the New York* NATION, *1865-1932* (Chapel Hill, 1953), chapter ii.
[4] *The American Commonwealth*, Vol. II, p. 45; see pp. 45-50 for a brief characterization of the Mugwump type.
[5] Grimes, op. cit., chapter iii.

to the masses against the plutocracy, and to appeal to them against the local bosses was usually fruitless. The Mugwump was shut off from the people as much by his social reserve and his amateurism as by his candidly conservative views. In so far as he sought popular support, he sought it on aristocratic terms.

One of the changes that made Progressivism possible around the turn of the century was the end of this insulation of the Mugwump type from mass support. For reasons that it is in good part the task of these pages to explore, the old barriers melted away. How the Mugwump found a following is a complex story, but it must be said at once that this was impossible until the Mugwump type itself had been somewhat transformed. The sons and successors of the Mugwumps had to challenge their fathers' ideas, modify their doctrinaire commitment to *laissez faire,* replace their aristocratic preferences with a startling revival of enthusiasm for popular government, and develop greater flexibility in dealing with the demands of the discontented before they could launch the movement that came to dominate the political life of the Progressive era.

But if the philosophy and the spirit were new, the social type and the social grievance were much the same. The Mugwump had broadened his base. One need not be surprised, for instance, to find among the Progressive leaders in both major parties a large number of well-to-do men whose personal situation is reminiscent of the Mugwumps of an earlier generation. As Professor George Mowry has remarked, "few reform movements in American history have had the support of more wealthy men."[6] Such men as George W. Perkins and Frank Munsey, who may perhaps be accused of joining the Progressive movement primarily to blunt its edge, can be left out of account, and such wealthy reformers as Charles R. Crane, Rudolph Spreckels, E. A. Filene, the Pinchots, and William Kent may be dismissed as exceptional. Still, in examining the lives and backgrounds of the reformers of the era, one is impressed by the number of those who had considerably more than moderate means, and particularly by those who had inherited their money. As yet no study has been made of reform leaders in both major parties, but the systematic information available on leaders of the

[6] George Mowry: *Theodore Roosevelt and the Progressive Movement* (Madison, 1946), p. 10.

Progressive Party of 1912 is suggestive. Alfred D. Chandler, Jr., sur-
veying the backgrounds and careers of 260 Progressive Party leaders
throughout the country, has noted how overwhelmingly urban and
middle-class they were. Almost entirely native-born Protestants, they
had an extraordinarily high representation of professional men and
college graduates. The rest were businessmen, proprietors of fairly
large enterprises. None was a farmer, only one was a labor-union
leader, and the white-collar classes and salaried managers of large
industrial or transportation enterprises were completely unrepresented. Not surprisingly, the chief previous political experience
of most of them was in local politics. But on the whole, as Chandler
observes, they "had had little experience with any kind of institutional discipline. In this sense, though they lived in the city, they
were in no way typical men of the city. With very rare exceptions,
all these men had been and continued to be their own bosses. As
lawyers, businessmen, and professional men, they worked for themselves and had done so for most of their lives. As individualists,
unacquainted with institutional discipline or control, the Progressive leaders represented, in spite of their thoroughly urban backgrounds, the ideas of the older, more rural America."[7] From the
only other comparable study, George Mowry's survey of the California Progressives, substantially the same conclusions emerge. The
average California Progressive was "in the jargon of his day, 'well
fixed.' He was more often than not a Mason, and almost invariably
a member of his town's chamber of commerce. . . . He apparently
had been, at least until 1900, a conservative Republican, satisfied
with McKinley and his Republican predecessors."[8]

[7] Alfred D. Chandler, Jr.: "The Origins of Progressive Leadership," in Elting
Morison, ed.: *The Letters of Theodore Roosevelt,* Vol. VIII (Cambridge, 1954),
pp. 1462-5. Chandler found the 260 leaders distributed as follows: business, 95;
lawyers, 75; editors, 36; other professional (college professors, authors, social
workers, and a scattering of others), 55. Chandler also found significant regional
variations. In the cities of the Northeast and the old Northwest, the role of the
intellectuals and professionals was large, while the businessmen were chiefly
those who managed old, established enterprises. In the South, however, a rising
social elite of aggressive new businessmen took part. In the West and the rural
areas, editors and lawyers dominated party leadership, while the businessmen
tended to be from businesses of modest size, like cattle, real estate, lumber, publishing, small manufacturing.

[8] George Mowry: *The California Progressives* (Berkeley, 1951), pp. 88-9; see
generally chapter iv, which contains an illuminating brief account of 47 Progres-

While some of the wealthier reformers were self-made men, like John P. Altgeld, Hazen Pingree, the Mayor of Detroit and Governor of Michigan, and Samuel ("Golden Rule") Jones, the crusading Mayor of Toledo, more were men of the second and third generation of wealth or (notably Tom Johnson and Joseph Fels) men who had been declassed for a time and had recouped their fortunes. Progressive ideology, at any rate, distinguished consistently between "responsible" and "irresponsible" wealth—a distinction that seems intimately related to the antagonism of those who had had money long enough to make temperate and judicious use of it for those who were rioting with new-found means.

A gifted contemporary of the Progressives, Walter Weyl, observed in his penetrating and now all but forgotten book *The New Democracy* that this distinction between types of wealth could often be seen in American cities: "As wealth accumulates, moreover, a cleavage of sentiment widens between the men who are getting rich and the men who *are* rich. The old Cincinnati distinction between the 'stick-'ems' (the actual pork-packers) and the rich 'stuck-'ems' is today reflected in the difference between the retired millionaires of New York and the millionaires, in process or hope, of Cleveland, Portland, Los Angeles, or Denver. The gilt-edged millionaire bondholder of a standard railroad has only a partial sympathy with timber thieves, though his own fortune may have originated a few generations ago in railroad-wrecking or the slave and Jamaica rum trade; while the cultured descendants of cotton manufacturers resent the advent into their society of the man who had made his 'pile' in the recent buying or selling of franchises. Once wealth is sanctified by hoary age . . . it tends to turn quite naturally against new and evil ways of wealth getting, the expedients of prospective social climbers. The old wealth is not a loyal ally in the battle for the plutocracy; it inclines, if not to democratic, at least to mildly reformatory, programs . . . the battle between the plutocracy and the

---

sive leaders. Three fourths of these were college-educated. There were 17 lawyers, 14 journalists, 11 independent businessmen and real-estate operators, 3 doctors, 3 bankers. Of the ideology of this group Mowry observed that they were opposed chiefly to "the impersonal, concentrated, and supposedly privileged property represented by the behemoth corporation. Looking backward to an older America [they] sought to recapture and reaffirm the older individualistic values in all the strata of political, economic, and social life." Ibid., p. 89.

democracy, which furiously wages in the cities where wealth is being actually fought for, becomes somewhat gentler in those cities where bodies of accumulated wealth exercise a moderating influence. Inheritance works in the same direction. Once wealth is separated from its original accumulator, it slackens its advocacy of its method of accumulation."[9]

Weyl realized, moreover, that so far as a great part of the dissenting public was concerned, the central grievance against the American plutocracy was not that it despoiled them economically but that it overshadowed them, that in the still competitive arena of prestige derived from conspicuous consumption and the style of life, the new plutocracy had set standards of such extravagance and such notoriety that everyone else felt humbled by comparison. Not only was this true of the nation as a whole in respect to the plutocracy, but there was an inner plutocracy in every community and every profession that aroused the same vague resentment: "The most curious factor," he found, in the almost universal American antagonism toward the plutocracy, was "that an increasing bitterness is felt by a majority which is not worse but better off than before. This majority suffers not an absolute decline but a relatively slower growth. It objects that the plutocracy grows too fast; that in growing so rapidly it squeezes its growing neighbors. Growth is right and proper, but there is, it is alleged, a rate of growth which is positively immoral. . . . To a considerable extent the plutocracy is hated not for what it does but for what it is. . . . It is the mere existence of a plutocracy, the mere 'being' of our wealthy contemporaries, that is the main offense. Our over-moneyed neighbors cause a relative deflation of our personalities. Of course, in the consumption of wealth, as in its production, there exist 'non-competitive groups,' and a two-thousand-dollar-a-year-man need not spend like a Gould or a Guggenheim. Everywhere, however, we meet the millionaire's good and evil works, and we seem to resent the one as much as the other. Our jogging horses are passed by their high-power automobiles. We are obliged to take their dust.

"By setting the pace for a frantic competitive consumption, our infinite gradations in wealth (with which gradations the plutocracy

[9] Walter Weyl: *The New Democracy* (New York, 1914), pp. 242-3.

is inevitably associated) increase the general social friction and produce an acute social irritation. . . . We are developing new types
of destitutes—the automobileless, the yachtless, the Newport-cottage-
less. The subtlest of luxuries become necessities, and their loss is
bitterly resented. The discontent of today reaches very high in
the social scale. . . .

"For this reason the plutocracy is charged with having ended our
old-time equality. . . . Our industrial development (of which the
trust is but one phase) has been towards a sharpening of the angle
of progression. Our eminences have become higher and more
dazzling; the goal has been raised and narrowed. Although lawyers,
doctors, engineers, architects, and professional men generally, make
larger salaries than ever before, the earning of one hundred thousand dollars a year by one lawyer impoverishes by comparison the
thousands of lawyers who scrape along on a thousand a year. The
widening of the competitive field has widened the variation and
has sharpened the contrast between success and failure, with resulting inequality and discontent."[1]

II. THE ALIENATION OF THE PROFESSIONALS

Whenever an important change takes place in modern society,
large sections of the intellectuals, the professional and opinion-
making classes, see the drift of events and throw their weight on
the side of what they feel is progress and reform. In few historical movements have these classes played a more striking role than
in Progressivism. While those intellectuals and professional men
who supported Progressive causes no doubt did so in part for
reasons that they shared with other members of the middle classes,
their view of things was also influenced by marked changes within
the professions themselves and by changes in their social position
brought about by the growing complexity of society and by the
status revolution.

In the previous era, during the industrial and political conflicts
of the 1870's and 1880's, the respectable opinion-making classes had
given almost unqualified support to the extreme conservative posi-

[1] Ibid., pp. 244-8.

tion on most issues. The Protestant ministry, for instance, was "a massive, almost unbroken front in its defense of the status quo."[2] Most college professors preached the great truths of *laissez faire* and the conservative apologetics of social Darwinism, and thundered away at labor unions and social reformers. Lawyers, except for a rare small-town spokesman of agrarian unrest or little business, were complacent. And while an occasional newspaper editor launched an occasional crusade, usually on a local issue, the press was almost as unruffled.

Beginning slowly in the 1890's and increasingly in the next two decades, members of these professions deserted the standpat conservatism of the post-Civil War era to join the main stream of liberal dissent and to give it both moral and intellectual leadership. The reasons for this reversal are complex. But if the professional groups changed their ideas and took on new loyalties, it was not in simple response to changes in the nature of the country's problems—indeed, in many ways the problems of American life were actually less acute after 1897—but rather because they had become disposed to see things they had previously ignored and to agitate themselves about things that had previously left them unconcerned. What interests me here is not the changed external condition of American society, but the inward social and psychological position of the professionals themselves that made so many of them become the advisers and the gadflies of reform movements. The alienation of the professionals was in fact a product of many developments, but among these the effects of the status revolution must be given an important place. Conditions varied from profession to profession, but all groups with claims to learning and skill shared a common sense of humiliation and common grievances against the plutocracy.

The contrast between the attitude of the clergy in the 1870's and that of the 1890's measures the change. When the hard times following the panic of 1873 resulted in widespread labor unrest, culminating in the railway strikes of 1877, the Protestant religious press was bloodthirsty in its reaction. The laborers were described as "wild beasts" and "reckless desperadoes," and some of the

---

[2] Henry F. May: *Protestant Churches and Industrial America* (New York, 1949), p. 91.

religious papers suggested that if they could not be clubbed into submission they should be mowed down with cannon and Gatling guns. During the social conflicts of the 1880's, ministers expressed an attitude only slightly less hysterical. By the 1890's, a liberal minority was beginning to express a far milder view of strikes, though the chief religious papers were still completely hostile, for instance, to the American Railway Union in the Pullman strike of 1894. By this time, however, a substantial reversal of opinion was under way, and the ideas of social Christianity and the social gospel had profoundly modified the outlook of many ministers in the major denominations. From 1895 through the Progressive era "the doctrines developed by the [early social-gospel] generation . . . increasingly dominated the most articulate sections of American Protestantism."[3]

The clergy were probably the most conspicuous losers from the status revolution. They not only lost ground in all the outward ways, as most middle-class elements did, but were also hard hit in their capacity as moral and intellectual leaders by the considerable secularization that took place in American society and intellectual life in the last three decades of the nineteenth century. On one hand, they were offended and at times antagonized by the attitudes of some of the rich men in their congregations.[4] On the other, they saw the churches losing the support of the working class on a large and ominous scale. Everywhere their judgments seemed to carry less weight. Religion itself seemed less important year by year, and even in their capacity as moral and intellectual leaders of the community the ministers now had to share a place with the scientists and the social scientists. In the pre-Civil War days, for example, they had had a prominent place in the control of higher education. Now they were being replaced on boards of trustees by businessmen, bankers, and lawyers,[5] and the newer, more

[3] Ibid., pp. 202-3.

[4] An interesting but by no means representative case was the controversy between W. S. Rainsford, rector of St. George's (Episcopal) Church in New York City, and one of his vestrymen, J. Pierpont Morgan. See Rainsford: *Story of a Varied Life* (Garden City, 1924), p. 281.

[5] In 1860, clergymen comprised 39 per cent of the governing boards of Earl McGrath's sample of private institutions; in 1930, 7 per cent. McGrath: "The Control of Higher Education in America," *Educational Record*, Vol. XVII (April 1936), pp. 259-72. During the Progressive era clergymen were also beginning to be replaced with laymen in the college and university presidencies.

secular universities that were being founded with the money of the great business lords brought with them social scientists whose word began to appropriate some of the authority that the clergy had once held. University learning, in many fields, carried with it the fresh and growing authority of evolutionary science, while the ministers seemed to be preaching nothing but old creeds.

The general decline in deference to the ministerial role was shown nowhere more clearly than in the failure of the lay governors of Protestant congregations to maintain the standard of living of their pastors under the complex conditions of urban life and the rising price level of the period after 1897. Not only were the clergy less regarded as molders of opinion, but they were expected to carry on the arduous work of their pastorates with means that were increasingly inadequate and to defer meekly to far more affluent vestrymen.[6]

In the light of this situation, it may not be unfair to attribute the turning of the clergy toward reform and social criticism not solely to their disinterested perception of social problems and their earnest desire to improve the world, but also to the fact that as men who were in their own way suffering from the incidence of the status revolution they were able to understand and sympathize with the problems of other disinherited groups. The increasingly vigorous interest in the social gospel, so clearly manifested by the clergy after 1890, was in many respects an attempt to restore through secular leadership some of the spiritual influence and authority and social prestige that clergymen had lost through the upheaval in the system of status and the secularization of society.

That the liberal clergy succeeded in restoring some of their prestige by making themselves a strong force in the Progressive ranks no student of the history of American social Christianity is likely to deny.[7] As practical participants and as ideologists and

---

[6] In 1918 a *Literary Digest* survey showed that only 1,671 of the 170,000 ministers in the United States paid taxes on incomes over $3,000. In 1920 a survey by the Interchurch World Movement found that the average annual pastoral income was $937. *Christian Advocate,* Vol. XCV (July 22, 1920), p. 985. Preachers were well aware that they had reached a point at which their wages were lower than those of many skilled workers, especially masons, plumbers, plasterers, and bricklayers. On preachers' salaries, see *Homiletic Review,* Vol. LXXXVI (December 1923), p. 437; Vol. LXXXVII (January 1924), p. 9.

[7] May, op. cit., chapter iv, "The Social Gospel and American Progressivism."

exhorters the clergy made themselves prominent, and a great deal of the influence of Progressivism as well as some of its facile optimism and naïveté may be charged to their place in its councils. Indeed, Progressivism can be considered from this standpoint as a phase in the history of the Protestant conscience, a latter-day Protestant revival. Liberal politics as well as liberal theology were both inherent in the response of religion to the secularization of society. No other major movement in American political history (unless one classifies abolitionism or prohibitionism as a major movement) had ever received so much clerical sanction. Jeffersonianism had taken the field against powerful clerical opposition; Jacksonianism had won its triumphs without benefit of clergy; but the new-model army of Progressivism had its full complement of chaplains.

The situation of the professors is in striking contrast to that of the clergy—and yet the academic man arrived by a different path at the same end as the cleric. While the clergy were being in a considerable measure dispossessed, the professors were rising. The challenge they made to the *status quo* around the turn of the century, especially in the social sciences, was a challenge offered by an advancing group, growing year by year in numbers, confidence, and professional standing. Modern students of social pyschology have suggested that certain social-psychological tensions are heightened both in social groups that are rising in the social scale and in those that are falling;[8] and this may explain why two groups

[8] Cf. Joseph Greenbaum and Leonard I. Pearlin: "Vertical Mobility and Prejudice," in Reinhard Bendix and Seymour M. Lipset, eds.: *Class, Status and Power* (Glencoe, Illinois, 1953), pp. 480-91; Bruno Bettelheim and Morris Janowitz: "Ethnic Tolerance: a Function of Personal and Social Control," *American Journal of Sociology,* Vol. IV (1949), pp. 137-45.

An amusing parallel to the professoriat is provided by the architects. Nothing could be clearer than that the standards and status of this profession had been much improved in the years before the turn of the century, yet we find one of its older members complaining in 1902 that when he was a boy "an architect was somebody. . . . He ranked with the judge, the leading lawyer, the eminent physician—several pegs higher in the social rack than the merely successful merchant or broker." F. W. Fitzpatrick: "The Architects," *Inland Architect,* Vol. XXXIX (June 1902), pp. 38-9. What could have been responsible for this false consciousness of a decline in the position of the profession but the fact that the rise of the architect and the development of urban business had brought him into intimate contact with a plutocracy that made him feel small? He was unhappy

with fortunes as varied as the professoriat and the clergy gave so much common and similar support to reform ideologies.

Unlike the clergy, academic men in America before 1870 had had no broad public influence, no professional traditions nor self-awareness, hardly even any very serious professional standards.[9] The sudden emergence of the modern university, however, transformed American scholarship during the last three decades of the century. Where there had been only a number of denominational colleges, there were now large universities with adequate libraries, laboratories, huge endowments, graduate schools, professional schools, and advancing salaries. The professoriat was growing immensely in numbers, improving in professional standards, gaining in compensation and security, and acquiring a measure of influence and prestige in and out of the classroom that their predecessors of the old college era would never have dreamed of. And yet there was a pervasive discontent. To overestimate the measure of radicalism in the academic community is a convention that has little truth. In the Progressive era the primary function of the academic community was still to rationalize, uphold, and conserve the existing order of things. But what was significant in that era was the presence of a large creative minority that set itself up as a sort of informal brain trust to the Progressive movement. To call the roll of the distinguished social scientists of the Progressive era is to read a list of men prominent in their criticism of vested interests or in their support for reform causes—John R. Commons, Richard T. Ely, E. R. A. Seligman, and Thorstein Veblen in economics, Charles A. Beard, Arthur F. Bentley and J. Allen Smith in political science, E. A. Ross and Lester Ward in sociology, John Dewey in philosophy, and (for all his formal conservatism) Roscoe Pound in law. The professors had their intimate experience with and resentments of the plutocracy— which illustrates Walter Weyl's apt remark that the benefactions

---

not because he had actually lost out but because the "reference group" by which he measured his position was a different one. There were, of course, elements of alienation from the clients based on professional considerations. See Fitzpatrick: "Architect's Responsibilities," ibid., Vol. L (October 1907), p. 41.

[9] Richard Hofstadter and Walter P. Metzger: *The Development of Academic Freedom in the United States* (New York, 1955), esp. chapters v, vi, ix.

of the millionaires aroused almost as much hostility as their evil works. Professors in America had always had the status of hired men, but they had never had enough professional pride to express anything more than a rare momentary protest against this condition. Now, even though their professional situation was improving, they found in themselves the resources to complain against their position;[1] not the least of their grievances was the fact that their professional affairs were under the control of the plutocracy, since boards of trustees were often composed of those very businessmen who in other areas of life were becoming suspect for their predatory and immoral lives. Further, academic men in the social sciences found themselves under pressure to trim their sails ideologically; and caste self-consciousness was heightened by a series of academic-freedom cases involving in some instances the more eminent members of the emerging social sciences—Richard T. Ely, Edward A. Ross, J. Allen Smith, and others. In 1915 this rising self-consciousness found expression in the formation of the American Association of University Professors.

If the professors had motives of their own for social resentment, the social scientists among them had special reason for a positive interest in the reform movements. The development of regulative and humane legislation required the skills of lawyers and economists, sociologists and political scientists, in the writing of laws and in the staffing of administrative and regulative bodies. Controversy over such issues created a new market for the books and magazine articles of the experts and engendered a new respect for their specialized knowledge. Reform brought with it the brain trust. In Wisconsin even before the turn of the century there was an intimate union between the La Follette regime and the state university at Madison that foreshadowed all later brain trusts. National recognition of the importance of the academic scholar

---

[1] Cf. the lament of John Dewey in 1902: "The old-fashioned college faculty was pretty sure to be a thoro-going democracy in its way. Its teachers were selected more often because of their marked individual traits than because of pure scholarship. Each stood his own and for his own." "Academic Freedom," *Education Review*, Vol. XXIII (January 1902), p. 13. This very idealization of the professional past was a product of the rise of the profession. For the falseness of this idealization, see Hofstadter and Metzger, op. cit., chapters v and vi, and *passim*.

came in 1918 under Woodrow Wilson, himself an ex-professor, when the President took with him as counselors to Paris that grand conclave of expert advisers from several fields of knowledge which was known to contemporaries as The Inquiry.

The legal profession, which stands in a more regular and intimate relation with American politics than any other profession or occupation, affords a good example of the changing position of the middle-class professional in the development of corporate society. The ambiguous situation of many lawyers, which often involved both profitable subservience to and personal alienation from corporate business, contributed significantly to the cast of Progressive thought and the recruitment of Progressive leaders. While many lawyers could participate in Progressive politics in the spirit of good counselors caring for their constituents, many also felt the impact of the common demand for reform as a response to changes in their own profession.

In the opening decades of the century the American legal profession was troubled by an internal crisis, a crisis in self-respect precipitated by the conflict between the image of legal practice inherited from an earlier age of more independent professionalism and the realities of modern commercial practice. Historically the American legal profession had had four outstanding characteristics. Where it was practiced at its best in the most settled communities, it had the position of a learned profession with its own standards of inquiry and criticism, its own body of ideas and ethics. A lawyer's reputation and fortune had been based upon courtroom advocacy, forensic skill, learning, and presence. It was, secondly, a professional group of exceptional public influence and power. Tocqueville's famous observation that in the absence of a fixed and venerable class of rich men the closest thing to an American aristocracy was to be found in the bench and bar may have been somewhat exaggerated, but it does justice to the mid-nineteenth-century position of this professional group—the nursery of most American statesmen and of the rank and file of practicing politicians. Thirdly, a sense of public responsibility had been present in the moral and intellectual traditions of the bar—a feeling embodied in the notion that the lawyer was not simply an agent of some litigant but also by nature an "officer of the court," a public servant. Finally, law had been, pre-eminently in the United States, one of the smoothest avenues along which a man who started with only moderate social advantages might, without capital, rise upward through the ranks to a position of wealth or power. Democratic access to the bar had been jealously protected—so much so that a peculiar notion of the "natural right" to practice law had developed and many professional leaders felt that the standards of admission to the profession had been set far too low.

At the turn of the century lawyers as a group were far less homogeneous than they had been fifty years before. The large, successful firms, which were beginning even then to be called "legal factories," were headed by the wealthy, influential, and normally very conservative minority of the profession that tended to be most conspicuous in the Bar Associations. In their firms were many talented young lawyers, serving their time as cheap labor. There was a second echelon of lawyers in small but well-established offices of the kind that flourished in smaller cities; lawyers of this sort, who were commonly attached to and often shared the outlook of new enterprisers or small businessmen, frequently staffed and conducted local politics. A third echelon, consisting for the most part of small partnerships or individual practitioners, usually carried on a catch-as-catch-can practice and eked out modest livings. As the situation of the independent practitioners deteriorated, they often drifted into ambulance-chasing and taking contingent fees. Much of the talk in Bar Associations about improving legal ethics represented the unsympathetic efforts of the richer lawyers with corporate connections to improve the reputation of the profession as a whole at the expense of their weaker colleagues.

A body of professional teachers of law, outside the ranks of practicing lawyers, was also developing as an independent force within the profession. The most effective type of legal education, then becoming dominant in the best university law schools, was Langdell's case method. It had been a part of Langdell's conception that the proper training for the teaching of law was not law practice but law study. As the part-time practicing lawyer became less conspicuous in legal education and the full-time *teaching* lawyer replaced him, the independent and professional consciousness of the guild was once again reinforced. Lawyers who were most attracted by the more intellectual and professional aspects of their field tended to go into teaching, just as those most interested in public service went into politics or administration. Young Charles Evans Hughes, for instance, temporarily deserted an extremely promising career in metropolitan practice for a relatively ill-paid job as a professor in Cornell's law school.[2] In the movement for broader conceptions of professional service, for new legal concepts and procedural reforms, for deeper professional responsibility, for criticism of the courts, the teaching side of the profession now became important. The teachers became the keepers of the professional conscience and helped implant a social view of their functions in the young men who graduated from good law schools.

With the rise of corporate industrialism and finance capitalism, the law, particularly in the urban centers where the most enviable prizes were to be had, was becoming a captive profession. Lawyers kept saying that the law had lost much of its distinctly professional character and had become a business. Exactly how much truth lay in their laments cannot be ascertained until we know more about the history of the profession; but whether or not their conclusions were founded upon a false sentimentalization of an earlier era, many lawyers were convinced that their profession had declined in its intellectual standards and in its moral and social position. Around the turn of the century, the professional talents of courtroom advocacy and brief-making were referred to again and again as "lost arts," as the occupation of the successful lawyer centered more and more upon counseling clients and offering business advice. General and versatile talent, less needed than in the old days, was replaced by specialized practice and the division of labor within law firms. The firms themselves grew larger; the process of concentration and combination in business, which limited profitable counseling to fewer and larger firms, engendered a like concentration in the law. Metropolitan law firms, as they grew larger and more profitable, moved into closer relationships with and became "house counsel" of the large investment houses, banks,

2 Merlo Pusey: *Charles Evans Hughes* (New York, 1951), Vol. I, pp. 95-104.

or industrial firms that provided them with most of their business. But the relation that was the source of profit brought with it a loss of independence to the great practitioners. The smaller independent practitioner was affected in another, still more serious way: much of his work was taken from him by real-estate, trust, and insurance companies, collection agencies, and banks, which took upon themselves larger and larger amounts of what had once been entirely legal business.[3] A speaker at the meeting of the Baltimore Bar Association in 1911 estimated that 70 per cent of the members of the profession were not making a suitable living. "Corporations doing our business are working . . . to our detriment," he said. "Slowly, but with persistence, the corporations are pushing the lawyer to the wall. They advertise, solicit, and by their corporate influence and wealth monopolize the legal field."[4]

That the dignity and professional independence of the bar had been greatly impaired became a commonplace among lawyers and well-informed laymen. "How often we hear," declared an eminent lawyer in an address before the Chicago Bar Association in 1904, "that the profession is commercialized; that the lawyer today does not enjoy the position and influence that belonged to the lawyer of seventy-five or a hundred years ago. . . ." He went on to deny—what many lawyers did not deny—that the alleged commercialization was serious; but he conceded that the lawyer had indeed suffered from what he called "the changed social and industrial conditions." These conditions, he observed, had "taken from the lawyer some of his eminence and influence in other than legal matters" and had also, for that matter, *in the same way and in no less degree affected the other learned professions, and indeed all educated or exceptional men.*"[5] Several years later another lawyer put it somewhat more sharply in an essay entitled "The Passing of the Legal Profession": "The lawyer's former place in society as an economical factor has been superseded by [the corporation]

[3] See Joseph Katz: *The American Legal Profession, 1890-1915,* unpublished M.A. thesis, Columbia University, 1953, for an illuminating discussion of trends in the profession during this period.

[4] "Corporate Monopoly in the Field of Law," 15 *Law Notes* (1911), p. 22.

[5] Lloyd W. Bowers: "The Lawyer Today," 38 *American Law Review* (1904), pp. 823, 829; italics added.

this artificial creature of his own genius, for whom he is now simply a clerk on a salary."[6]

Lord Bryce, in comparing the America of 1885 with the America of Tocqueville, had concluded that "the bar counts for less as a guiding and restraining power, tempering the crudity or haste of democracy by its attachment to rule and precedent, than it did." Shortly after the turn of the century he remarked that lawyers "are less than formerly the students of a particular kind of learning, the practitioners of a particular art. And they do not seem to be so much of a distinct professional class."[7] Commenting in 1905 on Bryce's observations, Louis D. Brandeis said that the lawyer no longer held as high a position with the people as he had held seventy-five or indeed fifty years before; but the reason, he asserted, was not lack of opportunity, but the failure to maintain an independent moral focus. "Instead of holding a position of independence, between the wealthy and the people, prepared to curb the excesses of either, able lawyers have, to a large extent, allowed themselves to become adjuncts of great corporations and have neglected the obligation to use their powers for the protection of the people. We hear much of the 'corporation lawyer,' and far too little of the 'people's lawyer.' "[8]

Thus internal conditions, as well as those outward events which

[6] George W. Bristol: "The Passing of the Legal Profession," 22 *Yale Law Journal* (1912-13), p. 590. For other discussions of this and similar issues, see George F. Shelton: "Law as a Business," 10 *Yale Law Journal* (1900), pp. 275-82; Robert Reat Platt: "The Decadence of Law as a Profession and Its Growth as a Business," 12 *Yale Law Journal* (1903), pp. 441-5; Newman W. Hoyles: "The Bar and Its Modern Development," 3 *Canadian Law Review* (1904), pp. 361-6; Henry Wynans Jessup: "The Professional Relations of the Lawyer to the Client, to the Court, and to the Community," 5 *Brief* (1904), pp. 145-68, 238-55, 335-45; Albert M. Kales: "The Economic Basis for a Society of Advocates in the City of Chicago," 9 *Illinois Law Review* (1915), pp. 478-88; Julius Henry Cohen: *The Law: Business or Profession?* (New York, 1916); John R. Dos Passos: *The American Lawyer* (New York, 1907); Willard Hurst: *The Growth of American Law: the Law Makers* (Boston, 1950), chapter xiii.

[7] Quoted by Louis D. Brandeis: *Business—a Profession* (Boston, 1927), pp. 333-4.

[8] Ibid., p. 337; cf. Woodrow Wilson: "The Lawyer and the Community," *North American Review*, Vol. CXCII (November 1910), pp. 604-22. Brandeis's interest in having the lawyers play a mediating role between social classes may be compared with the comments of Toqueville on this function of the profession: *Democracy in America*, Vol. I, chapter xvi.

any lawyer, as a citizen, could see, disposed a large portion of this politically decisive profession to understand the impulse toward change. That impecunious young or small-town lawyers or practitioners associated with small business, and academic teachers of law, should often have approached the problems of law and society from a standpoint critical of the great corporations is not too astonishing—though among these elements only one, the teacher, was consistently articulate. Somewhat more noteworthy is the occasional evidence of a mixed state of mind even among some of the outstanding corporation lawyers, for whom allegiance to the essentials of the *status quo* was qualified by a concern with its unremedied abuses and a feeling of irritation with its coarsest representatives. The top leaders of the law, in their strategic place as the source of indispensable policy advice to the captains of industry, probably enjoyed more wealth and as much power as lawyers had ever had. But their influence was of course no longer *independently* exercised; it was exerted through the corporation, the bank, the business leader. As A. A. Berle remarks, "responsible leadership in social development passed from the lawyer to the business man," and the principal function of the legal profession became that of "defending, legalizing, and maintaining this exploitative development."[9] The corporation lawyer lived in frequent association with businessmen who were oppressively richer, considerably less educated, and sometimes less scrupulous than himself. By professional tradition and training he saw things with much more disinterested eyes than they did; and although it was his business to serve and advise them, he sometimes recoiled. "About half the practice of a decent lawyer," Elihu Root once said, "consists in telling would-be clients that they are damned fools and should stop."[1] "No amount of professional employment by corporations," he wrote to a correspondent in 1898, "has blinded me to

9 A. A. Berle: "Modern Legal Profession," in *Encyclopedia of the Social Sciences.*

1 Willard Hurst, op. cit., p. 345; there are many complexities in lawyer-client relationships not dealt with here. On lawyer-client alienation, see David Riesman: "Some Observations on Law and Psychology," *University of Chicago Law Review,* Vol. XIX (Autumn 1951), pp. 33-4, and "Toward an Anthropological Science of Law and the Legal Profession," *American Journal of Sociology,* Vol. LVII (September 1951), pp. 130-1.

the political and social dangers which exist in their relations to government and public affairs. . . ."[2] Such men turned to public service with a sense of release. Root found that his work as Secretary of War under McKinley brought "a thousand new interests" into his life and that his practice seemed futile in comparison with his sense of accomplishment in Cabinet work.[3] Similarly, Henry L. Stimson told his Yale classmates at their twentieth reunion, in 1908, that he had never found the legal profession "thoroughly satisfactory . . . simply because the life of the ordinary New York lawyer is primarily and essentially devoted to the making of money —and not always successfully so. . . . It has always seemed to me, in the law from what I have seen of it, that wherever the public interest has come into conflict with private interests, private interest was more adequately represented than the public interest." After the last three years of his private practice, which were concerned with the affairs of "the larger corporations of New York," he reported that when he did turn to federal service as a United States attorney (his important early cases were prosecutions for rebating), his "first feeling was that I had gotten out of the dark places where I had been wandering all my life, and got out where I could see the stars and get my bearings once more. . . . There has been an ethical side of it which has been of more interest to me, and I have felt that I could get a good deal closer to the problems of life than I ever did before, and felt that the work was a good deal more worth while. And one always feels better when he feels that he is working in a good cause."[4]

It may be objected that the progressivism espoused by corporation lawyers on a moral holiday would be a rather conservative sort of thing. In fact it was, but this was not out of harmony with the general tone of the Progressive movement, especially in the Eastern states, where this kind of leadership played an important

[2] Hurst, op. cit., p. 369.

[3] Ibid., p. 369.

[4] Henry L. Stimson and McGeorge Bundy: *On Active Service in Peace and War* (New York, 1948), p. 17. Stimson's background provides an interesting insight into the moral atmosphere of the Mugwump type. His father, an old-family New Yorker, had been a banker and broker. After earning a modest fortune, he had quit business for the study and practice of medicine. He lived modestly and carried on his medical work in connection with philanthropic organizations. Ibid., p. xvii.

role. There Progressivism was a mild and judicious movement, whose goal was not a sharp change in the social structure, but rather the formation of a responsible elite, which was to take charge of the popular impulse toward change and direct it into moderate and, as they would have said, "constructive" channels— a leadership occupying, as Brandeis so aptly put it, "a position of independence between the wealthy and the people, prepared to curb the excesses of either."

III. FROM THE MUGWUMP TO THE PROGRESSIVE

What I have said thus far about the impact of the status revolution may help to explain the occurrence of the Progressive movement, but will not account for its location in time. A pertinent question remains to be answered: as the status revolution had been going on at least since the Civil War and was certainly well advanced by the 1890's, why did the really powerful outburst of protest and reform come only with the first fifteen years of the twentieth century? Why did our middle classes, after six years of civic anxieties and three years of acute and ominous depression, give Hanna and McKinley a strong vote of confidence in 1896? And then after this confidence seemed in fact to have been justified by the return of prosperity, when the nation's sense of security and power had been heightened by a quick victory in what John Hay called "our splendid little war," and when a mood of buoyant optimism had again become dominant, why should they have turned about and given ardent support to the forces that were raking American life with criticism?

First, it must be said that in some areas of American life those phenomena that we associate with the Progressive era were already much in evidence before 1900. In a limited and local way the Progressive movement had in fact begun around 1890. On the part of some business interests the movement for cheap transportation and against monopoly had already waxed strong enough to impel a reluctant Congress to pass the Interstate Commerce Act in 1887 and the Sherman Act in 1890.[5] Likewise the crusade for municipal

[5] The traditional emphasis on agrarian discontent has diverted attention from the pressure from business for such measures. See Lee Benson: *New York Merchants and Farmers in the Communications Revolution,* unpublished Ph.D. dissertation, Cornell University, 1952.

reform was well under way in the 1890's. A very large number of local organizations dedicated to good government and a variety of reforms had sprung into existence, and in some cities they had already achieved more than negligible changes.[6] Finally, the state legislatures had already begun to pass the sort of social legislation —regulation of hours and conditions of labor, for instance—that was later fostered more effectually by the Progressives.[7]

These were the timid beginnings of a movement that did not become nationwide until the years after 1901. One important thing that kept them from going further during the nineties was that the events of that decade frightened the middle classes so thoroughly that they did not dare dream of taking seriously ideas that seemed to involve a more fundamental challenge to established ways of doing things. The Progressive appeal was always directed very largely to people who felt that they did have something to lose. Populism, which was widely portrayed as "menacing socialism in the Western states," the Homestead and Pullman strikes with their violence and class bitterness, the march of Coxey's army, the disastrous slump in business activity, and the lengthening breadlines seemed like the beginnings of social revolution; and in the imagination of the timid bourgeois, Bryan, Altgeld, and Debs seemed like the Dantons, Robespierres, and Marats of the coming upheaval. Hence there was a disposition among the middle classes to put aside their own discontents and grievances until the time should come when it seemed safe to air them.[8]

More pertinent, perhaps, is the fact that the Progressive ferment was the work of the first generation that had been born and raised in the midst of the status revolution. In 1890 the governing genera-

[6] Clifford W. Patton: *The Battle for Municipal Reform* (Washington, 1940), chapter iv. William Howe Tolman: *Municipal Reform Movements in the United States* (New York, 1895) has a suggestive summary of over seventy such organizations.

[7] Legislation in this field before and after 1900 may be compared in Elizabeth Brandeis's treatment of the subject, John R. Commons, ed.: *History of Labor in the United States*, Vol. III (New York, 1935), pp. 399 ff. The chief fields that had been entered by state legislatures before 1900 were child labor, hours of women's labor, and employers' liability.

[8] There were, for instance, Eastern urban election districts, normally heavily Democratic, in which Bryan's support fell drastically in 1896 from its normal level both before and after.

tion still consisted of men born in the 1830's and 1840's, who through force of habit still looked upon events with the happier vision of the mid-nineteenth century. During the next twenty years the dominant new influence came from those who were still young enough in the nineties to have their thinking affected by the hard problems just emerging, problems for which the older generation, reared in the age of the great transcontinental settlement, had no precedents and no convincing answers. The crisis of the nineties was a searing experience. During the depression of 1893-7 it was clear that the country was being profoundly shaken, that men everywhere were beginning to envisage a turning-point in national development after which one could no longer live within the framework of the aspirations and expectations that had governed American life for the century past. Americans had grown up with the placid assumption that the development of their country was so much unlike what had happened elsewhere that the social conflicts troubling other countries could never become a major problem here. By the close of the century, however, younger Americans began to feel that it would be their fate to live in a world subject to all the familiar hazards of European industrialism. "A generation ago," said one of the characters in Henry Blake Fuller's *With the Procession* (1895), "we thought . . . that our pacific processes showed social science in its fullest development. But today we have all the elements possessed by the old world itself, and we must take whatever they develop, as the old world does. We have the full working apparatus finally, with all its resultant noise, waste, stenches, stains, dangers, explosions."[9]

The generation that went Progressive was the generation that came of age in the nineties. Contemporaries had often noticed how large a portion of the leaders at any Populist convention were the silver-haired veterans of old monetary reform crusades; Progressivism, however, passed into the hands of youth—William Allen White remembered them in his autobiography as the "hundreds of thousands of young men in their twenties, thirties, and early forties" whose "quickening sense of the inequities, injustices, and fundamental wrongs" of American society provided the motive

[9] Henry Blake Fuller: *With the Procession* (New York, 1895), p. 245.

power of reform.[1] The ascension of Theodore Roosevelt to the presidency, the youngest man ever to occupy the White House, was no more symbolic of the coming-of-age of a generation whose perspectives were sharply demarcated from those of their fathers and who felt the need of a new philosophy and a new politics.[2] T. R. himself had been thirty-two in 1890, Bryan only thirty, La Follette thirty-five, Wilson thirty-four. Most of the Progressive leaders, as well as the muckraking journalists who did so much to form Progressive opinion, were, at the opening of that crucial *fin de siècle* decade, in their early thirties, or perhaps younger, and hence only around forty when the Progressive era got under way.[3]

The Progressive leaders were the spiritual sons of the Mugwumps, but they were sons who dropped much of the ideological baggage of their parents. Where the Mugwumps had been committed to aristocracy, in spirit if not in their formal theories of government, the Progressives spoke of returning government to the people; and where the Mugwumps had clung desperately to liberal economics and the clichés of *laissez faire,* the Progressives were prepared to make use of state intervention wherever it suited their purposes. The Mugwumps had lacked a consistent and substantial support among the public at large. The Progressives had an almost rabidly enthusiastic following. The Mugwumps, except on sporadic occasions, were without allies among other sectors of the country. The Progressives had, on a substantial number of national issues, reliable allies in the very agrarian rebels for whom the Mugwumps had had nothing but contempt. In many ways the Mugwump type was refashioned into the Progressive by the needs and demands of its own followers. The circumstances that awakened the public and provided the Progressive leaders with large urban support are the subject of the next two chapters. But I may antici-

[1] White: *Autobiography,* p. 367.

[2] As a consequence of the sharp difference in the viewpoint of the generations, family conflicts around the turn of the century tended to take on an ideological coloring. For the treatment of this theme in the works of the most popular Progressive novelist, see Richard and Beatrice Hofstadter: "Winston Churchill: a Study in the Popular Novel," *American Quarterly,* Vol. II (Spring 1950), pp. 12-28.

[3] Cf. Mowry: "Compositely, the California progressive leader was a young man, often less than forty years old. . . . In 1910 the average age of ten of the most prominent Progressives was thirty-eight." *The California Progressives,* pp. 87, 313.

pate here at least one constellation of events that had vital importance, which centered on the reversal in the price trend. The unorganized middle class now found itself in the midst of a steady upward trend in the price cycle that was linked with the growing organization of American industry and labor. Prices, which began to go up after 1897, continued to go up steadily throughout the Progressive era, and indeed even more steeply during the war that followed. In the years between 1897 and 1913 the cost of living rose about 35 per cent. Those of us who have endured the inflation of the past fifteen years may smile at such a modest rise in prices; but the price movement of 1897-1913 was not accepted complacently by the generation that experienced it—particularly not by those who lacked the means to defend themselves against it by augmenting their incomes or by those who found the growth in their incomes largely eaten up by the higher lost of living. Just as the falling prices of the period 1865-96 had spurred agrarian discontents, so the rising prices of this era added to the strength of the Progressive discontents.

Rising prices in themselves were trouble enough; but the high cost of living took on added significance because it was associated in the public mind with two other unwelcome tendencies: the sudden development of a vigorous, if small, labor movement, and an extraordinary acceleration in the trustification of American industry. Both of these took place with alarming suddenness in the years from 1898 to 1904. John Moody singles out 1898 as "the year in which the modern trust-forming period really dates its beginning."[4] General business prosperity, rising prices, and an active securities market spurred on this burst of trust formation. Of the 318 trusts listed by Moody in 1904, 82, with a total capitalization of $1,196,700,000, had been organized before 1898. But 234, with a capitalization of over $6,000,000,000 had been organized in the years between January 1, 1898 and January 1, 1904.[5] Thus in this short period almost three quarters of the trusts and almost six sevenths of the capital in trusts had come into existence. It was

[4] John Moody: *The Truth about the Trusts* (New York, 1904), p. 486.
[5] Henry R. Seager and Charles A. Gulick, Jr.: *Trust and Corporation Problems* (New York, 1929), pp. 60-7.

during the last years of McKinley's administration and the early years of Roosevelt's that such frighteningly large organizations as the United States Steel Corporation, Standard Oil, Consolidated Tobacco, Amalgamated Copper, International Mercantile Marine Company, and the American Smelting and Refining Company were incorporated. Major local consolidations simultaneously took place in the fields of the telephone, telegraph, gas, traction, and electric power and light.

Far less spectacular, but none the less nettlesome to the middle-class mentality, were the developments in labor organization. During the long price decline of 1865-96 the real wages of labor had been advancing steadily at the average rate of 4 per cent a year.[6] But beginning with the upward trend of prices in 1897, these automatic gains not only ceased but were turned into losses, as unorganized workers found themselves unable to keep abreast of the steady advance in commodity prices. While real annual wages rose slightly during the period 1900-14, real hourly wages remained almost stationary.[7] Under the spur of rising prices and the favorable auspices of good business conditions, the young A.F. of L. seized its opportunity to organize skilled workers. By 1911 the membership of all American trade unions was five times what it had been in 1897; that of the A.F. of L. was almost seven times as large. Total union membership had grown from 447,000 to 2,382,000,[8] and, as in the case of industry, most of this new organization was concentrated in a sharp organizing drive between 1897 and 1904, a drive marked by a large increase in the number of strikes.

The price rise after 1897 was a part of a world-wide trend, connected with the discovery of new gold supplies and new refining processes. How much of it can properly be laid to the growing organization of industry is a moot point. What is most relevant here, however, is that the restive consuming public was not content to attribute the high cost of living to such impersonal causes. The

[6] Black: *Parity, Parity, Parity,* p. 74.

[7] Paul H. Douglas: *Real Wages in the United States, 1890-1926* (Boston, 1930), p. 111.

[8] Leo Wolman: *The Growth of Trade Unionism* (New York, 1924), p. 33. Figures for all unions are estimates; they exclude the membership of company unions.

average middle-class citizen felt the pinch in his pocketbook.[9] On
one side he saw the trusts mushrooming almost every day and
assumed that they had something to do with it. On the other he saw
an important segment of the working class organizing to protect
itself, and in so doing also contributing, presumably, a bit more
to higher prices. He saw himself as a member of a vast but unorganized and therefore helpless consuming public. He felt that he
understood very well what Woodrow Wilson meant when he declared that "The high cost of living is arranged by private understanding,"[1] and he became indignant. The movement against the
trusts took on new meaning and new power. To be sure, there had
always been antitrust sentiment, and the argument that the trusts
would squeeze the consumers after they had eliminated their competitors had been familiar for more than a generation. So long,
however, as prices were declining, this fear had lacked urgency.
Now that prices were rising, it became a dominant motif in American life.[2]

It was in the Progressive era that the urban consumer first stepped
forward as a serious and self-conscious factor in American social
politics. "We hear a great deal about the class-consciousness of
labor," wrote Walter Lippmann in 1914. "My own observation
is that in America today consumers'-consciousness is growing very
much faster."[3] Week after week the popular magazines ran articles
of protest or speculations about the causes of the difficulty, in which
the high protective tariff and the exactions of middlemen and dis-
tributors sometimes shared with the conspiratorial decisions of the
trust executives as objects of denunciation. While such men as
Theodore Roosevelt and E. A. Ross were decrying small families
among the "best" family stocks and warning about the dangers of

[9] Those portions of the middle classes that were on fixed salaries lost ground;
notable among them were postal employees, many clerical workers, government
employees, and ministers. Harold U. Faulkner: *The Decline of Laissez Faire* (New
York, 1951), p. 252.

[1] *The Public Papers of Woodrow Wilson,* Vol. II (New York, 1925), p. 462. For
a discussion of the cost-of-living issue by a contemporary, see Frederic C. Howe:
The High Cost of Living (New York, 1917).

[2] Cf. Walter Weyl, op. cit., p. 251: "The universality of the rise of prices has
begun to affect the consumer as though he were attacked by a million gnats. The
chief offense of the trust becomes its capacity to injure the consumer."

[3] Walter Lippmann: *Drift and Mastery* (New York, 1914), p. 73; cf. pp. 66-76.

"race suicide," women writers in the magazines were asserting that the high cost of rent, food, and fuel made smaller families inevitable.[4]

Of the actual organization of consumers there was very little, for consumers' co-operation was a form of action that had no traditional roots in the United States. In the absence of organizations, consumer discontent tended to focus upon political issues. This itself marked a considerable change. In 1897, when Louis D. Brandeis had testified against the Dingley tariff before the House Ways and Means Committee as a representative of the consumers, he was greeted with jeers.[5] By 1906, when the Pure Food and Drug Act was being debated, it had become clear that consumer interests counted for something at least in politics. By 1909, when the Republican insurgents were waging their battle against the Payne-Aldrich tariff bill in the name of "the American housewife," the sophistries of Senator Aldrich at the expense of the consumers ("Who are the consumers? Is there any class except a very limited one that consumes and does not produce?")[6] were altogether out of tune with popular feeling. The Payne-Aldrich tariff was as important as any other mistake in bringing about the debacle of the Taft administration.[7]

[4] Christine T. Herrick: "Concerning Race Suicide," *North American Review,* Vol. CLXXXIV (February 15, 1907), p. 407, argued that it was impossible to raise large families and maintain an adequate standard of living, especially for clerks, clergymen, newspapermen, and writers, on whom she felt the inflation worked the greatest hardship.

In 1907 the *Independent* published an article by a New York City woman who reported that she had been forced to go to work to supplement her husband's income. After submitting a detailed analysis of the family budget, she closed with this stark manifesto: "Now, gentlemen, You Who Rule Us, we are your 'wage slaves.' . . . You Who Rule Us may take our savings and go to Europe with them, or do sleight of hand tricks in insurance and railroading with them, so that we will not know where they are. You may raise our rent and the prices of our food steadily, as you have been doing for years back, without raising our wages to correspond. You can refuse us any certainty of work, wages, or provision for old age. We cannot help ourselves. But there is one thing you cannot do. You cannot ask me to breed food for your factories." "A Woman's Reason," *Independent* (April 4, 1904), pp. 780-4.

[5] Alpheus T. Mason: *Brandeis* (New York, 1946), pp. 91-2.

[6] Hechler, op. cit., p. 106.

[7] Cf. Henry F. Pringle: *The Life and Times of William Howard Taft,* (New York, 1939), Vol. I, chapter xxiv.

Vague as it was, consumer consciousness became a thing of much significance because it was the lowest common political denominator among classes of people who had little else to unite them on concrete issues. A focus for the common interests of all classes that had to concern themselves over family budgets, it cut across occupational and class lines, and did a great deal to dissolve the old nineteenth-century American habit of viewing political issues solely from the standpoint of the producer. In the discussion of many issues one now heard considerably less about their effects on the working class, the middle class, and the farmer, and a great deal more about "the plain people," "the common man," "the taxpayer," "the ultimate consumer," and "the man on the street." A token of a major shift in the American economy and American life from an absorbing concern with production to an equal concern with consumption as a sphere of life, this trend gave mass appeal and political force to many Progressive issues and provided the Progressive leaders with a broad avenue of access to the public.

HENRY PRINGLE

GREAT BIOGRAPHIES can be written only by men who are fundamentally in sympathy with the people they describe. Antagonism is apt to produce misunderstanding rather than insight and caricature rather than characterization. But respect for one's subject is hardly a guarantee of a true portrait. Indeed, more biographies have been distorted by unrestrained praise than by excessive criticism. Except for the professional "debunkers," authors are commonly led to a biographical subject by a feeling of sympathy. At the end of a period of difficult research, it is more natural to emphasize a man's constructive contribution than his limitations. Discovering a man's essential insignificance has never had the same appeal that comes from revealing his previously undetected importance.

The temptation toward favorable exaggeration is especially strong when the subject is a national hero whose patriotic achievements are a matter of historical record. The weight of the figure's generally accepted reputation lies heavily upon the biographer's mind. He may be intimidated into merely documenting his subject's virtues—or, on the other hand, he may be provoked into a search for faults which do not necessarily exist. Between these extremes is the independent judgment upon which all successful scholarship is based. When a natural rapport between author and subject takes the place of forced enthusiasm, insight is not limited to the description of praiseworthy episodes and approval is not made the equivalent of eulogy.

So conspicuous a figure as Theodore Roosevelt offers a difficult challenge to a biographer. Any new biography invites comparison with the many studies already produced, and even refreshes the memories of those of Roosevelt's contemporaries who are still alive. In attempting a fresh interpretation of Roosevelt's personality and an independent appraisal of his achievements, Henry Pringle had to compete in a crowded field.

The result of Pringle's labor is one of the best and most readable political biographies in American literature. Pringle's journalistic experience endowed him with a sense of the dramatic and the absurd which enabled him to make the Rooseveltian enthusiasms leap from the pages. The course of the President's political career was set down with incisive clarity. The Roosevelt who emerged in 1931 from Pringle's pen was essentially a conservative, whose genius it was to recognize that the most effective way to preserve the American system was to purge its abuses. Although he himself did not conceive the innovations with which his administration is credited, he not only publicized reform in an effective manner but also provided the political acumen necessary for the passage of legislation which the leaders of the Republican party generally opposed.

Although he recognizes Roosevelt's abilities and sympathizes with the measures which gave distinction to his presidency, Pringle's portrait is essentially less flattering than the traditional one. Others have emphasized the forceful man of action, but Pringle stresses the devious political maneuvers which Roosevelt was willing to engage in to gain a limited success. The line at which expediency turns to timidity and compromise to betrayal is difficult to draw, but Pringle locates it in such a way as to suggest Roosevelt's weakness rather than his strength. The exaggerated personal behavior which delighted a generation of Americans often becomes in Pringle's picture merely ridiculous.

Pringle is saved from caricature by a solid respect for facts and by his historical perspective. But if a complaint can be made about his work it would derive from the harshness of his criticism. Although Roosevelt may have been as absurd as the author occasionally makes him, the historical significance lies not in what his personality was intrinsically but in what his contemporaries thought of it. His immense popularity does not suggest that they thought him an object of ridicule. On a more serious level, it seems proper to suggest that the indirection and compromise which Roosevelt employed to achieve his purposes might as well be a subject of praise as of the condescension with which Pringle treats them. All successful Presidents have been guided as much by the thought of what was possible as by the principles of what was right.

But these are minor flaws in an outstanding work in American biography. Pringle has reproduced the excitement of the Roosevelt years and defined the essential significance of the period with a clarity which time cannot obscure. Few works are more successful in re-creating the past and making it meaningful to the present.

Malefactors of Great Wealth

I DO NOT like the social conditions at present," Roosevelt complained to Taft in March, 1906. "The dull, purblind folly of the very rich men; their greed and arrogance . . . and the corruption in business and politics, have tended to produce a very unhealthy condition of excitement and irritation in the popular mind, which shows itself in the great increase in the socialistic propaganda."[1]

The domestic policies of the President in his second term were largely a result of this apprehension. ". . . The growth of the socialistic

From *Theodore Roosevelt*, copyright, 1931, by Henry F. Pringle. Reprinted by permission of Harcourt, Brace & World, Inc.

[1] Roosevelt to Taft, Mar. 15, 1906.

party," he said, ". . . [is] far more ominous than any populist or similar movement in times past."[2] He was nervously anxious to cure the evils that existed; perhaps Roosevelt's genius lay in the fact that he realized their existence. The assets that gave him power were his gifts as a politician and his flair for arousing public interest. The liabilities that held him back were his sparsity of knowledge on economics, which approached ignorance, and his alliance with the Republican party. He had to work through such leaders as Speaker Cannon and Senators Aldrich, Allison, Foraker and Spooner. They were all of them conservatives, complacent and unafraid. They had no forebodings of the class war which, to Roosevelt, was an immediate possibility.

Always in the back of his mind, also, was the fear that if he went too far or too fast he faced the peril of business unrest. A panic might mean the defeat of his party. This was the worst of all possible dangers, for Roosevelt sincerely believed the Democratic party to be far less talented than his own in the science of government. It was permissible to appropriate theories and principles first conceived by Democracy, although wise to forget that this had been done. To subject the United States to the risk of Democratic rule was close to treason.

Roosevelt had often compromised, but hitherto his own political fortunes had been responsible. A higher expediency moved him in 1905 and 1906, and the first issue on which he surrendered was tariff revision. After the death of McKinley, Speaker Cannon wrote, the new President had been "full of revision," but had been handicapped by the fact that "economics was a subject of which he knew nothing."[3] On April 4, 1903, Roosevelt spoke on this troublesome issue at Minneapolis and his address, which avoided any positive recommendations, contained a phrase or two that had a familiar sound.[4] When David B. Hill, the New York State Democratic leader, pointed to a deadly parallel in sections of Roosevelt's speech and an address by Elihu Root in October of the previous year, the President confessed:

[2] Roosevelt to Charles F. Gettemy, Feb. 1, 1905.
[3] Busbey, L. W., *Op. cit.*, pp. 209-10.
[4] *Presidential Addresses*, Vol. I, pp. 294-302.

Alas! Hill has proved that I plagiarized from you. The worst of it is that I did, you know! I am now busy looking through your last tariff speech with the firm intention of plagiarizing from it, too.[5]

If he did, he took the precaution of changing the phraseology instead of again repeating Root word for word. But no suggestion for downward revision came from the White House. The tariff had become, as we have seen, a question "of expediency and not of morality." The 1904 campaign was approaching and, as Uncle Joe remarked, "no matter how much an improvement the new tariff may be, it almost always results in the party in power losing the following election."[6] Every one agreed that nothing should be done before or during the campaign, but after Roosevelt's victory even Root, who was hardly a radical on such matters, thought that the party could not successfully go before the voters in 1908 unless some action toward revision had been taken.[7]

Roosevelt, however, remained dubius. ". . . It is not an issue," he told James Ford Rhodes, "upon which I should have any business to break with my party."[8] His message to Congress on December 6, 1904, did not mention the tariff,[9] and all the rumors about changes to be made by the "friends of protection" came to nothing. It was Speaker Cannon whose influence predominated.

"Whence comes this so-called demand for tariff tinkering?" Uncle Joe demanded in November, 1905. "Aren't all our fellows happy?"[10]

In his annual message that year, Roosevelt said that there was "more need of stability than of the attempt to attain an ideal perfection in the methods of raising revenue"; his only reference was that Congress might well consider reciprocity agreements with other nations.[11] By 1906, Roosevelt had concentrated on other matters.

"I . . . believe that the tariff must be revised," he told Jacob Riis in April, ". . . but of course I am up to my ears in all the fighting that I can well undertake at the moment."[12]

[5] Roosevelt to Root, Apr. 23, 1903.
[6] Busbey, L. W., *Op. cit.,* p. 211.
[7] Root to Roosevelt, Nov. 16, 1904.
[8] Roosevelt to James Ford Rhodes, Nov. 29, 1904.
[9] *Works,* Vol. XV, pp. 215-66.
[10] Washington *Post,* Nov. 17, 1905.
[11] *Works,* Vol. XV, pp. 291-92.
[12] Roosevelt to Riis, Apr. 18, 1906.

Before long, however, he was wavering again; "If I were the legislative as well as the executive branch I would revise the tariff right away," he said in August. He doubted that anything could be done prior to the 1908 campaign. Then, he hoped, the Republican platform would "promise immediate action in the direction of a revision."[13]

Again, Uncle Joe forced his views upon the White House. From his home in Danville, Illinois, he wrote that a "promise now to revise would bring us defeat" in the approaching congressional election.[14] Roosevelt's apprehensions that, on the other hand, failure to make this pledge would result in a Democratic victory were not realized.[15] On February 28, 1907, the President admitted that the Speaker of the House had been right:

> For the last two years I have accepted your view as to just what we should say on the tariff—or rather as to what we should not say—and I am satisfied that it was wiser than the course I had intended to follow.[16]

By his agility, Roosevelt escaped the consequences of this vexatious issue. It had bothered him ever since, as a youth, he had abandoned his advocacy of free trade. He bequeathed it to Taft, who also learned, in 1910, that Uncle Joe had sound views, politically speaking, on tariff reform.

2

In selecting regulation of the railroads as an issue on which he was willing to fight, Roosevelt demonstrated his grasp of popular prejudices and popular limitations. "We *must* have legislation," he wrote in January, 1905.[17] "On the interstate commerce business, which I regard as a matter of principle," he told the editor of the Outlook "I shall fight."[18]

Hostility toward the railroads had been increasing since 1900. At first, probably until well past the middle of the century, the railroads basked in the sunlight of public approval. The new civilization they

13 Roosevelt to John A. Sleicher, Aug. 11, 1906.
14 Cannon to Roosevelt, Aug. 17, 1906.
15 Roosevelt to Root, Aug. 18, 1906.
16 Roosevelt to Cannon, Feb. 28, 1907.
17 Roosevelt to John J. McCook, Jan. 10, 1905.
18 Roosevelt to Lyman Abbott, Jan. 11, 1905.

were to bring had seemed very fair indeed and legislatures and municipal governments bid against each other in offering inducements to the promoters building the new lines. Heartache and bitter disappointment accompanied the expansion, of course, but they were limited to the villages and towns which had failed to make their offers attractive enough, which were left "off the railroad," and abandoned to the processes of industrial decay.[19] Even during the era of expansion in 1880 to 1890, however, it appeared that evils had arisen. The word "rebates" came to have a sinister meaning to the farmer and the workingman. It appeared that the railroads had been cutting their rates in order to strengthen powerful shippers at the expense of weaker competitors. A witness before the Cullom Committee, in 1886, explained:

> You can take hold of one man and build him up at the expense of the others, and the railroad will get the tonnage.
> Q. The effect is to build that one man up and destroy the others?
> A. Yes, sir; but it accomplished the purpose of the railroad better.[20]

Since there were certain to be numerous weak men who suffered at the expense of each beneficiary, this practice became a cause of denunciation. The abuse had an infinite variety of forms: allowances by the railroads for private freight cars owned by the shipper, free storage, free cartage, special carload rates. The railroads were soon as weary of rebating as the shipper who had been discriminated against. They learned, unfortunately too late, that an industry to which they had given rate concessions, and which had flourished, soon demanded further reductions. The Standard Oil Company, the worst of all the offenders, went so far as to insist that a surtax be added to the tariffs imposed on its competitors.[21] Out of these evils grew the Interstate Commerce Act of 1887, an ineffective measure. Insufferable delays followed the promulgation of its orders against secret rebates. By 1899, most of the old discriminations were being practiced again.[22] Moreover, the blessings that were to have followed the growth of the railroads had failed, in part, to materialize. For every farmer who "sold his pasture land" and took down, as innumerable rural ballads

[19] Sullivan, Mark, *Op. cit.*, Vol. II, pp. 260-61.
[20] Ripley, William Z., *Railroads; Rates and Regulation*, pp. 185-86.
[21] *Ibid.*, pp. 190-92.   [22] *Ibid.*, pp. 456-87.

told, his "gold-top walking cane," a dozen suffered from excessive freight rates.

In his first message to Congress, President Roosevelt pointed to defects in the act of 1887 and recommended changes that would bring fair rates to all shippers. But this was when Roosevelt was exceedingly cautious; he hurriedly added that the railroads were "the arteries through which the commercial life blood of this nation flows."[23] He left the details to Congress, and nothing was done. His action in bringing the Northern Securities suit in 1902, greatly as it distressed J. P. Morgan and the other railroad financiers, had nothing to do with the specific problem of rate regulation. By 1903, the railroads were again suffering from the demands made by large shippers, and they cordially endorsed amendments to the 1887 law sponsored by Senator Elkins of West Virginia. The important point to be remembered in judging Roosevelt's railroad regulation fight was that this bill did not relate to the main problem. It provided teeth for the original act against rebating, but it was not "even a preliminary skirmish" in the main struggle, for railroad rates that would be fair and reasonable.[24]

James J. Hill of the Great Northern made this clear in January, 1905. "Every railroad would be happy to have rebates abolished and the law against them enforced," he said. "Why does not the Interstate Commerce Commission prosecute . . . ? The law never has been enforced or anyone prosecuted." But government regulation of the tariffs was far different. "Competition," he insisted, forgetting that the Northern Securities Company would effectively have abolished this in the Northwest, "is the test which proves the survival of the fittest. . . . The laws of trade are as certain . . . as the laws of gravity."[25]

The impression has been given that President Roosevelt's message to Congress in December, 1904, recommended a law giving power to fix rates to the Interstate Commerce Commission.[26] This was not the case. His proposal was formulated in subsequent speeches or letters.

23 *Works,* Vol. XV, pp. 101-02.
24 Ripley, W. Z., *Op. cit.,* pp. 492-94.
25 New York *World,* Jan. 3, 1905.
26 Bishop, J. B., *Op. cit.,* Vol. I, p. 426; Ripley, W. Z., *Op. cit.,* p. 496.

In this case, he told Congress that "I am of the opinion that at present it would be undesirable, if it were not impracticable, finally to clothe the commission with general authority to fix rates." The commission should, however, have power, "where a given rate has been challenged and after full hearing found to be unreasonable . . . to decide what shall be a reasonable rate to take its place." This was to go into effect at once, subject to "judicial review."[27] The distinction is important because Roosevelt, after venturing somewhat further during one of the most bitter debates in congressional history, ultimately accepted as a compromise the Hepburn Bill providing virtually his first specifications. It was in the Union League Club address at Philadelphia on January 30, 1905, that the President called for control over rates by "some tribunal."[28] It was this speech, not the message to Congress, which aroused the respectables to apprehension concerning the President whom they had placed in the White House.

In May, 1904, President Butler of Columbia University warned Roosevelt that Governor Robert M. LaFollette of Wisconsin, whose reverberations against the corrupt alliance of business and politics had been echoing through the country, was a fanatic, and dangerous to Republican success in 1904.[29] "I agree with you . . . you read LaFollette exactly right," answered Roosevelt.[30] On June 5, 1908, he wrote to Lincoln Steffens:

> . . . you contend that Taft and I are good people of limited vision who fight against specific evils with no idea of fighting against a fundamental evil; whereas LaFollette is engaged in a fight against *the* "fundamental" evil. . . . LaFollette has been three years in the Senate. His "plan" . . . consists . . . of a string of platitudes and to adopt it wouldn't mean anything. . . . Like Tillman he has made great personal gains by what he has done as Senator, because he has advertised himself so that both he and Tillman are very popular in the Chautauquas where the people listen to them both, sometimes getting ideas that are right, more often getting ideas that are wrong, and on the whole not getting any ideas at all . . . and simply feeling the kind of

27 *Works,* Vol. XV, pp. 215-66.
28 *Presidential Addresses,* Vol. III, p. 222.
29 Butler to Roosevelt, May 19, 1904.
30 Roosevelt to Butler, May 21, 1904.

pleasurable excitement that they would at the sight of a two-headed calf, or of a trick performed on a spotted circus horse.

LaFollette, however, was not in the Senate when the rate fight started in 1905. His revelations in Wisconsin, combined with rising freight rates since 1900, caused the more liberal House of Representatives to pass a bill, the Townsend-Esch measure, by which the Interstate Commerce Commission could declare a freight or passenger rate unjust and could fix a substitute, which would go into effect in thirty days. Appeal could be taken to the courts.[31] This was Roosevelt's own bill, and its provisions were those of his message to Congress in 1904. No action was taken by the Senate, however, and as he drafted his message for 1905, the President approached, although he did not fully accept it, the principle of blanket rate-fixing. By November, he was sponsoring a bill that would grant authority to the Interstate Commerce Commission to specify maximum rates.

"The railroads have been crazy in their hostility," he wrote.[32]

". . . The most pressing need," the President said in his message on December 5, 1905, ". . . is the enactment into law of some scheme to secure to . . . the Government such supervision and regulation of . . . rates . . . as shall *summarily and effectively prevent the imposition of unjust or unreasonable rates.*" This was definitely more affirmative language than had appeared in his earlier messages. Although he again disavowed proposals to "initiate or originate rates generally," and said the control was to be limited to complaints brought on existing tariff schedules, the advance in Roosevelt's position was clear. ". . . The most important of all the powers I recommend," he said, was the right of the Interstate Commerce Commission or some similar body "to fix a maximum rate, which rate, after the lapse of a reasonable time, goes into full effect, subject to review by the courts." Even more indicative of the President's growing radicalism, perhaps, was his specification that there should be full publicity of all accounts of the common carriers. This caused additional apprehension in the breasts of the railroad men and their bankers, for they saw in it a threat of future action that could be defined only as sheer socialism. This was an impartial valuation of the railroad properties and the fixing of rates on the basis of a fair

[31] New York *World*, Feb. 10, 1905.
[32] Roosevelt to Ray Stannard Baker, Nov. 20, 1905.

return on capital invested. Roosevelt did not touch on this in his message but he added, characteristically:

"We desire to set up a moral standard."[33]

3

Both sides prepared for the battle during 1905. The railroads did so by flooding the newspapers of the country with propaganda. Their agents toured the country interviewing editors, and submitted reports as to the best method whereby these molders of public opinion could be influenced. One of them, who had confessed to anticorporation prejudices and who had revealed enthusiasm for Roosevelt, was a "weak and bibulous man. Tractable to R.R. suggestions." Such mythical organizations as the "Alabama Commercial and Industrial Association" held conventions for the adoption of resolutions denouncing rate regulation.[34]

Nor was Roosevelt idle. He made several addresses in the summer and fall of 1905 in which he emphasized the views he was to advance in his message to Congress. Incidents quite out of the President's hands brought public opinion to his side. Among them were the insurance scandals in New York during 1905, a general disruption of railway service due to bad management, and the revelation of rebating on the Santa Fe system. Then Roosevelt took action of his own to portray the corporations, in general, and the railroads, in particular, in dark tones before the country. The Elkins amendments, besides stiffening the penalties for rebating, provided that the shippers who received the concessions were culpable along with the railroads. On December 11, 1905, Attorney-General William H. Moody gave instructions that prosecutions were to be started by the Federal authorities of all jurisdictions.[35] Two days later, the Chicago grand jury returned an indictment which charged that the Chicago & Alton, and various of its officers, had given rebates to certain packing concerns.[36] Eight additional indictments were returned in Chicago on December 14, the Great Northern being among the latest defendants.[37] On December 15, a Federal grand jury in Kansas City

[33] *Works*, Vol. XV, pp. 274-80 (italics mine).
[34] Ripley, W. Z., *Op. cit.*, pp. 496-97.
[35] New York *Times*, Dec. 12, 1905.
[36] *Ibid.*, Dec. 14, 1905.   [37] *Ibid.*, Dec. 15, 1905.

accused such eminent Republican campaign contributors as the Armour Packing Company, Swift & Company, the Cudahy Packing Company, and Nelson Morris & Company, as well as the Burlington, the St. Paul, and the Chicago & Alton railroads, of having received or granted freight rebates.[38]

Further prejudice against the corporate interests had been aroused during the past three or four years by the muckrackers, those industrious and honest writers whose exposures sometimes disturbed Roosevelt as much as they disturbed the respectables. Miss Tarbell's history of the Standard Oil Company had started in 1902 in *McClure's Magazine*. Then had come the revelations by Lincoln Steffens and Ray Stannard Baker. Then, in February, 1906, Upton Sinclair published *The Jungle,* with its nauseating description of conditions under which meat was prepared.[39] On March 4, 1906, while the debate on railroad regulation was in progress in the Senate, the President made public the report of his Bureau of Corporations on the Standard Oil.

"The report shows," said Roosevelt, transmitting it to Congress, "that the Standard Oil Company has benefited enormously up almost to the present moment by secret rates. . . . This benefit amounts to at least three-quarters of a million a year." Roosevelt added that the Standard Oil was not the only corporation thus profiting. An investigation under way "as to shipments by the sugar trust over the trunk lines out of New York City tends to show that the sugar trust rarely, if ever, pays the lawful rate for transportation."[40]

It was to be a gaudy battle, this debate in which "liar," "unqualified falsehood," "betrayal," "surrender," and "chief cuckoos of the White House" were among the words and phrases scribbled by hurrying stenographers as they recorded for history the barrage of oratory. Roosevelt's bill was introduced by Representative Peter Hepburn of Iowa on January 4, 1906, and provided substantially his plan for railroad regulation contained in his message in December.[41] It was promptly passed by the House by the large majority of 346 to 7.[42]

[38] *Ibid.,* Dec. 16, 1905.
[39] Sullivan, Mark, *Op. cit.,* Vol. III, pp. 84-86.
[40] *Presidential Addresses,* Vol. V, pp. 742-43.
[41] New York *Times,* Jan. 5, 1906.
[42] Washington *Star,* Feb. 8, 1906.

Opposition so strong that defeat of the Hepburn Bill seemed probable was at once apparent in the Senate. On February 12, 1906, Senator Lodge made a long, scholarly address in which he said that more stringent penalties against rebating were doubtless needed as well as publicity for railroad earnings. But freight rates, on the whole, were not excessive.[43] This defiance on the part of Roosevelt's closest friend naturally started rumors of a break in the harmony that had lasted for so many years. But the President, in a letter to Lyman Abbott, conceded Lodge's sincerity.[44] It was not the only desertion; Senator Knox of Pennsylvania opposed the measure also. On February 18, 1906, he introduced an amendment providing for liberal court review of decisions in rate cases.[45]

The leaders of the opposition were Senator Aldrich, the Republican party whip, Foraker, and Elkins. The first of these, a son-in-law of John D. Rockefeller, was a dominating influence in the Senate. Elkins, the railroad Senator at whose suggestion the original Act of 1887 had been amended in 1903, was chairmen of the Senate Committee on Interstate Commerce. It was Aldrich and Elkins, apparently, who evolved what appeared to be an exceedingly clever scheme to embarrass Roosevelt. First, Elkins declined to sponsor the bill, although as the Republican chairman of a Senate committee this would be the usual course in relation to an administration measure. Then Aldrich, who also was a member of the Interstate Commerce Committee, secured adoption of a resolution that placed Senator Tillman of South Carolina, the famous "Pitchfork Ben" Tillman, in charge of Roosevelt's bill.[46] This was on February 23.[47]

Tillman, in addition to being a Democrat, was one of the Senators most disliked by Roosevelt. On February 24, 1902, the President had publicly withdrawn an invitation to dinner at the White House, where Prince Henry of Germany was guest of honor, because the South Carolinian had engaged in a brawl on the floor of the Senate.[48] A year later, referring to the Booker T. Washington incident, Tillman said that he never expected to go to the White House "while

[43] *Congressional Record*, Fifty-ninth Congress, pp. 2414-23.
[44] Lodge, H. C., *Op. cit.*, Vol. II, pp. 212-13.
[45] New York *Times*, Feb. 19, 1906.
[46] Sullivan, Mark, *Op. cit.*, Vol. III, pp. 228-29.
[47] New York *Commercial*, Feb. 24, 1906.
[48] New York *Tribune*, Feb. 25, 1902.

Roosevelt occupies it. . . . I do not blame any Southern man for opposing the practice of social equality, that is, if he is a white man."[49]

"I regarded the action as simply childish,"[50] Roosevelt said, on the Aldrich-Elkins maneuver, but it seriously jeopardized hope of success. Tillman was an ardent supporter of Roosevelt's rate bill, but how could he confer with the President? How could the President summon, at the peril of rebuke, the leader of the opposition? He went so far as to intimate that he believed Mr. Tillman to be a great and good man, after all. It was said that the White House latchstring had been hung out for his particular benefit.[51]

The final debate in the Senate was whether rates were to be regulated by an extension of the executive branch or by the judiciary. It is not difficult to understand why Roosevelt energetically supported the former theory, but it was on this point that he compromised, a compromise that brought heated charges of falsehood and bad faith. Late in March a solution was offered for the awkward situation of having a Democrat, who was also personally antagonistic to Roosevelt, in charge of the President's bill. A personal conference was not possible, but former Senator William E. Chandler of New Hampshire, holding a lame-duck appointive post at the capital, could serve as intermediary. On March 31, 1906, the President requested Chandler to call at the White House. An amusing, almost an idiotic, series of visits followed. Chandler hurried from the White House to the office of Pitchfork Ben and quoted Roosevelt as saying that Senators Knox, Spooner, and Foraker were attempting to defeat the bill. On April 1, Tillman shared this information with his colleague, Senator Joseph W. Bailey of Texas, and then Chandler brought word from the White House that there should be no difficulty about an agreement on the Hepburn amendments. The liaison activities continued until April 15, when Chandler, Bailey, and Tillman had a conference with Moody, Roosevelt's Attorney-General. The result of this was the drafting of an amendment that gave to the courts limited powers in passing on the rates fixed by the Interstate Commerce Commission.

Such, at least, was the story told by Senator Tillman when he

[49] Memphis *News*, Jan. 24, 1903.
[50] *Autobiography*, p. 435.
[51] Sullivan, Mark, *Op. cit.*, Vol. III, p. 233.

spoke in high indignation on May 12, 1906, and charged the President with breaking faith.[52] Meanwhile, as Roosevelt's letters prove and as soon became evident, the President had been negotiating with the conservative group. On April 12, he had written to Senator Allison of Iowa that he opposed an amendment providing interference with the commission by the injunction method. On the following day, he wrote that he was not certain that the Constitution would permit such an amendment because it limited the power of the courts.[53] On May 5, he announced that he would accept—not the Tillman amendment drafted by his own Attorney-General—but an amendment written by Senator Allison. It permitted the rates to be set aside by injunction proceedings and it represented victory, of a sort, for the railroad Senators.[54]

Thereupon Tillman exploded in the Senate that Roosevelt had made derogatory remarks regarding members of his own party. When the South Carolinian finished, Cabot Lodge presented a message from the President who, said the Massachusetts Senator, had declared the accusation "a deliberate and unqualified falsehood."[55] The quarrel, as Roosevelt's usually did, became even more violent before it ended. Articles appeared in the Chicago *Tribune* and the New York *Tribune* in which it was said that the President had been forced to desert Tillman because of the defection of his colleague, Senator Bailey. Undoubtedly these articles were inspired by the White House. They were written, said Bailey in the speech in which he, in turn, defended himself, by correspondents who were the "two chief cuckoos" of the administration. The statement that he had abandoned Tillman was "an unqualified, a deliberate and malicious lie."[56] Five years later President Taft, talking to Archie Butt, recalled that Roosevelt had occasionally "left his old friends," but soon returned to the fold:

. . . when he would get into hot water, he would send for the conservative members of the Cabinet and depend upon us to get him out of it. How well I remember the time he was pressing his rate bill.[57]

[52] *Congressional Record*, Fifty-ninth Congress, p. 6775.
[53] Roosevelt to John D. Kernan, Apr. 13, 1907.
[54] New York *Tribune*, May 6, 1906.   [55] Washington *Star*, May 13, 1906.
[56] Sullivan, Mark, *Op. cit.*, Vol. III, pp. 267-70; Chicago *Tribune*, May 15, 1906;
New York *Tribune*, May 16, 1906.
[57] Butt, Archie, *Op. cit.*, Vol. II, p. 346.

In all probability, despite his denials, Roosevelt had used derogatory terms in talking with Chandler about the opponents of his bill. It was his invariable custom to do so. "It's only *a* railroad law you want; not to cut the railroads out of the government," accused Lincoln Steffens, and to this Roosevelt agreed.[58] Such was his policy. Such, as he saw it, was the path of progress.

For all its defects, the Hepburn Act of 1906 was a step forward and without Roosevelt the Senate would never have passed the bill, as it did on March 18, 1906, by a vote of 71 to 3.[59] The Interstate Commerce Commission now had jurisdiction over pipe lines, express and Pullman operation, refrigeration, storage, and all the other aspects covered by the general term, transportation. The rate-making powers of the commission had been strengthened, although the courts were given more jurisdiction than Roosevelt desired. For violation of an order by the commission a penalty of $5,000 a day could be enforced. Prison penalties were also provided, but the clause requiring publicity of accounts was probably as important as any other. Honest accounting, now obligatory because the Government could examine the books of the railroads just as it could investigate the books of national banks, made for honesty of tariffs.[60]

But the plea of LaFollette, that fair rates could not possibly be determined unless the property of the carriers had first been evaluated,[61] had no effect for a good many years to come; not until Aldrich and Spooner and Allison and Lodge had seen their party wrecked by the upheaval of 1912. On May 8, 1907, Roosevelt confessed in a letter to Beveridge of Indiana that "events have moved so fast in the valuation business that I think it is impossible to avoid taking a conservative ground in its favor." On May 30, at Indianapolis, the President said that the Interstate Commerce Commission should undertake valuation of the roads, but he urged this in the name of "real . . . conservatism." He said that it would guard the carriers against "inadequate and unjust rates."[62] In his final message to Congress of December, 1908, Roosevelt called for "complete control over the issue of securities as well as over the raising or lowering of

58 Steffens, Lincoln, *Op. cit.,* Vol. II, p. 514.
59 Washington *Post,* May 18, 1906.
60 Ripley, W. Z., *Op. cit.,* pp. 499-508; 515-19.
61 New York *Press,* Apr. 20, 1906.
62 *Presidential Addresses,* Vol. VI, pp. 1249-56.

rates."[63] But he was soon to leave the White House. His political influence was ebbing.

4

They were busy years. The Russo-Japanese War, the Algeciras Conference, the possible menace of Japan, railroad regulation, the tariff: all these problems, technical and involved as they were, did not occupy fully the energies of the extraordinary personality in the White House. He had been attempting to view his country as a whole when he told Taft that "I do not like social conditions at present."[64] The very fact that Roosevelt groped for remedies that would benefit every one made the solution almost impossible. He said to Sir George Trevelyan that the corporations had to be controlled "without paralyzing the energies of the business community," while "tyranny on the part of the labor unions" had to be prevented and, at the same time, encouragement offered to "every proper effort made by the wage-workers to better themselves by combinations."[65]

The victory of the Government in the Northern Securities case had made valid again the provisions, whatever they may have been worth, of the Sherman antitrust law. In Roosevelt's mind this was not adequate protection against corporate power and on this, as much as on any issue, he worried his advisers. On December 24, 1904, as Roosevelt gave consideration to his trust-control program, Elihu Root begged him not to be precipitate regarding a proposal for Federal licensing of corporations. "It was Bryan's," he wrote, "and I think involves evils far greater than its benefits."

Roosevelt's corporation policy did not differ materially from his views as governor of New York. The remedy, he felt, lay in publicity of earnings and capitalization. At Chautauqua, New York, on August 11, 1905, the President said that certain of the large industrial combinations "by secret methods and . . . protracted litigation" sought to defeat the laws supposed to control them. He opposed "drastic action," but this might come "if . . . they foster the popular feeling which calls for such drastic action":

I believe that all corporations engaged in interstate commerce should

63 *Works,* Vol. XV, p. 491.
64 Roosevelt to Taft, Mar. 15, 1906.
65 Roosevelt to Sir George Trevelyan, Mar. 9, 1905.

be under the supervision of the national Government. . . . It may be that we shall . . . require all corporations . . . to produce proof . . . that they are not parties to . . . any violation of the anti-trust law and that . . . [they] shall agree, with a penalty of forfeiture of their right to engage in such commerce, to furnish any evidence of any kind as to their trade between the States whenever so required.[66]

Again, it is necessary to point to Roosevelt's fundamental belief, that the Federal Government was sovereign. In his message to Congress in December, 1905, he said that the corporations engaged in interstate business were "subjects without a sovereign," and that it might be essential to amend the Constitution to provide adequate control.[67] A year later he mentioned a national license law as a possible solution.[68] In 1907, he definitely advocated such a statute.

"This is not advocating centralization," he said, "it is merely looking facts in the face."[69]

But Roosevelt was again ahead of his time and it was impossible, even for him, to engage in battles comparable to the one on railroad rates on all these issues. Partly because the Government was handicapped by the law and thwarted by clever attorneys employed by the trusts, partly because Roosevelt was so busy on other matters, rather little was accomplished in actual prosecutions or in the dissolution of illegal combinations. Suits were instituted against the tobacco and packing trusts. The Interstate Commerce Commission put E. H. Harriman on the stand and a degree of public excitement was aroused by the unfortunately arrogant testimony of that railroad magnate. The New York Central Railroad was fined for rebates given to the American Sugar Refining Company. But it was not until the Taft Administration that the Standard Oil Company and the American Tobacco Company were ordered to dissolve. It was not until Woodrow Wilson came into power that the Clayton Act, an extension of trust control, became law.[70] Roosevelt's title as "Trust Buster" was, as he would have been the first to insist, an exaggeration. He started only twenty-five proceedings leading to indictments under the Sherman Act, while Taft began forty-five.[71] The signifi-

---

66 *Presidential Addresses*, Vol. IV, pp. 451-52.
67 Works, Vol. XV, pp. 272-74.
68 *Ibid.*, p. 364.   69 *Ibid.*, p. 415.
70 Beard and Beard, *Op. cit.*, Vol. II, p. 572.
71 *Ibid.*, p. 569.

cance of Roosevelt's corporation activities lay in what he said rather than what he did. Even the spectacular fine of $29,000,000 assessed by Federal Judge Kenesaw Mountain Landis on April 13, 1907, against the Standard Oil Company of Indiana[72] came to nothing. The higher courts set aside the penalty, and the Standard Oil Company paid nothing.

The fact is that Roosevelt would progress to a certain point in his program to ward off socialism and unrest, and then make energetic efforts to appease the right wing. Even the muckrakers, who had brought into the light so many of the evils on which Roosevelt acted, were to learn, in pained surprise, that he endorsed them with distinct reservations. In 1901, although he said nothing publicly, he expressed doubt that the indictment of Frank Norris against the Southern Pacific Railroad in California was accurate.[73] On March 17, 1906, when Speaker Cannon was the host at a dinner to the Gridiron Club, the President deprecated, quoting from *Pilgrim's Progress,* the man who fixed his mind only on things that were vile and debasing, on filth alone.[74] A few weeks later, he amplified his remarks, saying that he emphatically approved proper exposure of wrongdoing, but not sensationalism for its own sake.[75]

But one muckraker—the term was original with Roosevelt—inspired the President to another brisk fight with Congress. On March 9, 1906, Roosevelt wrote Upton Sinclair, whose *The Jungle* had recently been published, that "I shall read it with interest," although Commissioner of Corporations Garfield believed the conclusions regarding the Chicago packing houses "too pessimistic." At the same time he directed Secretary of Agriculture Wilson to appoint an investigator who would confer with Sinclair and begin an inquiry.[76] Two examiners were appointed, James Bronson Reynolds and Charles P. Neill, and their disclosures moved the President to horrified action. Beveridge of Indiana introduced a bill permitting effective inspection of the packing houses on May 22, 1906, and it passed the Senate three days later. Then it slumbered in the lower house.[77]

[72] New York *Times,* Apr. 14, 1907.
[73] Wister, Owen, *Op. cit.,* p. 83.
[74] Washington *Star,* Mar. 18, 1906.
[75] *Presidential Addresses,* Vol. V, pp. 712-20.
[76] Roosevelt to James Wilson, Mar. 12, 1906.
[77] Sullivan, Mark, *Op. cit.,* Vol. II, p. 538.

". . . Really, Mr. Sinclair, you *must* keep your head,"[78] begged Roosevelt while the author of *The Jungle* insisted upon immediate action and while press agents for the packers were insinuating that Roosevelt's animus was due to his failure as a cattleman in Medora in 1886.[79] The packers, who once had so gladly supported Roosevelt for office, continued to exert pressure against passage of the bill, and he struck at them on June 4, 1906, by making public a report compiled by Reynolds and Neill. It was a loathsome document. It told of filth, disease, and gross carelessness in the packing houses. Tuberculosis was prevalent among the workers. Old bits of rope had been discovered in chopped meat about to be placed in cans. The buildings in which the work was done were dark, damp, and badly ventilated.[80]

The folly of the packers was endless. Thomas E. Wilson, of the Nelson Morris Company, said that his plant was "as clean as any kitchen." He was confident that Reynolds and Neill, being men "of fine sensibilities," had been shocked into gross inaccuracies by the mere sight of blood.[81] Then the President let it be known that this was only a "preliminary report," and that additional facts might be published unless the packers told their agents in the House that the bill should be passed.[82] At the same time, because accounts of the Neill-Reynolds reports had been cabled abroad, it appeared probable that the export trade in American meat would suffer.[83] This economic argument, added to Roosevelt's threats of additional exposures, brought passage of the inspection bill on July 1, 1906.

The reform is illustrative of the degree to which the innovations for which Roosevelt received credit were suggested by others. Another instance was the battle for pure food. In 1883, Dr. Harvey Washington Wiley had been appointed chief chemist of the Department of Agriculture. By 1902 his "poison squad" of twelve young assistants was permitting experiments in the effect of adulterated foods and drugs to be made upon it.[84] Unfortunately, Dr. Wiley and

78 Roosevelt to Sinclair, Apr. 10, 1906.
79 New York *Tribune,* June 6, 1906.
80 *Presidential Addresses*, Vol. V, pp. 772-75.
81 New York *Tribune,* June 7, 1906.
82 Sullivan, Mark, *Op. cit.*, Vol. II, p. 540.
83 New York *Tribune,* June 7, 8, 1906.
84 Wiley, Harvey W., *Harvey W. Wiley, an Autobiography*, pp. 198-220.

the President irritated each other. Early in the administration, the pure-food enthusiast had been so foolish as to criticize Roosevelt's proposal for reduction of Cuban sugar tariffs and had very nearly been dismissed from the service.[85] He later felt that Roosevelt did not accord sufficiently firm support to those who enforced the law and that too much credit for its passage had been given to the White House.[86] On his part, the President believed that Dr. Wiley was a fanatic; but "I have such confidence in his integrity and zeal that I am anxious to back him up to the limit of my power wherever I can be sure that doing so won't do damage instead of good."[87]

A degree of justice undoubtedly lay in the position of each. Roosevelt was not bashful in taking credit to which his title was clouded. Dr. Wiley was probably overeager. Certainly the Pure Food Bill would not have been passed on June 23, 1906, had not Roosevelt recommended some such law in December, 1905.[88] The outcry over the Neill-Reynolds report, which did not concern the Pure Food Bill directly, was the final influence toward its passage.

Another aspect of his program for the suppression of socialistic unrest remains: protection for labor against the excessive use of the injunction. If the attitude of the New York *Sun* toward labor . . . becomes the attitude of the Republican Party," he told Knox just after Election Day in 1904, "we shall some day go down before a radical and extreme Democracy with a crash, which will be disastrous to the nation. We must not only do justice, but be able to show that we are doing justice."[89]

In 1905, in addition to suggesting employers' liability for the District of Columbia and an investigation of child labor, Roosevelt raised the question of limiting the power of the courts in defeating the aspirations of labor by means of the injunction.[90] In May, 1906, he said that he opposed having "any operation of the law turn into an engine of oppression against the wage worker."[91] In his message to Congress, the President pointed to "grave abuses" possible because of this weapon in the hands of capital.[92]

[85] *Ibid.*, p. 223.   [86] *Ibid.*, pp. 221, 231.
[87] Roosevelt to Peter Force, Jan. 7, 1909.
[88] *Works*, Vol. XV, p. 326.
[89] Roosevelt to Knox, Nov. 10, 1904.   [90] *Works*, Vol. XV, p. 284.
[91] Roosevelt to William H. Moody, May 12, 1906.
[92] *Works*, Vol. XV, p. 347.

5

Roosevelt's passionate interest in the national forests, in reclamation of arid Western lands by irrigation, in conservation of water power and other natural resources, may well be considered as part of his campaign against the malefactors of great wealth. There can be little controversy regarding Roosevelt's contribution to the cause of conservation, although he was faintly jealous of credit given to Senator Francis G. Newlands of Nevada, a Democrat and therefore a dubious source of constructive work for good.[93] It is probable, too, that Roosevelt minimized the contribution of Senator Hanna, who had first become interested in irrigation in 1897.[94] On all these important matters, however, there is credit enough for all. In a letter written on June 8, 1902, Roosevelt had appealed to Speaker Cannon —"I do not believe I have ever before written to an individual legislator in favor of an original bill"—not to oppose the Newlands Act for irrigation in the West.

Roosevelt's interest never slackened. As governor of New York he had emphasized the necessity for forest reserves.[95] As President, it was a subject dwelt upon at length in all of his annual messages to Congress. The preservation of the forests and the irrigation of desert lands were part of the heritage of Roosevelt's own years in the West. His opposition to exploitation of water power was based on the conception, novel in that day, that this was the property of the people and should redound to their benefit. In 1903, when the Fifty-seventh Congress passed a bill awarding to one N. J. Thompson the right to build a dam and construct a power station at Muscle Shoals, Alabama—thus ancient are the issues of American politics—the President vetoed the bill:

> . . . the ultimate effect of granting privileges of this kind . . . should be considered in a comprehensive way and . . . a general policy appropriate to the new conditions caused by the advance in electrical science should be adopted under which these valuable rights will not be practically given away, but will be disposed of with full competition in such a way as will best substantiate the public interest.[96]

93 Roosevelt to James Wilson, July 2, 1902.
94 Beer, Thomas, *Op. cit.*, p. 257.
95 *Works*, Vol. XV, pp. 21-22.
96 Toledo *Blade*, Mar. 4, 1903.

Roosevelt told the story of conservation, competently and without the distortions that sometimes marked his writings, in his autobiography. The influence of Gifford Pinchot, which started when Roosevelt was governor, was the dominant one in the great and significant changes whereby the forests were placed under adequate supervision. The Newlands Act, passed in 1902 with Roosevelt's energetic assistance, provided within four years the irrigation of some 3,000,000 acres, and engineering projects nearly as great as the Panama Canal.[97] In the opinion of Senator LaFollette, who had been one of the allies in the work, conservation would stand as Roosevelt's greatest work. He had, said the Wisconsin Senator, started a world movement "for staying territorial waste and saving for the human race the things . . . on which alone a peaceful, progressive and happy race life can be founded."[98]

[97] Muzzey, D. S., *Op. cit.*, Vol. II, p. 398.
[98] *Autobiography*, pp. 393-422.

ARTHUR LINK

〰〰

MUCH OF THE recent analysis of the Progressive movement in the federal government has used as its point of departure the differences between Theodore Roosevelt and Woodrow Wilson. These presidents are cited for representing—and nourishing —the two main strands of Progressive political thought.

Wilson's "New Freedom" is interpreted as reflecting the traditional antimonopoly ingredient, the Jeffersonian wish to free the individual. The chief purpose of government, and the focus of reform, was to do away with special privilege and the concentration of power. This old-fashioned program is contrasted with Roosevelt's "New Nationalism," which came to terms with great economic organizations and strove to regulate rather than destroy them. While Roosevelt himself is usually considered to have been limited in his reform objectives, others of his day envisioned extending the use of government to the sphere of social welfare legislation.

Historians have responded in a variety of ways to this alleged duality. Hofstadter emphasizes the backward-looking character of the Progressive movement as a whole, although he acknowledges the distinction. William Allen White, one of Theodore Roosevelt's staunchest supporters, described the two approaches as a case of Tweedledum and Tweedledee. Arthur Schlesinger, Jr. finds in the "New Nationalism" and the "New Freedom" the ideological origins of the first and second phases of the New Deal of the 1930's.

Two important books by Arthur Link examine the relevant

evidence in considerable detail. *Wilson, the New Freedom* (1956) is the second volume of a major biography; *Woodrow Wilson and the Progressive Era, 1910-1917* (1954) has a somewhat more general perspective. Link's basic thesis is that Wilson began his administration thoroughly committed to the "New Freedom" but that he changed rather abruptly into a "New Nationalist" in 1916. The first period saw the enactment of the Underwood Tariff, a standard attack on special privilege, and the passing of the Federal Reserve Act, which advanced Progressives found somewhat disappointing. In 1916, however, Wilson reversed himself to support such measures as federal funds for rural communities, the Keating-Owen Child Labor Bill, and the Adamson act establishing an eight-hour day for railroad employees.

There is some difficulty in fitting the general business legislation of 1914 into this pattern. Even the Clayton Antitrust Act, amending the antimonopoly Sherman act of 1890, contained special provisions for labor that would appear to stand outside Wilson's nineteenth-century liberalism. Link's solution is to reconcile this defense of unionism with the "New Freedom" by minimizing its importance. On the other hand he emphasizes the forward-looking character of the companion Federal Trade Commission Act. Rewritten and strengthened with Wilson's support, it rejected classic antitrust doctrine in favor of the control and supervision of business associated with "New Nationalism." Nevertheless, this was not the clear start of a new outlook, for it was followed by a period when Wilson was responsive to conservative influences and convinced that the reform program was completed.

Such problems of analysis are greatly reduced if the distinction between Wilson's two phases is minimized and the Progressive movement is treated as a whole. Roosevelt and Wilson are as easily brought together as separated. The extent to which Roosevelt shared the ideals of the "New Freedom" is suggested by his title, "trust-buster." Similarly, one could argue that

Wilson's liberalism always incorporated a willingness to regulate the economy as well as to free it from privilege. Certainly the Federal Reserve Act can be so understood. If Wilson came late to welfare legislation, sponsored by the federal government, the same may be said of the Progressive movement in general. However weak the labor provisions of the Clayton act, they surpassed anything enacted for unions in Roosevelt's administration. A basic point of unity is suggested by Link's characterization of the Progressive philosophy:

> To Wilson, as to most progressives of his time, progressivism meant a general attitude and a method of approach more than a finely spun ideology. It meant, in brief, the combining of a fundamental democratic philosophy with a certain dynamic quality and a willingness to experiment.

This is not to suggest that political reform did not contain within it several identifiable strands, among them preservation of competition, controlling intervention in the economy, and welfare devices. The question is rather whether at any time these elements were mutually exclusive or intrinsically antagonistic.

If these strands are regarded as part of an over-all Progressive outlook rather than as warring concepts, Wilson himself becomes more understandable. Pushed to the extreme, the two-phase interpretation of Wilson imposes the obligation of explaining the change. In writing of 1914, Link reports that "how the President was won over to the idea of a strong trade commission is nowhere evident." His explanation of Wilson's sudden conversion to social walfare in 1916 is similarly vague. Link suggests only that Wilson was "no inflexible dogmatist on methods or details" and hints that the change in outlook was motivated by a desire to keep the Democrats in power. To identify the President with the broad movement of progressivism, however, rather than specifically with the "New Freedom" would seem to make possible more plausible answers.

Link's suggestion of opportunism in Wilson is consistent with his rather unflattering portrait of the man, although somewhat at odds with the moral dogmatism that he also ascribes to the President. Wilson's dominant personal qualities emerge as egotism, self-righteousness, and naïveté. He was a poor judge of men, bored with details, yet "a scholar rather than an intellectual." He was not only ignorant of the facts of international life, but also "there is little evidence that Wilson had any deep comprehension of the far-reaching social and economic tensions of the time."

Yet Link never leaves the stature of the President in doubt. The other side of the coin converts defects into merits. The will to dominate bred courage and leadership. Aloofness to people went along with hospitality to ideas. The dogmatist was yet a synthesizer who could reconcile the conflicting proposals among the framers of the Federal Reserve Act. The idealist became the resourceful man of action when the Underwood Tariff was in jeopardy. Wilson emerges as a great man with large faults.

Link has mastered the intricacies of a turbulent and vital period of American life. However much remains unresolved about the Progressive era, he has made a permanent contribution to an understanding of it.

The New Freedom and the Progressive Movement, 1913-16

THE UNSUCCESSFUL struggle of the progressives to achieve a reserve banking and currency system owned and operated exclusively by the government underscored the dilemma in which the American progressive movement found itself during the

From "The New Freedom and the Progressive Movement" from *Woodrow Wilson and the Progressive Era, 1910-1917* by Arthur S. Link. Copyright 1954 by Harper & Brothers.

years immediately preceding the First World War. The great impulses of the several movements for social and economic justice were now pulsating more strongly than before; diverse groups were in the field, campaigning for stringent regulation of industry, woman suffrage, federal child labor legislation, and advanced governmental aid to labor, farmers, tenant farmers, and the unemployed. It was inevitable that these progressives[1] should sooner or later coalesce to put their program across. The important question was whether the New Freedom philosophy was sufficiently dynamic to accommodate the advanced progressive concepts; whether Wilson himself could abandon his liberal, *laissez-faire* rationale and become a progressive statesman; whether, in brief, there was room in the Democratic party for progressivism of this type.

Evaluating the New Freedom at the end of the first ten months of Wilson's incumbency, advanced progressives would have disagreed in their answer to that vital question. Most of them conceded that the Underwood tariff was a step in the right direction, even though it was in part based on *laissez-faire* assumptions. They viewed the Federal Reserve Act, however, with mixed reactions. Uncompromising progressives, like La Follette, and the irreconcilable agrarians denounced it because of the large measure of private control that it allowed,[2] while middle-of-the-road progressives approved it as beginning a new experiment in public regulation. Even so, they must have suspected that Wilson's concessions to the progressive concept had been made under duress and were not the result of any genuine convictions on his part.

[1] Diverse though they were, the several parts of advanced progressivism were clearly distinguishable by 1913. The more radical progressives included, first, the several important organized groups dedicated to the cause of social justice —the American Association for Labor Legislation, the Consumers' League, the organized social workers, the National Child Labor Committee, and the National Association for the Advancement of Colored People. The leaders of organized labor should also be included, even though they generally refused to associate themselves with the professional students of labor problems. Finally, there were the farm organizations, like the National Farmers' Union, and shortly afterward the Non-Partisan League, that were now demanding a dynamic program of governmental intervention in their behalf, especially the establishment of a governmental system of long-term rural credits.

[2] E.g., R. M. La Follette, "Legalizing the 'Money Power,'" *La Follette's Weekly*, V (Dec. 27, 1913), 1; Daniel T. Cushing, *The Betrayal of the People in the Aldrich-Wilson Federal Reserve Act and the Rural Credits Act* (Washington, 1916).

That this suspicion was well founded was demonstrated time and again from 1913 to 1916, by the manner in which the President either obstructed or refused to encourage the fulfillment of a large part of the progressive platform. There was, for example, the way in which he maneuvered on the important question of the application of the antitrust law to labor unions. Since 1906 the American Federation of Labor had waged a relentless campaign to obtain immunity from the application of the Sherman Law to its methods of industrial warfare, particularly the secondary boycott.[3] The Democratic platforms of 1908 and 1912 had endorsed labor's demands, and Democratic leaders in Congress from 1911 to March, 1913, had tried conscientiously, if unsuccessfully, to redeem their party's pledges.

Failing to get their contempt and injunction bills past the Republican opposition, the Democratic leaders had attached a rider to the Sundry Civil bill of 1913, prohibiting the Justice Department from using any funds therein appropriated in the prosecution of labor unions or farm organizations. President Taft promptly vetoed the bill, denouncing the rider as "class legislation of the most vicious sort." When the same measure came up again in the special session in April, Wilson intimated to Congressional leaders that he would not oppose the exemption. News of Wilson's apparent approval and passage of the bill with the rider attached evoked a flood of petitions and appeals to the President from practically every spokesman of organized capital in the country, and from many of his personal friends as well. "The most vicious bill ever enacted by a Congress of the United States now awaits your approval or your dissent," exclaimed George Harvey, perhaps the most authoritative conservative spokesman in the country.[4]

Under such pressure Wilson weakened and then reversed his position. He signed the bill on June 23 but at the same time issued a statement explaining that the rider was merely an expression of Congressional opinion and that he would find money in the general

[3] For a brief account of this campaign see "The Twenty-Year Struggle for Adequate Eight-Hour Legislation," *American Federationist*, XX (Aug., 1913), 590-616.

[4] "An Appeal to the President," *Harper's Weekly*, LVII (May 17, 1913), 3-4; also "Six Months of Wilson," *North American Review*, CXCVIII (Nov., 1913), 576-587.

funds of the Justice Department for the prosecution of any groups that broke the antitrust law. The explanation was not convincing, either to conservatives or to labor leaders. "He attempts to retain the support of those who insist upon this special privilege . . . by signing the bill," Taft commented, "and at the same time to mitigate the indignation of those who have regarded this as a test of his political character by condemning the rider in a memorandum and excusing his signature."[5] On the other hand, Samuel Gompers, president of the A.F. of L., had tried to make it plain that labor demanded nothing less than class legislation in its behalf; he later added that his union would not be satisfied until the principles embodied in the rider had been written into substantive law.

In this first critical test, however, Wilson had signified that he would adhere to the New Freedom doctrine of "special privileges to none," that he would no more approve special legislation on labor's behalf than such legislation in the interest of any other class. Using the New Freedom doctrine to thwart the demands of the farm groups was somewhat more difficult, however, as the agrarian spokesmen constituted perhaps a majority of the Democratic membership in Congress. Under heavy pressure, Wilson had consented to the addition of the short-term agricultural credit amendment to the Glass bill; but this had not involved federal subvention to farmers, nor did it satisfy farm groups throughout the country. Their chief objective was the establishment, underwriting, and operation by the federal government of a system of long-term credits. The question had been under discussion for many years; all three major parties promised some form of federal aid in their platforms of 1912. By 1913 the movement was so powerful that no one expected the new administration to resist it.

Indeed, at the beginning of the serious discussions of the rural credits question it appeared that no occasion for controversy would arise. In the spring of 1913 Congress authorized the appointment by the President of a Rural Credits Commission to study the problem and bring in a recommendation. The Commission studied rural credits systems in Europe during the summer; then its chairman, Senator Duncan U. Fletcher of Florida, framed a bill that

5 W. H. Taft to Gus J. Karger, June 25, 1913, the Papers of William Howard Taft, in the Library of Congress.

would establish a system of privately controlled land banks, operating under federal charter.[6] Secretary of Agriculture Houston endorsed the bill and Wilson added his warm approval. In fact, he conferred with the joint subcommittee of the House and Senate banking committees that had charge of the legislation and urged prompt passage of the Fletcher bill.

Encouraged by the President's friendly attitude, the joint subcommittee at once set to work and came up, around May 1, 1914, with a bill that adopted more or less the framework of the system proposed in the Fletcher plan but added a provision requiring the government to furnish the capital of the land banks, to purchase their bonds if private investors did not, and to operate the system. It was practically the same rural credit bill that was finally passed in 1916. The reporting of this, the so-called Hollis-Bulkley bill, set off a significant controversy in the administration, significant because it pointed up Wilson's limited view of the proper function of government. The root of the difficulty was that the farm spokesmen were convinced a rural credits system without governmental support and sponsorship would never succeed in making farmers independent of private moneylenders, while Wilson and Houston were just as strongly convinced this was no kind of business for the federal government to engage in.

Houston cogently expressed this sentiment in a speech before the National Grange at Manchester, New Hampshire, in November, 1913. "I am not impressed," he said, "with the wisdom and the justice of proposals that would take the money of all the people, through bonds or other devices, and lend it to the farmers or to any other class at a rate of interest lower than the economic conditions would normally require and lower than that at which other classes are securing their capital. This would be special legislation of a particularly odious type, and no new excursions in this direction would be palatable when we are engaged in the gigantic task of restoring the simple rule of equity."[7]

The controversy came to a head when Representative Robert J. Bulkley insisted on introducing the joint subcommittee's bill, in spite of the indignant protests of Carter Glass and other adminis-

[6] Introduced on August 9, 1913.
[7] Quoted in *Commercial West*, XXIV (Nov. 22, 1913), 7-8.

tration leaders. To head off the revolt, Majority Leader Underwood called a caucus of the House Democrats. To the assembled throng Glass read a fervent appeal from the President declaring he would gladly approve the Hollis-Bulkley bill without the governmental aid feature. But, Wilson added, "I have a very deep conviction that it is unwise and unjustifiable to extend the credit of the Government to a single class of the community." This, he continued, was a clear and permanent conviction, one that had come to him, as it were, "out of fire."[8] Obviously threatening a veto of the Hollis-Bulkley bill, Wilson's letter angered the agrarian spokesman, who avowed there would be no rural credits legislation at all until the President changed his mind. Nor was there any such legislation, until new political circumstances prevailed in 1916 and Wilson abruptly reversed his position.

Wilson's momentary defeat of the rural credits measure pleased the private investors, but it generated a good deal of bitterness among the rural leaders of the country. Efforts of Democrats like Glass and Bryan to justify the President's stand in terms of "sound Democratic doctrine"[9] made little sense to editors of farm papers and presidents of granges and farmers' unions. When Congress reconvened in December, 1914, Senator Henry F. Hollis warned the President that he and Bulkley planned to renew their campaign, even though Wilson's Annual Message had relegated rural credits legislation to the scrap heap.[10] Pressure from the rural sections mounted during the following months. Without warning to administration leaders, the Senate on February 25, 1915, adopted an amendment to the agricultural appropriation bill providing for

[8] Wilson to Glass, May 12, 1914, the Woodrow Wilson Papers, in the Library of Congress.

[9] Glass to D. C. Pryer, July 9, 1914, the Papers of Carter Glass, in the Library of the University of Virginia; Glass to Herbert Myrick, May 18, 1914, *ibid.;* "Rural Credits Legislation," *The Commoner,* June, 1914.

[10] Hollis to Wilson, Dec. 11, 1914, Wilson Papers. In his Annual Message of December 8, 1914, Wilson had declared: "The great subject of rural credits still remains to be dealt with, and it is a matter of deep regret that the difficulties of the subject have seemed to render it impossible to complete a bill for passage at this session. But it can not be perfected yet, and therefore there are no other constructive measures the necessity for which I will at this time call your attention to." Ray S. Baker and William E. Dodd (eds.), *The Public Papers of Woodrow Wilson* (6 vols., New York, 1925-27), *The New Democracy,* I, 220.

the establishment of a rural credits system in the Treasury Department. A few days later, on March 2, the House approved the Hollis-Bulkley bill, but the session expired before the conference committee could agree, and the President was spared the embarrassment of vetoing a bill that had overwhelming support in Congress and among the farmers of the country.

Thus Wilson successfully stood off the movements designed to swing the influence and financial support of the federal government to labor unions and farmers in their struggle for advancement. His strong conviction that there were definite limits beyond which the federal authority should not be extended was demonstrated, again, in the manner in which he thwarted the campaign of the social justice groups to commit the administration to a positive program of social legislation.

One of the chief objectives of the reformers, for example, was a federal child labor law. A model bill, drafted by the National Child Labor Committee, was introduced in the House by Representative A. Mitchell Palmer on January 26, 1914. It would be incorrect to say Wilson opposed it; he simply refused to support it because he thought it was unconstitutional.[11] And so long as he withheld his aggressive support the bill would never get past the Senate.

Another social justice objective was woman suffrage. Here, again, Wilson did not openly fight the cause but rather refused to aid it. And Southern opposition in Congress was so strong that without Wilson's most determined effort applied in its behalf a suffrage amendment could never obtain the necessary two-thirds vote. Wilson probably did not believe it was proper for a lady to vote, but the excuse he always gave the delegations of suffragettes who visited him was that he was bound hand and foot in the matter because the Democratic platform had not approved a suffrage amendment.[12]

[11] In early January, 1914, a delegation of leaders in the child labor reform movement requested an interview with the President. "Glad to see these gentlemen," Wilson replied, in a note to Tumulty, "but they ought to know, in all frankness, that no child labor law yet proposed has seemed to me constitutional." Wilson to Tumulty, inscribed at the bottom of Tumulty to Wilson, Jan. 24, 1914, Wilson Papers.

[12] *The New York Times, Dec. 9, 1914;* Elizabeth Glendower Evans, "An Audience at the White House," *La Follette's Weekly,* VI (Feb. 14, 1914), 5, 15.

Some of the interviews were not pleasant affairs, as the ladies could be brutally frank. For example, Mrs. Glendower Evans of Boston, who had escorted a large delegation of working women to the White House on February 2, 1915, reminded the President that in 1912 he had led her to believe he would support woman suffrage. Wilson replied that he had then spoken as an individual, but that he was now speaking as a representative of his party. "Of course," Mrs. Evans shot back, "you were gunning for votes then." Wilson's face turned red, but he managed a weak smile. On the occasion of the sixth visitation by petitioning females, however, he finally confessed that he was "tied to a conviction" that the states alone should control the suffrage.

A third item of the program supported by many leaders of the social justice movement was the imposition of some restriction on the enormous numbers of immigrants then coming to American shores. Restriction or, if possible, putting an end altogether to immigration had long been a prime objective of the A.F. of L. and other labor groups, whose spokesmen claimed unrestricted immigration operated to depress wages in the United States. Appalled by the dire effects of unrestrained immigration on American institutions, a number of leading sociologists and social workers supported the movement.[13] Moreover, the restrictionists were also strongly supported by anti-Catholic and anti-Jewish elements.

The device favored by the restrictionists and exclusionists of that day, the literacy test, was embodied in the Burnett general immigration bill, which the House approved on February 4, 1914, and the Senate on January 2, 1915. From the beginning of the debates in the House, Wilson had intimated he would veto the immigration bill if it included the literacy test. After the House passed the bill, he frankly warned Senate leaders that he would veto the measure if they did not strike out the disputed provision.[14] Whether he thus acted out of conviction or for reasons of expediency, it is im-

13 Among them were Henry P. Fairchild of Yale, Edward A. Ross of Wisconsin, Jeremiah W. Jenks of New York University, Thomas N. Carver of Harvard, Dean Leon C. Marshall of the University of Chicago, and Robert A. Woods of South End House, Boston. See H. P. Fairchild to Wilson, Mar. 17, 1914, Wilson Papers.
14 Wilson to Senator E. D. Smith, Mar. 5, 1914, *ibid.*

possible to say,[15] but when the Senate approved the Burnett bill *in toto* he replied with a ringing veto. "Those who come seeking opportunity are not to be admitted unless they have already had one of the chief of the opportunities they seek, the opportunity of education," he asserted. "The object of such provisions is restriction, not selection."[16] Two years later, in January, 1917, Congress re-enacted the Burnett bill. Wilson replied again with a stirring veto, but this time the forces of restriction were not to be denied victory, and the House on February 1 and the Senate on February 5 overrode the veto.

One great measure of social justice, the Seaman's bill, had the President's approval in the beginning, as its purpose was only to free American sailors from the bondage of their contracts and to strengthen maritime safety requirements. Any recital of how this measure was passed should begin by taking account of the devotion and twenty years' unrequited labor of the president of the Seamen's Union, Andrew Furuseth—"one of the heroes of the world, who . . . forfeited money, position, comfort and everything else to fight the battle of the common sailor."[17] Furuseth finally found sponsors

[15] Senator John Sharp Williams urged Wilson not to veto the Burnett bill. Wilson's reply indicated that political considerations were uppermost in his mind. He wrote: "I find myself in a very embarrassing situation about that bill. Nothing is more distasteful to me than to set my judgment against so many of my friends and associates in public life, but frankly stated the situation is this: I myself personally made the most explicit statements at the time of the presidential election about this subject to groups of our fellow-citizens of foreign extraction whom I wished to treat with perfect frankness and for whom I had entire respect. In view of what I said to them, I do not see how it will be possible for me to give my assent to the bill. I know that you will appreciate the scruple upon which I act." Wilson to Williams, Jan. 7, 1915, *ibid.*

[16] *The Public Papers, New Democracy,* I, 254.

It should be pointed out here that during this long controversy a number of the social justice leaders strongly opposed any form of restriction. See, e.g., Jane Addams to Wilson, Jan. 29, 1915, Wilson Papers; Stephen S. Wise to Wilson, Jan. 29, 1915, *ibid.; The Public,* XVIII (Feb. 5, 1915), 121.

The large employers of labor and their spokesmen, the spokesmen of the Italian-, Polish-, Hungarian-, and Russian-American societies, and the representatives of the Jewish community in the United States, however, were the real leaders in the fight against any form of restriction. The author could find no evidence that the Catholic Church entered the controversy on the political level.

[17] William Kent to Norman Hapgood, June 16, 1914, the Papers of William Kent, in the Library of Yale University.

for his bill in the Sixty-Second Congress, Representative William B. Wilson and Senator La Follette. It passed the House in 1912 and the Senate in 1913, only to receive a pocket veto from President Taft in the closing days of his administration.

Had the Seamen's Bill been merely a matter of domestic concern it would probably have been promptly re-enacted by the Sixty-Third Congress and signed by the President. Before the international ramifications of the measure were brought home to him, for example, Wilson was cordially disposed and promised to support the bill. Trouble arose, however, because the measure in effect abrogated the contractual obligations of alien seamen on foreign ships in American ports, thus violating treaties with all the maritime powers.[18] Moreover, the United States had consented to send delegates to an international conference on safety at sea in London in November, 1913; it seemed hardly courteous for the nation that had taken the initiative in calling the conference to act unilaterally before it could meet.

The envoys of several of the great powers expressed these objections emphatically to the Secretary of State, but Wilson was not disturbed until John Bassett Moore, Counselor of the State Department, called his attention to them on October 16, 1913. By this time it was too late to stop action by the Senate, which on October 23 adopted the Furuseth bill sponsored by La Follette. The administration blocked action by the House, however, and the American delegates, Furuseth among them, went to the London conference unembarrassed by any prior action by their government. Furuseth resigned and came home when the conference adopted safety requirements that did not meet the standards of his own bill. The rest of the American delegates stayed on, however, and helped draft a Convention that imposed uniform and generally rigid safety standards on the vessels of all maritime powers.

The administration was now in another dilemma. Should the United States ratify the Convention on Safety at Sea unconditionally, which would mean abandoning the Furuseth bill, or should it

[18] The United States had entered into treaties with the maritime powers providing for the arrest of foreign seamen who deserted while their ships were in American ports. The Seamen's bill would have unilaterally abrogated these treaties.

ratify with a reservation that would leave room for the passage of that measure? Wilson let the State and Commerce departments, which insisted on unconditional ratification, make the decision; and he reversed his own support of the Furuseth bill and applied administration pressure toward speedy ratification of the Convention. Thus a bitter controversy ensued between the administration and some of the progressive leaders in Congress. In the end the progressives won. The House passed a modified version of the Furuseth bill on August 27, 1914; the Senate in December ratified the Convention with a sweeping reservation; and three months later both houses ratified the conference report.

Events now moved swiftly to a conclusion. Bryan urged the President to give the bill a pocket veto,[19] and the newspapers on March 1, 1915, predicted that this would be the measure's fate. Furuseth appealed in a moving letter, begging Wilson to approve the legislation for which he had fought so long, and Wilson replied in words indicating he had no alternative but to follow the advice of the State Department. The same day, March 2, La Follette, Furuseth, and Senator Owen called on Bryan. Bryan had never heard of Furuseth, but he was so shaken by the old sailor's plea that he at once reversed his position.[20] La Follette added his personal promise that Congress would give the State Department ample time in which to abrogate old treaties and negotiate new ones. Wilson signed the Furuseth bill on March 4, but apparently not without considerable soul searching. "I debated the matter of signing the bill very earnestly indeed . . . ," he explained, "and finally determined to sign it because it seemed the only chance to get something like justice done to a class of workmen who have been too much neglected by our laws."[21]

The dearth in administration circles of any impelling passion

---

[19] On the grounds that passage of the bill would require the United States to denounce unilaterally some twenty-two treaties with maritime nations. Bryan to Wilson, Feb. 27, 1915, the Papers of William Jennings Bryan, in the National Archives. See also Bryan to Wilson, Mar. 1, 1915, Wilson Papers, and Robert Lansing to Bryan, Mar. 1, 1915, *ibid.*

[20] Bryan also urged the President to suggest that the Seamen's bill be amended so as to give the State Department time in which to abrogate the treaties. Bryan to Wilson, Mar. 2, 1915, *ibid.*

[21] Wilson to Newton D. Baker, Mar. 5, 1915, *ibid.*

for social justice was nowhere better illustrated than in the government's policy toward Negroes during Wilson's magistracy. During the campaign of 1912 Wilson had appealed for Negro support, and spokesmen for the cause of racial democracy, among them being Oswald Garrison Villard, William E. B. Du Bois, and William Monroe Trotter, had accepted his promises and worked for his election. Soon after Wilson's inauguration, Oswald Garrison Villard, one of the founders of the National Association for the Advancement of Colored People and publisher of the New York *Evening Post* and the *Nation,* called at the White House and presented a plan for the appointment of a National Race Commission to study the whole problem of race relations in the United States. Wilson seemed "wholly sympathetic" to the suggestion, and Villard left for a visit to Europe, confident Wilson would soon be ready to appoint the Commission.[22] He returned in July and tried several times to see the President, but Wilson refused to grant him an interview. Finally, when Villard appealed in personal terms, Wilson had to tell him that the political situation was too delicate for any such action, that the appointment of the Commission would incite the resentment of Southerners in Congress, whose votes he needed for the success of his legislative program.[23]

Villard's disappointment over Wilson's abandonment of the Race Commission was nothing, however, as compared with his consternation at the way in which Southern race concepts had gained acendancy in Congress and in the administration. Southerners were riding high in Washington for the first time since the Civil War, demanding segregation in the government departments and public services and the dismissal or down-grading of Negro civil servants.

Throughout his incumbency, Wilson stood firm against the cruder demands of the white supremacists, but he and probably all of his

22 O. G. Villard to R. H. Leavell, May 15, 1913, the Papers of Oswald Garrison Villard, in Houghton Library, Harvard University. Villard's plan was explained in *A Proposal for a National Race Commission to be appointed by the President of the United States, Suggested by the National Association for the Advancement of Colored People* (n.p., n.d.).
23 Villard to Wilson, Aug. 18, 1913, Villard Papers; Wilson to Villard, Aug. 21, 1913, *ibid*. Wilson made this point even clearer in a conversation with John Palmer Gavit on October 1, 1913, for an account of which see Gavit to Villard, Oct. 1, 1913, *ibid*.

Cabinet believed in segregation, social and official. The issue first arose on April 11, 1913, when Burleson suggested segregating all Negroes in the federal services. If there were any defenders of the Negro or any foes of segregation in the Cabinet they did not then or afterward raise their voice.[24] Shortly afterward the Bureau of the Census, the Post Office Department, and the Bureau of Printing and Engraving quietly began to segregate workers in offices, shops, rest rooms, and restaurants. Employees who objected were discharged.[25] Moreover, federal Post Office and Treasury officials in the South were given free rein to discharge and down-grade Negro employees. The postmaster of Atlanta, for example, discharged thirty-five Negroes. "There are no Government positions for Negroes in the South," the Collector of Internal Revenue in Georgia announced. "A Negro's place is in the cornfield."[26]

There had been segregation in the government departments before, to be sure, but it had been informal and unofficial. Now it seemed that for the first time since the Civil War the federal government had placed its approval on the Southern caste system. Needless to say, Negroes throughout the country were shocked and confused by this action of an administration that promised a new freedom for all the people. "I have recently spent several days in Washington, and I have never seen the colored people so discouraged and bitter as they are at the present time," the great leader of the Negroes wrote.[27] "We had looked forward in the hope that under your guidance all this would be changed," another Negro leader wrote the President, "but the cold facts presented to us show that these cherished hopes are to be dashed to the ground and that for a while longer we must continue to drink from this bitter cup."[28]

The anger of the Negro leaders at the new segregation policies was the natural reaction of a group who had hopefully supported

[24] The Diary of Josephus Daniels, in the Library of Congress, Apr. 11, 1913.
[25] May Childs Nerney to Oswald G. Villard, Sept. 30, 1913, Wilson Papers, is the report by an investigator for the National Association for the Advancement of Colored People. For other analyses see J. P. Gavit in New York *Evening Post*, Oct. 21, 1913, and William Monroe Trotter, "Federal Segregation Under Pres. Wilson," Boston *Guardian*, Oct. 25, 1913.
[26] Atlanta *Georgian and News*, Oct. 7, 1913.
[27] Booker T. Washington to O. G. Villard, Aug. 10, 1913, Wilson Papers.
[28] W. F. Powell to Wilson, Aug. 25, 1913, *ibid.*

the man they were sure would deal with them compassionately. More surprising, however, was the manner in which a large part of the progressive leadership of the North and Middle West rose in fervent protest. Villard and his *Nation* and New York *Evening Post* and the National Association for the Advancement of Colored People first sounded the alarm, and the storm of protests from editors, clergymen, and civic leaders that followed gave ample proof that the old spirit of equalitarianism was not dead.

Wilson was visibly surprised and greatly disturbed by the furor his subordinates had provoked. From the beginning of the controversy, however, he contended that segregation was being instituted in the interest of the Negroes, and throughout he stoutly maintained this position. "I would say that I do approve of the segregation that is being attempted in several of the departments," he wrote, for example, to the editor of the influential *Congregationalist*.[29] Moreover, when the militant Boston Negro spokesman, William Monroe Trotter, headed a delegation to carry a protest to the White House and spoke rashly, the President virtually ordered him out.

In every respect the whole affair was tragic and unfortunate— one of the worst blots on the administration's record. It was more than even Wilson's staunchest editorial supporter, Frank Cobb, could stomach. "It is a small, mean, petty discrimination," he cried in protest, "and Mr. Wilson ought to have set his heel upon this presumptuous Jim-Crow government the moment it was established. He ought to set his heel upon it now. It is a reproach to his Administration and to the great political principles which he represents."[30]

Although the President never set his heel upon Jim Crow, the forthright protests of the liberal North had some effect. The Treasury Department reversed its policy and began quietly to eliminate segregation. But more important was the fact that the segregation movement in other departments was entirely checked. Jim Crowism was not rooted out of the federal government, to be sure, but at least the white supremacists were less bold and far less successful after 1913.

[29] Wilson to Rev. H. A. Bridgman, Sept. 8, 1913, *ibid.*
[30] New York *World,* Nov. 13, 1914.

The segregation affair caused many progressives to wonder what kind of progressive Wilson was. Their confusion was compounded, moreover, by the perplexing reversals that Wilson executed when he proceeded to complete his legislative program by fulfilling his pledges to strengthen the antitrust laws.

Wilson had fabricated the New Freedom program in 1912 largely out of promises to destroy monopoly and restore free competition. He had, moreover, evolved a fairly definite remedy, which was to rewrite the rules of business practice so clearly that there could be no doubt as to their meaning, and to enforce these rules by the normal processes of prosecution and adjudication. Not until the middle of November, 1913, however, when the Underwood bill was passed and the Federal Reserve bill was safely on its way to passage in the Senate, did Wilson give any thought to details. On November 20 he began a long series of conferences with Democratic leaders in Congress, seeking their views and requesting them to submit their recommendations. The news that the President was determined to carry through with antitrust legislation also provoked the introduction of a bewildering variety of bills when Congress convened in December.

By the middle of December most of the recommendations were in, and it was evident that progressive opinion was divided over the remedy. The main body of Democrats desired merely an interpretative amendment of the Sherman Act, to define precisely the prohibitions against restraint of trade, to outlaw interlocking directorates of all kinds, and to narrow and clarify the "rule of reason," promulgated by the Supreme Court in 1911.[31] A minority of Democrats and practically all progressive Republicans, on the other hand, agreed with Theodore Roosevelt that this was a naïve solution, that it would be impossible to define by statute every

[31] The rule of reason, first promulgated by the Supreme Court in the Standard Oil case in May, 1911 (221 U.S. 1) and shortly afterward reaffirmed in the American Tobacco case (221 U.S. 106), represented a triumph for Chief Justice Edward D. White, who, since 1897, had contended that the framers of the Sherman Act had intended to outlaw only unreasonable, or direct, restraints of trade, not reasonable restraints that were normally ancillary to most contracts.
  Some Democats, notably John Sharp Williams and Bryan, wanted to abolish the rule of reason altogether and outlaw every restraint of trade, whether direct or ancillary. See J. S. Williams to Wilson, Jan. 13, 1914, Wilson Papers.

conceivable restraint of trade. They wanted instead a powerful, independent trade commission armed with broad authority and capable of suppressing unfair competition whenever it arose and under whatever guise.[32]

Wilson had to choose, therefore, between what he called the "two ways open to us"—in brief, to choose between the solution he had offered in 1912 and the program that Roosevelt and his friends championed. He pondered this question during his vacation at Pass Christian, Mississippi, over the Christmas holidays, and if there was any doubt in his mind, it was quickly resolved. He would press ahead for legislation along New Freedom lines, in spite of the great pressure that was being brought to bear upon him by personal friends and spokesmen of the great business interests to abandon his efforts, in spite of the seeming surrender of the House of Morgan, when it announced on January 2, 1914, its withdrawal from thirty directorships in banks, railroads, and industrial firms.[33]

Soon after his return to Washington, Wilson had full-dress conferences with Congressional leaders, who agreed to support the program the administration had formulated. Then, appearing for the fifth time before a joint session, the President explained in unusual detail the kind of legislation he had in mind. He brandished no flaming sword against business, however, but offered an olive branch of peace and the hope of permanent accommodation. "The antagonism between business and Government is over," he said several times, as if to emphasize that he was speaking for the best business thought of the country.[34]

Wilson's program was embodied in three bills, originally drawn by Chairman Henry D. Clayton of the House Judiciary Committee, which were soon combined into one measure, known as the Clayton bill. It enumerated and prohibited a series of unfair trade practices, outlawed in unqualified terms interlocking directorates and stockholdings, and gave private parties benefit of decisions in suits that the government had originated. A fourth bill, prepared by Representatives Clayton, James H. Covington, and William C. Adamson

[32] For an analysis of such proposals see J. E. Davies to Wilson, Dec. 27, 1913, and "Memorandum of Recommendations as to Trust Legislation by Joseph E. Davies, Commissioner of Corporations," both in *ibid*.

[33] *The New York Times*, Jan. 3, 1914.

[34] *The Public Papers, New Democracy*, I, 81-88.

THE NEW FREEDOM 305

and Senator Francis G. Newlands, created an interstate trade commission to supplant the Bureau of Corporations. The new commission would be no independent arbiter of business practices, however, but would serve merely as the right arm of the Justice Department in antitrust matters. Actually, it was the Bureau of Corporations, under a new name and with a little more power— as Wilson said, no "dangerous experiment," but a "safe and sensible" agency that all Democrats could approve. A final feature of the program was the bill prepared by Representative Sam Rayburn of Texas and Louis D. Brandeis, to give the Interstate Commerce Commission control over the issuance of new securities by the railroads.[35]

This, therefore, was the substance of the original Wilson program for trust reform. No sooner was it proposed, however, than there arose a storm of confusing dissent and criticism. The "Money Trust" expert, Samuel Untermyer, rushed to Washington and pointed to many weaknesses in the Clayton bill. Brandeis, who was now spending most of his time in Washington, was evolving an entirely new solution, the cornerstone of which was the strengthening of small business by fair-trade price laws. Progressives and the representatives of small business were up in arms in protest against the plan for a weak interstate trade commission. And to compound the difficulty, Democratic leaders in Congress began to quarrel among themselves over jurisdiction and details. It seemed no one knew what to do or how to do it.

The most serious controversy of all, however, was that which occurred when the labor leaders and spokesmen in Congress read the Clayton bill and found nothing in it to give labor unions exemption from the application of the antitrust laws. Gompers and his colleagues in the A.F. of L. had supported Wilson in 1912 and had confidently expected the administration to stand by the Democratic platform pledges to exempt labor and farm organizations from the penalties of the Sherman law. They were now up in arms, threaten-

[35] This measure passed the House on June 5, 1914, but later died in the Senate, in part a casualty of the panic that the war evoked. During the early months of the war the American security markets were in a chaotic condition; the New York Stock Exchange was closed; and the railroads were in a state approaching insolvency. Administration leaders decided, therefore, to drop the Rayburn bill entirely.

ing the Democrats with loss of labor's vote if these demands were not conceded. "Without further delay," Gompers declared, "the citizens of the United States must decide whether they wish to outlaw organized labor."[36]

In this bitter controversy Wilson and his Congressional leaders stood absolutely firm. The most they would concede was a compromise amendment providing for jury trials in cases of criminal contempt, circumscribing the issuance of injunctions in labor disputes, and declaring that neither farm nor labor unions should be considered as illegal combinations in restraint of trade when they lawfully sought to obtain legitimate objectives.[37] This did not go far enough to suit the labor leaders, whose spokesmen in Congress[38] went to the White House on April 30 and threatened to join the Republicans in defeating the administration's antitrust program if labor's demand for complete immunity were not granted. Wilson would not budge, however, and the labor congressmen and union officials had to accept the compromise, which was better than nothing.

With the compromise labor provision included, the House passed the Clayton bill, along with the interstate trade commission and railroad securities bills, by overwhelming majorities on June 5, 1914. The House's action brought to an end the New Freedom phase

[36] New York *World*, Mar. 1, 1914.

[37] Wilson was emphatic in declaring that the provision did not authorize labor unions to use methods of industrial warfare that had previously been condemned by the courts. *The New York Times*, June 2, 1914; New York *World*, June 2, 1914.

Representative E. Y. Webb of North Carolina, who framed the compromise provision, further explained:

"The framers of the Sherman law never intended to place labor organizations and farmers' organizations under the ban of that law. The existence of a labor or farmers' union never has been unlawful, and is not unlawful today, but it was decided to place in the statutory law of the country a recognition of the rights of those organizations to exist and carry out their lawful purposes.

"After the original Section 7 of the Anti-trust bill was drawn, certain representatives of labor contended that the section did not give labor all it was entitled to and demanded that we should make the section provide that the anti-trust laws should not apply to labor organizations. The acceptance of this amendment would have placed labor organizations beyond the pale of the anti-trust law entirely, which neither the president nor the members of the [Judiciary] committee would agree to." *The New York Times*, June 14, 1914.

[38] Representatives David J. Lewis of Maryland, Edward Keating of Colorado, Isaac R. Sherwood of Ohio, and John J. Casey of Pennsylvania.

of antitrust legislation, that is, of legislation based upon the assumption that all that was required was merely to make more specific the prohibitions against restraint of trade. From this point forward, progress away from this concept was uninterrupted, until in the end Wilson accepted almost entirely the New Nationalism's solution for the regulation of business by a powerful trade commission. The metamorphosis in administration policy was gradual, and the story of how it evolved is complicated; but the major reasons for the change are clear.

To begin with, there is much evidence that Wilson was growing uncertain as to the manner in which the broad objectives of his program should be accomplished. His attitude toward the industrial problem was conditioned by his belief that the vast majority of businessmen were honest and desired only the public good. Thus his objective was chiefly to strengthen the altruistic tendencies in the business community; and he began to wonder whether this could be done by rigid, inflexible laws that might only further alienate and confuse the honest businessman.

On the other hand, a large minority of the Democrats—the Southern agrarians and the Bryan followers—proposed legislation to destroy the oligarchical economic structure: stringent federal regulation of stock exchanges;[39] a graduated corporation tax that would bear so heavily on the great combinations as to put them out of business; limiting a corporation or holding company usually to about one-third the total product of any given industry;[40] abolition of the "rule of reason"; and the complete destruction of the complicated network of interlocking relationships among banks, railroads, corporations, and insurance companies.[41] This program

[39] This was one of the recommendations of the Pujo Committee and was strongly supported by Samuel Untermyer and Senator Robert L. Owen of Oklahoma. Early in the Congressional discussions of antitrust legislation the President let it be known he did not favor the stock exchange bill. *The New York Times,* Jan. 23, 1914.

[40] The report of the House committee, headed by A. O. Stanley of Kentucky, which investigated United States Steel in 1911-12, proposed that there should be a presumption of restraint of trade when a single corporation or holding company controlled at least 30 per cent of the output of a single industry. *House Report,* No. 1127, 62d Cong., 2d sess. (Washington, 1912), p. 214.

[41] This was the desire and determination, often voiced, of practically all the so-called radical Democrats in the House of Representatives.

went far beyond anything Wilson envisaged at any time. For example, he did not object to bigness per se; he only wanted to prevent the great interests from using their power to stifle new growth and competition. And he was beginning to doubt that the Clayton bill and the weak interstate trade commission bill offered an effective remedy.

In the second place, the spokesmen of the business community, particularly the United States Chamber of Commerce, had embraced the ideal of the "self-regulation" of business. What they desired most was legislation prohibiting unfair trade practices, with a trade commission to pass upon the legality of practices and to serve as a friendly adviser to businessmen. The suggestion found strong support in the Senate and among progressives generally, as it seemed to offer a simple solution to a perplexing difficulty.

Just at the moment when Wilson seemed most confused and uncertain, Louis D. Brandeis took up the strong trade commission idea and persuaded the President to adopt it also. Since October, 1913, Brandeis had been hard at work, in Boston and Washington, on the antitrust question. His close friend and associate, George L. Rublee of New York, had joined the "people's lawyer," and together the two men drafted a Federal Trade Commission bill that was introduced by Representative Raymond B. Stevens, Democrat of New Hampshire. The Stevens bill in general terms outlawed unfair trade practices and established a trade commission endowed with plenary authority to oversee business activity and by the issuance of cease and desist orders to prevent the illegal suppression of competition.

Wilson and Congressional leaders first learned the details of the Brandeis-Rublee plan in the latter part of April, 1914. The chairman of the House Commerce Committee, William C. Adamson of Georgia, was aghast at the proposal, declaring it proposed giving an administrative agency power to make law. Wilson said nothing at first, but after the antitrust bills were safely through the House he called Brandeis, Rublee, and Stevens to the White House on June 10 and told them he had decided to make the Stevens bill the cornerstone of his antitrust program. How the President was won over to the idea of a strong trade commission is nowhere evident. In any event, three days after the White House conference the

Senate Interstate Commerce Committee reported the Federal Trade Commission bill with the Stevens bill as an amendment. There then followed several weeks of debate in the Senate, during which time Wilson, Brandeis, and Rublee worked feverishly to overcome old-line Democratic and conservative opposition to Section 5, empowering the Commission to issue cease and desist orders. After adopting amendments guaranteeing broad court review of the Commission's orders, the Senate passed the bill on August 5 by a bipartisan vote of fifty-three to sixteen. The House agreed a month later, and the measure became law on September 10. "If the bill is wrong I shall be much to blame," Rublee wrote. "I drafted the conference report which was agreed to. Section 5 is exactly as I wanted it to be."[42]

Meanwhile, after he espoused the Brandeis-Rublee plan, Wilson seemed to lose all interest in the Clayton bill. It was cut adrift in the Senate, with the result that one after another of its strong provisions was so weakened as to make it in many particulars almost innocuous. For example, instead of forbidding exclusive selling contracts, interlocking directorates, or interlocking stockholdings outright, the words "where the effect may be to substantially lessen competition or tend to create a monopoly in any line of commerce," or words of similar purport, were inserted after all the prohibitions.[43]

"When the Clayton bill was first written," Senator James A. Reed of Missouri exclaimed, "it was a raging lion with a mouth full of teeth. It has degenerated to a tabby cat with soft gums, a plaintive mew, and an anaemic appearance. It is a sort of legislative apology to the trusts, delivered hat in hand, and accompanied by assurances that no discourtesy is intended."[44] Wilson, too, complained that Senator Culberson, chairman of the Judiciary Committee, had made the bill "so weak that you cannot tell it from water."[45] Of course

[42] Rublee to Brandeis, Oct. 6, 1914, the Papers of Louis D. Brandeis, in the Law School Library of the University of Louisville.

[43] For a good analysis of the weakening of the Clayton bill see Henry R. Seager and Charles A. Gulick, Jr., *Trust and Corporation Problems* (New York, 1929), pp. 420-422.

[44] *The New York Times*, Sept. 29, 1914.

[45] The Diary of Edward M. House, in the Papers of Edward M. House, in the Library of Yale University, Oct. 2, 1914.

this was largely true, but it was true because the administration had put all faith in the trade commission plan and had given up its effort to prohibit restraints of trade by statutory action.

Farm and labor leaders, meanwhile, had been striving mightily with the Senate to win the concessions the President and House of Representatives had denied them. On July 30, Gompers, Frank Morrison, secretary-treasurer of the A.F. of L., the legislative representatives of the railroad brotherhoods, the general counsel of the Farmers' Union, and the secretary of the Farmers' National Congress addressed an important appeal to the Senate Judiciary Committee. The letter reviewed the labor provisions of the Clayton bill, as it had passed the House, and pointed out specifically the changes that were necessary to satisfy labor and farm demands. The effect of the suggested changes would have been to give to labor and farm organizations the immunity from the penalties of the Sherman law they were seeking.

A comparison of the labor-farm demands with the labor provisions of the Clayton bill as it passed the Senate and conference committee reveals that the Senate, like the President and the House of Representatives, stood absolutely firm in resisting these demands. The Senate made one change that became famous but was not important. At the suggestion of Senator Albert B. Cummins, it amended the provision to read, "The labor of human beings is not a commodity or article of commerce," which phrase was nothing more than a pious expression of senatorial opinion and did not change labor's standing before the law.[46]

In any event, the labor provisions of the act apparently pleased everyone. Gompers hailed them as labor's "Magna Carta"[47] and afterward tried desperately to convince himself and the country that labor was freed from the restraints of the antitrust laws. On the other extreme, the general counsel of the American Anti-Boycott Association was also entirely satisfied with the legislation. "The bill

[46] That the labor provisions of the Clayton Act did not confer immunity from prosecution on farm and labor unions was the opinion of practically every responsible contemporary observer. See, e.g., the cogent essay, " 'Labor Is Not a Commodity,' " *New Republic*, IX (Dec. 2, 1916), 112-114, or W. H. Taft to G. W. Wickersham, Oct. 31, Nov. 8, 1914, Taft Papers.

[47] "Labor's Magna Carta—Demand It," *American Federationist*, XXI (July, 1914), 553-557; *ibid.* (Oct., 1914), 866-867.

makes few changes in existing laws relating to labor unions, injunctions and contempts of court," he observed, "and those are of slight practical importance."[48]

With the appointment of the Federal Trade Commission on February 22, 1915, the administration launched its experiment in the regulation of business enterprise. It is well, however, to understand the spirit in which the experiment was conceived and the purposes that Wilson and his colleagues hoped to accomplish. They were chiefly purposes friendly to business. As Redfield later put it, Wilson hoped to "create in the Federal Trade Commission a counsellor and friend to the business world. . . . It was no large part of his purpose that the Federal Trade Commission should be primarily a policeman to wield a club over the head of the business community. Rather the reverse was true and the restraining powers of the Commission were thought a necessary adjunct which he hoped and expected to be of minor rather than of major use."[49]

Progressives like Brandeis and Rublee, who hoped the Commission would become a dynamic factor in American economic life, were bitterly disappointed when it failed to do anything constructive during the first years of its life. Brandeis later correctly observed that Wilson had ruined the Commission by his choice of commissioners. "It was a stupid administration," he recalled.[50] The chairman, Joseph E. Davies of Wisconsin, lacked force and judgment. In fact, the only really competent appointee, Rublee, was prevented from serving because the Senate refused to confirm his nomination.[51] Davies proved so incompetent that in June, 1916, the majority of the Commission deposed him and made Edward N. Hurley, a Chicago industrialist, chairman. Hurley was certainly abler than Davies; but he devoted his talents to making the Commission useful

[48] Daniel Davenport, in Springfield *Republican,* Oct. 11, 1914.

[49] W. C. Redfield, "Woodrow Wilson: An Appreciation," in the Ray Stannard Baker Collection, in the Library of Congress; see also A. W. Shaw, MS of interview on Jan. 4, 1915, with Wilson, in Wilson Papers.

[50] R. S. Baker, interview with L. D. Brandeis, Mar. 23, 1929, Baker Collection.

[51] Jacob H. Gallinger of New Hampshire, minority leader in the Senate, objected to the appointment on personal grounds and the Senate refused to confirm Rublee, in spite of the President's strenuous efforts to obtain confirmation.

to businessmen and to preaching the doctrine of co-operation between government and business. And under his leadership, the
Commission practically abandoned its role as watchdog of business
practices. It was little wonder, therefore, that, on reviewing the
situation on the eve of America's entry into the war, Rublee concluded that the Commission was on the rocks.[52]

The weakening of the administration's antitrust program was
only the first sign of a general reaction that began to set in around
the beginning of 1914 and increasingly affected the administration
and the President. The chief cause of the ebbing of the reform
1913 and mounted in severity during the late winter and spring
of 1914. It was a world-wide phenomenon, the result of the tighten-
ing of credit in Europe because of the Balkan Wars and the fear
of a general war.[53] But in the United States the Republicans blamed
the Underwood tariff and Wilson's antitrust measures. Business
failures increased, production sagged, and unemployment was widespread and especially acute in the large cities.[54] Wilson and administration leaders like McAdoo tried to persuade themselves and the
public that no real depression existed. Actually, however, they were
seriously alarmed, and their concern inevitably evidenced itself in
administration policies.

To begin with, in the spring of 1914 the President embarked
upon a campaign calculated to win the friendship of businessmen
and bankers and to ease the tension that had existed between the
administration and the business community. The accommodation
of the antitrust program to the desires of the business world was the
first step, along with Wilson's repeated expressions of confidence in
and friendship for businessmen. Next the President began to welcome bankers and business leaders to the White House. In the

52 George Rublee to E. M. House, Jan. 26, 1917, Wilson Papers.
53 See the excellent analysis by S. S. Fontaine, in New York *World*, Jan. 3, 1915.
54 Incomplete surveys revealed that in New York 23.7 per cent of 115,960
families investigated in January-February, 1915, had members unemployed. The
Bureau of Statistics of Massachusetts reported that returns received from labor
organizations in the state, representing 66 per cent of the total trade-union
members, showed 18.3 per cent unemployed on December 31, 1914. See Mayor's
Committee on Unemployment, New York City, *Report of the Mayor's Committee on Unemployment* (New York, 1916), and Bureau of Statistics, Labor
Division, Commonwealth of Massachusetts, *Thirtieth Quarterly Report on Unemployment in Massachusetts, Quarter Ending June 30, 1915* (Boston, 1915).

palmy days of 1913 he had not wanted their advice; now he welcomed J. P. Morgan, delegations of businessmen and bankers from Illinois, and Henry Ford. Thirdly, Wilson let it be known in the financial circles of New York and Boston that he had never really been an enemy of big business, but only of business that grew "big by methods which unrighteously crushed those who were smaller."[55]

It was about this time, also, that Attorney General McReynolds, with Wilson's approval, began to use a new method in dealing with alleged combinations in restraint of trade. He announced that any large corporation that felt doubtful of the legality of its corporate structure might seek the friendly advice and help of the Justice Department in rearranging its affairs. Several great combinations, notably the American Telephone & Telegraph Company and the New Haven Railroad, came to terms with the administration and received its blessing.[56] Whether such policy was wise or foolish depended upon one's point of view; in any event, there was no trust-busting ardor in the Wilson administration.

Wilson climaxed his little campaign to win the friendship of the business classes by turning over control of the Federal Reserve Board, in effect, to their representatives, as if he were trying to prove the sincerity of his recent professions. For several months McAdoo and House had engaged in a tug of war over the selection

[55] Wilson to A. S. Burleson, July 27, 1914, Wilson Papers. See also Wilson to H. L. Higginson, Oct. 23, 1914, *ibid.*; E. M. House to J. C. McReynolds, Jan. 7, 1914, House Papers.

[56] For details and consequences of the A. T. & T. settlement, see *The New York Times*, Dec. 20, 21, 1913.

The New Haven settlement was reached only after long and bitter negotiations. There was first a thorough investigation into the affairs of the railroad by Joseph W. Folk, special prosecutor for the Interstate Commerce Commission. This was followed by an agreement for the dissolution of the vast New Haven empire, the terms of which were agreed to by railroad and Justice Department officials on January 10, 1914. *Ibid.*, Jan. 11, 1914. The New Haven officers objected, however, to the government's demand that they dispose of the Boston & Maine Railroad at once. *Ibid.*, July 21, 22, 23, 1914. The government replied by instituting a suit to compel dissolution, whereupon the railroad officials surrendered and accepted the Justice Department's terms. *Ibid.*, Aug. 12, 1914.

It should be added that when officials of the United States Steel Corporation, notably Henry C. Frick, endeavored to reach agreement with McReynolds, the Attorney General refused to approve the proposed settlement on the ground that it would not restore genuine competition in the industry. House Diary, Mar. 22, 24, 26, Sept. 30, 1913.

of the Board, McAdoo arguing that the appointees should be men in sympathy with the administration's broad policies, House advising that the President choose leading bankers and businessmen. Actually, there never was much doubt in Wilson's mind as to the wise course to follow; and when the membership of the Board was announced it evoked almost unanimous approval from bankers and business leaders. Progressives, on the other hand, were shocked and astonished. "Why, it looks as if Mr. Vanderlip [president of the National City Bank of New York] has selected them," one progressive Republican senator exclaimed.[57]

The degree to which Wilson had outraged progressive sentiment, however, did not become apparent until the President sent the nominations to the Senate on June 15. Insurgent anger in the upper house centered on two of the nominees—Thomas D. Jones of Chicago and Paul M. Warburg. A former trustee of Princeton University and a close friend of Wilson, Jones was one of the owners of the so-called Zinc Trust and a director of the International Harvester Company, then under state and federal indictment for being an illegal combination. Warburg was a partner in Kuhn, Loeb & Company, one of the great Wall Street banking houses.

In reply to attacks on his friend Jones, Wilson addressed a public letter to the Senate Banking Committee, defending him and explaining that he had become a director of the Harvester Trust to help bring that corporation into conformity with the law. Jones came before the Committee, however, and affirmed that he had not gone on the board of the corporation to reform it and approved everything the Trust had done since he became a director. The upshot was that the Banking Committee refused to approve Jones' nomination and Wilson had to ask him to withdraw from the contest. The Warburg affair, on the other hand, developed differently, and with certain comic aspects. Much insulted by the senatorial opposition, Warburg at first refused to appear before the Committee. Finally the President persuaded him to swallow his pride and the Senate confirmed his appointment.

The startling aspect of the Jones-Warburg affair, however, was Wilson's own reaction to it and the manner in which he came

[57] Boston *Advertiser*, May 6, 1914.

forward as the champion and defender of big business. "It would be particularly unfair to the Democratic Party and the Senate itself to regard it as the enemy of business, big or little," he declared, while the fight was in progress.[58] When it became obvious that the Senate would refuse to confirm Jones, Wilson's anger became intense. In a commiserating letter to Jones, he lashed out at the Senate insurgents, and at progressives in general. "I believe that the judgment and desire of the whole country cry out for a new temper in affairs," he wrote. ". . . We have breathed already too long the air of suspicion and distrust." In short, there was no room in this year of New Freedom grace for "class antagonism," for the very dynamic quality that had given impetus and force to the American progressive movement.[59]

Wilson's temper soon cooled, and a week later the attention of the country was diverted to other matters by the outbreak of the war in Europe. Then followed a period of political confusion, during which partisan passions subsided. As it turned out, these developments at home and abroad were a godsend to the Democrats during the ensuing Congressional campaign. The Republicans did not wage a vigorous fight, and there seemed to be a general disposition to stand by the President during a time of peril. The most important Democratic asset, however, was the continued disruption of the Republican party, with Roosevelt and the Progressives making one last and futile effort to establish themselves as a major party.[60]

In spite of all these advantages, the Democrats made such a poor showing in the state and Congressional elections on November 3 that their defeat in 1916 seemed almost certain. The Democratic majority in the House was reduced from seventy-three to twenty-five; there was no change of voting strength in the Senate; but the Republicans swept back into or stayed in power in states like New York, Illinois, Pennsylvania, Ohio, Kansas, New Jersey, Connecticut, Wisconsin and South Dakota. It seemed as if the progressive tide was beginning to recede and everywhere progressive

---

[58] *The New York Times,* July 9, 1914.
[59] Wilson to T. D. Jones, July 23, 1914, printed in *ibid.,* July 24, 1914.
[60] George E. Mowry, *Theodore Roosevelt and the Progressive Movement* (Madison, Wis., 1946), pp. 300-303.

leaders were disheartened. "The cataclysm was just about what I expected," Roosevelt lamented.[61] "We are saddened my many defeats," Brandeis added.[62] Wilson, too, was heartsick and wondered whether all the effort of the preceding two years had been worth while. "People are not so stupid not to know," he declared, "that to vote against a Democratic ticket is to vote indirectly against me."[63] He changed his mind soon, however, and boasted that the Democrats had won a great victory.

In the autumn of 1914 Wilson, moreover, thought his program to effect a fundamental reorganization of American economic life was complete and that the progressive movement had fulfilled its mission. "We have only to look back ten years or so to realize the deep perplexities and dangerous ill-humors out of which we have at last issued, as if from a bewildering fog, a noxious miasma," he wrote in a public letter to McAdoo in November, 1914, announcing the consummation of the New Freedom program. "Ten or twelve years ago the country was torn and excited by an agitation which shook the very foundations of her political life, brought her business ideals into question, condemned her social standards, denied the honesty of her men of affairs, the integrity of her economic processes, the morality and good faith of many of the things which her law sustained." And so things stood until the Democrats came to power and the New Freedom legislation righted fundamental wrongs. The nightmare of the past years was over now, and the future would be a time of co-operation, of new understanding, of common purpose, "a time of healing because a time of just dealing."[64]

Advanced progressives were puzzled by Wilson's remarkable letter. Did the President mean what he had said? Was the progressive movement over? If so, then where could the social justice element go? Herbert Croly, chief editor of the *New Republic,* which had just begun its distinguished career, voiced the apprehensions that many progressives felt when he wrote:

[61] Roosevelt to Archie B. Roosevelt, Nov. 7, 1914, the Papers of Theodore Roosevelt, in the Library of Congress.

[62] L. D. Brandeis to Gifford Pinchot, Nov. 4, 1914, Brandeis Papers.

[63] House Diary, Nov. 4, 1914.

[64] Wilson to W. G. McAdoo, Nov. 17, 1914, printed in *The New York Times,* Nov. 18, 1914. See also Wilson to Powell Evans, Oct. 20, 1914, Wilson Papers.

How can a man of . . . [Wilson's] shrewd and masculine intelligence possibly delude himself into believing the extravagant claims which he makes on behalf of the Democratic legislative achievement? . . . How many sincere progressives follow him in believing that this legislation has made the future clear and bright with the promise of best things? . . .

President Wilson could not have written his letter unless he had utterly misconceived the meaning and the task of American progressivism. After every allowance has been made for his justifiable pride . . . , there remains an ominous residue of sheer misunderstanding. Any man of President Wilson's intellectual equipment who seriously asserts that the fundamental wrongs of a modern society can be easily and quickly righted as a consequence of a few laws . . . casts suspicion either upon his own sincerity or upon his grasp of the realities of modern social and industrial life. Mr. Wilson's sincerity is above suspicion, but he is a dangerous and unsound thinker upon contemporary political and social problems. He has not only . . . "a single-track mind," but a mind which is fully convinced of the everlasting righteousness of its own performances and which surrounds this conviction with a halo of shimmering rhetoric. He deceives himself with these phrases, but he should not be allowed to deceive progressive popular opinion.[65]

Croly's analysis of the superficial character of Wilson's progressivism was essentially correct. There is little evidence that Wilson had any deep comprehension of the far-reaching social and economic tensions of the time. As Croly said, Wilson was intelligent and sincere. But that did not make him a prophet or a pioneer, or even a progressive of the advanced persuasion. He had not taken office to carry out a program of federal social reform. He had promised to lower the tariff, reorganize the currency and banking system, and strengthen the antitrust laws, in order to free the nation's energies and unleash the competitive urges of the people. He had done these things, and with a minimum of concession to advanced progressive concepts. He had, moreover, turned over control of the public agencies established by the new legislation—the Federal Reserve Board and the Federal Trade Commission—to cautious men. To try to portray such a man as an ardent social reformer is to defy the plain record.

This, however, is only one chapter in the history of the journey

[65] "Presidential Complacency," *New Republic,* I (Nov. 21, 1914), 7.

of the Democratic party on the road leading to the New Deal and the Fair Deal. Events and circumstances sometimes cause men to change their minds or to adopt policies they have previously opposed. The process of reform was but temporarily halted in 1914, only to be reactivated by 1916. But before we tell this story we must first give some account of other events more portentous for the immediate future of the American people.

PART IV

THE SECOND AFTERMATH

THOMAS A. BAILEY

THOMAS A. BAILEY's *Woodrow Wilson and the Peacemakers* is uniquely provocative among the literature describing America's role in the peace settlement following the First World War. It has given offense to both Wilson's friends and his enemies. Founded in a belief in the value of American participation in international organizations, it attacks the isolationists of 1919—indeed, it condemns isolationism in any year of the twentieth century. Yet it is a work whose main distinction lies in the blame it puts on Wilson's shoulders for the failure of the United States to ratify the Versailles Treaty. In short, while upholding vigorously Wilson's principles, it criticizes his actions.

The climax of the book is the Senate's rejection of membership in the League of Nations and the author's explanation of it. Bailey maintains that the crucial element in the situation was the character of the President. The same stubbornness and moral strength that enabled Wilson to persevere at Paris until he got the League established prevented him from accepting the compromises necessary for the ratification by the American government. This conclusion is based upon two fundamental assumptions: that these compromises—known as the Lodge Reservations—would not have destroyed the effectiveness of the League, and that they were acceptable to two thirds of the Senate, to the American people as a whole, and to the League members.

Bailey is firmly convinced of the truth of these assumptions. Blind to reality because of his moralism and his anger at the opposition, Wilson believed them to be false and opposed any modification of the League's provisions. It was the President's firmest supporters, joined in strange alliance with the extreme isolationists, who defeated the hopes of a Senate majority to accept the League with an amended covenant.

One of the curiosities of this theme is that it not only makes something of a villain of Wilson but also contributes to a rather flattering view of Henry Cabot Lodge, the Republican leader usually taken to embody the combination of partisanship and stunted vision responsible for the Senate's refusal to ratify. Bailey makes clear Lodge's political motivations but credits him with a greater willingness to compromise than Wilson showed. Further, since Bailey does not believe that the Lodge reservations crippled the League, he is led, consciously or unconsciously, to create an impression of the Senator as the League's friend rather than its opponent.

Obviously, this treatment of the battle over ratification has called forth numerous criticisms. It has seemed perverse to many that more distinction was not made between Wilson's possible errors of judgment as opposed to the mistaken principles of his antagonists. To create the impression that Wilson's tactical blunders are as responsible for the League's defeat as was the isolationist bloc of "Irreconcilables" is to reduce the historical scene to a focus so narrow as to destroy perspective.

The question inevitably arises concerning the relative importance of these particular men and the general atmosphere in which they worked. Bailey gives some attention to the matter of public opinion. But his conclusion that the country stood behind a League with reservations appears to some critics to be based upon an inadequate examination of the broad trends working against American participation on any terms.

In his discussion of the rather technical problem of the extent to which the proposed changes nullified the League's covenant, Bailey is aided by the hindsight which comes from knowing how ineffective the organization became. There is little doubt that Wilson's excessive expectations for the League's success, as well as his self-righteousness, conditioned his response to the plea to compromise. Nevertheless, the fact that the League was a failure does not preclude the possibility of its having been even more ineffectual. Although no one will deny that the membership of the United States would have strengthened the League, there are many who agree with Wilson that Lodge's reservations would have weakened it.

There is more agreement over the morals which Bailey intends to be drawn from his study than there is over the details of the narrative on which he bases them. By the time this book was published, in 1945, it was already reasonably clear to most that the United States could ill afford to withdraw after the Second World War as it had the First World War. Franklin Roosevelt was highly conscious of Wilson's tactical errors and determined not to repeat them. Although some historians may disapprove of the severity of Bailey's censure of the President, not many deny that Wilson contributed to the partisanship which permeated the debates of 1919. Even fewer wish to challenge the author's observation that domestic politics should not guide foreign policy and that compromise in unessentials helps to establish national unity.

The Supreme Infanticide

"As a friend of the President, as one who has loyally followed him, I solemnly declare to him this morning: If you want to kill your own child because the Senate straightens out its crooked limbs, you must take the responsibility and accept the verdict of history." SENATOR ASHURST *of Arizona (Democrat), March 11, 1920.*

1

THE TREATY was now dead, as far as America was concerned. Who had killed it?

The vital role of the loyal Democrats must be reemphasized. If all of them who professed to want the treaty had voted "Yea," it would have passed with more than a dozen votes to spare. If the strait-jacket of party loyalty had not been involved, the necessary two-thirds could easily have been mustered.

In the previous November, the Democrats might have voted against the treaty (as they did) even without White House pressure. But this time pressure had to be applied to force them into line, and even in the face of Wilsonian wrath almost half of them bolted. On the day of the final balloting the newsmen observed that two Cabinet members (Burleson and Daniels), possibly acting at the President's direction, were on the floor of the Senate, buttonholing waverers. The day after the fateful voting Hitchcock wrote Wilson that it had required the "most energetic efforts" on his part *to prevent a majority of the Democrats from surrendering to Lodge.*

Desertion of the President, as we have seen, is no light offense in the political world, especially when he has declared himself emphatically. Senators do not ordinarily court political suicide. Wil-

From *Woodrow Wilson and the Peacemakers,* by Thomas Bailey, copyright 1947 by The Macmillan Company and used with their permission.

son still had the patronage bludgeon in his hands, and having more than a trace of vindictiveness, he could oppose renegade senators when they ran again, and in fact did so.

Many of the loyal Democrats were up for reelection in 1920. They certainly were aware of the effects of party treachery on their political fortunes. They knew—or many of them knew—that they were killing the treaty; they made no real effort to revive it; they must have wanted it killed—at least until after the November election.

One striking fact stands out like a lighthouse. With the exception of Hitchcock of Nebraska, Johnson of South Dakota, and Thomas of Colorado, *every single one of the twenty-three senators who stood loyally with Wilson in March came from south of the Mason and Dixon line.* Only four of the "disloyal" twenty-one represented states that had seceded in 1860–1861. At the polls, as well as on the floor of the Senate, decent southern Democrats voted "the way their fathers shot." As between bothersome world responsibility on the one hand, and loyalty to President, party, section, and race on the other, there was but one choice. Perhaps world leadership would come eventually anyhow.

Democratic senators like Walsh of Montana and Ashurst of Arizona were not from the South. When the issue was clearly drawn between loyalty to party and loyalty to country, their consciences bade them choose the greater good. Ashurst had gone down the line in supporting Wilson; but several days before the final vote he declared, "I am just as much opposed to a White House irreconcilable as I am to a Lodge irreconcilable."

2

A word now about public opinion.

In March, as in November, more than 80 per cent of the senators professed to favor the treaty with some kind of reservations. All the polls and other studies indicate that this was roughly the sentiment of the country. Yet the senators were unable to scrape together a two-thirds vote for any one set of reservations.

The reaction of many newspaper editors, as before, was to cry out against the shame of it all—this indictment of the "capacity of our democracy to do business." We had astonished the world by our ability to make war; we now astonished the world with our "imbecility" in trying to make peace. How could we blame other countries for thinking us "a nation of boobs and bigots"? The Louisville *Courier-Journal* (Democrat), referring to our broken promises to the Allies, cried that we stood betrayed as "cravens and crooks," "hypocrites and liars."

Partisan Republican newspapers loudly blamed the stiff-backed Wilson and his "me-too" senators. Two wings of "irreconcilables"— the Wilsonites and the "bitter-enders"—had closed in to execute a successful pincers movement against the treaty. The New York *Tribune* (Independent Republican) condemned the "inefficiency, all-sufficiency and self-sufficiency of our self-named only negotiator," Woodrow Wilson. If the treaty died, said the *Tribune*, the handle of the dagger that pierced its heart would bear the "initials 'W. W.' "

If Republicans scolded Democrats, Democrats scolded Republicans. Lodge and his cheap political tricks were roundly condemned, and the general conclusion was that "the blood of the Treaty stains the floor of the Republican wigwam." A few of the less partisan Democratic journals openly conceded that Wilson's obstinacy had something to do with the final result. William Jennings Bryan asserted from the platform that this "most colossal crime against our nation and the civilized world in all history" made his "blood boil." He began a vigorous campaign against the two-thirds rule in the Senate. "A majority of Congress can declare war," he cried; "it ought to be as easy to end a war as to begin it."

The leading liberal journals, as before, were sadly happy. They rejoiced that the result would clear the way for a renovation of the treaty, but they regretted that the pact had been defeated as a result of partisanship rather than as a result of the betrayal of Wilson's promises.

An impressive number of the more discerning editors deplored the fact that the issue was now in the dirty hands of politicians. An electoral referendum, it was felt, would merely confuse the issue; such a canvass could not possibly reveal anything more than was already known, namely, that *an overwhelming majority of the people wanted the treaty with some kind of reservations.*

3

Is it true that the invalid in the White House really strangled the treaty to death with his own enfeebled hands?

It is seldom that statesmen have a second chance—a second guess. They decide on a course of action, and the swift current of events bears them downstream from the starting point. Only rarely does the stream reverse itself and carry them back.

In November, Wilson had decided that he wanted deadlock, because he reasoned that deadlock would arouse public opinion and force the Senate to do his bidding. The tidal wave of public opinion did surge in, and Wilson got his second chance. But he threw it away, first by spurning compromise (except on his terms), and then by spurning the Lodge reservations.

There had been much more justification for Wilson's course in November than in March. In November he was sick, secluded, was fed censored news, and was convinced by Hitchcock that the strategy of deadlock was sound. In March, he was much improved in health, far less secluded, more in touch with the press and with the currents of opinion, though probably still not enough. He consulted even less with the Senate, presumably because he had made up his mind in advance to oppose the Lodge reservations. In November, there was a fair possibility of reconsideration; in March, it was clear that the only possibility lay in making the League an issue in the coming campaign. Wilson, with his broad knowledge of government and politics, should have seen that this hope was largely if not completely illusory. Perhaps he would have seen it had he not been blinded by his feeling for Lodge.

The evidence is convincing that Wilson wanted the issue cast into the hurly-burly of politics. He could not accept Lodge's terms; Lodge would not accept his terms. The only possible chance of beating the senator—and this was slim indeed—was to win a resounding mandate in 1920.

Yet this strategy, as already noted, meant further delay. At Paris, the feeling at times had been, "Better a bad treaty today than a good treaty four months hence." Europe was still in chaos, and increasingly in need of America's helping hand. Well might the Europeans cry, "Better a treaty with the Lodge reservations today than a probable treaty without reservations after the election." Or as Dr. Frank Crane wrote in *Current Opinion,* "It is vastly more needful that some sort of League be formed, *any sort,* than that it be formed *perfectly.*" (Italics Crane's.)

Yet Wilson, for the reasons indicated, could not see all this clearly. Four days after the fatal vote he wrote Hitchcock, praising him for having done all in his power to protect the honor of the nation and the peace of the world against the Republican majority.

Mrs. Wilson, no doubt reflecting her husband's views, later wrote, "My conviction is that Mr. Lodge put the world back fifty years, and that at his door lies the wreckage of human hopes and the peril to human lives that afflict mankind today."

4

To the very end Wilson was a fighter. When the Scotch-Irish in him became aroused, he would nail his colors to the mast. He said in 1916 that he was "playing for the verdict of mankind." His conception of duty as he saw it was overpowering. He once remarked that if he were a judge, and it became his duty to sentence his own brother to the gallows, he would do so—and afterwards die of a broken heart.

It is well to have principles; it is well to have a noble conception of duty. But Wilson, as he became warmed up in a fight, tended to get things out of focus and to lose a proper sense of values.

The basic issue in 1920 was the Hitchcock reservations or the Lodge reservations. Wilson accepted those of Hitchcock while rejecting those of Lodge, which, he said, completely nullified the treaty and betrayed his promises to the Allies and to the American dead.

This, as we have seen, was a gross exaggeration. Minds no less acute than Wilson's, and less clouded with sickness and pride, denied that the Lodge reservations completely nullified the treaty. To the man in the street—in so far as he gave the dispute thought—there was little discernible difference between the two sets of reservations. How could one decry statements which merely reaffirmed the basic principles of the Constitution and of our foreign policy? To a vast number of Americans the Lodge reservations, far from nullifying the treaty, actually improved it. This was so apparent to even the most loyal Democrats in the Senate that Wilson could barely keep them in line.

In the final analysis the treaty was slain in the house of its friends rather than in the house of its enemies. In the final analysis it was not the two-thirds rule, or the "irreconcilables," or Lodge, or the "strong" and "mild reservationists," but Wilson and his docile following who delivered the fatal stab. If the President had been permitted to vote he would have sided with Borah, Brandegee, Johnson, and the other "bitter-enders"—though for entirely different reasons.

Wilson had said that the reservation to Article X was a knife thrust at the heart of the Covenant. Ironically, he parried this knife thrust, and stuck his own dagger, not into the heart of the Covenant, but into the entire treaty.

This was the supreme act of infanticide. With his own sickly hands Wilson slew his own brain child—or the one to which he had contributed so much.

This was the supreme paradox. He who had forced the Allies to write the League into the treaty, unwrote it; he who had done more than any other man to make the Covenant, unmade it—at least so far as America was concerned. And by his action, he contributed powerfully to the ultimate undoing of the League, and with it the high hopes of himself and mankind for an organization to prevent World War II.

5

The preceding dogmatic observations are of course qualified by the phrase, "in the last analysis."

Many elements enter into a log jam. Among them are the width of the stream, the depth of the stream, the swiftness of the current, the presence of boulders, the size of the logs, and the absence of enough lumberjacks. No one of these factors can be solely responsible for the pile-up.

Many elements entered into the legislative log jam of March, 1920. Among them were isolationism, partisanship, senatorial prerogative, confusion, apathy, personal pride, and private feuds. No one of them was solely responsible for the pile-up. *But as the pile-up finally developed, there was only one lumberjack who could break it, and that was Woodrow Wilson.* If at any time before the final vote he had told the Senate Democrats to support the treaty with the Lodge reservations, or even if he had merely told them that they were on their own, the pact would almost certainly have been approved. So "in the last analysis" the primary responsibility for the failure in March rested with Wilson.

What about Lodge? If the treaty would have passed by Wilson's surrendering, is it not equally true that it would have passed by Lodge's surrendering?

The answer is probably "Yes," but the important point is that Lodge had far less responsibility for getting the treaty through than Wilson. If Lodge had yielded, he probably would have created a schism within his ranks. His ultimate responsibility was to keep the party from breaking to pieces, and in this he succeeded. Wilson's ultimate responsibility was to get the treaty ratified, and in this he failed. With Lodge, as with any truly partisan leader, the party comes before country; with the President the country should come before party, though unhappily it often does not.

It is possible that Wilson saw all this—but not clearly enough. He might have been willing to compromise if his adversary had been any other than Lodge. But so bitter was the feeling between the two men that Wilson, rather than give way, grasped at the straw of the election of 1920.

Lodge did not like Wilson either, but he made more of a show of compromising than the President. He actually supported and drove through amendments to his original reservations which were in line with Wilson's wishes, and he probably would have gone further had the "irreconcilables" not been on his back. He fought the crippling Irish reservation, as well as others supported by the "bitter-enders." Finally, he gave the Democrats a fair chance to reconsider their vote and get on the bandwagon, but they spurned it.

If Lodge's words mean anything, and if his actions were not those of a monstrous hypocrite, he actually tried to get the treaty through with his reservations. When he found that he could not, he washed his hands of the whole business in disgust.

The charge is frequently made that, if Wilson had yielded to his adversary, Lodge would have gleefully piled on more reservations until Wilson, further humiliated, would have had to throw out the whole thing.

The strongest evidence for this view is a circumstantial story which Secretary Houston relates. During a Cabinet meeting Wilson was called to the telephone, and agreed to make certain concessions agreeable to Lodge. Before adjournment the telephone rang again, and word came that Lodge would not adhere to his original proposal.

This story is highly improbable, because Wilson attended no Cabinet meetings between September 2, 1919, and April 13, 1920. By the latter date, all serious attempts at compromise had been dropped; by the earlier date the treaty was still before the Senate committee, and the Lodge reservations, though in an embryonic stage, were yet unborn. But, even if the story is true, it merely proves that Lodge veered about, as he frequently did under "irreconcilable" pressure.

In March, as in November, all Wilson had to do was to send over Postmaster General Burleson to the Senate a few minutes before the final vote with the quiet word that the Democrats were to vote "Yea." The treaty would then have passed with the Lodge reservations, and Lodge could hardly have dared incur for himself or his party the odium of moving to reconsider for the purpose of screwing on more reservations. Had he tried to do so, the "mild reservationists" almost certainly would have blocked him.

6

A few days after the disastrous final vote, Wilson's only comment to Tumulty was, "They have shamed us in the eyes of the world." If his previous words said what he really meant, he was hardly more ashamed by the defeat of the treaty than by the addition of the Lodge reservations. In his eyes it all amounted to the same thing.

If the treaty had passed, would the President have been willing to go through with the exchange of ratifications? Would he not have pocketed it, as he threatened to do prior to the November vote?

Again, if Wilson's words may be taken at their face value, this is what he would have done. He had not backed down from his pre-November position. His Jackson Day message and his letter to Hitchcock made it unmistakably clear that he preferred the uncertainties of a political campaign to the certainties of ratification with the Lodge reservations. The addition of the indefensible Irish reservation provided even stronger justification for pocketing the entire pact.

It is probable that some of the loyal Democrats voted as they did partly because they were convinced that Wilson was going to pigeon-hole the treaty anyhow. From their point of view it was better that the odium for defeat should seemingly rest on Lodge rather than on their President. It also seems clear that Wilson preferred, as in November, to have the blood of the treaty on the Senate doorstep rather than on his. As he wrote to Secretary Colby, on April 2, 1920, the slain pact lay heavily on the consciences of those who had stabbed it, and he was quite willing to have it lie there until those consciences were either awakened or crushed.

Yet it is one thing to say, just before Senate action, "I will pocket the treaty." It is another, after the pact is approved and sent to the White House, to assume this tremendous responsibility. The eyes of the world are upon the President; he is the only man keeping the nation out of the peace which it so urgently needs; he is the one man standing in the way of the rehabilitation which the world so desperately demands. Public pressure to ratify in such a case would be enormous—probably irresistible.

Some years later Senator Hitchcock said that in the event of senatorial approval Wilson would possibly have waited for the November election. If he had won, he would have worked for the removal of the Lodge reservations; if he had lost, then the compulsion to go through with ratification would have become overpowering. By November more than six months would have passed, and by that time Wilson might have developed a saner perspective.

But this is all speculation. Wilson gave orders that the treaty was to be killed in the Senate chamber. And there it died.

7

One other line of inquiry must be briefly pursued. Is it true, as some writers allege, that the thirty-odd Allied signatories of the original treaty would have rejected the Lodge reservations when officially presented? We recall that under the terms of the preamble these nations were privileged to acquiesce silently or file objections.

One will never know the answer to this question, because Wilson denied the other signatories a chance to act. But it seems proper to point to certain probabilities.

One or more of the Latin American nations might have objected to the reservation regarding the then hated Monroe Doctrine. Yet the Monroe Doctrine would have continued to exist anyhow; it was already in the Covenant; and these neighboring republics might well have swallowed their pride in the interest of world peace.

Italy probably would have acquiesced, and the evidence is strong that France would have done likewise. The Japanese could not completely overlook the Shantung reservation, but it was generally recognized in their press as meaningless, and for this reason it might have been tolerated, though not without some loss of face. It is noteworthy that the most important Japanese newspapers regretted the Senate stalemate as an encouragement to world instability, particularly in China.

Great Britain probably would have been the chief objector. The reservation on Ireland was highly offensive but completely innocuous, for the British lion had long endured Irish-American tail-twistings in pained but dignified silence. The reservation on six-to-one was a slap at the loyal and sacrificing Dominions, but it did not mean that their vote was to be taken away. Moreover, the contingency envisaged by this proviso was unlikely to arise very often, and in the long run would doubtless have proved inconsequential.

In sum, there were only two or three reservations to which the outside powers could seriously object. If they had objected, it is probable that a satisfactory adjustment could have been threshed out through diplomatic channels. For when it became clear that only a few phrases stood between the United States and peace, the dictates of common sense and the pressure of public opinion probably would have led to an acceptable compromise. If the Senate had refused to give ground in such a case, then the onus would have been clearly on it and not on Wilson.

The World Court is a case in point. In 1926 the Senate voted to join, but attached five reservations, four of which were accepted by the other powers. By 1935 a compromise was worked out on the fifth, but an isolationist uprising led by William Randolph Hearst and Father Coughlin turned what seemed to be a favorable vote in the Senate into a narrow defeat for the World Court. The one-third minority again triumphed, with the aging Borah and Johnson and Norris and Gore still voting their fears and prejudices.

But the World Court analogy must not be pressed too far. In 1920 Europe was in a desperate condition; the only real hope for a successful League lay in American cooperation. Unless the United States would shoulder its obligations the whole treaty system was in danger of collapse. In 1926 the powers could afford to haggle over the World Court; in 1920 there was far less temptation to haggle while Europe burned. The European nations were under strong compulsion to swallow their pride, or at the very worst not to drive too hard a bargain in seeking adjustment.

But this again is pure speculation. Wilson never gave the other powers a chance to act on the reservations, though Colonel House and others urged him to. He assumed this terrific responsibility all by himself. While thinking that he was throwing the onus on the consciences of the senators, he was in fact throwing a large share of the onus upon his own bent shoulders.

8

What were the reactions of our recent brothers in arms on the other side of the Atlantic?

The British viewed the Senate debacle with mixed emotions. The result had been a foregone conclusion, and there was some relief in having an end to senatorial uncertainty—at least this stage of it. Some journals were inclined to blame the two-thirds rule; others, the unbending doctrinaire in the White House. The London *Times* sorrowfully concluded that all the processes of peace would have to be suspended pending the outcome of the November election.

The French were shocked, though hardly surprised. The Paris *Liberté* aptly referred to the state of anarchy existing between the executive and the legislative in America. Other journals, smarting under Wilson's recent blast against French militarism, blamed the autocrat in the White House. "At the most troubled moment in history," gibed the Paris *Matin*, "America has a sick President, an amateur Secretary of State, and no Treaty of Peace. A President in the clouds, a Secretary of State in the bushes, and a treaty in the cabbage patch. What a situation!"

But the French did not completely abandon hope that America might yet honor her commitments. Meanwhile they would keep their powder dry and pursue the militaristic course which widened the growing rift between Britain and France, and which proved so fatal to the peace of Europe in the 1930's. The French finally became disgusted with German excuses (which were probably encouraged by America's defection), and in April, 1920, the month after the Senate rejected the treaty, their tanks rumbled into the Ruhr and occupied several German cities as hostages for reparations payments. Bullets were fired, and some blood was shed. This was but a dress rehearsal for the catastrophic invasion of the Ruhr in 1923.

The action—or rather inaction—of the United States had other tragic consequences. It encouraged German radicals in their determination to tear up the treaty: they were finding unwitting collaborators in Senator Borah and President Wilson. It delayed by many months, as British Foreign Secretary Curzon openly charged, the treaty with Turkey, thus giving the "Sick Man of Europe" (Turkey) a chance to prove that he was the "Slick Man of Europe." It held up the economic and moral rehabilitation of the Continent, and even hampered the work of relief then going forward. It further disillusioned the liberals of Europe and others who had clung to Wilson as the major prophet of a new order. It gave new comfort to the forces of disorder everywhere. It left the United States discredited, isolated, shorn of its prestige, and branded as a hypocrite and renegade. It marked the first unbridgeable rift in the ranks of the victorious Allies, a coalition that might have kept the peace. Instead they now went their separate ways, perhaps not as enemies, but certainly no longer as close friends. The United States was the first to break completely away.

America—and the world—paid a high price for the collapse of the treaty-making process in Washington. We are still paying it.

9

One final question. Who won after all these months of parliamentary jockeying?

Lodge the master parliamentarian had not won—that is, if he really wanted the treaty with his reservations. As in November, he was unable to keep the "irreconcilables" in line on the crucial vote, and he was unable to muster a two-thirds majority. He finally had to confess failure of leadership, except in so far as he prevented a schism.

The Republican party had not won. Lodge had avoided a serious split with the "bitter-enders" by knuckling under when they laid down the law. But the Republican leaders did not really want the issue in the campaign, and they had made strong efforts to keep it out. Now it was on their hands to cause them no end of embarrassment.

Wilson had not won. He has been praised for having kept the party ranks intact, and for having retained undisputed leadership of his following. But the Democrats in the Senate split 21 for the treaty to 23 against it, and that is hardly holding one's followers in line. Wilson lost irreparably because he did not get his treaty, even with reservations, and because he was doomed to lose again by insisting on a referendum where there could be no referendum.

The Democrats had not won. The treaty issue had caused a serious rift in the Senate, and Bryan, who was still a great leader, was on the rampage. Except for Wilson and some of his "yes men," there were few Democratic leaders who wanted this troublesome issue catapulted into the campaign. Yet there it was.

The United States had not won. It had won the war, to be sure; but it was now kicking the fruits of the victory back under the peace table. We had helped turn Europe into a scrap heap, and now we were scrapping the treaty. We were going to stand by the Allies—with our arms folded. We were throwing away the only hope of averting World War II.

The real victor was international anarchy.

FREDERICK LEWIS ALLEN

As THE HISTORIAN comes closer to the present, he is confronted by both new opportunities and added obstacles. Whereas the chroniclers of remote times must search for every scrap of evidence, the recent past yields an embarrassing richness of material. Instead of worrying about whether his research has been exhaustive, the historian must concern himself with the development of sampling techniques which will permit him to get an accurate picture of the whole from a partial examination of the evidence.

Historians of the period after the First World War share the knowledge and insight which comes from having lived during the years they describe, but they have difficulty shedding the personal feelings which they experienced as participants. The record left by contemporary historians of other postwar periods does not inspire confidence in the ability of today's writers to be accurate in their analyses of the modern era. One recalls the patriotic distortion of the early accounts of the Revolution, the sectional prejudice of the Reconstruction historians, and the myopic nationalism which characterized the first narratives of the war with Spain. Such a series of failures suggests that the intention to be objective does not guarantee objectivity.

Nevertheless, one turns with at least a modicum of assurance to Frederick Lewis Allen's *Only Yesterday* for a description of life in America during the 1920's. Published in 1931, the book continues to enjoy a wide audience, and recent informal histories of the same period are surprisingly similar in their tone and emphasis. Further, since it is primarily descriptive rather than analytical, its usefulness is not dependent upon judgments, which might have been too quick, but upon a more durable foundation of facts.

In such a work, the author's individual interpretation does not lie on the surface but must be sought indirectly in his selection of material and the emphasis which he gives to some events at the expense of others. What interests Allen most is change rather than continuity, the individual characteristics of the 1920's rather than the long-term developments of American culture. With a sureness of touch revealing his journalistic training, he seizes upon the strange and the dramatic and presents a lively picture which most readers have found both entertaining and informative.

There is little doubt of the accuracy of the facts which he presents, but there is some question concerning their meaning. The world of Wall Street and Red Grange, of Bruce Barton, H. L. Mencken, and Al Capone was undoubtedly part of America—certainly the most publicized part. But can this part be taken for the whole? Apparently, Allen's view that the 1920's formed a distinct era in American history led him to overemphasize the conspicuous personalities and spectacular events which gave the period its distinctiveness. In describing what was unique, he does not entirely fulfill his promise to "reveal the fundamental trends in our national life and national thought." After the strikes of 1919, labor almost entirely disappears from his pages; the millions who spent their lives in farming communities are largely overlooked. There is little about domestic prices or American investments overseas.

The author's desire to set these years apart also leads him to a rather exaggerated emphasis on the prosperity of the era. By inference, one might come to believe that every closet housed a raccoon coat. An entire chapter is devoted to the Wall Street boom, but only a few paragraphs are concerned with the sick industries of the period. In the first chapter, the reader is introduced to a "Mr. Smith," whose daily routine is used to describe American society in 1919. But when "Mr. Smith" goes to luncheon at "his club" and joins his wife at a tea dance after work, it is obvious that most Americans could not follow him.

Yet the incompleteness of the work hardly destroys its value. When the book is considered for what it is, rather than for what it is not, one finds much to praise. If Allen describes the prosperousness of the 1920's, he is even more successful in depicting its spiritual poverty. Instead of presenting a fond reminiscence of the days of easy profits, he reveals the essential shallowness and the sense of insecurity which characterized many of the people who shared in those profits. Since it was Allen's intention to supply an obituary to an era, perhaps the study is necessarily fragmentary. What was healthy about these years is the other, larger fragment which constitutes America's permanent endowment.

Coolidge Prosperity

BUSINESS was booming when Warren Harding died, and in a primitive Vermont farmhouse, by the light of an old-fashioned kerosene lamp, Colonel John Coolidge administered to his son Calvin the oath of office as President of the United States. The hopeless depression of 1921 had given way to the hopeful improvement of 1922 and the rushing revival of 1923.

The prices of common stocks, to be sure, suggested no unreasonable optimism. On August 2, 1923, the day of Harding's death, United States Steel (paying a five-dollar dividend) stood at 87, Atchison (paying six dollars) at 95, New York Central (paying

From *Only Yesterday* by Frederick Lewis Allen, by permission of Harper & Brothers. Copyright, 1931, by Frederick Lewis Allen.

seven) at 97, and American Telephone and Telegraph (paying nine) at 122; and the total turnover for the day on the New York Stock Exchange amounted to only a little over 600,000 shares. The Big Bull Market was still far in the future. Nevertheless the tide of prosperity was in full flood.

Pick up one of those graphs with which statisticians measure the economic ups and downs of the Post-war Decade. You will find that the line of business activity rises to a jagged peak in 1920, drops precipitously into a deep valley in late 1920 and 1921, climbs uncertainly upward through 1922 to another peak at the middle of 1923, dips somewhat in 1924 (but not nearly so far as in 1921), rises again in 1925 and 1926, dips momentarily but slightly toward the end of 1927, and then zigzags up to a perfect Everest of prosperity in 1929—only to plunge down at last into the bottomless abyss of 1930 and 1931.

Hold the graph at arm's-length and glance at it again, and you will see that the clefts of 1924 and 1927 are mere indentations in a lofty and irregular plateau which reaches from early 1923 to late 1929. That plateau represents nearly seven years of unparalleled plenty; nearly seven years during which men and women might be disillusioned about politics and religion and love, but believed that at the end of the rainbow there was at least a pot of negotiable legal tender consisting of the profits of American industry and American salesmanship; nearly seven years during which the business man was, as Stuart Chase put it, "the dictator of our destinies," ousting "the statesman, the priest, the philosopher, as the creator of standards of ethics and behavior" and becoming "the final authority on the conduct of American society." For nearly seven years the prosperity band-wagon rolled down Main Street.

Not everyone could manage to climb aboard this wagon. Mighty few farmers could get so much as a fingerhold upon it. Some dairymen clung there, to be sure, and fruit-growers and truck-gardeners. For prodigious changes were taking place in the national diet as the result of the public's discovery of the useful vitamin, the propaganda for a more varied menu, and the invention of better methods of shipping perishable foods. Between 1919 and 1926 the national production of milk and milk products increased by one-third and that of ice-cream alone took a 45-per-cent jump. Between 1919 and 1928, as families learned that there were vitamins in celery, spinach, and carrots, and became accustomed to serving fresh vegetables the year round (along with fresh fruits), the acreage of nineteen commercial truck vegetable crops nearly doubled. But the growers of staple crops such as wheat and corn and cotton were in a bad way. Their foreign markets had dwindled under competition from other countries. Women were wearing less and less cotton. Few agricultural raw materials were used in the new economy of automobiles and radios and electricity. And the more efficient the poor farmer became, the more machines he bought to increase his output and thus keep the wolf from the door, the more surely he and his fellows were faced by the specter of overproduction. The index number of all farm prices, which had coasted from 205 in 1920 to 116 in 1921—"perhaps the most terrible toboggan slide in all American agricultural history," to quote Stuart Chase again—regained only a fraction of the ground it had lost: in 1927 it stood at 131. Loudly the poor farmers complained, desperately they and their Norrises and Brookharts and Shipsteads and La Follettes campaigned for federal aid, and by the hundreds of thousands they left the farm for the cities.

There were other industries unrepresented in the triumphal march of progress. Coal-mining suffered, and textile-manufacturing, and shipbuilding, and shoe and leather manufacturing. Whole regions of the country felt the effects of depression in one or more of these industries. The South was held back by cotton, the agricultural Northwest by the dismal condition of the wheat growers, New England by the paralysis of the textile and shoe industries. Nevertheless, the prosperity band-wagon did not lack for occupants, and their good fortune outweighed and outshouted the ill fortune of those who lamented by the roadside.

2

In a position of honor rode the automobile manufacturer. His hour of destiny had struck. By this time paved roads and repair shops and filling stations had become so plentiful that the motorist might sally forth for the day without fear of being stuck in a mudhole or stranded without benefit of gasoline or crippled by a dead spark plug. Automobiles were now made with such precision, for that matter, that the motorist need hardly know a spark plug by sight;

thousands of automobile owners had never even lifted the hood to see what the engine looked like. Now that closed cars were in quantity production, furthermore, the motorist had no need of Spartan blood, even in January. And the stylish new models were a delight to the eye. At the beginning of the decade most cars had been somber in color, but with the invention of pyroxylin finishes they broke out (in 1925 and 1926) into a whole rainbow of colors, from Florentine cream to Versailles violet. Bodies were swung lower, expert designers sought new harmonies of line, balloon tires came in, and at last even Henry Ford capitulated to style and beauty.

If any sign had been needed of the central place which the automobile had come to occupy in the mind and heart of the average American, it was furnished when the Model A Ford was brought out in December, 1927. Since the previous spring, when Henry Ford had shut down his gigantic plant, scrapped his Model T and the thousands of machines which brought it into being, and announced that he was going to put a new car on the market, the country had been in a state of suspense. Obviously he would have to make drastic changes. Model T had been losing to Chevrolet its leadership in the enormous low-priced-car market, for the time had come when people were no longer content with ugliness and a maximum speed of forty or forty-five miles an hour; no longer content, either, to roar slowly uphill with a weary left foot jammed against the low-speed pedal while robin's-egg blue Chevrolets swept past in second. Yet equally obviously Henry Ford was the mechanical genius of the age. What miracle would he accomplish?

Rumor after rumor broke into the front pages of the newspapers. So intense was the interest that even the fact that an automobile dealer in Brooklyn had "learned something of the new car through a telegram from his brother Henry" was headline stuff. When the editor of the Brighton, Michigan, *Weekly Argus* actually snapped a photograph of a new Ford out for a trial spin, newspaper-readers pounced on the picture and avidly discussed its every line. The great day arrived when this newest product of the inventive genius of the age was to be shown to the public. The Ford Motor Company was running in 2,000 daily newspapers a five-day series of full-page advertisements at a total cost of $1,300,000; and everyone who could read was reading them. On December 2, 1927, when Model A was unveiled, one million people—so the *Herald-Tribune* figured—tried to get into the Ford headquarters in New York to catch a glimpse of it; as Charles Merz later reported in his life of Ford, "one hundred thousand people flocked into the showrooms of the Ford Company in Detroit; mounted police were called out to patrol the crowds in Cleveland; in Kansas City so great a mob stormed Convention Hall that platforms had to be built to lift the new car high enough for everyone to see it." So it went from one end of the United States to the other. Thousands of orders piled up on the Ford books for Niagara Blue roadsters and Arabian Sand phaetons. For weeks and months, every new Ford that appeared on the streets drew a crowd. To the motor-minded American people the first showing of a new kind of automobile was no matter of merely casual or commercial interest. It was one of the great events of the year 1927; not so thrilling as Lindbergh's flight, but rivaling the execution of Sacco and Vanzetti, the Hall-Mills murder trial, the Mississippi flood, and the Dempsey-Tunney fight at Chicago in its capacity to arouse public excitement.

In 1919 there had been 6,771,000 passenger cars in service in the United States; by 1929 there were no less than 23,121,000. There you have possibly the most potent statistic of Coolidge Prosperity. As a footnote to it I suggest the following. Even as early as the end of 1923 there were two cars for every three families in "Middletown," a typical American city. The Lynds and their investigators interviewed 123 working-class families of "Middletown" and found that 60 of them had cars. Of these 60, 26 lived in such shabby-looking houses that the investigators thought to ask whether they had bathtubs, and discovered that as many as 21 of the 26 had none. The automobile came even before the tub!

And as it came, it changed the face of America. Villages which had once prospered because they were "on the railroad" languished with economic anæmia; villages on Route 61 bloomed with garages, filling stations, hot-dog stands, chicken-dinner restaurants, tearooms, tourists' rests, camping sites, and affluence. The interurban trolley perished, or survived only as a pathetic anachronism. Railroad after railroad gave up its branch lines, or saw its revenues slowly dwindling under the competition of mammoth interurban busses and trucks snorting along six-lane concrete highways. The whole country was covered with a network of passenger bus-lines. In thousands of towns, at the beginning of the decade a single traffic officer at the junction of Main Street and Central Street had been sufficient for the control of traffic. By the end of the decade, what a difference!— red and green lights, blinkers, one-way streets, boulevard stops, stringent and yet more stringent parking ordinances—and still a shining flow of traffic that backed up for blocks along Main Street every Saturday and Sunday afternoon. Slowly but surely the age of steam was yielding to the gasoline age.

3

The radio manufacturer occupied a less important seat than the automobile manufacturer on the prosperity band-wagon, but he had the distinction of being the youngest rider. You will remember that there was no such thing as radio broadcasting to the public until the autumn of 1920, but that by the spring of 1922 radio had become a craze—as much talked about as Mah Jong was to be the following year or cross-word puzzles the year after. In 1922 the sales of radio sets, parts, and accessories amounted to $60,000,000. People wondered what would happen when the edge wore off the novelty of hearing a jazz orchestra in Schenectady or in Davenport, Iowa, play "Mr. Gallagher and Mr. Shean." What actually did happen is suggested by the cold figures of total annual radio sales for the next few years:

```
1922—$ 60,000,000     (as we have just seen)
1923—$136,000,000
1924—$358,000,000
1925—$430,000,000
1926—$506,000,000
1927—$425,600,000
1928—$650,550,000
1929—$842,548,000     (an increase over the 1922
                       figures of 1,400 per cent!)
```

Don't hurry past those figures. Study them a moment, remembering that whenever there is a dip in the curve of national prosperity there is likely to be a dip in the sales of almost every popular commodity. There was a dip in national prosperity in 1927, for instance; do you see what it did to radio sales? But there was also a dip in 1924, a worse one in fact. Yet radio sales made in that year the largest proportional increase in the whole period. Why? Well, for one thing, that was the year in which the embattled Democrats met at Madison Square Garden in New York to pick a standard-bearer, and the deadlock between the hosts of McAdoo and the hosts of Al Smith lasted day after day after day, and millions of Americans heard through loud-speakers the lusty cry of, "Alabama, twenty-four votes for Underwoo—ood!" and discovered that a political convention could be a grand show to listen to and that a seat by the radio was as good as a ticket to the Garden. Better, in fact; for at any moment you could turn a knob and get "Barney Google" or "It Ain't Gonna Rain No More" by way of respite. At the age of three and a half years, radio broadcasting had attained its majority.

Behind those figures of radio sales lies a whole chapter of the life of the Post-war Decade: radio penetrating every third home in the country; giant broadcasting stations with nation-wide hook-ups; tenement-house roofs covered with forests of antennæ; Roxy and his Gang, the Happiness Boys, the A & P Gypsies, and Rudy Vallee crooning from antique Florentine cabinet sets; Graham McNamee's voice, which had become more familiar to the American public than that of any other citizen of the land, shouting across your living-room and mine: "*And* he did it! Yes, sir, he did it! It's a touchdown! Boy, I want to tell you this is one of the finest games . . ."; the Government belatedly asserting itself in 1927 to allocate wavelengths among competing radio stations; advertisers paying huge sums for the privilege of introducing Beethoven with a few well-chosen words about yeast or toothpaste; and Michael Meehan personally conducting the common stock of the Radio Corporation of America from a 1928 low of 85¼ to a 1929 high of 549.

There were other riders on the prosperity band-wagon. Rayon, cigarettes, refrigerators, telephones, chemical preparations (especially cosmetics), and electrical devices of various sorts all were in growing demand. While the independent storekeeper struggled to hold his own, the amount of retail business done in chain stores and department stores jumped by leaps and bounds. For every $100 worth of business done in 1919, by 1927 the five-and-ten-cent chains were doing $260 worth, the cigar chains $153 worth, the drug chains $224 worth, and the grocery chains $387 worth. Mrs. Smith no longer patronized her "naborhood" store; she climbed into her two-thousand dollar car to drive to the red-fronted chain grocery and save twenty-seven cents on her daily purchases. The movies prospered, sending their celluloid reels all over the world and making Charlie Chaplin, Douglas Fairbanks, Gloria Swanson, Rudolph Valentino, and Clara Bow familiar figures to the Eskimo, the Malay, and the heathen Chinee; while at home the attendance at the motion-picture houses of "Middletown" during a single month (December, 1923) amounted to four and a half times the entire population of the city. Men, women, and children, rich and poor, the Middletowners went to the movies at an average rate of better than once a week!

Was this Coolidge Prosperity real? The farmers did not think so. Perhaps the textile manufacturers did not think so. But the figures of corporation profits and wages and incomes left little room for doubt. Consider, for example, two significant facts at opposite ends of the scale of wealth. Between 1922 and 1927, the purchasing power of American wages increased at the rate of more than two per cent annually. And during the three years between 1924 and 1927 alone there was a leap from 75 to 283 in the number of Americans who paid taxes on incomes of more than a million dollars a year.

4

Why did it happen? What made the United States so prosperous?

Some of the reasons were obvious enough. The war had impoverished Europe and hardly damaged the United States at all; when peace came the Americans found themselves the economic masters of the world. Their young country, with enormous resources in materials and in human energy and with a wide domestic market, was ready to take advantage of this situation. It had developed mass production to a new point of mechanical and managerial efficiency. The Ford gospel of high wages, low prices, and standardized manufacture on a basis of the most minute division of machine-tending labor was working smoothly not only at Highland Park, but in thousands of other factories. Executives, remembering with a shudder the piled-up inventories of 1921, had learned the lesson of cautious hand-to-mouth buying; and they were surrounded with more expert technical consultants, research men, personnel managers, statisticians, and business forecasters than had ever before invaded that cave of the winds, the conference room. Their confidence was strengthened by their almost superstitious belief that the Republican Administration was their invincible ally. And they were all of them aided by the boom in the automobile industry. The phenomenal activity of this one part of the body economic—which was responsible, directly or indirectly, for the employment of nearly four million men—pumped new life into all the rest.

Prosperity was assisted, too, by two new stimulants to purchasing, each of which mortgaged the future but kept the factories roaring while it was being injected. The first was the increase in installment buying. People were getting to consider it old-fashioned to limit their purchases to the amount of their cash balance; the thing to do was to "exercise their credit." By the latter part of the decade, economists figured that 15 per cent of all retail sales were on an installment basis, and that there were some six billions of "easy payment" paper outstanding. The other stimulant was stock-market speculation. When stocks were skyrocketing in 1928 and 1929 it is probable that hundreds of thousands of people were buying goods with money which represented, essentially, a gamble on the business profits of the nineteen-thirties. It was fun while it lasted.

If these were the principal causes of Coolidge Prosperity, the salesman and the advertising man were at least its agents and evangels. Business had learned as never before the immense importance to it of the ultimate consumer. Unless he could be persuaded to buy and buy lavishly, the whole stream of six-cylinder cars, super-heterodynes, cigarettes, rouge compacts, and electric ice-boxes would be dammed at its outlet. The salesman and the advertising man held the key to this outlet. As competition increased their methods became more strenuous. No longer was it considered enough to recommend one's goods in modest and explicit terms and to place them on the counter in the hope that the ultimate consumer would make up his mind to purchase. The advertiser must plan elaborate national campaigns, consult with psychologists, and employ all the eloquence of poets to cajole, exhort, or intimidate the consumer into buying,—to "break down consumer resistance." Not only was each individual concern struggling to get a larger share of the business in its own field, but whole industries shouted against one another in the public's ear. The embattled candy manufacturers took full-page space in the newspapers to reply to the American Tobacco Company's slogan of

"Reach for a Lucky instead of a sweet." Trade journals were quoted by the *Reader's Digest* as reporting the efforts of the furniture manufacturers to make the people "furniture conscious" and of the clothing manufacturers to make them "tuxedo conscious." The salesman must have the ardor of a zealot, must force his way into people's houses by hook or by crook, must let nothing stand between him and the consummation of his sale. As executives put it, "You can't be an order-taker any longer—you've got to be a *salesman*." The public, generally speaking, could be relied upon to regard with complacence the most flagrant assaults upon its credulity by the advertiser and the most outrageous invasions of its privacy by the salesman; for the public was in a mood to forgive every sin committed in the holy name of business.

Never before had such pressure been exerted upon salesmen to get results. Many concerns took up the quota system, setting as the objective for each sales representative a figure 20 or 25 per cent beyond that of the previous year, and putting it up to him to reach this figure or lose his employer's favor and perhaps his job. All sorts of sales contests and other ingenious devices were used to stimulate the force. Among the schemes suggested by the Dartnell Company of Chicago, which had more than ten thousand American business organizations subscribing to its service, was that of buying various novelties and sending them to the salesman at weekly intervals: one week a miniature feather duster with a tag urging him to "dust his territory," another week an imitation cannon cracker with the injunction to "make a big noise," and so on. The American Slicing Machine Company offered a turkey at Christmas to every one of its salesmen who beat his quota for the year. "We asked each man," explained the sales manager afterward, "to appoint a child in his family as a mascot, realizing that every one of them would work his head off to make some youngster happy at Christmas. The way these youngsters took hold of the plan was amusing, and at times the intensity of their interest was almost pathetic." The sales manager of another concern reported cheerfully that "one of his stunts" was "to twit one man at the good work of another until he is almost sore enough to be ready to fight." And according to Jesse Rainsford Sprague, still another company invented—and boasted of—a method of goading its salesmen which for sheer inhumanity probably set a record for the whole era of Coolidge Prosperity. It gave a banquet at which the man with the best score was served with oysters, roast turkey, and a most elaborate ice; the man with the second best score had the same dinner but without the oysters; and so on down to the man with the worst score, before whom was laid a small plate of boiled beans and couple of crackers.

If the salesman was sometimes under pressure such as this, it is not surprising that the consumer felt the pressure, too. Let two extreme instances (both cited by Jesse Rainsford Sprague) suffice to suggest the trend in business methods. A wholesale drug concern offered to the trade a small table with a railing round its top for the display of "specials"; it was to be set up directly in the path of customers, "whose attention," according to *Printer's Ink*, "will be attracted to the articles when they fall over it, bump into it, kick their shins upon it, or otherwise come in contact with it." And *Selling News* awarded one of its cash prizes for "sales ideas" to a vender of electric cleaners who told the following story of commercial prowess. One day he looked up from the street and saw a lady shaking a rug out of a second-story window. "The door leading to her upstairs rooms was open. I went right in and up those stairs without knocking, greeting the lady with the remark: 'Well, I am here right on time. What room do you wish me to start in?' She was very much surprised, assuring me that I had the wrong number. But during my very courteous apologies I had managed to get my cleaner connected and in action. The result was that I walked out minus the cleaner, plus her contract and check for a substantial down payment." The readers of *Selling News* were apparently not expected to be less than enthusiastic at the prospect of a man invading a woman's apartment and setting up a cleaner in it without permission and under false pretenses. For if you could get away with such exploits, it helped business, and good business helped prosperity, and prosperity was good for the country.

5

The advertisers met the competition of the new era with better design, persuasively realistic photographs, and sheer volume: the amount of advertising done in 1927, according to Francis H. Sisson, came to over a billion and a half dollars. They met it with a new frankness, introducing to staid magazine readers the advantages of Odo-ro-no and Kotex. And they met it, furthermore, with a subtle change in technic. The copy-writer was learning to pay less attention to the special qualities and advantages of his product, and more to the study of what the mass of unregenerate mankind wanted—to be young and desirable, to be rich, to keep up with the Joneses, to be envied. The winning method was to associate his product with one or more of these ends, logically or illogically, truthfully or cynically; to draw a lesson from the dramatic case of some imaginary man or woman whose fate was altered by the use of X's soap, to show that in the most fashionable circles people were choosing the right cigarette in blindfold tests, or to suggest by means of glowing testimonials— often bought and paid for—that the advertised product was used by women of fashion, movie stars, and non-stop flyers. One queen of the films was said to have journeyed from California all the way to New York to spend a single exhausting day being photographed for testimonial purposes in dozens of costumes and using dozens of commercial articles, many of which she had presumably never laid eyes on before—and all because the appearance of these testimonials would help advertise her newest picture. Of what value were sober facts from the laboratory: did not a tooth-powder manufacturer try to meet the hokum of emotional toothpaste advertising by citing medical authorities, and was not his counter-campaign as a breath in a gale? At the beginning of the decade advertising had been considered a business; in the early days of Coolidge Prosperity its fulsome prophets were calling it a profession; but by the end of the decade many of its practitioners, observing the overwhelming victory of methods taken over from tabloid journalism, were beginning to refer to it—among themselves—as a racket.

A wise man of the nineteen-twenties might have said that he cared not who made the laws of the country if he only might write its national advertising. For here were the sagas of the age, romances and tragedies depicting characters who became more familiar to the populace than those in any novel. The man who distinctly remembered Mr. Addison Sims of Seattle. . . . The four out of five who, failing to use Forhan's, succumbed to pyorrhea, each of them with a white mask mercifully concealing his unhappy mouth. . . . The pathetic figure of the man, once a golf champion, "now only a wistful onlooker" creeping about after the star players, his shattered health due to tooth neglect. . . . The poor fellow sunk in the corner of a taxicab, whose wife upbraided him with not having said a word all evening (when he might so easily have shone with the aid of the *Elbert Hubbard Scrap Book*). . . . The man whose conversation so dazzled the company that the envious dinner-coated bystanders could only breathe in amazement, "I think he's quoting from Shelley." . . . The woman who would undoubtedly do something about B. O. if people only said to her what they really thought. . . . The man whose friends laughed when the waiter spoke to him in French. . . . The girl who thought filet mignon was a kind of fish. . . . The poor couple who faced one another in humiliation after their guests were gone, the wife still holding the door knob and struggling against her tears, the husband biting his nails with shame (When Your Guests Are Gone—Are You Sorry You Ever Invited Them? . . . Be Free From All Embarrassment! Let the Famous *Book of Etiquette* Tell You Exactly What to Do, Say, Write, or Wear on Every Occasion). . . . The girl who merely carried the daisy chain, yet she had athlete's foot. . . . These men and women of the advertising pages, suffering or triumphant, became a part of the folklore of the day.

Sometimes their feats were astonishing. Consider, for example, the man who had purchased Nelson Doubleday's *Pocket University*, and found himself, one evening, in a group in which some one mentioned Ali Baba:

> Ali Baba? I sat forward in my chair. I could tell them all about this romantic, picturesque figure of fiction.
> I don't know how it happened, but they gathered all around me. And I told them of golden ships that sailed the seven seas, of a famous man and his donkey who wandered unknown ways, of the brute-man from whom we are all descended. I told them things they never knew of Cleopatra, of the eccentric Diogenes, of Romulus and the founding of Rome. I told them of the unfortunate death of Sir Raleigh (*sic*), of the tragic end of poor Anne Boleyn. . . .
> "You must have traveled all over the world to know so many marvelous things."

Skeptics might smile, thanking themselves that they were not of the company on that interminable evening; but the advertisement stuck in their minds. And to others, less sophisticated, it doubtless opened shining vistas of delight. They, too, could hold the dinner party spellbound if only they filled out the coupon. . . .

By far the most famous of these dramatic advertisements of the Post-war Decade was the long series in which the awful results of halitosis were set forth through the depiction of a gallery of unfortunates whose closest friends would not tell them. "Often a bridesmaid but never a bride. . . . Edna's case was really a pathetic one." . . . "Why did she leave him that way?" . . . "*That's* why you're a failure," . . . and then that devilishly ingenious display which capitalized the fears aroused by earlier tragedies in the series: the picture of a girl looking at a Listerine advertisement and saying to herself, "This *can't* apply to me!" Useless for the American Medical Association to insist that Listerine was "not a true deodorant," that it simply covered one smell with another. Just as useless as for the Life Extension Institute to find "one out of twenty with pyorrhea, rather than Mr. Forhan's famous four-out-of-five" (to quote Stuart Chase once more). Halitosis had the power of dramatic advertising behind it, and Listerine swept to greater and greater profits on a tide of public trepidation.

6

As year followed year of prosperity, the new diffusion of wealth brought marked results. There had been a great boom in higher education immediately after the war, and the boom continued, although at a somewhat slackened pace, until college trustees were beside themselves wondering how to find room for the swarming applicants. There was an epidemic of outlines of knowledge and books of etiquette for those who had got rich quick and wanted to get cultured quick and become socially at ease. Wells's *Outline of History*, the best-selling non-fiction book of 1921 and 1922, was followed by Van Loon's *Story of Mankind*, J. Arthur Thomson's *Outline of Science* (both of them best sellers in 1922), the Doubleday mail-order *Book of Etiquette* and Emily Post's *Book of Etiquette* (which led the non-fiction list in 1923), *Why We Behave Like Human Beings* (a big success of 1926), and *The Story of Philosophy*, which ran away from all other books in the non-fiction list of 1927.

There was a rush of innocents abroad. According to the figures of the Department of Commerce, over 437,000 people left the United

States by ship for foreign parts in the year 1928 alone, to say nothing of 14,000 odd who entered Canada and Mexico by rail, and over three million cars which crossed into Canada for a day or more. The innocents spent freely: the money that they left abroad, in fact (amounting in 1928 to some 650,000,000), solved for a time a difficult problem in international finance: how the United States could continue to receive interest on her foreign debts and foreign investments without permitting foreign goods to pass the high tariff barrier in large quantities.

The United States became the banker and financial arbitrator for the world. When the financial relations between Germany and the Allies needed to be straightened out, it was General Charles G. Dawes and Owen D. Young who headed the necessary international commissions—not only because their judgment was considered wise, and impartial as between the countries of Europe, but because the United States was in a position to call the tune. Americans were called in to reorganize the finances of one country after another. American investments abroad increased by leaps and bounds. The squat limestone building at the corner of Broad and Wall Streets, still wearing the scars of the shrapnel which had struck it during the 1920 explosion, had become the undisputed financial center of the world. Only occasionally did the United States have to intervene by force of arms in other countries. The Marines ruled Haiti and restored order in Nicaragua; but in general the country extended its empire not by military conquest or political dictation, but by financial penetration.

At home, one of the most conspicuous results of prosperity was the conquest of the whole country by urban tastes and urban dress and the urban way of living. The rube disappeared. Girls in the villages of New Hampshire and Wyoming wore the same brief skirts and used the same lip-sticks as their sisters in New York. The proletariat —or what the radicals of the Big Red Scare days had called the proletariat—gradually lost its class consciousness; the American Federation of Labor dwindled in membership and influence; the time had come when workingmen owned second-hand Buicks and applauded Jimmy Walker, not objecting in the least, it seemed, to his exquisite clothes, his valet, and his frequent visits to the millionaire-haunted sands of Palm Beach. It was no accident that men like

Mellon and Hoover and Morrow found their wealth an asset rather than a liability in public office, or that there was a widespread popular movement to make Henry Ford President in 1924. The possession of millions was a sign of success, and success was worshiped the country over.

7

Business itself was regarded with a new veneration. Once it had been considered less dignified and distinguished than the learned professions, but now people thought they praised a clergyman highly when they called him a good business man. College alumni, gathered at their annual banquets, fervently applauded banker trustees who spoke of education as one of the greatest American industries and compared the president and the dean to business executives. The colleges themselves organized business courses and cheerfully granted credit to candidates for degrees in the arts and sciences for their work in advertising copy-writing, marketing methods, elementary stenography, and drug-store practice. Even Columbia University drew men and women into its home-study courses by a system of follow-up letters worthy of a manufacturer of refrigerators, and sent out salesmen to ring the door bells of those who expressed a flicker of interest; even the great University of Chicago made use of what André Siegfried has called "the mysticism of success" by heading an advertisement of its correspondence courses with the admonition to "DEVELOP POWER AT HOME, to investigate, persevere, achieve." . . . The Harvard Business School established annual advertising awards, conferring academic *éclat* upon well-phrased sales arguments for commercial products. It was not easy for the churches to resist the tide of business enthusiasm. The Swedish Immanuel Congregational Church in New York, according to an item in the *American Mercury*, recognized the superiority of the business to the spiritual appeal by offering to all who contributed one hundred dollars to its building fund "an engraved certificate of investment in preferred capital stock in the Kingdom of God." And a church billboard in uptown New York struck the same persuasive note: "Come to Church. Christian Worship Increases Your Efficiency. Christian F. Reisner, Pastor."

In every American city and town, service clubs gathered the flower of the middle-class citizenry together for weekly luncheons noisy with good fellowship. They were growing fast, these service clubs. Rotary, the most famous of them, had been founded in 1905; by 1930 it had 150,000 members and boasted—as a sign of its international influence—as many as 3,000 clubs in 44 countries. The number of Kiwanis Clubs rose from 205 in 1920 to 1,800 in 1929; the Lions Clubs, of which the first was not formed until 1917, multiplied until at the end of the decade there were 1,200 of them. Nor did these clubs content themselves with singing songs and conducting social-service campaigns; they expressed the national faith in what one of their founders called "the redemptive and regenerative influence of business." The speakers before them pictured the business man as a builder, a doer of great things, yes, and a dreamer whose imagination was ever seeking out new ways of serving humanity. It was a popular note, for in hundreds of directors' rooms, around hundreds of conference tables, the American business men of the era of Coolidge Prosperity were seeing themselves as men of vision with eyes steadfastly fixed on the long future. At the end of the decade, a cartoon in the *New Yorker* represented an executive as saying to his heavy-jowled colleagues at one of these meetings: "We have ideas. Possibly we tilt at windmills—just seven Don Juans tilting at windmills." It was a perfect bit of satire on business sentimentality. The service clubs specialized in this sort of mysticism: was not a speaker before the Rotarians of Waterloo, Iowa, quoted by the *American Mercury* as declaring that "Rotary is a manifestation of the divine"?

Indeed, the association of business with religion was one of the most significant phenomena of the day. When the National Association of Credit Men held their annual convention at New York, there were provided for the three thousand delegates a special devotional service at the Cathedral of St. John the Divine and five sessions of prayer conducted by Protestant clergymen, a Roman Catholic priest, and a Jewish rabbi; and the credit men were uplifted by a sermon by Dr. S. Parkes Cadman on "Religion in Business." Likewise the Associated Advertising Clubs, meeting in Philadelphia, listened to a keynote address by Doctor Cadman on "Imagination and Advertising," and at the meeting of the Church Advertising Department the subjects discussed included "Spiritual Principles in Advertising" and "Advertising the Kingdom through Press-Radio Service." The fact that each night of the session a cabaret entertainment was furnished to the earnest delegates from 11.30 to 2 and that part of the Atlantic City Beauty Pageant was presented was merely a sign that even men of high faith must have their fun.

So frequent was the use of the Bible to point the lessons of business and of business to point the lessons of the Bible that it was sometimes difficult to determine which was supposed to gain the most from the association. Fred F. French, a New York builder and real-estate man, told his salesmen, "There is no such thing as a reason why not," and continued: "One evidence of the soundness of this theory may be found in the command laid down in Matthew vii:7 by the Greatest Human-nature Expert that ever lived, 'Knock and it shall be opened unto you.'" He continued by quoting "the greatest command of them all—'Love Thy Neighbor as Thyself' "— and then stated that by following such high principles the Fred F. French salesmen had "immeasurably strengthened their own characters and power, so that during this year they will serve our stockholders at a lower commission rate, and yet each one earn more money for himself than in nineteen hundred twenty-five." In this case Scripture was apparently taken as setting a standard for business to meet—to its own pecuniary profit. Yet in other cases it was not so certain that business was not the standard, the Scripture complimented by being lifted to the business level.

Witness, for example, the pamphlet on *Moses, Persuader of Men* issued by the Metropolitan Casualty Insurance Company (with an introduction by the indefatigable Doctor Cadman), which declared that "Moses was one of the greatest salesmen and real-estate promoters that ever lived," that he was a "Dominant, Fearless, and Successful Personality in one of the most magnificent selling campaigns that history ever placed upon its pages." And witness, finally, the extraordinary message preached by Bruce Barton in *The Man Nobody Knows*, which so touched the American heart that for two successive years—1925 and 1926—it was the best-selling non-fiction book in the United States. Barton sold Christianity to the public by showing its resemblance to business. Jesus, this book taught, was not only "the most popular dinner guest in Jerusalem" and "an outdoor man," but a great executive. "He picked up twelve men from the bottom ranks of business and forged them into an organization that conquered the world. . . . Nowhere is there such a startling example of executive success as the way in which that organization was brought together." His parables were "the most powerful advertisements of all time. . . . He would be a national advertiser today." In fact, Jesus was "the founder of modern business." Why, you ask? Because he was the author of the ideal of service.

The Gospel According to Bruce Barton met a popular demand. Under the beneficent influence of Coolidge Prosperity, business had become almost the national religion of America. Millions of people wanted to be reassured that this religion was altogether right and proper, and that in the rules for making big money lay all the law and the prophets.

Was it strange that during the very years when the Barton Gospel was circulating most vigorously, selling and advertising campaigns were becoming more cynical and the American business world was refusing to exercise itself over the Teapot Dome disclosures and the sordid history of the Continental Trading Company? Perhaps; but it must be remembered that in all religions there is likely to be a gap between faith and works. The business man's halo did not always fit, but he wore it proudly.

8

So the prosperity band-wagon rolled along with throttle wide open and siren blaring. But what of the man on the driver's seat, the man whose name this era bore?

He did not have a jutting chin, a Powerful Personality, or an irresistible flow of selling talk. If you had come from Timbuctoo and found him among a crowd of Chamber of Commerce boosters, he would have been the last man you would have picked as their patron saint. He had never been in business. His canonization by the hosts of quantity production and high-pressure salesmanship was a sublime paradox—and yet it was largely justified. Almost the most remarkable thing about Coolidge Prosperity was Calvin Coolidge.

He was a meager-looking man, a Vermonter with a hatchet face, sandy hair, tight lips, and the expression, as William Allen White remarked, of one "looking down his nose to locate that evil smell which seemed forever to affront him." He was pale and diffident. In private he could be garrulous, but in public he was as silent as a cake of ice. When his firmness in the Boston police strike captured the attention of the country and brought him to Washington as Vice-President, not even the affable warmth of the Harding Administration could thaw him. The Vice-President has to go to many a formal dinner; Coolidge went—and said nothing. The hostesses of Washington were dismayed and puzzled. "Over the Alps lay Italy, they thought, but none of them had won the summit and so they couldn't be sure that the view was worth the climb," wrote Edward G. Lowry. Coolidge became President, and still the frost continued.

Nor did this silence cloak a wide-ranging mind. Coolidge knew his American history, but neither he nor his intellect had ever ventured far abroad. Go through his addresses and his smug *Autobiography,* and the most original thing you will find in them is his uncompromising unoriginality. Calvin Coolidge still believed in the old American copy-book maxims when almost everybody else had half forgotten them or was beginning to doubt them. "The success which is made in any walk of life is measured almost exactly by the amount of hard work that is put into it. . . . There is only one form of political strategy in which I have any confidence, and that is to try to do the right thing and sometimes be able to succeed. . . . If society lacks learning and virtue it will perish. . . . The nation with the greatest moral power will win. . . ." This philosophy of hard work and frugal living and piety crowned with success might have been brought down from some Vermont attic where *McGuffy's Reader* gathered dust. But it was so old that it looked new; it was so exactly what uncounted Americans had been taught at their mother's knee that it touched what remained of the pioneer spirit in their hearts; and Coolidge set it forth with refreshing brevity. So completely did it win over the country that if the President had declared that a straight line is the shortest distance between two points, one wonders if editorial pages would not have paid tribute to his concise wisdom.

He was not a bold leader, nor did he care to be. He followed no gleam, stormed no redoubt. Considering the fact that he was in the White House for five years and seven months, his presidential record was surprisingly negative. But it was just the sort of record that he preferred.

In its foreign policy, his Administration made little effort to persuade the American people that they were not happily isolated from the outside world. Bankers might engage in determining the amount of German reparations, unofficial observers might sit in on European negotiations, but the Government, remembering the decline and fall of Woodrow Wilson, shrewdly maintained an air of magnificent unconcern. Coolidge proposed, as had Harding before him, that the United States should join the World Court, but so gently that when the Senate eventually ratified the proposal with reservations which the other member nations were unable to accept, and the President went out of office without having achieved his end, nobody felt that his prestige suffered much thereby. A second naval conference was held at Geneva in 1927, but ended in failure. A Nicaraguan revolution was settled—after considerable turmoil and humiliation—with the aid of the Marines and of Henry L. Stimson's plan for a new election under American supervision. An even more bitter dispute with Mexico over the legal status of oil lands owned by American interests was finally moderated through the wisdom and tact of Coolidge's Amherst classmate and ambassador, Dwight W. Morrow. But the most conspicuous achievement of the Coolidge Administration in foreign affairs was the leading part it took in securing the Kellogg-Briand Treaty renouncing war as an instrument of national policy—a fine gesture which every nation was delighted to make but which had very little noticeable influence on the actualities of international relations. Aside from the belated solution of the Nicaraguan and Mexican difficulties and the championship of this somewhat innocuous treaty, the policy of the Coolidge Administration was to collect the money due it (even at the expense of considerable ill-feeling), to keep a watchful eye on the expansion of the American financial empire, and otherwise to let well enough alone.

Coolidge's record in domestic affairs was even less exciting. He was nothing if not cautious. When the Harding scandals came to light, he did what was necessary to set in motion an official prosecution, he adroitly jockeyed the notorious Daugherty out of the Cabinet, and from that moment on he exhibited an unruffled and altogether convincing calm. When there was a strike in the anthracite coal mines he did not leap into the breach; he let Governor Gifford Pinchot of Pennsylvania do it. On the one burning political issue of the day, that of prohibition, he managed to express no

opinion except that the laws should be enforced. There was dyna-
mite in prohibition; Calvin Coolidge remained at a safe distance
and looked the other way.

He maintained the *status quo* for the benefit of business. Twice he
vetoed farm relief legislation—to the immense satisfaction of the
industrial and banking community which constituted his strongest
support—on the ground that the McNary-Haugen bills were economically unsound. He vetoed the soldier bonus, too, on the ground
of its expense, though in this case his veto was overruled. His proudest boast was that he cut down the cost of running the Government
by systematic cheeseparing, reduced the public debt, and brought
about four reductions in federal taxes, aiding not only those with
small incomes but even more conspicuously those with large. Meanwhile his Secretary of Commerce, Herbert Hoover, ingeniously
helped business to help itself; on the various governmental commissions, critics of contemporary commercial practices were replaced, as
far as possible, by those who would look upon business with a lenient
eye; and the serene quiet which lay about the White House was
broken only by occasional flattering pronouncements upon business
and assurances that prosperity was securely founded.

An uninspired and unheroic policy, you suggest? But it was sincere: Calvin Coolidge honestly believed that by asserting himself as
little as possible and by lifting the tax burdens of the rich he was
benefiting the whole country—as perhaps he was. And it was perfectly in keeping with the uninspired and unheroic political temper
of the times. For the lusty business men who in these fat years had
become the arbiters of national opinion did not envisage the Government as an agency for making over the country into something
a little nearer to their hearts' desire, as a champion of human rights
or a redresser of wrongs. The prosperity bank-wagon was bringing
them rapidly toward their hearts' desire, and politics might block
the traffic. They did not want a man of action in the Presidency;
they wanted as little government as possible, at as low cost as possible, and this dour New Englander who drove the prosperity band-
wagon with so slack a rein embodied their idea of supreme statesmanship.

Statesmanship of a sort Calvin Coolidge certainly represented.
Prosperity has its undeniable advantages, and a President who is

astute enough to know how to encourage it without getting himself into hot water may possibly be forgiven such complacency as appears in his *Autobiography*. There is perhaps a cool word to be said, too, for the prudence which deliberately accepts the inevitable, which does not even try to be bolder or more magnanimous than circumstances will safely permit. The great god business was supreme in the land, and Calvin Coolidge was fortunate enough to become almost a demi-god by doing discreet obeisance before the altar.

ROBERT S. AND
HELEN MERRELL LYND

~~~~~~

ONLY IN RECENT YEARS have historians come to appreciate the contribution which other social sciences can make to an understanding of history. The reasons that an alliance was not made earlier are not difficult to see. Perhaps, fundamentally, there was need to wait until history ceased to be as preoccupied as it had been with past politics. But it must be remembered also that subjects such as sociology and anthropology did not assume their full dimensions and emerge as useful, independent disciplines until after the turn of the twentieth century.

The help which the historian receives from the kindred social sciences is of two kinds. Indirectly, he is assisted by the different concepts and the new methods which they have developed for handling materials. These may, with varying degrees of modification, be applied by historians to their own subject matter. But in the field of recent history, other social scientists can lend to the historian not only their technology but studies of immediate historical interest. Indeed, as the past merges with the present, the historian seems to lose his separate identity and becomes a combination of sociologist, political analyst, and economist.

Among the accounts of the 1920's now available to the history student, few are more valuable than Robert and Helen Lynd's *Middletown*, published in 1929. Based upon a field investigation conducted by the authors themselves, it is both a source book of primary materials and a secondary analysis of the facts collected. To those who think of the 1920's in terms of raccoon coats, stock-market booms, and Al Capones, *Middletown* comes as a sur-prise—even as a disappointment. The Lynds had no desire to be the lively chroniclers of a bizarre era. Instead, they attempted a clinical study of a typical American community, employing the scientific tools of the trained sociologist. If they were interested in what was new about the postwar period, they were equally concerned with the traditional patterns of action and thought.

It will be apparent at once that this book differs from Frederick Lewis Allen's *Only Yesterday* not only in method and purpose but also in the picture it gives of life in America during the years of "Coolidge Prosperity." The leisure of Middletown's citizens was conditioned by the same automobiles, radios, and motion pictures that loom so prominently in Allen's pages; their jobs were dependent on the same industrial developments that Allen describes. But the people of Middletown shared only a small amount of the prosperity and participated little in the desperate pursuit of pleasure which characterize Allen's 1920's. Theirs was not the insecurity which accompanied speculation in submerged Florida real estate, but that which comes from the chilling fear of unemployment. They could hardly have attended many all-night drinking parties, since most of them were on the way to work by seven o'clock in the morning.

Although *Middletown* and *Only Yesterday* have many points of dissimilarity, they are not necessarily contradictory. Allen's focus is essentially different from the Lynds' and wide enough to include subject matter which the Lynds do not consider. While Allen uses a broad panorama, leaping from New York to Florida and from the Waldorf-Astoria to Senate hearing com-mittees, the Lynds, using the technique of the sociologist, con-centrate their study on a small area, which they attempt to ex-plore intensively.

The obvious merits of *Middletown*, combined with the lack of an equally comprehensive parallel study, make it difficult for anyone to speak confidently of its deficiencies. As a historical study, its only apparent limitations derive from the modesty of the conclusions reached by the authors. One would wish to know what general meaning the Lynds ascribe to this analysis of one town. What portion of America is represented by Middletown and its citizens? How valid is the study for students of southern or New England history? That the answers to such questions lay outside the scope of the authors' intentions will continue to be a matter of regret to students of history.

Yet historians have more cause to rejoice over such a book than to carp at its failure to be designed perfectly for their purposes. Not only does it offer considerable assistance in itself; it suggests the enormous future contribution which the other social sciences can make toward a more mature and enlightened understanding of history.

The Long Arm of the Job

As one prowls Middletown streets about six o'clock of a winter morning one notes two kinds of homes: the dark ones where people still sleep, and the ones with a light in the kitchen where the adults of the household may be seen moving about, starting the business of the day. For the seven out of every ten of those gainfully employed who constitute the working class, getting a living means being at work in the morning anywhere between six-fifteen and seven-thirty o'clock, chiefly seven. For the other three in each ten, the business class, being at work in the morning means seven-forty-five, eight or eight-thirty, or even nine o'clock, but chiefly eight-thirty. Of the sample of 112 working class housewives reporting on this point, forty-eight (two out of five) rise at or before five o'clock, seventy-nine (nearly three-fourths) by five-thirty, and 104 (over nine-tenths) are up at or before six. Among the group of forty business class housewives interviewed, none rises before six, only six at six, fourteen at any time before seven, and twenty-six rise at seven or later.

This gap between the rising hours of the two sections of the population touches the interlocked complex of Middletown life at many points. A prominent citizen speaking on the curtailing of family life by clubs, committees, and other organized activities urged the parents of the city to "Help solve the boy problem by making breakfast a time of leisurely family reunion." He did not realize that such a solution could apply to only about one-third of the city's families, since in the other two-thirds the father gets up in the dark in winter, eats hastily in the kitchen in the gray dawn, and is at work from an hour to two and a quarter hours before his children have to be at school. Or take another local "problem"—the deadlock between north and south sides of the city in the spring of 1925 over daylight saving time; the working class majority overwhelmed the measure before the city officials on the plea that in summer their small dwellings cool off slowly, often remaining warm until after midnight, and that they can ill spare an hour of cool early-morning sleep before they must get up to work. The business men, on the other hand, urged the need of daylight time because of golf and because standard time put local business at a two-hour disadvantage in dealing with Eastern business. Each group thought the other unreasonable.

The rising hours of business and working class differed less thirty-five years ago, as early rising was then somewhat more characteristic of the entire city. Nowadays one does not find doctors keeping seven to nine o'clock morning office hours as in 1890. During the eighties retail stores opened at seven or seven-thirty and closed at eight or nine, a thirteen-hour day.[1] About 1890 a six o'clock closing hour,

[1] In the leading men's clothing store in 1890 the hours were 7 A.M. to 10 P.M. on Monday, 7 A.M. to 9 P.M. Tuesday to Friday, and on Saturday 7 A.M. to midnight. Stores were frequently open parts of such holidays as Thanksgiving and Christmas.

In 1890 the Middletown jewelry clerks "organized a union . . . and waited upon their employers and made known their desire of being off duty at 7.30 each

except on Saturdays, was tried by a few merchants, and gradually the practice prevailed. Today stores open at eight or eight-thirty and close at five-thirty.

Ten hours a day, six days a week, was the standard rhythm of work for Middletown industrial workers in 1890.[2] In 1914, 73 per cent. of them, according to the Federal Census, worked sixty hours a week or longer. By 1919 only 33 per cent. worked sixty hours or longer, although another 35 per cent. worked from fifty-five to sixty hours a week. The coming of the now almost universal Saturday half-holiday is the outstanding shift in industrial hours of work since 1890.

Year in and year out, about 300 working men work all night and sleep during the day. Periodically, however, a force of 3,000-4,000 men is either shifted from day work or recruited afresh by leading plants to work at night, thus establishing continuous day and night use of machinery.[3] These periods of night work continue usually five to six months, after which the workers are discharged or shifted to day work. The repercussion upon home, leisure time, community life, and other activities of these periodic dislocations of the rhythms of living, when anywhere from several hundred to three or four thousand heads of families "go on night shift," should be borne in mind; the normal relations between husband and wife, children's customary noisy play around home, family leisure-time activities, lodge life, jury duty, civic interest, and other concerns are deranged as by the tipping over of one in a long line of dominoes. "I work nights, judge, and sleep during the day, and I haven't been able to keep in touch with George," pled a father to the judge of the juvenile court in behalf of his son. The fact that, with few excep-

evening and allowed to attend all ball games." "We are glad to say," adds the press account, "that, rather than have trouble, the jewelry men have acceded to their demands."

[2] All four of the representative Middletown iron works and the four leading wood-working plants listed in the 1891 state *Biennial Report* had a ten-hour day. Among the glass workers, where there was a high degree of organization, two plants had a nine-hour day and two a ten-hour day.

[3] Only three times, for five or six months each, in the five years between January 1, 1920, and January 1, 1925, have "times" been sufficiently "good" in Middletown for this to happen generally throughout the major industries of the city. At other times night shifts are put on for short periods to meet the needs of individual plants.

tions, this dislocating factor affects only the working class has direct bearing upon the differential concern of the two groups for such things as the civic welfare of "Magic Middletown."

Not only does the accident of membership in one or the other of the two main groups in the city determine the number of hours worked and the liability to night work, but it also determines to a considerable degree whether one is allowed to get a living uninterruptedly year after year or is subject to periodic partial or total debarments from these necessary activities.[4] The most prosperous two-thirds of the business group, at a rough estimate, now as in 1890, are virtually never subject to interruptions of this kind so long as they do good work, while the other third is somewhat subject to cessation of work, though to a less extent than the working class. When "times were very bad" in 1924 the leading department store laid off small groups of clerks alternate weeks without pay. During 1923 the office force of a leading machine shop plant dropped at one time during the year to 79 per cent. of its peak number, while the wage-earners declined to 32 per cent. of the peak.[5]

Among the working class, however, the business device of the

[4] The institution of an annual vacation of one or two weeks with pay is another point at which the rhythms of work of working man and business man differ. Among the latter, vacations are today a well-nigh universal rule, but no working man gets vacations with pay, save an occasional foreman who may get a single week. Cf. discussion of the growth of the vacation habit since 1890 in Ch. XVIII [in *Middletown*].

[5] The relative seriousness of "bad times" to business and working class personnel is revealed in Willford I. King's *Employment Hours and Earnings in Prosperity and Depression* (New York; National Bureau of Economic Research, 1923), p. 53 ff., in the estimate for the continental United States of the percentage of maximum cyclical decline over the period of industrial strain from the beginning of 1920 through the first quarter of 1922 in the total hours actually worked, as follows:

	Enterprises having less than 21 employees	Enterprises having 21-100 employees	Enterprises having over 100 employees	Total enterprises of all sizes
Commerce and trade	1.27%	5.81%	9.94%	2.78%
Retail only	1.31	4.66	10.84	2.75
All factories	8.21	19.21	38.56	29.97
Metal and metal products only	17.89	52.10	52.65	50.25

In this connection the predominance of metal industries in Middletown should be borne in mind.

"shut-down" or "lay-off" is a recurrent phenomenon. If the number of working men employed in seven leading Middletown plants[6] on June 30, 1920, be taken as 100, the number allowed to get a living on December 31, 1921, was sixty-eight; on December 31, 1922, ninety-three; on June 30, 1923, 121; on December 31, 1923, 114; on June 30, 1924, seventy-seven; on December 31, 1924, sixty-one; on June 30, 925, eighty-one.[7] The month-by-month record of one of these plants, a leading machine shop, during 1923, again taking the number employed on June 30, 1920, as 100, was:

January 61	May 117	September 57
February 75	June 92	October 48
March 93	July 66	November 43
April 110	August 63	December 46

In one leading plant 1,000 is regarded as the "normal force." When interviewed in the summer of 1924, about 250 men were actually getting a living at this plant, though the bosses "think of about 550 [of the normal 1,000] as our men." The other 450 are floaters picked up when needed. In another large plant the number of men employed on December 31, 1923, was 802, and six months later, June 30, 1924, was 316, but only 205 of these men worked continuously throughout the entire six months with no lay-offs.

Of the sample of 165 working class families from whom data on steadiness of work was secured, 72 per cent. of the male heads of families lost no time at work in the twelve months of 1923 when "times were good," another 15 per cent. lost less than a month, and 13 per cent. lost a month or more; during the first nine months of 1924, throughout the last six of which "times were bad," only 38 per cent. of the 165 lost no time, another 19 per cent. lost less than a month, and 43 per cent. lost a month or more. Among the forty families of business men interviewed, only one of the men had been unemployed at any time during the two years, 1923-24—and that was not due to a lay-off.

It is difficult to say whether employment tends to be more or less regular in Middletown today than a generation ago. Sharper com-

6 These seven plants were used by a local bank as an index of local employment in its monthly summaries of local business.

7 These intervals are uneven because the data were available only for the dates given.

petition throughout markets that have become nation-wide, the rise of the new technique of cost-accounting, the resulting substantial overhead charges on expensive plant and machinery, and the imperturbability of machines in the doggiest of "dog-days" discourage today the easy custom of closing down the plant altogether which flourished among the flimsy factories and hand-workers of a generation ago. A characteristic summer news item in the Middletown *Times* for June 12, 1890, says: "Ninety per cent. of the glass houses in the U. S. A. close on Saturday until the first of September." Short shut-downs of two weeks or so at other times in the year were not uncommon. And yet, despite modern compulsions to maintain at least minimum production, and in fact because of such impersonal techniques as cost-accounting, lay-offs have become much more automatic than the reluctant personal decision of a sympathetic employer.[8] The sheer increase in the size of present-day plants[9] operates to make these periodic increases and curtailments in working force more obligatory when the need for them arises.[10]

As in the case of the lowering of the old-age deadline, described in Chapter V, the phenomenon of recurrent industrial unemployment assumes totally different aspects as it is viewed through the eyes of a business man or of a working man. For the dominant manufacturing group, the peremptory little figures on the cost sheets require that there shall always be on hand enough workers to take care of any fluctuations in business. The condition of there being

[8] "On the transition to the machine technology . . . the individual workman has been falling into the position of an auxiliary factor, nearly into that of an article of supply, to be charged up as an item of operating expenses." Veblen, *The Nature of Peace* (New York; Huebsch, 1919), pp. 320-321.

Cf. J. L. and Barbara Hammond, *The Town Labourer, 1760-1832* (London; Longmans, 1920), especially Chs. I, II, and VI.

[9] The Middletown press in 1890 hailed as "a gigantic concern" a new industry which was to have "when in full operation" 200 hands. The largest working group in the city in January, 1891, was 225. In 1923, eleven plants each employed more than 300—three of the eleven employed more than 1,000, while one of these three regards its "normal force" as over the 2,000 mark.

[10] See footnote 5 above regarding the relative impact of "hard times" on enterprises of different sizes. According to King's evidence, whether owing to the fact that "the small employer keeps less accurate accounts," to the fact that "the small employer, being well acquainted with his employees, is so much interested in the welfare of the latter that his relationships with them are not governed primarily by purely business considerations," or to other factors, the bump tends to hit the big enterprises several times as hard as the little fellows.

more men than available jobs, though dreaded by the working man, is commonly called by his bosses "an easier labor market."[11] In March, 1924, when the long slump of unemployment was commencing and employment in other cities ran "want ads." in the Middletown papers offering work, two special delivery letters were laid by the plate of the president of the Middletown Advertising Club at one of its weekly luncheons, asking the Club to use its influence to suppress such advertisement because they tended to draw unemployed machinists from town. The president of the club agreed that this was "something the Ad. Club certainly ought to back," and the representatives of all papers agreed to suppress the advertisements. The sentiment of the club was that it was important that plenty of skilled labor be kept in town.[12]

"People come to the house a great deal and tell me they can't get work," remarked the wife of a prominent business man. "Of course, I don't really believe that. I believe that any one who really tries can get work of some kind." This remark appears to sum up the philosophy of unemployment of many of the business class in

[11] This business men's psychology is well illustrated by the following statement by one of the city's influential manufacturers: "In 1922 we were so rushed with orders we couldn't possibly fill them or get enough men here in town to carry on, so we had to import some men from Kentucky and West Virginia. Our men from our local district here, born and bred on the farms near here, knowing the use of machinery of some sort from their boyhood, reliable, steady, we call 'corn-feds.' These men we brought in from the mountains we called 'green peas.' We brought two train loads of them down. Some of them learned quickly, and some of them didn't. Most of them have drifted back by now. We figured it cost $75-$200 to train each one of them, and there was such a demand for labor about town that they didn't stay with us. They drifted about from shop to shop, and of course when the slump came we fired them and kept our old men."

[12] To the bosses there is no "problem" in the abrupt posting, rarely more than a day in advance, of the announcement of a lay-off, or in the absence of any machinery for talking over with the men the reasons for the lay-off or its probable duration, or in the practice of "hiring at the gate."

During the depression of the summer of 1924 much press publicity was given to the announcement that a local plant would take on a thousand men the following Monday. The men crowded about the plant gates on the appointed day and a total of forty-eight were hired.

Cf. pp. 37-38 of Shelby M. Harrison's *Public Employment Offices* (New York; Russell Sage Foundation, 1924) for reasons why employers favor hiring at the gate. Cf. also Whiting Williams' *What's on the Worker's Mind* (New York; Scribner's, 1921), pp. 6-7, for the worker's view of this system.

Middletown. Others believe, as one outstanding business man put it, that "About the only thing that might be improved in the condition of working men today is unsteady employment. But that cannot possibly be helped. An employer cannot give employment to workmen if he cannot sell his goods."

To the workingmen, however, unemployment as a "problem" varies from a cloud the size of a man's hand when "times are good" to a black pall in a time of "easy labor market" that may overspread all the rest of their lives. It happened that times were not good during the late summer and fall of 1924 when the staff interviewed Middletown families. Over and over again, the wives interviewed answered the question, "What seems to be the future in your husband's job?" in terms of:

"He's to be laid off Saturday."

"He's just lucky if this job keeps up. He never knows from day to day whether his job will be there."

"He can't tell when he'll be laid off. One day he comes home thinking the work is over and then the next day he believes it will last a few weeks longer."

For many of them the dread had become an actuality:

"I know people that have been out of work since June," one woman said in October, "and they're almost crazy because of it. Maybe if more people understood what it means something could be done about it."

"Not even the foreman knew the lay-off was coming," said one quiet, intelligent-looking woman who with her husband had been laid off in a leading plant the night before, at the close of the first week in December. "Last week the whole plant worked overtime every night on straight time pay. A petition asking for more wages was circulated by the men, but my husband and two others wouldn't sign it because they thought it was no time to ask for a raise with so many out of work. Now we're told the lay-off came because of the petition, because orders have stopped coming in. We can't figure that out. . . . What'll we do? I don't know, but we must not take the boy out of school if we can any way get along."

"He's awfully blue because his job is gone," said another wife in November. "He's trying to get work at ——. He hopes his old job will open up again in the spring."

Several of these women, all of them having husbands over thirty-five, said that their husbands had taken or would want work that paid less and had less future if it seemed likely to be "steady" and less subject to lay-offs. Steady work appeared to be generally valued by these older workers above high wages.[13]

The commonest working class solution of the problem of unemployment is to "get another job." Of the 182 sample workers for whom data was secured on this point, including 124 with children of school age, over a quarter (27 per cent.) had been with their present employers less than a year, over a third (38 per cent.) less than two years, and over half (55 per cent.) less than five years.[14] This "getting another job" frequently involves leaving the city: "In the summer we took to the Ford and went looking for work." "He has a job now over in —— [twenty-five miles away] and likes it so much he may stay on there."[15]

Failing in finding another chance to get a living, the whole fam-

[13] Cf. Whiting Williams' statement: "If there is one thing I have learned on my labor travels it is that 'the job's the thing.' Wages are interesting, but the job is the axis on which the whole world turns for the workingman."

[14] These figures do not mean that these men had had no unemployment during these periods or had not in many cases worked temporarily in other plants until their regular jobs "opened up again."

Between January 1, 1919, and October 1, 1924, of 178 men for whom these data are tabulable, 46 per cent. had had one job, 20 per cent. two jobs, 22 per cent. three jobs, and the remaining 12 per cent. more than three. Here again brief fill-in jobs were not counted, provided a man returned to his old job when "work opened up."

It should be remembered that the interviewers had to rely upon the wife for these data in nearly every case, though every effort was made to see that she did not omit any pertinent data.

[15] This migratory tendency which modern industry invites and the Ford car enormously facilitates may be expected to have far-reaching influence throughout the rest of the workers' lives: e.g., the more frequent moving of working class families noted in Ch. IX [in *Middletown*] and the decline in neighborliness and intimate friends among the wives noted in Ch. XIX [in *Middletown*]. Cf. the statement by Roscoe Pound in *Criminal Justice in Cleveland:* "Some studies made during the war indicate that the moral implications of an increasingly migratory laboring population call for serious consideration. Our institutions presuppose a stable, home-owning, tax-paying population, of which each individual has and feels a personal interest in its legal and political institutions and bears his share in the conduct of them. Irregularity and discontinuity of employment and consequent migration from city to city, or back and forth between city and country, preclude the sort of society for which our institutions were shaped." (Cleveland; Cleveland Foundation, 1921; Part VIII), pp. 610-611.

ily settles down to the siege.[16] Of 122 housewives, who gave information regarding readjustments occasioned by unemployment,[17] eighty-three reported unemployment during the preceding fifty-seven months. Sixty-eight, the great majority of those reporting unemployment, had made changes in their routine habits to meet the emergency.[18] Of these,

47 cut on clothing;
43 cut on food;
27 of the wives worked for pay either at home or away from home;
14 of the sixty carrying some form of insurance got behind on payments;
6 moved to a cheaper home;
5 of the 20 having a telephone had it taken out;
4 of the 35 with children in high school took a child from school.[19]

Such comments as the following by some of these housewives reflect the derangement of established habits in "bad times":

As touching savings. "We had been saving to buy a home but lost all our savings paying rent while he was laid off." "We had to use up all our savings to keep going." "We lost both our auto and our house. We had paid $334.00 on the auto and had just a little over a hundred to pay. We had been paying on the house a little over a year." "My husband has just gone everywhere for work. We would have been out of debt now if he hadn't been out. It seems like a person just can't

16 At least two factors make the incidence of unemployment more difficult for the worker today than formerly: (1) The decline of trade unions and of neighborhood spirit (cf. Ch. VIII [*Middletown*]). (2) The extension of the precarious habit of leaning the present upon the future by long-term commitments to pay for the purchase of a home (cf. Ch. IX [*Middletown*]), insurance, household appliances, education of the children, and so on. To take but the case of life insurance: in the sixteen years between 1910 and 1926 the number of individual policies in force with one national company in Middletown and a portion of the surrounding county increased from 3,800 to 23,000; this number should be reduced by approximately 40 per cent. to get the number of policy holders.

17 These data are based upon the memory of the housewife; she had no opportunity to check up her recollection by talking to her husband. Undoubtedly certain minor lay-offs and times when work was reduced for short periods to three or four days a week were overlooked. These figures are therefore probably conservative throughout.

18 This does not include cessation of saving and inroads upon accumulated savings. If this factor be included, it is probably safe to say that unemployment affected the behavior of the entire group.

19 These changes did not usually come singly, and the families involved in the above categories therefore overlap.

save. We started to buy a house a couple of years ago and his company would have paid the first payment, but the very next day he got his arm broke. I never plan nothing any more." "We haven't lost our life insurance yet. Last year we had to let a thousand-dollar policy go when he was out."

As touching shelter. "We don't know where the rent for this month is coming from. We're out of coal, too." "We have cut down all we can on food and the phone is the next thing to go. I am not strong enough to wash as I used to when he was laid off. He hates to see the phone go. It's the only way we hear from our children."

As touching food. "Now they have a new man in the grocery and we're afraid he won't allow us to charge things so long. We had a $60.00 grocery bill when he went back to work in 1922." "We get on the cheapest we can. Our living expenses are never more than $5.00 a week" [family of five]. "We have been buying no fresh milk this year, using only canned milk" [a family including two boys age seven and nine]. "We just live as close as we can all the time. I tell the children if they get a little candy for Christmas this year they'll be lucky; they haven't had anything but clothes and things they absolutely need for the last two or three years." "We have cut our food all we can and have beans and potatoes two times a day with about $2.00 worth of meat scattered through the week. I don't know what we'll do if there isn't work soon." "Last winter our grocery bill ran eight or nine dollars a week. Now it is five or six dollars, partly because we trade at a cheaper place and partly because we're economizing."

As touching leisure time. "I haven't been able to afford a movie show since January" [ten months].

The forced choices during times of unemployment reveal sharply the things some of these working class people live by:

A woman who had just returned to the store a new winter coat because her husband had lost his job said she planned to cut down on "picture shows"—"but I'll never cut on gas! I'd go without a meal before I'd cut down on using the car."

Another woman said: "I'll give up my home last. A friend of mine belongs to several clubs and won't resign from any of them even though her husband has been laid off three months. She says she'll give up her home before her clubs."

One woman spoke for many others when she said: "We'll give up everything except our insurance. We just can't let that go." The head of a local insurance company reported that unemployment has relatively little effect upon insurance policies. Of the 100 working class families for whom income distribution on certain items was secured, all but seven reported money spent for life insurance in annual amounts ranging from $2.25 to $350.00.

To Middletown as a whole in its corporate group capacity, unemployment as a "problem" virtually does not exist. At most it becomes a matter for privately supported charity to cope with. In the extreme bad times of the winter of 1921-22 when local unemployment overwhelmed these charitable agencies, a supplementary fund of $40,000 was raised by popular subscription to be distributed in doles. And yet it was in February of this winter, when local hardship was most acute, that the City Council voted to discontinue support of the highly successful tax-supported free employment office launched during the War and in operation for two and one-half years.[20]

The mobility afforded by new modes of transportation combines with these periodic waves of employment, unemployment, and reemployment to diminish the tendency for the workers in a given factory to live together immediately about the plant. Everybody in Middletown in 1890 got to work by walking, and workers tended to settle in the immediate neighborhood of a given factory; as a new factory was located on the outskirts of the community it formed a magnet drawing new dwellings close about it.[21] Today, when one gets about the city and the country surrounding it by bicycle, fifteen-

[20] The failure of the Council to vote the $1,500 needed for the upkeep of the office caused its abandonment. Both Chamber of Commerce and Trades Council had favored the employment office and a leading local paper called it "one of the best investments ever made by the city and county." One powerful councilman, connected with a leading industry, is said to have led the opposition to the bureau, and is quoted as declaring the office of "no assistance whatever to the manufacturers or to the laboring man. If a man wants work in this city he can get it without going through the employment office." The office was abandoned and part of the director's salary left unpaid, although the State Attorney General ruled that the city was liable for it.

This incident affords an instance of the way much of the group business is conducted in Middletown and of the relative inarticulateness and helplessness of the group in the face of a powerful minority. The weaker of the two Middletown dailies called in vain for a frank statement of the nature of the "nigger in the woodpile" from "certain persons" who have made "a protracted effort . . . to end the official existence of the bureau."

[21] E.g., the following from the local press in 1890: "Work has commenced on the Westside Glass Works. The location of this factory at Westside has caused a great demand for residences in that vicinity."

minute street-car service, regular bus service, and five interurban lines, and approximately two out of every three families in the city own a passenger automobile, decentralization of residence is apparent. A check of the residences of all workers in the shops of three local plants, a total of 2,171, showed that 28 per cent. lived within one-half mile of their places of work and 55 per cent. less than a mile away, while 45 per cent. lived a mile or more away; 20 per cent. of the men lived outside the city and from three to forty-five miles away,[22] and 14 per cent. of the women lived from three to nineteen miles away. Two of these plants are old industries that have been in Middletown since gas boom days, while the third is a modern machine shop, located in Middletown more than a decade, of the sort that today dominates the city's industrial life. In the latter only 19 per cent. lived within one-half mile and only 43 per cent. within a mile, while 57 per cent. live over a mile away, and 29 per cent of the males lived three to forty-five miles away, the number of women employed being negligible.[23]

This trend toward decentralization of workers' dwellings means that instead of a family's activities in getting a living, making a home, play, church-going, and soon, largely overlapping and bolstering each other, one's neighbors may work at shops at the other end of the city, while those with whom one works may have their homes and other interests anywhere from one to two-score miles distant.

Meanwhile, in season and out, regardless of such vicissitudes as unemployment, everybody who gets a living in Middletown is theoretically in process of "getting there"; the traditional social philos-

[22] Five men went back and forth together in an automobile from a city of the same size forty-five miles distant.

Distances up to three miles were figured "as the crow flies" and are therefore somewhat underestimated.

[23] These addresses represent the summer force. In the machine shop, the bulk of whose employees require little training, the winter force is heavily recruited from farmers. (Cf. King, *op. cit.*, p. 91, for the reason agricultural labor flocks to the machine shops.) In response to a protest from local labor that they discriminated against city labor in the winter in favor of this cheaper-priced farm labor, Middletown manufacturers informed the Chamber of Commerce that they "consider [the] county a unit and not the city." The ease with which farmers can "when times are good" get work in machine shops and the general diffusion of Ford cars and surfaced roads is prompting some workers to return to small farms, preferably midway between Middletown and another small industrial city, where a garden can help out on food and work be drawn from either city.

ophy assumes that each person has a large degree of freedom to climb the ladder to ever wider responsibility, independence, and money income.[24] As a matter of fact, in six Middletown plants employing an average of 4,240 workers during the first six months of 1923[25] there were ten vacancies for foremen over a period of twenty-one months from January 1, 1923, to October 1, 1924.[26] This means that in a year and three-fourths there was a chance for one man in 424 to be promoted.[27] The total number of men estimated by the plants as of sufficient experience on January 1, 1923, to be eligible for consideration for promotion to foremanship was 531. Of this picked group one man in fifty-three got his chance in twenty-one months.[28]

The chance of promotion as it appears to the working class may be glimpsed from the answers of the wives in 105 of the 124 sample families to the question, "What seems to be the future in your husband's job?" It was a time of considerable local unemployment. Ten of the 105 husbands were already out of work, and "future" meant hope for the naked chance to begin getting a living again at anything; for twenty-two other wives future meant nothing beyond the possible date when "the mister" would be laid off—for two of them this future was no further off than "next Saturday"; to four

24 Thirty-four per cent. of 241 high school boys answered "true" to the extreme statement, "It is entirely the fault of a man himself if he does not succeed," while 16 per cent. more were "uncertain," and 49 per cent. thought the statement "false," the final 1 per cent. not answering. Forty-five per cent. of 315 girls thought the statement "true," while 9 per cent. were "uncertain," 44 per cent. marked it "false," and 2 per cent. did not answer.

25 Average of total payrolls as of December 31, 1922, and June 30, 1923, less estimated averages of 600 foremen and office workers.

26 One of the six plants reported vacancies over only eighteen months, from January, 1923, through June, 1924.

The condition of the Middletown labor market during these eighteen months can be seen in its setting from the index numbers of employment in seven leading plants given earlier in this chapter.

27 The job of assistant foreman is not considered here, as it apparently counts for little. Promotion to a foremanship is the real step up.

28 Not only were promotions infrequent, but during these twenty-one months a number of foremen were temporarily demoted to the ranks when forces were reduced, e.g., night shifts abandoned.

R. R. Lutz found that in the course of a year only one man in seventy-seven in a group of 618 eligible men in the metal trades in Cleveland had a chance of promotion. *The Metal Trades* (Cleveland; Cleveland Education Survey, 1916), p. 100.

others the future meant predominantly a fear of the old-age bread line; to eleven others a "good" future meant, "He'll probably have steady work"; nineteen others were hopeful in regard to their husbands' work and their chances in it;[29] while the remaining thirty-nine faced the future with no expressed hope of getting ahead. Of these thirty-nine, thirty-two, while not at the moment out of work or driven by an active fear of unemployment, voiced keen discouragement. Such answers as the following from this last group, to whom, with those unemployed or fearing a lay-off, the future shows no outlet toward greater security or recognition, reflect an outlook on life that probably conditions profoundly all their other activities:

(Husband a machinist, age thirty-eight.) "Well, he's been doing the same thing over and over for fifteen years, hoping he'd get ahead, and he's never had a chance; so I don't suppose he ever will."

(Husband a machinist, age twenty-six.) "There's nothing ahead where he's at and there's nothing to do about it."

(Husband a machine-tender, age forty-six.) "There won't never be anything for him as long as he stays where he is and I don't know where else he can go."

(Husband a foreman, age thirty-eight.) "He's been there nine years and there's no chance of promotion. The work is so hard he's always exhausted. He wants to get back on a farm. He's been lucky so far in not being laid off, but we're never sure."

(Husband a factory laborer, age thirty.) "He'll never get any better job. He'll be lucky if they keep him on this one."

And yet the chance of becoming a foreman, small as it is, would appear to be somewhat better than it was a generation ago. The experience of individual plants, cited below, suggests that foremen have increased more rapidly than the number of workmen. On the other hand, increasing technological complexity and the resulting tendency to insert college-trained technical men into a force between foremen and owners appear to hinder a workman's progress beyond a foremanship more than formerly.

[29] In one of these cases here counted as "hopeful" the wife said: "It's hard to say. There's not much opportunity for advancement but he is reading trade papers and studying his trade all the time to be able to take advantage of any opportunity that comes."

New technical developments such as the automobile and multiplied uses of electricity have opened new doors to some working men, enabling them to become owners of garages, filling stations, or electrical shops. The sharp increase in size, complexity, and cost of the modern machine-equipped shop, however, makes the process of launching out for oneself as a small manufacturer somewhat more difficult than a generation ago.

In general, the greater accessibility of those on the lower business rungs to sources of credit through lodge, club, church, and social contacts would seem to make fresh opportunities through the starting of a small industrial shop, retail store, or business of their own easier for them than for the working class. No direct study was made of the chance for promotion among the business group, and the local sentiment is such that one may not talk to business men and their wives about their personal advancement as one may to the working class. Close contact with Middletown's small shopkeepers and clerks as well as with the more powerful members of the business group throughout nearly a year and a half, however, yielded a distinct impression that psychologically the business families of the city tend to live, in the main, not on a plain stretching unbroken to the horizon, but on ground sloping upward, however gently. Contact with the working class, supplemented by interviews with the sample of wives and some of their husbands regarding the latter's chances of advancement, brought an equally clear impression that psychologically the outlook of the working class is somewhat flatter. The new rush of the children of the business man to college and of the working man's children to high school and college is increasing the vertical mobility of the children by offering all manner of short-cuts to the young man or woman with an education, but once established in a particular job, the limitations fixing possible range of advancement seem to be narrower for an industrial worker.

Vocational accidents are yet another differential accompaniment of getting a living for the two groups. Such accidents are practically unknown among the business class. For an average of 7,900 working men and women in the thirty-six factories constituting the industrial population of the city during the first half of 1923,[30] however,

30 Payrolls of 7,743 and 9,655 on December 31, 1922, and June 30, 1923, respectively, were averaged, and since none of the accidents recorded concerned a

824 accidents serious enough to involve a loss of time from work were recorded during this six-month period. If this period can be taken as representative, roughly one in each five persons of the working class employed in factories in Middletown has an accident serious enough to make him stop getting a living for a while each year. Fifty-seven per cent. of these injured workers lost less than eight days, 13 per cent. lost eight days to two weeks, 1 per cent. two to three weeks, and the remaining 29 per cent. three weeks or more. Three of the 824 injured during these six months were killed, one other was expected to die at the time the figures were tabulated, two lost one eye and three lost permanent partial use of an eye, three lost a hand and six partial use of a hand, eight lost a finger and sixteen partial use of a finger, and so on.

We can only infer a trend toward fewer accidents. In view of the fact that in the year ending September 30, 1920, there were only 922 amputations out of a total of 42,994 accidents reported throughout the entire state, numerous records like the following in the Middletown press in 1890 suggest a very different frequency: In one leading plant, employing about 200 hands, three men were injured in one day in three different accidents—one losing a hand, a second having a foot mashed, and a third losing a finger. The last-named is reported as "another to lose a finger in the machinery where no less than five have been nipped off in the past month or so." A superintendent in a leading plant employing about 200 men in 1890, when asked if working conditions then gave rise to a good many accidents, exclaimed:

"I should say they did! We kept a horse and buggy busy all the time taking men from the plant to the doctor."

"Not literally, of course?"

"No, not literally, but we used to have one almost every day."

The compulsory presence in each plant today of a first-aid kit

---

member of the office staff, an estimated total of 799 office employees was deducted from the payroll average of 8,699, the above figure of 7,900 resulting. A few very small industrial plants for whom records were not available are not included in the thirty-six above, also such groups of workers as the building trades, a few railroad mechanics, and other workers not in factories. The records of accidents were taken directly from the cards in the files of the State Industrial Board which administers the State Workmen's Compensation Law.

undoubtedly reduces infections;[31] hernias are fewer, as there is less heavy lifting; plants are better built and aired, and such conditions, conducive to pneumonia and rheumatism, as those described by a glass worker in 1890, are far less common: "We worked dripping with sweat, burning up on the side facing the pots and freezing on the other side in winter in the draughty old plants." On the other hand the speed of the iron man has brought new health hazards all its own—nerve strain due to noise and speed, new types of localized ailments due to specialization of activity curtailing movement in many cases from the larger body segments to a few small muscles used over and over. Two under-officials in the packing room of a large glass plant agreed in saying that "there have been several nervous breakdowns since the installation of the belt conveyor bringing the jars to the women packers." And one added, "This system may be good for the plant, but it certainly isn't good for the girls."

Prior to 1897, when the first factory inspector was appointed in the state, the workman carried the full burden of accident under the common law principles of "assumed risk," "contributory negligence," and the "fellow servant" doctrine. In 1915 the trend towards group participation in such matters eventuated in a State Workmen's Compensation Law under which the industrial plant, and thus ultimately the general public, bear a share of the burden.[32]

This process of the socialization of accident hazard is a phase of a larger trend towards impersonality in industrial operations in Middletown. Under the existing type of corporate ownership the presidents of three of the seven largest Middletown industrial plants today reside in other states, and two of the three plants are con-

---

[31] One plant has a doctor in attendance, a second a graduate nurse but no doctor, two others have practical nurses, another a matron but no nurse, and a number use the local Visiting Nurses' Association, the company paying for the service in each case. All this is new since 1890.

[32] The jungle of conflicting elements in a "social problem" is reflected in this case by two local situations: (1) The situation described in Ch. V [in *Middletown*] in which the adoption of casualty insurance has led in one large plant to a policy of "firing" all employees at sixty. (2) The fact that the company which is perhaps doing more than any other among the largest half-dozen in the city to care for its aging workers was reported by the State Industrial Board as "not in good standing"; this company, owned and operated by public-spirited citizens, had in 1925, according to the State Board, been carrying its own risk for three and a half years without the legal permission of the Board.

trolled by directors few of whom have ever even been in Middletown. This wide separation between a plant and the real authority over it combines with the increasing extent and complexity of the units of operation and the introduction of technically trained personnel to make it, in general, farther from the "floor" of a Middletown shop to the "office" today than a generation ago. Thus one plant whose sixty men in 1890 were officered by a president, a secretary who was also the chief engineer, a superintendent, and no foremen, today has for a force less than three times as large, a president, a vice-president (both largely inactive), a treasurer and general manager, a secretary who is also chief engineer, a superintendent, assistant superintendent, and three foremen. A second plant whose 200 men in 1890 were officered by a president, a vice-president who was also general manager, a secretary and treasurer, and two foremen, is operated today, with six times the original staff of workers, by a president, a vice-president and general manager, a treasurer, an assistant secretary, an assistant treasurer (largely inactive), an auditor, two superintendents, and thirty foremen. A third plant, a machine shop not locally owned and new since 1890, has a staff of 800 directed by a president (living out of the city), a resident vice-president who is also general manager, a second vice-president (inactive), a secretary, a comptroller, a factory manager, a general superintendent, three division superintendents, and twenty-five foremen.

More than one manufacturer said that he was no longer able to know his working force and their problems as he used to. One gains an impression of closer contact between many managers and their workers thirty-five years ago; we read in the press of 1890 of a plant closing down and owners and 176 workmen attending the funeral of one of the workers. On another occasion the management, unable to dismiss the force for a day at the county fair, ordered into the plant one hundred pounds of taffy from the fair grounds. Yet another old-time employer when he sold his plant a few years ago stipulated in his contract with the purchasers that the latter were to take over the entire force and keep all employees long enough to learn their worth before discharging any of them. This same man is reported to have sent $500 to each of his foremen when he sold out, and he endowed a room at the local hospital for his old workers and their families.

A few Middletown industrial plants make an attempt to bridge the gap between shop and office by such devices as shop committees and short term training groups, including lectures on engineering and metallurgy by extension lecturers from the state university. One factory has a safety committee and another a nominal "council of foremen," with an appointed head. The character of these groups appears in the exclamation of one leading manufacturer, representative in this respect of the entire group, when asked about his "shop committee": "You don't mean collective bargaining or anything of that sort, I hope? *We're* running this plant and want no mistake about that. We won't tolerate any shop councils or anything of that sort." This plant is reported on reliable authority to have "thrown all sorts of obstructions in the way of the insurance people getting together with their foremen to talk over safety means in the plant." Personnel and welfare managers, appointed by four plants, occasionally exercise a personal oversight of the workers' problems; in one prominent plant, however, the kind of personnel adjustment work done is reflected by the emphatic statement of the personnel manager: "If a man is fired by a foreman, he stays fired. A thing a man does once in a department he'll do again in another."

These various devices, together with the carrying by at least three plants of a blanket life-insurance policy for all employees, the passage of the State Workmen's Compensation Law, and the appointment of state factory inspectors, represent tendencies to diminish somewhat the disparity between the accompaniments of getting a living for the working class and for the business group. But, while these new devices are attempting to solve the "social problems" involved in getting a living, the long arm of the job in this swiftly changing culture is touching the lives of workers as well as business class with new problems.

PART V

THE NEW DEAL AND THE WORLD DIVIDED

ARTHUR M. SCHLESINGER, JR.

THE PASSING OF YEARS has reduced the urgency of partisanship in writing about the New Deal. Argumentation has declined in favor of analysis. Both attacks and defenses have gained depth and subtlety.

That Arthur M. Schlesinger, Jr., is a friend of the administration is unmistakable in the three massive volumes of *The Age of Roosevelt* already published, carrying the story to 1936. The portraits of most of the active participants—a major feature of the work—are drawn with affection and respect. The conclusion, that Franklin D. Roosevelt emerged as the savior of democracy and its leader in an era of totalitarianism, could not be more complimentary. Yet praise is mixed with criticism, some of it fundamental. Schlesinger's opinion of Roosevelt's philosophy, or lack of one, is essentially uncomplimentary, and his disappointment is evident over the New Deal's failure to persist in large-scale national planning.

Among the enduring concepts of the New Deal is the idea that it came in two phases. The first was occupied primarily with economy recovery and intended to be cordial to business; the second turned to reform and an alliance with labor. Schlesinger has made this change of outlook the focal point of his third volume, *The Politics of Upheaval*. The basic characteristic of the First New Deal, as he describes it, is not so much recovery itself as the means by which it was to be brought about. Urged on by Rexford Tugwell, Adolph Berle, Raymond Moley, and others, Roosevelt pursued the ideal of a cooperative economy, here epitomized by the National Industrial Recovery Act. Like Theodore Roosevelt's "New Nationalism," the First New Deal acknowledged the factors of business bigness and interdependence and sought to minimize competition as a market mechanism.

In 1935 comprehensive planning was discarded in favor of reform to revitalize the free market and restrain monopolistic tendencies. The counsel of Louis Brandeis and the memory of Wilson's "New Freedom" replaced the more ambitious schemes of the early "brain trust." Schlesinger is more sympathetic to the new political alliances with urban groups than to the innate economic conservatism of the Second New Deal: "In the end, the basic change in 1935 was in atmosphere—a certain lowering of ideals, waning of hopes, narrowing of possibilities, a sense that things were, not opening up, but closing in." Although trade unionists and other liberal elements gained an ascendency over the traditional northern city bosses and states' rights southern barons within the Democratic party, the ideology of the later period was "far more capitalistic" than that which dominated the first two years. Yet the author offers a glimmer of light. The "neo-Brandeisians" were "only the cutting edge of the Second New Deal," whose fundamental policies were to be determined eventually by the "spenders," who used fiscal policy to regulate and reform. Their activity will, presumably, form a major part of the next volume.

Why did the change come about? Schlesinger's narrative emphasizes a loss of momentum in the First New Deal in 1934, a despondency in Roosevelt as he saw his own popularity falling, the business community increasingly hostile, and demagogues like Huey Long and Father Coughlin growing in political strength. His more general analysis attributes the shift to an important degree to an economic recovery that destroyed the sense of crisis and, consequently, the opportunity for a massive reorientation of the American economy. Both explanations are consistent with the characterization of Roosevelt and his administrations as opportunistic, guided only by circumstance. "He had no philosophy save experiment, which was a technique; constitutionalism, which was a procedure; and humanity, which was a faith."

Schlesinger's major themes have achieved less than complete acceptance. The "two phases" interpretation, with which he agrees, may be answered by those who, from a variety of viewpoints, argue for the basic unity of the New Deal. Conservatives find a consistent effort to restrict private enterprise; the far left sees the opposite. The most favorable interpretation regards the difference between 1933 and 1935 fundamentally as a change in emphasis within a program that consistently sought to combine recovery with reform. The protection of labor's right to organize by Section 7a of the NIRA and the National Labor Relations Board preceded the alleged turning-point toward labor. Unemployment and old-age insurance and maximum-hour and minimum-wage legislation were all early incorporated and persisted in New Deal thinking. The same type of major agricultural reform was enacted in 1933, 1936, and 1938. Schlesinger's emphasis on planning versus competition will seem to some not so much an exaggeration of the importance of the NIRA as a minimizing of the extent to which the dual assumptions of private ownership and public supervision were continued throughout the Roosevelt years. Indeed, what was common to New Nationalism and New Freedom was more significant than their differences.

The statement that Roosevelt had no philosophy is a familiar one, but often challenged. It may be argued that Schlesinger's intermittent references to the President's beliefs are difficult to reconcile with his conclusion. He acknowledges that Roosevelt was both a humanist and a democrat, and that the New Dealers believed in capitalism and wanted to reform the system, not destroy it. He quotes "reasonable people" as affirming that this, in fact, was its achievement. That Roosevelt was pragmatic and experimental is undeniable, but such characteristics apply to changing means rather than persistent ends.

The final chapter of Schlesinger's third volume suggests two definitions of the New Deal's "middle way." Roosevelt is given credit for satisfactorily combining Wilson's "New Freedom" and Theodore Roosevelt's "New Nationalism." Then Schlesinger asserts, however, that Roosevelt also rejected "the platonic distinction between 'capitalism' and 'socialism' and led the way toward a new society which took elements from each and rendered both obsolescent." Some will see a problem in correlating these pairs of opposites. Can one simultaneously steer between Wilson and Theodore Roosevelt on the one hand and capitalism and socialism on the other? Further, that the New Deal made capitalism "obsolescent" is not comfortably compatible with the previous assertions that the New Deal believed in capitalism and "saved" it.

That *The Age of Roosevelt* both solves large questions and creates others is a measure of its size. It is a work rich in material and insights whose importance will persist.

The Ideology of the Second New Deal

THE YEAR 1935 marked a watershed. In this year the strategy and tactics of the New Deal experienced a subtle but pervasive change. The broad human objectives remained the same. But the manner in which these objectives were pursued—the techniques employed, the economic presuppositions, the political style, the vision of the American future itself—underwent a significant transformation.

The selection from Arthur M. Schlesinger, Jr., *The Politics of Upheaval,* 1960, is reprinted by permission of and arrangement with Houghton Mifflin Company, the authorized publishers.

The early New Deal has accepted the concentration of economic power as the central and irreversible trend of the American economy and had proposed the concentration of political power as the answer. The effort of 1933 had been to reshape American institutions according to the philosophy of an organic economy and a co-ordinated society. The new effort was to restore a competitive society within a framework of strict social ground rules and on the foundation of basic economic standards—accompanied, as time went on, by a readiness to use the fiscal pulmotor to keep the economy lively and expansive.

II

Those opposed to all forms of government intervention could see little difference whether the intervention was for the purpose of controlling concentration or resuscitating competition; such people continued to detest the New Deal as heartily as ever. But within the New Deal the alteration in course had sharp impact. The disappearance of the National Recovery Administration and, with it, the conception of overhead industrial planning, was only the most spectacular expression of the new departure. There were many other evidences of the change: the growing domination of the Agricultural Adjustment Administration and other agricultural agencies by the more prosperous farmers—*i.e.* by the clients rather than by the planners; the shift in the Tennessee Valley Authority from an experiment in regional planning into a corporation for the production of power and fertilizer; the defeat of the attempt to make the Reconstruction Finance Corporation an instrument of government capital allocation rather than simply of government commercial banking; the establishment of unemployment compensation as a federal-state rather than a national program; the measures of the 1935 session of Congress looking toward the breaking up of business bigness; the increasing, though as yet largely unconscious, reliance on spending as a substitute for structural reform.

This did not, of course, happen all at once. But the rapid fading out of what remained of NRA after its exorcism by the Supreme Court showed how hostile the new atmosphere was to the old assumptions. Various efforts were first made to continue NRA agreements on a voluntary basis. Then, in Septmeber 1935, Roosevelt appointed George L. Berry of Tennessee Co-ordinator for Industrial Co-operation, with the mission of organizing industrial conferences to carry on the partnership ideas of NRA. Berry was the president of the Pressmen's Union. He also personally owned a 30,000-acre farm in Tennessee, a quarry, and the largest color-label printing plant in the country (which he had started with union funds). These varied interests no doubt qualified him for the job of reconciling business, labor, and the consumer. It was his professed belief that 70 per cent of the old NRA could be saved through spontaneous co-operation. But the efforts of Berry's Council for Industrial Progress to redeem NRA by voluntary methods produced a paper organization, a draft legislative program, and nothing more. "So far as NRA and the Blue Eagle are concerned," said Hugh Johnson, "the poor, pale ghosts that spook around their ancient place have not even the dignity of the honored dead. They are just funny phantoms."[1]

III

Some of the changes of 1935 were at first hard to detect. But what was unmistakable was the change in personnel. The key figures of the First New Deal were Moley, Tugwell, Berle, Richberg, Johnson. From 1935, their influence steadily declined. The characteristic figures of the Second New Deal were Frankfurter, Corcoran, Cohen, Landis, Eccles, in time William O. Douglas, Leon Henderson and Lauchlin Currie. The shift in TVA from Arthur E. Morgan, the biographer of Edward Bellamy, to David Lilienthal, the protégé of Felix Frankfurter, was symptomatic.

The second New Deal was eventually a coalition between lawyers in the school of Brandeis and economists in the school of Keynes. But in 1935 the economists were still in the background; the neo-Brandeisian lawyers were at first the dominant figures in the new dispensation. As for the old Justice himself, he watched the events of the year with growing delight. Black Monday, the day the Supreme Court struck down NRA, seemed to him "the most important day in the history of the Court and the most benef-

[1] *Council for Industrial Progress* (Washington, 1937); Herbert Corey, "Up from a Dusty Road," *Nation's Business*, Oct. 1936; Hugh S. Johnson, *Where Do We Go From Here?* (New York, 1935), 10.

icent." The three decisions, he said, far from rushing the country back to "horse and buggy" days, only "compelled a return to human limitations." The time had come to correct the "lie" that the country could make an advance as a whole; it could advance, he said, only locally—in particular communities and particular industries. Everything was beginning to look better—the reversion of social security to the states, the holding-company battle, the tax message, the rise to influence of his disciples. "F.D. is making a gallant fight," he wrote Norman Hapgood early in August, "and seems to appreciate fully the evils of bigness. He should have more support than his party is giving him; and the social worker-progressive crowd seems as blind as in 1912."

Brandeis's cry of triumph did not mean the literal triumph of Brandeis's ideas. His faith in smallness was too stark and rigorous. To Milo Perkins of the Department of Agriculture he held forth, as Perkins reported to Tugwell, on "the sanctity of littleness in *all* fields of human activity." To place men in jobs calling for superhuman abilities, Brandeis suggested, was to corrupt or to destroy human nature. The transition back to small units would be worth any cost in dislocation or suffering. As Perkins rose to leave, the old man told him earnestly to go back to Texas—back to the hinterland, where the real movement to reshape America would originate.

When Brandeis talked in this mood, when he told Tom Corcoran to send his boys back to the state capitals, when he decried the automotive industry on the ground that Americans ought to walk more, he was speaking for an America that was dead. His words were morally bracing but socially futile. There was, indeed, a conflict in the heart of Brandeis's social philosophy. Much as he admired competition, he admired smallness even more; and, when the two principles clashed, it was competition which had to go under. Thus he wanted government action not only to destroy bigness but affirmatively to protect smallness—even, if necessary, at the expense of competition. He had long ascribed vast importance, for example, to resale price maintenance and other fair-trade laws—laws which denied consumers the benefits of price competition in the interests of keeping the corner grocer and shopkeeper in business. Here the neo-Brandeisians left him. They could never get excited over such measures and were content to leave their advocacy to the independent grocers' and druggists' lobbies. Where Brandeis, in short, exalted smallness and localism per se, men like Cohen and Corcoran were trying to make competition work in an economy which would be technologically advanced as well as socially humane.

Cohen and Corcoran were not economists, any more than Brandeis was. Their specialty was statutes, not programs. Elsewhere in government, however, program-minded economists were working on alternatives to the First New Deal. Leon Henderson, the vigorous and resourceful chief economist of NRA, viewing the economic future late in 1935 from the rubble of his agency, outlined one program to test the possibilities of competition. Though Henderson could not yet be counted a member of the Corcoran-Cohen group, his suggestions ably stated the direction in which the Second New Deal might go.

The key problem, as Henderson saw it, was to restore price competition. He appreciated the strength of the tendencies toward economic concentration and price inflexibility. "Indeed, at the NRA," Henderson said, "so insistent and so convincing were the arguments for price protection measures against cutthroat competition that I was often compelled to ask: Has the nature of competition changed?" This was a fruitful question; and Henderson might have been wise to consider it more seriously. But his disposition was rather to wonder whether one more effort was not in order to revitalize the market. The antitrust laws were not enough; they touched only a small part of the difficulties. More serious were the problems of productivity: obsolescent technology, as in textiles; unwieldly capital structures, as in steel; inflexible wage and transportation rate structures, as in construction; enforced scarcity as a result, for example, of tariff protection. "I favor a positive program for securing laissez faire," said Henderson—a multiple attack on concentration and price rigidity, including the active use of the taxing power; the revision of the patent laws; vigorous antitrust action; encouragement of co-operatives; yardstick competition; tariff reduction, and so on. "Perhaps the good old-fashioned kind of atomistic competition cannot exist everywhere in mass production," Henderson concluded. "If this be so, we need to know it realistically so that we may alter our concepts and our institutions to meet new demands. Certainly . . . a positive program to make it possible would liberate large areas for the agenda of market competition and reveal clearly those areas of production left for the agenda of the state."[2]

IV

Obviously the First New Dealers preferred the tempered and pragmatic spirit of a Henderson or Cohen to the extremism of a Brandeis. But in the end both were equally destructive to their

[2] A. T. Mason, *Brandeis: A Free Man's Life* (New York, 1946), 620, 622; Perkins to Tugwell, June 5, 1935, Tugwell Papers; interview with T. G. Corcoran, Oct. 21, 1957; Leon Henderson, "The Consumer and Competition," *Annals*, Jan. 1936.

The distinction between a First and Second New Deal was often noted by contemporaries, though rarely with agreement as to what the exact difference was. Basil Rauch brought the distinction into historical literature in his early and valuable *History of the New Deal* (New York, 1944); his conception, however, differs from the one presented here. Rexford G. Tugwell deals with the problem searchingly in *The Democratic Roosevelt* (New York, 1957). The distinction outlined in this chapter has won the assent of most veterans of both the First and Second New Deal kind enough to read these pages or to submit to interrogation. However, I would like to record a powerful *caveat* filed by Leon Keyserling (in a letter to me of April 9, 1958). With Mr. Keyserling's permission, I quote a few passages from his counterstatement:

"When Roosevelt came to Washington in 1933 he did not have what could be called a systematic economic program and he certainly had not spelled one out in his campaign. There did come to Washington in 1933, drawn by the crisis of the times, a great array of vigorous thinkers and doers of all kinds. It is perfectly feasible to pluck from the writings and speeches of some of these a series of statements which would seem to add up to the fairly coherent economic philosophy which you seem to attribute to the First New Deal. I suspect that it might be equally possible to pick from the writings and speeches of the same group a series of statements adding up to something quite different. In any event, the important thing seems to me to be that what Roosevelt adopted and the Congress approved during the First New Deal was highly experimental, improvised and inconsistent. . . .

"As the program of the First New Deal was largely incoherent, so the individuals whom you cite as the most important influences in the First New Deal were a medley of forceful people almost defying a single classification. Some of them were sincere people struggling for the ascendancy of their respective views; others were opportunists struggling for an ascendancy of personal power; still others were representatives of group interests struggling for the advancement of these interests. Those who stemmed from Mr. Baruch, such as General Johnson and George Peek, or who stemmed from Gerard Swope, can hardly be said, despite some of their polemics, to have desired structural changes or a transfer of fundamental power in the sense that Tugwell did. They were really crusaders

vision. The essence of the First New Deal was affirmative national planning. The men of 1933 believed that, in a modern industrial society, the problems of price-wage-profit behavior and of the allocation of resources could not be left to solve themselves. These problems could be handled, in their view, only by a considerable integration of private and public planning; and their

---

for the modification of the anti-trust laws toward the strengthening of business cartels. The National Recovery Act as they wanted it would not have included either Section 7(a) or the wage or hour or labor standard provisions. These emerged through a series of haphazard accidents reflecting the desire to get rid of the Black bill and to put something in to satisfy labor. . . .

"The reform measures of the First New Deal stemmed from entirely different sources and were its great achievement. They stemmed from all of the schools of reformers who for years had been working for social security systems, housing improvements, etc. Most of these, incidentally, did not flow from any of the people whom you classify as the primary influences of the First New Deal. . . .

"The period beginning with 1935 does not seem to me to represent primarily the kind of dividing point which you suggest. It represents rather a gradual weaking of the momentum and ideas of the Roosevelt Administration, and furthermore I think that this process was continuous (despite the election of 1936) from 1934 until World War II. This weakening was in part due to the natural political trends characteristic throughout American history. It was in part due to the fact that practically every type of experiment having been tried by 1935, there was not much more to offer in the absence of much coherence in any quarter. The President, personally, was inclined to slow down and draw back whenever things began to look a little better.

"The transfers in influence from those whom you call the First New Dealers to those whom you call the Second New Dealers does not seem to me to represent primarily a basic philosophic shift on the part of the President but rather to reflect what would have happened naturally in the course of the developments that I have just described. The First New Deal did so many things that so many powerful people disliked that the people who had been identified with them became whipping boys and were consequently eased out by the President. The practical, agile and vigorous people who took their places in influence were able to do so because fate had made them less vulnerable, and, of course they were smart enough to translate their drive for power into appealing generalizations. . . .

"Aside from the gradual wearing away of program and momentum, the real change from the First New Deal to the Second New Deal was a change in political strategy and semantics, illustrating the degree of improvisation and the lack of deep commitment to a fundamental program except for the general idea on the part of most to do what was right and to help the country. Political and economic conditions in 1933 were such as to call for effort to unite everybody. When the New Dealers found to their surprise that no program could unite everybody and that those who in some ways had benefited most were turning to bite the hand that fed them, they shifted from the political strategy of unity to the political strategy of division."

effort was to devise institutional means of associating business, labor, and government in this process. "For good or ill," as General Johnson said, "we are entering a managed economy. . . . It is not a question of whether we shall have a managed economy, but of who shall manage it. . . . The rout of laissez-faire is rampant through the world."

The First New Deal proposed to rebuild America through the reconstruction of economic institutions in accordance with technological imperatives. In the spring of 1934, Tugwell wrote with confidence, "We have turned our backs on competition and chosen control." But by autumn the bright hopes of 1933, when so much had seemed possible, were beginning to fade away. In October 1934 Tugwell mused in his diary about "the utter impossibility of achieving what it would be necessary to achieve in order to come close to solution of the socio-economic problem in our generation"; "we cannot," he said, "possibly move fast enough to stave off disaster."

Compared to the bold dream of making America over, the Brandeisian approach seemed mean and flat, a program of mending and tinkering. The New Dealers of 1935, Tugwell said, were denying the "operational wholeness," the intrinsic unity of the system. The running off into side issues, the constant tendency to escape from the structural problem into monetary manipulation or the redistribution of wealth through taxation or deficit spending—all this came, Tugwell thought, from a reluctance to take "the hard way," to accept the "harsh, relentless discipline" involved in a concerted national scheme "in which conflict disappears and the creative impulses of a people are fused in a satisfying effort." "Patching was all the [later] New Dealers knew how to do," he wrote subsequently, "—or, at any rate, all their enemies, as they regained their strength, would let them do." The result, he felt, was the trickling off of the energy of reform into painless—but for that reason, trivial—measures which left the basic structure of American capitalism untouched. So, too, Charles A. Beard, in Moley's *Today,* condemned Roosevelt as he had once condemned Wilson: "The cult of littleness and Federal impotence prevails. It is the cult of 'the new freedom' which hurries us on into greater bigness. Only the depth of the crisis in 1933 made it possible for the

President to abandon the admitted farce of trust-busting for a moment, and to seek the effective functioning of national economy." "The Anti-trust Acts," said Hugh Johnson, "are a throw-back to the Neolithic Age of statesmanship, and their blind sponsorship is a sort of jittering caveman ignorance."

Tugwell was always loyal and never vented his exasperation in public. Others among the First New Dealers were less restrained. "Think Fast, Captain!" said General Johnson in the *Saturday Evening Post* in the fall of 1935, blaming the trouble on what he called "the Harvard crowd" of "Happy Hot Dogs." Frankfurter, Johnson said in a burst of italics, was *the most influential single individual in the United States.* Tugwell, reaching back further, blamed it all on Brandeis, the "doctrinaire parading as an instrumentalist." As a justice of the Supreme Court, Brandeis had to operate discreetly; but he had found, Tugwell said, two powerful means of influence on the President. "The first of these means was his disciples; the second was the threat of unconstitutionality." His evangelism was implacable. "It is my firm belief," Tugwell concluded, "that it was responsible for the failure of the New Deal." By 1935 Moley, Johnson, Richberg, and Berle had left Washington. Tugwell remained, but he was shunted off to a siding: in 1937 he left, too. The First New Dealers had had their chance. Now others were taking over.[3]

V

From the viewpoint of the men of 1935, the partnership of 1933 —government, business, labor and agriculture, planning together for the common good—had been an experiment noble in purpose

[3] Hugh Johnson, "American Recovery and the European Situation," *Vital Speeches*, Jan. 1, 1937; R. G. Tugwell, *The Stricken Land* (New York, 1946), 22, 681; Tugwell, *Battle for Democracy* (New York, 1935), 264-67; Tugwell, "The Progressive Task," *Vital Speeches*, Nov. 16, 1935; Tugwell, "The Preparation of a President," *Western Political Quarterly*, June 1948; Tugwell, "The New Deal in Retrospect," *Western Political Quarterly*, Dec. 1948; Charles A. Beard, "America Must Stay Big," *Today*, Sept. 14, 1935; Johnson, *Where Do We Go from Here?* 13; Tugwell, "America Takes Hold of Its Destiny," *Today*, April 28, 1934; Tugwell, "After the New Deal," *New Republic*, July 26, 1939; Tugwell, Diary, Oct. 18, 1934; Ickes, *First Thousand Days*, 303; H. S. Johnson, "Think Fast, Captain!" *Saturday Evening Post*, Oct. 26, 1935; Tugwell, "New Deal Memoir," Part 8; Tugwell, *The Art of Politics* (New York, 1958), 247.

but doomed in result. The neo-Brandeisians rejected national planning because they thought it put impossible intellectual and administrative burdens on the planners. Even if it had proved technically feasible, however, they would still have rejected it because they believed that, in a controlled capitalism, capitalism was bound to capture the machinery of control.

Tugwell later noted that the concept of national economic co-ordination underlying the effort of 1933 was "congenial, fundamentally, only to big business." For Tugwell, this was an ironic paradox; for the Corcoran crowd, it was inevitable and, by virtue of its inevitability, an overriding disqualification. Tugwell could further write, "We lost our battles because, before long, they ceased to be our battles. Our allies became more powerful than ourselves." To the neo-Brandeisians, watching the manufacturers rise to power in NRA and the processors in AAA, this admission only further proved the Brandeisian point. Obviously business would take over any agency of central planning in a capitalist society: the alternatives were therefore socialism, which the neo-Brandeisians rejected as incompatible with freedom, or a restoration of control through the market. The political expectations of the First New Deal seemed to the Second New Dealers hopelessly naïve.

Yet if the politics of the First Deal were naïve, so, too, were the economics of the Second New Deal. Where the First New Deal sensed fundamental changes in the structure of the market and tried to adapt public policy to them, the Second New Deal too often supposed that the classical model of the market was somehow recoverable. It felt that government should confine itself to "general" policies, whether of ground rules or of fiscal stimulus, and that the pattern of resource use and the price-wage-profit relationship should be, within wide limits, "competitive" and unplanned. It was, as Corcoran correctly said, "ideologically far more 'capitalistic' than the First New Deal."

The basic conservatism of its economics was disguised by the aggressive radicalism of its politics. In part, this radicalism sprang from disenchantment with the experience of collaboration with business. In part, too, no doubt, it was an opportunistic improvisation, designed to neutralize the clamor on the left. And in part it emerged from a new conception of the problem. While the Second New Dealers wanted not a planned but a free economy, they felt that the way to restore the conditions of freedom was to use the powers of government to promote competitive enterprise in a society becoming increasingly interdependent; and this often seemed to involve the economic regulation and political chastisement of business.

In a memorandum to Hugh Johnson in 1933 Alexander Sachs had criticized the NRA approach as "monistic planning akin to state capitalism or state socialism" and proposed instead a system of "pluralistic planning . . . suited to a political and economic democracy." This distinction underlay the political philosophy of the Second New Deal. Where the First New Deal contemplated government, business, and labor marching hand in hand toward a brave new society, the Second New Deal proposed to revitalize the tired old society by establishing a framework within which enterprise could be set free. It was designed, Tugwell said, "to regulate industry, but not to require of it planning or performance."

A shift was taking place from a managed to a mixed economy: the one tried to convert business through new institutions, the other tried to discipline it through new laws. The First New Deal characteristically told business what it must do. The Second New Deal characteristically told business what it must *not* do.[4]

VI

The men of 1935 were somewhat different types from those of 1933. If, as Berle once remarked, Columbia was the "early intellectual home of the New Deal," the Harvard Law School was plainly its later home. The First New Dealers were characteristically social evangelists, with a broad historic sweep and a touch of the visionary, seeing America at a great turning of its history. The New Dealers of 1935 were characteristically lawyers, precise and trenchant, confining themselves to specific problems, seeing

[4] Tugwell, *Democratic Roosevelt*, 415, 454, 465; Tugwell, "New Deal Memoir," Part 8; T. G. Corcoran to author, April 1, 1958; Sachs to Johnson, May 20, 1933, C. F. Roos, *NRA Economic Planning* (Bloomington, Ind., 1937), 34.

America as off on a tangent but capable of being recalled to the old main road of progress.

These distinctions should not be pushed too far. Part of the change was the erosion of politics. One group had been on the firing line too long; some of its members were simply worn out, or had been subjected to a political hammering which had destroyed their public usefulness. It seemed time for a change. And to a degree, some of those involved might as well have ended up on one side as the other; only the accident of circumstance placed one man in the class of 1933 and another in the class of 1935. Nonideological figures like Hopkins and Ickes (not to mention Roosevelt) coexisted happily with both. In any case, the issues involved were those of economic program, not of religious principle, and reasonable men might swing back from one to another according to the pressures of the time. The leader of the neo-Brandeisians, Frankfurter, had himself been a follower of Theodore Roosevelt and the New Nationalism in 1912. Walter Lippmann, whose *Drift and Mastery* of 1914 was the most lucid statement of the case for the New Nationalism, was now beginning work on *The Good Society*, to be published in 1937, the most lucid statement of the tradition of the New Freedom. William O. Douglas who in 1933 rejected Brandeisianism as obsolescent, became in a few years almost its most effective champion, while David Lilienthal, a Brandeisian in 1933, ended as the prophet of bigness.

Yet, for all the happenstance involved, a difference remains between the intellectual style and texture of the two New Deals. Each, of course, saw the distinction in different terms. Tugwell saw it as between men who had social vision and men who lacked it; Corcoran saw it as between men who disdained legal exactitude and men who valued it—and no doubt both were right. As New Deal social thought lost richness and subtlety, its administrative thought was gaining clarity and precision. The two areas of economic analysis and legal draftsmanship best make the contrast.

In economics, the difference has been noted between the original and probing economic ideas of Berle, Means, and Tugwell and the free-market clichés of Brandeis and Frankfurter. The neo-Brandeisians often had not even thought through the economic implications of their own measures. Such enactments as the securities and exchange legislation, and especially the Public Utilities Holding Company Act, which were designed as exercises in "self-liquidating power" (in a phrase of Paul Freund's), often ended in government direction of precisely the sort to which the Second New Deal was theoretically opposed. "You start to set the patterns of right conduct," reflected Charles E. Wyzanski, Jr., years later, "and you may even get into the business that you have in the public utilities field of actually directing appropriate conduct through a public order enforcible through a judicial decree." He himself concluded that there was "no such thing as the mere elimination of improper practices, no such thing as the mere elimination of force and fraud. Whenever one goes into any area and purports to deal only with nefarious practices, one indirectly if not directly sets up standards of affirmative good conduct." Wyzanski wondered whether those who, like himself, were trained at the Harvard Law School were so clear about this as they should have been. (Cohen was an exception here, as to most generalizations; he well understood the subtle interplay of elements which made the differences between the First and Second New Deal, like those between the New Nationalism and New Freedom, less significant in practice than in principle. As Cohen later wrote, for example, "There was a measure of structural planning in the Holding Company Act which might have had more appeal to the First New Dealers if they had had clearer ideas of how they wished to give substance to their planning.")

In the field of law, however, the Second New Dealers were more accomplished and sophisticated. This difference, too, Wyzanski ascribed to the Harvard Law School and especially to the influence of Professor Thomas Reed Powell, whose exuberant insistence on the exact use of words made a generation of students, as Wyzanski put it, "think twenty times before you write that sentence quite that way." The difference emerged in the contrast between the sweeping and rhetorical legal strokes of, say, Donald Richberg, and the exquisite craftsmanship of Ben Cohen. Richberg, moved by a passionate feeling that the imperatives of history required drastic social reorganization, wanted to draft laws and fight cases in terms of prophetic affirmations; he resented the whole notion of pussy-footing around to avoid offending the stupid prejudices of reactionary judges. But Cohen, who felt it more important to make a particular statute stick than to promote a crusade, thought through every point with technical punctiliousness and always showed a meticulous regard for legal continuities. The laws drawn by the First New Deal tended to perish before the courts because of loose draftsmanship and emotional advocacy. The laws drawn by the Second New Deal were masterpieces of the lawyer's art; and they survived. Thus the National Recovery Act was, on the whole, a less complicated piece of legislation than the Holding Company Act; but, in the end, it turned out that one was, in the judgment of the Supreme Court, exhortation and the other, law.

VII

The First New Dealers, coming in at the bottom of the crisis, believing society to be almost on the verge of dissolution, attached a high value to social cohesion and viewed the governmental process as an exercise in conversion and co-operation. The Second New Dealers, coming in as things were on their way up, were less worried about the fragility of the system and saw the governmental process as an exercise in litigation and combat. They were quite prepared to risk straining the fabric of society in order to make their points and achieve their objectives. Moley ascribes a grim expression to Corcoran: "Fighting with a businessman is like fighting with a Polack. You can give no quarter." Corcoran does not remember saying this; it is perhaps the sort of thing he might have said without meaning it, with regard either to businessmen or Polacks; yet saying anything like this at all expressed the alteration in mood from 1933. Berle, deploring the change, tried to invoke the authority of Brandeis against "the would-be Brandeis follower of today," emphasizing Brandeis's ability "not only to attack an evil, letting the chips fall where they might; but to stand by and work out an appropriate arrangement by which all parties at the end could reach a stable relationship." Too often, Berle added, the neo-Brendeisian "has satisfied his lust for battle in mere punitive expeditions without having a clear picture of the result he intends to get; too often he has failed to recognize that the object is not winning a battle, but creating a socially workable result."

Arthur E. Morgan made a similar point in his bitter fight with

Lilienthal. He attacked those who "use any method at hand, including intrigue, arbitrary force, and appeal to class hatred. In my opinion," he continued, "such methods, while they may be effective toward achieving a reputation for political realism, do not contribute to the public welfare." The militants, he suggested, were forgetting the moral dimension of public policy. "The manner in which we achieve our ends," he said in a noble sentence, "may have a more enduring influence on the country than the ends we may achieve. The art of planting the seeds of mutual confidence and of giving the young plants a chance to grow is a great art. Most of Europe has not learned it. Let us hope that we in America may do so." The men of 1935 vigorously objected to Morgan's application of these principles. Yet Morgan had a profound point: a battle won at the cost of tearing the nation apart might not be worth the winning. Still, to this the Second New Dealers might have replied that the big interests were not the nation, and that they had no choice but to fight hard to save their adversaries from their suicidal policies. The correctness of this decision, they could later claim, lay in the extent to which even their one-time opponents eventually accepted the statutes of the Second New Deal.

Fundamentally, perhaps, the First New Deal was destroyed by success. The economic disintegration of 1932 could only be stopped by a concerted national effort and a unified national discipline. The method and approach of the Brandeis school would have been ineffective and irrelevant in 1933. But once the First New Deal had reversed the decline and restored the nation's confidence in itself, then the very sense of crisis which made its discipline acceptable began to recede. The demand for change slackened, the instinct toward inertia grew, the dismal realities of life and mediocrities of aspiration reasserted themselves. New methods were required, relying less on deathbed repentance and crisis-induced co-operation than on older and stabler incentives, such as the desire to make money and avoid the policeman. Most important of all, the First New Dealers had expended themselves; they had run out of policy; they had nothing further convincing or attractive to recommend; and, for an administration which thrived on action, this was the ultimate disqualification.

In the end, the basic change in 1935 was in atmosphere—a certain lowering of ideals, waning of hopes, narrowing of possibilities, a sense that things were, not opening out, but closing in. The Hundred Days had been a golden spring, like Versailles in 1919, when for a moment a passionate national response to leadership which asked great things made anything—everything—seem possible. The First New Dealers had a utopian and optimistic and moral cast of mind; the Second New Dealers prided themselves on their realism. The First New Dealers thought well of human rationality and responsibility. It was their faith that man was capable of managing the great instrumentalities he had invented. The Second New Dealers accepted Brandeis's maxim, "Man is weak and his judgment is fallible"; they said with Frankfurter, "We know how slender a reed is reason—how recent is emergence in man, how deep the countervailing instincts and passions, how treacherous the whole rational process." If man could not be relied on to assume responsibility for his own creations, he could be saved from his weakness only as these creations were cut down to his own size.

The shift from the First to the Second New Deal was not a whimsical change of direction so much as it was an almost inevitable response to the new necessities of the American situation. The problem had changed between 1933 and 1935, so policies changed, too, and men with them. The next wave of New Dealers, more skeptical, more hard-boiled, more tough-minded, ostensibly more radical but essentially more conservative, were prepared to work within the existing moral attitudes and the existing institutional framework and to generate by sheer vigor and combativeness the energy to fuel their more limited purposes. As children of light, the First New Dealers had believed in the capacity for justice which, in Niebuhr's phrase, makes democracy possible. As children of darkness, the Second New Dealers believed in the inclination to injustice which makes democracy necessary.[5]

VIII

The fight of 1935 was essentially between the planners and the neo-Brandeisians, the devotees of bigness and the devotees of competition. But it would be a mistake to regard this contest as de-

[5] Berle in *New York Times,* Aug. 17, 1933, and "The Way of an American," *Survey Graphic,* Nov. 1936; Charles E. Wyzanski, Jr., "Reminiscences" (Oral His-

fining the ultimate content of the Second New Deal. For the neo-Brandeisians were but the shocktroops of the 1935 coalition. They did the bureaucratic infighting and seized control of the strategic strong points. But they constituted only the cutting edge of the Second New Deal, not its inner essence. It was Marriner Eccles and the spenders, the silent partners of 1935, who eventually determined the fundamental policies.

The Second New Deal was not fully defined until the battle over spending in 1937-38. Still, the issue of fiscal policy did not go unperceived. It has been noted that Brandeis himself had favored government spending in 1933 and that Cohen from an early point was a thoughtful student of Keynes. The Supreme Court's condemnation of the structural approach of the First New Deal now heightened interest in a resort to fiscal policy. In 1934, when Frances Perkins had confided to Justice Stone her worries about the constitutionality of a social-security system, Stone whispered back, "The taxing power of the Federal Government, my dear; the taxing power is sufficient for everything you want and need." The same year Professor E. S. Corwin, in his *Twilght of the Supreme Court,* identified the independence of the spending power from constitutional control as the fatal weakness which threatened to envelop the entire institution of judicial review "in an atmosphere of unreality, even of futility." Thomas Reed Powell, reflecting on the NRA decision, now pointed out how the Supreme Court, without knowing it, had shoved the administration in new directions. "The waters dammed by judicial restrictions on the commerce power," Powell warned, "may break out in unwelcome fields of taxing and spending. What seems a great victory against national regulation may prove to be a Pyrrhic one. What is called the Ship of State has other controls than those with wires to where the Supreme Court is quartermaster."

And what was constitutionally possible might be socially de-

tory Research Office), 108, 110, 217; Paul A. Freund, "The Liberalism of Justice Brandeis," *American Jewish Archives,* April 1958; Brandeis, 285 U.S. 310; Felix Frankfurter, *The Public and Its Government* (New Haven, 1930), 128; Arthur E. Morgan, "Intelligent Reasonableness and the Utilities," *Vital Speeches,* Feb. 1, 1937; Moley, *After Seven Years,* 290; Raymond Moley, "There Are Three Brains Trusts," *Today,* April 14, 1934; Reinhold Niebuhr, *The Children of Light and the Children of Darkness* (New York, 1944), xi.

sirable as well. In a brilliant column a few days after the NRA decision, Walter Lippmann forecast the development of the Second New Deal. Indeed, Lippmann's own evolution showed something of the urgencies which caused the Second New Deal to displace the First. In the spring of 1933, he had written that, "for the idea of an automatic return to normalcy we have to substitute the idea of a deliberate attempt to plan, to organize, and to manage our own economic system." This meant, he explained, managing money and banking, managing foreign trade, managing new capital investment, bringing basic industries under greater social control; "there is no escape." The "ideal of a consciously controlled society," he said later in the year, challenged men at last with a transcendent purpose. "I say to you, my fellow students [he was speaking at the University of California], that the purpose to make an ordered life on this planet can, if you embrace it and let it embrace you, carry through the years triumphantly."

All this expressed the first exhilaration of the planning idea. In another year Lippmann drew back somewhat from the enthusiasm of 1933. He began his remarkable Godkin Lectures of 1934, published under the title *The Method of Freedom,* with his familiar demonstration of the failure of laissez faire. The self-regulating and self-adjusting character of the old order had been destroyed; under modern conditions the state had no choice except to intervene. But it could intervene, he now emphasized, in two radically different ways. Here Lippmann distinguished between what he called the Directed Economy and the Compensated Economy. The Directed Economy, in its extreme version, was the centrally planned and physically regimented economy of the totalitarian state. The Compensated Economy, on the other hand, retained private initiative and decision so far as possible but committed the state to act when necessary to "redress the balance of private actions by compensating public actions"—by fiscal and monetary policy, by social insurance, by regulation of business, by the establishment of minimum economic levels below which no member of the community should be allowed to fall.

In substance, the state undertakes to counteract the mass errors of the individualist crowd by doing the opposite of what the crowd is doing:

it saves when the crowd is spending too much; it borrows when the crowd is extravagant, and it spends when the crowd is afraid to spend . . . it becomes an employer when there is private unemployment, and it shuts down when there is work for all.

The shift from a Directed to a Compensated Economy forecast the directions in which the New Deal itself was beginning to move.

By 1935 Lippmann was sharply attacking the notion of detailed central planning. To him it seemed equivalent to trying to stop water from running through a sieve by plugging each hole. The principle of minute control, he had come to believe, was wrong; the economy needed only some form of "general social control"; and the most effective method would be, not to plug the individual holes in the sieve, but to control the flow of the water. What was necessary, he contended in his post-NRA column, were measures of "reflation"—government stimulus to promote expenditure— rather than measures of "regimentation." "If anything has been demonstrated in this depression which can be relied upon as a guide to policy, it is that reflation—not planning, not regimentation, and not laissez-faire—is the remedy." Not only woul fiscal policy produce results, but it was compatible with freedom. It "affects only the general purchasing power of the whole nation, and can be administered without detailed intervention in each man's affairs." It could be used without destroying the federal character of the American government or the private character of the American economy. And the authority to use it lay beyond challenge within the federal power. "The power to fix the wages paid for killing chickens is negligible and would be totally unnecessary, and would not even be desired, if the great power to stablize the total purchasing power of the nation were properly used."[6]

IX

The same issue had been considered at greater length a few months before when two Englishmen, Harold Laski and John Maynard

[6] Frances Perkins, *The Roosevelt I Knew* (New York, 1946), 286; E. S. Corwin, *Twilight of the Supreme Court* (New Haven, 1934), 178; T. R. Powell, "Commerce, Pensions and Codes," *Harvard Law Review*, Nov. 1935; and the following works by Walter Lippmann: "The New Deal," *American*, May 1933; *Interpretations, 1933-1935* (New York, 1936), 288-90; *A New Social Order* (New York, 1933), 16-17, 21-22, 24-25; *The Method of Freedom* (New York, 1934), 18, 46, 59, 74.

Keynes, debated for the doubtless astonished readers of *Redbook* the question, "Can America Spend Its Way Into Recovery?" For the Socialist, the answer was No. As Laski saw it, the only hope was structural change—in his view, the nationalization of the means of production. "It is to avoid this end that the United States has embarked upon its present experiment." Keynes could not have disagreed more. Was salvation possible through spending? "Why, obviously!" he wrote. ". . . No one of common sense could doubt it, unless his mind had first been muddled by a 'sound' financier or an 'orthodox' economist." An economy produces in response to spending; how absurd to suppose that one can stimulate economic activity by declining to spend! When individuals fail to spend enough to maintain employment, then government must do it for them. "It might be better if they did it for themselves, but that is no argument for not having done it at all." While productive would be better than unproductive expenditure, "even pure relief expenditure is much better than nothing. The object must be to raise the total expenditure to a figure which is high enough to push the vast machine of American industry into renewed motion."

For Keynes, this was part of a larger argument. He was opposed to any system which would subject most of the economic life of the community to physical controls. "If the State," he believed, "is able to determine the aggregate amount of resources devoted to augmenting the instruments [of production] and the basic rate of reward to those who own them, it will have accomplished all that is necessary." The central controls necessary to influence these aggregates of economic activity would unquestionably mean an extension of state power; but a wide field remained for private initiative and responsibility. In this field, Keynes said, the traditional advantages of individualism—the decentralization of decision; the exercise of individual choice; variety and freedom— would still hold good. In stating this faith in indirect over direct planning, Keynes was putting in a more inclusive way what would become the ideals of the Second New Deal.

Of all the minds contending against dogmatism, both of right and left, and asserting the possibility of reasoned change, that of Keynes was the most luminous and penetrating. The Cambridge economist, indeed, represented almost the culmination of the British analytical tradition. He had grown up in the high noon of British rationalism—Cambridge before the First World War, G. E. Moore and Alfred North Whitehead and Bertrand Russell. But he tempered rationalism with rich cultivation; and he strengthened it with extraordinary practical instincts about public issues.

Keynes made clear his skepticism about laissez-faire capitalism in the twenties. That condition of perfect equilibrium imagined by the classical economists, in which the interest of each ministered to the interest of all, seemed to him a phantasm. The state obviously had to intervene all the time to keep the economy going; more than that, big enterprise was growing away from the old individualistic economic motives; it was socializing itself. What lay ahead was a new economic society, moving far ahead of the doctrines of both right and left. Classical socialism, indeed, seemed to him quite as stupid as classical capitalism. The socialist program was "little better than a dusty survival of a plan to meet the problems of fifty years ago, based on a misunderstanding of what someone said a hundred years ago." He marveled at how a doctrine "so illogical and so dull" as Marxism could ever have influenced anyone.

"For my part," Keynes said, "I think that Capitalism, wisely managed, can probably be made more efficient for attaining economic ends than any alternative system yet in sight." He proposed to manage capitalism "by the agency of collective action"—in particular, by a larger measure of public control over currency, credit, and investment, so that basic economic decisions would no longer be left entirely to the chances of private judgment and private profits. Such extensions of public authority need not, he felt, impair private initiative. But all this represented only theoretical possibilities. In the mid-twenties Keynes was pessimistic about actually reforming the system. "There is no party in the world at present," he ruefully concluded, "which appears to me to be pursuing right aims by right methods. . . . Europe lacks the means, America the will, to make a move."

By 1929 Keynes had succeeded in converting the Liberal party and Lloyd George to his doctrines. *We Can Conquer Unemployment,* a Liberal tract for the General Election that year, set forth an ambitious program of "national development," calling for public action to build roads and houses, to promote electrification, and to reclaim land. (A heckler asked how Keynes could support the man whom he had charged a decade earlier with wrecking the peace. "The difference between me and some other people," Keynes blandly replied, "is that I oppose Mr. Lloyd George when he is wrong and support him when he is right.") In a defense of the Liberal platform, entitled *Can Lloyd George Do It?* Keynes sharply distinguished the expansionist program from socialism. For their part, the Socialists attacked the Keynes program as a "quack remedy" and as "madcap finance" which would only increase the public debt.

Keynes was quick to recognize the depression as no passing squall, but rather a protracted storm which would test all democratic resourcefulness. He rejected the counsels of impotence so fashionable among his academic colleagues. "Our destiny is in our own hands," he said. In his *Treatise on Money* in 1930, he worked out the theory of a policy, arguing in effect that, when investment exceeded savings, the result was prosperity, and when savings exceeded investment, the result was depression. If this were so, then recovery required restoring the volume of investment to a point where it would once again offset savings; and this, as he saw it, called for a drastic reduction in the interest rate, a general rise in prices, and extensive government programs of public works.

But these policies presupposed more than ever political parties that were free, as he put it, of both the influence of Die-Hardism and of Catastrophe. Where were such parties to be found? Evidently not in Great Britain. The economic ideas of J. H. Thomas, the Labourite, seemed to Keynes as senseless as those of Neville Chamberlain, the Conservative. Ramsay MacDonald's Economy Report struck him as "the most foolish document I have ever had the misfortune to read." Both left and right retaliated in kind. The Tory Sir John Simon said it was tragic to see how Keynes had taken leave of his wits; the right-wing Socialist Philip Snowden called him a fool; and the left-wing Socialists considered him preposterous.

Shortly after Roosevelt's inauguration Keynes spoke once again in a brilliant pamphlet called *The Means to Prosperity*. Here he argued with new force and detail for public spending as the way out of depression. Employing the concept of the "multiplier" introduced by his student Richard F. Kahn, Keynes contended that deficit spending for public works would employ two additional men indirectly for each man directly employed in public projects. He even called for tax reduction; "given sufficient time to gather the fruits, a reduction of taxation will run a better chance, than an increase, of balancing the budget." The budget could only be balanced, after all, by enlarging the national income, and this could only be done by expanding employment. Make bank credit cheap and abundant; lower the interest rate; above all, demand massive and organized government action "to break the vicious circle and to stem the progressive deterioration." But would any government do this? "Unfortunately," Keynes wrote in April 1933, "it seems impossible in the world of today to find anything between a government which does nothing at all and one which goes right off the deep end! the former leading, sooner or later, to the latter."[7]

X

Then Roosevelt's message to the London Economic Conference in July 1933 came to cheer him. Here, perhaps, was a leader prepared to emancipate his nation from enslavement by defunct economists. In September, though, he confessed a certain disappointment. "I fear that the hesitation in American progress today," he said, "is almost entirely due to delays in putting loan expenditure in effect. . . . It seems to have been an error in choice of urgencies to put all the national energies into the National Recovery Act." Still, the flexibility and courage which lay behind New Deal policies continued to hearten him. Later in the autumn

[7] J. M. Keynes and H. J. Laski, "Can America Spend Its Way Into Recovery?" *Redbook,* Dec. 1934; J. M. Keynes, *The General Theory of Employment, Interest and Money* (London, 1936), 378-80; and *The End of Laissez-Faire* (London, 1926), 34, 43, 45, 48, 52, 53; and *Essays in Persuasion* (New York, 1932), 306, 329; Liberal Party, *We Can Conquer Unemployment* (London, 1929); Keynes and Hubert Henderson, *Can Lloyd George Do It?* (London, 1929); Labour Party, *Labour's Reply to Lloyd George* (London, 1929), 5, 9; R. F. Harrod, *Life of John Maynard Keynes* (New York, 1951), 390-413, 438-39; Keynes, *The Means to Prosperity* (London, 1933); *London Times,* April 27, 1933; Hugh Dalton, *Back to Yesterday* (London, 1953), 261, 290; Keynes, "The Dilemma of Modern Socialism," *New Republic,* April 13, 1932; Seymour E. Harris, *John Maynard Keynes: Economist and Policy Maker* (New York, 1955), Chs. 9-10.

Keynes had talks with Frankfurter, who was then at Oxford; and in December Frankfurter forwarded to Roosevelt an advance copy of an open letter to the President scheduled for publication in the *New York Times* at the end of the year.

In this eloquent document Keynes summed up the vivid hope with which he viewed the American experiment. The problem, as he saw it, was Roosevelt's conflict of purpose between recovery and reform. "For the first, speed and quick results are essential. The second may be urgent, too; but haste will be injurious, and wisdom of long-range purpose is more necessary than immediate achievement." Too much emphasis on reform, Keynes suggested, might upset business confidence. It might weaken the existing motives to action before Roosevelt had time to put other motives in their place. And it might, in addition, confuse the administration by giving it too much to think about and do all at once. This was why Keynes considered concentration on NRA, despite its admirable social objectives, the wrong choice in the order of priorities.

Keynes questioned, moreover, the administration's devotion to raising prices as an end in itself. The techniques seemed to him bad: whether limiting production (though he approved the social purposes of NRA and "the various schemes for agricultural restriction. The latter, in particular, I should strongly support in principle"); or increasing the quantity of money ("like trying to get fat by buying a larger belt"; or fooling around with exchange depreciation and the price of gold ("the recent gyrations of the dollar have looked to me more like a gold standard on the booze than the ideal managed currency of my dreams"). In any case, the right way to get prices up was to stimulate output by increasing aggregate purchasing power; and not the other way round. Deficit spending was the answer; "nothing else counts in comparison with this." In the past, Keynes told Roosevelt, orthodox finance had regarded war as the only legitimate excuse for creating employment by government expenditure. "You, Mr. President, having cast off such fetters, are free to engage in the interests of peace and prosperity the technique which has hitherto only been allowed to serve the purposes of war and destruction."

There is no record of Roosevelt's reaction to this document.

A few months later Keynes came to the United States to receive an honorary degree at Columbia. Frankfurter armed him with a note to the President; and on May 28, 1934, Keynes came to tea at the White House. The meeting does not seem to have been a great success. Keynes was a formidable person, and his urbanely arrogant manner may have annoyed Roosevelt. He was capable, for example, of saying publicly (as he did later that year), "The economic problem is not too difficult. If you will leave that to me, I will look after it." Such an attitude might well irritate statesmen. In addition, he was hopelessly quick and patronizing. "Annihilating arguments darted out of him with the swiftness of an adder's tongue," Bertrand Russell once wrote. "When I argued with him, I felt that I took my life in my hands, and I seldom emerged without feeling something of a fool." Still, Tugwell recalled Keynes's attitude in conversations with Roosevelt as "more that of an admiring observer than that of an instructor."

What is more certain is that Roosevelt shared the resentment which old Wilsonians felt toward Keynes ever since *The Economic Consequences of the Peace*. In 1923, for example, Roosevelt congratulated the author of a piece in *Foreign Affairs*; "I particularly love the way you hand things to Mr. Keynes." And in 1941, when Bernard Baruch, who had helped negotiate the reparations clauses which Keynes condemned as folly, warned Roosevelt against him, Roosevelt replied, "I did not have those Paris Peace Conference experiences with the 'gent' but from much more recent contacts, I am inclined wholly to agree." To Frankfurter, Roosevelt politely wrote after the first meeting that he had had "a grand talk" with Keynes and liked him "immensely"; and Tugwell mentions subsequent meetings in which Roosevelt talked to Keynes with "unusual" frankness. But to Frances Perkins Roosevelt complained strangely, "He left a whole rigamarole of figures. He must be a mathematician rather than a political economist."

For his part, Keynes, as was his custom, looked first at Roosevelt's hands and found them disappointing—"firm and fairly strong, but not clever or with finesse, shortish round nails like those at the end of a business-man's fingers." Also, they seemed oddly familiar; for some minutes Keynes searched his memory for a forgotten name, hardly knowing what he was saying about silver and balanced budgets and public works. At last it came to him: Sir Edward Grey!—more solid, cleverer, much more fertile, sensitive and permeable, but still an Americanized Sir Edward Grey. When Roosevelt got down to economics, Keynes's disappointment persisted. He told Frances Perkins later that he had "supposed the President was more literate, economically speaking"; to Alvin Johnson, "I don't think your President Roosevelt knows anything about economics."

XI

Keynes found others in Washington more receptive. Steered around by Tugwell, he met a number of the younger men and told them to spend—a monthly deficit of only $200 million, he said, would send the nation back to the bottom of the depression, but $300 million would hold it even and $400 million would bring recovery. A few days later he sent Roosevelt the draft of another *New York Times* article entitled "Agenda for the President." Here he continued his running review of the New Deal, saying he doubted whether NRA either helped or hurt as much as one side or the other supposed and again defending the agricultural policies. As usual, the best hope remained an increase in public spending; $400 million, through the multiplier, would increase the national income at least three or four times this amount. In detail, Keynes advocated special efforts in the housing and railroad fields. "Of all the experiments to evolve a new order," he concluded, "it is the experiment of young America which most attracts my own deepest sympathy. For they are occupied with the task of trying to make the economic order work tolerably well, whilst preserving freedom of individual initiative and liberty of thought and criticism." With this, Keynes, pausing only to make astute investments in the depressed stocks of public utilities, returned home.

Newspapermen were quick but wrong to ascribe the increase in spending in the summer of 1934 to Keynes. No doubt Keynes strengthened the President's inclination to do what he was going to do anyway, and no doubt he showed the younger men lower down in the administration how to convert an expedient into a policy. But it cannot be said either that spending would not have taken place without his intervention or that it did take place for his reasons. In 1934 and 1935 the New Deal was spending in spite of itself. The deficit represented a condition, not a theory. What was happening was a rush of spending for separate emergency purposes. "I think that 95 per cent of the thinking in the administration is how to spend money," said Henry Morgenthau in a morose moment in the summer of 1935, "and that possibly 5 per cent of the thinking is going towards how we can work ourselves out of our present unemployment." Certainly, except for Marriner Eccles, no leading person in Roosevelt's first administration had much notion of the purposeful use of fiscal policy to bring about recovery; and Eccles's approach, with its rough-and-ready empiricism, lacked the theoretical sophistication and depth of Keynesianism. Roosevelt's own heart belonged—and would belong for years—to fiscal orthodoxy. "I doubt if any of his reform legislation," wrote Stanley High, a close adviser in 1936, "would give him as much satisfaction as the actual balancing of the budget."

In 1935 Keynes was a potential rather than an actual influence. But circumstances were making the atmosphere increasingly propitious for his ideas—ideas which received their classic statement in February 1936, in his *General Theory of Employment, Interest and Money*. If Keynes's direct impact on Roosevelt was never great, his ideas were becoming increasingly compelling. They pointed to the alternatives to the First New Deal, and they provided an interpretation of what worked and what didn't in American economic policy. As no one knew better than Keynes, "The ideas of economists and political philosophers, both when they are right and when they are wrong, are more powerful than is commonly understood. Indeed, the world is ruled by little else."[8]

8 *Time,* Sept. 25, 1933; *New York Times,* Dec. 31, 1933; F.D.R. to G. P. Auld, Oct. 13, 1923, Frankfurter to F.D.R., Dec. 16, 1933, May 7, Keynes to Marvin McIntyre, June 5, F.D.R. to Frankfurter, June 11, 1934, Wallace to F.D.R., May 8, 1936 (with memorandum by A. P. Chew of talk with Keynes), Baruch to F.D.R., July 9, F.D.R. to Baruch, July 11, 1941, Roosevelt Papers; Bertrand Russell, "Portraits from Memory," *Harper's,* Jan. 1953; J. M. Keynes, "Shaw on Wells on Stalin," *New Statesman and Nation,* Nov. 10, 1934; Tugwell, *Democratic Roosevelt,* 375; Perkins, *Roosevelt I Knew,* 225-26; Harrod, *Keynes,* 20, 447-50; Alvin Johnson, *Pioneer's Progress* (New York, 1952), 244; Harris, *Keynes,* Ch. 24; J. H. Williams, "Federal Budget: Economic Consequences of Deficit Financing," *American Economic Review,* Feb. 1941; Morgenthau, Diary, July 3, 1935; Stanley High, *Roosevelt—and Then?* (New York, 1937), 9; Keynes, "A Self-Adjusting Economic System?" *New Republic,* Feb. 20, 1935; Keynes, *General Theory,* 383.

ALFRED KAZIN

〜〜〜

ALFRED KAZIN'S *On Native Grounds* is a book for which historians are particularly grateful. It deals with the literary history of the period since the 1890's in a way which historians understand—that is, as an expression of American society. Based upon a huge fund of specialized knowledge and a highly developed insight into literary expression, it does for historians what they could not do for themselves.

A comparison of this study with Vernon L. Parrington's *Main Currents in American Thought* suggests itself at once. Both authors have a sociological point of departure. Yet Parrington was ultimately concerned with the political and economic meaning of literary works, whereas Kazin is interested in constructing from them the contours of the general intellectual environment. Indeed, Parrington was so insistent upon compressing literature into categories labeled "liberal" and "conservative" that he had little time for considering individual books of any kind on their own merits, and no space at all for works labeled "belletristic"—that is, which offer no substantial evidence of their author's social views. Avowedly a "Jeffersonian" by conviction and a Populist by training, Parrington approached his writing with deep feeling and a thesis which divided all writers into two groups—friends of democracy and its enemies.

Kazin's mood is calmer. As a critic, he chooses to place himself in a middle position between the two extremes of the Marxists, "who could study a work of art only in terms of its social relations," and the Formalists or New Critics, "who study literature precisely because it has no social relations at all." Rejecting both of these naïve totalitarianisms, Kazin holds the moderate view that although literature proceeds from a society, it is the product of men and not of trends, constituting a series of distinct even if representative creations.

The cohesive element in Kazin's study does not approach the definiteness of Parrington's theme. The author is well aware that he has less a thesis than a starting-point—the need to describe comprehensively the consequences apparent in literature of the disruptive change from an agricultural society to an industrialized, urban culture. In performing this task, Kazin is balanced and trustworthy, yet he lacks Parrington's intensity and originality.

However judicious, *On Native Grounds* is neither dull nor dispassionate. Its author's mind is too quick, its diction too incisive and energetic to permit a lag. And although Kazin has no very explicit propositions to prove, he has moral convictions which guide his judgments and break down the sense of detachment. Perhaps this is why he is so often disappointed in American literature. In any case, his standards are high and he seems more ingenious in laying bare our literary deficiencies than our achievements.

The economic collapse after 1929 ushered in a period of crisis, the intellectual repercussions of which are still being felt. Writing in 1942, Kazin was certainly in no position to tell what the final outcome would be, or even to see the various elements in the literary scene in their correct proportion. For example, his emphasis upon the Marxist school of criticism now seems exaggerated. On the other hand, he has captured the sense of insecurity which blended with the realism of the decade. Perhaps even more significantly, he has given an extended treatment to the affirmative note which arose in the midst of great problems. The rediscovery of the American past, the rising awareness of a need to know American culture—indeed, the discovery that there *was* an American culture—are a part of the history of this decade often lost sight of by historians whose eyes are fastened on employment charts and political reforms. Kazin succeeds in communicating to the reader a sense of the limitations of this affirmation, its frequent sentimentalism and uncriticalness, yet also something of the excitement and positive values implicit within it.

Whatever its errors—and there are not many apparent to a historian—*On Native Grounds* reveals to historians their weaknesses as students of the literary aspects of the American past and at the same time offers substantial help in overcoming them.

America! America!

"Do you know that European birds have not half the melody of ours?"
—ABIGAIL ADAMS *to John Adams*

UNDERLYING the imaginative life in America all through the years of panic, depression, and the emergence of international civil war was an enormous body of writing devoted to the American scene that is one of the most remarkable phenomena of the era of crisis. That literature has hardly run its course, and it may even dominate the scene for many years to come; but for all its shapelessness and often mechanical impulse, it is a vast body of writing that is perhaps the fullest expression of the experience of the American consciousness after 1930, and one that illuminates the whole nature of prose literature in those years as nothing else can. For that literature of nationhood, beginning with

From *On Native Grounds*, copyright, 1942, by Alfred Kazin. Reprinted by permission of Harcourt, Brace and Company, Inc.

the documentation of America in the depression and reaching a thunderous climax in an effort to seek out the American tradition, is largely the story of the American people as they came to understand it for themselves in a period of unprecedented crisis. It is the story of that now innocent, now calculating, now purely rhetorical, but always significant experience in national self-discovery which had its origin in the same obsession with society that led to the social novels of the period, but went on to create original or to reclaim traditional forms in a passionate effort to make a living record of contemporary American experience. It is the story of a vast new literature in itself, some of it fanatical or callow, some of it not writing at all, much of it laboriously solid and curious and humble, whose subject was the American scene and whose drive always was the need, born of the depression and the international crisis, to chart America and to possess it. It is the story of a literature of collective self-consciousness, a people's and a nation's biography; a story of physical and human geography, composed under pressure, often testifying only to the immediacy of that pressure, yet for all its occasional opportunism or naïveté, never without some fundamental joy in the study of America and the pride taken in its aroused self-comprehension.

Whatever form this literature took—the WPA guides to the states and roads; the reaction against the skepticism and now legendary "frivolity" of the twenties; the half-sentimental, half-commercial new folklore that manufactured or inflated comic demigods out of the reclaimed past; the endless documentation of the dispossessed in American life—it testified to so extraordinary a national self-scrutiny, signified so widespread and insistent a need, that all other considerations of it seem secondary. As if it marked a release of energies more thwarted in the past than anyone had suspected, a release of powers of affirmation crying for expression, whole divisions of writers now fell upon the face of America with a devotion that was baffled rather than shrill, and an insistence to know and to love what it knew that seemed unprecedented. Never before did a nation seem so hungry for news of itself, and not since those early years of the nineteenth century when the American had been the world's eighth wonder to European observers did America—if only the very texture of the country—seem so magnetic a subject in itself to so many different minds. The question now was no longer posed from afar—"What is an American?" Here the intelligence was native, as the subject was its very self, and by that very token a moving and always astonishing hunger for self-knowledge, since it seemed to express a profoundly innocent unanimity of spirit.

On the eve of this new nationalism, in 1932, Albert Jay Nock published a sardonic paper, "Return of the Patriots," in which he foretold that the "license of indiscriminate negation" during the twenties would be followed by a "license of indiscriminate affirmation" in the thirties. He saw ahead a literature of mechanical patriotism modeled upon the worst of the old—"it will be turgid, superficial, unintelligent, truculent." Yet though the spirit of the new nationalism did result in unprecedented affirmation, it was not at all what anyone in 1932 could have expected, for at its center lay a devotion to the heroic example, a need to question contemporary failure and demoralization, that had its roots in the same impulse which drove so many writers to report on the country all through the thirties. Obviously, of course, much of this writing represented the reflex patriotism and hungry traditionalism of a culture fighting for its life as it moved into war. Obviously, too, Hitler made nationalists out of many American writers almost as easily as Mencken had once made them scornful of the most commonplace national allegiance. The nationalist trend was marked here and there by a sentimentality that found its appropriate expression in the historical romance, and a certain comfortable smugness that showed in even ambitious histories and biographies and documentary studies. In a period when Hollywood found it so necessary to take a flyer on the Spirit of '76, a period when too many people thought they were writing history when they were only searching their attics, a period in which wistful souls who had in the twenties revenged themselves on their fathers now sought only the solid comfort of their grandfathers, the need to reclaim the past made for a certain complacency and swooning antiquarianism.

Often exploited, this new nationalism was, however, something profoundly more than a fashion, and to understand the spirit in which so many writers turned to recover America and to understand it is to appreciate how compelling was the drive toward national inventory which began by reporting the ravages of the depression and ended by reporting on the national inheritance. In his sequel to *The Flowering of New England,* a prime example of this new nationalism, Van Wyck Brooks rejoiced that "the golden-rod rises again in its season, and the folk-poem recovers its meaning, when the heart of a nation, grown old, returns to its youth." But as Brooks's own passionate attacks on certain modern "misleaders" later proved, his kind of devotion to the past was reminiscent with a purpose beyond reminiscence. For whatever the elegiac piety of this new traditionalism, its longing for the past was curiously in agreement with what André Malraux had meant when he said that a cultural inheritance does not consist in works which men must respect, but in works which help them to live. Nothing proves how well the leaders of the new nationalism believed that as the fury with which writers like Brooks and Archibald MacLeish, Howard Mumford Jones and Lewis Mumford, now began to excoriate so much of the modernism that had flowered between two world wars. Theirs was the rhetoric of haste, but in their own minds their haste was that of the demiurge; and the most significant aspect of the new traditionalism, whatever its inevitable narrowness or bigotry, was always its insistence upon reclaiming the past for the strengthening of the present.

So far from being merely a blind and parochial nationalism, this experience in national self-discovery was largely shaped by the sudden emergence of America as the repository of Western culture in a world overrun by Fascism. America may have been cut off from Europe after 1933, but the migration of so many European intellectuals to America meant, as John Peale Bishop said, that the European past was now confided to us, since we alone could "prolong it into the future." This was a profound influence on the reawakening to America's own tradition, since it meant a study of the national past conducted in the light of the European example in America, in the light of a new—if frantically enforced—sense of world responsibility. In an America which had either received or enrolled among its own so many of Europe's finest spirits from Thomas Mann to Jacques Maritain, from Albert Einstein to Sigrid Undset, the pride of helping to breed a new cosmopolitan culture gave a healthy stimulus to the searching of our own culture. To believe, as one German émigré wrote so wistfully, that "in America the word still has real value; in Europe it is only make-believe," was to give an unprecedented importance to the consciousness of the word in America and an appropriate dignity.

For better or worse this new nationalism was a pervasive force, a new historic consciousness that gave new meaning to contemporary experience and thought, and to appreciate that is to see something in the experience of the times that we are perhaps not now fully prepared to understand. For here, in the revealing—especially revealing because it was so often mechanical—effort of so many American writers to seek out the reality of America in a time of crisis, is an authentic and curiously unconscious characterization of a tragic period. Here, in the vast granary of facts on life in America put away by the WPA writers, the documentary reporters, the folklorists preparing an American mythology, the explorers who went hunting through darkest America with notebook and camera, the new army of biographers and historians—here, stocked away like a reserve against bad times, is the raw stuff of that contemporary mass record which so many imaginative spirits tried to depict and failed to master. What we study here is all too often only a sub-literature, perhaps only a preparation for literature—evidence of a nostalgia too easily content with the trappings of sentimental autobiography and romance; evidence of a need to retreat into the solid comfort of descriptive facts, of a social awareness that found its appropriate expression in photographic details and sociological captions. Yet in that signal literature of empiricism which embodies the failure of so many to discriminate between the pen and the camera, between the need for the past and the comforting surface of that past, is the record of what most deeply interested the contemporary imagination.

Here, in this body of writing, is evidence of how deeply felt was the urge born of the crisis to recover America *as an idea*—and perhaps only thus to build a better society in the shell of the old; only thus to prepare a literature worthy of it. Out of the decade of unrelieved crisis and failure, of fumbling recovery and tension and war; out of the panic and extremism of so many of its finest talents; out of the desire to assess what could be known and to establish a needed security in the American inheritance, came the realization of how little, for all its now world-famous triumphs, American writing had served the people and how little it had come to grips with the subject that lay closest at hand—the country itself.

2

There is a profound significance in the fact that this need to search out the land, to compile records, to explain America to itself, found its most abundant expression in a literature of formal social exploration and descriptive journalism. The novel, as Allen Tate said just a little contemptuously, may be an impure literary form because it is so much like history; but in a period when society is changing too rapidly and too violently for literature even to command the necessary detachment for imaginative truth, the serious novel itself will suffer in its effort to dominate what is not yet really known. In times of crisis people prefer to take their history straight, and on the run; and the documentary journalist who writes it on the run will give them history in terms which they are prepared to understand. If we ask why so many documentary journalists did more with their material than the social novelists who seemed to be working with the same material, the fact seems inescapable that because of the very nature of the crisis and the explosive strains it imposed, too many contemporary imaginations were simply not equal to it. Nothing proves that so well, perhaps, as the readiness of so many novelists today to desert the novel altogether, or the palpable fact that so many writers enjoyed a greater certainty and ease when they no longer felt it necessary to impose an imaginative unity upon their work.

For what emerges so unmistakably from the enormous descriptive and historical literature of our day is how unready so many writers have been to seek its imaginative truth, how lacking they have been in the requisite confidence or detachment to dominate as artists what they suffer as citizens seeking to survive. Why is it, as so many have felt, that a job of straight left-wing reporting like Ruth McKenny's study of the rubber workers in Akron, *Industrial Valley*, is so much better a study (so much better a proletarian novel, as Malcolm Cowley said) than most proletarian novelists achieved? Why is it that so sensitive and scrupulous a work of reporting the depression scene as George Leighton's *Five Cities* is so much richer and more authentic than most novels of the period? Why is it that in a period of unprecedented literary interest in the South, a period when the sharecropper haunted the imagination, the most moving and illuminating testimony of life in the South came from a WPA record of case histories, *These Are Our Lives?* Why is it that so much of the literature of the thirties and early forties must seem in retrospect a literature of Fact—one of those periods in which, despite the emergence of so many brilliant individual sensibilities, the chief effort of many writers seemed bent only on reporting, reporting; on running not too far behind the phenomena of the times?

The decline of the novel all through the period, a moral and physical decline, tells its own story in this respect. In so curious and difficult a revolutionary period as our own, so peculiarly hazardous a period, no one needs to be told how difficult it is for the imaginative spirit to command a necessary poise. Yet while the preponderance of descriptive nonfiction can be attributed partly to those who can appreciate reality only in terms of public events, there is an advantage the typical social reporter of the period enjoyed that explains why, as it happens, he often did succeed brilliantly within his sphere. For there is a sense in which the reality of our time *has* been composed of public events—a series of shattering shocks and tremors that has pounded away mercilessly at the mind. In such a period, marked by so pervasive and unexampled a sense of insecurity, the social reporter did not have to affect certainty; he was only a spectator of the passing show, a taker of notes. And because of the very nature of those repeated shocks, the moral and intellectual climate of the time seemed to call for nothing more than so passive (at most passively indignant) and even sardonic a spirit as the documentary literature of the thirties provided.

Like the effect Henry James sought in *The Princess Casamassima,* the reporting mind that opened the way for this new nationalism might be described as one "of our not knowing, of society's not knowing, but only guessing and suspecting and trying to ignore what goes on irreconcilably, subversively, beneath the vast smug surface." The surface was now anything but smug and, far from trying to ignore what went on beneath it, the world of contemporary opinion was haunted by its subterranean revolution. Yet that conviction of "our not knowing, of society's not knowing," was the field in which the documentary reporter and traveler now operated with ease and a certain serene humility that in that "not knowing" lay his usefulness as an observer and his ability to satisfy his readers on the same level.

> We don't know
> We aren't sure
> We wonder
> We're asking

In that "not knowing, of society's not knowing," indeed, was the test of his participation in the great contemporary experience, for society, which knew only that it did not know, would respond to and believe in only those writers who pressed it on—not too hard, certainly—to grasp the first facts about itself.

The two great associations of this literature of social description —the New Deal and the camera—help to illuminate its character in this respect. For rather like the New Deal itself, which opened so many new fields of investigation for this documentary school and even subsidized the WPA contributions to it, this new literature symbolized the effort of the inquiring mind, living in a period when the New Deal represented all the manifold adjustments of crisis government, to approach the problem of democratic survival. And just as the New Deal was weakest in philosophy, most transparently lacking in some centrality of direction and belief, so this documentary literature of the New Deal era represents a profound yet significantly indirect process of education. It was, indeed, a literature just as profound as the New Deal, no more and no less; a plastic literature, with all America for its subject, that became, as Dixon Wecter said of President Roosevelt, "a rare seismograph for all the social tremors of his time"; a crisis literature moving by an explosion of quick yet uncertain starts within the framework of the established order; a literature in which the sense of movement and of perpetual search was always more dynamic than any conception of the ends toward which it moved.

Franklin Roosevelt, considered as one national leader among others, may seem distinctive enough, since he was the leader of a mass movement greater than any Jackson, Lincoln, T. R., or Wilson led. But what is significant here—it may yet seem a fact of the first importance to future students of New Deal America—is not the power or resourcefulness of his leadership, but the extent to which his famous malleability, his "statesmanship as adjustment," was the focus of the great national experience under the New Deal. Everyone was learning in the thirties (well, nearly everyone), learning and groping at a time when the learning process had become a major experience in itself; and H. G. Wells's description of Roosevelt—"a ganglion for reception, expression, transmission, combination, and realization"—expresses one of the great truths of a time that found its appropriate expression in a literature of responsive social description. As Max Lerner said, the importance of Roosevelt's own responsiveness to public opinion is that he had to educate not only himself, but the whole country, to the forces remaking the world. But in a larger sense Roosevelt was responsive to more than "public opinion." How else are we to understand the world of the thirties that raised him to world leadership, raised him from the amiable but seemingly not too profound land-squire of Hyde Park, the pedestrian Admiralty law specialist, the former vice-president of the Fidelity Deposit Company, the complaisant Governor of New York?

What the documentary literature provided, then, was a register of the learning process, an example of a new social consciousness in America whose greatest distinction was the very fact of that consciousness in itself, the sense of a grim and steady awareness rather than of great comprehension. In this respect none of the devices the documentary and travel reporters used is so significant as their reliance upon the camera. Ever since the daguerreotype had come into American life, writers had been affected by the photographic standard, but now they became curiously abject before it. Nothing in this new literature, indeed, stands out so clearly as its attempt to use and even to imitate the camera. In a whole succession of books—Erskine Caldwell's and Margaret Bourke-White's *You Have Seen Their Faces and Say, Is This the USA;* Dorothea Lange's and Paul S. Taylor's *An American Exodus;* Archibald MacLeish's *Land of the Free* (pictures by courtesy of the Farm Security Administration); James Agee's and Walker Evans's *Let Us Now Praise Famous Men,* the new genre developed by Pare Lorentz in *The*

River, and the rest—the words and pictures were not only mutually indispensable, a kind of commentary upon each other, but curiously interchangeable. In a postscript to his *Land of the Free,* Archibald MacLeish wrote:

> [It] is the opposite of a book of poems illustrated by photographs. It is a book of photographs illustrated by a poem. . . . The book is the result of an attempt to give these photographs an accompaniment of words. . . . The original purpose had been to write some sort of text to which these photographs might serve as commentary. But so great was the power and the stubborn inward livingness of these vivid American documents that the result was a reversal of that plan.

So Dorothea Lange and Paul S. Taylor wrote of their *An American Exodus: A Record of Human Erosion* that it was neither a book of photographs nor an illustrated book, in the traditional sense. "Its particular form is the result of our use of techniques in proportions and relations designed to convey understanding easily, clearly, and vividly. . . . Upon a tripod of photographs, captions, and text we rest themes evolved out of long observations in the field." And even the unillustrated books of social "reportage," like Edmund Wilson's *The American Jitters* and *Travels in Two Democracies,* James Rorty's *Where Life is Better,* Nathan Asch's *The Road: In Search of America,* Louis Adamic's *My America,* showed that their authors were always seeking to catch reality on the run, as it were; to identify the object seen by etching it sharply on the mind; to give it a kind of wry objective irony or bitterness. Indeed, the technical and psychological fascination of the camera may be considered even to have given a new character to contemporary prose, a transformation which can be appreciated only in terms of its moral example, since it was the camera's essential passiveness that made for its technical influence over so many writers.

As a few great Americans have proved so well, the camera can be an extraordinary medium for the sensitive imagination; but in the crisis-begotten literature of the documentary school it served to give the general appearance of what Lincoln Kirstein described as the function of the candid camera in our time, to make up "in quantitative shock what it lacks in real testimony. . . . Its only inherent characteristic is the accidental shock that obliterates the essential nature of the event it pretends to discover." The photographs in most

of the documentary books were anything but candid-camera shots, of
course. Few artists today have created anything so rich and meaningful as the photographs Walker Evans contributed to *Let Us Now
Praise Famous Men* and his own volume of *American Photographs,*
and the photographs in the documentary books by photographers
like Ben Shahn, Dorothea Lange, Carl Mydans, and others were
often of extraordinary merit. But the extent to which the camera
as an idea affected documentary and travel reporters and served them
as a prime symbol of a certain enforced simplicity and passivity of
mind, is still little appreciated.

Margaret Bourke-White put it with wonderful simplicity when
she said: "Whatever facts a person writes have to be colored by his
prejudice and bias. With a camera, the shutter opens and closes and
the only rays that come in to be registered come directly from the
object in front of you." It follows from all that has been said of
the documentary reporters that the appeal of the camera was not to
their superficiality but to their spiritual fatigue, as it were; to their
"not knowing . . . society's not knowing." The "keen historic spasm
of the shutter," as James Agee called it, served not only "to portray
America," but also to answer subtly to the writer's conscious or unconscious unwillingness or inability to go beyond his material. As
Agee put it in that documentary book written to end all documentary books, *Let Us Now Praise Famous Men,*[1] with the camera
"everything is to be discerned, for him who can discern it, and
centrally and simply, without either dissection into science, or
digestion into art . . . all of consciousness is shifted from the
imagined, the revisive, to the effort to perceive simply the cruel
radiance of what is."

In the vast flood of social reports there were naturally a good
many books which merely exploited the camera technique on its
lowest level, books as superficial as the average weekly picture magazine or as loud as a tabloid headline. But while there were necessarily

[1] Agee's text has a special importance not merely because it is an unusually
sensitive document and a work of great moral intensity, but particularly because
it represents a revolt against the automatism of the documentary school. It was
begun as a typical documentary assignment and ended by being an attack on the
facile mechanics and passivity of most documentary assignments. Agee went so
far in his revulsion, in fact, that his book even took on the deep personal suffering of Faulkner's novels.

a good many books of this order, books which merely pandered to public excitement, the real significance of the literary use of the camera is that many serious writers were so affected by its use—or symbolism—that they seemed interested only in photographing the country on the run, in giving to the accumulated weight of a thousand different details and impressions of the national texture the solid testimony of their "education." In this respect the camera served to give documentary prose a hard, wry, noncommittal character—a character entirely appropriate to its obsession with the surface drama of the times, its stabbed and stab-like consciousness, its professed contempt for "illusion." What the fascination of the camera represented, in a word, was a kind of sick pride in its fiercely objective "realism." The camera did not fake or gloss over; it told "the truth of the times"; it was at once so aggressive and uncertain that it highlighted an awakened, ironic, militant, yet fundamentally baffled self-consciousness. Most important, the camera reproduced endless *fractions* of reality. In itself so significant a medium of tension, it fastened upon the atmosphere of tension. And if the accumulation of visual scenes seemed only a collection of "mutually repellent particles," as Emerson said of his sentences, was not *that* discontinuity, that havoc of pictorial sensations, just the truth of what the documentary mind saw before it in the thirties?

Reveling in a land so rich in descriptive facts, content with a kind of fever brilliance or anger or wit in the presence of so stupendous and humiliating a disorder as the depression scene provided, the documentary-travel reporter thus had his happiness. America lay all before him, his to choose; and how much there was to see and how little to annotate! The sharecropper, for example, fascinated the writer out to see the country, since he embodied so visual a conception of all that had to be recognized and redeemed in America. He provided an occasion for catharsis; he was a special contemporary phenomenon that fixed the general sense of outrage and quickened the sensibility of fellowship. Yet one had only to look at him (Margaret Bourke-White having taken his picture, imprisoning his agony for all history to gape at) to know how little there was to say. One had only to look at his South to believe that what one saw was the American drama of this day and age, all the pressures of the time brought together at the point of maximum curiosity and rage. Yet having looked, what was there to say that the Farm Security Administration did not have down in its files, the sociologist in his statistics? Here was America, all of it undoubtedly America—but America in a gallery of photographs, an echo of the people's talk, a storehouse of vivid single impressions.

Here was America—the cars on the unending white ribbon of road; the workers in the mills; the faces of farmers' wives and their children in the roadside camp, a thousand miles from nowhere; the tenant farmer's wife with her child sitting on the steps of the old plantation mansion, where the columns were gray and crumbling with age. Here was the child in the grimy bed, the Okies crossing the desert in their jalopy, the pallor of August in the Dust Bowl, the Baptist service in the old Negro church. Here was the greatest creative irony the reportorial mind of the thirties could establish— a picture of Negro farmers wandering on the road, eating their bread under a billboard poster furnished by the National Association of Manufacturers—"America Enjoys the Highest Standard of Living in the World." Here was the migrant family sleeping on sacks in the roadside grass, above them the railroad legend "Travel While You Sleep." Here was the Negro sitting in the fields near Memphis (more men than jobs at the Bridgehead labor market), saying: "They come off the plantations 'cause they ain't got nothin' to do. . . . They come to town and they *still* got nothin' to do." Here was the treeless landscape in southwestern Oklahoma, a country strewn with deserted and crumbling houses, the farmers driven off by the tractors, a picture of land where the tractors now kneaded the earth right "to the very door of the houses of those whom they replace."

Here, indeed, was an America that could only be quoted and photographed, described in pictures or in words that sought to be pictures. "America today is the scene of a mighty drama," Erskine Caldwell wrote in *Say, Is This the USA,* "the like of which we have never before experienced." There was no audience; everyone was on the stage playing his part. And if there were doubts as to what the play meant, "in the meantime, there is action on top of action, there is action galore. . . . All these people, all this abundance, all these things, is this America we live in; but none of us knows what to do about it. This is us, this is what we have; but nobody knows what to do next." Like Thomas Wolfe, who was reduced to making lists of all those things and scenes in the world he tried vainly to bind together, the documentary reporter, precisely because he was unable or unwilling to bind anything together, was driven to make lists of single impressions, lists of objects and names, above all lists of all those people scattered in the lava flow of the thirties who had stories to tell. America was everywhere, in everything; America was people everywhere; people on farms and on relief; people on the road; farmers in town standing before store windows; the girl on the bus who was going from town to town looking for work; the anonymous sharecropper who told his woes and said sharply, "These things are a pressin' on us in the state of Mississippi"; the migrant farmer in California who said of Oklahoma: "No, I didn't *sell* out back there. I *give* out"; the Negro boy Erskine Caldwell met who built coffins underground because he had served three years on a chain gang in Georgia for owing a white man $11, and had said he would let daylight burn itself out—*he* would never look at it —before he would get caught in such a jam again.

   Yes, America lay all before the documentary reporter, his to choose; and what did it matter if the America he saw was often only the America he came prepared to see? He made up his pattern, and the country—so rich in patterns for different minds—always lived up to it. Sherwood Anderson, who early in the thirties published a book appropriately entitled *Puzzled America,* had one pattern. Theodore Dreiser, who published another on *Tragic America,* had his pattern, the Dreiser pattern, always tragic. In *The "Argonauts,"* a book by five leftist college students who went out to see the country "for themselves"—the rootlessness of young people without jobs had long since made a virtue out of necessity—one saw an America that consisted rather exclusively of CIO organizers, chain gangs, sharecroppers, ugly native Fascists, leftist movie stars. In Edmund Wilson's early book of this type—*The American Jitters,* published in the worst year of the depression—all the savagery and inchoate bitterness of 1932 went into coruscating snapshots of police fighting hunger marchers, Tammany Hall, the Fish Committee investigating the Red Menace, suicides in Brooklyn, and the unhappy depositors of the Bank of United States. In his *Travels in Two Democracies* all the nervous brilliance so latent in the travelogue report went into a portrait of extraordinary density, yet one in which everything in America from Hull House to Radio City looked as if it had been photographed on Inauguration Day, 1933, with all the banks closed and the country running a high fever.

From Portland to Portland, from Detroit to the Gulf, from New York to Hollywood, there were patterns for all. In Louis Adamic's *My America,* a sprawling book of impressions by a writer whose immigrant past had given him an outsider's curiosity and a vibrant democratic fraternalism, America appeared as a strange but promising land that was essentially "a process—long and endless." Nathan Asch's highly introspective *The Road* bore no relation to the cautious unpanicky middle-class Indiana of the Lynds' *Middletown in Transition;* Benjamin Appel's studiously leftist *The People Talk* was not the same America that Rollo Brown found in *I Travel by Train;* but it was all America nevertheless. In *Where Life Is Better: An Unsentimental American Journey* (the main title was ironic), James Rorty described an America built on fear and ignorance and hatred, an America "building the stockades of fascism with which to protect what was left of its grandiose acquisitive dream." He saw an America, all retching ugliness and class conflict, that moved him to cry in despair: "What profound failure of American life did this drift of human atoms signify and embody, and to what would it lead? . . . The people had not possessed the landscape, nor had the landscape possessed them. The balance was indeed broken." Yet though what he saw seemed only "some profound profanation of the human spirit," in the end he was moved to confess that he did not know what America was. "I suspect that no one knows. Certainly I am in no position to make any categorical pronouncement."

No. No one knew. The girl in the bus, groping her way in the darkness from job to job; the boy in the road waiting for a lift; the salesman in the store, his baffled eyes belying his professional smile; the hotel clerk who said of the titled refugees from Fascism: "I used to think America would always stay the same, but now with all kinds of people coming here it's bound to change." What were they trying to say that only all America could say for them? Did they know? Did anyone know, when the pictures said so much, when one's whole experience on the road was a succession of pictures on the mind?

3

Yet something always remained: the shadow of the past on the land the Okies had left behind; the land itself that lay everywhere ready to be discovered and reclaimed; the framework of a whole American civilization, richer and more curious than many in the depression generation knew, greater than any crisis, waiting and begging to be known. The paradox of the crisis, as Lewis Mumford said, was that in a period of abnormal stress Americans began for the first time to learn many of the things that should have been normal to them as a people. Playgrounds and schools were built that prosperity could not afford; a new folk art and regionalism, and with it a reawakening to the forgotten cultural resources of the country, were developed out of the make-work programs of the WPA; only when writers had gone on relief was America charted in the great New Deal Baedeker of the states and roads; searching only for facts, a whole army of social reporters and travelers recovered an American sense of history and began to chant the rich diversity and beauty of the country as if America had never been really known before. Reporters of crisis, the documentary and travel writers now stumbled almost unwittingly into history; working and living on the surface of contemporary migration and poverty and unrest, they pieced together the broad outlines of a national civilization.

So Pare Lorentz, preparing his documentary film on floods and erosion in the Mississippi Valley, suddenly caught the image of the river, the spinal cord of the nation, in a chanting litany of American river names, caught it in a burst of celebrant American splendor unparalleled since Whitman. Here was the national center, as Sherman had caught the vision from it of a central union so long before at Vicksburg—here, in the gallery portrait of migration and erosion, the central and symbolic agony of the times. Yet how strange that anything so seemingly "descriptive" could be so beautiful!

> Down the Judith, the Grand, the Osage, and the Platte,
> The Rock, the Salt, the Black and Minnesota,
> Down the Monongahela, the Allegheny Kanawha and
>   Muskingum,
> The Miami, the Wabash, the Licking and the Green . . .

("Monongahela," Whitman had said admiringly; "it rolls like venison off the tongue.")

So the WPA state guides, seemingly only a makeshift, a stratagem of administrative relief policy to tide a few thousand people along and keep them working, a business of assigning individuals of assorted skills and interests to map the country, mile by mile, resulted in an extraordinary contemporary epic. Out of the need to find something to say about every community and the country around it, out of the vast storehouse of facts behind the guides—geological, geographic, meteorological, ethnological, historical, political, sociological, economic—there emerged an America unexampled in density and regional diversity. Were the state guides, as some felt, only a project for research workers rather than for writers? Perhaps; but the literary merit of some of them was greater than most people have appreciated, and their coverage of the country anything but mechanical. More than any other literary form in the thirties, the WPA writers' project, by illustrating how much so many collective skills could do to uncover the collective history of the country, set the tone of the period. As the first shock and panic of the depression passed, and the social reporters settled down to cover the country with a growing eagerness and interest in the epic unfolding out of their investigations, the WPA guides became something more than a super-Baedeker (America had been too much for the Baedeker industry itself, which had quit after one guide): it became a repository as well as a symbol of the reawakened American sense of its own history.

The facts in the guides were only the underpinning of history, but as they began to pour out of the presses, accompanied by the research notes of the Survey of Federal Archives, the Historical Records Survey, the historical notes of the students collecting American folk songs for the Music Project, they had an extraordinary charm in themselves, and a good many surprises to offer. This, like so much in the descriptive and historical literature of the thirties, was perhaps only the raw stuff of history, America put away into a long succession of files, a formal uninterpreted table of statistics on a civilization. But as Robert Cantwell pointed out, the guides went so far and so deep into every corner of the American land that they uncovered an America that nothing in the academic histories had ever prepared one for, and very little in imaginative writing. Road by road, town by town, down under the alluvia of the industrial culture of the twentieth century, lay an America that belied many of the traditional legends about itself. For here, under the rich surface deposits of the factory and city world, lay the forgotten stories of all those who had failed rather than succeeded in the past, all those who had not risen on the steps of the American dream from work bench to Wall Street, but had built a town where the railroad would never pass, gambled on coal deposits where there was no coal, risked their careers for oil where there was no oil: all the small-town financiers who guessed wrong, all those who groped toward riches that never came. And here, too, was the humorous, the creepy, the eccentric side of the American character: the secret rooms and strange furtive religions; the forgotten enthusiasms and heresies and cults; the relics of fashion and tumbling mansions that had always been someone's folly; the grandiose projects, like the ersatz Venice of so many seaside realtors' dreams in the twenties. Here, as Cantwell said in his essay on the America revealed in the state guides, was a chronicle not of the traditional sobriety and industry and down-to-earth business wit of the American race, but rather of a childlike, fanciful, impulsive, and absent-minded people —"a terrible and yet engaging corrective to the success stories that dominate our literature."

But there was something more than a history of secret failure to be uncovered. Important as the WPA guides were in themselves, they pointed even more significantly to a reawakened interest in the whole of the American past, a need to give the whole spirit of social inventory in New Deal America a basic foundation in the reclaimed American inheritance. Now, as the tide of Fascism mounted higher and higher in Europe, and it looked as if Americans had been thrown back on their own resources as never before, the whole emphasis of the early depression literature on national self-scrutiny became a thundering flood of national consciousness and self-celebration. Suddenly, as if it marked a necessary expiation of too rapid and embittered a disillusionment in the past, American writing became a swelling chorus of national affirmation and praise. Suddenly all the debunkers of the past, who had long since been on relief, became the special objects of revulsion and contempt. Suddenly all the despised catchwords of the democratic rhetoric took on a brilliant radiance in a Hitler world; in the emotional discovery of America the country once more became, as Jefferson had long ago foreseen, "this government: the world's best hope."

No longer could one even believe, as Archibald MacLeish had written in *Land of the Free,* that

> We wonder whether the dream of American liberty
> Was two hundred years of pine and hardwood
> And three generations of the grass
>
> And the generations are up: the years over
>
> We don't know.

No, the dream of American liberty was here; it was now. Americans, MacLeish now let himself go in *The American Cause,* were people "who had the luck to be born on this continent where the heat was hotter and the cold was colder and the sun was brighter and the nights were blacker and the distances were farther and the faces were nearer and the rain was more like rain and the mornings were more like mornings than anywhere else on earth—sooner or sweeter and lovelier over unused hills." *"O my America—my new-found-land . . . / How blest am I in this discovering thee!"* Chanting America, loving it, celebrating it, there was suddenly a whole world of marvels on the continent to possess—a world of rivers and scenes, of folklore and regional culture, of a heroic tradition to reclaim and of forgotten heroes to follow. America was here, now, a continent to be surveyed as Lincoln had surveyed the prairie sod where a civilization would follow, an inheritance to rejoice in and to find strength in. America was, indeed, again what Whitman had seen in the first preface to his great poem:

> The Americans of all nations at any time upon the earth, have probably the fullest poetical nature. The United States themselves

are essentially the greatest poem. In the history of the earth hitherto, the largest and most stirring appear tame and orderly to their ampler largeness and stir. Here at last is something in the doings of man that corresponds with the broadcast doings of the day and night. Here is action untied from strings, necessarily blind to particulars and details, magnificently moving in masses.

After the hard-crusted social novels, the crusading polemics, and the exacerbated social reportage of the thirties, the new nationalism now flowered in a literature of solid and affectionate history and biography. As the great affirmative testaments of this new spirit began to appear in endless anthologies of "the democratic spirit," in Sandburg's Lincoln and Carl Van Doren's Benjamin Franklin, in the lyrical history of the New England nineteenth-century mind produced by Van Wyck Brooks, in the tremendous literature that fought the Civil War over as if it had never been fought before, in hundreds of historical novels, in whole tons of folklore material, the hunger for the past—with all it signified of a yearning for stability in the American tradition—told a story greater and more moving in itself than any of the capacious new biographies and histories and novels could suggest. This was a crisis-begotten nationalism, yes; a fever glow of patriotism, quick to rise and perhaps quick to sicken; an army of open-mouthed tourists who seemed to regard America as one vast national park, full of interesting boulders, quaint bits of Indian folklore, and meteorological wonders. Perhaps. Here, as one liked, was either the ironic epilogue to half a century of critical modernism in America or the happy emergence of a real maturity and profound national allegiance among American writers. Yet whatever its virtues or crudities, historical services or pieties, how great a story it did tell in itself!

"In times of change and danger when there is a quicksand of fear under men's reasoning," John Dos Passos now wrote in his tribute to the democratic tradition, *The Ground We Stand On,* "a sense of continuity with generations gone before can stretch like a lifeline across the scary present." In that contemporary sense of danger and the historical sense it invoked lay the moving force of the new nationalism. There had been a flood of historical novels in the eighteen-nineties, but that had been a purely middle-class romanticism, a desire for sentiment and romance that testified not to an interest in history but to a desire to invest the solidity of the rich self-conscious prosperity of the industrial epoch with the trappings of an adventurous and glorious past. So in the great era of American historical writing represented by Prescott and Parkman, Bancroft and Motley, the pride in the independence and stability of the young republic had led men to look back with a fresh and confident pleasure on its early struggles and on the history of the American continent, cradle of a great civilization. But the historical writing that became so preponderant in the thirties was not so much a self-conscious reading of the past as a supplication to it. All history is self-conscious; all true history, as Croce said, is "contemporary history." But what distinguishes the historical writing of the thirties in most of its forms is its curious solidity, its attempt not to "escape" into the past but to pack the whole of the past into the present. What distinguishes it is a curious literalness, a veneration of the past at once grim and uncritical, a desire actually to use the past as if it had never been used before.

Uncritical *and* unsentimental. Inevitably, some of this historical literature was sentimental, as a good deal of Van Wyck Brooks's New England history, for example, was a sentimental transcription of Concord sights and sounds. Yet the most illuminating quality of this new writing was precisely its objectivity, since its great aim was not to prettify the past but to recover it bodily, as it were; to take possession of it and to enjoy it on the fullest possible scale. The cry now, as in the social journalism of the period, was for facts, facts; but facts on how men *in the past* had lived, on how they had withstood the pressure of their times, on how they had survived. Even the many historical novels, despite their own tradition of romanticism, despite the inevitable confectionery of the sword-and-cape romance, were distinguished by their general tone of sober matter-of-fact realism. In fact, so many of these new historical novels seemed to be written in the best tradition of American scholarship, replete with historical apparatus and bibliographies, that they testified as nothing else could to the demand of the period for solidly grounded and tirelessly accumulated monuments of historical fact. So the new histories and biographies, all so palpably built out of enormous labor and affection, all so objective and massive and even a little pious, revealed the taste for scrupulous and inclusive portraiture of the past.

Nowhere in the enormous descriptive literature of the thirties did this new spirit reveal itself so vividly as in biography, where it had its triumph. Carl Sandburg spoke not only for his fellow craftsmen in the field, but also for a whole generation, when he wrote bitterly of the debunkers that they had written "books where men of shallow wisdom and showman's tricks had subverted and falsified so as to fool young people regarding events and characters where the reality is better than the myth." Odell Shepard, another leading biographer of the period, wrote in reviewing a new, solid, and definitive life of Timothy Dwight (so many of the biographies were now "solid and definitive"):

> During recent years and months . . . we have begun to realize that there was something quite indispensable in those virtues that once seemed parochial and outworn. We are now learning once more to respect those orthodoxies and fidelities which are the products not of ease but of danger. Now and then we look back a little wistfully at the heroes of our national past, wishing that the attitude of hero-worship had not been quite so violently assailed in the presence of those who are now called upon to be themselves heroic. What this amounts to is that our pose of ultra-sophistication, a familiar trait of adolescence, is no longer fashionable. We are now making rapid progress toward the simplicity of really mature minds.

What this "simplicity" meant stood clearly revealed in the foreword that Henry Steele Commager wrote to his glowing biography of Theodore Parker:

> Where [Parker] was vain I have not sought to rebuke his vanity, where he was inconsistent I have not thought it necessary to remark his inconsistency, where he was ungenerous I have not taken him to task, where he was violent I have not tried to abate his violence, where he was mistaken I have not attempted to set him right.

Shades of Joseph Wood Krutch's brilliant psychoanalytical dissection of Poe, of W. E. Woodward's *Meet General Grant,* of Van Wyck Brooks's *The Ordeal of Mark Twain!* The reaction had set in, and with Lytton Strachey departed forever, along with all those easy and deliciously scornful epigrams that had once provoked an irreverent generation to laughter, the taste now was all for an objectivity that not merely fulfilled its function in scholarship but became a search for the very "feel" of the past. It was this pressing need to recover as much of the past as possible, to steep oneself in it, that explains why the staggering detail of these books, with their rich and eagerly proffered accumulation of data, made them seem anything but pedestrian. The stress of biography was no longer on distinction of style, on a calculated evocation of atmosphere and character; given the facts, the biographer seemed to say, the story would tell itself, aided only by common sense, the necessary sympathy for one's subject (this was of the first importance), and a decent respect for the merit and dignity of the world to be described.

With the return of "fat, full, old-fashioned biography, rich in facts and lean in random speculation," the very literary character of modern American biography seemed to change, as indeed it did. But the reaction was not simply a return to the "life-and-letters" school of the Victorian tradition. Books like Carl Van Doren's Franklin, Douglas S. Freeman's Lee, Lloyd Lewis's Sherman, Allan Nevins's Grover Cleveland and Rockefeller and Frémont (among others), Marquis James's Sam Houston and Andrew Jackson, Carl Sandburg's Lincoln, Claude Bowers's Jefferson, were all scholarly books—biography was now nothing if it was not scholarly—but they were books to be read and enjoyed, books that had been written to restore their subjects—"in grand dimensions," as Carl Van Doren wrote of his Franklin—to the world. The "reality was better than the myth," and it had only to be described in all its incomparable fullness. And since there was so much to give back, the writers of these books generally adopted a loose-ranging, convenient bluntness of style that served to shovel the whole of the past into their books. The highest aspiration now was to be as humble and attentive as Boswell; no one ever thought to be as magnificently wrong as Dr. Johnson. A full-dress description of a Civil War battle, as in Douglas S. Freeman's Lee or Lloyd Lewis's Sherman, was now worth a hundred epigrams; a laborious recreation of the subject's background, solidly documented and affectionately written, as in George F. Whicher's notable Emily Dickinson, easily surpassed the most brilliant flights of character speculation. To live with Lincoln in Carl Sandburg's six volumes, face to face with the people he met, the things he saw and wrote, hearing again almost every one of the thousand stories he told, was to know the supreme happiness of being alive again in the past.

The immense distinction of Sandburg's book made it the monument of the new biography, a peculiarly transparent example of a new historical consciousness. Built up through the years like a coral reef, loosely written and at times even slovenly—it was curious to note how the conscious, faintly sentimental lyricism of the early chapters in *The Prairie Years* soon broke into a businesslike trot under the flood of data in *The War Years*—the book revealed a studiously negative artistry. Under the pressure of that whole Civil War world to recreate, the very effort of Sandburg's imagination was subtly transformed into a supreme historical sensitiveness, a capacity for embracing the whole stupendous past. Where in *The Prairie Years* one could still see a certain self-conscious (and appealing) "poetizing" of the facts, with Sandburg, as it were, plotting the chronicle of Lincoln's growth, the measure of Lincoln now became the measure of that whole American civilization that would find its apotheosis in him. The past came rushing back in a torrent, all of it, seemingly; the story began to tell itself. Out of the recovery of a period in time, a period restored day by day, month after month, layer on layer, a mound heap of human stories, Lincoln arose before the reader like a massive shadow of the racked civilization he had held together, a stupendous aggregation of all those American traits that were to find so ambiguous and moving an expression in him. And this was the distinction of Sandburg's portrait: Lincoln did not live in himself, he lived because an epoch had to be pieced together slowly and laboriously to reclaim him; he lived because the very pang of democracy, rising out of so much struggle and aspiration, now resided in him. More than a symbol of a distinct American experience, he had become the propulsion of a great symphonic poem; more than a leader, the people's legend of him now seemed the greatest of all American works of art.

5

Slowly and hopefully, this new historical spirit was now edging its way into the unabashed recovery of an American mythology. The past was not always glorious, but no matter; its glory lay in its being past. A golden haze now lay over "the age of confidence" —a term which Henry Seidel Canby used as the title of his memoir of life in the eighteen-nineties, but which could have been used with equal nostalgia and affection by most of the numerous biographers and historians, autobiographers and historical novelists, who now turned to describe scene after scene out of that past which lay beyond the stain of contemporary instability and terror. Remembering the nineties, Canby wrote of it as a time when "you belonged—and it was up to your own self to find out how and where. There has been no such certainty in American life since." *"In that last epoch of American stability of which I write . . ."* Any epoch which a man could remember as different from the present now seemed "the last epoch of American stability." A wave of remembrance had set in, and all the queer country grandfathers, all the joys of life with father, all the solid, folksy virtues came back—less out of a pride in their forbears, as Lewis Gannett suggested, than out of an inferiority complex. So even Harold E. Stearns, who had made a reputation for himself in the twenties by mobilizing contemporary intellectuals in the fashionable expatriate scorn for Babbitt America, now became a heated propagandist of the national virtues. So even H. L. Mencken, who had taken to writing his memoirs, now wrote with an almost touching sentimental pleasure of the great days, the good old days, that lay before. What times! What endless gaiety and confidence!

The past now lay everywhere ready to be reclaimed, waiting to be chanted and celebrated. The old ballads began to come back, all the dear familiar legends, all the fine rawboned heroes of the frontier epic—Davy Crockett and Paul Bunyan, Mike Fink and John Henry, Johnny Appleseed and Daniel Boone, and with them a host of new supermen and gargantuan jokers and work giants—Whiskey Jack, Johnny Inkslinger, Pecos Bill. "From a nation lean in folk annals and too short-lived to boast an heroic age," as one folklore specialist wrote, there had suddenly sprung a knavish, comic, blustering, yet proudly titanic race of superheroes. Often transparently synthetic heroes, they yet all testified to the fascination with the prodigal carelessness, the strong pride in the homemade myths of a lusty day, now felt by their uneasy urbanized descendants. From its first beginnings

American folklore had always been the tribute paid in reminiscence by a late generation to an earlier. So even Mike Fink, the Mississippi river god, was supposed to have cried when he was turned out to pasture in a world of canals and factories: "What's the use of improvements? Where's the fun, the frolicking, the fighting? Gone! All gone!" Now the impulse to collect folklore was more poignantly than ever a longing for a heroic tradition, and the stories so many students now begin to pick up were of fabricated giants (what did it matter that they were fabricated?) dreaming and fighting and loving like young gods in the visible Homeric heavens. All other mythical heroes, as Max Eastman said, were serious; ours had come too late to be serious, and that was their charm. They were not plaster casts in a pantheon of greatness; they were the embodiment of a jealous American aspiration, the recovered stuff of a forgotten American laughter. "They were born in laughter," as Eastman said; "they are consciously preposterous; they are cockalorum demi-gods. That is the natively American thing—not that her primitive humor is exaggerative, but that her primitive exaggerations were humorous." And in their humorous strength lay what was wanted.

So the new literature of American folkways, of the river legends and regional cultures, while often shallow enough, was anything but museum-like. Often only too eager to claim a distinctive cultural tradition for every corner of the country, the many descriptive-historical books that now poured out of the presses testified to a need to tag and index and literally possess the country. Everything that lay at hand cried to be photographed and recorded and admired; everything that was past was now interesting and charming and radiantly alive: costumes and houses, manners and people, Benedict Arnold's first great services, cracker-barrel legends, all the stuff of a hundred forgotten political conflicts, *American* conflicts. Even the Loyalists of the Revolutionary period were restored to favor in Kenneth Roberts's slick *Oliver Wiswell,* and everyone sighed over their misfortunes and loved them in the same spirit that they now loved Tom Paine and Sam Adams. Even Ezra Pound, in one of the last cantos he wrote before he went to work for the Axis, paid his tribute to John Quincy Adams. And Daniel Webster, of whom Emerson and Whittier had had another opinion, now appeared in Stephen Vincent Benét's charming story as a *big* man, a pillar of virtue, a gigantic folk hero, fit to rescue Yankee souls from the Devil and beat him easily at his own game. "No American citizen may be forced into the service of a foreign prince."

What all this was leading to, as the trend in biography had shown and the rage of the historical novel now proved, was a desire to enter bodily into the past, to make a great, comforting, yet authentic pageantry out of it. What did it matter that Kenneth Roberts described the Revolutionary patriots as a "rabble," or that Margaret Mitchell won the peace as if the North had never won the Civil War? All the lost causes now came back through the historical novel, that favorite home of the lost causes, and no one—least of all the millions of readers in the North and the West gulping up one Confederate romance after another—cared whether the South had lost at all. South or North, West or East, it all added up to everything the contemporary world was not, a kind of seamless web of heroic and exhilarating legend. What the historical novelists now sought was an image of the past made whole, an image of a world modern readers could enter into completely and possess in all its parts; and they generally found it on the basis of an imitative modern realism in the novel. For only a meticulous realism could now reproduce the past as it needed to be reproduced; photographed, as it were, in a succession of glowing scenes. The new historical novel, at once so conscientiously antiquarian and self-consciously contemporary, therefore had no need of the old romantic apparatus of the historical novel; it made a romance out of its recovery of the past. Too deeply interested in their own world to fool with the old conventional idealizations, too sophisticated to want anything less than an authentic transcription of how other people had really lived, the historical novelists were at the same time interested only in making the past come alive, in giving it a realistic quality that would illuminate, rather than deny, the riches of the past it tried to evoke.

It was in this same vein of historical portraiture and pageantry, significantly enough, that popular histories and anthologies of "the American spirit" now began to appear. Even so solidly respectable a historian as Allan Nevins launched an appeal, in *The Gateway to History,* for a more colorful history, a history richer in human interest and literary skill. He paid tribute to the great American historians of the past who had thought of history as the creator and inspirer of nations, and recalled the spirit of Treitschke, who had resolved to revive the national spirit of the Germans by writing history. So even John Dos Passos, sketching the history of the Anglo-American tradition in *The Ground We Stand On,* was moved to a new and startling eloquence in his contemplation of Thomas Jefferson on his hill at Monticello, dreaming the promise of a "future that like a great convex mirror magnified every act and gesture of the men working their fields and building their farms in the tiny settlements along the Eastern seaboard." Describing the lives of Roger Williams and Sam Adams, Tom Paine and Jefferson, of Joel Barlow and Hugh Henry Brackenridge, Dos Passos seemed to recover so exhilarating a sense of pride in the American tradition —"we must never forget that we are heirs to one of the grandest and most nearly realized worldpictures in all history"—that the very writing of history now became for him a series of picturesque and exciting vignettes of the past—Roger Williams bringing the great tradition of Puritan liberalism to New England; Franklin shining in all his natural grace at the French court; Jefferson building his republican projects at Monticello; Sam Adams plotting the Revolution in Boston. Reaching, as it were, for an image of the repose and nobility that so few characters in any Dos Passos novel ever knew, he now found it in the portraiture of the fresh and burgeoning world of eighteenth-century America: the iron forges, the deer in the woods, Jefferson's classic integrity, the moment when the flag was first raised over Fort Pitt at the gateway to the Alleghenies, and it was felt that "the level land of the lakes and rivers would be the nursery of a new century of the young republic."

A golden haze indeed now lay over the past, and with the triumphant popular success of *The Flowering of New England* and *New England: Indian Summer*—the first two volumes in Van Wyck Brooks's projected history of American literature—it became clear that even literary history could now be written with all the ceremonious pageantry of the historical novel. For what was so distinctive about Brooks's loving portrait of the nineteenth-century New England mind was that for all its incidental brilliance of observation, it was the work of a critic who was fundamentally no longer interested in criticism. His history was an affectionate pilgrimage to the great shrines of the past, a radiant and mellifluous avowal of love and pride in a tradition, and it was just Brooks's ability to touch all the departed figures in his work with his own radiance that made his work so eloquent a testament. Where another writer would have described the lives of his characters in an effort to understand their books better, Brooks seemed almost more interested in the authors than in their books. What he was aiming at, as had already been clear in *The Life of Emerson,* was not a desire to meet Emerson—and Emerson's time—as contemporaries, but a sweet and shining epic of a lost heroic tradition, a kind of American Nibelungenlied in which all the gods were literary men and women and all their passions revolved around a distinctive moral idealism. What he was aiming at, in a word, was an epic in heroic tone, an uncovered tradition of ancient dignity and Emersonian sweetness, of aspiration and culture, of a certain delicious quaintness and inspiring integrity, in which author, background, and book were commingled.

So strong was Brooks's desire to make this past come alive in the spirit of the historical novel that he even called his second volume a "sequel" to his first, and wrote in explanation of his emphasis on Boston in that second volume that he had done so partly because he wished to give the book "a unity of place." The writers who streamed through his pages were all characters in a great historical drama, perhaps the noblest and most commanding in American history, and what they had written served to characterize them as actors in it. The emphasis was all on personalities and friendships, the evocation of atmosphere and scenes. One of the chapters in *New England: Indian Summer* was significantly titled "Country Pictures," and all through the two volumes one could see Brooks aiming at "effects" and dramatic revelations and climaxes—a succession of brilliant and often moving scenes, felicitous recreations of lost moments in time, that could be (most explicitly in the chapter on Emily Dickinson) totally unrelated to the writer's work. The scenes, the scenes were the great thing: Washington Allston moving like a great sage through the Boston of 1815; John Quincy Adams remembering proudly that he had said the Lord's Prayer

every night of his life and "had never mumbled it once"; Emerson
listening to the Aeolian harp receiving the winds on his porch;
Thoreau in the woods; Howells and James walking up and down
the streets of Cambridge at night dreaming of future conquests
in the novel; Francis James Child, the sailmaker's son, collecting his
ballads and tending his roses; Francis Parkman, blind and broken
with illness, fighting like a wounded knight to finish his books.

Here, America, here, Brooks seemed to be saying in exultant
pride on every page, is your tradition, and what a tradition! What
men! What faith! What scholars! In tribute to Emerson's great
generation he wrote:

> As heirs of the Revolution they spoke for the liberal world-com-
> munity. As men who loved the land and rural customs, they shared
> the popular life in its roots, at its source. As readers and students of
> the classics, they followed great patterns of behaviour, those that
> Europeans followed also. . . . If they believed in progress, and felt
> that America led the way, they professed their faith in a fashion that
> commanded respect, for they had known doubts and struggles, wars
> and vigils. . . . They had cultivated their gardens, they knew the
> country, the seacoast and the homestead, the lakes and mountains.

Lost that great world might be, lost in time; yet by recreating its
pageantry, by learning from its accumulated example, there was sus-
tenance for contemporary spirits. What was so moving as the
memory of John Quincy Adams (so much a greater man than his
querulous grandson Henry), diplomat, scholar, poet, scientist,
teacher, Secretary of State, President of the United States, an old
Roman who had not been ashamed to return to Congress after leaving the White House, nor too tired to journey to Cincinnati on a
flatboat in the dead of winter to dedicate an observatory to the
spirit of science that should flourish in the young republic? What
heroic example out of the past did any contemporary nation possess
as fine as the moral devotion of Wendell Phillips, the purity of
Emerson, the courage of Thoreau, the scholarship of Prescott and
Parkman, the flinty idealism of Whittier, the radiant spirit of Long-
fellow?

For Brooks himself, as had been clear ever since he had written
his preliminary idyll in *The Life of Emerson,* the wheel had come
full circle. In a period of unparalleled crisis of spirit, a period

when the whole modern movement he had once helped to shape had reached its climax, he had fashioned for himself a purpose seemingly beyond criticism and even creative literature: he had become, like Fichte or Treitschke, the celebrator of a national tradition, the historian who delved into the past so that he could sustain and arm his countrymen in time of danger. For thirty years and more he had written criticism, as the great nineteenth-century masters he loved had written criticism—as a form of moral instruction, a guide to spiritual fulfillment. For thirty years and more he had lamented the alienation of American writers from their native roots, but had documented and illuminated that rootlessness in a spirit of tragic justification. And all through those years he had been the prophet of only one central, all-pervading idea: that the great writer is only the voice of the culture to which he belongs, the culture in which he is rooted and which he accepts. In the words of D. H. Lawrence, with which Brooks now crowned *The Flowering of New England:* "Men are free when they are in a living homeland . . . free when they are obeying some deep, inward voice of religious belief . . . free when they belong to a living, organic, believing community, active in fulfilling some unfulfilled, perhaps unrealized purpose." Now he had no longer any reason to lament the absence of that spirit in America. He had found it, like buried treasure, under the ground men walked in America, found it in their own past—a standard, an image of belief and security.

Most significantly, out of his rapture in that recovered past Brooks had found a fighting faith for himself, and he now turned it furiously upon all those modern writers in France and England, as well as in America—the Eliots, the Joyces, the Prousts—who had dominated letters in the period between two wars. For it was at this point, with the emergence of so self-consciously contemporary an American mythology, that Brooks passed from his renewal of faith in the native tradition to a bitter attack on all that which in his mind had departed from it and corrupted it, all that which now seemed to impede the mobilization of the democratic spirit at a time when democracy needed every available resource to survive. It was not merely for Brooks himself that the wheel had come full circle; in so unparalleled a crisis the whole tradition of modernism to which Brooks had once contributed was now called into question. Along with writers like Archibald MacLeish, Howard Mumford Jones, Lewis Mumford, Brooks now protested that too many modern writers had failed themselves, failed or even betrayed the democratic hope, failed in their responsibility as humanists and citizens. In the light of the tradition he had recovered Brooks could now see only a degeneracy of will and spirit, an egotism and a subtle corruption, on the part of those who should have been at the very least leaders in the mobilization against Fascism.

Brooks's attack, particularly in such a book as *The Opinions of Oliver Allston*, was primarily a call to arms; but it was significant also because it brought to a head a certain self-disgust that had been evident in contemporary writing. Where Archibald MacLeish fell upon the antiwar novels written in the twenties, and Howard Mumford Jones complained that the irreverence of modern letters had produced a race of young people who had no "mythology" with which to fight the Fascist mythology, Brooks's attack was leveled against what he felt to be the moral irresponsibility of contemporary literature. And it was just here that his stridency exposed him to the charge by T. S. Eliot that he "might have been interested in not merely denouncing modern art, but in enquiring *why* it is what it is." For Brooks's intense personal attacks confused the issue and served no purpose. There is sickness in contemporary literature, a very great sickness; but it is hardly self-willed, and it is bound up with the situation of contemporary humanity. Brooks, by calling some writers "rattlesnakes" in the narrowly censorious fashion with which an Irving Babbitt had so often been moved to call them degenerates, missed the laborious integrity of modern writers, their will to understand, to live, to create insofar as the world will allow them to. He missed, in his attack on Proust, the profound moral structure and genius of Proust's great work; in his attack on Eliot, Eliot's extraordinary services in behalf of the continuity of the Western tradition and of a new language for poetry; in his attack on Joyce, Joyce's passionate devotion to the life of art, to mention nothing more, in a world where art was as never before the embodiment of the life of reason. Brooks saw his own morality and belief in humanity; he forgot that one does not have to intone a standard to live and write by one, and that those who intone too self-righteously may have nothing left but a standard.

There was nothing in Brooks's attack writers could learn from; he had simply withdrawn his sympathy and understanding from them, and his message was too abstract, too hollow in its evangelicism. The moral paralysis that can be found in certain writers today is real enough, and with it the self-contentment of those who do not know that literature lives by something more than literature. But you cannot relieve that paralysis by calling it wickedness; and Tolstoy and John Greenleaf Whittier, while noble men both, do not mix very well for a writer talking about writing. What was particularly lamentable in Brooks's attack was its essential remoteness from literature. Literature will live fully again when the world is able to live fully again; the "primary" virtues in literature may come back only when men are bound up again in the indivisible moral life of humanity. But if they do come back, it will be not merely because the world has attained some semblance of order, but even more because, in times of terror and human hazard like our own, men have kept their responsibility to literature and to themselves. Literature lives by faith and *works*. Joyce may be the "dead ash of a burnt-out cigar," but the Joyce who worked away at *Ulysses* during the last war kept something alive in the European tradition that those who merely spoke in the name of that tradition did not. Brooks defeated his own best purpose by yielding to an impatience with writers as writers, to the panicky call to action and conformism that had been depressingly familiar in literature after 1930. The pressure of the times was too great for him; it made for so confused a sense of urgency that he forgot that writers are never of any use to themselves, or to society, when they are beaten into shape.

Yes, the pressure of the times is too great; it beats upon all of us. Literature today lives on the narrow margin of security that the democratic West, fighting for its life, can afford; and that margin may grow more narrow every day. The pressure of that struggle beats upon us and all our culture; it beats upon the Hemingways and the Eliots, the Joyces and the Prousts, the wasteland and the grandeur; it beats upon the ardors and accidents, the laborious struggles for realism and realization that make up our modern American literature; it beats equally upon the modernism that dazzled the world between wars and the facile expiation that would wipe it all away. It beats upon us in America as it beats upon all the nations and all the living and the dead; and our whole modern democratic culture is being tried by it. Never was it so imperative as it is now not to sacrifice any of the values that give our life meaning; never was it so imperative for men to be equal to the evil that faces them and not submissive to its terror. The world seems to be waiting, waiting for its new order; everything we do, everything we believe in this moment of climacteric, can help to shape the future toward which men are moving in such agony today. It is not for us, then, but for the Axis Ministers of Culture—the half-men, the death's-heads grinning over their spoil of our time—to impose an external unity upon culture; it is only those who have no culture and no belief in culture who resent differences among men and the explorations of the human imagination. For the rest, the past is what it is; the record of modern literature in America is what men have made it. *"They will have seen the new truth in larger and larger degree; and when it shall have become the old truth, they will perhaps see it all."* We have seen it become the "old truth." We have not even begun to see it all—and what it may become.

ROBERT E. SHERWOOD

As one of America's great dramatists, Robert Sherwood showed, when *Abe Lincoln in Illinois* made its appearance, in 1938, how the creative insight of a literary artist could be used to inject meaning and life into historical situations. *Roosevelt and Hopkins* displays the same talent applied to the much more complicated subject of the Second World War. Despite the epic nature of the action, a sense of intimacy remains. The forces of history are overwhelming, but the author never permits the reader to forget that it is individual men with personal reactions who are caught up in them.

The framework upon which the story has been built is the figure of Harry Hopkins, New Dealer and Franklin Roosevelt's close associate during the crucial war years. The book took its departure from the voluminous records which Hopkins had gathered and from which he was preparing to write his own account when lingering illness brought him to his death in 1946. Sherwood agreed to complete the task, which had not progressed beyond a preliminary sorting of materials.

With this mass of evidence as a core, Sherwood proceeded to buttress his research by a series of interviews with people who had known Hopkins in his various capacities and who had shared with him the top secrets of the war itself. As a frequent visitor at the White House and as the Director of the Overseas Branch of the Office of War Information, Sherwood was able to add his personal observations. With so impressive a fund of information available to a man of Sherwood's consummate literary ability, the result could not be other than it was: one of the most distinguished books yet produced in a field already crowded with significant works.

Although the future may produce more comprehensive accounts of the war years, it is doubtful that anyone will duplicate Sherwood's delineation of key personalities. The anecdotes and the glimpses he gives of what was happening behind the scenes not only humanize the narrative but make understandable a good deal that documents can never reveal. The major portion of the book concerns the years of conflict, but a prefatory section traces Hopkins' career in Washington, from his appointment as Relief Administrator in 1933. Because Hopkins and many of the war leaders were in the limelight during the 1930's, Sherwood's story extends back from Pearl Harbor into the domestic phases of the New Deal.

Sherwood's purpose is to tell how men thought and acted rather than to give a critique of American diplomacy. Nevertheless, he makes certain assumptions which color a considerable part of his findings. In the field of foreign policy, his comments are premised upon the idea that America was so intimately involved in the world crisis that no species of isolationist policy was proper to follow. Whereas more formal historians might undertake to examine alternative views, Sherwood assumes that credit should be given to anyone who shared his own preconception.

Even though Sherwood was fundamentally sympathetic to the New Deal and to the President's war policies, he was interested in telling the whole truth as he understood it rather than in presenting a documented eulogy. Instead of minimizing the conflicts within the New Deal family—for example, between Hopkins and Harold Ickes and between Cordell Hull and Sumner Welles—Sherwood exposes them to view and clarifies them with illustrative episodes. No effort is made to disguise Hopkins' pacifistic misconceptions during the period of American neutrality; instead, Sherwood expresses the opinion that Hopkins shared

Roosevelt's interventionist ideas only because of his faith in the President's judgment. Roosevelt himself is brought to task for publicly talking about his hopes for peace when he privately anticipated quite the opposite.

Yet it is evident that Sherwood is writing about people whom he admired. Certainly Hopkins and Roosevelt had faults, but faults which Sherwood saw were far outweighed by their virtues. If he reveals their weaknesses, it is not to condemn them but to share with the reader his understanding of men who do not need the defense of expurgated testimony. Although Hopkins is the central figure, Roosevelt dominates the book. As an American, Sherwood is proud of Roosevelt's contribution to the world and believes that his stature will grow instead of diminish as the historical record unfolds. But as a democrat rather than a hero-worshipper, he adds an expression of his concern that one man could become so important to the country's safety.

The Phony War

WHEN the Second World War started the defenses of the United States consisted primarily of a scrap of paper called the Neutrality Law, which the Congress had passed and which President Roosevelt had signed "with reluctance." That piece of legislation, passed originally in 1936, was carefully designed to prevent us from getting into war in 1917. It was purely retroactive, as though its framers believed that it would restore life to the brave men who had died at Chateau Thierry and in the Argonne. It was born of the belief that we could legislate ourselves out of war, as we had once legislated ourselves out of the saloons

From *Roosevelt and Hopkins* by Robert E. Sherwood, by permission of Harper & Brothers. Copyright, 1948, by Robert E. Sherwood.

(and into the speakeasies). Like Prohibition, it was an experiment "noble in motive" but disastrous in result.

The Second World War started with Hitler's brutal invasion of Poland from the West, followed by the Soviet Union's march into Poland from the East. Britain and France declared war on Germany, in fulfillment of their pledge to Poland, but for nearly eight months there was no fighting by the Western Allies except for isolated naval engagements. The Soviet Union attacked Finland and gained certain territorial advantages thereby, but Hitler remained quiescent and allowed his neighbors to continue in a state of quivering suspense during the autumn and winter of 1939-40. This became known as the period of "the Phony War" and it was the heyday of isolationism in the United States. It was one crisis in Roosevelt's career when he was completely at a loss as to what action to take—a period of terrible, stultifying vacuum.

In October, 1939, Hopkins wrote from his sickbed to his brother Emory in Portland, Oregon. He said:

> The only interest here, as everywhere, is the war and I believe that we really can keep out of it. Fortunately there is no great sentiment in this country for getting into it although I think almost everyone wants to see England and France win.

In those two sentences Hopkins unconsciously stated the greatest problem that Roosevelt had to face in his entire Administration, the greatest problem any President had faced at least since Lincoln made the determination against the urgent advice of almost all of his Cabinet to send relief to Fort Sumter. I believe that Hopkins' tendency was naturally isolationist, he was certainly a pacifist, as were so many other liberals; he had only the vaguest concept of the deadly peril to American security that Roosevelt saw in the world situation.

In his speech to a Canadian audience at Queens University in Kingston, Ontario, a year previously, Roosevelt had said:

> We in the Americas are no longer a far away continent to which the eddies of controversies beyond the seas could bring no interest or no harm. Instead, we in the Americas have become a consideration to every propaganda office and to every general staff beyond the seas. The vast amount of our resources, the vigor of our commerce and the

strength of our men have made us vital factors in world peace whether we choose it or not.

When Roosevelt said that, as when he made the Quarantine Speech, he was accused by the isolationists of exaggerating dangerously for the purpose of creating undue alarm. "What European general staff," they asked, "could possibly be concerned with the Western Hemisphere?" But Roosevelt in his own mind was not exaggerating in any of his prewar speeches: he was erring on the side of understatement. Although he was no great authority on military strategy, and gave almost unqualified freedom of decision during the war to his Chiefs of Staff, the knowledge that he did possess was basic. The first point in his military credo was that an ocean is not necessarily a barrier—it is a broad highway. His considerable knowledge of geography and of navigation gave him understanding of the importance of the bases from which traffic on that highway could be controlled. His thinking was, of course, essentially naval, which meant that he did not look very far beyond the bridgeheads secured by Marines; however, he knew what the essential bridgeheads were— the British Isles, France, the Iberian Peninsula, the North and West Coasts of Africa and, in the Pacific, the Netherlands East Indies, the Philippines and the Marianas. Early in 1939, some unidentified Senator told the press that, in the course of a secret White House conference on the European situation, the President had said, "Our American frontier is on the Rhine." That quotation was hailed joyously in Britain and in France, and with threatening indignation in Nazi Germany and Fascist Italy. The isolationists at home set up angry howls of protest. When questioned about it at a subsequent press conference, Roosevelt denounced the quotation as a "deliberate lie" and referred to the anonymous informant as "some boob." Nevertheless, whether or not Roosevelt actually made the statement, he most certainly did believe that America's eastern frontier was on the Rhine and it was on this belief that he acted when he risked political suicide in his efforts to break through the Neutrality Law and to get aid to those who fought against Axis aggression. He was unable to get such aid through effectively in time to keep the frontier on the Rhine; but he was able to help incalculably in keeping it on the English Channel and the Straits of Gibraltar.

When the war actually broke out in Europe, Roosevelt was tame enough in his first public statements to satisfy the most timid. He said:

> This nation will remain a neutral nation, but I cannot ask that every American remain neutral in thought as well. Even a neutral has a right to take account of facts. Even a neutral cannot be asked to close his mind or his conscience. . . .
>
> I hope the United States will keep out of this war. I believe that it will. And I give you assurance and reassurance that every effort of our Government will be directed toward that end.

This last may be denounced as, at worst, deliberately misleading or, at best, as wishful thinking. The inescapable fact is that this was what Roosevelt felt compelled to say in order to maintain any influence over public opinion and over Congressional action. Two weeks after the war started he called Congress into extraordinary session to repeal the arms embargo provisions of the Neutrality Law and thus permit the sale of war matériel to England and France on a "cash and carry" basis. Even this meager concession had to be asked for on the grounds that the embargo provisions were, "in my opinion, most vitally dangerous to American neutrality, American security and, above all, American peace." It is my belief—and this is pure speculation—that at this time and up to the fall of France Roosevelt was wishfully hoping that Britain and France would prove indomitable in the West, that the Soviet Union would keep Germany contained in the East, that this stalemate would last until the German people would become fed up with "guns before butter" and revolt, thereby bursting the Nazi bubble so that peace would be restored without the need for American armed intervention. It seems quite evident that Roosevelt did not have full comprehension of the real, paralyzing force of the Nazi fury, nor of the imminence of the danger to the United States, until the Blitzkrieg was hurled into France in the spring of 1940. At that point, I am sure, he became convinced—and this is not speculation—that if Britain fell disastrous war for the United States would be inevitable, that Germany would attack the Western Hemisphere, probably at first in Latin America, as soon as she had assembled a sufficient naval force and transport and cargo fleet (not too long a process, with all the shipbuilding facilities of Europe at Germany's disposal) and that Japan would concurrently go on the rampage in the Pacific.

One major factor in Roosevelt's thinking as the war began is a matter of certainty: his greatest fear then and subsequently was of a negotiated peace, another Munich. Here again was demonstration of the fear of fear itself. He communicated his concern to the British Government through extra-official channels (specifically, Lord Beaverbrook) and he started his historic correspondence with Winston Churchill—whom he addressed as the "Naval Person"—recognizing in him his foremost British ally in awareness of the folly of any attempt to do business with Hitler. (Churchill's cables to Roosevelt were usually addressed to "POTUS," the initials of "President of the United States.") Roosevelt's fear of a negotiated peace was based on the conviction that it would be dictated by the same craven considerations that dictated the surrender at Munich—fear of Nazi might and fear that, if Nazi might were eliminated, Germany would no longer be a buffer state between Russia and the West. It was obvious to Roosevelt as it should have been to any other informed observer that Hitler wanted a negotiated peace because it would work in so many ways to his advantage:

(1) It would further strengthen his position in Germany, providing conclusive proof to the German people that he could hoodwink Britain and France into selling another small country into slavery (in this case, Poland) rather than to risk actual war.

(2) It would give Germany time to consolidate her gains in Czechoslovakia and Poland and further to increase her rearmament, particularly in the building of submarines, airplanes and the Siegfried Line.

(3) It would tend to push public sentiment in Britain and France —and most of all in the United States—back into the peacetime isolationist ruts, and thereby retard if not nullify all efforts in the democracies to prepare for war.

(4) It would convince the Russians—and the Japanese—that the Western democracies were completely spineless and decadent, as Hitler and Mussolini had so long and so loudly proclaimed them to be.

Thus, Roosevelt was on sure ground when he urged that a negotiated peace would give Hitler the one or two years' respite that he needed to prepare for conquest of Europe, Africa, the Middle East and the major part of the Atlantic world; but, when the European

Allies asked Roosevelt, as France in effect did, "What will *you* do to back us up?"—he could only reply that he had virtually nothing to offer more tangible than his personal good will. He could utter brave words but, when deeds were called for, he was hogtied by the prevailing isolationist sentiment.

Since I use the word "isolationists" frequently in these pages, perhaps it would be well to clarify it. Actually, in the first year or more of war, the ranks of the isolationists included the overwhelming majority of the American people who would have been glad to see the European war end on almost any inconclusive terms merely as a guarantee that the United States would not be drawn into it. Public opinion on this score was much more nearly unanimous and more clearly expressed than it had been in 1914-17. It is true that in the First World War there was substantially more pro-German sentiment in the United States: large numbers of German-Americans then still held close cultural and emotional ties with the Fatherland, for the Hohenzollern brand of imperialism, while objectionable to the average American, did not inspire the same horror and loathing as Nazism. The American people were, in a way, more truly neutral in 1914 than they were twenty-five years later. However, Americans in 1939 were fortified with the experience that the previous generation had conspicuously lacked, the experience of involvement in European war, and they wanted no more of it. The impulse to let "Europe stew in its own juice" was a very powerful one and an entirely understandable one, for there were too many Americans who considered that their country's only reward for coming to the aid of Britain and France in 1918 was to be given the name of "Uncle Shylock." (As Roosevelt remarked many times, "We fortunately never had a chance to find out what our 'reward' would have been if Germany had won that war.") Thus, isolationist sentiment in 1939 was not limited to Americans of German birth or descent, or to those who loved German music and admired German science and industry, or to those who were pure pacifists: it was representative of the entire American people save for a diminutive minority of those who believed that a victory for Hitler would put the security of our own country and our own constitutional democracy in deadly peril. The first wartime Roper poll taken in September, 1939, gave eloquent testimony to the state of the nation's thinking.

It will be seen that the extreme interventionist sentiment was limited to 2.5 per cent of the population. Isolationist sentiment was, of course, much stronger among women than among men. The sectional breakdown of this analysis showed very little difference between the New England and Middle Atlantic States and those in the Middle West but far more interventionist sentiment below the Mason-Dixon Line and, somewhat surprisingly, in the Rocky Mountain and Pacific Coast States. (It should be remembered that this public opinion poll did not contemplate the possibility of war with Japan, the Rome-Berlin-Tokyo Axis not having been formed at that time.)

Which of these comes closest to describing what you think America should do about the present European war?

	Total	Sex		Age	
		Male	Female	Under 40	Over 40
	%	%	%	%	%
Enter the war at once on the side of England, France and Poland ...	2.5	3.6	1.3	2.1	2.8
Find some way of supporting Germany	.2	.2	.1	.1	.3
Take no sides and stay out of the war entirely, but offer to sell to anyone on a cash-and-carry basis	37.5	43.0	32.2	37.8	37.2
Do not enter the war but supply England, France and Poland with materials and food, and refuse to ship anything to Germany	8.9	9.0	8.7	8.8	9.0
Stay out for now and for as long as we can, but go into war on the side of England and France if they are in real danger of losing, and in the meantime help that side with food and materials ...	14.7	16.1	13.3	15.4	14.0

Have nothing to do with any warring country—don't even trade with them on a cash-and-carry basis	29.9	23.6	36.1	29.9	29.9
Other—Pro-Ally	.6	.8	.6	.7	.6
Other—Pro-Germany ..	—	—	—	—	—
Other—Favoring neither side	1.8	1.8	1.9	1.5	2.2
Don't know	3.9	1.9	5.8	3.7	4.0

The all-out isolationist faction which would have "nothing to do with any warring country" was close to thirty per cent and this remained a pretty constant figure through all of the opinion tests that were made over such issues as Selective Service, the destroyers-for-bases deal, Lend Lease, etc. This thirty per cent represented the hard core of isolationists and included in it were such strange bedfellows as all the native Fascist organizations, which hailed Hitler as the champion against Bolshevism, and all the members of the Communist party and their fellow travelers; for this was the age of that colossal anomaly, the Nazi-Soviet mutual nonaggression pact. The Fascist groups and individuals were unimportant numerically but they had an altogether disproportionate capacity for noisemaking (like the Communists) and they were by no means a negligible force in spreading the propaganda line as dictated by Goebbels from Berlin.

Immeasurably stronger were the racial and religious groups who favored extreme isolationism. I do not believe that the German-Americans should be included among these for the great majority of them were appalled by what Hitler had done to the land of their forefathers and those who joined or even tolerated the German-American Bund were fortunately few in number. The Scandinavians, particularly in the North Middle West, were considerably more emphatic than the Germans in championing strict neutrality but this sentiment was later affected by the invasions of Denmark and Norway. The Italian-Americans as a group were not necessarily in favor of Fascism but they admired the seeming accomplishments of Mussolini in restoring Italy to the dignity of a great power and there were many of them who were mortally offended by Roosevelt's reference to the "stab in the back." The more rabid Irish-Americans who constituted a potent political force in some of the larger metropolitan areas were, as always, inclined to cheer for anyone who was fighting against England and they were at this time given effective leadership by the violent pamphleteer and radio star, Father Charles E. Coughlin. Because of Father Coughlin and the activities of such subversive organizations as the Christian Front, as well as the sentiments of so many Irish- and Italian-Americans, the Catholic Church became identified to a certain extent in the public mind with the cause of extreme isolationism. However, the Polish-Americans, who formed an important part of the Catholic community, were of course bitterly anti-Nazi as well as anti-Communist.

Organized labor, the greatest unit of support for Roosevelt, was now an uncertain quantity. The unions under Communist domination dutifully followed the party line of all-out isolationism and so did those under the control of John L. Lewis, the bitterest Roosevelt-hater of them all. The great bulk of labor while unquestionably anti-Nazi was also anti-war, fearing that United States involvement would retard or even destroy the gains made by labor under the New Deal. I believe that much the same sentiment had prevailed in the Labor party in Great Britain before the war; it had certainly prevailed in the C.G.T. in France.

The chief leadership and the essential financing of isolationism as a political faction were provided by men and women who belonged to no particular group: there were a number of businessmen, like General Robert E. Wood, Jay Hormel, and James D. Mooney, who simply believed that Hitler was going to win and that the United States had better plan to "do business" with him; and there were technicians, of whom the arch example was Colonel Charles A. Lindbergh, who were so impressed with the technological achievements of Hitler's regimented state, as contrasted with the hopeless inefficiency of democracy, that they believed Fascism constituted "the wave of the future." It was such as these, together with assorted sufferers from the virulent xenophobia of the Hearst-Patterson-McCormick press, who formed the America First Committee, the ultimate spearhead of isolationism.

There were, in addition, considerable numbers of liberals, and many of them in the Roosevelt Administration itself, who opposed the President's unneutral policy because of a pacifistic fear that involvement in war, or even preparation therefor, would produce an interruption in social progress and an assault upon civil liberties such as that which occurred under A. Mitchell Palmer, Alien Property Custodian and Attorney General in the Wilson Administration. As I have indicated, Harry Hopkins would undoubtedly have been included with his friends Senator Robert M. La Follette and Robert M. Hutchins in this category of liberal isolationists had it not been for his fervent conviction that Roosevelt could not possibly be wrong on any major issue. It was the liberal group—and, to a much lesser extent, the Communists—who made the greatest appeal to youth in the country and inspired so many "Keep Us Out of War" demonstrations on so many campuses.

There was another and extremely important element in the thinking of liberals and of countless middle-of-the-road Americans whose political affiliations were hazy but whose impulses were essentially decent: that was profound distrust of the reactionary leaders in Britain and France who had gone to Munich once and might well go there again. Here was an honest and intelligent sentiment which dishonest and dangerously stupid men could exploit. The records of calculated British propaganda in America in the First World War as they had been set down by such thoughtful and reasonable writers as Walter Millis and Quincy Howe evoked too many malodorous memories. Before the advent of calamity in Western Europe and of Winston Churchill, the Allied cause did not have a good smell even in the nostrils of those who hated Fascism and all its evil works. The same general sentiment applied—although to a far lesser extent, because of public ignorance of the area—to the Kuomintang regime in China. It was not easy to answer the question: should American boys die fighting Fascism in Europe and Asia in order to defend neo-Fascism? The unworthy Frenchmen who raised the cry, "Why should we die for Danzig?" raised more echoes in American hearts than Goebbels or Gayda ever did. Early in 1939 that understanding, objective, sharp-witted Scot, Robert Bruce Lockhart, author of *British Agent* and many other books, went on a lecture tour of the United States. In a later book, *Comes the Reckoning,* he wrote:

> The effect of my lectures, like that of most British lecturers, was insignificant, if not indeed harmful, and the only benefit of my tour was self-education.

Lockhart summarized the average American's attitude toward Britain's problems in these words:

> "We Americans went into the last war to save democracy. We pulled you out of a hole and we received very grudging thanks. At Versailles and after Versailles you trampled on democratic ideals. Now, largely through your own fault, you are in trouble again and you want our help. Well, we've learnt our lesson."

Lockhart later became Director General of the Political Warfare Executive, which was attached to the Foreign Office and the Ministry of Information. Perhaps because of his own experience and his remarkably realistic appraisal thereof, the British sent no lecturers to the United States during the entire war, except when specifically requested to do so by the American authorities. The mistakes of the First World War were not repeated.

What Lockhart encountered may be described as the essential "grass roots" sentiment, which was strongly represented in the Congress together with all the various prejudices and fears that always beset little men. There was another powerful influence in the Congress: this was the kind of crossroads chauvinism which afflicts minor politicians who know they can always get applause by indulging in eagle-screaming—the kind of picayune parochialism which contends that all "furriners," particularly Englishmen and Frenchmen, are slick deceivers who are out to pull the wool over the eyes of poor, innocent, gullible Uncle Sam the while they deftly extract the gold from his teeth. I am not suggesting that Congress was dominated by this spirit, nor that the Republicans had any more of it than the Democrats; but it was always there and always highly vocal and such forceful isolationist leaders as Senator Burton K. Wheeler (Democrat, of Montana), and Representative Joseph W. Martin, Jr. (Republican, of Massachusetts), knew well how to mobilize it.

When I speak of the "isolationists," from now on, I shall refer particularly to those in the Congress who were in a position to block the Roosevelt measures and, from their rostrum on Capitol Hill, to publicize what they considered his attempts to dupe the American people into a war which they believed was none of our business. It was a curious fact that these extreme isolationists were not pacifists in the sense that they opposed war, as such; indeed, their attitude toward the Soviet Union—and also, in some cases, toward Japan—

was one of extreme belligerency. They seemed to be in favor of fighting under two essential conditions: (1) that all battles be staged on our own home grounds, in the Western Hemisphere (otherwise, it would be a "foreign" war); and (2) that in the war we keep ourselves pure, and therefore "100 per cent American," by having no allies whatsoever. Evidently it was felt that we had made a terrible mistake in 1918 by fighting in France together with Allies who had turned out to be ingrates, and so we must be careful never to do that again. The Roosevelt doctrine was that if we were to get into a war we should fight it as far from our own shores as possible and with the greatest number of allies, regardless of ideology, that we could enlist, accepting whatever risks there might be of potential ingratitude after the common enemies had been disposed of.

The myopic form of Congressional isolationism can best be expressed by two quotations of the period. The first was from Representative John G. Alexander, a Minnesota Republican. In a letter to the President on Selective Service, he wrote:

> Why take our youth from their homes and out of the wholesome environment in which most of them are living, and transplant them into the lonely inhospitable and disturbing and discouraging arena of a training camp? Their mental, moral and physical well-being is too important to be disregarded in that way. . . . Mr. President, we want no foreign wars, we want none of our American boys to fight in foreign lands or seas, we want only to prepare to protect and defend our own shores and border.

The other quotation was from Senator Robert A. Taft:

> I do not know what the Germans may do, and no one knows what they may do until they are freed from the present war and have an opportunity to show. When they do, we can adopt the same methods. We can take the same steps that may be necessary to meet the particular kind of German "blitzkrieg," if there is such a blitzkrieg, at the time we find out what it is.

In other words, we were to fight only (1) when the enemy, having previously disposed of all of our potential allies, had arrived at our shores or "border" and (2) after he had revealed to us all of the new weapons and tactics that he proposed to employ for our destruction. These two quotations might well be printed at the start of the most elementary textbook used at West Point and Annapolis in order to teach student officers what they must first contend with in their careers of service to the United States.

In his constantly delicate and difficult relations with the Congress in matters of foreign policy, Roosevelt was constantly careful to avoid what Tolstoy called "the irrevocable act." He now carried a heavy share of responsibility for the future history of the world. If he were to go before the Congress with a request for action on an issue of international importance and were defeated, it would involve more than gleeful editorials in the *Chicago Tribune* and possible losses for the Democratic party at the next elections; it could well involve utter, world-wide disaster. The melancholy story has been told of the meeting in the President's study one evening a few weeks before war broke out in Europe at which Roosevelt and Cordell Hull told Vice President Garner, Senator William E. Borah and other Senators of their conviction that war might be averted by immediate amendment of the Neutrality Act. Hull argued the point with tears in his eyes, but Borah brushed him off with the statement that his private sources of information assured him there would be no war ("Germany isn't ready for it"); and Garner ended the meeting by saying, cheerfully, to Roosevelt: "Well, Captain, we may as well face the facts. You haven't got the votes, and that's all there is to it." Roosevelt did not forget that experience and neither did Hull, who had more respect than Roosevelt did for the dignity and authority of the Congress. Before Roosevelt asked for anything else in the next two years, he was extremely careful to make sure that he had "the votes." He hesitated to take a chance which might result in an adverse vote—or even a fairly close vote—in the Congress and thereby render aid and comfort to the Germans and Japanese and discouragement and demoralization to those who fought them. It is not easy for the average citizen to appreciate the extent to which every word, every implication, uttered by the President of the United States, as well as every action committed by him, may bolster the courage or deepen the despair of hundreds of millions of people in lands overseas. But Roosevelt appreciated it. His cautious policy of one step at a time often infuriated the extreme interventionists who often asked, "Why doesn't he go to Congress and demand a declaration of war *now*?" Had he done so in the summer of 1940, for example, when Britain was fighting alone, he would undoubtedly have been repudiated by the Congress and that might well have been the signal to the British people that their cause was hopeless and that they had no choice but surrender. I think that the criticism aimed at Roosevelt by the interventionists caused him more temporary irritation than that hurled at him day after day by the isolationists. Shortly before Christmas, 1939, someone sent him a copy of a poem written by Joseph Warren in 1775, the first verse of which was as follows:

> Lift up your hands, ye heroes,
> And swear with proud disdain;
> The wretch that would ensnare you
> Shall lay his snares in vain.
> Should Europe empty all her force
> We'll meet her in array
> And fight and shout and fight for free Amerikay.

The correspondent—name unknown to me—who sent that to the President explained that "according to Carl Sandburg, the pronunciation 'Amerikay' was customary with both Lincoln and Jeff Davis."

Roosevelt sent a copy of this verse to Hopkins with the following letter:

> Those verses by Joseph Warren, written in 1775, are interesting as showing that a matter of four million people with few resources thought even in those days that they could lick the world. I fear that today altogether too many people in Amerikay want, as they did then, to "fight and shout and fight." Some of us believe there would be more shouting than fighting.

Roosevelt, normally one who interpreted his constitutional powers in the broadest possible terms, might have used the immediate impact of European war to assume authority far beyond that of the normal peacetime President. But he did just the opposite. In a press conference following his Proclamation of Limited Emergency, on September 8, 1939, he clarified his intentions by saying:

> There is no intention and no need of doing all those things that could be done. . . . There is no thought in any shape, manner or form, of putting the Nation, either in its defenses or in its internal economy, on a war basis. That is one thing we want to avoid. We are going to keep the Nation on a peace basis, in accordance with peacetime authorizations.

Those were probably the weakest words that Roosevelt ever uttered. He was outdoing even Warren G. Harding by getting the country "back to normalcy" before the war had really started. He was revealing the woeful weakness of his own Administration, especially in the three Departments that mattered most in a time of international crisis—the State Department, War Department and Navy Department.

It is always easy to poke fun at the State Department—indeed, it ranks second only to the Congress as a target for those who like to indulge in the inexpensive pastime of ridiculing our government—but it is considerably less easy to understand the peculiar difficulties which afflicted the Department in 1940 and thereafter. Cordell Hull had set as his worthy goal the prevention of a Second World War. He was deeply injured when Borah contemptuously dismissed the Department's information as inferior to his own; for Hull, any reflection on his Department constituted an affront to his personal honor and pride—and, as an old soldier of Tennessee, he had plenty of both. Hull's admirable crusade for reciprocal trade was frustrated by the war, and he found himself largely restricted to the maintenance of hemispheric solidarity—in itself a form of isolationism, according to the Roosevelt concept—as a means of keeping the State Department a factor of importance in the Federal Government. While the British Foreign Office was organized on a basis that contemplated the constant possibility of war as "continuation of policy by other means," the State Department was compelled by twenty years of isolationism to operate on the principle that the Alpha and Omega of American foreign policy is to *keep out of war.* When this became impossible, the functions of the State Department, except in regard to neutral countries, became atrophied. This was a bitter pill for Hull to swallow, and he never did fully digest it. He was extremely jealous of his reputation as one officer of the Administration who had been guilty of no conspicuous blunders and who had been spared the criticism lavished on all the others, including the President himself. However, in times of desperate emergency when drastic, daring action had to be taken quickly, Roosevelt was bound to become impatient with anyone whose primary concern was the maintenance of a personal record of "no runs—no hits—no errors." To an ever greater extent, Roosevelt bypassed Hull to deal directly with

Sumner Welles, or to assign what should have been State Department functions to the Treasury Department, the War Department, or to any other agency or individual who might get things done, including eventually Harry Hopkins, the archetype of what Hull called "the extreme left fringe" surrounding the President. Hull believed that he had been selected by Roosevelt as the man to succeed him at the end of the second term, and this belief was assiduously cultivated and encouraged by James A. Farley—as is discussed elsewhere in these pages. Although Hull had conducted no campaign in his own behalf (Farley was doing that for him) he felt that he had been betrayed, if not by Roosevelt, then by Hopkins and the "extreme left fringe." However, unlike Farley, he finally stood by Roosevelt in the campaign of 1940 and was a powerful force in his re-election; and Roosevelt did not forget this.

Unquestionably, the most lasting and most deplorable element in the distant relations between the White House and its next-door neighbor to the west was the President's close association with Sumner Welles—an association based on long friendship and genuine admiration. I cannot pretend to give the reasons for the animosity that existed between the Secretary and Under Secretary of State. But there is no question of doubt that their conflict became so ugly and so extremely dangerous that it eventually compelled the resignation of Welles, which was a serious loss to Roosevelt, for he placed great dependence on Welles's judgment particularly in all matters relating to the framing of the ultimate peace. These are circumstances of which it is not agreeable to write, and impossible for a contemporary to write without evidence of bias in one form or another. However, history will achieve no complete understanding of Franklin Roosevelt's Administration without knowledge of the intramural feuds which so frequently beset it. (I do not believe that even history will ever be able to understand why he tolerated them to the extent that he did.)

The War Department was weakened by a more obvious and even more impolite running battle between the Secretary, Harry H. Woodring, and Louis A. Johnson, Assistant Secretary. Woodring was isolationist at heart while Johnson believed in all-out armament. Their severe clashes were hardly helpful to the Army at a time when its needs were most desperate.

The Navy Department was in much better shape although its Secretary, Charles Edison, was frail in health and insufficiently enthusiastic about his job. Furthermore, Edison appears to have been singularly complacent about the world situation. On June 21, 1940— the very day when Hitler dictated his armistice terms to Pétain's stunned representatives in the forest of Compiègne—Edison wrote to Hopkins urging the use of airships (dirigibles) for the increase of trade with South America. The following words in this letter were underscored by Hopkins:

We may safely assume, I feel, that as soon as the present situation clears in Europe, Germany will immediately resume her South American airship service, even despite her lack of helium or possibly with Russian helium.

The Navy, like the War Department, was to a lamentable extent cowed by the force of isolationist sentiment on Capitol Hill and was trained to be timid in requests for appropriations. The officers most successful in the Department in peacetime were those whom Congress identified as the most economy minded—and sailors or soldiers who are economy minded rarely win wars.

The officer personnel in both services were anything but blind in devotion to the policies of their Commander in Chief. In the Army, there was a tendency among officers of both ground and air forces to admire Germany for her achievements in building up these arms. This led in some extreme cases to the hope that Germany would conquer England thereby providing historic demonstration of the superiority of land and air power over sea power. Obviously, these sentiments were not shared by Navy officers but, for many of them, the main interest was in the Far East, rather than Europe, and it was their hope that if the United States must go to war the main battleground would be the Pacific.

There was another reason for the weakness of Roosevelt's position during the period of the Phony War, and it was probably the most important reason of all: he was in the last year of his second term as President, and it is one of the classical weaknesses of our American constitutional system that a President who is approaching the end of his tenure of office can exercise little authority in the conduct of foreign affairs. The old theory that politics "ends at the waterline" is nonsense. In times of partisan struggle for power there is no point at which politics ends and this was particularly true in 1939-40 when all domestic issues became indistinct and insignificant in the shadow of war. If Roosevelt had indicated in 1939 or early 1940 that he *would* run for a third term, then he would have become a candidate rather than a President; his own party would have been divided into pros and cons and the Republicans would have been united in attacking his every policy, foreign and domestic. If he had indicated he would not run again, then his authority would have become negligible at home and nonexistent abroad. His only solution was to shroud his intentions in mystery; in addition to which, it is apparent that for a long time he himself did not know just what these intentions were. This was a period of impotence when, with all of civilization in peril, the leader of the most powerful nation on earth had to wait, day after anxious day, for his own course of action to be shaped by events over which he had no control. It was particularly agonizing for one of his venturesome spirit to be unable to act boldly or even cautiously to plan action in face of impending calamity, of which the Blitzkrieg in Poland had given a suggestion. The world now knew how the Nazis could strike—how their Air Force could paralyze communications—that their tanks were not, as had hopefully been reported, made of ersatz steel. But the French could only crouch behind the Maginot Line, and the British behind the Royal Navy, and the Americans behind the Neutrality Law. And Roosevelt was, for once in his life, deedless and, so far as he was able to say anything of any consequence, speechless. Early in January, 1940, he sent for Sumner Welles, who has written, "He admitted frankly that the chances seemed to him about one in a thousand that anything at all could be done to change the course of events." The one chance as Roosevelt then saw it was to send Welles to Europe to talk to the heads of government in Germany, Italy, France and Britain to determine "the possibilities of concluding any just and permanent peace" but not any "temporary or tentative armed truce." If Roosevelt believed there was any possibility that Hitler would agree to disarm— or even to give up one acre that Germany had seized—he most certainly was thinking wishfully. Welles returned from his mission with discouraging reports about everything except the temper of the British, but with much useful information on the personalities of the men he had met, and Roosevelt was one who knew how to use such information. It was always of tremendous importance to him to be able to size up the characters of the leaders of both enemy and friendly states.

One may wonder why Welles did not also go to the Soviet Union at the time, but Roosevelt "did not feel that a visit to Moscow would serve any useful purpose." Indeed, then, the prestige of the Soviet Union was so low that it was counted as only a potential victim of Germany and not as a valid aggressive factor. Russia was then involved to the discredit of its arms in the Winter War with little Finland and was making a woefully unimpressive showing. There was no hint revealed of the eventual magnificence of the Red Army in action. Many people have assumed that this was an act of deliberate deception on Russia's part—simulating weakness in order to mask her real strength—but a remark made by Joseph Stalin, printed later in this book, indicated that the weakness then was real.

The war in Finland caused intensification of the isolationist activities of the Communist party in the United States and led to a singular episode at the White House: An American Youth Congress held a convention in Washington in February, 1940, and the delegates assembled on the south lawn of the White House on a raw, rainy day to hear a speech by the President. It was one of the few occasions in his life when Roosevelt was booed and hissed to his face by an audience of Americans. He referred to a resolution, passed by one of the councils of this Youth Congress, against the granting of American aid to Finland on the ground that such action was "an attempt to force America into the imperialistic war." Roosevelt said:

> More than twenty years ago, while most of you were very young children, I had the utmost sympathy for the Russian people. In the early days of Communism, I recognized that many leaders in Russia were bringing education and better health and, above all, better opportunity to millions who had been kept in ignorance and serfdom under the imperial regime. I disliked the regimentation under Communism. I abhorred the indiscriminate killings of thousands of innocent victims. I heartily deprecated the banishment of religion—though I knew that some day Russia would return to religion for the simple reason that four or five thousand years of recorded history have proven that mankind has always believed in God in spite of many abortive attempts to exile God.
>
> I, with many of you, hoped that Russia would work out its own problems, and that its government would eventually become a peace-

loving, popular government with a free ballot, which would not interfere with the integrity of its neighbors.

That hope is today either shattered or put away in storage against
some better day. The Soviet Union, as everybody who has the courage to face the fact knows, is run by a dictatorship as absolute as any
other dictatorship in the world. It has allied itself with another
dictatorship, and it has invaded a neighbor so infinitesimally small
that it could do no conceivable possible harm to the Soviet Union, a
neighbor which seeks only to live at peace as a democracy, and a
liberal, forward-looking democracy at that.

It has been said that some of you are Communists. That is a very
unpopular term these days. As Americans you have a legal and constitutional right to call yourselves Communists, those of you who do.
You have a right peacefully and openly to advocate certain ideals of
theoretical Communism; but as Americans you have not only a right
but a sacred duty to confine your advocacy of changes in law to the
methods prescribed by the Constitution of the United States—and you
have no American right, by act or deed of any kind, to subvert the
Government and the Constitution of this Nation.

Those words, which appear to have been very carefully chosen,
and the boos that greeted them, provide eloquent testimony to the
weirdness of the atmosphere that prevailed during the Phony War.
For Roosevelt was the President who had first established friendly
relations with the Soviet Union, after sixteen years of attempts by
the U.S. Government to ignore its existence, and who subsequently
rendered decisive aid to the Russians when they became victims of
the savage forces they had sought to appease.

During this winter of the Phony War, Churchill paid his respects
to the neutral nations of Europe who sought to buy immunity from
German aggression by appeasement. He said, "Each one hopes that
if he feeds the crocodile enough, the crocodile will eat him last."
Churchill evidently liked to use the crocodile as the symbol of Nazi
voracity. Years later, when he was explaining the North African
operation to Stalin, he drew a picture of a crocodile on a sheet of
Kremlin paper and said, "We shall strike him here, in the soft under-
belly [the Mediterranean] while at the same time we hit him here,
in the snout" [Northern France].

In March, 1940, Hopkins was sufficiently recovered to get out of
bed for a few hours each day and go downstairs and even, when the
weather was sunny and warm, go out for an occasional drive. But he

was still very weak. He wrote to Henry Wallace, Secretary of Agriculture, asking for help in obtaining some seeds for his garden. Among them were petunias, begonias, ageratums, candy tufts, sweet alyssum, pansies, forget-me-nots, calliopsis, bachelor buttons and white and yellow rose bushes. He told Wallace, "This is to be the extent of the kind of thing I am going to be able to do this spring." (In the years that I knew Hopkins I never saw him take any interest in a flower.)

GEORGE F. KENNAN

~~~~~~

THE FIELDS of scholarship and active politics, usually widely separated, are attractively joined in the career of George Kennan. A professional diplomat, he is also a student of foreign affairs who sees in history a key to a better understanding of today's problems.

It is not, however, the scholarship of *American Diplomacy, 1900–1950,* that impresses the historian. Rather, it is the analysis which Kennan has added to facts which are for the most part familiar and dealt with elsewhere more comprehensively. Although he is moderate in tone and generous in his judgments of American diplomats, his point of departure is essentially negative. Primarily concerned with the errors which help to account for the series of international catastrophes in which the country has participated, he condemns both the principle and practice of American diplomacy.

Kennan's basic complaint is against the legalistic-moralistic approach to foreign policy, apparent as early as 1899 in the pronouncement of the "Open Door" policy in China. This method consists in getting a purely verbal commitment among differing powers to pursue a course of action based neither on the realities of the situation nor upon America's willingness to back up its moral sponsorship with force. The view that the morality of nations is similar to that of individuals and, further, that American standards are universal has led to false hopes and illusions of international order. Thus, over a period of years we counted on Japan's formal agreement to principles which she not only had no intention of living up to but which demanded action so far removed from her real needs as to be virtually impossible irrespective of her moral fiber.

Kennan believes that this moral absolutism has had the unfortunate consequence in times of war of leading the United States to insist upon such demands as "unconditional surrender" and "total victory." These war cries, he thinks, are a poor substitute for a careful analysis of the conditions necessary for a lasting peace. Since the world cannot be remade, only limited objectives are possible to achieve. Similarly, the United States should realize that the idea of complete triumph is at odds with its limited military potential. The victory in the Second World War could have been won only by an alliance with a totalitarian power with quite different objectives which would inevitably share the control of the postwar world.

In substition, Kennan offers a foreign policy based upon realities and a frank appraisal of what is necessary to maintain a favorable balance of power. This policy should not embarrass our friends or underestimate our enemies. It should not insist even that our allies conform to our national ideals. As an example, he suggests that the United States should "contain" Russia within its present limits rather than attempt either to ignore or to annihilate her.

Kennan's well-mannered but devastating attack on American diplomacy has seemed to some to be more accurate in its factual detail than it is justified in its conclusions. Unless one assumes that the foreign policy of the United States was in some sense crucial, this analysis loses most of its force. Yet many would contest this assumption and argue that the pattern of events was shaped by forces and by nations over which the wisest of American policies could not have triumphed. The author is, of course, aware of these implications of his theme and somewhat hesitant about suggesting exactly what would have happened in world politics had this country acted differently. Yet his diffidence can hardly be accepted as a proof; and it may be that by laying such store by our policy, he is guilty in some measure of the nationalistic orientation of which he accuses others.

Further, one wonders how amoral Kennan, and the United States government, could be in a crisis. Would he have us select our friends solely on the basis of their power status? Would he recommend that we act in time of war totally without regard to international law and justice? To assume that the United States could behave in this manner is to base its foreign policy on an illusion quite as dangerous as the idealistic one he deplores. Indeed, the persuasiveness of Kennan's prose, and the justice of his criticism of the past tend to obscure the incompleteness of his formula for the present and the future. For example, the difficulties of adjusting a balance of power in which there are only two great powers were not present in previous centuries. Moreover, to try to solve a crisis based importantly upon moral issues precisely by avoiding moral judgments seems less than completely practical.

Almost no one who has criticized *American Diplomacy, 1900–1951* has raised the slightest question concerning its worth. Kennan has put questions to our diplomatic history which have called forth deeply searching answers. At a time when so many areas of international tension call for immediate decisions, he has made us pause and consider the importance of having a philosophy of international relations which will save us from errors of sudden heat and confusion. Whatever steps are taken to meet this need and to base it in the realities of our diplomatic history will be the more informed for this able and stimulating study.

World War II

T HE Cambridge historian, Herbert Butterfield, recently wrote: "Behind the great conflicts of mankind is a terrible human predicament which lies at the heart of the story: . . . Contemporaries fail to see the predicament or refuse to recognize its genuineness so that our knowledge of it comes from later analysis. It is only with the progress of historical science on a particular subject that men come really to recognize that there was a terrible knot almost beyond the ingenuity of man to untie."

I do not suppose that this was any more true of World War II than of any other great conflict. But the fact remains that it was a war poorly understood by the peoples who fought it on the democratic side, and particularly ourselves; and I am sure that this lack of understanding of what was involved in the conflict itself has much to do with the great bewilderment and trouble we seem now to be experiencing in our attempts to adjust ourselves to the situation it left in its train.

It occurs to me that perhaps the most helpful thing to understand about this recent war is the extent to which it was prejudiced, as a military encounter, before it was begun—the extent to which, you might say, it was not fully winnable.

Let me explain how this was. Before the war began the overwhelming portion of the world's armed strength in land forces and air forces had accumulated in the hands of three political entities— Nazi Germany, Soviet Russia, and Imperial Japan. All these entities were deeply and dangerously hostile to the Western democracies. As things stood in the late thirties, if these three powers were to combine their efforts and stick together in a military enterprise, the remaining Western nations plainly had no hope of defeating them on the land mass of Europe and Asia, with the armaments

From *American Diplomacy, 1900-1950* by George Kennan, by permission of The University of Chicago Press. Copyright 1951 by the University of Chicago.

at hand or even those in prospect. In Europe and Asia, Western democracy had become militarily outclassed. The world balance of power had turned decisively against it.

I am not claiming that this was perceived, or would have been easy to perceive, by Western statesmen. But I believe it was a reality. And, as such, it plainly limited the actual prospects for the West, if war were to come. Of the three totalitarian powers, Japan was the only one which could conceivably be defeated by the democracies without invoking for this purpose the aid of one of the other totalitarian powers. In the case of Germany and Russia, circumstances were bitter. Together, they could not be defeated at all. Individually, either of them could be defeated only if the democracies had the collaboration of the other.

But such collaboration, if permitted to proceed to the point of complete victory, would mean the relative strengthening of the collaborating power and its eventual appearance as a greedy and implacable claimant at the peace table. Not only that: any war in which one of these two powers was fighting on the side of the democracies could scarcely be fought to a complete and successful finish without placing the collaborating totalitarian power in occupation of large parts of eastern Europe simply by virtue of the sweep of military operations.

As things stood in 1939, therefore, the Western democracies were already under the handicap of being militarily the weaker party. They could hardly have expected to avoid paying the price. Theirs were no longer the choices of strength. The cards were so stacked against them that any complete, unsullied democratic victory in a new world war was practically impossible to foresee.

Now it may be asked, from the vantage point of hindsight, whether, if this was the case, Western statesmen would not have been wiser in the years prior to hostilities to have shaped their policies in such a way as to embroil the totalitarian powers with one another in order that they might exhaust themselves and leave the security of the Western democracies undiminished. This is of course precisely what Soviet propaganda has charged Western statesmen with doing in the thirties, and indeed some of their actions were so ambiguous and ill advised as to seem to lend substance to the charge. Actually, it would be flattering to the vigor and incisiveness of Western policy in those unhappy years of the late thirties if we could believe that it was capable of such desperate and Machiavellian undertakings. I personally can find no evidence that any substantial body of responsible opinion in any of the Western countries really wished for war at all at that time—even one between Russia and Germany. It was plain that a war between the Nazis and the Russian Communists could take place only over the prostrate bodies of the small states of eastern Europe. And, notwithstanding the tragedy of Munich, the extinction of the independence of these eastern European states was something no one wished for. If other evidence of this were lacking, one had the bald fact that it was, after all, the issue of the independence of Poland for which the French and British finally went to war in 1939.

The fact is that a policy aimed deliberately at the embroilment of the totalitarian powers against each other was, for subjective reasons, never really a practical alternative for democratic statesmen. People who wish well for the democratic idea can find in that fact a source of hope or despair, depending on how they look at it. And as the shades of war closed down over Europe in the summer of 1939, the dilemma of Western statesmen, as we now see it in retrospect, was clear and inescapable. There was no prospect for victory over Germany, unless it were with the help of Russia. But for such help, even if it were forthcoming, the Western democracies would have to pay heavily in the military consequences of the war and in the demands that would be raised at the peace table. Their military purposes, in other words, were mortgages in advance. They might be achieved, as far as Germany was concerned; but there would be a heavy political charge against them. This was not, incidentally, merely a matter of collaboration with Soviet Russia. The tortured compromises the democracies were destined eventually to make with Vichy and with Franco Spain and elsewhere were all part of this pattern. They were part of the price of Western military weakness.

It is important that these things be recognized; for when we look at the problem of Western powers in this light, bearing in mind the unpromising nature of the military undertaking on which they were embarking in 1939, we begin to wonder whether the great mistakes of Western statesmen in connection with this world war were really those of the wartime period at all—whether they were not rather the earlier mistakes, or perhaps we ought to say earlier "circumstances"—which had permitted the development of a situation so grievously and fatefully "loaded" against Western interests. This is of course the problem of the deeper origins of the war; and I think we have no choice but to face it, for the thought at once suggests itself that the best way to win so inauspicious a war might have been to find some way in which one would not have had to fight it at all. By September, 1939, it was of course too late for this. By that time the French and British had no choice, any more than we had in the Pacific in the days following Pearl Harbor. But was there a time when it was *not* too late?

The question as to what Western statesmen might have done to avoid World War II is not an easy one. It is a little disconcerting to find respectable scholars, such as the French historian Bainville, claiming as early as 1920 to see a peculiar logic in the situation flowing from World War I and predicting quite accurately, on the basis of this logic, the general course of events up to and including the outbreak of World War II. It is disconcerting because it leads you to ask whether World War II was not perhaps implicit in the outcome of World War I; in the fact that England and France had been injured and weakened far more deeply than they knew in that first encounter; in the fact that Austria-Hungary and Russia were both lost for the maintenance of European stability, Austria-Hungary because she had disappeared entirely, Russia because her energies and resources had been captured by people violently hostile to capitalist democracy in general; and in the fact that the Germans —frustrated, impoverished, stung with defeat, uncertain in the breakdown of their traditional institutions—were nevertheless left as the only great united people in Central Europe. Looking at these things, it is easy to conclude that World War II just could not help but develop, that it was nothing more than the inevitable aftermath of World War I. You then start poking back into the origins of the earlier war to discover the real sources of the instability of our time. And from this standpoint it is only a step to absolving the Western statesmen of the twenties and thirties of all responsibility for the second war and to regarding them exclusively as the actors in a tragedy beyond their making or repair.

This is of course an extremism. Statesmen, it is true, generally inherit from their predecessors predicaments and dilemmas to which they can see no complete solutions; their ability to improve situations by action over the short term is often quite genuinely limited; but over the long term (and two decades is a respectable length of time) there are always some choices at their disposal. I think it fair to say that World War I was a genuine tragedy which left the Western world much worse off afterward than it had been before and significantly narrowed the choices of Western statesmen in the postwar period; but it did not eliminate those choices entirely. There were, in other words, still things that "could have been done" and which we may assume would at least have been helpful and have had greater possibilities of preventing further tragedy than the things that were done. In so far as we are talking about Germany, there are two such things that strike me as of obvious importance, and in both of them we Americans could, had we wished, have taken a considerable part. First, we could have tried to give greater understanding, support, and encouragement to the modern forces in the Weimar Republic. And if that did not succeed in preventing the rise of naziism, then we could have taken a stiffer and more resolute attitude against Hitler's earlier encroachments and provocations.

It is the last of these two possibilities, that of a stronger stand against Hitler at an earlier date, that has received most prominence in Western thought and has constituted the source of most reproaches to democratic statesmanship between the wars. Unquestionably, such a policy might have enforced a greater circumspection on the Nazi regime and caused it to proceed more slowly with the actualization of its timetable. From this standpoint, firmness at the time of the reoccupation of the Rhineland in 1936 would probably have yielded even better results than firmness at the time of Munich. But I wondered whether we do not tend to exaggerate the relative importance of this question of stopping Hitler once he was in power, as compared with the importance of seeing to it that a person of his ilk should not come into power at all in a great Western country. It was a defeat for the West, of course, that Hitler was able to consolidate his power and be successful in the years 1933–39. But actually the West had suffered an even greater defeat on the day when the German people found itself in such a frame of mind that it could, without great resistance or remonstrance, accept a Hitler as its leader and master.

A stiffer attitude on the part of the Western democracies might, it is true, have resulted in Hitler's overthrow and his replacement by a less obnoxious regime before war could come; in fact, there is evidence that a revolt might well have been attempted had the British and French had the perceptiveness to stand firm at the time of Munich. But great uncertainties lay along this path. The hypnotic charm of naziism was already strong upon the German people. If anyone had overthrown Hitler, presumably it would have been the generals. Whether they would have been able to control the situation subsequently, to lay the ghost not only of naziism but of German aggressiveness in general, and to adjust peaceably their relations with the West, is not certain. The great misfortune of the West, I suspect, was not Hitler but the weakness of German society which made possible his triumph. And it is this which takes us back to this question of the attitude of the Western democracies toward the Weimar Republic.

Events have moved so fast that we have almost lost sight of this intensely interesting period in German history—the period before 1933, with its amazing cultural and intellectual flowering, so full of hope and yet so close to despair. In the decade of the twenties Berlin was the most alive of the capitals of Europe, and things were taking place there from which the Western democracies might have derived profit and instruction. It is true that the peace treaty we Americans concluded with Weimar Germany was nonpunitive. Americans cannot be justly charged with any political offensiveness toward the new Germany. We even financed her lavishly, though foolishly. But what I am thinking of pertained not just to us but to the Western democracies in general, and it was something more than political or financial: it was a general attitude of distaste and suspicion, intermingled with a sort of social snobbery so grotesque that as late as 1927 a German could still be prohibited from using the golf links at Geneva, the seat of the League of Nations. We did nothing to harm Weimar Germany; but we left it very much to its own devices. There are times when that is a good policy toward another country. But I fear that this was not one of those times. Here, in any case, were lost opportunities; and it is significant that they lay as much in the cultural and intellectual as in the political field.

Now a word about Russia, the second totalitarian party. Was there nothing we could have done, prior to 1939, to keep this great country out of the camp of our adversaries? I am sorry that we cannot devote an entire lecture to this subject, for it is an interesting one and close to my heart. I do not feel that we in this country always conducted ourselves in the manner best calculated to reduce the dimensions of the Soviet threat. I think we might have done more to win the respect, if not the liking, of the Russian Communists; and the respect of your enemies—as we are apt sometimes to forget—is nothing to be sneezed at. But I know of little that we could have done to alter basically the political personality of the Bolshevik leadership or to moderate the violent preconceptions against Western democracy on which it was reared and with which it came into power. These things had deep psychological roots, lying in specifically Russian phenomena. Whether the capitalist democracies of the West had done things prior to 1917 to deserve this burning hostility, I do not know. But I am sure that, once developed, it was hardly to be altered by anything the West might do directly; and the best reaction to it on our part would have been at all times an attitude of great reserve, consistency, and dignity.

As for Japan, the problem of whether she had also to be ranged against us in war in the early 1940's was of course primarily our problem, not that of the French and British. I would wish that we could skip it entirely for purposes of this discussion; for it is a tremendous subject in itself, relatively remote from the causes of the war in Europe, and not easy to treat in a few words. But the fact of our simultaneous involvement with Japan and Germany was so important an element in the course and outcome of the war that I think one cannot simply pass the question by.

To discuss this problem at all adequately would be to discuss the entire sequence of American-Japanese relations over the half-century preceding the outbreak of war in the Pacific; and that we obviously cannot do here. To this we must add the disturbing fact that there can never be any certainty about these post mortems on history. It does seem plain that, as the earlier decades and years of this century went by and the hour of Pearl Harbor approached, the choices of American statesmen that held promise of averting a war with Japan became narrower and narrower, and no one can be sure, I suppose, that anything we might have done or failed to do in the final years and months before the Japanese attack could really have forestalled the final outcome. If there were happier possibilities, they were surely more abundant in the more distant past, when our allotment of time was more generous and our area of diplomatic maneuver greater. But whether such possibilities really existed must remain a matter of opinion. My own feeling, for whatever it is worth, is that a policy carefully and realistically aimed at the avoidance of a war with Japan and less encumbered with other motives would certainly have produced a line of action considerably different from that which we actually pursued and would presumably have led to quite different results.

But I think it is enough for us to record that here again, as in the European theater, if there were ways in which this war might have been avoided altogether, they were probably ways that did relate to the more distant past: to a period when people were not thinking about war at all and had no idea that the things they were doing or failing to do were creating for them this tremendous predicament of the future.

So we are back again to our fundamental fact that by the year 1939 affairs were really quite inauspicious for the Western democracies. The situation which they had allowed to arise was one for which there were no complete cures. Whether they realized it or not, the war could be for them, in the deeper sense, at best a war of defense: a war that might bring immediate survival but could scarcely bring an improvement in the stability of the world they lived in, and certainly not the advance of any of the more positive and constructive purposes of democracy. When this is borne in mind, the great decisions of the war years themselves appear for the most part in a more charitable light.

The first of these great decisions which deserves mention seems to me to have been our own decision—if we may call it that—not to enter the European war until the Germans declared war upon us. This was of course comparable to our behavior in World War I, when we refrained from entering until an overt German action, namely, the declaration of unrestricted submarine warfare, brought us in. And what seems to me most interesting about our conduct in each of these cases is the marked change in our emotional attitude toward the struggle itself, once we had become formally involved in it. Theoretically, if the issues involved in the European struggle were really as vital to us as we persuaded ourselves they were in the years 1942–45, they were surely no less important from 1939 to 1941. Actually, in that earlier period, before the German attack on Russia, the cause of the British and French could really be called the cause of freedom and democracy, for very little else was involved on the Western side; whereas later, when we did discover that our vital stake in the anti-German cause warranted great military sacrifice on our part, it was at a time when that cause had been rendered ambiguous, as anything more than a defensive undertaking, by the participation of the U.S.S.R. on the side of the democracies.

Now I mention this, because, making all due allowance for the deliberateness of the opinion-forming process in a democracy, it does look as though the real source of the emotional fervor which we Americans are able to put into a war lies less in any objective understanding of the wider issues involved than in a profound irritation over the fact that other people have finally provoked us to the point where we had no alternative but to take up arms. This lends to the democratic war effort a basically punitive note, rather than one of expediency. I mention this because, if there is anything in this thought, it goes far to explain the difficulty we have in employing force for rational and restricted purposes rather than for purposes which are emotional and to which it is hard to find a rational limit.

Once we had come into the European war, and granted the heavy military handicaps with which the Western powers were then confronted in that theater, the decisions taken throughout the remainder of the war years were those of harried, overworked men, operating in the vortex of a series of tremendous pressures, military and otherwise, which we today find it difficult to remember or to imagine. I think that some injustice is being done both to the men in question and to the cause of historical understanding by the latter-day interpretations which regard specific decisions of the wartime years as the source of all our present difficulties. The most vociferous charges of wartime mistakes relate primarily to our dealings with the U.S.S.R., and particularly to the wartime conferences of Moscow, Teheran, and Yalta. As one who was very unhappy about these conferences at the time they were taking place and very worried lest they lead to false hopes and misunderstandings, I may perhaps be permitted to say that I think their importance has recently been considerably overrated. If it cannot be said that the Western democracies gained very much from these talks with the Russians, it would also be incorrect to say that they gave very much away. The establishment of Soviet military power in eastern Europe and the entry of Soviet forces into Manchuria was not the result of these talks; it was the result of the military operations during the concluding phases of the war. There was nothing the Western democracies could have done to prevent the Russians from entering these areas except to get there first, and this they were not in a position to do. The implication that Soviet forces would not have gone into Manchuria if Roosevelt had not arrived at the Yalta understanding with Stalin is surely nonsense. Nothing could have stopped the Russians from participating in the final phases of the Pacific war, in order to be in at the kill and to profit by an opportunity to gain objectives they had been seeking for half a century.

It is similarly incorrect to portray the Yalta agreement as a terrible betrayal of Nationalist China. The agreement was that we should recommend certain things to the Chinese government. The leaders of that government were not averse to these things at the time. They had asked us, long before Yalta, to help them to arrange their affairs with the Soviet government. They later expressed themselves as well satisfied with what we had done. And in the subsequent negotiations which they themselves conducted independently with the Russians and which actually constituted the controlling arrangements for the future of Manchuria, they went in some respects further in the way of concessions to the Soviet Union than anything that had been agreed upon at Yalta and recommended to them by us. They did this despite the fact that they were specifically warned by us that in doing so they were acting on their own responsibility and not at our recommendation.

The worst that can fairly be said about the wartime conferences from the practical standpoint, therefore, is that they were somewhat redundant and led to a certain number of false hopes here and elsewhere. But we must remember, in this connection, that these conferences had a distinct value as practical demonstrations of our readiness and eagerness to establish better relations with the Soviet regime and of the difficulties we encountered in our effort to do so. Like other evidences of patience and good will, they were important for the record. Had we not gone into them, it is my guess that we would still be hearing reproachful voices saying: "You claim that cooperation with Russia is not possible. How do you know? You never even tried."

A more substantial charge against our wartime policy toward Russia, although one we hear less about, is that which relates to the continuation of lend-lease during the latter period of the war, and specifically subsequent to midsummer of 1944. By that time, as you will recall, Russia's own territory had been freed of the enemy; our own talking position vis-à-vis the Russians had been considerably improved by the creation of a successful second front; and from there on out whatever the Russian forces did was bound to have important political consequences for European peoples other than the Germans—consequences which went far beyond the mere defeat of Germany. I think it can be well argued that there was no adequate justification for refusing to give any attention to these developing political problems and for continuing a program of lavish and almost indiscriminate aid to the Soviet Union at a time when there was increasing reason to doubt whether her purposes in eastern Europe, aside from the defeat of Germany, would be ones which we Americans could approve and sponsor.

But in all these matters we must bear in mind both the overriding compulsion of military necessity under which our statesmen were working and also the depth of their conviction that one had no choice but to gamble on the possibility that Soviet suspicions might be broken down and Soviet collaboration won for the postwar period, if there were to be any hope of permanent peace. Many of us who were familiar with Russian matters were impatient with this line of thought at the time, because we knew how poor were the chances of success, and we saw no reason why a Western world which kept its nerves, its good humor, and a due measure of military preparedness should not continue indefinitely to live in the same world with the power of the Kremlin without flying to either of the extremes of political intimacy or war. In the light of what has occurred subsequently, I can see that our view, too, was not fully rounded. We were right about the nature of Soviet power; but we were wrong about the ability of American democracy at this stage in its history to bear for long a situation full of instability, inconvenience, and military danger. Perhaps Harry Hopkins and F.D.R. had more reason than we then supposed to believe that everything depended on the possibility of changing the attitude of the Soviet regime. But, if so, this is then only an indication that the dilemma was crueler than any of us really appreciated, and the crisis of our time one of such profundity that even the vast dislocations of World War II were only a partial symptom of it.

And there is no reason to suppose that, had we behaved differently either with respect to lend-lease or with respect to the wartime conferences, the outcome of military events in Europe would have been greatly different than it was. We might have wasted less money and material than we did. We might have arrived in the center of Europe slightly sooner and less encumbered with obligations to our Soviet allies. The postwar line of division between East and West might have lain somewhat farther east than it does today, and that would certainly be a relief to everyone concerned. But we were still up against the basic dilemma that Hitler was a man with whom a compromise peace was impracticable and unthinkable and that, while "unconditional surrender" was probably not a wise thing to talk a lot about and make into a wartime slogan, in reality there was no promising alternative but to pursue this unhappy struggle to its bitter end, whether you were acting in agreement with your Russian allies or whether you were not; and this meant that sooner or later you would end on some sort of a line in eastern or Central Europe, probably more central than eastern, with ourselves on one side and Soviet forces on the other, and with the understanding between us just about what it has proved to be in these six years since the termination of hostilities.

Remembering these things, I think we are justified in asking whether the greatest mistakes of World War II were really these tortured and hard-pressed decisions which defined military operations and gave shape to inter-Allied relations in the stress of military operations—whether they were really, in other words, the errors of decision on the part of a few highly placed individuals—whether they were not rather the deeper mistakes of understanding and attitude on the part of our society in general with respect to a military venture in which we were engaged. First of all, there was the failure to remember the essentially and inescapably defensive nature of this particular war, as one in which we in the West were at first the weaker party, capable of achieving only a portion of our aim and of achieving that portion only in collaboration with a totalitarian adversary and at a price. This failure stemmed from our general ignorance of the historical processes of our age and particularly from our lack of attention to the power realities involved in given situations.

But beyond that, it seems to me, there lay a deeper failure of understanding, a failure to appreciate the limitations of war in general—any war—as a vehicle for the achievement of the objectives of the democratic state. This is the question of the proper relationship of such things as force and coercion to the purposes of democracy. That they have a place in the international as well as the domestic functioning of democracy I would be the last to deny. That will continue to be true until the world is an entirely different world from what we have known it to be throughout our national history. But I would submit that we will continue to harm our own interests almost as much as we benefit them if we continue to employ the instruments of coercion in the international field without a better national understanding of their significance and possibilities. It is essential to recognize that the maiming and killing of men and the destruction of human shelters and other installations, however necessary it may be for other reasons, cannot in itself make a positive contribution to any democratic purpose. It can be the regrettable alternative to similar destruction in our own country or the killing of our own people. It can conceivably protect values which it is necessary to protect and which can be protected in no other way. Occasionally, if used with forethought and circumspection and restraint, it may trade the lesser violence for the greater and impel the stream of human events into channels which will be more hopeful ones than it would otherwise have taken. But, basically, the democratic purpose does not prosper when a man dies or a building collapses or an enemy force retreats. It may be hard for it to prosper *unless* these things happen, and in that lies the entire justification for the use of force at all as a weapon of national policy. But the actual prospering occurs only when something happens in a man's mind that increases his enlightenment and the consciousness of his real relation to other people—something that makes him aware that, whenever the dignity of another man is offended, his own dignity, as a man among men, is thereby reduced. And this is why the destructive process of war must always be accompanied by, or made subsidiary to, a different sort of undertaking aimed at widening the horizons and changing the motives of men and should never be thought of in itself as a proper vehicle for hopes and enthusiasms and dreams of world improvement. Force, like peace, is not an abstraction; it cannot be understood or dealt with as a concept outside of the given framework of purpose and method. If this were better understood, there could be neither the sweeping moral rejection of international violence which bedevils so many Americans in times of peace nor the helpless abandonment to its compulsions and its inner momentum which characterizes so many of us in times of war.

It is hard for me to say how different would have been our situation today had our public opinion and the mental outlook of our leading persons comprised a comprehension of these realities throughout the entire period of the thirties and forties which we associate with World War II. It is easy to imagine that war might never have come upon us in the form that it did had this been the case. Or, perhaps, even if it had come upon us, we might have been prepared to enter it sooner and in greater force, and thus have been able to end it in a way more favorable to the interests of moderation and stability in world affairs. But these are only conjectures. The historian can never prove that a better comprehension of realities would have prevented any specific calamity or obviated any of the major human predicaments. He can only say that in the law of averages it should have helped.

At the very worst, we can be sure that, had we understood better the elements of our predicament during World War II, we would be calmer and more united and less irritated with one another today in this country, for we would have been better prepared for the things that have happened since 1945 and less inclined to mistake them for the product of somebody else's stupidity or bad faith. But actually it is my belief, which I cannot prove, that the benefits would have gone much farther than this. The possibilities which lie in human understanding, like those that lie in darkness and ignorance, are seldom hypothetically demonstrable; but sometimes they are surprising.

PART VI

AFFLUENCE AND CONFORMITY

JOHN KENNETH GALBRAITH

THE THEME of *The Affluent Society* is the failure of economic theory and public policy to take into account the sufficiency of America's productive capacity and the inadequacy of its public services. Our ability to build cars outdistances the roads to carry them; television aerials fill the sky over urban landscapes lacking in playgrounds; there is an excess of food but not enough colleges and hospitals.

John Kenneth Galbraith, one of the country's leading economists, first takes his colleagues to task for continuing to base their analyses of contemporary America on ideas that arose out of conditions no longer present or relevant. The poverty, the inequality, and the economic peril to which nineteenth-century writers like David Ricardo and Thomas Malthus responded quite understandably led to theories that presumed a scarcity of goods and masses of people living on the verge of starvation. Galbraith shows how this orientation has persisted in today's "conventional wisdom," which makes increased production the central economic goal.

The error of this view is the subject of Galbraith's systematic attack. He begins with a refutation of the need for a fundamental concern with economic equality and insecurity. The widespread increase in general standards of living and the diminution through taxes of both the power and the income of the rich have provided an effective answer to the demands of earlier reformers. "Equality" is therefore no longer a pressing economic issue, and a program for removing poverty by a redistribution of concentrated wealth has lost whatever meaning it once had. Similarly, the insecurity of previous eras has been insured against by both business and government, through such devices as private research, price agreements, social welfare, and agricultural price supports. The existence of such safeguards leads him to believe that the elimination of economic insecurity can be "a finished business."

Those who acknowledge that "equality" and "security" are no longer vitally important issues are apt, in defending the primary importance of production, to fall back upon "consumer demand" as the controlling factor. Galbraith believes that this too has an exaggerated importance. Production has long since satisfied the consumer's self-induced wants and now must create others. One cannot defend the urgency of production by pointing to the urgency of wants created only by production itself, through advertising and salesmanship. He points out that the willingness of economists to acknowledge the marginal utility of individual goods has not been extended to a recognition of the crucial fact that there may be a diminishing utility from new and different goods taken as a whole.

Finally, the author attempts to refute the basic notion that a focus on production can be justified because of a direct correlation between national military power and total economic output. Even in the last war, he argues, it was the ability of the economy to expand rather than to divert existing facilities from consumer goods that proved effective. In the future, total production will be relevant neither to limited wars of the Korean type or to total nuclear war, which would allow no time for conversion.

Despite the fundamental fallacy of their position, Galbraith finds near-unanimity among business conservatives and liberal intellectuals in favor of a production-oriented economy—as an end in itself or as a means of insuring full employment. Since their analysis is grounded on a false premise, he warns, their remedies for economic problems are inadequate. For example, the installment buying by which consumption is now nourished cannot be expanded indefinitely. Further, to operate industry at the high level of capacity sought by labor, management, and the economists is continually to encourage inflation. Neither efforts to control inflation by monetary policy—the conservative remedy—nor by fiscal policy—the liberal solution—can be successful.

Galbraith then turns from criticism to construction, attempting to set forth both a general theoretical framework and specific proposals based upon it. The point of departure is affluence, a sufficiency of consumer goods that makes unnecessary a concern for production. He substitutes instead the need to consider another primary problem—an "inherent tendency for public services to fall behind private production." This tendency destroys the "social balance" that exists when these two factors are abreast—a goal around which Galbraith declares public policy should be oriented. In place of today's profound preoccupation with production per se, he recommends a direct concern for individual happiness and well-being and a minimization of social tensions.

Yet such change of emphasis would call for an alternative to full production as a guarantee of individual incomes. The solution he suggests is an enlarged and flexible system of unemployment compensation, called "Cyclically Graduated Compensation," under which individual benefits would increase as unemployment increased and decrease as unemployment fell. This plan would permit the economy to function at less than capacity and reduce the pressure toward inflation when combined with wage and price controls.

The basic problem of improving public services and achieving "Social Balance" would be met by taxation, which would automatically make "a *pro rata* share of increasing income available to public authority." The cure for remaining poverty would be provided chiefly by improved services. For unlike past poverty, which rested on the failure of society to provide a sufficient quantity of goods, those in want today are apt to be individual cases of maladjustment or groups in "islands" of poverty—whole communities suffering in the midst of plenty. In these situations better education, housing, and other public services would offer a more certain cure than a national increase in production.

The reactions of readers of *The Affluent Society* will vary according to their preconceptions. Those who lean to the left of the political spectrum will note a curious disparity between the sweeping criticism of economy theory and practice and the relatively few, and ever familiar, reform measures offered to adjust the situation. Indeed, Galbraith's proposals suggest a respect for the existing system that his complaints obscure. Even the most stalwart defenders of private enterprise should be impressed with the assumption that an abundance of consumer goods is assured, even with factories operating below "near capacity." But they will be bothered by a second assumption that substantial tax increases, wage and price controls, and the large expansion of public services will not have a deleterious effect upon the operation of business. Those at the "center" will wonder whether sufficient safeguards have been provided for individual incomes, full employment, and security against inflation and depression.

Yet few will wish to deny that the book is illuminating and provocative both as an essay in economic theory and as a commentary on modern America. It combines bold originality with an incisive elaboration of what has been commonly but only dimly perceived.

The Theory of Social Balance

It is not till it is discovered that high individual incomes will not purchase the mass of mankind immunity from cholera, typhus, and ignorance, still less secure them the positive advantages of educational opportunity and economic security, that slowly and reluctantly, amid prophecies of moral degeneration and economic disaster, society begins to make collective provision for needs which no ordinary individual, even if he works overtime all his life, can provide himself.

—R. H. TAWNEY[1]

THE FINAL PROBLEM of the productive society is what it produces. This manifests itself in an implacable tendency to provide an opulent supply of some things and a niggardly yield of others. This disparity carries to the point where it is a cause of social discomfort and social unhealth. The line which divides our area of wealth from our area of poverty is roughly that which divides privately produced and marketed goods and services from publicly rendered services. Our wealth in the first is not only in startling contrast with the meagerness of the latter, but our wealth in privately produced goods is, to a marked degree, the cause of crisis in the supply of public services. For we have failed to see the importance, indeed the urgent need, of maintaining a balance between the two.

This disparity between our flow of private and public goods and services is no matter of subjective judgment. On the contrary, it is the source of the most extensive comment which only stops short of the direct contrast being made here. In the years following World War II, the papers of any major city—those of New York

The selection from John Kenneth Galbraith, *The Affluent Society*, copyright 1961, is reprinted by permission of and arrangement with Houghton Mifflin Company, the authorized publishers.

[1] *Equality* (4th revised ed.), pp. 134-35.

were an excellent example—told daily of the shortages and short-comings in the elementary municipal and metropolitan services. The schools were old and overcrowded. The police force was under strength and underpaid. The parks and playgrounds were insufficient. Streets and empty lots were filthy, and the sanitation staff was underequipped and in need of men. Access to the city by those who work there was uncertain and painful and becoming more so. Internal transportation was overcrowded, unhealthful, and dirty. So was the air. Parking on the streets had to be prohibited, and there was no space elsewhere. These deficiencies were not in new and novel services but in old and established ones. Cities have long swept their streets, helped their people move around, educated them, kept order, and provided horse rails for vehicles which sought to pause. That their residents should have a nontoxic supply of air suggests no revolutionary dalliance with socialism.

The discussion of this public poverty competed, on the whole successfully, with the stories of ever-increasing opulence in privately produced goods. The Gross National Product was rising. So were retail sales. So was personal income. Labor productivity had also advanced. The automobiles that could not be parked were being produced at an expanded rate. The children, though without schools, subject in the playgrounds to the affectionate interest of adults with odd tastes, and disposed to increasingly imaginative forms of delinquency, were admirably equipped with television sets. We had difficulty finding storage space for the great surpluses of food despite a national disposition to obesity. Food was grown and packaged under private auspices. The care and refreshment of the mind, in contrast with the stomach, was principally in the public domain. Our colleges and universities were severely overcrowded and underprovided, and the same was true of the mental hospitals.

The contrast was and remains evident not alone to those who read. The family which takes its mauve and cerise, airconditioned, power-steered, and power-braked automobile out for a tour passes through cities that are badly paved, made hideous by litter, blighted buildings, billboards, and posts for wires that should long since have been put underground. They pass on into a countryside that has been rendered largely invisible by commercial art. (The goods which the latter advertise have an absolute priority in our value system. Such aesthetic considerations as a view of the countryside accordingly come second. On such matters we are consistent.) They picnic on exquisitely packaged food from a portable icebox by a polluted stream and go on to spend the night at a park which is a menace to public health and morals. Just before dozing off on an air mattress, beneath a nylon tent, amid the stench of decaying refuse, they may reflect vaguely on the curious unevenness of their blessings. Is this, indeed, the American genius?

II

In the production of goods within the private economy it has long been recognized that a tolerably close relationship must be maintained between the production of various kinds of products. The output of steel and oil and machine tools is related to the production of automobiles. Investment in transportation must keep abreast of the output of goods to be transported. The supply of power must be abreast of the growth of industries requiring it. The existence of these relationships—coefficients to the economist —has made possible the construction of the input-output table which shows how changes in the production in one industry will increase or diminish the demands on other industries. To this table, and more especially to its ingenious author, Professor Wassily Leontief, the world is indebted for one of its most important of modern insights into economic relationships. If expansion in one part of the economy were not matched by the requisite expansion in other parts—were the need for balance not respected—then bottlenecks and shortages, speculative hoarding of scarce supplies, and sharply increasing costs would ensue. Fortunately in peacetime the market system operates easily and effectively to maintain this balance, and this together with the existence of stocks and some flexibility in the coefficients as a result of substitution, insures that no serious difficulties will arise. We are reminded of the existence of the problem only by noticing how serious it is for those countries —Poland or, in a somewhat different form, India—which seek to solve the problem by planned measures and with a much smaller supply of resources.

Just as there must be balance in what a community produces, so there must also be balance in what the community consumes. An increase in the use of one product creates ineluctably, a require-ment for others. If we are to consume more automobiles, we must have more gasoline. There must be more insurance as well as more space on which to operate them. Beyond a certain point more and better food appears to mean increased need for medical services. This is the certain result of the increased consumption of tobacco and alcohol. More vacations require more hotels and more fishing rods. And so forth. With rare exceptions—shortages of doctors are an exception which suggests the rule—this balance is also main-tained quite effortlessly so far as goods for private sale and con-sumption are concerned. The price system plus a rounded condition of opulence is again the agency.

However, the relationships we are here discussing are not confined to the private economy. They operate comprehensively over the whole span of private and public services. As surely as an increase in the output of automobiles puts new demands on the steel industry so, also, it places new demands on public services. Similarly, every increase in the consumption of private goods will normally mean some facilitating or protective step by the state. In all cases if these services are not forthcoming, the consequences will be in some degree ill. It will be convenient to have a term which suggests a satisfactory relationship between the supply of privately produced goods and services and those of the state, and we may call it social balance.

The problem of social balance is ubiquitous, and frequently it is obtrusive. As noted, an increase in the consumption of automobiles requires a facilitating supply of streets, highways, traffic control, and parking space. The protective services of the police and the highway patrols must also be available, as must those of the hospitals. Although the need for balance here is extraordinarily clear, our use of privately produced vehicles has, on occasion, got far out of line with the supply of the related public services. The result has been hideous road congestion, an annual massacre of impressive proportions, and chronic colitis in the cities. As on the ground, so also in the air. Planes collide with disquieting conse-quences for those within when the public provision for air traffic control fails to keep pace with private use of the airways.

But the auto and the airplane, versus the space to use them, are merely an exceptionally visible example of a requirement that is pervasive. The more goods people procure, the more packages they discard and the more trash that must be carried away. If the appropriate sanitation services are not provided, the counterpart of increasing opulence will be deepening filth. The greater the wealth the thicker will be the dirt. This indubitably describes a tendency of our time. As more goods are produced and owned, the greater are the opportunities for fraud and the more property that must be protected. If the provision of public law enforcement services do not keep pace, the counterpart of increased well-being will, we may be certain, be increased crime.

The city of Los Angeles, in modern times, is a near-classic study in the problem of social balance. Magnificently efficient factories and oil refineries, a lavish supply of automobiles, a vast consumption of handsomely packaged products, coupled with the absence of a municipal trash collection service which forced the use of home incinerators, made the air nearly unbreathable for an appreciable part of each year. Air pollution could be controlled only by a complex and highly developed set of public services—by better knowledge stemming from more research, better policing, a municipal trash collection service, and possibly the assertion of the priority of clean air over the production of goods. These were long in coming. The agony of a city without usable air was the result.

The issue of social balance can be identified in many other current problems. Thus an aspect of increasing private production is the appearance of an extraordinary number of things which lay claim to the interest of the young. Motion pictures, television, automobiles, and the vast opportunities which go with the mobility, together with such less enchanting merchandise as narcotics, comic books, and pornographia, are all included in an advancing gross national product. The child of a less opulent as well as a technologically more primitive age had far fewer such diversions. The red schoolhouse is remembered mainly because it had a paramount position in the lives of those who attended it that no modern school can hope to attain.

In a well-run and well-regulated community, with a sound school system, good recreational opportunities, and a good police force— in short a community where public services have kept pace with private production—the diversionary forces operating on the modern juvenile may do no great damage. Television and the violent mores of Hollywood and Madison Avenue must contend with the intellectual discipline of the school. The social, athletic, dramatic, and like attractions of the school also claim the attention of the child. These, together with the other recreational opportunities of the community, minimize the tendency to delinquency. Experiments with violence and immorality are checked by an effective law enforcement system before they become epidemic.

In a community where public services have failed to keep abreast of private consumption things are very different. Here, in an atmosphere of private opulence and public squalor, the private goods have full sway. Schools do not compete with television and the movies. The dubious heroes of the latter, not Miss Jones, become the idols of the young. The hot rod and the wild ride take the place of more sedentary sports for which there are inadequate facilities or provision. Comic books, alcohol, narcotics, and switchblade knives are, as noted, part of the increased flow of goods, and there is nothing to dispute their enjoyment. There is an ample supply of private wealth to be appropriated and not much to be feared from the police. An austere community is free from temptation. It can be austere in its public services. Not so a rich one.

Moreover, in a society which sets large store by production, and which has highly effective machinery for synthesizing private wants, there are strong pressures to have as many wage earners in the family as possible. As always all social behavior is part of a piece. If both parents are engaged in private production, the burden on the public services is further increased. Children, in effect, become the charge of the community for an appreciable part of the time. If the services of the community do not keep pace, this will be another source of disorder.

Residential housing also illustrates the problem of the social balance, although in a somewhat complex form. Few would wish to contend that, in the lower or even the middle income brackets, Americans are munificently supplied with housing. A great many families would like better located or merely more houseroom, and no advertising is necessary to persuade them of their wish. And the provision of housing is in the private domain. At first glance at least, the line we draw between private and public seems not to be preventing a satisfactory allocation of resources to housing.

On closer examination, however, the problem turns out to be not greatly different from that of education. It is improbable that the housing industry is greatly more incompetent or inefficient in the United States than in those countries—Scandinavia, Holland, or (for the most part) England—where slums have been largely eliminated and where *minimum* standards of cleanliness and comfort are well above our own. As the experience of these countries shows, and as we have also been learning, the housing industry functions well only in combination with a large, complex, and costly array of public services. These include land purchase and clearance for redevelopment; good neighborhood and city planning, and effective and well-enforced zoning; a variety of financing and other aids to the housebuilder and owner; publicly supported research and architectural services for an industry which, by its nature, is equipped to do little on its own; and a considerable amount of direct or assisted public construction for families in the lowest income brackets. The quality of the housing depends not on the industry, which is given, but on what is invested in these supplements and supports.

III

The case for social balance has, so far, been put negatively. Failure to keep public services in minimal relation to private production and use of goods is a cause of social disorder or impairs economic performance. The matter may now be put affirmatively. By failing to exploit the opportunity to expand public production we are missing opportunities for enjoyment which otherwise we might have had. Presumably a community can be as well rewarded by buying better schools or better parks as by buying bigger automobiles. By concentrating on the latter rather than the former it is failing to maximize its satisfactions. As with schools in the community, so with public services over the country at large. It is scarcely sensible that we should satisfy our wants in private goods with reckless abundance, while in the case of public goods, on the evidence of the eye, we practice extreme self-denial. So, far from systematically exploiting the opportunities to derive use and pleasure from these services, we do not supply what would keep us out of trouble.

The conventional wisdom holds that the community, large or small, makes a decision as to how much it will devote to its public services. This decision is arrived at by democratic process. Subject to the imperfections and uncertainties of democracy, people decide how much of their private income and goods they will surrender in order to have public services of which they are in greater need. Thus there is a balance, however rough, in the enjoyments to be had from private goods and services and those rendered by public authority.

It will be obvious, however, that this view depends on the notion of independently determined consumer wants. In such a world one could with some reason defend the doctrine that the consumer, as a voter, makes an independent choice between public and private goods. But given the dependence effect—given that consumer wants are created by the process by which they are satisfied—the consumer makes no such choice. He is subject to the forces of advertising and emulation by which production creates its own demand. Advertising operates exclusively, and emulation mainly, on behalf of privately produced goods and services.[2] Since management and emulative effects operate on behalf of private production, public services will have an inherent tendency to lag behind. Automobile demand which is expensively synthesized will inevitably have a much larger claim on income than parks or public health or even roads where no such influence operates. The engines of mass communication, in their highest state of development, assail the eyes and ears of the community on behalf of more beer but not of more schools. Even in the conventional wisdom it will scarcely be contended that this leads to an equal choice between the two.

The competition is especially unequal for new products and services. Every corner of the public psyche is canvassed by some of the nation's most talented citizens to see if the desire for some

---

[2] Emulation does operate between communities. A new school or a new highway in one community does exert pressure on others to remain abreast. However, as compared with the pervasive effects of emulation in extending the demand for privately produced consumer's goods there will be agreement, I think, that this intercommunity effect is probably small.

merchantable product can be cultivated. No similar process operates on behalf of the nonmerchantable services of the state. Indeed, while we take the cultivation of new private wants for granted we would be measurably shocked to see it applied to public services. The scientist or engineer or advertising man who devotes himself to developing a new carburetor, cleanser, or depilatory for which the public recognizes no need and will feel none until an advertising campaign arouses it, is one of the valued members of our society. A politician or a public servant who dreams up a new public service is a wastrel. Few public offenses are more reprehensible.

So much for the influences which operate on the decision between public and private production. The calm decision between public and private consumption pictured by the conventional wisdom is, in fact, a remarkable example of the error which arises from viewing social behavior out of context. The inherent tendency will always be for public services to fall behind private production. We have here the first of the causes of social imbalance.

IV

Social balance is also the victim of two further features of our society—the truce on inequality and the tendency to inflation. Since these are now part of our context, their effect comes quickly into view.

With rare exceptions such as the post office, public services do not carry a price ticket to be paid for by the individual user. By their nature they must, ordinarily, be available to all. As a result, when they are improved or new services are initiated, there is the ancient and troublesome question of who is to pay. This, in turn, provokes to life the collateral but irrelevant debate over inequality. As with the use of taxation as an instrument of fiscal policy, the truce on inequality is broken. Liberals are obliged to argue that the services be paid for by progressive taxation which will reduce inequality. Committed as they are to the urgency of goods (and also . . . to a somewhat mechanical view of the way in which the level of output can be kept most secure) they must oppose sales and excise taxes. Conservatives rally to the defense of inequality—although without ever quite committing themselves in such uncouth terms—and oppose the use of income taxes. They, in effect, oppose the expenditure not on the merits of the service but on the demerits of the tax system. Since the debate over inequality cannot be resolved, the money is frequently not appropriated and the service not performed. It is a casualty of the economic goals of both liberals and conservatives for both of whom the questions of social balance are subordinate to those of production and, when it is evoked, of inequality.

In practice matters are better as well as worse than this statement of the basic forces suggests. Given the tax structure, the revenues of all levels of Government grow with the growth of the economy. Services can be maintained and sometimes even improved out of this automatic accretion.

However, this effect is highly unequal. The revenues of the federal government, because of its heavy reliance on income taxes, increase more than proportionately with private economic growth. In addition, although the conventional wisdom greatly deplores the fact, federal appropriations have only an indirect bearing on taxation. Public services are considered and voted on in accordance with their seeming urgency. Initiation or improvement of a particular service is rarely, except for purposes of oratory, set against the specific effect on taxes. Tax policy, in turn, is decided on the basis of the level of economic activity, the resulting revenues, expediency, and other considerations. Among these the total of the thousands of individually considered appropriations is but one factor. In this process the ultimate tax consequence of any individual appropriation is *de minimus,* and the tendency to ignore it reflects the simple mathematics of the situation. Thus it is possible for the Congress to make decisions affecting the social balance without invoking the question of inequality.

Things are made worse, however, by the fact that a large proportion of the federal revenues are pre-empted by defense. The increase in defense costs has also tended to absorb a large share of the normal increase in tax revenues. The position of the federal government for improving the social balance has also been weakened since World War II by the strong, although receding, conviction that its taxes were at artificial wartime levels and that a tacit commitment exists to reduce taxes at the earliest opportunity.

In the states and localities the problem of social balance is much more severe. Here tax revenues—this is especially true of the General Property Tax—increase less than proportionately with increased private production. Budgeting too is far more closely circumscribed than in the case of the federal government—only the monetary authority enjoys the pleasant privilege of underwriting its own loans. Because of this, increased services for states and localities regularly pose the question of more revenues and more taxes. And here, with great regularity, the question of social balance is lost in the debate over equality and social equity.

Thus we currently find by far the most serious social imbalance in the services performed by local governments. The F.B.I. comes much more easily by funds than the city police force. The Department of Agriculture can more easily keep its pest control abreast of expanding agricultural output than the average city health service can keep up with the needs of an expanding industrial population. One consequence is that the federal government remains under constant pressure to use its superior revenue position to help redress the balance at the lower levels of government.

V

Finally, social imbalance is the natural offspring of persistent inflation. Inflation by its nature strikes different individuals and groups with highly discriminatory effect. The most nearly unrelieved victims, apart from those living on pensions or other fixed provision for personal security, are those who work for the state. In the private economy the firm which sells goods has, in general, an immediate accommodation to the inflationary movement. Its price increases are the inflation. The incomes of its owners and proprietors are automatically accommodated to the upward movement. To the extent that wage increases are part of the inflationary process, this is also true of organized industrial workers. Even unorganized white collar workers are in a milieu where prices and incomes are moving up. The adaption of their incomes, if less rapid than that of the industrial workers, is still reasonably prompt.

The position of the public employee is at the other extreme. His pay scales are highly formalized, and traditionally they have been subject to revision only at lengthy intervals. In states and localities inflation does not automatically bring added revenues to pay higher salaries and incomes. Pay revision for all public workers is subject to the temptation to wait and see if the inflation isn't coming to an end. There will be some fear—this seems to have been more of a factor in England than in the United States —that advances in public wages will set a bad example for private employers and unions.

Inflation means that employment is pressing on the labor supply and that private wage and salary incomes are rising. Thus the opportunities for moving from public to private employment are especially favorable. Public employment, moreover, once had as a principal attraction a high measure of social security. Industrial workers were subject to the formidable threat of unemployment during depression. Public employees were comparatively secure, and this security was worth an adverse salary differential. But with improving economic security in general this advantage has diminished. Private employment thus has come to provide better protection against inflation and little worse protection against other hazards. Though the dedicated may stay in public posts, the alert go.

The deterioration of the public services in the years of inflation has not gone unremarked. However, there has been a strong tendency to regard it as an adventitious misfortune—something which, like a nasty shower at a picnic, happened to blight a generally good time. Salaries were allowed to lag, which was a pity. This is a very inadequate view. Discrimination against the public services is an organic feature of inflation. Nothing so weakens government as persistent inflation. The public administration of France for many years, of Italy until recent times, and of other European and numerous South American countries have been deeply sapped and eroded by the effects of long-continued inflation. Social imbalance reflects itself in inability to enforce laws, including significantly those which protect and advance basic social justice, and in failure to maintain and improve essential services. One outgrowth of the resulting imbalance has been frustration and pervasive discontent. Over much of the world there is a rough and not entirely accidental correlation between the strength of indigenous communist parties or the frequency of revolutions and the persistence of inflation.

VI

A feature of the years immediately following World War II was a remarkable attack on the notion of expanding and improving public services. During the depression years such services had been elaborated and improved partly in order to fill some small part of the vacuum left by the shrinkage of private production. During the war years the role of government was vastly expanded. After that came the reaction. Much of it, unquestionably, was motivated by a desire to rehabilitate the prestige of private production and therewith of producers. No doubt some one who joined the attack hoped, at least tacitly, that it might be possible to sidestep the truce on taxation vis-à-vis equality by having less taxation of all kinds. For a time the notion that our public services had somehow become inflated and excessive was all but axiomatic. Even liberal politicians did not seriously protest. They found it necessary to aver that they were in favor of public economy too.

In this discussion a certain mystique was attributed to the satisfaction of privately supplied wants. A community decision to have a new school means that the individual surrenders the necessary amount, willy-nilly, in his taxes. But if he is left with that income, he is a free man. He can decide between a better car or a television set. This was advanced with some solemnity as an argument for the TV set. The difficulty is that this argument leaves the community with no way of preferring the school. All private wants, where the individual can choose, are inherently superior to all public desires which must be paid for by taxation and with an inevitable component of compulsion.

The cost of public services was also held to be a desolating burden on private production, although this was at a time when the private production was burgeoning. Urgent warnings were issued of the unfavorable effects of taxation on investment—"I don't know of a surer way of killing off the incentive to invest than by imposing taxes which are regarded by people as punitive."[3] This was at a time when the inflationary effect of a very high level of investment was causing concern. The same individuals who were warning

[3] Arthur F. Burns, Chairman of the President's Council of Economic Advisers, *U. S. News & World Report,* May 6, 1955.

about the inimical effects of taxes were strongly advocating a monetary policy designed to reduce investment. However, an understanding of our economic discourse requires an appreciation of one of its basic rules: men of high position are allowed, by a special act of grace, to accommodate their reasoning to the answer they need. Logic is only required in those of lesser rank.

Finally it was argued, with no little vigor, that expanding government posed a grave threat to individual liberties. "Where distinction and rank is achieved almost exclusively by becoming a civil servant of the state . . . it is too much to expect that many will long prefer freedom to security."[4]

With time this attack on public services has somewhat subsided. The disorder associated with social imbalance has become visible even if the need for balance between private and public services is still imperfectly appreciated.

Freedom also seemed to be surviving. Perhaps it was realized that all organized activity requires concessions by the individual to the group. This is true of the policeman who joins the police force, the teacher who gets a job at the high school, and the executive who makes his way up the hierarchy of Du Pont. If there are differences between public and private organization, they are of kind rather than of degree. As this is written the pendulum has in fact swung back. Our liberties are now menaced by the conformity exacted by the large corporation and its impulse to create, for its own purposes, the organization man. This danger we may also survive.

Nonetheless, the postwar onslaught on the public services left a lasting imprint. To suggest that we canvass our public wants to see where happiness can be improved by more and better services has a sharply radical tone. Even public services to avoid disorder must be defended. By contrast the man who devises a nostrum for a nonexistent need and then successfully promotes both remains one of nature's noblemen.

---

[4] F. A. Hayek, *The Road to Serfdom* (London: George Routledge & Sons, 1944), p. 98.

DAVID RIESMAN

〜〜〜

DESPITE A FORMAL TRAINING in law and, at times, unorthodox professional methods, David Riesman easily takes his place among the nation's leading sociologists. *The Lonely Crowd,* written in collaboration with Nathan Glazer and Reuel Denney, has supplied a generation of Americans with concepts by which they can look at themselves and even a technical vocabulary that has entered common usage. Indeed, the popularity of the book is, itself, a significant historical fact to put alongside the authors' observations on mid-century society.

That such studies will continue to increase the scope and depth of historical writings cannot be doubted. But to receive maximum benefit from the sociologists, historians must not only incorporate sociological data but equip themselves to understand clearly the methods used to gather them and the concepts used to explore their meaning.

The Lonely Crowd concerns a subject that has long intrigued historians and commentators on the contemporary scene—the idea of national character and national types. It proposes categories that theoretically could be used to analyze many societies, and Riesman's illustrations come from a wide selection of historical periods and national settings. But it is obviously from the American experience that most of the material comes, gathered from interviews, polls, and a great variety of written material—but mainly, as the authors acknowledge, "our experiences of living in America."

Despite this principal reliance on contemporary observations, the basic ideas of *The Lonely Crowd* are set forth and best understood in terms of an historical evolution. Riesman suggests three basic "social characters" adopted by Western man since the Middle Ages. The first, of somewhat limited meaning in America, is the "tradition-directed" type typical of a period of relatively unchanging customs and social structure. Individual behavior is minutely controlled through traditions that insure conformity. Such a society existed in Europe in the Middle Ages; it also may be considered as the dominant behavior pattern among the Zulus in Africa, the Hopi Indians in Southwest United States, the Chinese and the Balinese.

With the Renaissance there arose a new character, the "inner-directed" man, who came to dominate America. He appeared in response to an era of expansion—geographical, industrial, cultural, and political. One thinks immediately of a Leonardo da Vinci, a Daniel Boone, or a John D. Rockefeller—all with new worlds to conquer through individual initiative. Yet "inner-direction" is not to be considered synonomous with "autonomy." It indicates only that patterns of behavior are "implanted early in life by the elders and directed toward generalized but nonetheless inescapably destined goals." Thus, "inner direction," like "tradition-direction," secures the kind of conformity in individuals appropriate to a particular set of circumstances.

A knowledge of these two predecessors makes clear what, in fact, is the main substance of *The Lonely Crowd,* the analysis of the "other-directed" persons—still a minority—who have emerged in upper-middle-class, urban, mid-twentieth-century America. If the "inner-directed" individual has a "psychic gyroscope" set going by his parents and responsive thereafter to similar advice, the "other-directed" man acquires a "radar" that reacts continually to a wide range of influences in his environment. He openly embraces a conformity that the other seemingly, and only seemingly, rejects. "Adjustment," "getting along with others," "tolerance," "security"— these represent the values of "other direction."

Riesman's explanation of the causes of this evolution are much less developed than his definitions of types and analysis of their consequences in various areas of human activity. The most explicit reference to cause is contained in his discussion of stages of population growth. But he acknowledges that this is a "kind of shorthand for referring to the myriad institutional elements that are also—though usually more heatedly— symbolized by such words as 'individualism,' 'folk society,' 'monopoly capitalization,' 'urbanization,' 'rationalization,' and so on." In short, he seems not concerned in any depth with cause, either within the United States or outside it. For the same reason, the historical portions of the book are the least valuable, except insofar as they make clearer the incisive analysis of contemporary society.

Living in an era of "mass culture," Riesman admits a preference for the "inner-directed" man, with clearer and more persistent values, and with anxieties arising more from his failures to satisfy himself than to appease others. Yet he is, on the whole, far more sympathetic to the culture of mid-twentieth-century America than many of his colleagues are. An excessive concern for human relations in modern industry is much to be preferred, he believes, to the brutalization of men in the early days of the industrial revolution. He notes an improvement in "movies" and in popular taste in art and furniture, and suggests the term "class-mass" to describe products more varied and of higher quality than those of the handicraft era. Unlike most observers, he believes the nation is becoming less materialistic, less grasping, and more amiable as a consequence of "other direction."

Neither does he believe that the future dignity of the individual should be sought in a return to "inner-directedness." Instead he proposes the goal of the "autonomous" social character whose "adjustment" to society would not be based on coercion nor require the suspension of independent judgment.

The Other-Directed Round of Life:
From Invisible Hand to Glad Hand

*Since sociability in its pure form has no ulterior end, no content and
no result outside itself, it is oriented completely about personalities.
. . . But precisely because all is oriented about them, the personalities
must not emphasize themselves too individually.*
— GEORG SIMMEL, *The Sociology of Sociability*

THE INNER-DIRECTED PERSON is not only chained to the endless
demands of the production sphere; he must also spend his
entire life in the internal production of his own character.
The discomforts of this internal frontier are as inexhaustible as the
discomforts of the frontier of work itself. Like the fear of being retired or unemployed in the economic realm, apathy in many sectors
of his inner or outer life is felt as underemployment of characterological resources. The inner-directed man has a generalized need
to master resource exploitation on all the fronts of which he is
conscious. He is job-minded.

The frontiers for the other-directed man are people; he is people-
minded. Hence both work and pleasure are felt as activities involving people. Many of the job titles that exist today existed in
the earlier era; many recreations likewise. My effort is to see how
change of character is connected with change of meaning in the
same pursuits as well as with development of new pursuits.

I. THE ECONOMIC PROBLEM: THE HUMAN ELEMENT

As the phase of transitional growth drew to an end in America,
the "no help wanted" sign was posted on the frontier in 1890,

From *The Lonely Crowd* by David Riesman, with Nathan Glazer and Reuel
Denny, copyright 1950, Yale University Press. Reprinted in Doubleday Anchor
Books edition, 1953, abridged and corrected.

in imagination if not in actual land-grant practice, and the same sign was hung out on our borders in 1924 with the virtual cutting off of immigration from Europe. With these valedictories a great symbol of hope and movement in the western world was destroyed. The combination of curtailed immigration and a falling birth rate eventually altered the population profile of the country; and, in the ways already hinted at, its characterological profile as well. Today it is the "softness" of men rather than the "hardness" of material that calls on talent and opens new channels of social mobility.

Whereas the production frontier, and even the land frontier, may actually be roomy even in the phase of incipient population decline, it nevertheless feels crowded; and certainly the society is no longer felt as a wilderness or jungle as it often was earlier.

This is particularly true in industry and the professions. Take, for example, the position of the foreman. He no longer stands alone, a straw boss in a clear hierarchy, but is surrounded with people. He is a two-way communication channel between the men under him and a host of experts above and around him: personnel men, safety directors, production engineers, comptroller's representatives, and all the rest of the indirect managerial work force. The plant manager is hardly better off for emotional elbowroom: he is confronted not only with the elaborate intra-plant hierarchy but with the public outside: the trade association group, the unions, consumers, suppliers, the government, and public opinion. Likewise, the professional man feels surrounded by a swarm of competitors, turned out by the vastly expanded educational system of a society whose capital plant is in such good shape that it can afford to devote—in fact, can hardly help devoting—a large share of the national income to the service trades and professions and to education for their proper use.

People, therefore, become the central problem of industry. This does not mean that the older revolutions in tooling, the machine process, and factory organization come to a halt. Rather, advances here are increasingly routinized; the continuing increment in productivity becomes a by-product of institutional forms. However, the newer industrial revolution which has reached its greatest force in America (although it is also beginning to be manifest elsewhere, as in England) is concerned with techniques of communication and control, not of tooling or factory layout. It is symbolized by the telephone, the servomechanism, the IBM machine, the electronic calculator, and modern statistical methods of controlling the quality of products; by the Hawthorne counseling experiment and the general preoccupation with industrial morale. The era of economic abundance and incipient population decline calls for the work of men whose tool is symbolism and whose aim is some observable response from people. These manipulators, of course, are not necessarily other-directed in character. Many inner-directed people are successful manipulators of people; often, their very inner-direction makes them unaware of how much they do manipulate and exploit others. Nevertheless, for manipulating others, there is a somewhat greater compatibility between characterological other-direction and sensitivity to others' subtler wants.

This can be explained more clearly by reference to one of our interviews. The man interviewed is the vice-president for sales and advertising of a large west coast machine-tool company, and he is also head of one of the leading trade associations for his industry. In origin he is the son of a Congregationalist preacher in a small midwestern town. His background, his mobility drive, his initial technical orientation are typical for the inner-directed; but his situation calls for the negotiating skill and interpersonal sensitivity more characteristic of the other-directed. This conflict produces strain. Asked about political issues on which he has recently changed his mind, he says:

> . . . I don't think this fits the category you're working on now, but I've become a great deal more tolerant of labor leaders and organizers [then catching himself]—not agitators, necessarily. I've come to appreciate what they're doing. They don't have much choice in taking the particular methods and means sometimes. I need a psychoanalyst.

He also told the interviewer that his principal worry is that he does not get along too well with another top executive of his company. He was troubled when a suggestion of his that was rejected later turned out to be right—and the other chap knew it was right. In such a situation he felt exposed. He cannot eat before going into a board meeting, and wondered to the interviewer whether he might not be better off running his own small company rather than as an official of a large one. For recreation he plays golf, though he does not seem to care for it and, in good inner-directed style, or perhaps simply good American style, does "a little fooling around with tools in the basement."

Material from interviews is, of course, open to a variety of possible interpretations, and I have no great confidence that those here suggested are correct. It would surely be erroneous to conclude that this executive has doubts about himself because he is not fully other-directed or inner-directed (by the very definition of these terms, no one is fully one or the other). The point is rather that the modern executive, regardless of the blend of the two modes of conformity he displays, is put under constant social pressure, in and out of the office. This executive is perhaps better able than most to verbalize the strain this pressure sets up.

FROM CRAFT SKILL TO MANIPULATIVE SKILL

The pressure toward social competence, with its concurrent playing down of technical competence, suggests another aspect of this executive's history which is typical for the emergence of a new pattern in American business and professional life: *if one is successful in one's craft, one is forced to leave it.* The machine-tool man began in the shop; as V.P. for sales and advertising he has become an uneasy manipulator of people and of himself. Likewise, the newspaperman who rises becomes a columnist or deskman, the doctor becomes the head of a clinic or hospital, the professor becomes a dean, president, or foundation official, the factory superintendent becomes a holding company executive. All these men must bury their craft routines and desert their craft companions. They must work less with things and more with people.

To be sure, business was always work with people. But when the size of enterprises was small, the head could remain a colleague among other colleagues; he did not cut connections entirely and enter a new milieu. William Allen White's *Autobiography* shows that he was able to maintain all his life the amiable fiction that he was only a working newspaper man. Similarly, the older generation of college presidents was composed largely of men who continued to think of themselves as scholars. So, too, the older generation of business executives kept their hats on in the office, chewed tobacco, and otherwise tried to retain their connections with the shop. Today, however, the familiar organizational concepts of "staff and line" symbolize the cutting off of direct contact between the executive and the working staffs of both staff and line. To sit at his new big desk—or to get there—he has to learn a new personality-oriented specialty and unlearn or at least soft-pedal his old skill orientation.

To the point is a story of an engineer who is offered the far more lucrative job of sales manager.[1] He loves engineering, but his wife won't let him turn down the promotion. His sponsor in the organization tells him it is now or never: does he want to be wearing a green eyeshade all his life? He reluctantly accepts. That night he has a dream. He has a slide rule in his hands, and he suddenly realizes that he does not know how to use it. He wakes in panic. The dream clearly symbolizes his feeling of impotence in a new job where he is alienated from his craft.

The executive who has moved up from a professional position can hardly help feeling that his work is air conditioned: fine only so long as the machinery below runs smoothly. Those colleagues whom he has left behind will not be slow, in their envy, to remind him that he can no longer consider himself a competent craftsman among his fellow craftsmen, that he does not fool them if, as an editor or by-line columnist, he occasionally attends a presidential press conference; or, as a college administrator, an occasional scholarly convention; or, as a sales manager, occasionally makes a mark on a drawing board.

Indeed, a society increasingly dependent on manipulation of people is almost as destructive of the craft-oriented professional and businessman as a society in the earlier stages of industrialization is destructive of the handicraft-oriented peasant and artisan. The professional of the more recent period is pushed upstairs into the managerial class while the artisan of the earlier period was pushed into the proletariat; and this testifies to a profound difference in the two historic situations. Yet in both cases the industrial process advances by building into machines and into smooth-flowing organiza-

1 Professor Everett Hughes of the University of Chicago, who has guided me in the analysis of changing career lines in business and the professions, tells this story.

tions the skills that were once built, by a long characterological and apprenticeship process, into men.

Despite this pattern, there are many positions in business, and in particular in the older professions, that offer comfortable places to inner-directed types. In medicine and law the ideology of free enterprise is strong. The attempt to apply objective criteria in selecting personnel persists, and is strengthened by the otherwise odious emphasis on grades in the educational and licensing system. In a hospital, a law firm, a university, there is room not only for those who can bring people together but for those who can bring together chemicals, citations, or ideas. There are many niches for the work-minded craftsman who does not care to learn, or cannot learn, to move with the crowd.

Even in big industry some such areas can continue to exist because not all technological problems—problems of the hardness of the material—have been solved or put on a routine problem-solving basis. Moreover, there are certain key spots in big business and big government where at times it is precisely an inner-directed rate-buster who is needed—for instance, a man who can say no without going through an elaborate song and dance. At the same time the values characteristic of other-direction may spread at such a rate as to hit certain sectors of the economy before these sectors have solved their technological problems. In the United States the lure of other-directed work and leisure styles cannot be everywhere modulated to the uneven front of economic advance.

FROM FREE TRADE TO FAIR TRADE

Very soon after the Federal Trade Commission Act of 1914 outlawed unfair competition it became clear that what was unfair was to lower the price of goods, though this view was concealed under attacks against cheating or mislabeling of goods. But in the NRA period this covert attitude received government and public sanction, and it became libelous to call someone a price cutter. With the passage of the Robinson-Patman Act and state fair-trade laws, free trade and fair trade became antithetical terms. Prices come to be set by administration and negotiation or, where this is too likely to bring in the Antitrust Division, by "price leadership." Relations that were once handled by the price mechanism or fiat are now handled by negotiation.

Price leadership often looks to the economist simply as the manipulation of devices to avoid price wars and divide the field. But price leadership has other aspects as well. It is a means by which the burden of decision is put onto the "others." The so-called price leaders themselves look to the government for clues, since cost —that mythical will-of-the-wisp—is no longer, if it ever really was, an unequivocal guide. Follow-the-leader is also played in arriving at the price and working conditions of labor; and unions have profited from their ability to play on the wishes of top management to be in stride with the industry leaders, and to be good fellows to boot. As we shall see, later, the other-directed pattern of politics tends to resemble the other-directed pattern of business: leadership is in the same amorphous state. Moreover, both in business and in politics, the other-directed executive prefers to stabilize his situation at a level that does not make too heavy demands on him for performance. Hence, at various points in the decision-making process he will vote for an easier life as against the risks of expansion and free-for-all competition.

Such a business life does not turn out to be the "easy" one. For one thing, the other-directed people do not have things all their own way in business any more than they do in politics. Free trade is still a powerful force, despite the incursions of the fair traders. Many observers, judging the degree of monopoly by looking at the percentage of assets controlled by the large, administered-price corporations, overlook the fact that even a small percentage of companies outside the range of the glad hand can have a leverage quite disproportionate to their assets. Rubber may be a monopoly, but will we always need rubber? Movies may be monopolistic, but what about television? In the small and marginal industries, the monopolies not of today but of tomorrow, there is often no need to be a good fellow. What is more, the dynamics of technological change remain challenging; whole departments within industries, as well as whole industries themselves, can become obsolete, despite their ability to negotiate repeated stays of technological death sentence. Even within the great monopolistic industries there are still many technologically oriented folk as well as many technologically oriented departments; no management planning in any one company can completely smooth out and routinize the pressure resulting from their innovations.

To the extent that the businessman is freed by his character and situation from cost considerations, he must face the problem of finding new motives for his entrepreneurship. He must tune in to the others to see what they are saying about what a proper business ought to be. Thus, a psychological sensitivity that begins with fear of being called a price cutter spreads to fear of being unfashionable in other ways. The businessman is as afraid of pursuing goals that may be obsolete as of living a style of life that may not be stylish. Oriented as he is to others, and to the consumption sphere, *he views his own business as a consumer.*

By and large, business firms until World War I needed only three kinds of professional advice: legal, auditing, and engineering. These were relatively impersonal services, even when, in the case of the lawyers, the services included buying—for cash on the barrelhead—a few legislators or judges. Since the number of available specialists was fairly small in comparison with demand, they could be absorbed into either or both of the two types of prevailing nexus: one, the family-status-connection nexus which persisted from earlier times in the smaller communities and does so even today in these communities and in the South; the other, the cash nexus based on performance, or on "character" in the older sense. Today the buyer is, first of all, not sure which of many services to buy: shall he get a lawyer *or* a public relations man *or* a market research agency *or* call in a management consulting firm to decide; second, he is not sure of his choice among the many potential suppliers of each of these services—none of whom must he accept either for family-status-connection reasons or for obviously superior character and performance. Thus choice will turn on a complex of more or less accidental, whimsical factors: a chance contact or conversation, a story in *Business Week* or a "confidential" newsletter, the luck of a salesman.

We can see the shift in many corporate histories. A business that begins as a small family enterprise, whose founders have their eye on the main chance—with a focus on costs and a "show me" attitude about good will and public relations—often alters its aims in the second generation. *Fortune* is put on the table, a trade association is joined, and the aim becomes not so much dollars as the possession of those appurtenances which an up-to-date company is supposed to have. We see a succession of demi-intellectuals added to the staff: industrial relations directors, training directors, safety directors. A house organ is published; consultants are called in on market research, standard operating procedures, and so on; shop and store front have their faces lifted; and in general status is sought, with profits becoming useful as one among many symbols of status and as the reserve for further moves toward a status-dictated expansion.

In many cases this shift is accompanied by a conflict of the older, more inner-directed with the younger, more other-directed generation. The older men have come up through the shop or through a technical school with no pretensions in the field of human relations. The younger ones are imbued with the new ethic. They seem still to be concerned about making money, and to some extent they are, but they are also concerned with turning their company into the model which they learned at business school. Businessmen recognize this new orientation when they speak of themselves, as they frequently do, as trustees for a variety of publics. And while they try to manipulate these publics and to balance between them, they, like the political leaders, are manipulated by the expectations the public has, or is thought to have, of them.

If one had to set a date for the change, one might say that the old epoch ended with the death of Henry Ford. After his death the firm, a last stronghold of older ways, completed the installation of new labor, accounting, and other management techniques and orientations.

The word *fair* in part reflects a carry-over of peer-group values into business life. The peer-grouper is imbued with the idea of fair play; the businessman, of fair trade. Often this means that he must be willing to negotiate matters on which he might stand on his rights. The negotiator, moreover, is expected to bring home not only a specific victory but also friendly feelings toward him and toward his company. Hence, to a degree, the less he knows about the underlying facts, the easier it will be to trade concessions. He is like the street-corner salesman who, reproached for selling for four cents apples that cost him five, said "But think of the turnover!" Here again craft skill, if not an actual drawback, becomes less important than manipulative skill.

Obviously, much of what has been said applies to the trade unions, the professions, and to academic life as well as to the business world. The lawyer, for instance, who moves into top positions inside and outside his profession is no longer necessarily a craftsman who has mastered the intricacies of, let us say, corporate finance, but may be one who has shown himself to be a good contact man. Since contacts need to be made and remade in every generation and cannot be inherited, this creates lucrative opportunities for the mobile other-directed types whose chief ability is smooth negotiation.

FROM THE BANK ACCOUNT TO THE EXPENSE ACCOUNT

In this phrase Professor Paul Lazarsfeld once summed up some recent changes in economic attitudes. The expense account is tied in with today's emphasis on consumption practices as firmly as the bank account in the old days was tied in with production ideals. The expense account gives the glad hand its grip. In doing so it still further breaks down the wall that in the era depending on inner-direction separated the paths of pleasure and of work. The successful other-directed man brings to business the set of attitudes learned in the consumption sphere not only when he appraises his own firm with a customer's eye but also when he is "in conference."

Business is supposed to be fun. As World War II inflation cooled off, the business pages repeatedly carried speeches at conventions on the theme: "Now selling will be fun again!" The inner-directed businessman was not expected to have fun; indeed, it was proper for him to be gloomy and even grim. But the other-directed businessman seems increasingly exposed to the mandate that he enjoy the sociabilities that accompany management. The shortening of hours has had much greater effect on the life of the working class than on that of the middle class: the executive and professional continues to put in long hours, employing America's giant productivity less to leave for home early than to extend his lunch hours, coffee breaks, conventions, and other forms of combining business with pleasure. Likewise, much time in the office itself is also spent in sociability; exchanging office gossip ("conferences"), making good-will tours ("inspection"), talking to salesmen and joshing secretaries ("morale"). In fact, depleting the expense account can serve as an almost limitless occupational therapy for men who, out of a tradition of hard work, a dislike of their wives, a lingering asceticism, and an anxiety about their antagonistic cooperators, still feel that they must put in a good day's work at the office. But, of course, Simmel would not admit, in his brilliant essay from which I quoted at the head of this chapter, that this kind of sociability, carrying so much workaday freight, was either free or sociable.

For the new type of career there must be a new type of education. This is one factor, of course not the only one, behind the increasing vogue of general education and the introduction of the humanities and social studies into technical high school and university programs. The educators who sponsor these programs urge cultivating the "whole man," speak of training citizens for democracy, and denounce narrow specialisms—all valuable themes. Indeed this book grows in part out of the stimulation of teaching in a general social science program. But while it may be doubtful that engineers and businessmen will become either better citizens or better people for having been exposed to these programs, there is little question that they will be more suave. They may be able to demonstrate their edge on the roughnecks from the "tech" schools by trotting out discourse on human relations. Such eloquence may be as necessary for professional and business success today as a knowledge of the classics was to the English politician and high civil servant of the last century.

Meanwhile, I do not wish to exaggerate the emphasis on human relations even in the bureaucratized sectors of the economy. There is much variety still: some companies, such as Sears Roebuck, seem to be run by glad handers, while others like, let us say, Montgomery Ward, are not; some, like Anaconda, are public relations conscious; others, like Kennecott, are less so. Much current progress in distribution, even in selling, tends to reduce the importance of the salesman. This is clear enough in the Automat. Moreover, the personality aspects of selling can be minimized wherever a technician is needed: for instance, salesmen of specialized equipment which requires a reorientation of the customer's work force. Though IBM salesmen have to be go-getters, they also have to know how to wire a tabulating machine and, still more important, how to rationalize the information flow within a company. Hence, although they are facilitators of the communications revolution, they must be no less craft oriented than the salesmen of the less complex equipment of an earlier era. Within most such industries there is a great need for technically minded people who are, to a considerable degree, protected by their indispensable skills from having to be nice to everybody, with or without an expense account.

II. THE MILKY WAY

In the preceding chapter, I symbolized the ambition of the inner-directed man by referring to a frequent motto of his period: ad astra per aspera. The inner-directed man, socialized with reference to an older model, might choose for emulation a star from the heroes of his field. By contrast, the other-directed person does not so often think of his life in terms of an individualized career. He seeks not fame, which represents limited transcendence of a particular peer-group or a particular culture, but the respect and, more than the respect, the affection, of an amorphous and shifting, though contemporary, jury of peers.

To attain this goal he struggles not with the hardness of the material but with the very antagonistic cooperators who are engaged in the same pursuit and to whom he looks at the same time for values and for judgments of value. Instead of referring himself to the great men of the past and matching himself against his stars, the other-directed person moves in the midst of a veritable Milky Way of almost but not quite indistinguishable contemporaries. This is partly a tribute to the size of the educated middle class in the phase of incipient decline of population.

The uncertainty of life in our day is certainly a factor in the refusal of young people to commit themselves to long-term goals. War, depression, military service, are felt today as obstacles to planning a career far more than in the period prior to World War I. But these changes are not the whole story: the type of man who will not commit himself to long-range goals rationalizes his perspective on the future and his deferral of commitment by pointing to the all too evident uncertainties. We can conceive of people living at a time of equal uncertainty who would, out of ignorance and insensitivity as much as out of strength of character, plow ahead in pursuit of extensive aims. Doubtless, many other factors are also in the air: such as the fact, mentioned in a preceding section, that mobility often depends on leaving one's craft skill behind; and this very fork in the road which separates avenues within a craft from those achievable only by leaving the craft, suggests itself at an early stage of occupational life and complicates the career planning of the mobile youth.

There are certain positive sides to this development. The seemingly sure commitment of many inner-directed youths was based on an unquestioning acceptance of parental orders and parental ranking of occupations. The other-directed youth of today often asks more of a job than that it satisfy conventional status and pecuniary requirements; he is not content with the authoritative rankings of earlier generations. The age of other-direction does open up the possibilities of more individual and satisfying career choice, once society's pressure for an early decision, and the person's feeling of panic if he can make no decision, can be relaxed.

It follows from all this that the heavens of achievement look quite different to the other-directed youth than to his inner-directed predecessor. The latter found security in moving to the periphery of the various frontiers and establishing an isolated and recognizable claim on a new piece of territory—often with quite grandiose and imperialistic trappings. If he founded a firm, this was his lengthened shadow. Today the man is the shadow of the firm. Such long-term aims as exist as built into the firm, the institution; this is also the repository of the imperialist drives that sometimes take shape as the institution harnesses the mild and tractable wills of many other-directed people who are competing for places of marginal differentiation on the Milky Way.

To outdistance these competitors, to shine alone, seems hopeless, and also dangerous. To be sure, one may try to steal a march—to work harder, for instance, than the propaganda about working would permit—but these are petty thefts, not major stick-ups. They do, however, keep the competition for a position on the major streamlined runs of occupational life from being entirely cooperative. Yet even such behavior that may marginally flout the prevailing concepts of fairness looks to the peer-group for its norms of what is to be desired. And since each projects his own tendencies to unfair play onto the others, this, too, requires living in a state of constant alert as to what the others may be up to.

Hence the Milky Way is not an easy way, though its hardships differ from those of the earlier era. Obliged to conciliate or manipulate a variety of people, the other-directed person handles all men as customers who are always right; but he must do this with the uneasy realization that, as Everett Hughes has put it, some are more right than others. This diversity of roles to be taken with a diversity of customers is not institutionalized or clear cut, and the other-directed person tends to become merely his succession of roles and encounters and hence to doubt who he is or where he is going. Just as the firm gives up the one-price policy for an administered price that is set in secrecy and differs with each class of customer depending on the latter's apparent power and "good will" requirements, so the other-directed person gives up the one-face policy of the inner-directed man for a multiface policy that he sets in secrecy and varies with each class of encounters.

United with others, however, he can seek a modicum of social, economic, and political protection. The peer-group can decide that there are certain outcasts, in class or ethnic terms, to whom the glad hand need not be extended, or who can (like the Negro in the South) be forced to personalize without the privilege of demanding a reciprocal response. A class of customers can be politically created who are by definition wrong. Yet no amount of exclusiveness, though it may make life a bit easier for the insiders, can completely guarantee continuance in a place of visibility and approval in the Milky Way.

The Other-Directed Round of Life
(Continued):
The Night Shift

But it must not be supposed that in the midst of all their toils the people who live in democracies think themselves to be pitied; the contrary is noticed to be the case. No men are fonder of their own condition. Life would have no relish for them if they were delivered from the anxieties which harass them, and they show more attachment to their cares than aristocratic nations to their pleasures.
— TOCQUEVILLE, *Democracy in America*

THE ONLY THING that has changed since Tocqueville wrote (no small change, it is true) is that the sphere of pleasures has itself become a sphere of cares. Many of the physical hardships of the older frontiers of production and land use have survived in altered, psychological form on the newer one of consumption. Just as we saw in the previous chapter that the day shift of work-mindedness is invaded by glad-hand attitudes and values that stem in part from the sphere of leisure, so the night shift of leisure-mindedness is haunted by the others with whom one works at having a good time.

First of all, however, with the rise of other-direction, we see the passing both of the acquisitive consumers and of the escapists of the earlier era. The passion for acquisition diminishes when property no longer has its old stability and objective validity; escape diminishes by the very fact that work and pleasure are interlaced. We can see these new tendencies, in what is perhaps their most extreme form, the attitudes toward food and sexual experience prevailing among some upper middle-class groups.

I. CHANGES IN THE SYMBOLIC MEANING OF FOOD AND SEX

From the Wheat Bowl to the Salad Bowl. Among inner-directed types there is of course great variation as to interest in food. In America—the story is different among the food-loving peoples of the rest of the world—puritans and nonpuritans of the recent past might use food for display, with relatively standardized menus for company and for dining out; what was put on display was a choice cut of meat, an elegant table, and good solid cooking. All this was an affair largely of the women, and in many circles food was not a proper topic for dinner conversation. Having the proper food was something one owed to one's status, one's claim to respectability, and more recently to one's knowledge of hygiene with its calories and vitamins. (This last pattern did not spread to the South, where an older, more gastronomically rugged tradition of ceremonial fondness for food prevailed.) The earlier editions of the *Boston Cooking School Cookbook* breathe this air of solidity, conservatism, and nutrition-mindedness.

The other-directed person of the midtwentieth century in America, on the contrary, puts on display his taste and not directly his wealth, respectability, cubic capacity, or caloric soundness. Indeed we saw in Chapter IV how the radio begins the other-directed person's training in food taste even before the child goes to school and how seriously he takes his lessons. While well-educated upper middle-class parents are becoming hesitant to tell children to eat something because it is good for them—lest they create oral complexes—they join the radio in discussion of what is "good" as a matter of taste. Often, in fact, this merely disguises the emotion focused on the child's eating habits, almost as much emotion as their parents concentrated on the regimen of no-nonsense plate cleaning. The other-directed person is thus prepared for the search for marginal differentiation not only in what he sets before his guests but in how it is talked about with them.

Earlier there existed a small coterie of gourmets; fastidious enjoyment of food was one hobby, among others, that inner-directed people might choose. Today, in wide circles, many people are and many more feel that they must be gourmets. The abundance of America in the phase of incipient population decline is perhaps the most important factor in this development; it has made the good foods available to nearly everybody. The seasonal and geographic limitations that in the earlier period narrowed food variations for all but the very rich have now been largely done away with by the network of distribution and the techniques of food preservation—both being legacies from the phase of transitional population growth. The consumer's choice among foods need therefore no longer be made on the basis either of tradition or of Malthusian limits.

As a result, both the setting of the meal and its content are affected. Informality breaks down the puritan inhibition against talking about food and drink, just as Mexican casseroles and copper kettles replace the white napery and classic decor of the nineteenth-century middle-class table. More important still, the housewife can no longer blame the preferential and limited cuisine offered by a kitchen servant for her failure to personalize her own tastes in food. In the period of incipient population decline servants disappear from the middle-class home, and where they do not, they lack any traditional pattern of prerogatives that allows them, rather than the host and hostess, to control the menu and its stylized serving. No walls of privacy, status, or asceticism remain to protect or prevent one from displaying personalized taste in food and decor as an element in one's competition with others. The diner has the power, unlike Jiggs, to decide that corned beef and cabbage is an amusing dish; he can ransack immigrant cookeries or follow the lead of food columnist Clementine Paddleford toward exoticism. Only at conventional conventions can one still find the uniform menu of steak or chicken, potatoes, and marbled peas. And at home, in place of the staple menu, the hostess today is encouraged to substitute her own specialty, such as lasagna or rüstoffel. Men are involved almost as much as women, and in the kitchen as well as at the backyard grill.

The most popular cookbook today is said to be *The Joy of Cooking,* and the number of specialized cookbooks—ethnic, chatty, and atmospheric—constantly increases to meet the demand for marginal differentiation. The very change in titles—from the *Boston Cooking School Cookbook* to *How to Cook a Wolf* or *Food is a Four Letter Word*—reveals the changing attitude. For the other-directed person cannot lean on such objective standards of success as those which guided the inner-directed person: he may be haunted by a feeling that he misses the joy in food or drink which he is supposed to feel. Mealtime must now be "pleasurable"; the new *Fireside Cookbook* is offered to "people who are not content to regard food just as something one transfers periodically from plate to mouth." And if one still fails to get much joy out of the recipes given there, he may search in books like *Spécialité de la Maison* to see what "others" are eating—to get the "favorite recipes" of such people as Noel Coward and Lucius Beebe, Fred MacMurray and Claudette Colbert testify to the delights of new concoctions such as "The Egg and I Julep"; and "There is nothing," writes MacMurray in a little collection of his favorite egg recipes, "so appealing as a pair of fried eggs with their limpid golden eyes gazing fondly at you from the center of a breakfast plate, festooned with strips of crisp bacon or little-pig sausage. Or poached, gaily riding a raft of toast." The most popular translation of an old French cookbook, *Tante Marie,* is also extremely chatty, and *The Joy of Cooking* explains its chattiness by saying that originally the recipes were collected and written down for the author's daughter, who in turn thought "other daughters" might like them. (As there is today less teaching of daughters by mothers, the daughter must rely on the instruction of an outsider, if she is to cook at all.) In short, the other-directed person in his approach to food, as in his sexual encounters, is constantly looking for a qualitative element that may elude him. He suffers from what Martha Wolfenstein and Nathan Leites call "fun-morality."[1]

Of course, putting matters this way exaggerates the disadvantages of the shift: undeniably, many more people today really enjoy food and enjoy talk about food than was the case when the monotony of the American diet was notorious.

Many people, to be sure, follow the new fashions in food without being other-directed in character, just as many personnel directors in industry are zealous inner-directed believers in the glad hand. Even so, if we wanted to demarcate the boundaries of other-direction in America, we might find the analysis of menus to provide a not too inaccurate index. As tossed salads and garlic, elaborate

[1] In *Movies* (Glencoe, Illinois, The Free Press, 1950).

sauces, dishes en casserole, *Gourmet* magazine, wine and liqueurs, spread west from New York and east from San Francisco, as men take two-hour lunch periods and exhibit their taste in food and wine, as the personalized cookbook tends to replace the Boston Cooking School type—in all these signs of the times we see indications of the new type of character. Recently, Russell Lynes, in his article, "Highbrow, Lowbrow, Middlebrow,"[2] sought to delineate the contemporary urban American social system in terms of similar consumption indexes. Thus, the tossed salad is the sign of the high-brow, who may also be tagged by his taste in cars, clothes, and posture. What we really see emerging is an embryonic social system whose criteria of status are inconsistent with the criteria of the more traditional class system. This has been seen by Lloyd Warner, who actually defines class less in terms of wealth or power and more in terms of sociability habits and consumption styles. These observers, however, are exceptional; as we shall see in Chapter XI, most Americans continue to see their social structure in terms of an older one based on wealth, occupation, and position in the society-page sense. But beneath these older rubrics, I believe that a much more amorphous structure is emerging in which taste leadership is increasingly important, and in which the "brow" hierarchy competes for recognition with the economic and production hierarchies.

Sex: the Last Frontier. In the era depending on inner direction sex might be inhibited, as in classes and areas affected strongly by the Reformation and Counter Reformation. Or its gratification might be taken for granted among men and within given limits, as in Italy, Spain, and the non-respectable elements, such as the "riverbottom people," in every population. In both cases there was a certain simplification of sex, in the one instance by taboos, in the other by tradition. Economic or power problems, problems of mere existence or of "amounting to something," were uppermost; and sex was relegated to its "proper" time and place: night, the wife or whore, occasional rough speech, and daydreams. Only in the upper classes, precursors of modern other-directed types, did the making of love take precedence over the making of goods (as

2 *Harper's, 198* (1949), 19.

alleged in France) and reach the status of a daytime agenda. In these circles sex was almost totally separated from production and reproduction.

This separation, when it goes beyond the upper class and spreads over almost the whole society, is a sign that a society, through birth control and all that it implies, has entered the population phase of incipient decline by the route of industrialization. In this phase there is not only a growth of leisure, but work itself becomes both less interesting and less demanding for many; increased supervision and subdivision of tasks routinize the industrial process even beyond what was accomplished in the phase of transitional growth of population. More than before, as job-mindedness declines, sex permeates the daytime as well as the playtime consciousness. It is viewed as a consumption good not only by the old leisure classes but by the modern leisure masses.

The other-directed person, who often suffers from low responsiveness, may pursue what looks like a "cult of effortlessness" in many spheres of life. He may welcome the routinization of his economic role and of his domestic life; the auto companies may tempt him by self-opening windows and self-shifting gears; he may withdraw all emotion from politics. Yet he cannot handle his sex life in this way. Though there is tremendous insecurity about *how* the game of sex should be played, there is little doubt as to *whether* it should be played or not. Even when we are consciously bored with sex, we must still obey its drive. Sex, therefore, provides a kind of defense against the threat of total apathy. This is one of the reasons why so much excitement is channeled into sex by the other-directed person. He looks to it for reassurance that he is alive. The inner-directed person, driven by his internal gyroscope and oriented toward the production problems of the outer world, did not need this evidence.

While the inner-directed acquisitive consumer could pursue the ever receding frontiers of material acquisition, these frontiers have lost much of their lure for the other-directed person. As we saw in Chapter III, the latter begins as a very young child to know his way around among available consumption goods. He travels widely, to camp or with his family. He knows that the rich man's car is only marginally, if at all, different from his own—a matter at best of a few additional horsepower. He knows anyway that next year's model will be better than this year's. Even if he has not been there, he knows what the night clubs are like; and he has seen television. Whereas the deprived inner-directed person often lusted for possessions as a goal whose glamour a wealthy adulthood could not dim, the other-directed person can scarcely conceive of a consumption good that can maintain for any length of time undisputed dominance over his imagination. Except perhaps sex.

For the consumption of love, despite all the efforts of the mass media, does remain hidden from public view. If someone else has a new Cadillac, the other-directed person knows what that is, and that he can duplicate the experience, more or less. But if someone else has a new lover, he cannot know what that means. Cadillacs have been democratized. So has sexual glamour, to a degree: without the mass production of good-looking, well-groomed youth, the American pattern of sexual competition could not exist. But there is a difference between Cadillacs and sexual partners in the degree of mystery. And with the loss or submergence of moral shame and inhibitions, but not completely of a certain unconscious innocence, the other-directed person has no defenses against his own envy. He is not ambitious to break the quantitative records of the acquisitive sex consumers like Don Juan, but he does not want to miss, day in day out, the qualities of experience he tells himself the others are having.

In a way this development is paradoxical. For while cookbooks have become more glamorous with the era of other-direction, sex books have become less so. The older marriage manuals, such as that of Van der Velde (still popular, however), breathe an ecstatic tone; they are travelogues of the joy of love. The newer ones, including some high school sex manuals, are matter of fact, toneless, and hygienic—Boston Cooking School style. Nevertheless, much as young people may appear to take sex in stride along with their vitamins, it remains an era of competition and a locus of the search, never completely suppressed, for meaning and emotional response in life. The other-directed person looks to sex not for display but for a test of his or her ability to attract, his or her place in the "rating-dating" scale—and beyond that, in order to experience life and love.

One reason for the change is that women are no longer objects for the acquisitive consumer but are peer-groupers themselves. The relatively unemancipated wife and socially inferior mistresses of the inner-directed man could not seriously challenge the quality of his sexual performance. Today, millions of women, freed by technology from many household tasks, given by technology many "aids to romance," have become pioneers, with men, on the frontier of sex. As they become knowing consumers, the anxiety of men lest they fail to satisfy the women also grows—but at the same time this is another test that attracts men who, in their character, want to be judged by others. The very ability of women to respond in a way that only courtesans were supposed to in an earlier age means, moreover, that qualitative differences of sex experience— the impenetrable mystery—can be sought for night after night, and not only in periodic visits to a mistress or brothel. Whereas the pattern of an earlier era was often to make fun of sex, whether on the level of the music hall or of Balzac's *Droll Stories,* sex today carries too much psychic freight to be really funny for the other-directed person. By a disguised asceticism it becomes at the same time too anxious a business and too sacred an illusion.

This anxious competitiveness in the realm of sex has very little in common with older patterns of social climbing. To be sure, women still use sex as a means to status in spheres controlled by men. But they can do this chiefly in industries that are still competitive in the pre-monopolistic patterns. Thus until recently the theater and the movies were controlled by *novi homines* who remind us of those early nineteenth-century British mill owners who, before the Factory Acts, relied on their mills as a harem.[3] And Warner, Havighurst, and Loeb in *Who Shall Be Educated?*[4] describe how women schoolteachers may still cabin-date their way up the relatively unbureaucratized hierarchies of local school systems. These, however, are exceptional cases; the search for experience

[3] See G. M. Young, *Portrait of an Age* (London, Oxford University Press, 1936), p. 16, n. 1.

[4] W. Lloyd Warner, Robert J. Havighurst, and Martin Loeb, *Who Shall Be Educated?* (New York, Harper, 1944), e.g., p. 103.

on the frontier of sex is, in the other-directed era, generally without ulterior motives.

II. CHANGES IN THE MODE OF CONSUMPTION OF POPULAR CULTURE

ENTERTAINMENT AS ADJUSTMENT TO THE GROUP

In Chapter IV we saw how the inner-directed youth was made ready to leave home and go far both by directly didactic literature and by novels and biographies that gave him a sense of possible roles on the frontiers of production. In contrast to this, the other-directed person has recourse to a large literature that is intended to orient him in the noneconomic side of life. This orientation is needed because, with the virtually complete disappearance of tradition-direction, no possibility remains of learning the art of life in the primary group—a possibility that persisted even in the mobile families of the era dependent on inner-direction. The child must look early to his mass-media tutors for instruction in the techniques of getting life directions as well as for specific tricks of the trade.

We can trace an edifying sequence that runs from the success biography of the Samuel Smiles or the Horatio Alger sort to the contemporary books and periodicals that deal with peace of mind. The earlier books are directly concerned with social and economic advance, dealt with as achievable by the virtues of thrift, hard work, and so on. Then we find in the first years of this century the development in America of the now almost forgotten "New Thought" movement. As described by A. Whitney Griswold, the movement's motto was: "Think Your Way to Wealth."[5] That is, wealth was to be achieved no longer by activity in the real world but by self-manipulation, a kind of economic Couéism. But wealth itself as a goal was unquestioned.

From then on, inspirational literature becomes less and less exclusively concerned with social and economic mobility. Dale Carnegie's *How to Win Friends and Influence People,* written in 1937, recommends self-manipulative exercises for the sake not only

[5] "The American Cult of Success" (Doctor's thesis, Yale University, 1933); abstracted in *American Journal of Sociology,* XL (1934), 309-318.

of business success but of such vaguer, leisure goals as popularity. Perhaps it is not only the change from depression to full employment that led Carnegie to write *How to Stop Worrying and Start Living* in 1948, in which self-manipulation is no longer oriented toward some social achievement but is used in a solipsistic way to adjust one to one's fate and social state. The same tendencies can be found in a large group of periodicals, with an interlocking directorate of authors and with titles such as *Journal of Living, Your Personality, Your Life,* which testify to the alteration of mobility paths and hopes and the increase of anxiety as a spur to seeking expert help. The *New York Times Book Review* of April 24, 1949, advertises *Calm Yourself* and *How to be Happy While Single;* the latter deals according to the advertisement with such problems as "how to handle the men in your life (heavy dates, office companions, friends, drunks) . . . making conversation . . . liquor, boredom—just about every problem you'll encounter on your own." Certainly, there are many positive sides to a development that substitutes for the older, external, and often pointless goals such as wealth and power, the newer, internal goals of happiness and peace of mind, though of course, one must always ask whether, in changing oneself, one is simply adapting to the world as it is without protest or criticism.

Here, however, I am not evaluating these trends but am interested in showing how popular culture is exploited for group-adjustment purposes not only in the form of manifestly didactic literature and services but also in fictional guise. There is nothing new in the observation that people who would rather not admit their need for help, or who prefer to spice it with fun, look to the movies and other popular media as the sources of enlightenment. In the studies of the movies made under the Payne Fund twenty years ago, much evidence was gathered concerning use of the movies by young people who wanted to learn how to look, dress, and make love.[6] The combination of learning and excitement was clear in these cases, especially among children of lower-class origin suddenly brought face to face with sex and splendor. Today, however, as

---

[6] See, for example, Herbert Blumer and Philip Hauser, *Movies, Delinquency, and Crime* (New York, Macmillan, 1933), pp. 102 et seq.

audiences have become more sophisticated, the mixture of messages has become more subtle.

From a sample of a group of women's magazines, *Ladies' Home Journal, American, Good Housekeeping,* and *Mademoiselle,* for October, 1948, I concluded that a good many stories and features and of course, far less subtly, many ads, dealt largely with modes of manipulating the self in order to manipulate others, primarily for the attainment of intangible assets such as affection. Two stories will illustrate: "The Rebellion of Willy Kepper" by Willard Temple in *Ladies' Home Journal* and *"Let's Go Out Tonight"* by Lorna Slocombe in the *American* magazine.

Handling the office. "The Rebellion of Willy Kepper" is unusual in that it deals with a work situation rather than a domestic and leisure one. It is the story of a paint salesman, Willy, a shy young man who has worked himself up through the factory. There is a pretty file clerk whom Willy wants to know better but does not know how to approach. At this point the stockholder's son enters the business, gets the promotion Willy hoped for, and makes time with the file clerk. Willy, previously so mild, loses his temper and becomes gruff and rasping with people in the office and shop. This is his "rebellion." This change of mood is of course noticed at once.

Willy, however, has built up an enormous capital of good will by his previous good temper, so that plant people, instead of turning on him, try to find out what the trouble is; it cannot be Willy's fault. They discover that the stockholder's son is to blame, and they set out to hex him—he trips into paint, gets orders mixed up, and rapidly learns how dependent he is on others' liking him if he is to do his job. Willy, in fact, saves him from his worst jam with a customer, and after a few knocks of this sort the son decides to start at the bottom in the factory, in order to earn his own capital of good will. Thus the road to Willy's promotion is reopened. At the end Willy asks the stockholder's son what techniques he used with the file clerk. He tells Willy to compliment her on her eyes; he does so and succeeds in making a date.

There are some fairly obvious things to be said about this story. In the first place, though it is set in the sphere of production, it deals with the sales end of a factory which is a net of interpersonal relations that will deliver paint to the customer only against a bill of lading marked "good will." The work situation is seen in terms of its human element and its noneconomic incentives. There are no problems about paint, but only about people. In the second place, the stockholder's son was able to date the girl not because of his wealth and position but because of his line, his skill in the leisure arts of language. Language is presented as a free consumers' good; one, moreover, of which the consumer is also a producer; there is no patent or monopoly on lines. Finally, we have a picture of the "antagonistic cooperators" of the same sex—Willy and the son—whose rivalry for job and girl is so muted that they can exchange advice on how to win both; in a way, they are more interested in each other's approval than in victory. In the end, Willy has regained his lost good temper and his rival has given up his early arrogance.

Handling the home. "Let's Go Out Tonight" pictures the consumption frontier of a young, college-bred suburban matron. Her husband is a good provider and faithful; her two children are healthy; she has everything—except enough attention from her tired businessman spouse. The latter comes home, reads a paper, goes to bed, and his wife complains to her friend in their morning telephone chat that they never go places and do things any more. She looks back nostalgically on her college days when he was courting her and when life seemed glamorous. Suddenly she decides to go back to her college to see just what the magic was in those days.

When she gets to her old room she realizes that only in retrospect was her college dating effortless. Actually, she recalls, she slaved to arrange parties for her future husband, to manipulate him into kissing her and finally into proposing. She concludes that she just has been loafing on her job as a housewife, and returns full of tolerant understanding for her husband and enthusiasm for new and improved manipulation. By buying a new dress, arranging with a sitter to have the children taken care of, and similar measures, she inveigles her husband into a theater date and is able to report success to her friend on the telephone.

In the era of inner-direction, stories of a similarly orientational cast often encouraged the reader to aspire to distant horizons, to play for big stakes; many such stories today strike us as escapist and sentimental. In contrast, the type of "realism" in modern magazine fiction is neither uplifting nor escapist. There is an all too sensible refusal, in a story like "Let's Go Out Tonight," to admit that there can be decisively better marriages than this one, with its continuous petty deception. The reader of these stories will by no means always find his ideals and ways of life approved—it is a mistake to suppose that such magazines as *Ladies' Home Journal* are edited by a formula of giving "the public what it wants"— but he is seldom stimulated to make great demands on life and on himself. In both of the stories I have used here as illustration, the assumption is made that a solution of conflict is available that involves neither risk nor hardship but only the commodities— interpersonal effort and tolerance—that the other-directed person is already prepared to furnish.

"Conspiracy" theories of popular culture are quite old, summed up as they are in the concept of "bread and circuses." In "The Breadline and the Movies" Thorstein Veblen presented a more sophisticated concept, namely, that the modern American masses paid the ruling class for the privilege of the very entertainments that helped to keep them under laughing gas. Such views assume the culture to be more of a piece than it is. Group adjustment and orientational influence in contemporary popular culture does not serve the interest of any particular class. In fact, pressures for other-directed conformity appear strongest in the better educated strata. The form these pressures take may be illustrated by a few examples.

Heavy harmony. The head of a progressive boarding school in the East recently addressed the parents of its children as follows:

The music department at X School wishes to provide for every child, as rich a musical experience as possible.
  We believe that music is a necessary part of life and its influence is felt in every phase of living. Singing and playing together can bring

understanding and good-will and it seems to me that this world needs more of this kind of harmony.

At X, we try to provide some kind of music participation for every child and wish to encourage more musical activity, especially that of playing with a group in an orchestra.

This letter does not betray much interest in music as such. It sees music primarily as a way of bringing people together locally and internationally too. Music as a way of escape into one's individual creative life—a private refuge—would strike many such school authorities today as selfish.

A similar theme appears in more refined form in Helen Howe's novel of Harvard academic life, *We Happy Few*.[7] The heroine Dorothea is viewed by Miss Howe as a selfish woman who, during the war, escapes from her social duties by having a love affair and by playing Bach and Mozart to herself on the piano. She is taken in the novel through a series of group-adjustment experiences that deflate what Miss Howe regards as her intellectual snobbery. Becoming a nurse's aid, she meets other nurse's aids socially; they are fine and dull. Traveling to Coeur d'Alene to be near her son in training, she "sees" America: in the stench of the ladies' room, the sadness of platform partings, the goodheartedness of midwesterners. The townsfolk of Coeur d'Alene are another group-adjusting experience; they, too, are fine and dull. At the end Dorothea returns to Cambridge a sadder and wiser woman: her pride is gone, and she has learned humbly to admire the great open spaces and the open sentiments usually associated with them in song and story.

As a symbol of the learning process, Miss Howe writes that Dorothea, while a nurse's aid staggering through agonizing days at the hospital, learns in her few off hours to enjoy Schumann as well as her beloved Bach and Mozart: "Her aesthetic as well as her human taste was stretching, too—cruder, possibly, but warmer and more inclusive."

This quotation hardly needs comment. Instead of permitting the heroine to escape either up or down from the exasperating

[7] I have dealt with the implications of this book in more detail in "The Ethics of We Happy Few," *University Observer*, I (1947), 19; I draw on this article in what follows.

human contacts of a nurse's work day, Dorothea must move sideways. She must acquire warmer, group-adjusted musical tastes— she would be forgiven even more, doubtless, if she learned to like Ethelbert Nevin.[8]

Yet granting Dorothea should learn this interpersonal art as a benefit to her work as a nurse's aid—perhaps the sick are a special case and do need warmth of this sort—it is striking that she must bring the identical attitude into her leisure time: no change of roles is permitted. Leisure and work must, like Dorothea herself, be stretched (assuming, falsely, that Schumann's sentimentality is "warmer") until they completely overlap. The theme of both is group adjustment.

What I have said is not to be understood as a polemic for coldness as against warmth or as a criticism of the genuine elements in the other-directed person's concern for warmth, in himself and in others. Certainly it is an advance from the compulsory emotional constriction, the frightening coldness, of many inner-directed Americans, to open up group sociability to a wider and more outgoing responsiveness.

Lonely successes. In our discussion of the comics, of *Tootle,* and of "Willy Kepper," we saw how modern popular culture stresses the dangers of aloneness and, by contrast, the virtues of group-mindedness. In a thoughtful article, "The Gangster as Tragic Hero," Robert Warshow deals with a number of recent gangster films from this perspective.[9] He notes that, inevitably, the gangster's success spells his undoing. For it cuts him off from the group— not only the law-abiding community but also his own gang. At the peak of success he is therefore miserable and frightened, waiting to be cut down from the heights.

We can interpret this as a cautionary tale about what happens

---

[8] The reference to warmth is especially significant in the analysis of peer-group preferences in people. In a very interesting set of experiments, Solomon E. Asch has shown that the warm-cold axis is for his student subjects the controlling dimension of personality: people who are said to be warm are positively valued no matter what other traits they have, while people who are cold are distrusted no matter how honorable and brave they may be. See Solomon E. Asch, "A Test for Personality," *Journal of Abnormal and Social Psychology, 41* (1946), 258-290.

[9] *Partisan Review,* XV (1948), 240.

if one goes off on one's own pursuits. Success is fatal. According to the code of the movies one is not permitted to identify with the lonely escapist; his lot is pictured, like that of Dorothea in the novel, as a set of miseries and penances. The movie *Body and Soul* points a similar moral. The hero is a Jewish boy from the East Side who gets to be boxing champion and proceeds to alienate all surrounding groups: his family circle and faithful girl; his unambitious, devoted retinue; the East Side Jews who see him as a hero. He agrees for a large sum to throw his last fight and bets against himself; his losing will complete his alienation from these groups. En route to the fight he is told that the Jews see him as a hero, a champion in the fight against Hitler. Recalled to "himself," he double-crosses his gangster backers by winning the fight; and poor again, he is restored to the primary group of family, girl, and Jews.

A movie or book occasionally comes along that departs from this formula. *The Fountainhead,* by Ayn Rand, a popular book and movie, pictures its architect hero as standing out, in violent integrity, against the pressure for group adjustment and, in the end, success-fully bringing the jury of his peers along with him. He *does* take all: the heights of fame, his rival's wife, the death of his rival. What is most striking in all this, however, is the unintended caricature, both of group adjustment and of group resistance. The group is made out not tolerant but mean, inartistic, and corrupt. And group resistance is seen in terms of nobility on the part of the sadistic hero, who wants to deny any ties to humanity, any dependency. This superman for adults is the very apotheosis of the lonely success, to be admired perhaps by the reader but too stagey to be imitated.

In all likelihood, moreover, the Ayn Rand audience that applauds fiery denunciations of group-mindedness and submission to others is quite unaware of its own tendencies to submission in the small, undramatic situations of daily life. In that sense *The Fountainhead* is escapist.

GOOD-BYE TO ESCAPE?

So far, in these illustrations, we have seen little that would cor-respond to the unambiguous escapes of the inner-directed. Rather, we have seen popular culture used, often quite desperately, for train-ing in group adjustment. In the same way, we may find popular culture used as training in consumer orientation, which is hardly a less serious problem (in many ways it is the same problem) for the other-directed person. Despite appearances the other-directed person seems often unable to get away from himself or to waste time with any gestures of abundance or abandon. (Of course, if we compared patterns of alcoholic escape, we might come up with somewhat different results.)

The inner-directed person, if influenced by Protestantism, is of course also unable to waste time. The mobile youth from the lower classes shows his commitment to inner-direction by cutting himself off from hard-drinking, horse-play-indulging pals: he continues the production of an inner-directed character through practicing a kind of mental bookkeeping by which the demons of Waste and Sloth are ruthlessly driven out. Such a person has little leisure, unless he can justify it as self-improving, and a life that has never an idle moment must have many a tense one. On the face of it the other-directed person is no puritan; he seems much less preoccupied with waste; his furnishings, manners, and morals are more casual. But an attenuated puritanism survives in his exploitation of leisure. He may say, when he takes a vacation or stretches a weekend, "I owe it to myself"—but the self in question is viewed like a car or house whose upkeep must be carefully maintained for resale purposes. The other-directed person has no clear core of self to escape from; no clear line between production and consumption; between adjusting to the group and serving private interests; between work and play.

One interesting index of this is the decline of evening dress, especially among men, and conversely, the invasion of the office by sport clothes. This looks like an offshoot of the cult of effortlessness, and of course men say "it's too much trouble" in explaining why they don't change for dinner or the evening. But the explanation lies rather in the fact that most men today simply do not know how to change roles, let alone mark the change by proper costuming. Another reason may be the fear of being thought high-hat; one can wear gaudy shirts but not stiff ones. Thus the sport shirt and casual dress show that one is a good fellow not only on the golf course or on vacation but in the office and at dinner too.

Women are still permitted to dress for the evening, a sign, perhaps, of their laggard response to changing modes. They are more involved than men in the dying patterns of conspicuous consumption. However, they probably make more of an actual shift from housework and babies to dinner party than many men do, who exchange office gossip both at work and play: moreover, they really like the shift, dragging the men, who would just as soon be in the office, along with them. I have observed that women's shop talk of children and domestic matters is often—though certainly not always!—conducted with more skill, interest, and realism than that of men since the change of role refreshes both work and play.

What is it that drives men who have been surrounded with people and their problems on the day shift to seek often exactly the same company (or its reflection in popular culture) on the night shift? Perhaps in part it is the terror of loneliness that the gangster movies symbolize. But certainly it makes for strain. Though popular culture on one level "fills in" between people so as to avoid any demand for conversational or sexual bambits, on another level the popular-culture performance is not simply a way of killing time: in the peer-group situation, it makes a demand that it be appraised. The other-directed girl who goes in company to the movies need not talk to the others during the picture but is sometimes faced with the problem: should she cry at the sad places or not? What is the proper reaction, the sophisticated line about what is going on? Observing movie audiences coming out of a "little" or "art" theater, it is sometimes apparent that people feel they ought to react, but how?

In contrast to this, the inner-directed person, reading a book alone, is less aware of the others looking on; moreover, he has time to return at his own pace from being transported by his reading—to return and put on whatever mask he cares to. The poker game in the back room, with its praise of masks, fits his habituation to social distance, even loneliness. His successor, dreading loneliness, tries to assuage it not only in his crowd but in fantasy pursuits that, like a mirror, only return his own concerns to him.

III. THE TWO TYPES COMPARED

We have completed our direct confrontation of the two types; and it now becomes necessary to redress the balance against other-direction, which, I know, has come off a bad second in these pages. It is hard for us to be quite fair to the other-directed. The term itself suggests shallowness and superficiality as compared to the inner-directed, even though direction in *both* cases comes from outside and is simply internalized at an early point in the life cycle of the inner-directed.

There are factors outside of terminology that may lead readers to conclude that inner-direction is better. Academic and professional people are frequently only too pleased to be told that those horrid businessmen, those glad-handing advertisers, are manipulative. And, as we all know, the businessmen and advertisers themselves flock to plays and movies that tell them what miserable sinners they are. Of course it is especially gratifying to look down one's nose at Hollywood, soap opera, and other mass-culture phenomena.

Inner-directed persons of high status, moreover, are associated with the Anglo-Saxon tradition and with the reverence we pay to those among the aged who are still powerful. Furthermore, since the inner-directed face problems that are not the problems of the other-directed, they seem to be made of sterner and more intrepid stuff. As we already find the Victorians charming, so we can patronize the inner-directed, especially if we did not personally suffer from their limitations, and view the era depending on inner-direction with understandable nostalgia.

Furthermore I do not want to be understood as saying it is wrong to be concerned with the "others," with human relations. That we can afford to be concerned with such problems is one of the important abundances of a high technology society. We must ask anyone who opposes the manipulation of men in modern industry whether he prefers to return to their brutalization, as in the early days of the industrial revolution. In my scheme of values, persuasion, even manipulative persuasion, is to be preferred to force. There is the danger, in fact, when one speaks of the "softness of the personnel," that one will be understood to prefer hardness. On the contrary, one of the main contentions of this book is that the other-directed person, as things are, is already too hard on himself in certain ways and that his anxieties, as child consumer-trainee, as parent, as worker and player, are very great. He is often torn between the illusion that life should be easy, if he could only find his way to the proper group-adjustment practices, and the half-buried feeling that it is not easy for him. Under these conditions it would only complicate his life still further to hold up the opposite illusion of stern inner-direction as an ideal, though this is just what many people propose. In fact, just because he is other-directed he is often overready to take some intransigent and convinced person as a model of what he himself ought to be like; his very sympathy and sensitivity may undo him.

It is easy to score verbal triumphs over American personnel practices and popular culture, for age-old snobberies converge here. Thus, a critique of the glad hand can be made from many points of view, radical or reactionary. The context out of which I have written is, however, somewhat different—it is an effort to develop a view of society which accepts rather than rejects new potentialities for leisure, human sympathy, and abundance. Both the glad hand and the search for adjustment lessons in popular culture are themselves often poignant testimonials to these potentialities. The values of the era of the invisible hand accompanied scarcity, and thus require re-interpretation before they become relevant to an era of abundance. The promising alternative to other-direction . . . is not inner-direction, but autonomy.